readings in psychology today
third edition

Selected and introduced by
James B. Maas, Ph.D.

CRM BOOKS

Del Mar, California

Library of Congress Catalog Card Number: 74-76093

Standard Book Number: 87665-221-6

Manufactured in the United States of America

9 8 7 6 5 4 3 2

introduction

Psychologists are interested in understanding, predicting, and controlling human behavior. To pursue these interests, they engage in a broad range of activities. If you were to take a guided tour at a university to watch psychologists in action, you would see some implanting electrodes in animal brains, some administering personality tests, others lecturing on Freudian theory, a few counseling those students who are having problems coping with their lives, and some taking notes on the behavior of people waiting in line for a concert. You can gain some idea of the diversity of psychology if you know that the American Psychological Association now has thirty-three divisions, representing the members' various interests. A few of those divisions are: Consumer Psychology, Psychopharmacology, Developmental Psychology, Educational Psychology, Clinical Psychology, Psychology and the Arts, Community Psychology, Experimental Analysis of Behavior.

Besides the contrasting interests represented by the divisions of the discipline, there is in psychology much controversy about the value of various theoretical approaches and wide debate about what research strategies are appropriate. But there are forces that hold the elements of this developing science together. One integrative factor is the discipline's concern with fundamental issues that have their heritage in philosophy, religion, physics, physiology, and biology. No matter what subject area a psychologist chooses to investigate, his work usually aims to shed light on such substantive issues in human thought and action as nature versus nurture, good versus evil, free will versus determinism, mind versus body, and subjectivity versus objectivity (Wertheimer, 1972). An introduction to the field of psychology should reflect the discipline's concern with these focal issues, and the articles in this collection of readings were selected on that basis.

A student is usually introduced to psychology by means of a textbook. Textbooks, however, have drawbacks. Although they do provide a wide overview of the field, they often lack depth or fail to emphasize the most important aspects of the field. The author or authors usually report on hundreds of studies, often many years after the research was completed.

Textbooks rarely attempt to integrate findings and theories because there is simply too much material to cover in a few hundred pages.

One other means of introduction to psychology, especially for students who want the intellectual stimulation of dealing with fundamental issues and recent research, might be to read scientific journals. But most students' initial enthusiasm would soon be blunted by wading through the psychological jargon, uninspiring prose, and statistical and methodological details that are often characteristic of scientific articles.

One viable alternative for the beginning student is a collection of articles describing pivotal research and written expressly for the lay person—such as the articles collected in this volume. *Psychology Today* magazine seeks the most respected thinkers in the field, researchers who are currently involved in doing studies seminal to the understanding of behavior. The magazine asks psychologists to share their ideas and concerns with people who are, in general, unacquainted with the field. Because it is often difficult for scientists to express themselves in terms that the uninitiated can easily understand, *Psychology Today* editors and illustrators work with the scientists to produce articles that are both academically sound and easily understood. Over the more than seven years of its publication, the magazine has produced a substantial library of outstanding articles. Selected collections of these writings have appeared in two earlier editions of *Readings in Psychology Today*. Many colleges and universities have adopted these books for both introductory and upper-division courses.

Readings in Psychology Today, Third Edition, represents a substantial revision of the earlier editions; a different pedagogical framework was used to determine articles' inclusion. The criteria for selection included: (1) an article's overall interest level (determined by pretesting in a university course in introductory psychology); (2) its importance in the *Zeitgeist* (spirit of the times); and (3) the potential value of the work it represents, even though the article may challenge traditional thinking. Many articles appear in the collection for the first time; others were in previous editions and have withstood the test of time, in terms of both scientific value and reader interest. The selection is meant especially to try to represent important controversy in the field—to reflect debate over theoretical issues, interpretation of findings, and ethical problems. These intellectual battles give the field its excitement and present the challenges at the frontiers of psychological inquiry.

This collection of readings is divided into eight major units. Each unit is preceded by an introductory statement that describes focal issues and specifies the relationship between these issues and the readings that follow. While not all issues of importance to psychologists are represented, those issues that are raised are among the most stimulating and recent. You may also find useful the cross-references to other *Psychology Today (PT)* articles.

Unit I, Psychology: The Science of Behavior, looks into the issues of pure versus applied research, of experimental versus clinical data, of bias in psychological research, and of ethics in the psychological laboratory.

Unit II, Brain and Behavior, provides an exciting journey into the realm of electronic control of behavior, of drugs and the mind, of conscious control of brain waves and body functions, of the nature of sleep and dreaming, of extrasensory perception, of hypnosis, and of the ethics of controlling behavior.

Unit III, The Sensory World, explores research into the nature of sensation and perception. This unit includes studies on illusions and the perception of the visual world, on photographic memory, on acupuncture, and on the sensory mechanisms of lower animals.

Unit IV, Learning, Memory, and Language, presents the work of contemporary learning theorists and shows how their approaches are applied to analyses of behavior. Memory storage and retrieval is investigated on a molecular and behavioral basis, and a report on some special feats of memory is included. The controversy over theories of language is developed in two articles by leading psycholinguists.

Unit V, Psychological Development, focuses on issues in cognitive and social-emotional development. The thought processes of children and the social development of primates are explored in the context of the heredity-environment controversy. Cross-cultural comparisons are made between our own child-rearing practices and those of other cultures.

Unit VI, Individual Differences and Personality, outlines the current controversy over the nature of intelligence and its measurement. The unit raises ethical questions about personality testing. Socially relevant problems are investigated in studies on locus of control, feminism, and aggression.

Unit VII, Disorders and Therapy, deals with mental illness, therapeutic techniques, and the relative effectiveness of treatment by various procedures. The controversy over the nature of mental disorders and the role of therapists and mental institutions is portrayed in a series of articles that present conflicting theoretical orientations and paradoxical research results.

Unit VIII, Social Psychology, samples research in person perception, attitude formation, leadership, and reactions in crises, among other topics. The articles point up the difficulties of doing research outside the controlled laboratory environment and the problems of generalizing research findings from the laboratory situation to behavior in the outside world.

Readings in Psychology Today, Third Edition, is designed to provide a stimulating and challenging exposure to the field of psychological knowledge. It reflects the field's diversity and concerns. Its readers will find that there are few pat answers to questions of why people behave as they do.

The book is dedicated to the thousands of students in introductory psychology at Cornell University who have taken the time to comment on the readings in psychology that they consider valuable. I also wish to express my gratitude to David Bellinger, Andra Putenis, Anne Maas, Violet Shepardson, and Caroline Ulbing, who provided invaluable assistance in preparing background materials.

James B. Maas, Ph.D.
Associate Professor of Psychology and Director of the Center for the Improvement of Undergraduate Education, Cornell University

contents

iv. learning, memory, and language 112

v. psychological development 158

vi. individual differences and personality 218

I. psychology: the science of behavior

Many would agree that the human condition improves as people increase their understanding of themselves and their environment. Because psychology is a science that seeks to improve understanding, many people are interested in its subject matter. But they are often wary of psychologists' motives because they fear that such understanding can also be used to control behavior. Psychologists who wish to maintain public trust must therefore constantly consider the implications of their findings; they should ask themselves: Who shall decide what are worthwhile topics for investigation? What is the nature of psychological research, and what are its ultimate consequences for society? Who shall decide how the new knowledge is to be applied, especially where the possibilities of control exist? Are the products of psychology as potentially powerful as, for instance, the products of nuclear physics?

Many contemporary psychologists have been concerned with the image and purpose of psychology. One of them, George Miller, a former president of the American Psychological Association, feels that understanding and prediction are the essential goals of psychology, and he finds little value in research and action programs that emphasize only the control of behavior. Instead, psychologists should engage in programs designed to improve human welfare and society, and they should disseminate their findings to all who need and ask for them. Psychology can best contribute to the human condition if it can be practiced by nonpsychologists, that is, by anyone. This, in essence, is Miller's conception of the primary purpose of psychology as a discipline. He believes that psy-

chologists will be developing new conceptions of people as individuals and as members of society.

If psychological research is to contribute to the understanding of human beings, it must employ the appropriate methodology. The techniques of nineteenth-century scientists, so useful to the physical and biological sciences, might not apply to the complex realities of human development and behavior. B. G. Rosenberg argues that, while laboratory studies permit precise observation and measurement, most behavior in nonlaboratory, "natural" settings is quite different from behavior in the laboratory. He believes that many behavioral scientists focus on the general laws of overt human functions and neglect unique private realms of experience; instead, behavioral scientists should develop a new model for studying behavior that treats a person as an open system, capable of change and endless growth. Rosenberg's arguments support the views of many psychologists who feel that findings from the experimental laboratory are too molecular and too systematic to explain the complex patterns of behavior that are found outside the laboratory.

Some aspects of the scientific model have limited people's understanding of themselves, as David Bakan demonstrates in his history of the scientific approach to psychology. He distinguishes between experimental research and empirical research and discusses the relevance of both for establishing a psychology that is authentic. Bakan, like Rosenberg, emphasizes the need for studying the psychological processes of thought and emotion, phenomena not easily investigated using the experimental methods of natural science.

Whether psychologists make their observations in the laboratory or outside the laboratory, whether they use human or animal subjects, or whether they have strong theoretical biases or not, they all seek uncontaminated, reliable data and strive for absolute objectivity. Robert Rosenthal, in a brilliant series of studies, shows how even scientists with the utmost integrity can unconsciously influence the outcome of their research: The investigators' expectancies influence the subjects' responses in the direction of what the investigators expect to happen. Rosenthal's findings must be taken into consideration in assessing the validity of any research that may have been affected by the interaction of researcher and subject.

Ralph Rosnow, who has collaborated with Rosenthal, focuses on the behavior of subjects in psychological experiments, who often try to please the experimenters by complying with what seem to be the experimenters' desires. Rosnow warns of other dangers in laboratory experimentation. For instance, volunteer subjects tend to be more sensitive and accommodating to implicit experimental demands than are captive nonvolunteers. But perhaps most important is the fact that *80 percent of the psychological research reported in scientific journals is based on the behavior of college undergraduates,* a mere 3 percent of the total United States population. How far can psychologists generalize the results of their research with undergraduates to the behavior of the total population? Does psychology portray only the behavior of college students and little else? Rosenthal's and Rosnow's questions about the social psychology of the psychological experiment have contributed to recent improvement in research methodology and experimentation.

Very much related to the problems of experimenter expectancies and too-willing subjects is the notion of contrived human behavioral research. Psychologists can perform their investigations by observing behavior as it unfolds in natural settings (for example, by making unobtrusive recordings of people's interactions in crises); by systematically assessing behavior through questionnaires, tests, and interviews; or by experimental manipulation of pertinent variables in a laboratory setting. Most psychological research, by its very nature, falls into the category of experimental manipulation. Laboratory experimenters have frequently resorted to deception because subjects have a tendency to react in socially acceptable ways if they know that their reactions are being observed or if they know the purpose of the experiment. If subjects were naive about the variables under consideration, they might respond differently. Zick Rubin reviews a host of questionable practices in social-psychological experiments and urges psychologists to consider more straightforward methods of gathering data whenever possible. Rubin has challenged psychologists to develop reliable measurement techniques for studying uninhibited behavior in a natural setting, and in many cases they have. Perhaps these efforts will strengthen public interest and trust in the findings of psychologists.

ON TURNING PSYCHOLOGY OVER TO THE UNWASHED

by George A. Miller

I will begin by saying publicly something that I think psychologists all feel, but seldom talk about. Scientific psychology is potentially one of the most revolutionary intellectual enterprises conceived by the mind of man. If we were to achieve substantial progress toward our stated aim—toward the understanding, prediction and control of mental and behavioral phenomena — the implications for every aspect of society would make brave men tremble.

Responsible spokesmen for psychology seldom emphasize this revolutionary possibility. One reason is that the general public is all too ready to believe it, and public resistance to psychology would be all too easy to mobilize. Knowing that revolutionary pronouncements might easily do more harm than good, a prudent spokesman finds other drums to march to.

I believe there is another reason for our public modesty. Anyone who claims that psychology is a revolutionary enterprise will face a demand from his scientific colleagues to put up or shut up. Nothing that psychology has done so far, they will say, is very revolutionary. They will admit that psychometric tests, psychoanalysis, conditioned reflexes, sensory thresholds, implanted electrodes and factor analysis are all quite admirable, but they can scarcely be compared to gunpowder, the steam engine, organic chemistry, radiotelephony, computers, atom bombs, or genetic surgery in their revolutionary consequences for society. Our enthusiastic spokesman would have to retire in confused embarrassment.

But I do not believe the psychological revolution is still pie in the sky. It has already begun.

One reason the psychological revolution is not more obvious may be that we have been looking for it in the wrong place. We have assumed that psychology should provide new technological options, that a psychological revolution will not occur until someone in authority exercises those options to attain socially desirable goals. One reason for this assumption, perhaps, is that it follows the model we have inherited from all previous applications of science to practical problems. An applied scientist is supposed to provide instrumentalities for modifying the environment — instrumentalities that can then, under public regulation, be used by wealthy and powerful interests to achieve certain goals. The psychological revolution, when it comes, may follow a very different course, at least in its initial stages.

Kingsley Davis has explained the difference between applied social science and applied natural science in the following way:

Applied science, by definition, is instrumental. When the human goal is given, it seeks a solution by finding what effective means can be manipulated in the required way. Its function is to satisfy human desires and wants; otherwise nobody would bother. But when the science is concerned with human beings—not just as organisms but as goal-seeking individuals and members of groups—then it cannot be instrumental in this way, because the object of observation has a say in what is going on and, above all, is not willing to be treated as a pure instrumentality. Most so-called social problems are problems because people want certain things or because there is a conflict of desires or interests.

Davis goes on to argue that once conflicts of interest have developed, applied social science is helpless; that it is only when people are agreed on their goals that our information can be usefully applied.

Although I agree with Davis that behavioral and social science cannot be applied to people and institutions in the same way that physical and biological science are applied to objects and organisms, I do not agree with his view that we must remain impotent in the face of conflict. We know a great deal about the prevention and resolution of conflicts, and that information could certainly be put to better use than it has been. Indeed, sometimes what is needed is not to resolve conflict but to foster it, as when entrenched interests threaten segments of the public that have no organizational identity. And there, in turn, we know a great deal about the creation of appropriate constituencies to defend their common interests. Behavioral and social scientists are far from helpless in such situations.

More important, however: I believe that the real impact of psychology will be felt, not through the technological products it places in the hands of powerful men, but through its effects on the public at large, through a new and different public conception of what is humanly possible and what is humanly desirable.

I believe that any broad and successful application of psychological knowledge to human problems will necessarily entail a change in our conception of ourselves and of how we live and love and work together. Instead of inventing some new technique for modifying the environment, or some new product for society to adapt itself to however it can, we are proposing to tamper with the adaptive process itself. Such an innovation is quite different from a "technological fix." For my part, I can see very little reason to believe that the traditional model for scientific revolutions should be appropriate.

Consider, for example, the effect that Freudian psychology has already had on Western society. It is obvious that its effects, though limited to certain segments of society, have been profound, yet I do not believe that one can argue that those effects were achieved by providing new instrumentalities for achieving goals socially agreed upon. As a method of therapy, psychoanalysis has had limited success even for those who can afford it. It has been more successful as a method of investigation, perhaps, but even there it has been only one of several available methods. The impact of Freud's thought has been due far less to the instrumentalities he provided than to the changed conception of ourselves that he inspired. Most important in the scale of history has been his effect on the whole intellectual community and through them, on the public at large. Today we are much more aware of the irrational components of human nature and much better able to accept the reality of our unconscious impulses. The true importance of Freudian psychology derives far less from its scientific validity than from the effects that it has had on our shared image of man himself.

One might argue that changes in man's conception of himself under the impact of advances in scientific knowledge are neither novel nor revolutionary. For example, Darwin's theory changed our conception of ourselves, but not until the past decade has it been possible to mount a truly scientific revolution based on biological science. One might argue that we are now only at the Darwinian stage in psychology, and that the real psychological revolution is still a century or more in the future. I do not, however, find this analogy appropriate.

To discover that we are not at the center of the universe, or that our remote ancestors lived in trees, does indeed change our conception of man and society, but such new conceptions can have little effect on the way we behave in our daily affairs and in our institutional contexts. A new conception of man based on psychology, however, would have immediate implications for the most intimate details of our social and personal lives. This fact is unprecedented in any earlier stage of the Industrial Revolution.

The heart of the psychological revolution will be a new and scientifically based conception of man as an individual and as a social creature. When I say that the psychological revolution is already upon us, what I mean

is that we have already begun to change man's self-conception. If we want to further that revolution, not only must we strengthen its scientific base, but we must also try to communicate it to our students and to the public. It is not the industrialist or the politician who should exploit these new ideas, but Everyman, every day.

The enrichment of public psychology by scientific psychology constitutes the most direct and important use of our science to promote human welfare. Instead of trying to foresee new psychological products that might disrupt existing social arrangements, therefore, we should be self-consciously analyzing the general effect that our scientific psychology may have on popular psychology.

The Control of Behavior. One of the most admired truisms of modern psychology is that some stimuli can serve to reinforce the behavior that produces them. The practical significance of this familiar principle arises from the implication that if you can control the occurrence of these reinforcing stimuli, then you can control the occurrence of adaptive behavior intended to achieve or avoid them. This principle has been demonstrated in many studies of animal behavior, where environmental conditions can be controlled, or at least specified, and where the results can be measured with some precision.

Something similar holds for the human animal, of course, although it is complicated by man's symbolic proclivities and by the fact that the disparity between experimenter and subject changes when the subject is also a man. Between men, reinforcement is usually a mutual relationship, and each person controls the other to some extent. This relation of mutual reinforcement, which man's genius for symbols has generalized in terms of money or the promise of money, provides the psychological basis for our economic system of exchange. Psychologists did not create this economic system for controlling behavior, of course. What we have tried to do is to describe its psychological basis and its limits in terms sufficiently general to hold across different species, and to suggest how the technique might be extended to educational, rehabilitative, therapeutic, or even po-

litical situations where economic rewards and punishments would not normally be appropriate. Once a problem of behavior control has been phrased in these terms, we may then try to discover the most effective schedule of reinforcements.

My present concern has nothing to do with the validity of these ideas. I am concerned with their effect on the public at large, for it is there, if I am right, that we are most likely to achieve a psychological revolution.

In the public view, I suspect, all this talk about controlling behavior comes across as unpleasant, if not actually threatening. Freud has already established in the public mind a general belief that all behavior is motivated. The current message says that psychologists now know how to use this motivation to control what people will do. When our scientific colleagues hear this, of course, they are likely to accuse us of pseudoscientific claims; less scientific segments of the public are likely to resent what they may perceive as a threat to their personal freedom. Neither reaction is completely just, but neither is completely unjustifiable.

I believe these critics see an important truth, one that a myopic concentration on techniques of behavior control may cause us to overlook. At best, control is but one component in any program of personal improvement or social reform. Changing behavior is pointless in the absence of any coherent plan for how it should be changed. It is our plan for using control that the public wants to know about. Too often, I fear, psychologists have implied that acceptable uses for behavior control are either self-evident or can be safely left to the wisdom and benevolence of powerful men. Psychologists must not surrender the planning function so easily. Humane applications of behavior control must be based on intelligent diagnosis of the personal and social problems we are trying to solve. Psychology has at least as much to contribute to the diagnosis of personal and social problems as it has to the control of behavior, probably more.

Regardless of whether we have actually achieved new, scientific techniques of behavior control that are effective with human beings, and regardless of whether control is of any value in the absence of diagnosis and

5

planning for its use, the simple fact that so many psychologists keep talking about control is having an effect on public psychology. The average citizen is predisposed to believe it. Control has been the practical payoff from the other sciences. Control must be what psychologists are after, too. Moreover, since science is notoriously successful, behavior control must be inevitable. Thus the layman forms an impression that control is the name of the road we are traveling, and that the experts are simply quibbling about how far down that road we have managed to go.

Closely related to this emphasis on control is the frequently repeated claim that living organisms are nothing but machines. A scientist recognizes, of course, that this claim says far more about our rapidly evolving conception of machines than it says about living organisms, but this interpretation is usually lost when the message reaches public ears. The public idea of a machine is something like an automobile, a mechanical device controlled by its operator. If people are machines, they can be driven like automobiles. The analogy is absurd, of course, but it illustrates the kind of distortion that can occur.

If the assumption that behavior control is feasible in some precise, scientific sense becomes firmly rooted in public psychology, it could have unfortunate consequences, particularly if it is coupled with an assumption that control should be exercised by an industrial or bureaucratic elite. Psychologists must always respect and advocate the principle of *habeas mentem*—the right of a man to his own mind. If we really did have a new scientific way to control human behavior, it would be highly immoral to let it fall into the hands of some small group of men, even if they were psychologists.

When the evolution of species was a new and exciting idea in biology, various social theorists took it up and interpreted it to mean that capitalistic competition, like the competition between species, was the source of all progress, so the great wealth of the new industrialists was a scientifically necessary consequence of the law of the survival of the fittest. This argument, called "social Darwinism," had unfortunate consequences, both for social science and society generally.

If the notion should now be accepted that it is a scientifically necessary consequence of the law of reinforcement that industrialists or bureaucrats must be allowed the same control over people that an experimenter has over his laboratory animals, I fear that a similar period of intolerable exploitation might ensue—if, indeed, it has not already begun.

The dangers that accompany a science of behavior control have been pointed out many times. Psychologists who study motivation scientifically are usually puzzled by this widespread apprehension that they might be successful. Control is not something invented by psychologists. Everyone is controlled all the time by something or other. All we want is to discover how the controls work. Once we understand that, society can use the knowledge in whatever manner seems socially advantageous. Our critics, on the other hand, want to know who will diagnose our problems, who will set our social goals, and who will administer the rewards and the punishments.

All that I have tried to add to this familiar dialogue is the observation that the social dangers involved need not await the success of the scientific enterprise. Behavior control could easily become a self-fulfilling prophecy. If people generally should come to believe in the scientific control of behavior, proponents of coercive social programs would surely exploit that belief by dressing their proposals

"Understanding and prediction are better goals for psychology than is control — better both for psychology and for the promotion of human welfare."

in scientific costumes.

If our new public conception of human nature is that man's behavior can be scientifically controlled by those in positions of power, governments will quickly conform to that conception. Thus, when I try to discern what direction our psychological revolution has been taking, some aspects of it disturb me deeply and lead me to question whether in the long

run these developments will really promote human welfare.

This is a serious charge. If there is any truth to it, other approaches are open to us.

Personally, I believe there is a better way to advertise psychology and to relate it to social problems. Reinforcement is only one of many important ideas that we have to offer. Instead of repeating constantly that reinforcement leads to control, I would prefer to emphasize that reinforcement can lead to satisfaction and competence. And I would prefer to speak of understanding and prediction as our major scientific goals.

Understanding and prediction are better goals for psychology than is control — better both for psychology and for the promotion of human welfare—because they lead us to think, not in terms of coercion by a powerful elite, but in terms of the diagnosis of problems and the development of programs that can enrich the lives of every citizen.

Public Psychology: Two Paradigms. It should be obvious by now that I have somewhere in the back of my mind two alternative images of what the popular conception of human nature might become under the impact of scientific advances in psychology. One of these images is unfortunate, even threatening; the other is vaguer, but full of promise.

The first image is the one I have been describing. It has great appeal to an authoritarian mind, and fits well with our traditional competitive ideology based on principles of coercion, punishment and retribution. The fact that it represents a serious distortion of scientific psychology is exactly my point. In my opinion we have made a mistake by trying to apply our ideas to social problems and by trying to gain acceptance for our science within the framework of this ideology.

The second image rests on the same psychological foundation, but reflects it more accurately; it allows no compromise with our traditional social ideology. It is assumed, vaguely but optimistically, that this ideology can be modified so as to be more receptive to a truer conception of human nature. How this modification can be achieved is one of the problems we face; I believe it will not be achieved if we continue to advertise the control of behavior through reinforcement as our major contribution to the solution of social problems. I would not wish to give anyone the impression that I have formulated a well-defined social alternative, but I would at least like to open a discussion and make some suggestions.

My two images are not very different from what Douglas McGregor once called Theory X and Theory Y. Theory X is the traditional theory that holds that, because people dislike work, they must be coerced, controlled, directed, and threatened with punishment before they will do it. People tolerate being directed, and many even prefer it, because they have little ambition and want to avoid responsibility. McGregor's alternative Theory Y, based on social science, holds that work is as natural as play or rest. External control and threats are not the only means for inspiring people to work. People will exercise

"Psychology must be practiced by nonpsychologists. We are not physicians; the secrets of our trade need not be reserved for highly trained specialists."

self-direction and self-control in the service of objectives to which they are committed. Their commitment is a function of the rewards associated with the achievement of their objectives. People can learn not only to accept but to seek responsibility. Imagination, ingenuity and creativity are widely distributed in the population, although these intellectual potentialities are poorly utilized under the conditions of modern industrial life.

McGregor's Theory X and Theory Y evolved in the context of his studies of industrial management. They are rival theories held by industrial managers about how best to achieve their institutional goals. A somewhat broader view is needed if we are to talk about public psychology generally, and not merely the managerial manifestations of public psychology. So let me amplify McGregor's distinction by referring to the ideas of Jacobo A. Varela, a remarkable engineer in Montevideo, Uruguay, who uses scientific psychology in the solution of a wide range of personal and social problems.

Varela contrasts two conceptions of the social nature of man. Following Thomas Kuhn's discussion of scientific revolutions, he refers to these two conceptions as paradigms.

The first "paradigm" is a set of assumptions on which our social institutions are presently based: All men are created equal. Most behavior is motivated by economic competition, and conflict is inevitable. One truth underlies all controversy, and unreasonableness is best countered by facts and logic. When something goes wrong, someone is to blame, and every effort must be made to establish his guilt so that he can be punished. The guilty person is responsible for his own misbehavior and for his own rehabilitation. His teachers and supervisors are too busy to become experts in social science; their role is to devise solutions and see to it that their students or subordinates do what they are told.

The second paradigm that Varela offers is based on psychological research: There are large individual differences among people, both in ability and personality. Human motivation is complex and no one ever acts as he does for any single reason, but in general, positive incentives are more effective than threats or punishments. Conflict is no more inevitable than disease and can be resolved or, still better, prevented. Time and resources for resolving social problems are strictly limited. When something goes wrong, how a person perceives the situation is more important to him than the "true facts," and he cannot reason about the situation until his irrational feelings have been toned down. Social problems are solved by correcting causes, not symptoms, and this can be done more effectively in groups than individually. Teachers and supervisors must be experts in social science, because they are responsible for the cooperation and individual improvement of their students or subordinates.

It seems obvious to me that the psychologically based paradigm is incompatible in several respects with the prevailing ideology of our society.

Here then, is the real challenge. How can we foster a social climate in which some such new public conception of man, based on psychology, can take root and flourish? In my opinion, this is the proper translation of our more familiar question about how psychology might contribute to the promotion of human welfare.

I cannot pretend to have an answer to this question, even in its translated form, but I believe that part of the answer is that psychology must be practiced by nonpsychologists. We are not physicians; the secrets of our trade need not be reserved for highly trained specialists. Psychological facts should be passed out freely to all who need and can use them. And from successful applications of psychological principles the public may gain a better appreciation for the power of the new conception of man that is emerging from our science.

If we take seriously the idea of a peaceful revolution based on a new conception of human nature, our scientific results will have to be instilled in the public consciousness in a practical and usable form so that what we know can be applied by ordinary people. There simply are not enough psychologists, even including nonprofessionals, to meet every need for psychological services. The people at large will have to be their own psychologists, and make their own applications of established principles. Of course, every one of us practices psychology. I am proposing that we should teach people to practice it better, to make use self-consciously of what we believe to be scientifically valid principles.

Our responsibility is less to assume the role of experts and try to apply psychology ourselves than to give it away to the people who really need it—and that includes everyone. The practice of valid psychology by non-psychologists will inevitably change people's conception of themselves and what they can do. When we have accomplished that we will really have caused a psychological revolution.

How To Give Psychology Away. I am keenly aware that giving psychology away will be no simple task. In our society there are depths of resistance to innovation that have to be experienced to be believed.

Solving social problems is generally considered to be more difficult than solving scientific problems. A social problem usually involves many more independent variables, and it cannot be finally solved until society has been persuaded to adopt the solution. Many who have tried to introduce sound psychological practices into schools, clinics, hospitals, prisons or industries have been forced to retreat in dismay. They complain, and with good reason, that they were unable to buck The System, and often their reactions are more violent than sensible. The System, they say, refuses to change even when it doesn't work.

Perhaps pressure toward internal coherence lies at the root of public resistance to many of our innovative suggestions. It often seems that any one of our ideas taken alone is inadequate. Injected into the existing social paradigm it is either a foreign body, incompatible with the other presuppositions that shape our social institutions, or it is distorted and trivialized to fit the pre-existing paradigm.

One of the most basic ideas in all the social sciences is the concept of culture. Social anthropologists have developed a conception of culture as an organic whole, where each particular value, practice or assumption must be understood in the context of the total system. They tell terrible tales about the consequences of introducing Western reforms into aboriginal cultures without understanding the social equilibria that would be upset.

Perhaps cultural integrity is not lim-

ited to primitive cultures, but applies also to our own society here and now. If so, then our attempts at piecemeal innovation may be doomed either to fail or to be rejected outright.

I label these thoughts pessimistic because they imply a need for drastic changes throughout the whole system and changes that could only be imposed by someone with dangerous power over the lives of others.

"I am keenly aware that giving psychology away will be no simple task. In our society there are depths of resistance to innovation that have to be experienced to be believed."

And that, I have argued, is not the way our psychological revolution should proceed.

In my more optimistic moments, however, I recognize that you do not need complete authority over a social organization in order to reform it. The important thing is not to control the system, but to understand it. Someone who has a valid conception of the system as a whole can often introduce relatively minor changes that have extensive consequences throughout the entire organization. Lacking such a conception, worthwhile innovations may be total failures.

For example, if you institute a schedule of rewards and punishments in the psychiatric ward of a veterans hospital, you should not be indignant when the American Legion objects to your withholding food and clothing from veterans. If you had a more adequate understanding of the hospital as a social system, you would have included the interests and influence of the American Legion in your diagnosis, and you would have formulated a plan to gain their endorsement as part of your task as a social engineer. Understanding must come first.

In my optimistic moments, I am able to convince myself that understanding is attainable, the task is manageable, and that social science is already at a stage where successful applications are possible. Careful diagnosis and astute planning based on what we

already know can often resolve problems that at first glance seemed insurmountable. Many social, clinical and industrial psychologists have already demonstrated the power of diagnosis and planning based on sound psychological principles.

We are in serious need of many more psychological technologists who can apply our science to the personal and social problems of the general public, for it is through them that the public will eventually discover the new paradigm that psychologists are developing. That is to say, it is through the success of such practical applications that we have our best hope for revolutionizing public psychology.

There is no possibility of legislating the changes I have in mind. Education would seem to be our only possibility, education shaped to fit the perceived needs of the general public, something they can use. Lectures suitable for graduate seminars are seldom suitable for laymen, and for a layman facing a concrete problem they are usually worse than useless. Abstract theories, however elegant, or sensitivity training, however insightful, are too remote from the specific troubles they face. We must begin with people where they are, not assume we know where they should be.

If a supervisor is having trouble with his men, perhaps we should teach him how to write a job description and how to evaluate the abilities and personalities of those who fill the job; perhaps we should teach him the art of persuasion or the time and place for positive reinforcement. If a ghetto mother is not giving her children sufficient intellectual challenge, perhaps we should teach her how to encourage motor, perceptual and linguistic skills. The techniques involved are not some esoteric branch of witchcraft that must be reserved for those with Ph.D. degrees in psychology. When the ideas are made sufficiently concrete and explicit, the scientific foundations of psychology can be grasped by sixth-grade children.

There are many obvious and useful suggestions that we could make and that nonpsychologists could exploit. Not every psychological problem in human engineering has to be solved by professional psychologists; engineers can rapidly assimilate psychological facts and theories that are relevant to their own work. Not every teaching program has to be written by a learning theorist; principles governing the design and evaluation of programmed materials can be learned by content specialists. Not every personnel decision has to be made by a psychometrician, not every interview has to be conducted by a clinical psychologist, not every problem has to be solved by a cognitive psychologist, not every reinforcement has to be supervised by a student of conditioning. Psychological principles and techniques can be usefully applied by everyone. If our suggestions actually work, people should be eager to learn more. If they don't work, we should improve them. But we should not try to give people something whose value they cannot recognize, then complain when they don't return for a second meeting.

Consider the teaching of reading, for example. Here is an obviously appropriate area for the application of psychological principles. So what do we do? We assemble experts who decide what words children know, and in what order they should learn to read them; then we write stories with those words and teachers make the children read them, or we use them in programmed instruction that exploits the principles of reinforcement. But all too often the children fail to recognize the value of learning these cleverly constructed lessons.

Personally, I have been impressed with the approach of Sylvia Ashton-Warner, who begins by asking a child what words he wants. Mummy, daddy, kiss, frightened, ghost, their own names — these are the words children ask for, words that are bound up with their own loves and fears. She writes each child's words on large, tough cards and gives them to him. If a child wants words like police, butcher, knife, kill, jail and bomb, he gets them.

And he learns to read them almost immediately. They are *his* words, and each morning he retrieves his own words from the pile collected each night by the teacher. Each child decides where he wants to start, and each child learns something whose value he can recognize.

Could we generalize this technique discovered by an inspired teacher in a small New Zealand school? In my own thinking I have linked it with something that Robert White has called competence motivation. In order to tap this motivational system we must use psychology to give people skills that will satisfy their urge to feel more effective. Feeling effective is a very personal thing, for it must be a feeling of effectiveness in coping with personal problems in one's own life. From that beginning some might want to learn more about the science that helped them increase their competence, and then perhaps we could afford to be more abstract. But in the beginning we must try to diagnose and solve the problems people think they have, not the problems we experts think they ought to have, and we must learn to understand those problems in the social and institutional contexts that define them. With this approach we might do something practical for nurses, policemen, prison guards, salesmen—for people in many different walks of life. That, I believe, is what we should mean when we talk about applying psychology to the promotion of human welfare.

How can we do it? I can see some promise for innovations in particular subcultures. If we can apply our new paradigm in particular institutions—in schools, hospitals, prisons, industries —we can perhaps test its validity and demonstrate its superiority. Many such social experiments are, of course, already in progress. And much of the recent surge of interest in community psychology has been stimulated by the realization that we really do have something to contribute to community life. Perhaps all this work will eventually have a cumulative effect.

One trouble, of course, is that we are trying to reverse the natural direction of influence. Ordinarily an institution or a community models its own subculture more or less automatically on the larger culture in which it is embedded, and new members require little indoctrination in order to

understand the tacit assumptions on which the institution is based. Whether the new paradigm will be powerful enough to reverse this direction is, I suppose, a matter for pure speculation at the present time. It seems unlikely that we will succeed, however, if each application of the new paradigm is viewed as unrelated to every other, and no attempt is made to integrate these experiments into a paradigm for society as a whole.

It is possible, however, that our society may not be quite as resistant as we anticipate. The demand for social relevance that many psychologists have been voicing is only one aspect of a general dissatisfaction with the current state of our society. On every hand we hear complaints about the old paradigm. People are growing more and more alienated from a society in which a few wise men behind closed doors decide what is good for everyone. Our system of justice based on punishment and retribution is not working. Even those most blessed by economic rewards are asking for something more satisfying to fill their lives. We desperately need techniques for resolving conflicts, and for preventing them from becoming public confrontations from which reasonable retreat is impossible. Anyone who reads the newspapers must realize that vast social changes are in the making, that they must occur if civilized society is to survive.

Vested interests will oppose these changes, of course, but as someone once said, vested interests, however powerful, cannot withstand the gradual encroachment of new ideas. If we psychologists are ready for it, we may be able to contribute a coherent and workable philosophy, based on the science of psychology, that will make this general agitation less negative, that will make it a positive search for something new.

It will not be easy, but difficulty is no excuse for surrender. There is a sense in which the unattainable is the best goal to pursue. So let us continue our struggle to advance psychology as a means of promoting human welfare, each in his own way. For myself, however, I can imagine nothing we could do that would be more relevant to human welfare, and nothing that could pose a greater challenge to the next generation of psychologists, than to discover how best to give psychology away.

9

Psychology Through the Looking Glass

by B.G. Rosenberg

I**N PERSPECTIVE** it seems that psychology has divided the estate of human behavior between the two quarrelsome sisters of Lewis Carroll's *Through the Looking Glass*. The decision of the founding fathers to make psychology a science instead of an art—to adopt the strict methodology of a *Naturwissenschaft* rather than the imaginative approach of a *Geisteswissenschaft* — has restricted psychological research to the observation of regular patterns of human behavior, and as a consequence, to selected negative aspects of that behavior.

While the rigorous standards of 19th-Century science, including our orientation toward the highly mechanistic animal model of behavior and medical concept of symptom treatment, have contributed significantly to our understanding of human behavior, it is time we recognized the limitations of this approach. Psychology is heir to a legacy of precision that has little application to the complex realities of clinical practice, or for that matter, to most events of our daily activity. If we are to progress toward a more complete and useful view of man, we must realize that psychological thought tends to neglect the developmental potential of human behavior.

Source. It is not surprising that the most comprehensive theories of human behavior originate in nonlaboratory settings. The research psychologist, in an attempt to systematize what he is able to learn, necessarily assumes that man is like other phenomena studied by science. Therefore, the behavioral scientist tries to isolate the characteristics and activities shared by *all* men, and expects individuals to behave in a pre-determined, orderly manner according to experimental findings. The clinical psychologist, having encountered the private, idiosyncratic facets of human behavior, knows that the discoveries of the laboratory are no match for the spontaneous inventions of his patients.

The obstacles to clinical use of psychological research are the very assumptions that guide the research in the first place. The behavioral scientist believes: 1. that man *can* be studied the way other animals or physical phenomena are; 2. that what is regular and orderly is important; 3. that what occurs with a degree of frequency will continue unabated at the same frequency; and 4. that knowledge of the major parameters of behavior will guide our study of other processes characteristic of man.

Drama. It is easy to understand why we focus on regular patterns in behavior and on the isolated disruptions we call symptoms. Irregularities are usually dramatic and they command our attention. In therapy, irregularities often become less frequent or less intense, and the patient is in a more comfortable state. Successful therapy reinforces the medical or disease model of research. In a sense we can comprehend and control regular behavior through principles discovered in the study of behavior disruption.

Unfortunately, a focus on the aspects of behavior that we can observe and manipulate directs our attention away from the details of behavior that are covert and elusive. The insistence that the study of orderly behavior, and the appearance of common traits, is essential to psychology precludes attention to the exceptional, the infrequent, the spontaneous creative response. Fantasy or image-making, for example, while they are immediately inexplicable, may hold the key to what and how man experiences. It is difficult to argue that the limited aspects of behavior we are able to study in the laboratory are more than peripheral aspects of human experience.

Science is reductive; it can less well address itself to the total fabric of human experience. The mechanical model of scientific tradition presents behavior as a system of compensations and conflict resolutions. The psychologist interprets human activity in terms of logical cause and effect. For instance, dreams are outlets for wishes that cannot be gratified in waking hours. One takes food to compensate for deprivation at the tissue level. Such a view is partial at best. Scientific logic simply does not take into account what might be called emergent creative processes, self-determination and developmental transformations. In a study of the long-range data collected at the Institute of Human Development at the University of California, Berkeley, Jean Macfarlane frequently found that individuals who had been quite disturbed in adolescence were able to lead stable, productive lives as adults *without* therapeutic intervention. It may well be that healthy behavior simply emerges at different stages in development and we cannot predict such changes on the basis of what we know about the individual's history.

The conflict-resolution model impels us to see activity in terms of the immediate situation. For instance, fantasy is the necessary compensation for lack of fulfillment in other spheres. Fantasy may be compensatory, but we must realize that it also is an integrative function. Fantasy is fulfilling as a process, as well as being a vehicle for the contents of conflict resolution. We should study fantasy as a broad aspect of human activity, a generative condition of the individual, rather than as a response to conflict.

Run. Another restriction on the study of behavior is the concept of adaptation that we have taken from biology. Like the conflict-resolution model, it views man mechanistically, in terms of the immediate situation. The concept has been useful in accounting for animal behavior in a natural environment, but it is too simple for human behavior. The fact is that human beings do more than adapt. Equilibrium is not the natural order of man, no matter how appealing we find the theories of tension reduction or homeostatic process. Psychologists have neglected the White Queen's remark to Alice that we have to run to stay in the same place and to get somewhere else we have to run twice as fast.

We have not studied the steady states that reasonably characterize man. Steady states comprise the bulk of human behavior, and though they are transient, they mark the movement of the organism toward progressively higher levels of development. The organism must change constantly if it is to maintain its level of stability. Disequilibrium is the natural order. Life is not simply an attempt at adaptation—it is a realization of potential at varying stages of development. The potential for higher levels of functioning exists from the beginning, and it is not necessarily the consequence of the situation.

Open. One of the major errors psychology continues to make is that it treats the human organism as a *closed system*, a mechanical model of fixed inputs and predictable responses. I would like to suggest that the human being is an open system, capable of change and endless growth. We should abandon the mechanical model for what might be called the process model.

In a sense psychology has created the individual in its own image. In the course of his development an individual learns the customs and roles that his society values. His first choice of role is based on the *saliency* of one or more signs, and it often is a haphazard thing. Once he makes the choice, he seeks regularities in manner, habit and custom that will allow others to identify him in them. These regularities, however, are not the totality of what a person is; the limited aspects of behavior studied by psychology are not the totality either. The feelings, thoughts and actions that make up one's behavior and experience as a father, husband, or friend are seldom open to inspection or study.

The individual is essentially a private experience that cannot easily be categorized.

I suggest that the hidden regularities that make up the fabric of the individual are no less important or lawful than those that are observable. They are simply more elusive; they require greater inference for study. The regularity of such underground behavior may well be revealed to us in the exceptional cases of behavior that we treat as abnormal. Rather than spend time on the stable continuities visible in everyday life, we should attend to the discontinuities.

Leap. The holistic picture of man does not lend itself to careful, precise study of total man. To satisfy our need for a comprehensive theory we often make vast and indiscriminate leaps from our knowledge of aspects of behavior to a set of verbal constructs regarding the interaction of the underlying processes. We term such constructs "personality."

The idea that personality can be developed through instruction or behavior modification is popular at the moment. A classical study by Mary Cover Jones demonstrated a child's acquisition of fear of an object that had not been frightening before. Scholars thought that this causal model was adequate to explain the development of all emotions. Certainly, children learn some types of behavior through rewards and punishments manipulated by parents, but it is ludicrous to try to account for all development with this model.

We ignore the spontaneous, accidental education that occurs outside of the Skinner Box of family relations. Psychologists tend to neglect the steady states, the stages in which most growth occurs. Unquestionably the scope and content of nonparental instruction are greater than the behavior that parents intentionally foster. It is probable that the most relevant behavior is *not* learned through instruction. Contemporary thinkers suggest that the variety of social roles results from learning, not from teaching, and from an absence of drive reduction. Man is essentially self-directed, or perhaps self-selective.

Change. This view clearly undercuts theories on the nature and purpose of cultural patterning, of socialization techniques, and of training preadaptive to adult status in society. Another legacy inherited from biology is the concept of cultural evolution. According to those who studied the behavior of lower animals, lower animals were on the way to becoming human. The modern view argues that animals are on the way to becoming something else, different in each case. Psychologists assume that the child is on his way to becoming a human adult, like us. Yet each generation emerges at a different point in time, confronted by a different store of cultural information and possessed of a different gene pool. We cannot really predict the direction of self-development that each generation will take. The creative aspects of change provide the base of daily human experience. Obviously no parent trained his children for the long-hair, unisex, drug culture of today's young. The child does not necessarily ape his elders in becoming a human adult.

Science studies man as he is, but renders him a static, atemporal object. Treatment of the irregular disruptions of behavior seeks to relieve suffering and to return the subject to his former, normal, state. Psychology ignores the possibility that, in his steady states, man creates himself. Life is a process of change, of creation, not the static existence of a mechanical object.

Afoot. I suggest that rigorous science as it is presently applied is not the road to understanding human behavior. To study the typewriter that a novelist used is no way to understand his novel. We must develop a paradigm that reconciles the laboratory and the clinic if we are to hear man, observe his behavior, and examine the unique generalities of every man and his fellows. We must study man as he is on the way to becoming, rather than as he is. The clinical psychologist must abandon the notion that when we remove a noxious stimulus or a conflict situation, a man automatically returns to his initial condition, what we call normality or health. Man does not return to that condition; and we have no exact language to describe what that state of normal existence is.

We must learn to apply the methodology of science to aspects of behavior that are more representative of daily life. We must acknowledge that much of human behavior involves the private, spontaneous and innovative attempts of the individual to become something more than what he has been. We must have new models that will enable us systematically to study adequacy, love and fulfillment. The psychologist then can tune in on the changing social conditions that surround us.

The human organism is a viable, changing object of study. Experience brings about cognitive and emotional restructuring of the organism in a continuous process of differentiation and integration at higher levels of development. This conception of man unstrings most of the present models used to study behavior. Behavioral regularities, it should be clear, may be lawful, but the criterion of relevance is more important. And relevance, in the study of man, is the study of behaviors that are a central, functioning part of the generative state of man.

Psychology Can Now Kick the Science Habit

by David Bakan

Psychology is not an autonomous discipline, but many psychologists behave as if it were. They often are unaware of the social and historical forces that have shaped psychology—unaware especially of the ways in which the development of the university, and the natural sciences within it, have shaped their attitudes and interests. This lack of awareness has handicapped the field internally, in its emergence as an authentic discipline, and externally, in its usefulness to society.

In the beginning, the American colleges were tied to the Protestant churches and were intended largely to serve religiously based values. Psychology was a largely philosophical and moral enterprise, a handmaiden to religion. It purposed to raise moral virtue.

By the middle of the 19th century, however, the academy began to part from the Church. That separation was closely associated with the growth of natural science and the relevance of natural science to the Industrial Revolution. In 1862 Congress passed the first Morrill Act to establish land-grant colleges, partly as a response to the need for increased agricultural productivity. Great industrial fortunes began to support new private universities, because business benefited from scientific research. The church colleges also made room for the natural sciences.

By the late 1800s science had become a vocation. Until then, only gentlemen with resources and leisure could engage in their scientific interests: men such as Charles Darwin, Thomas Jefferson, Benjamin Franklin. But then the professional scientist emerged—one who was paid to develop theories and run experiments. Applications derived from the theories and experiments were left to craftsmen.

Split. A two-step approach to science grew: the acquisition of knowledge was one thing; its application was another. This notion is now so deeply entrenched that we forget how recent it is. Craftsmen were refining petroleum well before Berthelot's 1867 research on the effect of heat on hydrocarbons. The practical need for minerals and the flourishing of construction projects were associated with major advances in geology. Craftsmen had developed ingenious methods of precision-shaping of metals and mechanical power transmission with little benefit from theory —Oliver Evans, for example, automated a flour mill as early as 1785.

Electricity was the important exception that promoted the acceptance of the two-step notion. Laboratory findings were essential to the development of power plants and electrical-distribution systems. The popularity of the two-step approach heightened the prestige of the academy and the natural sciences. Business and industry, through extensive financial contributions, came to control academic governing boards.

Import. Against this backdrop, psychology searched for ways to establish itself as a natural science in the late 19th and early 20th centuries. The German laboratory model appeared to be the perfect alternative to the American moral-philosophic model. Young American students eagerly set out for Germany to study German psychology and bring it home; and universities imported German-educated professors such as E. B. Titchener and Max Meyer.

The natural-science ideal flourished in the years between the great wars. The behavioristic learning psychology of E. L. Thorndike and John Watson prevailed, supported by a belief that the scientific method in psychology would release untold potentialities in man. During the crash and Depression, when America was filled with competing ideologies, the scientific model acquired renewed social value as a shield against propaganda. Other persuasions of psychology—especially the Freudian—flourished principally outside of the academy, in America's popular literature; they went underground as far as academic psychology was concerned.

Bomb. World War II vindicated the two-step notion. Scientists, including psychologists, mobilized to solve war problems; they applied theory and research fast and well. Psychologists contributed to the selection and training of personnel for the armed forces. Natural scientists developed new ways to help man, other means to kill him—from penicillin to more-effective bomb fuses. The most dramatic scientific contribution was the atom bomb.

The creation of the bomb taught policy makers an important lesson: *scientists could contribute significantly without knowing how those contributions would be used.* Research could be split up, assembly-line fashion, with someone else responsible for putting the pieces together and using it. This division of labor accorded comfortably with the scientists' belief that they were interested in truth for its own sake.

Fear. After the war the awesome displays of the power of science cre-

---

"If psychology continues to rely on experiment and ignores or disparages the larger empiricism, it will go nowhere."

---

ated a backlash. The Government attempted to bind such power, out of its fear of unknown Russian scientific activities and fretfulness about the American scientists' activities. To keep the Russians away from its secrets—inscribed in the notebooks and neurons of the researchers—the Government launched an effort to control American science and scientists. It used compulsory loyalty oaths, surveillance, and other methods to keep scientists in line. The scientists, in turn, were surprised by the practical and political consequences of their work—and, as a result, many became interested in social policy. As scien-

tists became involved in policy, the Government redoubled its efforts to keep them in their place.

Return. It soon became clear that efforts to control scientists were interfering with recruitment and productivity. When Russia exploded the atom bomb and launched Sputnik, the country made a vigorous return to the two-step strategy. Support for so-called basic research, the first step, increased. The Government relieved scientists of the burden of secrecy and gave them money without visible strings. The scientists felt that they could work autonomously; the Government could stockpile scientific research and talent for industrial, military, or political purposes.

This strategy seemed very well and good, but it had its effect on the kind of research that was done. Research money went for projects that were small in scope, aimed at getting fast results, while ambitious or exploratory or humanistic studies were less likely to get funds. Scientists labored to create fact-modules—bits of information that could be stored, retrieved, and applied as needed.

The university supported the narrow-scope, fact-module orientation, since this brought in Government money. It rewarded rapid publication, and if one did research on small problems, it was easy to produce a multitude of papers. It promoted the professors who brought in support funds, tolerated poor teaching—especially of undergraduates—and did not object to narrowing the curriculum.

Ride. American psychology was part of this process, riding the coattails of the fact-module approach. It had the necessary credentials from its tradition: an emphasis on measurement and statistics, a history of laboratory experimentation.

Further, its parametric view of human nature meshed easily with the fact-module approach. That is, psychology saw human functioning in terms of specific variables, each of which could be studied separately, yet which in conjunction would ultimately "explain" man and predict his behavior. With statistical tests of significance, one presumably could identify the relationships among vari-

ables, factoring out the noise of other uncontrolled variables. It was believed that when psychologists identified all possible relationships, of course all such noise would be eliminated.

The natural sciences were presumed to have progressed on the basis of this parametric assumption, and psychologists adopted it without question. Nor did anyone seriously doubt the use of statistical tests of significance in pursuit of perfect understanding. These statistical methods dovetailed with the fact-module approach; that was enough.

Gadfly. The bureaucracy of the university, the narrowing of its focus, and the hardening of orthodox experimental psychology, meant that underground psychology had to stay underground. Its concepts and its values, however, appeared in literature—and the popular imagination eagerly accepted them.

Fiction played gadfly to Establishment ideology and impersonal bureaucracy. Modern American literature asserts, almost invariably, that personality is more important than role. It enthusiastically portrays the struggle of the individual against the system, the thinking man against the mindless mass, e.g., *Catch-22, One Flew Over the Cuckoo's Nest.*

Psychoanalytic concepts meshed with the writer's belief in human uniqueness. There was great appeal in Freud's arguments that internal repression results from external oppression, that repression causes neurosis, that healing requires a fight against repression, and that man's psychic life is more rich and complicated than the social order admits.

Such concepts, quite beyond statistical methods, were far more popular with laymen than with orthodox psychologists. From time to time academic psychologists made pious efforts to tame psychoanalysis with experimental research, but generally they scorned its ideas and its practitioners.

In virtually every introductory course in psychology, there was war between experimental (academic) and underground (clinical) psychology. Behavioristically minded professors sought to convert their underground-informed students, to exorcise heresies from their minds. Students who wanted good grades, admission to graduate school, and, ultimately, faculty appointments, managed to abjure the errors of their youth and became true believers. Heretics rarely made it to graduate school.

Ambivalence. World War II stimulated the growth of clinical psychology. Veterans needed help, and the public endorsed funds for clinical psychology. But psychology departments accepted such funds with considerable ambivalence: clinical psychology might, after all, corrupt scientific quality. They compromised by accepting the funds and by keeping clinical psychology in second-class status, subject to the control of the dominant experimental ideology.

The new clinical Ph.D.s were in an awkward situation. Few universities wanted to hire them for their clinical wisdom and understanding; psychology departments sought their skill only in running experiments that hinted vaguely at clinical significance. The new clinicians kept bumping into opposition from the medical profession. Mental hospitals, for example, employed many of the new clinicians, but kept them subordinate to medical doctors. At the same time, medicine opposed the licensing and certifica-

---

"Psychology now has an opportunity to free itself from the natural-science model, to pursue intrinsically relevant goals."

---

tion that would allow clinical psychologists to work in private practice.

Bind. The American Psychological Association became a locus of this struggle. It had the power to give clinical psychologists a professional seal of approval, but experimentalists argued that this would downgrade the whole organization. APA eventually compromised by subdividing into special-interest groups; universities tried to do the same thing.

Clinicians were caught on both sides. They had academic credentials;

they admired the scientific method that had insured those credentials; they even knew statistics, which they felt gave them an edge over research-incompetent physicians. But they had been indoctrinated: they could not forge ahead freely to develop methods appropriate to clinical problems; they were afraid to draw on, and build from, the psychology of the underground.

Insight. Psychologists often treat the terms *experimental research* and *empirical research* as though they were synonymous. In fact they are different, the experiment being only one form of empiricism. An *experiment,* says one dictionary, is "an operation carried out under controlled conditions in order to discover an unknown effect or law, to test or establish a hypothesis, or to illustrate a known law." *Empirical,* by contrast, means "originating in or based on observation or experience." The sciences have progressed more on the basis of broad empirical work than on experimental work. Darwin and Freud were arch-empiricists; virtually all of the sciences, from geology and astronomy to zoology and medicine, have depended on insight and observation at least as much as on experiment. If psychology continues to rely on experiment and ignores or disparages the larger empiricism, it will go nowhere.

Letdown. I think that now we are in a period of transition—for the status of the sciences in general and for psychology itself. In the last decade we have begun to question the unquestioned belief that fact-module experimental research is a panacea for man's problems; the payoffs of this research have been smaller than we had hoped. Huge amounts of money produced many frivolous results. We made it to the moon, but did less to improve the earth. Research in quality control allowed manufacturers to sell products at the margin of market acceptability. Medical research has not appreciably affected the death rate or lowered the infant-mortality rate in recent years. Military research produced defoliants, napalm, and poison gases but did not end the conflict in Vietnam. Indeed,

the association between the military and science meant that as the prestige of the one fell, so did that of the other. By early 1970 the reaction against science was considerable. The Government, again following the public mood, began to withdraw its previously enthusiastic support for so-called basic research.

Psychology, which once sought to free itself from its philosophic-religious tradition, now has an opportunity to free itself from its reliance on the natural-science model, to pursue intrinsically relevant goals.

Obstacle. The marriage between psychology and natural science brought a critical attitude to the study of psychological phenomena, and this was an important step forward. But the attempt to transfer other features of the natural sciences also had negative effects. Principally, this alliance: 1) deflected psychology away from its primary subject matter—thinking, feeling and willing; and 2) perpetuated an unwillingness to recognize the special quality of psychological phenomena that I call *reflexivity.*

A major obstacle to the development of an authentic psychology is man's intrinsic *psychophobia*—man's fear of acknowledging the truth about his own mind—which Freud called repression. The natural sciences study matter; so academic psychologists, who wanted to borrow the methods and guiding principles of hard science, chose to emphasize man's corporeality. They tended to ignore true psychological processes such as thought and emotion, since these were not easily investigated by the particular methods of natural science.

Process. An authentic psychology must also concern itself with *reflexivity:* the effect of thinking, feeling and willing on these processes themselves. Reflexivity played little part in the great successes of the natural sciences. Natural scientists were content to let their knowledge affect their thoughts and desires, but they did not think that this process itself was worth study.

Psychology's unwillingness to explore reflexivity, a process unique to man and critical to the study of man, did more than hobble the discipline. It made psychology a manipulative enterprise. Psychologists assumed that the power of natural science to predict and control natural phenomena could be translated into human terms. But that lost something in translation: it became prediction and control of *others,* an aim that is both odious and ineffective.

In an attempt to keep their experiments "scientific," psychologists tried to study "naive" subjects. This simple, mindless effort to ignore reflexivity required the use of deception in research, and the active concealment of information about psychological processes. By the most elementary canons of the scientific method, psychologists should have realized that generalizations based on naive subjects would apply only to naive subjects and not necessarily to so-phisticated ones. But the dogged pursuit of the natural-science ideal precluded such awareness.

Psychologists did not see that the experimental manipulation of unreflexive phenomena such as rocks, cells or plants is not the same thing as the experimental manipulation of reflexive human beings. Behaviorism's ideal of prediction and control not only fails on scientific grounds but makes the psychologist appear monstrous and contemptuous.

Goal. It would be wrong to reject the scientific model in its entirety; to dismiss the grand history of science and its role in increasing man's understanding of himself and his environment; or to disparage the potential of science to change man's future. Instead we must learn how social forces have restricted the freedom of the scientific enterprise. Science falters now because extrinsic forces have misshaped it. If we are smart, we will use the current unpopularity of science to confront the negative factors that have put us in our present state—and correct them.

We cannot preempt the future, of course, nor should we try to dictate the direction that psychology should take. But we can begin from one strategic premise: *the major function of social science, including psychology, should be to make man aware of the forces that operate on him.* (In psychology, for example, Freud identified some of the internal forces that affect man's emotions and behavior; in sociology, Emile Durkheim explored the social facts in society that control his behavior.) This simple goal will help assure the independence of psychology as a field of study, will reawaken public respect for the discipline, and will contribute to man's freedom and betterment. ⏹

Self-Fulfilling Prophecy

By Robert Rosenthal

Much of our scientific knowledge is based upon careful observation and recording of events. That the observer himself may have a biasing effect on his observations has long been recognized. There are two basic types of experimenter effects. The first operates without affecting the event or subject being studied. It occurs in the eye, the hand and the brain of the researcher. The second type is the result of the *interaction* between the experimenter and the subject of the experiment. And when the research deals with humans and animals, as it does in the behavioral sciences, this interaction actually can alter the responses or data that are obtained.

Quite unconsciously, a psychologist interacts in subtle ways with the people he is studying so that he may get the response he expects to get. This happens even when the person cannot see the researcher. And, even more surprisingly, it occurs when the subject is not human but a rat.

If rats became brighter when expected to by their researcher, isn't it possible that children become brighter when their teachers expect them to be brighter?

Lenore Jacobson, of the South San Francisco Unified School District, and I set out to see if this is so. Every child in an elementary school was given an intelligence test, a test described by us as one that would predict "intellectual blooming."

The school was in a lower socioeconomic neighborhood on the West Coast. There were three classrooms for each grade—one for children of above average ability, one for average ability, and one for below average ability. About 20 per cent of the children in each classroom were chosen at random to form the experimental group. The teachers were given the names of this group and told that these children had scored high on the test for intellectual blooming and would show remarkable gains in intellectual development during the next eight months.

In reality, the only difference between these children and their classmates was *in the minds* of their teachers.

At the end of the school year, all the children were again given the same I.Q. test. In the school as a whole, the children who had been designated as "bloomers" showed only a slightly greater gain in verbal I.Q. (two points) than their classmates. However, *in total* I.Q., the experimental group gained four points more on the average than their counterparts did, and in reasoning I.Q., the average gain was seven points more.

Usually, when educational theorists talk of improving scholastic achievement by improving teacher expectations, they are referring to children at the lower levels of achievement. It was interesting to find that teacher expectations affected children at the highest level of achievement as much as it did children at the lowest level.

At the end of the school year, we asked the teachers to describe the classroom behavior of all their pupils. The children in the group designated as the bloomers were seen as more interesting, more curious, and happier. The teachers also found "blooming" children slightly more appealing, better adjusted, and more affectionate, and with less need for social approval.

Many of the other children in the classes also gained in I.Q. during the year, but teachers reacted negatively to *unexpected* improvement. The more the undesignated children gained in I.Q. points, the more they were regarded as *less* well-adjusted, *less* interesting, and *less* affectionate. It appears that there may be hazards to unpredicted intellectual growth—at least in the eyes of the teacher. This is particularly true of children in the low-ability groups.

The effects of teacher expectation were most evident in reasoning I.Q. gains. But only the girls in the group designated as "bloomers" showed greater gains than the rest of the class. The boys designated as bloomers actually gained less than their classmates. Partly to check this finding, Judy Evans and I repeated the experiment with schoolchildren in a small Midwestern town. The children here were from substantial middle-class families.

Again we found that teacher expectations affected reasoning I.Q. gains in pupils. However, this time it was the boys who tended to show greater gains than girls. These results underline the effects of teacher expectations, but they also indicate the complexity of these effects as a function of the pupil's sex, social status, and very likely other variables as well.

In another study, conducted by Lane K. Conn, Carl N. Edwards, Douglas Crowne and me, we selected an East Coast school with upper-middle-class pupils. This time we also measured the children's accuracy in judging the emotion conveyed in tone of voice. The children who were more accurate in judging the emotional tone of an adult female's voice benefited most from favorable teacher expectations. And in this school, both the boys and girls who were expected to bloom intellectually showed greater reasoning I.Q. gains than their classmates.

W. Victor Beez of Indiana University conducted an experiment in 1967 which sheds some light on the phenomenon of teacher expectancy. His pupils were 60 preschoolers from a summer Head-Start program. Each child had one teacher who taught him the meaning of a series of symbols. Half of the teachers were led to expect good symbol learning, and the other half were led to expect poor learning.

Nearly 77 per cent of the children designated as good intellectual prospects learned five or more symbols. Only 13 per cent of the children designated as poor prospects learned five or more symbols. A researcher from the outside who did not know what the teachers had been told about the children's intellectual prospects assessed the children's actual performance.

What happened in this study was that the teachers with favorable expectations tried to teach more symbols to their pupils than did teachers who had unfavorable expectations. This indicates that the teacher's expectations may not only be translated into subtle vocal and visual nuances, but also may cause dramatic alterations in teaching style. Surprisingly, however, even when the amount of teaching was held constant, the children who were expected to learn more did learn more.

Teacher expectancy effects are not limited to the teaching of intellectual tasks. Recent research reported by J. Randolph Burnham and Donald M. Hartsough of Purdue University indicates that the teaching of motor skills also may be affected by teacher expectations. At a camp for underprivileged children from the Philadelphia area, Burnham administered a test to nonswimmers that ostensibly would predict psychological readiness to swim. He then randomly selected children from various age groups and gave their names to the waterfront counselors as those who were "ready" to swim. He found that the children designated as "ready" tended to pass more of the tests in the Red Cross beginning swimmer's course than the average for their peer group.

If the expectancy effect occurs in the laboratory and in the classroom, then it

is not surprising to find it occurring in everyday life. Your expectation of how another person will behave often may become a self-fulfilling prophecy. We know that nonverbal and unintentional communication between people does take place. What we don't know is *how* such communication occurs. Further research on the interaction of the experimenter and the subject may eventually teach us more about dyadic interactions in general.

The interaction of experimenter and his subject is a major source of knowledge in the behavioral sciences. Until recently, however, this interaction has been an uncontrolled variable in psychological research. But the demonstration of experimenter effects does not necessarily invalidate a great deal of behavioral research. It does mean, however, that we must take extra precautions to reduce "expectancy" and other unintended effects of the experimenter.

Just what does a behavioral scientist unintentionally do in gathering his data so that he unwittingly influences his sub-

jects' responses? This question must be answered satisfactorily if we want to have dependable knowledge in the behavioral sciences.

In our research, we have distinguished five categories of interactional effects between the experimenter and his subjects: the *Biosocial, Psychosocial, Situational, Modeling* and *Expectancy Effects*.

Biosocial Effects

The sex, age and race of investigators all have been found to affect the results of their research. It is tempting to assume that the subjects simply are responding to the biosocial attributes of the investigator. But the investigator himself, because of sex, age or race, may respond differently to male or female, young or old, white or Negro subjects. And even a slight change in behavior alters the experimental situation.

Our evidence suggests, for example, that male and female experimenters conduct the same experiment quite differently. The different results they obtain are not due to any error as such, but may well be due to the fact that they have unintentionally conducted different experiments.

In one study of the effect of the characteristics of subjects on the experimenter, the interaction between experimenters and subjects was recorded on sound film. Only 12 per cent of the investigators smiled even a little at male subjects, but 70 per cent smiled at female subjects. These smiles may well have affected the results of the experiment. It may be a heartening finding to know that chivalry is not dead, but as far as methodology is concerned it is a disconcerting finding. In general, the experimenter treated his male subjects and female subjects differently, so that, in a sense, men and women really were not in the same experiment at all.

Moreover, when we consider the sex of both the experimenter and the subject, other interaction effects emerge. In the study recorded on film, we found that the experimenters took more time to collect some of their data from subjects of the opposite sex than from subjects of the same sex.

The age of the investigator may also affect the subject's response. Studies suggest that young subjects are less likely to say "unacceptable" things to much older investigators, indicating that an "age-barrier" may exist in at least some behavioral studies.

The skin color of the investigator also may affect response, even when the response is physiological.

A number of studies have found that Negroes tend to control their hostility more when contacted by a white rather than a Negro experimenter and give more "proper" responses to white than black interviewers.

Psychosocial Effects

Experimenters are people, and so they differ in anxiety, in their need for approval, in personal hostility, authoritarianism, status and in personal warmth. Experimenters with different personalities tend to get different responses from their experimental subjects. For example, researchers higher in status—a professor as compared to a graduate student, or a captain as compared to a corporal —tend to obtain more responses that *conform* to the investigator's suggestions. And investigators who are warmer toward people tend to obtain more *pleasant* responses.

Situational Effects

Investigators experienced in conducting a given experiment usually obtain responses different from those of less experienced investigators. This may be because they behave differently. Also, experimenters who are acquainted with the people in the experimental group get results that differ from those obtained by researchers who have never met their subjects before.

What happens to the experimenter during the course of his experiment can influence his behavior, and changes in his behavior may lead to changes in the subjects' responses.

For instance, if the first few subjects respond as expected (*i.e.*, confirming the experimenter's hypothesis), the behavior of the researcher alters, and he influences subsequent subjects to respond in a way that supports his hypothesis.

Modeling Effects

Sometimes before an experimenter conducts a study, he first tries out the task he will have his research subjects perform. For example, if the task is to rate a series of 10 photos of faces according to how successful or unsuccessful the persons pictured appear to be, the experimenters may decide to rate the photos themselves before contacting their

subjects. Though evidence is not yet definite, it appears that at least sometimes the investigator's own ratings become a factor in the performance of his subjects. In particular, when the experimental stimuli, such as photos, are ambiguous, the subjects' interpretation may agree too often with the investigator's interpretation, even though the latter remains unspoken.

Some expectation of how the research might turn out is virtually a constant factor in all scientific experiments. In the behavioral sciences, this expectancy can lead the investigator to act unconsciously in such a way that he affects the responses of his subjects. When the investigator's expectancy influences the

responses in the direction of what the investigator expects to happen, we can appropriately regard his hypothesis as a *self-fulfilling prophecy*. One prophesies an event, and the expectation of the event then changes the behavior of the prophet in such a way as to make the prophesied event more likely.

In the history of psychology, the case of *Clever Hans* is a classic example of this phenomenon. Hans was a horse owned by a German mathematics instructor named Von Osten. Hans could perform difficult mathematical calculations, spell, read and solve problems of musical harmony by tapping his foot.

A panel of distinguished scientists and experts on animal behavior ruled that no fraud was involved. The horse was given no cues to tell him when to start or when to stop tapping his foot.

But, of course, there *were* cues. In a series of brilliant experiments reported in 1911, Oskar Pfungst showed that Hans could answer questions only when the questioner himself knew the answers and when the horse could see the questioner. Finally, Pfungst learned that a tiny forward movement of the experimenter's head was the signal for Hans to start tapping. A slight upward movement of the head, or even a raised eyebrow, was the signal for the horse to stop tapping.

Hans's questioners expected him to give the right answers, and their expectation was reflected in their unwitting signals to start and stop tapping. The horse had good eyesight, and he *was* a smart horse.

Self-fulfilling Prophecies

To demonstrate experimenter effects in behavioral research, we must have at least two groups of experimenters with different expectations. One approach is to take a survey of investigators in a certain area of research and ask those with opposite expectancies to conduct a standard experiment. But the differences in the results could be due to factors other than expectancy, and so a better strategy is required.

Rather than trying to find two groups of experimenters with different expectations, we could *create* such groups. In one experiment, we selected 10 advanced undergraduate and graduate students of psychology as our researchers. All were experienced in conducting research. Each was assigned a group of 20 participating students as his subjects. The experiment consisted of showing 10 photographs of people's faces one at a time to each subject. The participant was to rate the degree of success or failure reflected in the facial expression of the person in the photo. Each of the faces could be rated from −10 (extreme failure) to +10 (extreme success). The faces in the photos were actually quite neutral, and on the average the total ratings should have produced a numerical score of zero.

All 10 experimenters had identical instructions to read to their subjects, and they also had identical instructions on how to conduct the experiment. They were specifically cautioned not to deviate from these instructions.

Finally, we informed our researchers that the purpose of the experiment was to see how well they could duplicate results which were already well-estab-

lished. We told half of the experimenters that the "well-established" finding was that people rated the faces in the photos as successful (+5). And we told the other half that people rated the faces in the photos as unsuccessful (−5). And thus informed, they began their research.

The results were clear-cut. Every researcher who was led to expect that the photographed people were successful obtained a higher average rating of success from his group than did any experimenter who expected low-success ratings.

We repeated this experiment twice with different groups with the same results. Research in other laboratories has shown much the same thing. Although not every experiment showed a significant effect, probability that results of all these experiments occurred by chance is less than one in a thousand billion.

Having found that what the experimenter expects to happen can affect the outcome of his research, we then began to look for some clues as to *how* the experimenter unwittingly communicates his expectancy to his subjects.

Through the use of accomplices who acted as subjects in an experiment, we learned how the responses of the first few subjects affected the experimenter's behavior to subsequent subjects. If the responses of the first few subjects confirmed the experimenter's hypothesis, his behavior to subsequent participants somehow influenced them also to confirm his hypothesis. But when the "planted" accomplices contradicted the expectations of the experimenter, the following subjects were affected by the experimenter's behavior so that they, too, tended to disconfirm his hypothesis. It seems, then, that the early returns of data in behavioral research can affect and possibly shape the final results.

Reverse Effects

In some of our experiments, when we offered too-obvious incentives or too-large rewards to investigators to bring in "good" data, the expectancy effect was reduced, and in some cases even reversed. Both the autonomy and the honesty of the researchers may have been challenged by the excessive rewards offered. It speaks well for the integrity of our student-researchers that they would not be bribed. In fact, they

tended to bend over backwards to avoid the biasing effect of their expectation. But they often bent so far backward that the results of their experiments sometimes were the opposite of what they had been told to expect.

The process by which an experimenter unintentionally and covertly communicates instructions to his subjects is very subtle. For six years we have studied sound films of research interviews in an attempt to discover the cues that the experimenter unwittingly gives to the subject, and for six years we have failed, at least partly.

We know, however, that visual cues *are* important. Placing a screen between the investigator and the person he is interviewing reduces the investigator's influence on the results. But the expectancy effect is not eliminated completely, indicating that auditory cues are also important.

This was dramatically demonstrated by John G. Adair and Joyce Epstein of the University of Manitoba in their tape-recording experiment. They first duplicated the expectation effects study in which 10 photographs of people's faces are rated successful or unsuccessful. Half of the investigators were told to expect a success response and half a failure response. Adair and Epstein tape-recorded each of the sessions. The results matched those of the original studies.

Next, with a new group of subjects a second experiment was conducted. But instead of having live investigators, the subjects listened to the tape-recording of an investigator reading the standard instructions to the previous group. Again the results were much the same. Self-fulfilling prophecies, it seems, can come about as a result of the prophet's voice alone. Since in the experiment all prophets read standard instructions, self-fulfillment of prophecies may be brought about by the tone in which the prophet prophesies.

Early in our research on self-fulfilling prophecies, we thought that some form of operant conditioning might be the explanation. It could be that when the investigator obtained a response consistent with his expectations, he would look more pleasant, or smile, or glance

A dull rat

at the subject approvingly. The investigator could be entirely unaware of these reinforcing responses. We analyzed many experiments to see if this type of operant conditioning was present. If indeed it was, then the subject's responses should gradually become more like those expected by the investigator—there would be a "learning curve" for subjects.

But no learning curve was found. On the contrary, it turned out that the first responses of the subject were about as much affected by the investigator's expectations as the last responses.

Further analysis revealed that while there was no learning curve for the subjects, there seemed to be a learning curve for the investigators. As the investigator interviewed more and more subjects, the expectancy effect grew stronger. It appeared possible that the subject's response was the reinforcing event. The subjects, then, may quite unintentionally shape the investigator's behavior. So not only does the experimenter influence his subjects to respond in the expected manner, but the subjects may well influence the experimenter to behave in a way that leads to fulfillment of his prophecies.

Perhaps the most significant implication of this research is that human beings can engage in highly effective and influential unintended communication with one another—even under controlled laboratory conditions.

But do expectancy effects occur when the experimental subjects are not human? We designed a study to find out. Twelve experimenters were each given five rats that were to be taught to run a maze with the aid of visual cues. Six of the experimenters were told that their rats had been specially bred for maze-brightness; the other six were told that their rats had been bred for maze-dullness. Actually, there was no difference between the rats.

At the end of the experiment, researchers with "maze-bright" rats found superior learning in their rats compared to the researchers with maze-dull rats.

A second experiment made use of the special training setup designed by B. F. Skinner of Harvard. Half the researchers were led to believe that their rats were "Skinner box bright" and half were told that their rats were "Skinner box dull." Initially, there were not really such differences in the rats, but at the end of the experiment the allegedly brighter animals *were* really brighter, and the alleged dullards *really* duller.

How can we reduce the expectancy effect in behavioral research?

One way is to design procedures that enable us to assess whether the expectancy effects have altered the results of an experiment. In addition, the experimenter could employ investigators who have not been told the purpose of the study, or automated data-collection systems could be used.

Perhaps a new profession of fulltime experimenters could be developed, who would perform others' experiments without becoming involved in setting up a hypothesis or interpreting the results. Precedents for such professionals are found in both medical research and public-opinion surveys.

Dependable Knowledge

Because of the general nature of expectancy and other experimenter effects, it would be desirable to use more experimenters for each study than we presently use. Having a larger number of returns we could assess the extent to which different experimenters obtained different results, and in any area of psychological research this is worth knowing.

Scientists have long employed control groups in their experiments. Usually the experimental group receives some kind of treatment while the control group receives no treatment. To determine the extent of the expectancy effect, we could add two special "expectancy control" groups to the experiment. In one of these special groups, the investigator would be told that the group's subjects had received some treatment, when in fact it had not. The experimenter in the other group would be told the subjects had not received treatment when in fact it had. Such a research design would permit us to assess the magnitude of the effect of experimenter's expectancy.

To the extent that we hope for dependable knowledge in the behavioral sciences, we must have dependable knowledge about the psychological experiment and the interaction of experimenter and subject. We can no more hope to acquire accurate information for our disciplines without understanding the experimenter effect than astronomers or zoologists could hope to acquire accurate information without understanding the effects of their telescopes and microscopes. And behavioral scientists, being as scientifically self-conscious a group as they are, may one day produce a psychology of those psychologists who study psychologists.

Then, in the laboratory, in the classrooms, in every sector of our lives we will come closer to understanding the effect of a smile.

When He Lends a Helping Hand, Bite It

by Ralph L. Rosnow

The Good Subject for behavioral research, like the proverbial Boy Scout, makes a habit of being useful to others. If he has not helped any little old ladies across the street lately, it may be that no experimenter has asked him to. His creed might be a paraphrase of the song about Lola—"Whatever experimenters want, experimenters get."

Not everyone is willing to play the Good Subject. But many college undergraduates—the favorite research subjects because psychology students are so available—are more than willing to cooperate in psychology experiments. The extent to which some students will collaborate sometimes surprises even the experimenter. At one point in his hypnosis research, Martin Orne, a University of Pennsylvania psychiatrist, tried to devise a set of dull, meaningless tasks that nonhypnotized persons would either refuse to do or would try for only a short time. One task was to add hundreds of thousands of rows of two-digit numbers. Five and a half hours after the subjects began, the experimenter gave up. When the subjects were told to tear each work sheet into a minimum of 32 pieces before going on to the next, they *still* persisted.

Stake. Orne suggests that the students were so compliant because they placed meaning in a meaningless chore. Perhaps they thought that no matter how trivial and inane the task seemed to them the experimenter certainly had an important scientific purpose that justified their work. Feeling that they had a stake in the outcome of the study, the students may have rationalized that they were making a useful contribution to science by acquiescing in the experimenter's implicit demands. This motive is not uncommon among research subjects, Orne contends. The Good Subject tries to comply with what he sees as the experimenter's scientific desires.

Subjects' ideas about what the researcher wants are a mixture of various hints in the experimental procedure. Presumably the subjects evaluate these cues in the context of other information, such as the instructions, the setting, rumors about the purpose of the experiment, and especially their impressions of the experimenter. The typical research subject is an active, aware human being who may be quite interested in the experimenter's results. Thus his behavior will be determined largely by the different cues he sees in the particular situation. Yale psychologist Chris Argyris says that the subject who does not like the experimenter may "enjoy botching the works with such great skill that the experimenter is not aware of this behavior." But if he likes the experimenter, on goes the Boy Scout uniform and out steps the Good Subject.

Foot. In contrast, Milton Rosenberg, a University of Chicago social psychologist, believes that the average subject is afraid that the experimenter plans to evaluate him psychologically and will evaluate his performance unfavorably. Because most people like to look good in front of people they respect, the Good Subject puts his best foot forward. When he gives in to implied demands, probably it is to persuade the experimenter to think favorably of him. Social psychologists Harold Sigall, Elliot Aronson and Thomas Van Hoose have shown that if there is a conflict between the experimenter's scientific desires and giving a good appearance, the subject may prefer to look good rather than cooperate with the experimenter.

Some situations, such as psychological testing, are highly conducive to a fear of evaluation. Experiments that contain an element of surprise or have an aura of mystery may also arouse intense feelings. If a subject is told about the quality of his performance, it is likely that the Good Subject will act to elicit the social approval he wants.

Personality psychologists Douglas Crowne and David Marlowe suggest that when there is a high need for approval, the subject's image may have "something of the quality of the masks worn by the characters in Eugene O'Neill's play, *The Great God Brown*—masks that the characters wear in self-protection and conceal-ment of their inner selves from others." Rosenberg has discovered that when the cues are made explicit, the results will be biased from an ap-prehension of being evaluated. The same is true if the experimenter grants approval or if the subject needs little effort to respond.

Mix. The compliance that Orne found and the apprehension that Rosenberg discovered are not necessarily con-tradictory; they may be pitted against each other or they may interact in a complementary way. This happened in a recent experiment done by Irwin Silverman, a social psychologist at the University of Florida. He randomly assigned undergraduates to four groups that read a 250-word argu-ment in favor of using closed-circuit TV tapes to give lectures to large classes. Silverman predicted that the students would be more persuaded by the argument when they were told that they were subjects in an experi-ment than they would if they were not told, and that they would comply more with the inherent demands if they had to sign their opinions than they would if they were tested anony-mously. This is exactly what occurred.

If we add to this the findings of David Holmes, a University of Texas psychologist, that subjects who have previously participated in experiments are more cooperative than those who

---

"Because most people like to look good in front of people they respect, the Good Subject puts his best foot forward."

---

have not, then it becomes clear that the Good Subject's behavior can be the result of a complex mixture of dif-ferent factors.

Not all subjects are equally com-pliant with experimental demands. But perhaps the most consistently coop-erative is the volunteer, the person who willingly chooses to become a research subject.

Cues. In a series of studies that Har-vard psychologist Robert Rosenthal and I conducted with the help of graduate students Roberta Marmer McConochie and Robert Arms, we compared the reactions of undergrad-uates who had volunteered for a psy-chology experiment with the reactions of a comparable group of nonvolun-teers in experimental tasks in which they were all captive participants.

Volunteer subjects appeared to be more sensitive and accommodating to implicit experimental demands than captive nonvolunteers did. This is complicated by the hints of what is expected in the experiment. When the cues are simple and straightforward but not patently obtrusive, volunteers tend to be more compliant. At the other extreme, when the demands are not readily apparent, differences in the results between experiments us-ing volunteers and those using non-volunteers are negligible. To play Boy Scout in a psychology experiment re-quires the desire *and* a knowledge of what is useful.

When the cues confuse the subjects, interesting differences result. In one study, we gave two statements to female volunteers and nonvolunteers at Boston University, one in favor of fraternities and one opposing them. Each statement was read to a sepa-rate group that contained both non-volunteers and verbal volunteers by a person the subjects regarded as moderately anti-fraternity. The volun-teers were more responsive to the anti-fraternity arguments while the nonvolunteers were more responsive to the pro-fraternity arguments.

Since both volunteers' and nonvol-unteers' opinions about college fra-ternities were initially about the same, we could not attribute the differences after the experiment to attitudes held before it. Our guess is that the volun-teers who heard the pro-fraternity arguments were more accommodat-ing to what they probably saw as the dominant demand—the attitude of the person reading the argument—than they were to the more blatant cues of the argument.

The implication that volunteers are more easily influenced is consistent with other data. Crowne and Marlowe have shown that the need for approval and the ability to be influenced may be directly related. Since volunteers often score higher than nonvolunteers on tests of the need for social ap-proval, again it follows that volunteers may be more easily influenced.

Fear. For several years social psy-chologists have debated whether a person's vulnerability to persuasion increases or decreases according to the amount of fear aroused by emo-tional statements. Irwin Horowitz of the University of Toledo found that experiments supporting the view that more fear increases influenceability were based mainly on volunteer sub-jects. Studies supporting the opposite view were based mainly on captive samples, which may have been com-posed largely of nonvolunteer types.

"If a subject is told about the quality of his performance, it is likely that the Good Subject will act to elicit the social approval he wants."

Horowitz then studied the differ-ence in persuadability of volunteer and nonvolunteer undergraduates. The subjects were assigned randomly to two groups—one in which a high level of fear would be aroused and one in which there would be a low level of fear. The high-fear group read pamphlets on the abuse and effects of drugs and watched two Public Health Service films on the hazards of LSD and other hallucinogens and the dangerous effects of ampheta-mines and barbiturates. The low-fear group did not see the film; they read pamphlets on the hazards of drug abuse, but the vivid verbal descrip-tions of death and disability were omitted. Horowitz found that the vol-unteers in the high-fear group were more persuadable than those in the low-fear group. The nonvolunteers, however, were more persuadable in the low-fear group than in the high-fear group. Apparently, volunteers complied more with the demands they felt from the experiment. Since the nonvolunteers have less need for ap-proval, they are more resistant to demands.

No-Show. The person who volunteers to take part in an experiment and then does not show up poses a prob-lem for research on volunteers and nonvolunteers. The same motive that impels a person to volunteer can sometimes turn him into a no-show.

A person with a high need for social approval might agree impulsively to serve as a subject, just to avoid appearing uncooperative or implying that he had something to hide. After he has thought about the possibility that he might perform poorly, his fear of unfavorable evaluation might lead him to invent some excuse for failing to appear for the experiment. This pseudo-volunteer is a difficulty for research that compares verbal volunteers with nonvolunteers. As Sigall, Aronson and Van Hoose put it, "How do we know that the data we are using to discuss possibly biased data are not, in and of themselves, biased?"

Unfortunately we know very little about the causes and effects of volunteering and then not showing. The little information that is available suggests that people who don't show may be more like nonvolunteers than volunteers who do keep their appointments. If this is true, we may actually be underestimating the real effect of whether a subject has volunteered or not because our volunteer groups may have included people who under other circumstances would not have shown up.

Kinsey. Bias resulting from volunteer subjects is also a hazard in survey research. The question was particularly important in the early 1950s when the Kinsey sex reports were pub-

lished. Alfred Kinsey's subjects, because they were willing to be interviewed, might have had other characteristics that made them different from people who were unwilling to be interviewed. If this was the case, then the results could not be generally applied to the rest of the population. In 1952 Abraham Maslow and James Sakoda suggested that for two reasons Kinsey's subjects may have had different sexual behavior from those who refused to be interviewed. First, persons who were willing to partici-

pate in a Kinsey-type interview tended to have higher self-esteem than those who were unwilling. Second, persons who have high self-esteem tend to have unconventional sexual attitudes and behavior.

Self-esteem and the need for approval are not the only variables that distinguish willing subjects from unwilling ones. In our recent reviews of the extensive and sometimes contradictory published results on research bias in this area, we noted that volunteers tend to score higher on I.Q. tests than nonvolunteers. Standardizing an intelligence test on volunteers will probably produce artificially higher norms. The same is true for standardizing tests of the need for social approval and self-esteem. There are other characteristics that apparently are reliable differences between volunteers and nonvolunteers. Volunteers tend to be better educated and to hold positions of higher status than nonvolunteers. They are also less authoritarian, more sociable, more unconventional, more often first-born and younger, and they seek arousal more than nonvolunteers.

Pitchmen. Although it is possible to speculate that each of these other characteristics may possibly bias research results, it is difficult to predict them because volunteering is partly determined by the situation. Stanley Schachter and Robert Hall have shown, for example, that when an associate volunteers, others will follow more easily. The same technique, they point out, is used by pitchmen who employ stooges to make a conspicuous first purchase and by fund-raisers who stimulate contributions by announcing generous donations from others.

Milton Rosenbaum has shown a similar effect in other situations. Students at the University of Texas were asked to be subjects in psychological research. Significantly more students agreed to participate when Rosenbaum's accomplice agreed than when there was no accomplice. And fewer students would take part when there was an accomplice who refused than when there was no accomplice. A person will have more than one motive for volunteering and may be pushed by internal forces while simultaneously being pulled by external ones.

Bias. The problem facing the experimenter is to increase the representativeness of his subjects and at the

same time eliminate the Good-Subject reaction and encourage authentic response. Not having a representative sample is a ubiquitous source of bias.

Reginal Smart, a Canadian psychologist, estimated that four out of five published psychological studies of nonpsychiatric adults in the United States have college undergraduates as subjects. This means that 80 per cent of the research is based on the three per cent of the population that is in college. Smart asks, "How do we know that the majority of our research on social processes, attitudes,

verbal learning, and personality is doing any more than exploring the vicissitudes of the present...college population?"

Chris Argyris mentions that several graduate students have considered forming a student organization that would provide human subjects for hire as Manpower, Inc. provides secretaries. Undergraduates would be promised more money, better and greater feedback about their performance. If the enterprise succeeds, the old saw about psychology being a science of the behavior of the college sophomore may prove to have been too liberal a view. The psychology of the future would be a science with research restricted to those highly motivated college students who volunteer and who are fully aware of what the experimenter is seeking.

Fortunately, these difficulties are at least recognized and an effort is being made to try to solve them. Research of the social psychology of the psychological experiment has become increasingly popular. The result is that several control procedures have already been devised to estimate the effects of various sources of bias. The problem of complete control is proving to be exceedingly complex. It turns out to be very difficult to keep a Boy Scout-Good Subject from being prepared, courteous, loyal and very helpful. Ω

Jokers Wild In the Lab

by Zick Rubin

Two young men, college sophomores, sit at a table facing a screen, electrodes clamped to their wrists. A tall young man explains to them that he is a graduate student in psychology and that he is investigating homosexual arousal: the students are to watch pictures of men projected on the screen while a galvanometer hooked to the electrodes monitors subtle changes in their skin conductivity. These responses will measure the extent of their homosexual arousal. The more the needle jumps, the more homosexual they are. And, as the students watch photographs of seminude men, they find to their dismay that the needles do a lot of jumping. . . .

The tall young man was indeed a graduate student—named Dana Bramel—then working on his Ph.D. thesis at Stanford. But nothing else Bramel told the sophomores was true. The electrodes were not connected to the galvanometer. Bramel controlled it from a hidden switchboard. And he was *not* studying homosexual arousal, but rather the mechanisms underlying the defensive projection of undesirable traits to others. (One conclusion:

students who thus "learn" that they are homosexual often decide that their friends are too.)

The sophomores, serving as experimental subjects to meet a requirement of their introductory psychology course, invariably fell for Bramel's story. Afterward, of course, he told them what he was really up to. Some of his subjects thought it was a good joke. Others probably did not.

Tricks. This experiment typifies a popular mode of social-psychological research that many psychologists don't like to talk about. It centers on trickery that ranges from harmless clownery to the downright diabolical.

Take an example from Ohio State: the trusting subject sits in front of a large steel machine with an impressive array of push buttons, lights and toggle switches. The experimenter says he is studying motor learning and that the subject's task will be to turn lights on and off consecutively by pushing appropriate buttons. After demonstrating the procedure the experimenter explains that, "All my research money is tied up in this contraption and I'll never get my master's degree if it doesn't function properly." Forewarned, the subject starts pushing buttons carefully—but, as the script dictates, never carefully enough. Soon he hears a deafening bang followed by a shrieking whistle and swirling clouds of thick white smoke. The experimenter now speaks in a broken voice, "I'll never get my master's now . . . (choke) . . . What did you do to the machine? . . . (sob) . . . Well, I guess that ends the experiment . . . (long pause and then solemnly) . . . The machine is broken."

On this tragic note, the subject mumbles his apologies and prepares to leave. But before he can do so the experimenter suddenly brightens and asks a favor. "I'm a member of the Young Democrats and have to circulate this petition," he says. "As long as you're here, would you sign it?" The petition reads: "The tuition at Ohio State University should be doubled to improve the quality of the faculty and the physical condition of the university." It is a safe bet (which was confirmed with control subjects) that virtually no sane Ohio student would sign such a declaration. But 56 per

cent of the guilt-stricken experimental subjects did.

Bias. Some social psychologists argue that such techniques are essential in studying such phenomena as persuasion, conformity, aggression and embarrassment. One cannot simply ask people about such things and expect objective answers. It is to counteract these biasing effects that the experimenter resorts to deception. By creating a believable cover story and catching the subject off guard, the experimenter increases the likelihood that his results will reflect real social behavior.

There is little doubt that trumped-up laboratory happenings can yield valuable information. A classic example is the series of psychodramas staged in the late 1940s by Solomon Asch at Swarthmore. The studies pretended to deal with visual acuity but they were in fact concerned with conformity. In one variant of the script, seven students were asked in turn which of three lines was identical in length to a comparison line. Actually only one of the students was really a subject and he was maneuvered into the next-to-last position. The other six were paid confederates instructed to make judgments that were clearly, often ludicrously, incorrect. The key question was: How often would the subject go along with the crowd?

Critics. Asch's experiments were widely applauded by social scientists. But during the 1950s and particularly the 1960s, laboratory playwrights proliferated. As they have gained in popularity, the productions have evolved from unexciting skits into dazzling—often terrifying—extravaganzas.

And they have been criticized. Members of the profession decry what they consider to be a move from science to fun and games. Kenneth Ring of the University of Connecticut has noted that "There is a distinctly exhibitionistic flavor to much current experimentation, while the experimenters often seem to equate notoriety with achievement." Also, the deception involved has been called dehumanizing and some experimenters have been accused of doing serious psychological harm to unsuspecting and unconsenting subjects.

The theater where the dramas take

place is usually a suite of soundproof rooms equipped with one-way mirrors, an intercom system, and an assortment of electrical gadgetry. The cast includes experimenter, subject, and often an additional performer popularly known as a stooge. The stooge is an assistant of the experimenter who advances the plot in the guise of a fellow subject or an uninvolved bystander.

In Asch's studies, for example, the stooge's major task was to keep a straight face while making ridiculous perceptual judgments. In recent years stooge assignments have become more diverse. They have had to insult subjects (while the subjects watch through a one-way mirror), to impersonate deaf people (in a study of attitudes toward the deaf), and to exhibit spontaneous and unrestrained euphoria (in a study dealing with the contagion of emotion), among other chores.

Date. Other stooges are cast in more melodramatic roles. The drift toward soap opera is illustrated by an experiment conducted by Elaine Walster, now a professor at the University of Wisconsin. Walster wondered whether a young woman's self-esteem affects her propensity to fall in love.

The cast consisted of 37 Stanford and Foothill Junior College coeds, and the romantic lead was played by Gerald Davison, a matinee-idol-type graduate student. As the drama opened, each girl arrived at an empty reception room where a sign asked her to wait for the experimenter. Then Davison, smooth and well-dressed, came out and explained that he was waiting for another experimenter. After a few moments of silence, Davison casually began a conversation, and in 32 out of 37 cases, was able to make a date with the subject.

The experimenter then arrived and escorted each happily deluded subject to another room, where she explained that the purpose of the study was to compare various personality tests. The subject had previously taken a test and now she saw an evaluation of her own personality prepared by a "therapist" in San Francisco. Half of the girls got the great news that they possessed, among other things, "sensitivity to peers, per-

sonal integrity, originality and freedom of outlook." The remaining girls received far-less-glowing reports, such as, "Although she has adopted certain superficial appearances of maturity . . . her basically immature drives remain. . . . She shows a weak personality, antisocial motives, a lack of flexibility and originality, and a lack of capacity for successful leadership . . . Her feelings of inadequacy led her constantly to overestimate many of her own characteristics." (If these girls hadn't had feelings of inadequacy before the experiment began, they surely had at this point.)

Next the girls were asked to rate how much they liked certain persons, including a teacher, a friend, "and, since we have one space left, why don't you also rate that fellow from Miss Turner's study whom you were waiting with?" This evaluation was the point of all the preceding rigamarole. The result: subjects with lowered self-esteem (the ones told that they were immature, etc.) reported that they liked Davison more than did the girls with raised self-esteem.

Curtain. In the final act of the melodrama, Walster confessed to the young innocents that the personality appraisal was phony, that they were not really all that bad or all that good, and finally—the crushing blow—that the date must be broken. "I was just so upset," Walster told me when I discussed the experiment with her. "It wasn't just breaking the date, but that they might be embarrassed that a guy could con them to that extent." To reassure her subjects she stressed the fact that *nobody* turned Gerry down, and that even if he wanted to, Gerry was forbidden to date any subject. Finally, the girls were sworn to secrecy. According to Walster, virtually all of them went away happy.

I asked Davison, who is now a professor at the State University of New York at Stony Brook, how he felt about his stooging experience. His answer: "I have regretted ever participating in it. Looking back on the study now, I have concluded that the importance of the results did not justify the magnitude and/or the quality of the manipulations."

Shock. Equally troubling questions are raised by the widely reported

studies of obedience done at Yale by Stanley Milgram. His subjects were men from a wide range of occupations who were told that they were to take part in a study of the effects of punishment on memory.

First a pair of subjects drew straws to decide who was to be the teacher and who was to be the learner. The learner was then taken into an adjacent room (out of the teacher's sight) and strapped into the laboratory version of an electric chair, where electrodes were attached to his arms. The teacher, meanwhile, was seated behind a precision-made shock generator, ostensibly capable of delivering painful jolts to the learner. The generator had 30 clearly marked voltage levels with switches ranging from 15 to 450 volts, and with labels ranging from "Slight Shock" to "Danger: Severe Shock." Two additional switches were designated only as "XXX."

The learner's task was to memorize a list of word pairs. Whenever he made a mistake the teacher was to punish him by administering a shock, increasing the intensity one step each time. Before they began, the teacher himself was given a "mild" shock of 45 volts, to make it painfully clear that the shocks were real. As the session went on, the learner made many mistakes and had to be given increasingly severe shocks. The pain seemingly became excruciating. As the level of the shocks increased, the learner grunted, moaned and hollered, demanding to be released. After 315 volts the learner no longer answered, but groaned whenever a shock was administered and finally stopped making any sounds at all.

The learner was, of course, a stooge. The shock generator was phony and the learner's protests were really on tape. The teacher, who was the only real subject (the drawing was fixed), didn't know this. The object of the study was to find out at what point he would refuse to obey the experimenter's commands.

Wreck. For many subjects, the experience was terrifying. "I observed an initially poised businessman enter the laboratory smiling and confident," one of Milgram's observers reported. "Within 20 minutes he was reduced to a twitching, stuttering wreck, who was rapidly approaching a point of nervous collapse. He constantly pulled on his earlobe and twisted his hands. At one point he pushed his fist into his forehead and muttered, 'Oh God, let's stop it.' And yet he continued to respond to every word of the experimenter, and obeyed to the end." (Sixty per cent did so.)

Some psychologists contend that Milgram's procedures may have caused severe psychological harm. Herbert Kelman of Harvard suggests that "at least some of the obedient subjects came away from this experience with lowered self-esteem, having to live with the realization that they were willing to yield to destructive authority to the point of inflicting extreme pain on a fellow human being."

Many experiments have been at least as ghoulish as Milgram's. For example, a group of Army psychologists at the then-called Leadership Human Research Unit in Monterey, California has studied reactions of new recruits to extreme stress. Unwitting subjects were made to believe, among other things, that they were on a plane about to make a crash-landing, and that they were personally responsible for an explosion that had seriously injured a soldier.

Value. Milgram's work has a social importance that, in my view, vastly overweighs any psychological harm it may have inflicted, and which was probably minimal. He carefully screened his subjects before the experiment, painstakingly dehoaxed them afterward, and had a psychiatrist follow up on them.

There is a question, however, whether much of the work of laboratory manipulators is science at all. The orientation toward fun-and-games, as Ring has noted, is often antithetical to the proper scientific goals of increasing knowledge and, ultimately, serving the public good. Worse, many experimental social psychologists have taken deception for granted. They have assumed that the

moral value of honesty, which they subscribe to in virtually all other contexts, is simply irrelevant to their behavior in the laboratory. This, in my view, is an unjustified conceit.

Kelman has argued cogently that tricks in the laboratory help to create an image of man as "an object to be manipulated at will." As he puts it, "Deception has been turned into a game, often played with great skill and virtuosity. . . . In institutionalizing the use of deception in psychological experiments we are contributing to a historical trend that threatens values most of us cherish."

"Pretend." To eliminate all deceptive experiments would be a mistake. I am convinced that many are of potentially great scientific and social importance. However, psychologists should first consider more straightforward methods of gathering data— even if they seem to be less fun.

Such reflection has recently come into vogue, and there has been a discernible trend toward nondeceptive role-playing procedures. In such studies, subjects are asked in effect to *pretend* that they are taking part in an experiment. The procedures of the pseudoexperiment are carefully explained to them, and they are asked to behave as they think they would if they were really in the experimental situation.

Many social psychologists doubt the validity of such an approach, however. A characteristic opinion is that of Columbia's Jonathan Freedman, who calls most role-playing studies "a return to the prescientific days when intuition and consensus took the place of data." Although Freedman may be right, the potential value of such procedures certainly deserves to be explored systematically.

At the same time that they are being beset by a storm of ethical criticism, social psychologists have also been required to refine their methods in response to pragmatic concerns. Students on many campuses have be-

come increasingly alert to deceptive techniques. As a result, experimenters have been resorting to increasingly complex deceptions and double-deceptions. "It's like bugs and DDT," one researcher told me. Others seek new sources of uncorrupted subjects, including nursery-school students, mental patients, and church groups.

Real. Still another way to combat subject sophistication is to stage experiments in real-life settings. The New York City subway stretch from 59th Street to 125th Street in Manhattan was the scene of a naturalistic study of altruism conducted recently by Irving and Jane Piliavin of the University of Pennsylvania and Judith Rodin of New York University. A young male rider simulated collapse on the subway-car floor, while observers recorded who came to his aid and how quickly they did so. And James Bryan of Northwestern and Mary Ann Test of Mendota State Hospital in Wisconsin set up shop on a Los Angeles thoroughfare to study the role of imitation in altruistic behavior—in this case, helping a stooge change a flat tire. Such real-life experiments are becoming increasingly popular, and they are of potentially great value in helping to span the gulf between studies of social behavior in the laboratory and in real life.

Nevertheless the vast majority of laboratory playwrights continue to stage their performances in the soundproof rooms with the flashing lights and the one-way mirrors, and their stars continue to be unsuspecting— they hope—college students. As ethical criticism intensifies and the credibility gap widens between experimenter and subject, some observers foresee an early end to psychology's theater of the absurd. "It might just die," Milgram said ruefully, "like acupuncture and bloodletting." But others are convinced (and they are probably right) that the battle of wits between experimenter and subject will go on— like bugs and DDT. ∩

II. brain and behavior

For years scientists have studied various inputs to and outputs of the brain, but the activity of the brain itself had been beyond the reach of scientific observation. Now researchers using modern neurophysiological and psychological techniques have begun to unravel the mysteries of the brain's mechanisms; their discoveries will undoubtedly revolutionize scientific theory and psychiatric practice.

One of the techniques now used to study the brain is electrical stimulation. José Delgado, a foremost practitioner of electrical stimulation of the brain (ESB), reviews the recent history of psychophysiological research using ESB and shows how different behavioral responses can be evoked by stimulating specific cortical and subcortical structures. Delgado also discusses the therapeutic use of ESB in cases of mental and physiological illness and related ethical controversies, such as the concern that ESB, in the hands of a well-meaning neurosurgeon—or a ruthless dictator—could shape a person's personality.

While the lay person hears of ESB as a possible cure for the mentally ill or reads novels about computer-controlled minds, scientists attempt to separate fact from fiction by rigorously delineating the characteristics of electrically induced behavior: Are electrically induced responses similar to spontaneous responses? And which patterns of behavior can be elicited by electrode stimulation? Psychophysiologist J. Anthony Deutsch, for example, specifies the differences in rats' behavior produced by natural rewards, such as food, and stimulation of the brain's so-called pleasure centers. Deutsch is concerned with discovering which type of reward is more effective in creating drive states and other activity and with postulating some future uses of electrical pleasure.

Electrical stimulation is by no means the only method of stimulating or directly altering brain activity. Although the idea of implanting electrodes within the human brain to change undesirable behavior is repulsive to many, there seems to be less opposition to modifying the antisocial or abnormal reactions of mental patients through the use of drugs. Psychopharmacologist Murray Jarvik reviews the use of drugs and provides a description of the methodology used to determine the effectiveness of various tranquilizers and stimulants. He makes a strong argument for collaborative research among biochemists, neurophysiologists, and psychologists in drug research.

Still another technique for regulating the brain and behavior is illustrated by the work of Joe Kamiya, who has taught individuals to consciously control their brain waves. With his noted research program on the feasibility of alpha-wave conditioning, Kamiya has begun to explore human consciousness and its relationship to the autonomic nervous system. He sees such investigations of consciousness as the possible key to unifying the subjective and objective aspects of psychology and psychiatry. He also hopes to determine whether training individuals to control their bodily states increases their ability to learn or to cope with anxiety.

Peter Lang, using an operant feedback method similar to that used by Kamiya, has demonstrated that visceral responses can be shaped in the same way as any other behavior. The work of Lang and others has now destroyed the traditional dichotomy of voluntary and involuntary responses and has altered theoretical conceptions of human emotion. Visceral learning has the potential of becoming an important therapeutic method, especially if individuals can be trained to manipulate their heart rates and blood pressure to avoid or overcome emotional disturbance or systemic disease.

Michael Chase sounds a warning to those who feel that visceral or brain-wave conditioning is already of therapeutic value and stresses that the use of biofeedback machines should be regulated. The brain controls every organ in the body, and when electrical activity is modified in one part of the body, potentially harmful changes may occur elsewhere.

Perhaps the most exciting discoveries in the last few years of research on the brain have been in the area of sleep and dreaming. For centuries theologians, philosophers, and physiologists have pondered the functions and outputs of the sleeping brain. Ralph Berger describes a recent breakthrough achieved by psychologists and physiologists who have identified the various stages of sleep and dreaming that occur throughout a typical night's rest. Knowing the physiological indices of each stage, researchers can wake dreaming subjects and capture dream reports that might otherwise have been forgotten by morning. It is now possible for researchers to proceed with important investigations into the frequency and duration of dream periods, the degree to which eye movements during dream periods indicate the content of the dream, and the physiological and emotional functions of sleep.

Typical of the research sparked by the discovery of sleep indicators is the work of Montague Ullman and Stanley Krippner. They have attempted to influence the dreams of a sleeping subject by having their agent send telepathic messages to the sleeper. They have obtained results that statistically confirm the existence of a telepathic effect, and now they are trying to determine if paranormal experiences are indeed within the realm of scientific explanation.

Hypnosis, like telepathic communication, has long fascinated the lay person; demonstrations of hypnosis by theatrical performers have been presented on television and in night-club acts. However, psychologists have been unable to agree on an operational definition of hypnotism, and Theodore Barber even doubts its existence as a discrete state of consciousness. There is little scientific evidence for a "hypnotic trance" that enables individuals to accomplish feats supposedly impossible for them to perform in the waking state. Barber, in a series of ingenious experiments, has tested his notions against the evidence offered by those who believe in hypnosis.

Gardner Murphy, a former president of the American Psychological Association, abstracts some of the more reliable findings in parapsychological research and encourages his colleagues to accept this pioneer field as worthy of serious study. He proposes a framework for the collection of scientific evidence but suggests that parapsychological theories and research programs do not necessarily need to dovetail with traditional physical concepts and facts.

With so much interest and research in the mechanisms of the brain, it is inevitable that questions of social control should arise. Psychosurgery and drug therapy are two components of a psychotechnology that Stephen Chorover feels is being fraudulently advanced as a proper approach to the solution of social conflicts. Chorover, a physiological psychologist, warns of an apparent predisposition to use technological advances to control social deviance and political dissent in ways that are essentially totalitarian. Control through psychotechnology must not be used as a substitute for dealing with social issues, he says, and human behavior must be recognized as part of a complex sociobiological system.

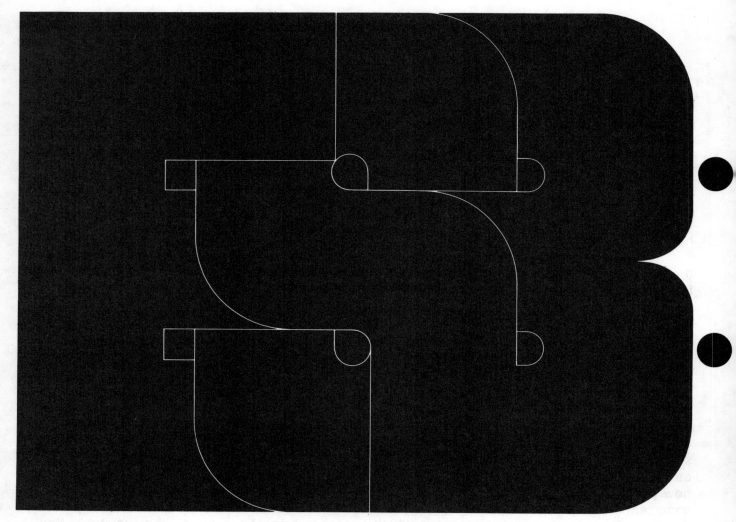

Electrical Stimulation of the Brain can put human beings through the paces from fear, anxiety, rage, aggression, pain, alertness, volubility and euphoria to near-orgasm. ESB prevails over free will. It is a foot in the door of an infinitely bigger world.

by José M. R. Delgado

The history of Electrical Stimulation of the Brain (ESB) is very recent, but already there is much information about its effectiveness and much fear about the dangers of its social misuses. Could a ruthless dictator stand at a master radio transmitter and stimulate the brains of a mass of hopelessly enslaved people? This Orwellian nightmare may provide a good plot for a novel but fortunately it is beyond the theoretical and practical limits of ESB. We cannot, by means of ESB, substitute one personality for another nor can we make a behaving robot of a human being. It is true that we can influence emotional reactivity and make a patient more aggressive or amorous, but in each case the details of behavioral expression are related to an individual history that cannot be created by ESB.

THE CHRONICLE OF CIVILIZATION is the story of a cooperative venture consistently marred by self-destruction, and every advance has been accompanied by increasingly efficient violent behavior. Firearms have made unskilled individuals more powerful than mythical warriors of the past. The technology for destruction has placed at the disposal of man a vast arsenal of ingenious weapons that threaten the very existence of civilization.

Violence is a product of cultural environment and is an extreme form of aggression, distinct from self-expression required for survival and development under normal conditions. Man may react to unpleasant or painful stimuli with violence—but only if he has been taught by his culture to react in this manner. We should remember that it is normal for an animal to urinate when the bladder is full and to mount any available female during mating season, but that these behaviors may be controlled in man through training.

Aggression. Human aggression may be considered a behavioral response characterized by force intended to inflict damage on persons or objects. The phenomenon may be analyzed in three components: *inputs,* environmental circumstances perceived through sensory receptors; *throughputs,* the personal processing of these circumstances through the intracerebral mechanisms; and *outputs,* the expressions of individual and social behavior that constitute observable aggression. The essential link in the nervous system often is forgotten. It is however an incontrovertible fact that the environment is only the provider of sensory inputs that must be interpreted by the brain. Any kind of behavior is the result of intracerebral activity. Sociologists as well as biologists therefore should recognize that experimental investigation of the cerebral structures responsible for aggressive behavior is an essential counterpart of social studies.

Rage. In animals, the first demonstration that offensive activity could be evoked by ESB was provided by W. R. Hess. It has subsequently been confirmed by numerous investigators. Cats under electrical stimulation of the periventricular gray matter acted "as if threatened by a dog," responding with unsheathed claws and well-aimed blows. Is this a false or sham rage containing the motor components of offensive display without actual emotional participation? These issues have been debated over the years, but today it is clear that both sham rage and true rage can be elicited by ESB, depending on the location of stimulation.

Monkeys are more interesting subjects than cats for study because of their more numerous and skillful spontaneous activities. Monkey colonies constitute autocratic societies in which one animal establishes itself as boss, claiming a large portion of the territory, feeding first. He is avoided by the others, who express their submissiveness by grimacing, crouching and offering sexual play. Radio stimulation of specific points in the thalamus or central gray in the boss monkey increased his aggressiveness and induced attacks against other members of the group. His hostility was oriented purposefully and according to his previous experience; he usually attacked the other male who represented a challenge to his authority and always spared the little female who was his favorite partner.

Fury. Would the social inhibitions of lower-ranking members of the colony block electrically induced hostility? We investigated this question in one colony by changing its composition to increase progressively the social rank of a female

named Lina. In the first grouping of four animals Lina ranked lowest; she progressed to number three in the second group, and to number two in the third. On two successive mornings in each colony, Lina was radio stimulated for five seconds each minute for one hour in the nucleus posterolateralis of the thalamus. In all three colonies, these stimulations induced Lina to run across the cage, climb to the ceiling, lick, vocalize and—according to her social status—to attack other animals. In the group where Lina was submissive, she attacked another monkey only once, and she was threatened or attacked 24 times. In group two she became more aggressive (24 occurrences) and was attacked only three times. In group three Lina attacked other monkeys 79 times and was not threatened at all. No changes in the number of antagonistic acts were observed in any group before or after the stimulation hour, showing that alterations in Lina's aggressive behavior were determined by ESB.

Input. It is interesting that electronic stimulation of the brain modified the interpretation of the environment, changing the peaceful relations of a group of animals into sudden overt hostility. The same sensory inputs provided by the presence of other animals—which were neutral during control periods—were under ESB the cues for a ferocious and well-directed attack. Apparently brain stimulation introduced an emotional bias that altered interpretation of the surroundings.

While neurophysiological activity may be influenced or perhaps even set by genetic factors and past experience, the brain is the direct interpreter of environmental inputs and the determinant of behavioral responses. Electricity cannot determine the target for hostility or direct the sequences of aggressive behavior. Artificially and spontaneously provoked aggression have many elements in common, suggesting that in both cases similar areas of the brain have been activated.

While acts of violence may seem distant from the electrical discharges of neurons, we should remember that personality is not in the environment but in the nervous tissue. Possible solutions to undesirable aggression obviously will not be found in the use of ESB. But without knowledge of the brain it will be difficult to correlate social causality with individual reactivity.

Fear. The direct induction of fear in humans without any other accompanying

sensation has been reported by several investigators. Lesions in the medial thalamus give effective pain relief with minimal sensory loss, and for this reason the thalamus often has been explored electrically in cancer patients. In some cases it has produced acute anxiety attacks, which one patient vividly described: "It's rather like the feeling of having just been missed by a car and leaping back to the curb and going B-r-r-r." The unpleasant sensation of fear was felt in one side of the body, contralateral to the brain stimulation.

In one of our female patients stimulation of the dorsolateral nucleus of the thalamus induced a fearful expression and she turned to either side, visually exploring the room behind her. When she was asked what she was doing she replied that she felt a threat and thought that something horrible was going to happen. The response started with a delay of less than one second, lasted for as long as the stimulation, and did not leave observable after-effects. The patient remembered her fear but was not upset by the memory.

Fear is a cerebral interpretation of reality that depends on a variety of cultural and experiential factors with logical or illogical reasons. The fact that it can be aroused by stimulation of a few areas of the brain allows us to explore the neuronal mechanisms of anxiety. As a working hypothesis we may suppose that the emotional qualities of fear depend on the activation of determined structures located probably in the thalamus, amygdala and a few other as yet unidentified nuclei. Knowledge of intracerebral mechanisms of anxiety and fear will permit the establishment of a more rational pharmacological and psychiatric treatment of many suffering patients, and may also help us to understand and ameliorate the increasing level of anxiety in our civilization.

Anger. It is known that in some tragic cases abnormal neurological processes may cause unreasonable and uncontrollable violence. Those afflicted may often hurt or even kill strangers or close family members. J. P. was a charming and attractive 20-year-old girl with a history of encephalitis at 18 months and crises of temporal lobe seizures and *grand mal* attacks for the last 10 years. Her main social problem was frequent, unpredictable rage, which on more than a dozen occasions resulted in her assaulting another person with a knife or scissors. The patient was committed to a ward for the criminally insane, and

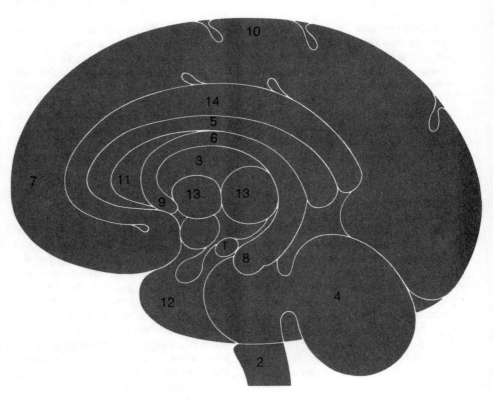

1 amygdala
2 brain stem
3 caudate nucleus
4 cerebellum
5 corpus callosum
6 fornix
7 frontal lobe
8 hippocampus
9 hypothalamus
10 motor cortex
11 septal region
12 temporal lobe
13 thalamus
14 transitional cortex

electrodes were implanted in her amygdala and hippocampus for exploration of possible neurological abnormalities. She became one of the first clinical cases instrumented with a stimoceiver, which made it possible to study intracerebral activity without restraint. Depth recordings taken while the patient moved freely around the ward demonstrated marked electrical abnormalities in both amygdala and hippocampus. Spontaneous periods of aimless walking coincided with increased high voltage sharp waves. At other times the patient's speech was inhibited for several minutes although she retained partial comprehension and awareness. The patient read papers, conversed with others and walked around without causing noticeable alteration in the telemetered intracerebral electrical activity.

Assaultive behavior similar to the patient's spontaneous bursts of anger could be elicited by radio stimulation of contact three in the right amygdala. This point was stimulated while she was playing the guitar and singing with enthusiasm. At the seventh second of stimulation she threw away the guitar and in a fit of rage attacked the wall and then paced the floor for several minutes. Then she gradually quieted down and resumed her usual cheerful behavior. This effect was repeated on two different days. That only the contact located in the amygdala induced rage suggested that the neuronal field around contact three was involved in the patient's behavior problem. This finding was of great clinical significance in subsequent treatment.

Although the patient seemed out of control in this electrically induced aggression she did not attack the interviewer, indicating that she was aware of her social situation. This is reminiscent of the stimulated monkeys who directed their aggressiveness according to previous experience and social rank. Apparently ESB can induce a state of increased violent reactivity that is expressed in accordance with individual structure and environmental circumstances.

Hedonism. In psychological literature pleasure has been considered a subjective name for the diminution of drive, the withdrawal of strong stimulation or the reduction of pain. This pain-reduction theory has been fruitful as a basis for psychological investigations, but it is gloomy to think that we live in a world of punishment in which the only reality is suffering and that our brain can perceive different degrees of pain but no real pleasure.

Recent experimental studies have renewed interest in earlier ideas of hedonism. According to this theory pain and pleasure are relatively independent sensations and can be evoked by different stimuli that are recognized by separate cerebral mechanisms. Behavior is considered to be motivated by stimuli that the organism tries to minimize (pain) or by stimuli that the organism tries to maximize (pleasure). The discovery of two anatomically distinct mechanisms in the brain, one for punishment and one for reward, provided a physiological basis for the dualistic motivation postulated in hedonism.

Animals of different species have vol-untarily chosen to press a lever that provided electrical stimulation of specific cerebral areas. The demonstrations are highly convincing because animals that initially pressed a lever to obtain sugar pellets later pressed at similar or higher rates when electrical stimulation was substituted for food. Watching a rat or monkey stimulate its own brain is a fascinating spectacle. Usually each pressing of the lever triggers a brief brain stimulation that can be more rewarding than food. Hungry rats ran faster to reach the self-stimulation lever than to obtain pellets, and they persistently pressed this lever, ignoring food that was within easy reach. Rats have removed obstacles, run mazes and even crossed electrified floors to reach a lever that provided cerebral stimulation.

Systematic analysis of the distribution of pleasurable areas in the rat shows that 60 per cent of the brain is neutral, 35 per cent is rewarding and only five per cent may elicit punishing effects. The idea that far more brain is involved in pleasure than in suffering offers the optimistic hope that this predominance of the potential for pleasurable sensations can be developed into a more effective behavioral reality.

Any idea about the kind of pleasure animals experience during ESB is a matter of speculation. There are some indications, however, that the perceived sensation could be related to anatomical differentiation of primary rewards of food and sex, because hungry animals stimulated themselves more in the middle hypothalamus, while castrated rats that received sex hormones did more lever-pressing in the more lateral hypothalamic points.

The controversial issue of how these findings in animals may relate to human behavior has been resolved by the information obtained in patients with implanted electrodes.

Orgasm. Studies in human subjects with implanted electrodes have demonstrated that electrical stimulation of the depth of the brain can induce pleasurable manifestations, as shown by spontaneous verbal reports of patients, their facial expressions and general behavior, and their desire to repeat the experience. In a group of 23 patients suffering from schizophrenia, electrical stimulation of the septal region, located deep in the frontal lobes, produced enhanced alertness sometimes accompanied by increased verbal output, euphoria or pleasure. In a more systematic study one man suffering from narcolepsia was given a small stimulator and a built-in counter that recorded the number of times he voluntarily stimulated each of several selected points in his brain. During a period of 17 weeks the highest score was recorded from one point in the septal region and the patient declared that pushing this particular button made him feel good, as if he were building up to a sexual climax, although he was not able to reach the end-point, or orgasm, and often felt impatient and anxious. His narcolepsia was greatly relieved by pushing this septal button. Another patient with psychomotor epilepsy also enjoyed septal self-stimulation, which again had the highest rate of button-pressing and often induced sexual thoughts.

Giggles. In our own experience pleasurable sensations were observed in patients with psychomotor epilepsy. One case was V. P., a 36-year-old woman with a long history of epileptic attacks that could not be controlled by medication. Electrodes were implanted in her right temporal lobe and upon stimulation of a contact located in the superior part about 30 millimeters below the surface the patient reported a pleasant tingling sensation in the left side of her body. She giggled and made funny comments, stating that she enjoyed the sensation very much. Repetition of these stimulations made the patient more communicative and flirtatious and she ended by openly expressing her desire to marry

the therapist. Stimulation of other cerebral points failed to modify her mood and indicated the specificity of the evoked effect. During control interviews, her behavior was quite proper, without familiarity or excessive friendliness.

Morals. Placing electrodes inside the brain, exploring the neuronal depth of personality, and influencing behavior by electrical stimulation have created a variety of problems, some shared with general medical ethics and others more specifically related to moral and philosophical issues of mental activity.

A main objective of animal research is the discovery of new principles and methods that can be applied for the benefit of man. Their potential advantages and risks cannot be ascertained until they have been extensively tested in human subjects, and preliminary trials must always be considered experimental.

Knives. The historical demonstration by J. F. Fulton and C. F. Jacobsen that frustration and neurotic behavior in the chimpanzee could be abolished by destruction of the frontal lobes was the starting point of lobotomy, which was widely used for treatment of several types of mental illness in human patients. This operation consisted of surgical disruption of the frontal lobe connections and demonstrated that psychic manifestations can be influenced by physical means as bold as the surgeon's knife.

In spite of initial acclaim, lobotomy was soon severely criticized as a therapeutic procedure because it often produced concomitant undesirable alterations of personality. More conservative treatments were actively sought and implantation of electrodes in the brain offered promising possibilities. In monkeys stimulation or limited destruction of the caudate nucleus produced several of the symptoms of frontal lobotomy with more discrete behavioral changes. Implantation of electrodes in man permitted access to any cerebral structure for recording, stimulation or destruction. Their potential clinical application raised controversial issues about risks, rationale and medical efficacy, but there is general agreement that depth recordings may provide significant information that cannot be obtained by other means, information that is essential for the proper diagnosis and treatment of patients who have some cerebral disturbances. However, the therapeutic use of electrodes in cases of mental illness has been more doubtful and must be considered to be in an experimental phase.

Voltage vs. Will. The most alarming aspect of ESB is that psychological reactivity can be influenced by applying a few volts to a preselected area of the brain. This has been interpreted by many people as a disturbing threat to human integrity. In the past the individual could face risks and pressures with preservation of his own identity. His body could be tortured, his thoughts and desires could be challenged by bribes, by emotions and by public opinion; his behavior could be influenced by environmental circumstances. But he always had the privilege of dying for an ideal without changing his mind. Fidelity to our emotional and intellectual past gives each of us a feeling of transcendental stability—perhaps of immortality—more precious than life itself.

New neurological technology, however, has a refined efficiency. The individual is defenseless against direct manipulation of the brain, because he is deprived of his most intimate mechanisms of biological reactivity. In experiments, electrical stimulation of appropriate intensity always prevailed over free will. For example flexion of the hand evoked by stimulation of the motor cortex cannot be voluntarily avoided. Destruction of the frontal lobes produced changes in affectiveness that are beyond any personal control.

Control. Scientific annihilation of personal identity or, even worse, its purposeful control, has sometimes been considered a future threat more awful than atomic holocaust. The prospect of any degree of physical control of the mind provokes a variety of objections: theological objections because it affects free will, moral objections because it affects individual responsibility, ethical objections because it may block self-defense mechanisms, philosophical objections because it threatens personal identity.

These objections are debatable. Prohibition of scientific advance is obviously naive and unrealistic. It could not be universally imposed and, more importantly, it is not knowledge itself but its improper use that should be regulated. A knife is neither good nor bad; it may be used by a surgeon or an assassin. Science may be neutral, but scientists should take sides.

The mind is not a static, inborn entity owned by the individual and self-sufficient; it is the dynamic organization of sensory perceptions of the external world, correlated and reshaped through internal anatomical and functional structure of the brain. Personality is not an intangible, immutable way of reacting but a flexible process in continuous evolution, affected by its medium. Culture and education are meant to shape patterns of reaction that are not innate in the human organism; they are meant to impose limits on freedom of choice.

Alarm. This is precisely the role of electrical stimulation of the brain: to add a new factor to the constellation of behavioral determinants. The result—as shown experimentally in animals—is an algebraic summation, with cerebral stimulation usually prepotent over spontaneous reactions. It is accepted medical practice to try to modify the antisocial or abnormal reactions of mental patients. Psychoanalysis, insulin or electroshock, such drugs as energizers and tranquilizers, and other varieties of psychiatric treatment are all aimed at influencing the abnormal personality in order to change undesirable mental characteristics. Therefore the possible use of implanted electrodes in mental patients should not pose unusual ethical complications if the accepted medical rules are followed. Perhaps the limited efficiency of standard psychiatric procedures is one reason that they have not caused alarm among scientists or laymen. Although electrical stimulation of the brain is still in the initial stage of development, it is in contrast far more selective and powerful; it may delay a heartbeat, move a finger, bring a word to memory, or set a determined behavioral tone.

Inviolate Bodies. Even if our conduct is entirely within the law, we cannot escape the intervention of the state in our private lives and in our most intimate biology. In general we are not even aware of it. Many free societies, including the United States, do not allow a bride and groom to marry legally until blood has been drawn from their veins and a medical officer has certified the absence of syphilis—a procedure that casts insulting doubt on their past integrity and intelligence. In order to cross international borders, it is necessary to document that our skin has been scarified and injected with smallpox. In many cities, by government regulation, the drinking water floods our bodies with chlorine for safety reasons and with fluoride for strengthening our teeth. The table salt that we buy usually is fortified with iodine to aid the physiology of our thyroid glands. These intrusions into our private blood, teeth and glands are accepted, practiced and enforced. They

have been legally introduced, are useful for the prevention of illness and generally benefit society and individuals. But they also have established the precedent of official manipulation of our personal biology.

To evaluate the rationale of governmental intervention in our bodies we must realize that civilization represents a considerable degree of biological artificiality: the intelligent escape from a primitive natural fate that was characterized by the death of countless babies, the short span of life and the high incidence of illness and physical misery. Human health has improved in a spectacular way precisely because official agencies have had the knowledge and power to influence our personal biology. It should be emphasized that health regulations are similar in dictatorial and in democratic countries.

Our own existence from birth to death must be properly certified to be officially recognized. We are surrounded by government-regulated industrial manipulations that extend to the food we eat, the water we drink and the conditioned air we breathe. We are in a highly organized age in which social and individual needs often conflict and social ruling usually prevails. From the medical point of view this organization is highly beneficial, but the loss of personal self-determination is one of the problems of civilized life that must be carefully confronted if we are to reach reasonable compromises. Even if we agree that individual freedom should in general bow to community welfare, we enter a new dimension when we consider the social implications of the new technology that can influence personal structure and behavioral expression by surgical, chemical and electrical manipulation of the brain. We may tolerate the practicality of being innoculated with yellow fever when visiting Asia, but shall we accept the theoretical future possibility of being

forced to take a pill or submit to electric shock for the socially protective purpose of making us infertile, more docile, better workers, or just happier?

Both the medical benefits and the social implications of cerebral research depend on the acquisition of knowledge about brain physiology, the possibility of investigating the mechanisms of the mind experimentally, the understanding of the determinants of reward and punishment in relation to human emotions and desire, and the unveiling of the neuronal basis of personal identity.

Understanding of biology, physics and other sciences enables man to use his intelligence and skills to impose a human purpose on earth. We are now on the verge of a process of mental liberation and self-domination that continues our evolution. Its experimental approach is based on the investigation of the depth of the brain in behaving subjects. Its practical applications do not rely on direct cerebral manipulation but on the integration of neurophysiological and psychological principles leading to a more intelligent education. That education must start from the moment of birth and continue throughout life, with the preconceived plan of escaping the blind forces of chance and of influencing cerebral mechanisms and mental structure. We must create a future man with greater personal freedom and originality—a member of a psychocivilized society, happier, less destructive and better balanced than present man.

BRAIN REWARD, ESB & ECSTASY

By J. Anthony Deutsch

Anyone who has observed electrical stimulation of the brain in the laboratory knows why it generates controversy. We watch the rat continually press a lever that will send electrical current through its brain; it will do virtually anything we demand in order to get the stimulation—run mazes, press bars, cross highly charged grids. If we give the rat unlimited access to the switch that allows current to flow into the electrodes in its head, it will press the bar thousands of times—perhaps for 16 hours a day—until it is exhausted. Nothing deters it from the ecstatic frenzy, not even food, which a hungry male rat prefers to a receptive female.

This extraordinary phenomenon was the serendipitous finding of James Olds, in collaboration with Peter Milner. Olds had implanted electrodes in rats to study the reticular formation of the brain. One such electrode landed in an area he had not intended it to hit, and the rat kept returning to the place on the table where Olds had stimulated that part of its brain. To his and his colleagues' surprise and incredulity, Olds soon demonstrated that the rat would learn to run mazes to get the electrical current—to get brain reward.

Horns. The technique we use to implant electrodes is much easier and less painful than it sounds. We modified a method developed some 40 years ago by Walter R. Hess, a Swiss neuroscientist. We anesthetize the rat and fix its head in a stereotaxic instrument that allows us to find any point within the skull in relation to bony landmarks, such as the ear canals, that have constant spatial relation to the brain's internal parts. We drill tiny holes and insert the electrodes—stiff, thin, stainless-steel pins—and set them in place with quick-drying plastic. When the rat awakens, it is barely aware of its new steel horns; it may live to ripe old age without ill effects from them.

The stimulation of some pathways in the brain, positive sites, will reward the rat; stimulation of other, negative, sites will be aversive or punishing. Some of the positive sites are in the hypothalamus and ventral tegmentum; some negative sites are in the spinothalamic tract and the periaqueductal grey. Researchers have found, however, that the medial forebrain bundle (MFB)—a large mass of nerve fibers that run close to the base of the brain—is the principal positive pathway; its stimulation produces reward behavior.

We know little about the MFB other than where it is; we cannot specify what it does or how it does it. There are many types of fibers in the MFB; perhaps they are accidental neighbors in the wiring diagram of the brain, each responsible for different behaviors; or perhaps they all are essential, related links in a reward circuit. We do know that if we stimulate the MFB with weak currents, we can induce a rat to eat, drink, copulate, and act in other instinctive ways. Even greater stimulation of the MFB acts as a reward, and will produce as wide a range of behaviors as such other reinforcers as food.

Fun. Because the rat that is stimulated in this fashion becomes wildly excited (human beings interpret this state as ecstasy), and because it will cross all sorts of hurdles to get the brain reward, some researchers suggest that the electrode stimulates an unknown pleasure center in the animal's brain. To be sure, pleasure center has a catchy sound, and the rat certainly seems to be having fun. But I think that this simple explanation of the phenomenon is incorrect. Electrical stimulation of the brain can indeed reinforce behavior, but there are three important differences between this type of reward and others:

1) When animals learn to perform for brain reward, they will stop the activity as soon as we discontinue the brain stimulation—as quickly as 30 seconds thereafter. By contrast, if they learn to perform for a normal reward—food—their behavior will persist for many hours when we stop the reward, though eventually it will cease—undergo extinction. Because animals that work for brain reward stop their activities as soon as we stop the stimulation, we first thought that extinction in this case was simply very rapid. But the abrupt extinction was most puzzling—it was inconsistent with the extreme persistence and strength of the rats' ecstatic behavior while we stimulated their brains.

2) When rats learn a task based on a food reward, they remember it from trial to trial, regardless of the length of time that elapses between tests. But a curious feature of brain reward is its overnight decrease: rats that respond well at the end of a day's session seem to have forgotten their lesson when we put them in the same situation the next day. It is possible, however, to cure this apparent loss of memory in these rats. If we give each a free electrical jolt through the electrode, it will behave as if it had never been away from the task.

3) Animals will work for brain reward in the absence of any identifiable drive, even though they seem to be extremely motivated to get the electrical charges. They will, as I said, press levers at a feverish rate, race through mazes at top speeds, and tolerate shocks from charged grids to get brain reward. A rat would have to be terribly hungry or thirsty to work that hard for food or water, a normal reward.

Drive. While performance for brain reward may be independent of drive states, drives do influence ESB behavior in some circumstances. A rat typically will not press a bar for a brain reward unless we give it that reward with every response. If it works for food, on the other hand, it will press a bar vigorously even if it gets the food a small proportion of the time.

We can increase the number of bar-presses of the brain-rewarded rat, however, by making sure that it is hungry. A brain-rewarded rat that is sufficiently hungry or thirsty will not stop working when we stop the reward. Instead, extinction will take about as long as it does for rats that work to get food or water. In this case, the drive—hunger or thirst—maintains the behavior that procured brain reward. Moreover, the rats show no overnight "forgetfulness" when we keep them hungry. Hungry or thirsty rats do not forget the task they learned for brain reward.

If drive states influence ESB behavior, the reverse is also true. Many animals—not all—want to eat or drink when they are stimulated electrically, if food or water is available. And some rats show normal motivated behavior, like that of food-rewarded rats, when they work for brain reward. It may be that the electrodes in such animals are so placed that they interact with unsatisfied drives.

How then does brain reward function? We could argue that it is independent of drive state, since animals will work for electrical stimulation even when they are not thirsty, hungry, or sexually aroused. But I have noted some ways in which drive state affects brain-rewarded behavior, so they must be connected in some way. The question is very much open.

One hypothesis is that an electrode that produces brain reward also evokes drive: the drive is, so to speak, injected into the brain along with the reward. In the absence of hunger or thirst or such deprivation that would maintain it, the drive decays very quickly. The animal has no real appetite for the reward, hence it loses interest quickly if there are long pauses between stimuli. This loss of interest looks to us like rapid forgetfulness.

By contrast, before we train the animal with normal rewards we create real physiological needs: we deprive the rat of food or water. Consequently it will keep working at a task that it thinks will alleviate that deprivation—at least until it realizes that no matter how well or how often it runs the maze, no food will be forthcoming.

Two. We suggest that each brain stimulus has a double function: to reward the rat's last response and to produce a drive for the next reward. If this is true, we must assume that the electrode is stimulating two sets of connections in the medial forebrain bundle. (This assumption is not unlikely, since we have evidence that the same electrode that produces brain reward also produces a tendency for the rat to eat, drink, copulate, or gnaw.) To explain why brain-rewarded behavior persists when the animal is hungry, we need only suppose that the nerve fibers that are being stimulated electrically carry messages of hunger or thirst. In such a case, a drive or appetite is already present; not all of it must come from the electrical jolt. Consequently the drive is much more persistent, and the brain-rewarded activity looks more like normal, food-rewarded behavior.

Considerable experimental work is in progress to determine whether the dual-function theory of ESB is correct. For example, if it were accurate, we would expect the tendency to seek brain reward to weaken rapidly as time elapses between rewards. The tendency should decay—not to zero but to a level dependent on the drive pathways that also are stimulated by

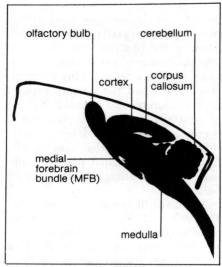

RAT'S BRAIN. Drawing shows the location of olfactory bulb, cortex, corpus callosum, cerebellum, medial forebrain bundle (MFB) and medulla. Electrical stimulation of the MFB makes the rat wildly excited; it will cross hurdles to get this reward.

the electrode. Thus the tendency will persist so long as the pathways carry messages of hunger or thirst.

Some of my students and I trained rats to run in a T-maze. They got water on one bar of the T and electrical stimulation on the other. We made sure they were thirsty and gave them a choice of the two rewards. Whichever side they chose, we would then hold them for varying amounts of time (up to 60 seconds) and send them through the maze again.

As it turned out, if we released the rats immediately after they chose brain reward, that would be their choice again 100 percent of the time. But if we detained them for 60 seconds, they would go to the water reward almost every time. In short, the tendency to seek out brain reward does decrease as a function of elapsed time between stimuli.

Charles R. Gallistel came to the same conclusion. He trained rats to run a straight runway to get brain reward at the end. When he released the rat immediately after the reward, it would run quickly to obtain the reward. If he held it for five minutes, the rat typically would not run at all. This decline in reward-seeking does not happen when a rat works for natural rewards.

Such experiments show that the fast extinction that supposedly occurs with brain reward is not really extinction. In normal reward circumstances, extinction is independent of lapsed time between rewards; it depends on the number of unrewarded responses. By

contrast, the rat's tendency to stop brain-rewarded activity is due not to its unrewarded responses, but to elapsed time.

Such findings accord with the view that drive for brain reward decays. However, one might argue that it is rather the memory of brain reward that decays so rapidly; that one need only remind the animal by giving it another reward. Gallistel's experiments do not support this objection. Gallistel gave his rats free brain stimuli—reminders—before he let them run down a straight alley to the brain reward. In one condition, he varied the length of the free stimulus; in another condition, he varied the length of the reward stimulus. In the first condition—varied-length free stimulus—the rat's speed of running increased directly as Gallistel increased the length of the reminder stimulus—but only up to a minute. Any increases in the length of the stimulus beyond one minute produced no further increases in running speed.

In the second condition—varied-length reward stimulus—extending the length of brain reward also produced faster running—but only up to half a second. With brain rewards longer than that, Gallistel produced little increase in running speed.

If the free brain reward serves as a reminder to a rat that treats await it at the end of the alley, Gallistel's experiments disagree. It is difficult to understand why the effectiveness of brain stimulation as a reminder should increase up to a minute in length, while its effectiveness as a reward does not increase beyond half a second.

Pain. The exact processes behind brain reward are still unknown. Nor do we have a good sense of how brain reward works in human beings, although ESB has been applied in clinical work [José Delgado, on page 30, discusses some of its human applications and implications]. The human patient generally is more casual and lackadaisical under ESB than the experimental animal; there is no direct human parallel to the excitement and single-minded frenzy that we have seen in the rat. But then the human brain is far more complex and highly evolved than the rat's brain.

We have much to learn. While we may hope that brain reward eventually will be used to relieve intractable pain, we are a long way from becoming an implanted people who pursue electrical pleasure and neglect all else. ∩

By MURRAY E. JARVIK

THE PSYCHOPHARMACOLOGICAL REVOLUTION

ONE HOT August evening in 1955, Helen Burney sat listlessly on her bed in the violent ward of the large Texas hospital where she had been confined for the past four months. During most of that unhappy time, Helen had been highly vocal, abusive, and overactive. Only the day before she had tried to strike a ward aide, but immediately several burly attendants had grabbed her, roughly tying her into a straitjacket and pinioning her arms against her chest. But today Helen's behavior was very different. Her incessant talking and shouting had stopped; all day long she spoke only when spoken to; most of the time she lay on her bed with her eyes half closed, moving little, and looking rather pale. However, she was unusually cooperative with the nursing personnel, got out of bed·when told to, and went to the dining room without resisting. What had happened to bring about this remarkable change?

That morning she had received an injection of a new synthetic drug, chlorpromazine, which had been discovered a few years earlier in France. On the same day thousands of mental patients throughout the world were receiving the same drug, many of them for the first time. News of the drug's usefulness had spread rapidly in the preceding months, and it was being tried in mental hospitals throughout the world. Few of those taking or administering the drug realized that they were participating in a revolution in psychiatric treatment. In fact, many psychiatrists felt that this drug would be no more effective in treating schizophrenia than the other drugs which had previously been tried with little success. But they were wrong —and luckily, too—for there was little else they could offer the masses of impoverished patients who clogged the mental institutions all over the world. Soon it would be difficult to find a psychotic patient who was not receiving a drug of some kind for the treatment of his illness. The era of clinical psychopharmacology had begun, and the new

drugs were hailed as the first real breakthrough in the treatment of one of man's most serious and mysterious afflictions —psychosis.

Until it was discovered that drugs could help the severely disturbed, almost the only recourse in the management of such patients was physical restraint. Philippe Pinel, the famous French psychiatrist, campaigning for humane treatment of the insane at the end of the 18th century, freed the inmates of the grim Bicetre mental hospital from their iron chains. Unfortunately, other physical restraints had to be substituted when patients became assaultive or destructive, and though the padded cell and the camisole, or straitjacket, may have been softer than chains, they allowed no greater freedom. Not until the mid-1950's did drugs finally promise total emancipation from physical restraint for

most patients. Despite the fears of some psychiatrists, psychologists, and social workers that the social and psychological factors contributing to mental illness would be ignored, the use of psychopharmaceuticals radically improved the treatment of the mentally ill within and without the hospital. Indeed, only with their use has it been possible for some families to be held together, for some individuals to be gainfully employed, and for some patients to be reached by psychotherapy.

Since 1955, psychopharmacology has burgeoned as an important scientific discipline in its own right. In the past 15 years, many new chemical agents have been developed for the treatment of each major category of mental illness. These drugs include phenothiazines, rauwolfia alkaloids, butyrophenones, propanediol and benzodiazepine compounds, monoamine oxidase (MAO) inhibitors, dibenzazepine derivatives, and many more. They have been found useful in the treatment of psychoses, neuroses, and depressions. Even autistic behavior, psychopathy, sexual deviation, and mental retardation have been attacked with drugs, but clinical psychopharmacologists feel that the surface has only been scratched in these areas. The search continues, though presently on a smaller scale than in the past, for more effective agents.

Folk-Psychopharmacology

Although as a full-fledged scientific discipline psychopharmacology is less than 15 years old, the psychological effects of drugs have piqued the curiosity of occasional researchers for almost a hundred years. Indeed, it is surprising that interest was so slow in  developing, for man's empirical knowledge of the effects of drugs on behavior is both ancient and widespread.

The records of mankind, going back thousands of years, are filled with anecdotal and clinical reports of the psychological action of drugs obtained from plants. Though we can be sure that most of these folk remedies were merely placebos, a few have demonstrable me-

dicinal properties and are still in use today. The cuneiform tablets of ancient Assyria contain numerous references to medicinal preparations with psychological effects. For more than 5000 years, the Chinese have used the herb Ma Huang (yellow astringent), which contains the potent stimulant, ephedrine, and in the earliest writings of China, Egypt, and the Middle East there are references to the influence of various drugs on behavior.

In the first century before Christ, the Roman poet Horace wrote lyrically of the psychological effects of **alcohol:** "What wonders does not wine! It discloses secrets; ratifies and confirms our hopes; thrusts the coward forth to battle; eases the anxious mind of its burthen; instructs in arts. Whom has not a cheerful glass made eloquent! Whom not quite free and easy from pinching poverty!" And "In vino veritas" was already a familiar Roman adage when it was cited by Pliny.

Opium, an effective folk remedy, is mentioned in the Ebers papyrus, and Homer tells us that Helen of Troy took a "sorrow-easing drug" obtained from Egypt—probably opium. Although the analgesic and sedative properties of opium were extensively described in classical literature, little was said about its addictive properties until Thomas de Quincy hinted at them, early in the 19th century, in his *Confessions of an English Opium Eater.* And while the chemical isolation of morphine and the invention of the hypodermic needle, in the middle of the 19th century, made profound addiction truly feasible, morphine is still considered by many physicians the most

essential drug they use — "God's own remedy."

Morphine and its derivatives and analogs (for example, heroin) are self-administered by countless thousands of people throughout the world, although in many countries, especially in the West, such use is illegal. The practice persists, nevertheless, perhaps for the reasons given by the French poet, Jean Cocteau, who was himself an addict: "Everything that we do in life, including love, is done in an express train traveling towards death. To smoke opium is to leave the train while in motion; it is to be interested in something other than life and death."

Like morphine, **cocaine** is another vegetable product discovered by primitive man. It is clearly not a placebo, and its use is illegal. The Indians of Peru have chewed coca leaves for centuries, and still do, to relieve hunger, fatigue, and the general burdens of a miserable life. The alkaloid cocaine was isolated in 1859, and its systematic use was not only practiced but advocated by such respected figures as Sigmund Freud and William Halsted, as well as by the legendary Sherlock Holmes. It is highly doubtful that the continued use of cocaine produces a physiological dependence. Today, cocaine-taking is relatively uncommon in the northern hemisphere.

On the other hand, an ancient drug which remains exceedingly popular, though its medical uses today are nil, is **marijuana,** the dried leaves of the hemp plant *Cannabis sativa.* Cannabis is so ubiquitous, and grows so easily, that its widespread use is not surprising. Marco Polo is credited with bringing the "Green Goddess" to the Occident, although Herodotus tells us that the Scythians inhaled the vapor, obtained by heating hemp seeds on red-hot stones, and then "shouted for joy." To this day, cannabis is almost always smoked; this allows its active ingredients to be absorbed into the pulmonary blood circulation and, avoiding the liver, to be promptly carried to the brain. Similarly, the active ingredients of opium and tobacco are usually self-administered by inhalation of the vapors from heated plant products.

Hashish, derived from cannabis, and

smoked, chewed, or drunk, has been widely used for centuries throughout the Middle East. The Arabic term for a devotee of hashish is "hashshash;" from the plural, "hashshashin," comes the English word "assassin," for at the time of the Crusades, the Hashshashin were a fanatical secret Moslem sect who terrorized the Christians by swift and secret murder, after having taken hashish to give themselves courage. Richard Burton, the famous traveler, adventurer, and writer, described his experiences with hashish during a pilgrimage to Mecca at the end of the 19th century. About 50 years earlier, Moreau de Tours suggested that physicians should take hashish in order to experience mental illness and thereby understand it better. Claude Bernard, the great French physiologist, is said to have declared that "hashish is the curare of the mind." Today we know a great deal about the mode of action of curare and almost nothing about that of hashish, but Bernard suggested a working hypothesis. Perhaps cannabis, like curare, blocks some vital neurohumor in the brain.

Quantitative, objective studies of cannabis are rare, even today. However, a recent report by Carlini indicates that cannabis facilitates maze-learning in rats. In the absence of comparative studies, it is difficult to say how cannabis resembles or differs from other drugs; anecdotal reports suggest that it resembles lysergic acid diethylamide (LSD).

Another drug with a long history of use is **mescaline** or **peyote,** which the Aztecs are credited with having used five centuries ago, and which has been and still is used by certain Indians of Central America and the Southwest United States. Its effects resemble those of marijuana and LSD; they have also been compared with those of **psilocybin,** a drug which the Aztecs derived from a psychotogenic mushroom they called "teonanacatl," or "God's flesh."

The Chemical Era

Until the 19th century, the only drugs known to affect behavior were those de-

rived from plants and long familiar to mankind. With advances in chemistry during the first half of the 19th century, however, the general anesthetics, including nitrous oxide, diethyl ether, and chloroform were discovered and brought into widespread use; and by the time Emil Kraepelin began his psychopharmacological investigations in the 1880's, a few new sedatives, including the bromides and chloral hydrate, were available.

Nitrous oxide, an artificially prepared inhalation anesthetic, was investigated by Sir Humphrey Davy, who described its effects thus in 1799: "I lost all connections with external things; trains of vivid images rapidly passed through my mind and even connected with words in such a manner as to produce perceptions perfectly novel. I existed in a world of newly connected and newly modified ideas."

Inhaling nitrous oxide soon became a favorite student diversion, and enterprising showmen charged admission for public demonstrations of its effects; the popular interest in this gas reminds one very much of the current preoccupation with LSD. But though nitrous oxide was beguiling to thrill seekers, it never became as popular as LSD, perhaps because the gas is difficult to transport. Although **diethyl ether** was originally prepared in 1543 by Valerius Cordus when he distilled alcohol with sulfuric acid, its potential as an anesthetic remained unknown for 300 years until Crawford Long and William Morton first used it clinically in the 1840's. Ether parties subsequently became popular among students, although the drug's extreme flammability probably discouraged more widespread and persisting popular use. **Chloroform** was introduced about the same time as ether, but its toxic effects upon the heart, recognized almost immediately, discouraged its nonmedical use. It was not known for many years that the liver, also, is severely damaged by this drug.

Chloral hydrate, a powerful sleep-producing drug, was introduced into medicine in 1869 but has been generally ignored by experimental psychologists—though not by the underworld where, in the form of "knockout drops" mixed with alcohol, it has been the active in-

gredient of the "Mickey Finn." **Paraldehyde,** first used in 1882, has similarly been eschewed by psychological investigators, perhaps because of its extremely unpleasant odor; nevertheless, it has been used extensively for many years in mental institutions for producing temporary narcosis in dangerously violent patients, especially those with delirium tremens from alcohol withdrawal.

Bromides, particularly potassium bromide, slowly gained popularity during the 19th century to the point where millions of people were taking them as sedatives. Unlike the barbiturates, however, the bromides produce psychoses involving delirium, delusions, hallucinations, as well as a variety of neurological and dermatological disturbances. For a time, chronic toxicity resulting from continued use of these compounds became a leading cause of admission to mental hospitals. Bromide is still a common ingredient in headache remedies, "nerve tonics," and over-the-counter sleeping medications.

The Antipsychotic Drugs

With the antipsychotic drugs, as happens more often than is supposed, use preceded research. The ancient preparation, Indian snakeroot powder, mentioned more than 2500 years ago in the Hindu Ayurvedic writings, deserves at least as much credit for ushering in the era of clinical psychopharmacology as does the modern synthetic drug, chlorpromazine. According to the ancient doctrine of signs, since the roots of the plant *Rauwolfia serpentina* were snake-like, they were administered for snakebite. Snakeroot was also used for insomnia and insanity—quite rational uses,

in view of modern findings—as well as for epilepsy and dysentery which it actually aggravates, and for a host of other conditions for which its value is questionable.

The first scientific intimation that Indian snakeroot might be useful in mental illness came in 1931 when Sen and Bose published an article in the *Indian Medical World* entitled "*Rauwolfia serpentina*, a new Indian drug for insanity and high blood pressure." But this suggestion was not confirmed for almost a quarter of a century. Rauwolfia began to attract the attention of the Western world only in 1949, when Rustom Valkil advocated it for hypertension, and the Swiss pharmaceutical firm, Ciba, subsequently isolated the active ingredient which they named **reserpine.** In 1953 a Boston physician, Robert Wilkins, confirmed that reserpine was effective in the treatment of hypertension, and a year later a New York psychiatrist, Nathan Kline, announced that he had found reserpine useful in the treatment of psychotic disorders. Soon numerous psychiatrists in other parts of the world corroborated Kline's results, and the use of reserpine spread with amazing speed. When Frederick Yonkman at Ciba used the term "tranquilizing" to describe the calming effect of reserpine, the word "tranquilizer" entered all modern languages to designate a drug which quiets hyperactive or anxious patients.

The subsequent clinical history of reserpine is a strange one. Reserpine and chlorpromazine were twin heralds of the dawn of psychopharmacological treatment, but the popularity of reserpine in the treatment of mental disease has dwindled until today, a decade and a half later, its use has been practically abandoned for such therapy while chlorpromazine is still the leading antipsychotic drug. Yet there are many studies which attest to the efficacy of rauwolfia and its derivatives in the treatment of psychiatric disorders; probably its tendency to produce depression was one of

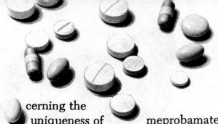
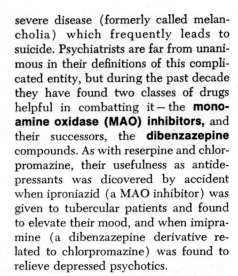

the chief reasons for its near demise. Furthermore, chlorpromazine has spawned scores of offspring-phenothiazines, widely used for the mentally ill.

Like reserpine, **chlorpromazine's** usefulness as an antipsychotic drug was discovered more or less by accident. In the early 1950's the French surgeon, Henri Laborit, introduced chlorpromazine into clinical anesthesia as a successor to promethazine, known to be a sedative antihistamine capable of heightening the effect of other drugs. It was noticed that chlorpromazine reduced anxiety in surgical patients and enabled them to face their ordeal with indifference. This led to its trial with agitated psychotics, whom it calmed with dramatic effectiveness. In 1954 the drug was released commercially in North America by Smith, Kline and French as an anti-emetic, but shortly thereafter it was tried with psychiatric patients. Large-scale controlled studies by the United States Veterans Administration and by the Psychopharmacology Service Center of the National Institute of Mental Health showed chlorpromazine and the related phenothiazines to be useful in the treatment of acute schizophrenia. Other studies show that phenothiazines help discharged mental patients to stay out of the hospital. A drug with ubiquitous actions on all body systems, chlorpromazine has been used in the treatment of anxiety and tension, depression, mental retardation, senility, drug addiction, pain, nausea and vomiting, and spasticity. Since its mechanisms of action are still not known, it is difficult to delimit the validity of these applications.

Anti-Anxiety Drugs

Anxiety is such a common experience that everyone reading this article has a subjective understanding of the term. It may be defined as an unpleasant state associated with a threatening situation, and is closely allied to fear. Sedative hypnotic drugs including alcohol, barbiturates, bromides, and chloral hydrate, have frequently been employed for the treatment of anxiety. In 1955 a number of new drugs with properties common to the sedative hypnotics were introduced for the treatment of anxiety, but the most successful of these, by far, was **meprobamate,** popularly known as Miltown or Equanil. Many of the arguments con-

cerning the uniqueness of meprobamate revolve around its similarity or dissimilarity to the barbiturates. But since the properties of the various barbiturates differ from one another, it is not easy to compare the whole class to meprobamate. All, however, tend to produce sleep when used in large doses, to produce effects reported as pleasant, and to produce convulsive seizures as a consequence of sudden withdrawal after the prolonged administration of large doses. Giving meprobamate to a patient suffering from neurotic anxiety is not quite the same as inserting a nail into a broken bone to hold it together, or giving insulin to a diabetic. In giving meprobamate, we are employing a drug with a poorly defined action to treat a poorly defined condition. But the condition is widespread, important, and demands action, and the drug seems to help.

In any case, meprobamate's standing as the most popular tranquilizer was soon usurped by **chlordiazepoxide** (Librium). This compound strongly resembles meprobamate and the barbiturates, but there do appear to be differences which the experimentalist can measure. For example, Leonard Cook and Roger Kelleher recently reported an experiment in which rats could postpone a punishing shock by pressing a lever. Cook and Kelleher found that at some doses chlordiazepoxide will produce an increase in the rate of lever pressing whereas meprobamate does not. Also it has been shown with a Lashley jumping stand that rats will sometimes become "fixated" if the discrimination problem is made insoluble. Chlordiazepoxide seems to eliminate this fixated behavior whereas meprobamate does not. The possible differences in the behavioral effects of sedative hypnotic drugs have not yet been fully explored, and the study of these differences should tell us a great deal about the drugs themselves.

Anti-Depression Drugs

While depression, at least in a mild form, is an experience perhaps as common as anxiety, it can also constitute a severe disease (formerly called melancholia) which frequently leads to suicide. Psychiatrists are far from unanimous in their definitions of this complicated entity, but during the past decade they have found two classes of drugs helpful in combatting it—the **monoamine oxidase (MAO) inhibitors,** and their successors, the **dibenzazepine** compounds. As with reserpine and chlorpromazine, their usefulness as antidepressants was dicovered by accident when iproniazid (a MAO inhibitor) was given to tubercular patients and found to elevate their mood, and when imipramine (a dibenzazepine derivative related to chlorpromazine) was found to relieve depressed psychotics.

In attempting to understand the etiology of depression, it is ironic that biochemists have not hesitated to rush in where experimental psychologists fear to tread. What has emerged, based on a combination of clinical observations and animal studies, is the *catecholamine theory* of depression. Broadly interpreted, the theory says that a state of well-being is maintained by continuous adrenergic stimulation of certain receptors in the brain by catecholamines like norepinephrine and dopamine (hormones produced in the brain). For example, reserpine's so-called tranquilizing effect—indifference to surroundings, lack of appetite, and apparent lassitude—is attributed to depletion of catecholamines. Another compound, alphamethyltyrosine, which decreases the synthesis of catecholamines, has been found to produce "depression" in animals. On the other hand, some compounds have been found which produce an increase in the level of brain catecholamines. Administration of MAO inhibitors, which inactivate MAO and thus prevent catecholamine from being destroyed, produce increased levels of catecholamines and greater alertness, activity, and degree of electrical self-stimulation (in animals implanted with electrodes in "reward" areas of the brain). Administering the precursors of catecholamines—for example, dihydroxyphenylalanine (DOPA)—or MAO inhibitors, will prevent or reverse the depression caused by reserpine [see illustration opposite page].

The dibenzazepine compounds, typified by **imipramine** (Tofranil), do not change the level of brain catecholamines in animals, yet they are effective antidepressants. However, the mode of action of these compounds may be compatible with the theory. Studies show that the catecholamine level in the brain is reduced, not only by enzymatic de-

struction, (for example, by MAO), but also by reabsorption of the catecholamines into the neurons. It has been hypothesized that the dibenzazepine compounds potentiate the action of normally present catecholamines by preventing this reabsorption.

LSD

LSD shares the responsibility with reserpine and chlorpromazine for ushering in the psychopharmacology era. Albert Hofmann's accidental discovery of this substance at Sandoz Pharmaceuticals in Basel, Switzerland in 1943 is now well known. LSD is a semi-synthetic compound of plant origin, a derivative of ergot (a fungus which infects rye). Although its effects are similar to those of marijuana and mescaline, its outstanding characteristic is its extreme potency, and its ability to produce bizarre mental states picturesquely described by Humphrey Osmond as psychedelic or "mind-expanding." The ability of LSD to block 5-hydroxytryptamine (another amine resembling the catecholamines in some respects, abbreviated 5HT) and thus to change brain levels of 5HT, has excited interest. More recently Maimon Cohen has reported the frightening finding that LSD can damage chromosomes. The role of LSD in producing a psychotic state has not been established. Despite thousands of papers dealing with this substance, we have very little idea of what LSD does, and we don't know how it does it. It is unfortunate that legal restrictions and the manufacturers' understandable diffidence make this fascinating chemical inaccessible for research.

There is something in the use or action of psychotogenic or "hallucinogenic"

drugs which appeals to certain towering if unconventional figures in literature and the arts. From the time of Toulouse-Lautrec through the era of the expatriates (Gertrude Stein, James Joyce, Ernest Hemingway), bohemian Paris was not exactly abstemious nor did it restrict itself to alcohol for thrills or new sensations. Though the virtues of illicit drugs do not appear in paid advertisements in the public press, nevertheless very talented "copywriters" have turned out glowing testimonials to promote the use of these drugs. Thomas de Quincey and Samuel Coleridge, at the beginning of the 19th century, recommended opium, and Paolo Mantegazza in 1859 gave highly colored accounts of the beatific effects of coca. Freud also approved of cocaine and advised his fiancée to take it. Charles Baudelaire, called the "De Quincey of hashish," was supported

by Arthur Rimbaud and Paul Verlaine in acclaiming the beneficence of this drug; more recently Aldous Huxley declared that the "doors of perception" could be opened by mescaline and LSD. Many jazz, swing, bop, and other musicians claim that marijuana and other stimulant drugs enhance their playing or composing.

Whether drugs truly enhance creativity is a moot point. Artists, poets, scientists, and inventors will testify that LSD or marijuana or amphetamine inspired them to produce works of value, but controlled experiments to test these claims are lacking. Who would not like to find a magic drug that would turn an ugly frog into a handsome prince, or a Cinderella into a princess? Drugs can sometimes seem to have magic powers, but they do not ordinarily instill beauty, wisdom, and virtue into the taker. Yet estrogens can change a skinny adolescent girl into a beauty queen and, if one can extrapolate from cases of precocious puberty (or infant Hercules), super-androgens must be responsible for Clark Kent's transformation into Superman.

Drugs do change our perception of the world, and when this perception becomes unbearable, as in terminal cancer, drug use is clearly justified. The question is whether it is justified for the relief of unhappiness, dissatisfaction, or boredom. The religious uses of wine and peyote for sacramental purposes have, in part, inspired Timothy Leary to found a new religion, the League for Spiritual Discovery (LSD), which advocates the use of LSD and other so-called psychedelic drugs. The legal difficulties of this organization have spurred city, state, and federal legislative and enforcement bodies to enter the field of psychopharmacology in order to control the distribution and use of behavior-affecting drugs. But the government is trying to make rules about substances which are still poorly understood, and it rests with psychopharmacologists to clarify the action of psychotogenic drugs so that such rules can be made on a more rational basis.

The Birth of Scientific Psychopharmacology

Without the spur of clinical success, it is doubtful that basic research in the effects of drugs on behavior could have advanced very rapidly. During the first half of the 20th century, drugs were seldom used in the treatment of mental illness, since morphine, cocaine, barbiturates, and other sedative hypnotics had already been tried and proven generally ineffective. Other more physical

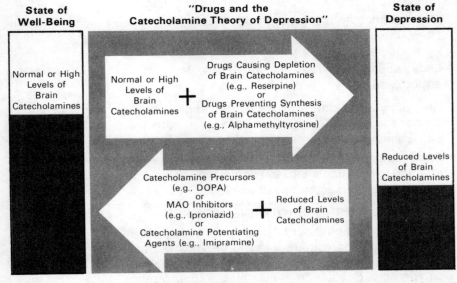

Relationships between drug-produced changes in brain catecholamine levels and changes in mental states provide evidence for the "catecholamine theory of depression."

41

The classification of some major drugs and their properties are outlined in this table. Complex psychological and pharmacological effects require some multiple listings. Only one trade name is listed for each drug. The question mark (?) indicates unknown information.

approaches to therapy, including hydrotherapy, occupational therapy, and psychosurgery had been employed with varying results. Only electroconvulsive shock (ECS) seemed to be very successful, but its administration required considerable skill. Psychiatrists depended chiefly, therefore, on psychological methods (primarily communicative interactions) which, unfortunately, were usually inefficient and ineffective for the majority of severely psychotic individuals.

Experimental psychologists showed only an intermittent and desultory interest in the effects of drugs on behavior. A handful of drugs had already been investigated, but the results were of very little interest to the most influential psychologists who were busy, in the 1930's and 1940's, building their own psychological systems or attacking rival systems.

In fact, however, psychopharmacology had already been born more than half a century earlier. In 1879 the first laboratory of experimental psychology had been established at Leipzig by Wilhelm Wundt. One of Wundt's most famous students was Emil Kraepelin, sometimes called the father of modern psychiatry because he invented a widely used system for classifying mental disorders. Kraepelin might also be called the father of scientific psychopharmacology, for he applied Wundt's new experimental methods to investigate the influence of drugs on psychological functions. Kraepelin studied pharmacology at Tartu in Estonia, then a center of research in this field. During his stay there he demonstrated that alcohol, morphine, and other drugs impair reaction time and the mental processes involved in associational learning. It is an ironic coincidence that Kraepelin was interested in the two areas which finally coalesced 75 years later—basic, quantitative, experimental psychopharmacology, and the treatment of mental disease.

Though psychopharmacology had little scientific status at the beginning of the 20th century, Kraepelin's early work was continued by a few psychologists who studied the effects of alcohol, caffeine, cocaine, strychnine, and nicotine. In 1908 the Englishman, W. H. R. Rivers, reported on the influence of drugs

Drug Class	Group
PSYCHOTHERAPEUTICS These drugs are typical of many used in the treatment of psychological and psychiatric disorders. **Anti-psychotic** drugs are used primarily to treat major psychoses, such as schizophrenia, manic depressive psychoses, and senile psychoses.	**ANTI-PSYCHOTIC:** Rauwolfia alkaloids Phenothiazines
Anti-anxiety drugs are used to combat insomnia, induce muscle relaxation, treat neurotic conditions, and reduce psychological stress.	**ANTI-ANXIETY:** Propanediols Benzodiazepines Barbiturates
Anti-depressant drugs are effective in the treatment of psychiatric depression and phobic-anxiety states.	**ANTI-DEPRESSANT:** MAO Inhibitors Dibenzazepines
Stimulants (see **STIMULANTS**, below)	**STIMULANT:**
PSYCHOTOGENICS These drugs produce changes in mood, thinking, and behavior. The resultant drug state may resemble a psychotic state, with delusions, hallucinations, and distorted perceptions. These drugs have little therapeutic value.	Ergot derivative Cannabis sativa Lophophora williamsii Psilocybe mexicana
STIMULANTS These drugs elevate mood, increase confidence and alertness, and prevent fatigue. Analeptics stimulate the central nervous system and can reverse the depressant effects of an anesthetic drug. Caffeine and nicotine, found in beverages and tobacco, are mild stimulants.	Sympathomimetics Analeptics Psychotogenics Nicotinics Xanthines
SEDATIVES AND HYPNOTICS Most of these drugs produce general depression (sedation) in low doses and sleep (hypnosis) in larger doses. They are used to treat mental stress, insomnia, and anxiety.	Bromides Barbiturates Chloral derivatives General
ANESTHETICS, ANALGESICS, AND PARALYTICS These drugs are widely used in the field of medicine. **General anesthetics** act centrally to cause a loss of consciousness.	General anesthetics
Local anesthetics act only at or near the site of application.	Local anesthetics
Analgesic drugs, many of them addicting, typically produce euphoria and stupor, and are effective pain-relievers.	Analgesics
Paralytic drugs act primarily at the neuro-muscular junction to produce motor (muscular) paralysis, and are commonly used by anesthesiologists.	Paralytics
NEUROHUMORS (NEUROTRANSMITTERS) Adrenergic and cholinergic compounds are known to be synaptic transmitters in the nervous system. Other natural compounds (e.g., 5-HT, γ-aminobutyric acid, Substance P) may also be neurotransmitters.	Cholinergic Adrenergic Others (?)

Example	Trade or Common Name	Natural or Synthetic	Usage	How Taken	First Used	Evidence of Addiction?
reserpine	(Serpasil)	nat	greatly diminished	injected ingested	1949	no
chlorpromazine	(Thorazine)	syn	widespread	injected ingested	1950	no
meprobamate	(Miltown)	syn	widespread	ingested	1954	yes
chlordiazepoxide	(Librium)	syn	widespread	ingested	1933	yes
phenobarbital	(see SEDATIVES)					
tranylcypromine	(Parnate)	syn	diminished	ingested	1958	no
imipramine	(Tofranil)	syn	widespread	ingested injected	1948	no
amphetamine	(see STIMULANTS)					
lysergic acid diethylamide	(LSD, Lysergide)	syn	widespread?	ingested	1943	no
marijuana	(hemp, hashish)	nat	widespread	smoked	?	no
mescaline	(peyote button)	nat	localized	ingested	?	no
psilocybin		nat	rare	ingested	?	no
amphetamine	(Benzedrine)	syn	widespread	ingested injected	1935	yes
pentylenetetrazol	(Metrazol)	syn	rare	ingested injected	1935	no
lysergic acid diethylamide	(see PSYCHO— TOGENICS)					
nicotine		nat	widespread	smoked ingested	?	yes
caffeine		nat	widespread	ingested	?	yes
potassium bromide		syn	widespread	ingested	1857	no
phenobarbital	(Luminal)	syn	widespread	ingested injected	1912	yes
chloral hydrate		syn	rare	ingested	1875	yes
alcohol		nat	widespread	ingested	?	yes
nitrous oxide	("laughing gas")	syn	rare	inhaled	1799	no
diethyl ether		syn	greatly diminished	inhaled	1846	no
chloroform		syn	rare	inhaled	1831	no
cocaine	(coca)	nat	widespread	applied ingested	?	yes
procaine	(Novocaine)	syn	widespread	injected	1905	no
Opium derivatives	(morphine, heroin)	nat	widespread	injected smoked	?	yes
d-tubocurarine	(curare)	nat	widespread	injected	?	no
acetylcholine		nat syn	laboratory	injected	1926	no
norepinephrine		nat syn	laboratory	injected	1946	no
5-hydroxytryptamine	(5-HT, Serotonin)	nat syn	laboratory	injected	1948	no

on fatigue; in 1915 the Americans, Raymond Dodge and Francis Benedict, and Harry Hollingsworth (1912, 1924) examined the effects of drugs on motor and mental efficiency. In 1924 even Clark Hull, one of the most influential psychologists of the mid-20th century, studied the effect of pipe smoking and coffee drinking on mental efficiency, before he turned his attention to building theoretical systems.

Psychopharmacological research was spurred in the 1930's and 1940's by the imminence and advent of World War II, which aroused military interest in the applications of drugs, particularly the amphetamines, and concern about the psychological consequences of anoxia, i.e., severe oxygen deficiency. Both allied

and German soldiers were given amphetamines to combat sleeplessness and fatigue; these drugs were found to diminish fatigue, but whether they could raise performance above normal levels was an open question which is still not fully answered. Insufficient supply of oxygen to the brain was shown to adversely affect reasoning, memory, and sensory functioning; for example, it renders the subject less sensitive to visual stimuli, and prolongs the time needed for the eyes to adapt to the dark. Such impairment was particularly serious in military pilots for whom the loss of judgment and sensory function resulting from lack of oxygen at high altitudes could be disastrous.

More recently a number of factors have converged to make psychopharmacology a popular field for research. During the mid-1950's, Europe and the United States were prospering, and governmental support for health services and medical research began to expand at an unprecedented rate. Spurred by therapeutic success and the possibilities of large profits, and as yet unencumbered by severe governmental restrictions concerning drug safety and efficacy, pharmaceutical companies were eager to discover new drugs prescribable to millions of waiting patients. Support for research on new psychotherapeutic drugs became big business. In addition, the Psychopharmacology Service Center, established within the National Institute of Mental Health, contributed millions of dollars for research on the psychological effects of drugs.

With the rise of psychopharmacology, clinical psychologists immediately began to devise methods, such as rating scales and questionnaires, to evaluate the effects of the new drug therapies. However, some of the psychotherapeutic achievements credited to the action of drugs may also be attributed to reforms in mental hospitals and better programs of community mental hygiene.

Psychological Methods in Psychopharmacological Research

To screen out potentially useful drugs and characterize their action, psychopharmacologists have used a variety of procedures in studies carried out with rats and mice. Measures of spontaneous motor activity are widely employed, as are other observational and rating techniques. Among the most favored procedures are those based on operant conditioning, because they are objective, automatic, generally quite reliable, and permit extended investigation of a single animal. The chief apparatus is the Skinner box, a cage containing a lever-pressing mechanism. Depending on the experimental conditions, depression of this lever can produce either a positive reinforcement (food) or a negative reinforcement (electrical shock). Some investigators feel that the schedule, and not the kind or amount of reinforcement, determines a particular drug susceptibility. Some schedules require that the animal respond quickly, or slowly, or in certain patterns, in order to obtain food

or avoid shock. On the other hand, even before the phenothiazines and reserpine appeared on the market, it was shown that these drugs seemed to selectively impair conditioned responses controlled by aversive consequences (that is, punishing shock) but had less effect upon unconditioned responses. It appears that the strength of the stimulus and the nature of the motor response required are vital factors determining the relative susceptibility to different drugs.

Many psychopharmacologists not trained in the Skinnerian approach use discrimination boxes and mazes to study the effects of drugs, and a number also use classical conditioning procedures; maze-learning was used in a recent study which demonstrated that analeptics (such as strychnine) facilitate learning. Similarly, work on the amnesia produced by intracerebral antibiotics was based on results obtained with mazes and shuttleboxes. Even single-trial learning procedures are being increasingly used to study the effects of drugs. Psychological research has not yet reached a point at which any one method of measuring behavior can be considered superior to any other.

Chemistry and the Brain

Psychologists have subdivided behavior in different ways, but they are in general agreement about certain broad categories of functions. If different psychological functions depend upon discrete chemical substances, then we

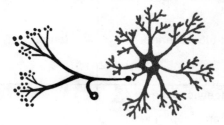

might expect to find specificity of drug action—that is, that certain drugs selectively affect certain functions. If the localization of psychological functions involves a grosser type of organization—if it depends, say, on complex neural connections—then we would not necessarily expect to find such specific relations between drug action and psychological function.

Certain sensory structures are clearly chemically coded. Taste and smell receptors obviously are and respond to specific drugs. Sodium dehydrochlorate and saccharin, even when injected into an antecubital vein, respectively produce a characteristic bitter or sweet taste on reaching the tongue and are used for measuring blood circulation time. Streptomycin and dihydrostreptomycin selectively, though not exclusively, attack the eighth nerve; visual effects are produced by santonin, digitalis, and LSD. Haptic sensations are said to be produced by cocaine ("cocaine bug"), but there is no good evidence that somesthetic sensory pathways are selectively affected by any chemical substance. Histamine and polypeptides, such as substance P or bradykinin, will at times produce itch or pain, and hint that sensory chemical specificity is a possibility.

Motor structures are also chemically coded and enable curariform drugs to have a selective paralyzing action. Similarly, autonomic ganglia can be affected selectively by different drugs and the vast field of peripheral neuropharmacology rests on such specificity.

We are beginning to learn how the central nervous system is organized neuropharmacologically. Histochemical, radioautographic, and fluorescent techniques are making such mapping possible. For example, it is known that the central nervous system pathways which control motivational mechanisms such as hunger, thirst, and sex, are susceptible to cholinergic, adrenergic, and hormonal substances. Further mapping of this kind is bound to result in better understanding of the relationship between drug action and functional localization in the central nervous system.

One can inhibit activity with a wide variety of depressant drugs or activate animals with stimulant drugs. No simple role can be ascribed to acetylcholine, norepinephrine, or 5-hydroxytryptamine (serotonin) in the control of behavior. What part, if any, these substances play in learning is even more mysterious. Some theorists have proposed an inhibitory cholinergic system balanced by an excitatory adrenergic system, and the facts seem to fit thus far. Of course, the brain is full of all species of chemicals which are waiting to be investigated by psychologists. Nucleic acids and particu-larly ribonucleic acid (RNA) have been assigned a special role in learning by some, but evidence is conflicting. Proteins seem a more likely candidate, and such inhibitors of protein synthesis as puromycin and cyclohexamide do interfere with both memory and learning. The production of retrograde amnesia

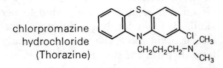

lysergic acid diethylamide (LSD)

chlorpromazine hydrochloride (Thorazine)

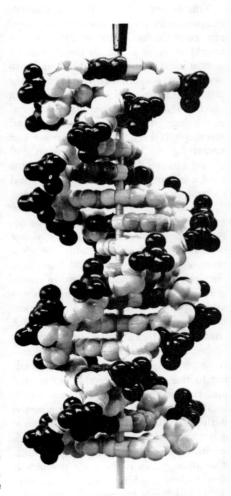

deoxyribonucleic acid (DNA)

reserpine (Serpasil)

and the post-trial facilitation of learning by drugs provide evidence for a consolidation process. [See "Amnesia: A World Without Continuity," PT, May 67]. But the experiments are difficult to perform, and many unspecified sources of variability will have to be identified before general mechanisms can be revealed.

The Future of Psychopharmacology

Ever since Loewenhoek's invention of the microscope, scientists have tended to believe that in the "ultra-fine structure" of an organism lie the explanations for its functioning. Hence it is not surprising that attempts to explain drug action are couched in terms of chemical binding to specific molecular receptors. However, behavior can no more be seen in a test tube full of brain homogenate, than can the theme of a mosaic be determined from an analysis of its stones. The Gestalt principle that the whole is something more than the sum of its parts is not always recognized by physical scientists who tend to be very analytical, to look at "parts" in their approach to explanation. The psychologist has an increasingly important role to play in psychopharmacology, for he must determine whether the particular sedative, antidepressant, psychotogenic, or facilitating drug which the biochemists and neurophysiologists want to study, really has the behavioral properties they think it does.

In the future it should be possible to say in what ways each important psychopharmaceutical influences behavior, and thus to characterize it by a behavioral profile, just as we can now describe a chemical in terms of its chromatographic pattern. Ultimately, it ought to be possible to look at the chemical structure of any new drug and predict whether it will be useful as an antipsychotic, an antifatigue agent, an appetite stimulant, and so forth. By the same token, the physiological determinants of behavior will be so well worked out that we will understand why a drug which causes alertness also depresses hunger, or why one that causes difficulty in doing arithmetic also causes peculiar sensations in the skin. One can envisage the day when drugs may be employed not only to treat pathological conditions (reduce pain, suffering, agitation, and anxiety), but also to enhance the normal state of man — increase pleasure, facilitate learning and memory, reduce jealousy and aggressiveness. Hopefully such pharmacological developments will come about as an accompaniment of, and not as a substitute for, a more ideal society.

Conscious Control of Brain Waves

By Joe Kamiya

A YOUNG GIRL SITS ALONE. Her eyes are closed and electrodes are pasted to her skull. By consciously producing a particular brain wave, she turns on a steady tone that fills the darkened room. When she ceases to produce the brain wave, the room falls silent.

This is not a scene from a science-fiction drama, but an experiment in operant conditioning. Just as rats can be taught to press a bar, so people can be taught conscious control of their brain activity in a relatively short time. My studies indicate that by combining methods adapted from experimental psychology, computer technology and electrophysiology, we can increase our knowledge of the brain's function and of the elusive dimensions of consciousness, and can teach man to perceive and to control some of his brain functions.

The brain produces electrical activity from the moment of birth, and this activity can be recorded easily by means of the electroencephalograph. An electroencephalogram, or "EEG," shows a continuously changing series of wave patterns, waxing and waning in both size and rapidity of fluctuations and produced in seemingly random sequence. A number of these wave patterns—the alpha, beta, theta and delta rhythms—have been identified and named according to the number of cycles per second and the amplitude of the wave.

My experiments have been concerned with the alpha wave, a rhythm between eight and 12 cycles per second, with an amplitude up to about 50 microvolts. The alpha wave is the most prominent rhythm in the whole realm of brain activity and tends to come in bursts of a few waves to many hundreds. When one opens his eyes and reads or stares at something, the alpha rhythm disappears and is replaced by a random, low-voltage, mixed-frequency rhythm. Alpha rhythm is recorded most prominently from silver disk electrodes pasted to the scalp at the back of the head. These

MONITORING EEGS. Author Kamiya traces subject's control of alpha rhythms.

electrodes are connected to equipment in another room by means of wires.

While conducting experiments in sleep in 1958 at the University of Chicago, I compared EEGs made during the sleeping and waking states. I became fascinated by the alpha rhythms that came and went in the waking EEGs and wondered if, through laboratory experiments with this easily traced rhythm, a subject could be taught awareness of an internal state.

We began with a single subject. He was placed in a darkened room, told to keep his eyes closed, and his EEGs were monitored continually with equipment in an adjacent room. He was told that a bell would ring from time to time, sometimes when he was in state A (alpha) and at other times when he was in state B (non-alpha). Whenever he heard the bell, he was to guess which of the two states he was in. He was then told whether he was right or wrong.

The first day, he was right only about 50 per cent of the time, no better than chance. The second day, he was right 65 per cent of the time; the third day, 85 per cent. By the fourth day, he guessed right on every trial—400 times in a row. But the discrimination between the two states is subtle, so subtle that on the 401st trial, the subject deliberately guessed wrong to see if we had been tricking him. In order to be sure that he was differentiating between the two states from internal clues, we tried the experiments again without the bell. Perhaps, we speculated, since alpha and non-alpha are physiological states, they are connected with the threshold of hearing. But again he discriminated between the two states, saying A or B as he changed from one to the other.

We investigated the possibility that eye position might be related to alpha activity. We found that whenever our subject raised his eyes, there was a burst of alpha. Another test was run. This time he was required to look straight ahead, and his performance dropped from 100 per cent accuracy to 80 per cent. Yet within 40 trials he was back up to 100 per cent. Whatever relationship had existed between his eye position and his discernment of the alpha state was now destroyed.

These tests were repeated with 11 other subjects, and eight reached a significant proportion of correct guesses within seven sessions of about an hour each, although none reached the level of performance of our first subjects. These results suggested that a conditioned, introspective response had been established. When asked to describe the difference between the two states, all those who had taken part in the experiment described various kinds of visual imagery or "seeing with the mind's eye" as occurring in the non-alpha state. The alpha state commonly was reported as "not thinking," "letting the mind wander," or "feeling the heart beat." The task demanded focused attention, for when trained subjects were asked to repeat the alphabet backward during the trials, their discrimination of alpha dropped dramatically.

Interestingly we found that when subjects had successfully learned to discern the two states, they were able to control their minds to the extent of entering and sustaining *either* state upon our command.

Our studies here at Langley Porter Neuropsychiatric Institute in San Francisco have been on a somewhat different basis. The goal of these experiments has been to see if subjects can learn to control their alpha waves without first going through discrimination training. With the aid of digital logic components, we devised a circuit to respond to the occurrence of alpha waves by sounding a tone. As long as the alpha waves per-

sisted, the tone sounded. When the alpha waves stopped, so did the feedback.

The volunteer was seated in a darkened, sound-deadened room and challenged to find a way to keep the tone sounding. It was explained only that certain mental states produced the tone. Overt muscular movements were not allowed. At the end of each minute-long trial, he was told the per cent of time that he had been able to sustain the tone. After five such trials, his task was reversed. He was to suppress the tone for five additional one-minute trials. After 40 such tests, eight of the 10 subjects were able to control the tone, emitting

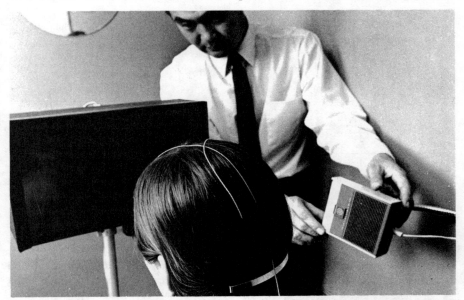

ALPHA CONDITIONING, control. Electrodes record when subject consciously produces particular brain wave. Graph, following page, shows result of five one-minute trials in conditioning; graph on far right shows mean performance of 10 subjects in frequency control.

or suppressing alpha waves in accordance with our instructions. [*See illustration, p. 48, right.*] Again, visual imagery was reported as effective in decreasing the tone—and the alpha—while an alert calmness, a singleness of attention, and a passive "following" of the tone sustained it—and the bursts of alpha activity. Alpha waves apparently result from an alert, non-drowsy state, devoid of concrete, visual imagery.

This experiment on trained self-control of alpha waves has been confirmed at several other laboratories. Dr. Barbara Brown of the Sepulveda Veterans' Administration Hospital has successfully used a light instead of a tone to help people turn on their alpha waves with their eyes *open*. Each time the alpha train was interrupted, the light dimmed and went out. Even though visual imagery has an initial suppressive effect on alpha activity, her subjects also learned to control their alpha waves.

People describe themselves as being

tranquil, calm and alert when they are in the alpha state, and about half of our subjects report the alpha state as very pleasant. Some of them asked us to repeat the tests so that they could experience once again the high alpha condition.

The reports, so closely resembling descriptions of Zen and Yoga meditation, were so provocative that we invited seven practiced Zen meditators to participate in our experiments. These men, who were experienced in Zen meditation, learned control of their alpha waves far more rapidly than did the average person. Meditation means long periods of sitting still, of turning the attention inward, and of learning to control the mind and body, and so the conditions required for the experiment were perhaps not strange to this special group.

The work of Tomio Hirai and of Akira Kasmatsu of Tokyo University is especially interesting in this context. They found a high correlation between EEG patterns and the number of years of Zen practice and the proficiency rating of Zen masters. These two researchers described progressive changes in the EEG of Zen masters during meditation: prominent alpha activity (with eyes open); increased alpha amplitude, particularly in the central as opposed to the posterior cortical regions; the slowing of alpha frequency; and—in mystics with 20 years or more of Zen practice—the appearance of trains of theta activity. (The theta wave is even slower than the alpha wave and has a rhythm of five to seven cycles per second.) In another study, B. K. Anand, G. S. Chhina and Balden Singh of the All-India Institute of Medical Sciences in New Delhi, found that beginning Yoga students with pronounced alpha activity in their EEG patterns while they were at rest had an unusual aptitude for the practice of Yoga.

The great interest at present in comparing various subjective states with that state produced by psychedelic drugs—and the deliberate use of these drugs to alter states of consciousness—indicates a possible value in studies of alpha wave control during the LSD experience. A study by Barbara Brown indicates that, by listening to the subject's report of his drug experience, one can predict the

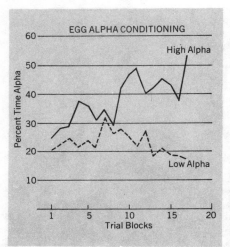

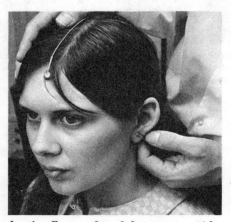

drug's effect on his alpha activity. If he reports only diffused states of feeling, his EEG will reveal little or no change; if he reports visual hallucinations, his EEG will show low alpha activity.

It must be stressed that there is no connection between alpha waves and extrasensory perception. People tend to associate the two because radio waves are involved in communication, but radio waves are generated at several thousand cycles per second, while brain waves range between a fraction of a cycle and about 100 cycles per second, with most of the energy limited to about 15 cycles per second. Also, the amount

of energy involved is so infinitesimal that a powerful receiver placed half an inch from the skull could never detect it. There is thus no evidence of electromagnetic radiation to the outside world by brain activity.

While the alpha rhythm covers the range from eight to 12 cycles per second, the dominant alpha frequency for each person is different and probably varies no more than half a cycle at any time. With this in mind, we tested the ability of 10 volunteers to increase or decrease consciously the frequency of their alpha rhythm. [*See illustration, below.*] Each volunteer heard a series of clicks instead of a steady tone. With digital logic devices we compared single alpha cycle durations with a standard duration preselected for the subject, so that about half of his cycle would be shorter than this standard. If the alpha rhythm took longer to complete its cycle than the individual's standard (fewer cycles per second), he heard a high-pitched click; when the rhythm was completed before his standard (more cycles per second), he heard a low-pitched click. The subject was told only that the clicks were generated by his brain waves and that his job was to increase the number of high clicks. Most people managed to control their average alpha frequency by this method, although they found it difficult to describe precisely what they did to gain control.

Since we first began experimenting at the University of Chicago, we have tested over 100 people. A few produced no alpha waves at all. Of those who did produce alpha waves, 80 to 90 per cent learned to control them to at least some degree. We found that people who were relaxed, comfortable and cooperative tended to produce more alpha waves than those who felt tense, suspicious and fearful, or who actively thought of what

was going to happen next. We found that people peak and then level off in the extent to which they can control the emission of alpha waves. Most of the people with whom we worked have been young, college-educated adults, from 18 to 45 years old. The youngest person we tested was 15, the oldest, 60.

More work needs to be done with other groups to determine what results can be obtained with uneducated people, people with low I.Q.s, and with professional groups such as bankers or insurance salesmen. It would be revealing to do a study with young children, who do not have a differentiated, sophisticated vocabulary and who lack abstract concepts for these internal states. They might give us a fresh look at what goes on inside our bodies, and they might prove even more skilled at controlling their own brain waves than adults.

We have only scratched the surface of a challenging new field. These studies need to be expanded even further into what might be called a "psychophysiology of consciousness." Each of the different brain rhythms could be investigated as we have studied the alpha wave. The activity of the autonomic nervous system is now being explored in my laboratories. The heart rate, visceral contractions, palm sweating, and muscle tension can be brought under control by this method. Our preliminary studies already indicate that the systolic blood pressure of some hypertensive patients may be subject to learned control.

Dimensional analysis of the specific psychological states associated with the control of physiological processes seems to be a worthy goal. This would require a computer that can store information, compare the relation among several measures in a single subject, and produce an instantaneous feedback. The fact that for many centuries mystics have been doing something measurably real suggests that the meditative tradition is worth examination. Learning the essence of this obscure, dimly comprehended tradition might strip it of much of its mystical quality.

We have expended very little systematic effort in our culture on teaching people to discern and control the inner workings of their bodies. Once we are able to control these body functions, immense possibilities suddenly lie before us. We then will have the tools for an intensive exploration of the consciousness of man. Different subjective states —anxiety, misery, euphoria or tranquility—might be mapped with the aid of trained subjects. Their reports of these

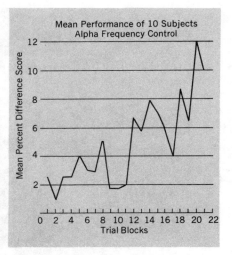

various internal states could be related to their EEGs and to the various reactions of their autonomic nervous systems. Perhaps, through methods like factor analysis, we can discover that anxiety consists of a particular proportion of beta and a wave not yet identified, together with specific degrees of certain measurable autonomic responses. We suspect that tranquility and alpha activity somehow are connected.

Psychiatrists and psychologists, today's specialists on matters of the mind, disagree on most of the fundamental issues concerning consciousness. Through an intensive investigation such as we have proposed, the discontinuity between the subjective and the objective aspects of psychology and psychiatry might dissolve, and we would have a unified science. Someday it might be possible to examine a patient's physio-

logical states and diagnose his neurosis just as the physician now detects tuberculosis by examining an X-ray. And if certain mental states can be defined, people can be trained to reproduce them. Instead of gulping a tranquilizer, one might merely reproduce the state of tranquility that he learned by the kind of training used in our studies. Perhaps our increasing concern over control of the individual by psychological persuasion could be diminished. People with full control of their internal states might be better prepared to resist external control. Studies of learning as a physiological process might disclose ways to increase the efficiency of learning in our schools and colleges. Trained control of bodily states might well be added to the curriculum, perhaps beginning as early as elementary school.

Suppose that we can measure the ef-

fect of a Beethoven concerto or a Shakespearean sonnet or a painting by Van Gogh. Would critics of the future be replaced by psychologists? They might at least be compelled to use a precise language. For the first time we might have a precise language for them to use because, to the extent that brain waves and other physiological states represent various states of mind, man would at last have an exact vocabulary for interpersonal communication.

Today we are little better informed about human consciousness than were Plato and Aristotle. By combining the methods of modern psychology and the advances in electronics and data-processing, perhaps one day we will make the same kind of stride physics has taken since the days of Democritus. ∩

AUTONOMIC CONTROL

by Peter J. Lang

"Recently I was asked to treat a nine-month-old boy who regularly vomited his entire meal immediately after eating. When I first saw him he was in an advanced state of dehydration and malnutrition. He weighed less than 12 pounds, was being fed through a stomach pump, and was not expected to live.

"Extensive medical tests showed that his condition was not organic. I'm still not sure how he learned this response, but we know that what is learned usually can be unlearned. I measured the muscle potentials along the infant's esophagus and found that on the graph paper I could detect the first wave of reverse peristalsis that just preceded regurgitation. I arranged an apparatus to give aversive electric shocks to his leg whenever his esophagus started to back up, which continued until vomiting had ceased. After only a few meals with this therapy the infant ceased to vomit. He is now a healthy toddler."

BEFORE HARRY HOUDINI performed one of his famous escapes, a skeptical committee would search his clothes and body. When the members of the committee were satisfied that the Great Houdini was concealing no keys, they would put chains, padlocks and handcuffs on him.

Of course, not even Houdini could open a padlock without a key, and when he was safely behind the curtains he would cough one up. He could hold a key suspended in his throat and regurgitate it when he was unobserved.

The trick behind many of Houdini's escapes was in some ways just as amazing as the escape itself. Ordinarily when an object is stuck in a person's throat he will start to gag. He can't help it—it's an unlearned, automatic reflex. But Houdini had learned to control his gag reflex by practicing for hour after hour with a small piece of potato tied to a string.

In more recent years scientific investigators have studied men with unusual body control. The Russian psychologist A. R. Luria described a mnemonist who in addition to his remarkable memory could control his skin temperature and heart rate. Merely by visualizing himself as asleep or as vigorously active, he could abruptly alter his heart rate over a range of nearly 40 beats per minute. And he could raise the skin temperature of his right hand by imagining it was on a hot stove, while simultaneously lowering the temperature of his left hand by imagining that it was holding an ice cube.

Classes. Houdini and the mnemonist run counter to our ordinary conceptions of what the human body can do. Tradition divides human responses into two neat classes—voluntary and involuntary—that correspond to two distinct parts of the nervous system.

Walking, hitting a tennis ball or clapping hands are voluntary responses—a person can learn to do these whenever he wants. The muscles that control these responses have striped fibers and are activated by the central nervous system.

Salivating and vomiting, heart rate, skin temperature, stomach secretions, and perspiration are involuntary responses—unlearned reflex actions. The nervous system that trips these responses is not under the control of the will—it is autonomous and for this reason is known as the autonomic nervous system. One can learn to give autonomic responses to a new stimulus—Pavlov's dogs learned to salivate to the sound of a metronome—but it has been assumed that one could have no voluntary control over them.

Undirected. The fact that we need not control autonomic events is a great convenience in day-to-day life. We do not have to take time out from other activities to digest a meal—it happens without our direction. When we wield pen or hammer, our attention is not diverted by the task of moving blood to the relevant muscles. On the other hand, our inability to control these internal events is often discouraging. It would be a blessing if a seasick voyager could calm his stomach at will. And how helpful it would be if a patient with hypertension could lower his own blood pressure.

Our visceral organs act without our conscious control, and usually without our knowledge. Except in marked arousal, one has no idea whether his heart is beating faster or slower than usual, or what changes are going on in his intestines.

Feedback. It is the absence of continuous information about visceral responses that makes them so different from the action of striated muscle. We ordinarily learn to guide our behavior by watching the consequences of what we do, and by making appropriate adjustments. Thus, a person is not expected to drive a car blindfolded —he needs to see the road and the front of the car.

Of course, the feedback need not be visual. Airplane pilots have learned to fly the beam, adjusting the position of an aircraft to changes in an auditory signal. If we could similarly perceive the consequences of visceral change, we might learn to guide these responses in the same way that we learn to control our hands, a car, or a plane.

The first researcher to produce serious evidence that

human beings might be able to control their own visceral organs was the Russian psychologist, M. I. Lisina. In 1958 she reported in this country that she had tried to train her subjects to dilate or constrict the blood vessels in their arms in order to avoid electric shock. At first she was unsuccessful, but when a subject was permitted to watch his own vascular changes displayed on a recording device, he quickly learned how to control them.

A few years later Donald Shearn, working in this country under the direction of the pioneer psychophysiologist R. C. Davis, taught subjects to control their own heart rates. A subject listened to amplified feedback of his heartbeat, and learned to avoid a mild electric shock by increasing his heartbeat to a specified rate at scheduled times during the experiment.

Drive. In 1962 I started work on the problem of autonomic conditioning in my laboratory at the University of Pittsburgh, and later at the University of Wisconsin in Madison. With Michael Hnatiow, I built an apparatus that permitted a subject to "drive" his own heart. The machine was reminiscent of the driving-skill booths in penny arcades. A subject had to keep the variability of his heartbeat within a specified range. For example, one subject's heart beat about 60 times a minute, so there was about one second between one beat and the next. Of course, this was just the average. Actually, the time between two beats might vary by a half-second or more during a minute, even while the overall rate remained at 60 per minute. The subject watched a small spot of light on a screen in front of him. Whenever the interval between two heartbeats was exactly one second, the light appeared on a vertical line in the center of the screen. When the interval was longer or shorter, the light moved off to the right or left. The subject was told to keep the light within a narrow "road" often less than 90 milliseconds wide—from 955 to 1,045 milliseconds. He soon was quite skilled at keeping the light on the road, and his ability improved with practice.

Previous investigators had used shock avoidance in feedback studies (and occasionally, positive rewards such as money), but we found that the students could achieve considerable heart-rate control without special incentives. The game was its own reward.

Wordless. When we asked the students to explain *how* they had learned, their replies were diverse and inarticulate. This was not unexpected—the English language has almost no words to describe how our bodies feel. I am just as inarticulate in trying to describe the muscles and movements I use in making a forehand shot in tennis as my subjects are in describing how they control their heart rates. In post-experiment interviews our subjects often said that they used idiosyncratic mental routines—counting backward, thinking of emotional events—or small ritualistic movements that they superstitiously believed were causing heart-rate changes.

The fact that our subjects were able to control their heart rates did not necessarily mean that we had demonstrated learning in the autonomic nervous system. One

can make one's heart beat faster by breathing deeply or by tensing certain muscles that are under voluntary control. To illustrate: Marion Wenger and his associates took polygraph recordings of Indians who were expert in Yoga. While none could actually cause his heart to stop (as had been claimed for them) some could slow their heart rates drastically. Wenger did not consider that he had found evidence for direct autonomic control, however. He speculated that the Indians exercised voluntary control over their breathing and chest muscles and that these actions produced heart-rate changes.

Dual Control. With this in mind, we monitored our subject's breathing and found no evidence that they were using breath control. However, a relationship might have been obscured by our method of recording or analysis, so Alan Sroufe of our laboratory made a more explicit test. First he trained his subjects to breathe at specified rates and depths. When they had learned this, he added the heart-rate feedback device to the experiment. The subjects were told to continue the respiration task and to control their heart rates at the same time. Despite the difficulty of steering two systems at once, the subjects also achieved good heart-rate control. Thus, although breath control such as that used by yogis may be a practical way to change heart rate, it does not appear to be necessary.

Manipulation of any large muscle group can also alter heart rate, however, and it would be impossible to control all the muscle options available to an intact human subject. But one can achieve such control in animals with injections of curare, which causes all the striated movement muscles to relax completely. The drug causes an animal to lie limp and motionless, though its brain and internal organs continue to function normally. Its breathing is done by an artificial respirator and this removes any possibility that heartbeat is controlled by breathing or muscular movement.

Rat Focus. When he was at Yale, psychologist Neal Miller and his associates administered curare to rats and rewarded certain heart-rate changes with electrical stimulation of pleasure centers in their brains. Soon the animals' hearts were going at the rate that would produce the most stimulation. Miller found that training rats under the drug was easier than training undrugged rats. He speculated that curare reduced external distractions and allowed the animals to focus on the activities in their organs.

After doing this experiment, Miller and his colleagues went on to demonstrate similar operant conditioning of contractions in the stomach, the volume of blood in the ears, even the rate of urine formation in the kidneys. They have also shown that the findings were not simply the result of activating the autonomic nervous system as a whole. For example, their rats learned to dilate the blood vessels in one ear only.

Other researchers have used operant-feedback methods to demonstrate that a human being can learn to control his own blood pressure, sweat-gland activity, and

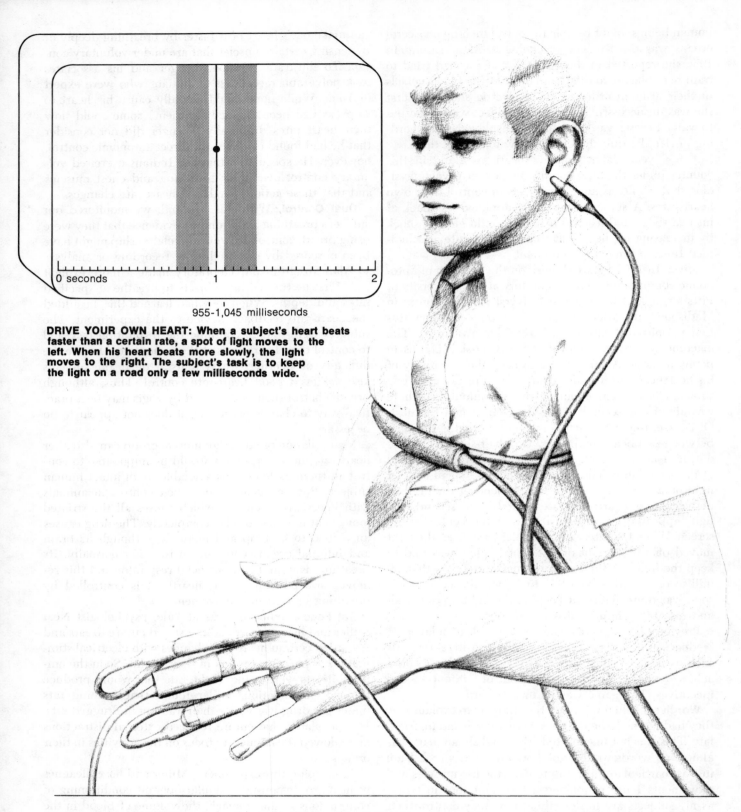

955–1,045 milliseconds

DRIVE YOUR OWN HEART: When a subject's heart beats faster than a certain rate, a spot of light moves to the left. When his heart beats more slowly, the light moves to the right. The subject's task is to keep the light on a road only a few milliseconds wide.

brain waves [*see "Conscious Control of Brain Waves" by Joe Kamiya, page 46*]. Last year Eberhard Fetz of the University of Washington demonstrated reward learning in a single neuron in a monkey's brain.

On the Screen. Now that we know it is possible to train autonomic functions, we are eager to test the limits of the operant-feedback procedure. We now use a digital computer to process physiological data instantly and dis-play it on a screen for the subject. As soon as a subject's heart beats, he sees moving across the screen from the left a horizontal line that is stopped by his next heart-beat. His job is to make the line stop between two stable, vertical lines positioned by the computer. The computer scores the hits and the misses on a scoreboard. When the subject achieves a certain number of successes the computer compliments him and then automatically readjusts target lines to require more control for success.

The computer is helpful and understanding. A subject who can't succeed at first gets an easier problem to work on until his success rate entitles him to a more difficult game. The machine is programmed to turn off in the event of unusual changes in respiration or muscular activity. Thus, striated-muscle "cheating" is discouraged and only heart-rate changes are reinforced.

Out the Window. Work on voluntary control of the autonomic nervous system has forced psychologists to some profound theoretical considerations. In the first place, the traditional neat dichotomy of voluntary and involuntary responses is now out the window. And we must now revise our conceptions of human emotion. For many psychologists the visceral activity of emotion was its primary defining property. In fear, one's mouth goes dry, the pupils dilate, breathing quickens, hands sweat, the heart beats harder and faster. One may deny he is afraid, but supposedly these autonomic signs will give him away. The belief that affect is immutably tied to the autonomic nervous system is so well-established that the instrument for detecting autonomic change is called a lie detector. But if visceral responses can be shaped in the same way as any other behavior, the lie detector is no sure route to emotional truth.

This is not to deny that visceral arousal normally accompanies strong emotion. Indeed, the autonomic arousal may itself contribute to the emotions. It is difficult to be calm, even in a safe and comfortable situation, when the heart pounds and the hands sweat. Reducing nervous symptoms directly may help to reduce the anxiety—the function of a tranquilizer. Perhaps one day we can do this voluntarily.

Relax. Systematic desensitization, which is one very effective type of therapy for fear [see "For Phobia: A Hair of the Hound," Joseph Wolpe, PT, June 1969], works with analogous principles. A patient is trained to relax muscles all over his body and to remain relaxed while a therapist describes scenes that would ordinarily arouse anxiety in him. Operant-feedback methods may one day permit a patient to calm his own heart rate, blood pressure and intestinal activities—even his brain waves—while the therapist describes the scary scene.

In our laboratory we are working on an experimental version of systematic-desensitization therapy in which the therapist is actually a digital computer. During treatment the computer analyzes the subject's physiological state continuously and the results may be used to adjust the pattern of his exposure to fear materials. Preliminary work suggests that a machine is in some ways more efficient than a live therapist. We plan to improve the effectiveness of computer therapy by training patients to relax their internal organs as well as their skeletal muscles.

Accidents. It has been assumed that psychosomatic diseases arise as a result of interpersonal stress, although it is difficult to explain why some individuals who lead relatively placid lives develop disease, while some who lead stressful lives do not. The new visceral-learning data suggest that some body abnormalties may arise through accidental reinforcement learning. A child who is repeatedly allowed to stay home from school when he has an upset stomach may be learning the visceral responses of chronic indigestion. If family arguments always erupt at the beginning of a meal, the food could reinforce the elevated blood pressure of the antagonists. This process may lay the ground work for many cases of essential hypertension.

A number of investigators are on the autonomic-learning frontiers. They apply research findings to human problems. Bernard Engel of the Baltimore City Hospital uses operant-feedback methods to teach patients to control cardiac arrhythmia. His results are very promising although it is not yet clear that the therapeutic changes he has achieved are due solely to the feedback program. Research groups at Harvard and the University of Tennessee are looking at high blood pressure and disturbances of blood flow to see if they can be brought under voluntary control with operant-feedback therapy.

Light. Francis M. Forster and his associates have reported some success in using analogous methods to treat epileptic patients. One patient who developed seizures when he was exposed to a specific rate of flickering light was treated successfully with a computer-controlled feedback system. In this procedure therapists exposed the subject to flickers at frequencies progressively closer to the critical rate. The computer analyzed changes in the electrical activity of the patient's brain. Whenever his brain waves began to look like those that typically precede a seizure the computer turned off the light and presented auditory clicks to disrupt the seizure pattern. The technique was effective in eliminating the patient's epileptic reactions.

While some researchers have reported dramatic success, it is not yet clear that visceral learning will actually become an important therapeutic method. No one has yet achieved consistent, large changes in cardiovascular or intestinal activity. Most learned changes in human heart rate and blood pressure have been modest—below the level of significant therapeutic effect. And it is doubtful that any learning can overcome autonomic abnormalities that result from physical damage in the organ tissues. Also, it may be that only a few autonomic athletes will be able to achieve important control—early data indicate as much. Work by Jasper Brener and Bob Stern suggests that actors may be able to learn heart-rate and sweat-gland control more readily than ordinary folk. And of course, it is possible that the patients who are unable to control their visceral responses are the ones who develop systemic diseases in the first place.

It is, nevertheless, clear that operant-feedback research has taught us much that we previously did not know about control of the human body. Whether we will be able to use the control to develop practical therapies for emotional disturbance or systemic disease is, I think, one of the most exciting questions in psychology today. ∩

The Matriculating Brain

Through operant-conditioning techniques, the human brain can learn to fire its own neurons singly or in complex patterns. Can it be taught to still the tremors of Parkinson's disease or wield an artificial limb?

THE HUMAN BRAIN, for all our intimacy with it, has surrendered less to scientific research than have the distant moon, stars and ocean floor, or such intimate processes as genetic coding, immune reactions or muscle contraction. This complex organ, with its more than 10 billion neurons, has had the incredibly difficult task of understanding itself. Perhaps the task has been so difficult because even thinking about thinking is like picking oneself up by the boostraps—one process negates the other.

The brain interacts with every system in a person's body. Experiments to determine how the brain controls body movements (motor responses) date back hundreds of years. Recently, we have begun to understand how the brain controls our internal organs (visceral processes). We had assumed that, unlike body movements, the brain regulated the internal organs automatically—that the muscles of the heart, for instance, were beyond conscious control.

Our assumption turned out to be wrong. Within the last six years we have discovered that one can condition the processes of his internal organs, *and we now know that the brain can actually learn to control its own pattern of activity*. With simple conditioning techniques a person can learn to increase or decrease his rate of urine formation, to dilate or constrict his blood vessels, to raise or lower his blood pressure. This discovery fundamentally altered our perception of how the brain can be trained to control the function of other organs, and has suggested a new approach to brain research: *operant conditioning of the brain*. With this methodology, which applies the same behavioral principles that B. F. Skinner developed, we can teach the brain to alter its patterns of electrical activity. We can even teach it to fire one neuron and not to fire an adjacent neuron, or to alternate their firing in a complex pattern.

The scientific and clinical implications of this new research technique are staggering. For the first time we will be able to determine the limits of brain function in a rather direct manner. What neural activity is necessary or sufficient for certain behaviors to occur? What happens to behavior when certain neural patterns are conditioned? What are the limits of the brain's ability to modify its own patterns of electrical discharge? What are the mechanisms by which this control is made possible?

This information should have a number of important clinical implications. It may give physicians the facts they need to develop new treatments for illnesses, like Parkinson's disease, that involve an abnormal neural control of body movements. It may also lead to a whole new technology in artificial limbs by making it possible to control them with electrical impulses sent from the brain.

My colleagues and I are involved in a variety of research projects which involve conditioning the brain's activity.

Brain-Wave Machines. In traditional operant conditioning, the subject performs a task, such as pressing a lever, which brings him a reward that increases the probability that he will make the same response again. The reward is the subject's feedback. It tells him that he is performing the task correctly. In the typical situation, both the investigator and the subject can *see* the response and feedback.

Operant conditioning of the brain works the same way, except that the response, being an electrical pattern of activity, is invisible. So we hook the subject up to a machine that graphs electrical impulses. But these impulses occur at a rate of hundreds per second. Taken together, they result in complex by Michael H. Chase

electrical wave forms. We therefore need a computer, or "black box" (biofeedback machine) of some nature to ring a bell or flash a light to tell the subject when he has performed the desired response—that is, when he has produced the neural activity the experimenter wants. The bell or light provides the subject with feedback by telling him whether his performance has improved.

We can monitor the broad electrical patterns, called electroencephalographic (EEG) activity, that the brain generates which last for hundredths of a second. Or we can monitor the activity of a single neuron, or a discrete group of neurons, which lasts for only thousandths of a second.

Alpha waves, a hot commercial item these days, are one category of broad-based EEG activity. From the amount of publicity about them—the miracles guaranteed the consumer who buys a $99.99 machine and makes it go beep by producing the right brain waves—it would be reasonable to surmise that there has been a major breakthrough in brain research. Not true. There has been only the development of a powerful new methodology for the study of brain activity with a great, but unproven, clinical potential.

Since Joseph Kamiya, the leading alpha researcher, published his work in 1968 [see "Conscious Control of Brain Waves" on page 46] the claimed benefits of producing alpha waves have escalated. Many persons today vaguely associate alpha waves with exalted states of consciousness; alpha waves, they believe, are a short cut to sudden enlightenment.

The Facts About Alpha Waves. Alpha waves, however, represent a pattern of electrical activity of the visual cortex that occurs when this area of the brain is not processing visual information. Alpha waves are generated by visual cortical neurons, or by the connecting points between these neurons, or by both. Usually a person produces alpha waves when his eyes are shut, but he can generate them with open eyes, as long as he is not processing visual information.

By operant-conditioning procedures, we can increase or decrease a subject's alpha-wave amplitude, and accelerate or decelerate its frequency. If a subject's baseline alpha activity is 10 cycles per second with an amplitude of approximately 50 microvolts, we can investigate what happens to him when he sustains this pattern for a period of time. We can also try to find out what happens to him when he increases or decreases his alpha-wave amplitude, or changes its frequency.

I believe that there is little difference between being drowsy and relaxed and being in the alpha state. A drowsy, relaxed subject who is not processing visual information produces alpha waves. Those who proselytize for alpha concede that it is like being sleepy, but they argue that something more happens, something tied to creativity, other-worldly sensations and occasional psychic phenomena, or that it improves the general state of mind. Current data are not sufficient to allow us to accept this argument, and there are no known therapeutic effects from prolonged periods of conditioned alpha activity.

Subjects trained to produce long periods of high-amplitude alpha report that they experience a decrease in visual imagery and that they feel very calm and relaxed. I have no quarrel with the accuracy of the feelings reported. But I do object to the conceptual framework that many investigators have built on the basis of these subjective statements. It is possible that the "alpha state" underlies unique physiological and psychological experiences, but I doubt it.

Besides alpha waves, other common electroencephalographic patterns have been identified: beta, theta and delta waves, each categorized by a specific amplitude and frequency. Beta waves occur during wakefulness and generally signify that the brain is active—solving a problem, worrying, perceiving. They also occur during REM (rapid eye movement—active) sleep, when the most dramatic dreaming occurs. Beta waves (15 to 30 cycles per second) are generally faster and of smaller amplitude than alpha waves (about 10 cycles per second). Theta and delta waves, on the other hand, are very slow (below eight cycles per second) and of high amplitude. They usually occur only when a person is extremely weary or in NREM (quiet) sleep. Each of these wave forms can be conditioned, and we can analyze the subject's responses to their conditioned occurrence.

The Hippocampus and Movement. The theta rhythm in lower animals is the predominant electrical pattern of the hippocampus, a structure deep within the brain that is associated with a variety of functions ranging from memory to sex to simple movement. Abraham Black of McMaster University, Ontario, Canada, is studying the hippocampus by using operant conditioning to increase and decrease the amplitude and frequency of theta waves. Black wants to find out which motor behaviors correspond to which theta-range frequencies in the hippocampus. He conditions an animal to increase the frequency of theta toward its upper limit, and finds that the animal vigorously moves its leg or turns its head. When the animal stops producing these high-frequency theta waves, it holds still.

Black tried, but was unable, to train animals to produce high-frequency theta without moving. This indicates an in-

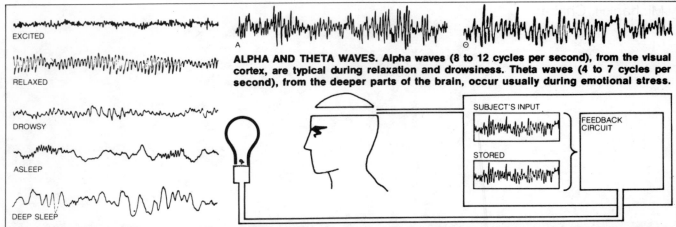

EXCITED

RELAXED

DROWSY

ASLEEP

DEEP SLEEP

EEG. Electroencephalographic records of brain activity during excitement, relaxation and varying degrees of sleep.

A   ©

ALPHA AND THETA WAVES. Alpha waves (8 to 12 cycles per second), from the visual cortex, are typical during relaxation and drowsiness. Theta waves (4 to 7 cycles per second), from the deeper parts of the brain, occur usually during emotional stress.

SUBJECT'S INPUT

STORED

FEEDBACK CIRCUIT

OPERANT CONDITIONING OF THE BRAIN. Electrodes attached to skull pick up brain waves. These waves are then compared to information stored in a computer. When the two match a light flashes to tell the subject he has produced the waves the experimenter wants.

timate link between the hippocampus and body movements.

I have used operant conditioning to change the electrical activity of localized areas of the cerebral cortex in cats. The purpose is to find out if specific conditioned rhythms lead to specific changes in a cat's behavior, and to see if, with conditioning, each area of the cerebral cortex can generate all rhythms.

Pavlovian Cats. When a cat is immobile, it occasionally produces a spontaneous EEG pattern of 12 to 14 cps from its sensory-motor cortex, a part of the brain concerned with the conscious evaluation and control of sensory and motor functions. This EEG pattern occurs when the animal is in a state of behavioral inhibition—that is, when it actively withholds a response, or when the animal is motionless. Pavlov theorized that an animal that maintained this state would eventually fall asleep. When we used operant conditioning to produce an EEG pattern of 12 to 14 cps in a cat's sensorymotor cortex, we found that the cat's somatic reflexes, muscle tone, eye movements and heart rate mirrored those of the initial stages of sleep. In short, Pavlov was probably right.

Since the EEG is an index of the normal or abnormal activity of cortical neurons, the operant control of the cerebral cortical EEG appears to have direct clinical applications. By modifying the symptom (the EEG) it may be possible to alleviate the underlying problem.

For example, we can record the EEG of an insomniac while he is asleep, or falling asleep. Then, while he is fully awake, we may be able to teach him to change his EEG activity in the direction of his "sleep" pattern; and thus condition a presleep or drowsy state. Or we could condition a decrease in heart rate, a decrease in muscle tone and very regular respiration—all of which occur during sleep. Perhaps prolonged alpha conditioning would achieve this same end. Our goal, regardless of specific strategy, would be to treat the person by decreasing the neural pattern that accompanies his sleeplessness or by augmenting a sleep pattern.

The opposite of insomnia is narcolepsy, or uncontrollable sleeping. Its most extreme and traumatic aspect is cataplexy. Just prior to a cataplectic attack a person is awake and feels entirely normal; then, in an instant, usually in conjunction with a strong emotion, the person loses all muscle tone and collapses. According to William Dement of Stanford University, there are an estimated 100,000 narcoleptics in the United States, many of whom also suffer from cataplexy. The number of fatal accidents that occur as a result of this condition is unknown, but probably high. If we could teach these patients to generate an electrical pattern in the motor cortex that normally accompanies heightened muscle tone, it might be possible for cataplectic patients to avoid attacks. During the short precataplectic period, after cortical conditioning, they might be able to sustain muscle tone and thus avoid an attack or diminish its severity.

Epilepsy also originates as an abnormal neuronal discharge. By conditioning a person to reduce the electrical brain pattern that is responsible for the attack, or by conditioning him to generate an EEG rhythm incompatible with the epileptic pattern, we might be able to reduce his seizures. We might also be able to condition the "epileptic" neurons to stop firing. In cases of Parkinson's disease, if we could determine the neuronal discharge that is responsible for the tremor, we might be able to use similar conditioning strategies to reduce or eliminate the abnormal motor activity.

Theoretically, the use of operant-conditioning techniques lets us attack a wide variety of clinical problems by influencing the central nervous system. But this kind of therapy has its dangers. The brain controls every system in the body, every physical and psychological state and process. If we change the electrical activity in one part of the brain, we affect almost all other areas of the brain and almost all other organ systems. Much basic brain research remains to be done before such procedures become safe and then common.

Blueprinting the Brain. The brain is still a conglomerate of extraordinary and elusive puzzles. EEG research is an aid to the intricacies of these puzzles, but, by itself, cannot provide all of the solutions. We cannot tell what a person is thinking by looking at his EEG, nor can we describe his physical state in other than very generalized terms. There is no way, at the present time, to condition EEG waves of any more specificity than those correlated with very gross approximations of sleep, wakefulness, movement, excitement, etc.

However, operant conditioning has given researchers a new way to draw a blueprint of the brain. Our research strategy is to change the firing pattern of a single neuron, small groups of neurons, or widespread masses of neurons. We then examine the consequent physiological and psychological condition of the animal.

Eberhard Fetz, of the University of Washington, Seattle, for example, places microelectrodes next to single neurons in a monkey's cerebral cortex. He finds that the monkey always makes a very specific movement—for instance, lifting one finger—when that neuron fires. Fetz then conditions the monkey not to make that movement when that specific neuron discharges. His conclusion: neurons that normally accompany a movement can fire without that movement taking place.

Fetz has yet to determine if the converse is true, i.e., if specific movements can take place without the firing of specific neurons; or whether there is a minimum number of related neurons that must fire to produce a given movement. But Fetz's work demonstrates that we can now investigate the processes that govern the firing of neurons and their relationship to behavior by manipulating patterns of neuronal output. This approach will lead to a clearer understanding of the functioning of the body's motor systems, and to their control, for both scientific and clinical purposes.

At Baylor University in Waco, Texas, LaNelle Linnstaedter is using an operant technique to condition a pattern of electrical activity that normally accompanies eye movement. She has been able to induce increases or decreases in this type of neuronal discharge, irrespective of a monkey's eye movements. In this case, operant conditioning has successfully separated normally linked patterns of neuronal discharge and motor activity.

Electric Limbs. John Hanley of the University of California, Los Angeles, is applying a system originally developed to track satellites to brain research. Hanley uses the "phase-locked loop" electronic circuit to compare EEG signals from a person's brain with an EEG pattern that is stored in a computer. When the two signals match, a switch is thrown electronically. This procedure can be used to provide reinforcement in operant conditioning. Hanley is attempting to use a miniaturized version of this technique to help amputees operate their artificial limbs. His system picks up EEG signals from the scalp of the amputee and feeds the signals into a phase-locked loop that allows the person to substitute subliminal control of the device for the usual method of conscious control.

Another group of researchers—including Stephen Fox, J. Peter Rosenfeld, and David Walker—is trying to determine the extent to which the brain can manipulate the activity of discrete groups of neurons that lie along sensory pathways. They condition responses to specific stimuli—a flashing light, for example, or a clanging bell.

These researchers may place electrodes along the visual pathway in the brain of an animal. They then flash a light in the animal's eyes. The nervous system carries this information from the external sensory receptor (the eye, in this case) through subcortical relay neurons, to the cortical receiving area. The implanted electrodes are used to monitor the amplitude and frequency of the discharging neurons, which form a regular pattern. This type of electrical pattern is called an evoked potential, an electrical discharge (potential) that is caused by a known stimulus. The next step is to condition the animal to alter this pattern of response with operant-conditioning techniques. This is done by using a biofeedback machine to determine when parts of the evoked potential activity change to a predetermined configuration.

So powerful is the operant-conditioning technique that the waves of activity in the sensory pathway can be doubled in amplitude or completely suppressed. The potential can even be manipulated so that very small parts of it can be changed without disrupting its basic configuration.

Further experimentation with operant techniques will tell us how an animal reacts to an evoked potential that is suppressed, augmented, inverted or changed in any manner. We also need to find out if the complete suppression of the electrical activity evoked by a stimulus will cause the animal to react as if the stimulus did not exist. Or will he become more aware of an augmented potential? This information should help us to understand the reception and integration of sensory information.

Altering the Brain's Activity. We have just begun to understand how to alter electrical activity in the brain—EEG activity, spontaneous neuronal discharges and the neuronal discharges we evoke with specific stimuli.

With operant-conditioning techniques, we can, in a sense, turn the electrical activity of the brain as a whole, or specific parts selectively, on and off like a faucet. Since the brain interacts with every organ system in the body, it might seem that mind control, in the manner of 1984, might be within our grasp. The therapeutic benefits would appear at first glance to be incredibly far-reaching. But, unfortunately, this is not the reality. Our knowledge of the significance and underlying functional properties of the electrical rhythms of the brain places a strict limitation upon the operant modification of brain activity. Operant techniques are limited by our lack of data relating behavior to brain activity.

I cannot stress too strongly that the brain controls every organ system in the body. When one modifies the electrical activity of one part of the brain, changes occur in almost every other area.

Biofeedback Machines Are Dangerous. The dangers involved in the utilization of operant techniques to modify central neural patterns of activity are exemplified by the large and aggressive commercial enterprises that market alpha-conditioning machines for home use. It is my belief that these machines should be regulated in the same manner as any medical procedure, prescription drug, or piece of electronic equipment that is subject to governmental regulation authorizing its use by licensed practitioners only. Once an individual has a machine in his possession there is no way for him to calibrate it; no way to make sure that it is continuing to detect the specific brain-wave patterns for which it was designed. An even greater danger to the free and frequent use of these machines is that we have not yet evaluated the effects prolonged periods of conditioned EEG activity may have upon a subject's physical or psychological state.

The fact remains that a marvelous new method for exploring the central nervous system, with great potential for clinical application, has been discovered in the last few years. Like any other new discovery, there were at first many fantastic predictions for its use. I believe that we have reached a stage where the first bursts of enthusiasm have been consumed by the flames of reality, so that we can now get on with the serious business of further exploring the central nervous system with operant techniques in a reasoned and critical fashion. We can fully expect that the results of these explorations will alleviate a host of clinical problems. ◘

This article is based upon a conference which was organized and supported by the Brain Information Service, UCLA and The KROC Foundation, Santa Ynez, California.

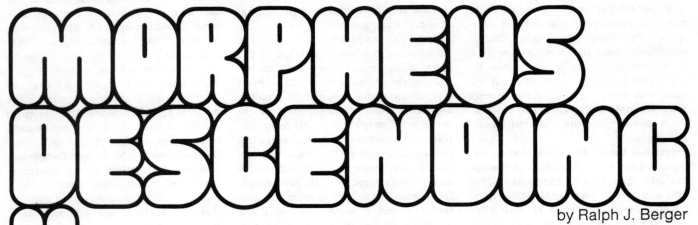

MORPHEUS DESCENDING

by Ralph J. Berger

UNTIL RECENTLY it was thought that when a tired man hit the sack, he slept like a log, not stirring until he awoke in the morning. By attaching electrodes to his scalp, forehead, chin, chest and penis, and connecting them to an electroencephalograph (EEG machine), we have found this is not the case. At regular intervals throughout sleep he tosses and turns, his eyes waggle to-and-fro under his closed eyelids, his penis becomes erect and his heart may beat as rapidly as it does when he runs a race.

From electrical recordings of the brain and body we have learned more about sleep and dreaming in the last 15 years than we had learned in all of time up to then.

In the mid-1950s Eugene Aserinsky and Nathaniel Kleitman found that the state of sleep is actually two states that are quite distinguishable from each other.

Four to six times a night, at intervals of about an hour and a half, we enter a sleep state in which the eyes dart and roll around under the lids. This state is called *REM* sleep because of these rapid eye movements. The REMs are clearly visible beneath the closed lids and can be observed by anyone who looks closely at a sleeping person, especially during the early morning. The first REM period of the night typically starts an hour or so after going to sleep. It is usually only five to 10 minutes long, much shorter than the 25-minute REM periods that occur later in the night. While the eye muscles are hard at work and the heart and breathing rates speed up, the rest of the body is extremely relaxed—muscle tension is lower than at any other time asleep or awake—so the REM stage is sometimes called paradoxical sleep.

Adults sleep with REMs only about 25 per cent of the night. During the rest of our sleep the eyes roll slowly from side to side or are completely still, so this state is called non-REM sleep *(NREM)*. Sleepwalking occurs only in this NREM sleep and most other activities like sleeptalking, snoring and bedwetting are also primarily NREM phenomena.

Dreaming. After the basic dichotomy of sleep was discovered, Aserinsky and Kleitman published an even more intriguing research discovery. People awakened from REM sleep often said that they had just been dreaming—much more often than when they were awakened from NREM sleep. The presence of rapid eye movement seemed to mean that the sleeper was dreaming.

Few respectable scientists were interested in dreams before these discoveries, because dreaming was considered a subjective, personal experience, unobservable by anyone other than the dreamer, and therefore not open to study by scientific methods. Dreaming was classed with folklore, psychoanalysis and such subterranean phenomena as extrasensory perception.

The new discoveries meant that if a night's mental meanderings could be correlated with the tracings of pens on EEG paper, then the elusive phenomena of dreams could be studied in the psychological laboratory.

Unfortunately scientific discoveries are rarely as dramatic and clear-cut as they first seem. We now know that dreaming can and does occur during every state of sleep. It is true that dreams are *reported* more often when people are awakened from REM sleep than when they are awakened from NREM sleep, but this is not the same as saying that dreams *occur* more often in REM sleep.

Chase. What is a dream? For one thing, it depends on how *dreaming* is defined. The kind of bizarre, active

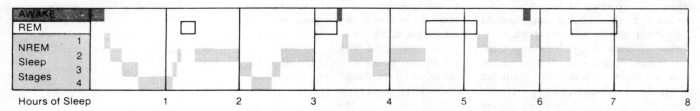

A YOUNG ADULT'S SLEEP PATTERN. There are four different stages of NREM sleep identifiable by characteristic electrical tracings of eyes, muscles and brain. First REM period is usually shortest and NREM periods get shorter toward latter part of the night.

dream recalled at the breakfast table is reported after 80 per cent of awakenings from REM sleep but only after seven per cent of awakenings from NREM sleep. Being chased through a supermarket by a gang of Hell's Angels is an example of this type of dream.

But if we allow fragmentary reports of mental activity — nonvisual, plotless, everyday thoughts — to be called *dreams*, then as many as 70 per cent of the awakenings from NREM sleep will be accompanied by dream-recall. In such a dream, one might be thinking out a mathematical problem, simply lifting an arm or bending down to put a dime in a soft-drink machine.

Dream investigators can judge with 90 per cent success whether a dream report was from a REM awakening or a NREM awakening when they read reports that are jumbled together. However, reports from either type of awakening become "dreamier" in content as they are obtained later and later toward the end of the sleep period in the morning.

Initially it was thought that the mental activity reported in NREM sleep might simply be the vague recall of dreams that had occurred during the previous REM periods. However, later studies by David Foulkes and his associates showed convincingly that there were some reports of vivid and visual dreams that occurred during the initial NREM stage, before any REM phases had appeared. Most investigators now agree that mental activity occurs continuously throughout sleep.

Memory. It is possible that the ability to remember one's dreams may be different in the different stages of sleep. The short-term memory of dream events is a fragile thing. Who has not awakened sure that he has just had a dream but not at all sure what it was about?

People differ in their ability to remember dreams. Some claim they have never had a dream in their lives. Yet when they sleep in the laboratory and are awakened from REM sleep, they report dreams 50 per cent of the time. It appears that "nondreamers" probably dream as often as dreamers but merely have poorer recall.

The small number of dream reports that follow NREM awakenings may also be the results of poor recall. Gregory Portnoff and his associates have been studying the consolidation period that appears to be necessary for an experience to enter long-term memory. Portnoff would awaken an experimental subject in the middle of the night, show him some written material, and then the next morning test his memory of it. He found that the subject's memory was better when he had been awake for a few minutes after reading the material than when he was allowed to fall straight back into NREM sleep. The period of wakefulness apparently provided an opportunity for the memory to consolidate: This apparently did not occur with immediate return to NREM sleep.

Another related finding is that dream recall drops off sharply within five to 10 minutes after the end of the REM period. A subject who is awakened say five minutes after the end of a REM period is typically less likely to remember a dream than is a subject awakened three minutes after a REM period. It is possible that we dream all through the night, but that the state of consciousness during NREM sleep is such that stimuli do not jell or set into permanent memories.

A Test. This memory-consolidation theory of the differences between REM and NREM reports would be supported if it could be shown that memory is better when a period of REM sleep immediately follows the presentation of the material. The problem in testing this is that people usually go directly into NREM sleep after being awake. There are exceptions—newborn infants, who may spend as much as 50 per cent of their sleep time in the REM state, often enter a REM phase as soon as they fall asleep. So do persons who are being withdrawn from certain drug addictions and persons with narcolepsy, who fall asleep without wanting to, even in mid-conversation. Ian Oswald is now trying to test the memory-consolidation theory with narcoleptic patients.

State Dependence. Another possibility is that in order to recall a dream the brain must be in the same physiological state it was in when the dream occurred. Many drug studies have shown that if an animal learns to navigate a maze under the influence of a drug, he may be unable to do so again until he is again in the drugged state. This phenomenon has been called state-dependent learning [see "High Education" by Donald A. Overton, *P.T.*, November 1969].

The state of brain activity in REM sleep is similar to wakefulness, whereas the brain-wave tracings from NREM sleep are quite different from those from the waking state. Thus, although vivid dreaming might occur continuously during NREM sleep, the dreams might not be available to memory when the subject is awake.

Subjects in NREM sleep sometimes *appear* to be dreaming, or having conscious experiences of some sort. People talk and walk in their sleep during NREM, and it would seem reasonable that sleepwalkers are having some conscious experiences. Yet when they are awakened they are usually mystified about why they are out of bed. Possibly the mental experiences are not registered in memory storage, or cannot be retrieved on awakening. Therefore the question of whether a sleepwalker is acting out a dream remains to be answered.

Watching. When sleep researchers thought that dreams came only during REM sleep, the natural theory was that a dreamer's eyes were darting around rapidly because he was watching a dream. Howard Roffwarg and his associates tested this theory by looking at a subject's dream reports and predicting what his eye-movement tracings would look like if he were watching such a dream. Then they compared their predictions with the actual eye-movement tracings which they had not seen previously.

When the dream reports were vivid, the experimenters considered their predictions to be good 70 to 80 per cent of the time. One subject recalled a dream in which she walked up five stairs, which she glanced up at with every step. The prediction that there would be five vertical eye movements corresponded closely to the actual eye-movement record.

Blindness. Some support for the scanning hypothesis also came from studies of blind persons' dreams. Persons who lose their sight late in life say that they can still visualize things. They have visual dreams and normal REM periods. But the congenitally blind are not able to visualize; they have no eye movements during otherwise typical REM periods. They dream, but they usually describe their dreams in auditory or tactual terms.

It may be that there is no direct connection between a blind person's loss of REMs and his loss of visualization; both may independently go with blindness. Gilbert Meier and I found that infant monkeys blinded at birth without ever having seen anything still had eye movements during their REM-sleep periods, though the number of eye movements became fewer as the monkeys got older.

Eric Moskowitz and I have tried to find the correspondence between eye movements and dream content that Roffwarg reported, but we introduced an experimental design that eliminated any possibility of experimenter bias in the matching of eye-movement records with dream reports. In these conditions the number of correct matchings was no greater than would be expected by chance. And we found several instances in which the recorded eye movements were totally inappropriate to the events in the dream. One subject said she had been dreaming of looking at a vertical row of buttons from a distance of about two feet. "I was looking vertically," she insisted, but her eye-movement record was almost totally horizontal.

Further, if the scanning hypothesis is correct, how can we account for the visual imagery often found during NREM periods? We also find that each person's eye movements tend to have characteristic rates and directions, even though the content of his dreams varies from night to night.

Dream Time. At one time it was thought that dreams could occur in a flash. We now know, at least for REM periods, that dream events take as long to occur as real events. Voices, bells, sirens and tactile stimuli are often woven into dreams. William Dement and Edward Wolpert found that when water was sprayed on the skin of a sleeping subject, he might later report that he was dreaming about a rain shower. I found that spoken names would produce "clang" associations in dreams. For example when I said the name "Robert" to a sleeping subject, she later reported a dream about a distorted rabbit. When "Sheila" was spoken, the subject reported a dream about a book by Schiller. And when subjects are asked to estimate how long it would take for their dream events to occur, their estimates correspond closely to the actual amount of time between the stimulus and when the subject was awakened.

Recharge. Explaining REM sleep is clearly connected with an understanding of the function of sleep in general. Perhaps the oldest theory of sleep is that it is nature's restorative—it keeps our brains and bodies from becoming exhausted by continuous activity. Since some lower vertebrates without a cortex, such as fish and amphibians, do not appear to sleep at all, the need to let our cerebral cortex rest and recharge itself was considered especially important.

Studies of individual nerve cells show, however, that the brain is never really asleep in the sense of shutting down its activity. The number of nerve cells that are active is about the same in REM sleep, NREM sleep and wakefulness, but the pattern of nervous activity is different. During NREM sleep the nerve cells fire simultaneously in synchronized bursts, but in the REM and waking states they fire independently and randomly.

Physiologically, the REM state can be more active than wakefulness. Heart rate and blood pressure go up. Breathing becomes faster, using up more oxygen. Males often experience erections, regardless of what they are dreaming about.

The theory that sleep is nature's restorative is also inconsistent with the sluggishness and fatigue many persons report after over-sleeping. John Taub has confirmed this subjective impression in our laboratory: persons who regularly sleep eight hours function best on vigilance tasks when they have had just that amount of sleep. If they have either more or less sleep, their performance is

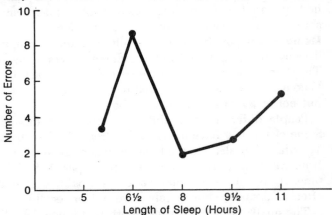

SLEEP VARIATION. Vigilance-task errors made after different lengths of sleep in eight subjects who regularly slept eight hours.

worse. We are following up these results by studying people who regularly sleep six or 10 hours a night to see if they function optimally when they have had just that amount of sleep.

Theories. Some investigators suggest that REM sleep may be involved in the sorting and storing of memories, possibly involving the synthesis of proteins. Others have postulated that it accelerates the growth and development of the nervous system in the fetus and the infant. Still others think that REM sleep serves a sentinel function, keeping the brain aroused so that when an animal awakens after a REM sleep period it can scan the environment for any threat to its survival.

There is evidence to support each of these theories. They have much in common and are not mutually exclusive, so one or all might be valid. To add to the pot, I have suggested the hypothesis that REM sleep maintains efficient binocular coordination of the two eyes. For maximum depth perception, our eyes must move together. Without the periodic exercise of conjugate eye movements during sleep, one's eyes might be out of alignment briefly on awakening, and depth perception would be considerably impaired. We might even see the world as double.

One bit of evidence in support of this hypothesis is that stereoscopic depth perception is present only in mammals, and so is REM sleep in its complete manifestations. In animals with 3-D vision, there is a striking

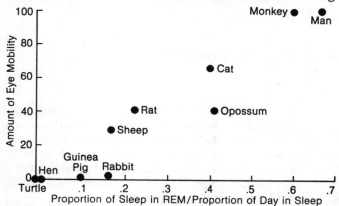

REM SLEEP. Correlation between amount of eye mobility in various species and proportion of REM sleep, normalized for total sleep time. Man's eye mobility was assigned a value of 100.

correlation between the amount of eye mobility in different species and the proportion of their sleep occupied by REM periods. Our research has even taken us to the study of tree shrews because they have very few eye movements and poor binocular coordination—their eyes sometimes move almost independently of each other. We found that the REM-sleep periods of these small primates are very poorly integrated compared to those of other mammals.

In another test of the hypothesis of REM sleep and oculomotor control, we have looked at the accuracy of subjects' depth perception when they are awakened from various periods of sleep. In eight subjects we found, as predicted, that binocular depth perception was significantly *better* at the end of REM periods than it was at their beginning, whereas the accuracy of monocular depth perception showed no systematic difference. In addition we found that binocular depth perception was significantly better a few minutes after one's awakening in the morning than it was just before one's going to sleep the night before. In contrast, monocular depth perception was significantly worse. On most performance tasks, people are typically somewhat poorer just after waking than they are before going to sleep, so the finding of an *improvement* in binocular vision after a night's sleep is especially interesting.

Hallucinations. Many drugs have a definite effect on REM sleep. Barbiturates and other sleeping pills act oppositely to amphetamines and other stay-awake pills in their actions on the waking brain. But they affect sleep sim-

ilarly, so that a person who takes either type of drug has shorter and fewer REM periods than usual in his sleep. If he uses one of these drugs regularly and then suddenly stops, the amount of REM sleep increases massively. A person in withdrawal from a serious drug addiction may spend nearly the entire night in REM sleep and spontaneously wake up several times to report terrifying nightmares.

Amphetamine addicts who tend to go for long periods without sleep often develop psychological disturbances such as paranoid delusions and hallucinations, that sometimes resemble the psychotic features of schizophrenia. Persons who have gone on marathons of sleeplessness without the help of amphetamines often show similar psychological disturbances. Ian Oswald and I observed a medical-student volunteer who had gone without sleep for 96 hours. He thought he heard voices while a water faucet was running and turned off the water "to hear them better." While walking along a main street he peered and pointed at the jacket of a friend, saying it had handwriting on it. He insisted that his companion remove his jacket for closer inspection. He later thought that his drinking water had been drugged and that he was going to be locked up in a hospital. He was normal after a good night's sleep.

Psychoses. These psychotic derangements are typical of dreaming—indeed, dreams have frequently been referred to as model psychoses. Because of these similarities between dreams and psychoses, William Dement thought that the psychotic features of sleep deprivation might be caused specifically by the loss of REM sleep. A pressure for REM sleep might build up until the dream hallucinations that were lost would break through into waking thought. In one study Dement deprived subjects of REM sleep by waking them up as soon as the REM periods began, but allowing them to get all the NREM sleep they wanted. He reported that his subjects showed increased appetite, anxiety, irritability and lack of concentration as a result of this procedure, but he saw no evidence of hallucinations or delusions. Later studies on REM deprivation have for the most part failed to confirm the production of psychological disturbances. Ian Oswald and I found that when volunteers went to bed after four nights and five days without sleep, NREM sleep took priority over REM sleep, so that REM sleep was less than normal.

People who have been awake for more than 60 hours are known to take frequent microsleeps—catnaps only a few seconds long—and these undoubtedly cause some lapses of performance and derangements of thinking. Vivid hallucinations and dream experiences often occur as a person is falling asleep. A sleep-deprived subject who is repeatedly falling into microsleeps may eventually fail to distinguish between these dream experiences and reality and thereby exhibit a syndrome not unlike schizophrenia.

One thing is sure: regardless of what specific functions the REM or NREM states may serve, we must sleep in order to stay sane.

ESP
IN THE NIGHT

By Montague Ullman and Stanley Krippner

Our interest in telepathy and dreams can be traced back to 1950 when Montague Ullman was treating a 40-year-old woman in psychoanalysis. She had been in analysis for over a year when she told of the following dream:

I was at home with David [her ex-husband]. There was a bottle on the table containing part alcohol and part cream. It was sort of white, foamy stuff. David wanted to drink it. I said no, you can drink it later. I looked at the label. It read "Appealing Nausea." I meant to drink it when we went to bed, although we seemed to be in bed at the time.

She then presented another dream that occurred the same night:

I had a small leopard. It was very dangerous. I wrapped him up and put him in a large bowl. Mother told me to take him out or he would die.

She was unable to think of any explanation for the symbols in the dream, though in searching for the usual sexual meanings, she said that the label "Appealing Nausea" reminded her of her own revulsion to sex: "When I get sexually excited," she said, "I get sick."

Ullman was struck not so much by the sexual symbolism as by the close correspondence to an experience of his own a few days earlier. With his wife he had attended a meeting of the New York Academy of Medicine to hear Dr. Jules Masserman give a talk about animal neuroses. Part of his presentation was a film outlining techniques for creating alcohol addiction in cats. In contrast to the normal cats in the movie, an alcoholic cat would pass up a glass of milk for a glass containing half milk and half alcohol. The correspondence of the

movie to the patient's dream of a bottle containing part alcohol and part cream was striking, and was emphasized by the additional dream about a leopard. Ullman asked the woman when she had experienced the dreams. It was the previous Friday night, she said. That was the same night Ullman was watching the movie about alcoholic cats.

Was it possible that telepathic communications could occur during dreams? Scientists had looked for ESP in daytime experiments with cards and dice and statistical tables, but their evidence left many scientists unconvinced. Might ESP be more demonstrable in the state of dreaming? Dreaming is an altered state of consciousness resembling in many ways the dissociated states frequently linked with para-normal events, and dreaming is highly related to a person's strongest current motivations, another resemblance to the anecdotal accounts of spontaneous telepathy.

In 1953 Ullman began a series of experiments with Mrs. Laura A. Dale of the American Society for Psychical Research. They kept daily diaries of their dreams and compared them every week to search for correspondences. On some nights their dream-diaries showed curious similarities, but the method was crude and had many weaknesses.

When the relationship of rapid-eye-movement (REM) sleep to dreaming was first recognized in the mid-50s, dream research gained respectable objectivity and impetus. Each dream could be studied immediately; it was no longer necessary to wait for fragmentary morning-after diary entries.

The REM technique was first applied

to the study of telepathy and dreams in 1960 at the Parapsychology Foundation, and later under more formal conditions at the Maimonides Medical Center in New York when a Dream Laboratory was established there in 1962.

In one exploratory study the subject was a psychoanalytic colleague. When electroencephalograph (EEG) tracings indicated that he was starting a REM period, an agent made a freehand drawing of a circle and concentrated on it. When the subject was awakened 13 minutes later he reported the following dream:

I feel as if I was sort of floating to sleep at the time. I had an image of a, oh, it wasn't really like a dream. It was sort of like being on a round road, like the bottom half of a large tube, such as if you would be going into the Holland Tunnel or something—sort of like a road. As I was traveling, there seemed to be people there but it didn't seem to be like a typical dream. Sort of falling asleep I caught an image and I was conscious of just having started to fall asleep. I was on a road shaped like the curve of a trough.

Our first formal study was essentially a screening device. Each night a young adult volunteer reported to the Dream Laboratory at his usual bedtime. We studied a different volunteer each night for 12 nights. An experimenter applied five electrodes from the EEG machine—a ground electrode to the subject's ear, two at the outside corners of his eyes to register rapid eye movements, and two in the parietal and occipital areas to record the electrical activity signifying the different stages of sleep.

The subject slept in a sound-isolated room, while his EEG tracings were monitored by the experimenter in a nearby room. A third person, the agent, spent the night in a third room, also acoustically isolated, 32 feet away from the sleeping room. (In later experiments the agent's room was across the building from the sleep room, 98 feet away. We are now using a soundproof facility where the agent's room is in a different building entirely.) The agent had 12 sealed manila envelopes with him, each containing a reproduction of a famous painting.

After the subject had gone to sleep, the agent selected one envelope at random, opened it and removed the art print. He looked at it, drew pictures of it and wrote down any associations he had to it, trying to communicate the content of the picture to the dreams of the sleeping subject in the other room. Two staff members, one male and one female, alternated as agents. The agent could open the envelope at any time after he received a signal from the experimenter that the subject was asleep. The agent continued to concentrate on the same print for the rest of the night. (In later experiments we included props in the envelopes to heighten the agent's involvement with the art print. For example, the packet that contained Max Beckmann's *Descent from the Cross* also contained a crucifix, a picture of Christ and a red pen, so that the agent could color Christ's wounds.)

When the EEG showed that the subject was starting a dream period, the subject was allowed to dream for about 10 minutes. The experimenter then awakened the subject with a buzzer and asked through an intercom that he report his dreams into a tape recorder next to the bed. Through another intercom, the agent could listen in on the subject's dream report but could not communicate with him.

The subject was then allowed to go back to sleep until another period of REMs appeared, when he was re-awakened and again asked to report his dreams. On the next night, with a new subject, the alternate agent randomly selected an art print from one of the 11 envelopes that remained.

In one instance, the randomly selected art print was Schlemmer's *Bauhaus Stairway*. It depicts several schoolboys

Oskar Schlemmer, *Bauhaus Stairway* (1932). Oil on canvas. 63⅞" x 45"

ascending a staircase. The subject, a young male psychologist, included the following observations in one of his dream reports that night:

Ascending. Very unclear. I was ascending some sort of road. . . . Going upward toward a hill . . . . I was going up a road, driving my car . . . but still going upward, you know, ascending this mountain. . . . One of the elements that pervaded almost everything was this conical shape, pointed conical mountain-like . . . shape.

On the morning after the experiment, the subject was asked to record any associations or comments he had about the night's dreams. He was then given copies of the 12 pictures, in a predetermined random order, so that the correct picture could appear anywhere in the series. The pictures were presented by a new experimenter who did not know which print had been selected the night before.

The subject was asked to select the picture that most reminded him of his dreams. He then ranked the rest of the pictures, in order, down to the one he thought least resembled his dreams. When the correct picture was ranked in the upper half of the 12-picture distribution, we called it a hit. When it was ranked among the six least likely pictures, we considered it a miss.

By chance, one would expect 50 per cent hits and 50 per cent misses. After

12 experimental nights we had studied 12 dreamers with 12 different art pictures and we had scored 10 hits and two misses, a statistically significant indication that we could influence a person's dreams in a manner that did not use any of the usual known senses.

We also had three independent judges look at the transcripts of each subject's dream reports and the subject's morning-after reflections and rank the art prints from most likely to least likely for each subject. The judges' overall hit-rate was not significantly greater than 50 per cent, but they were able to match dreams and pictures from the male agent's six subjects with significantly more accuracy than for the female agent's six subjects.

The best subject of the 12 was William Erwin, a young psychologist and psychoanalyst. He agreed to participate in a seven-night series, exclusively with the male agent.

After this series, Erwin received transcripts of his dream reports and for each transcript, he ranked the art prints according to their resemblance to his dream record. He was able to match up the prints and dreams with a significant degree of accuracy. Three outside judges were accurate to a highly significant degree when they matched the correspondences between target pictures and Erwin's dreams.

One night the print selected was Dali's *The Sacrament of the Last Supper*. During the night Erwin had eight dream periods. The fourth, fifth and sixth dreams dealt with doctors and healing, but otherwise had no apparent refer-

Salvador Dali, *The Sacrament of the Last Supper* (1955).

ences to the subject of Dali's painting. Here are excerpts from the rest of his dream report that night:

1) There was one scene of an ocean . . . It had a strange beauty about it and a strange formation.

2) I haven't any reason to say this but somehow boats come to mind. Fishing boats. Small-size fishing boats . . . There was a picture in the Sea Fare Restaurant that came to mind as I was describing it. It's a very large painting. Enormous. It shows, oh, I'd say about a dozen or so men pulling a fishing boat ashore right after having returned from a catch.

3) I was in a room all night, and it seemed like it was an analytic session . . . And I think then it led into the other dream . . . I was looking at a catalog . . . it was a Christmas catalog. Christmas season.

7) The only part that comes to mind is the part where I'm in a kitchen, and there is a restaurant that I was planning to go to.

8) I was sampling these different articles that looked like spices. Herbs. Grocery store. Place to eat. Food of different types.

When he was asked to associate to his dreams next morning, Dr. Erwin said: . . . The fisherman dream makes me think of the Mediterranean area, perhaps even some sort of Biblical time. Right now my associations are of the fish and the loaf, or even the feeding of the multitudes . . . Once again I think of Christmas.

Several other studies in our Dream Laboratory have yielded dreams that corresponded closely to selected art prints. One night the subject was a male artist. The picture selected was Dempsey and Firpo by George Bellows, which shows two boxers and a referee in a boxing ring. One of the boxers has been knocked through the ropes into the audience. The subject gave four dream reports that night, from which the following three statements are excerpted:

1) . . . something about posts . . . just posts standing up from the ground, and nothing else . . . There's some kind of a feeling of moving . . . Ah, something

George Bellows, *Dempsey and Firpo* (1924). Oil on canvas. 51" x 63¼"

about Madison Square Garden and a boxing fight. An angular shape, as if all these things that I see were in a rectangular framework. That angular right-hand corner of the picture is connected with Madison Square boxing fight . . . I had to go to Madison Square Garden to pick up tickets to a boxing fight, and there were a lot of tough punks . . . people connected with the fight—around the place . . .

2) I'm unclear if there are two or three figures in the dream because there seems to be the presence of other people . . . These people seem to have met in a social situation but they were there for some other purpose anyway, and they came together, but when they came together it was apparently the only reason that they came together. Now it seems to be clearer. There's one older figure of an old man and two younger ones that I can remember, and there certainly is an awareness of a third person.

3) A hexagonal cube appeared. It's a cube with a number of sides. I don't know exactly how many, but something like six or eight . . .

In another study, the art print selected was *Mystic Night* by Millard Sheets. The painting shows five female figures in a night-time ritual in a wooded area; a greenish-blue color pervades the mountains, grass and foliage. Our subject was a woman psychologist. Here are excerpts from her dreams:

Being with a group of people . . . It had to do with participating in something . . . and there's a woman in it. She's . . . in the country . . . I see lots of mountains and trees . . . The mountains are like those up near Bear Mountain and it's very, very green . . . The blue—this kind of sky blue color and the foliage—I mean, there was so much greenery and country atmosphere throughout. I remember the green and blue being terribly bright . . . I have the feeling that it's some sort of . . . a jungle scene or something with very lush foliage . . . There's some sort of primitive aspect to whatever was in that target. I can almost see it as some sort of tribal ritual in a jungle.

Since hypnosis is often allied to the dreaming state, we wondered whether the telepathic transmission of information would be facilitated if the dreamlike imagery were hypnotically induced.

Millard Sheets, *Mystic Night* (20th Century).

We had eight subjects in a hypnosis group—they were hypnotized and told to let their minds wander into dreamlike reverie. The eight subjects in the control group were given the same instructions, but were not hypnotized.

Meanwhile, one of the four agents in this experiment was attempting to transmit the content of an art print. After this brief test the subjects went home and kept a dream diary for the next seven days, during which time the agent concentrated each night on the same art print, trying to get a reference to the picture to appear in the subject's dream diary. After seven days the subjects brought their dream diaries into the lab.

Three outside judges attempted to match the images, the dream diaries and the art prints. For the hypnosis group, the imagery that was produced after hypnotic induction in the lab yielded statistically significant data, while their dream diaries at home did not. For the nonhypnosis group, the results were reversed; their laboratory images contained very few correspondences to the paintings, but their dream diaries produced significant results.

One member of the hypnosis group was a jewelry store proprietress. The agent selected, at random, Hiroshige's *A Bridge Across the Nishigawa*. These were the subject's images, produced after hypnotic induction:

Ropes. Sort of hanging. Cables of a bridge. The ropes led me on to the bridge. A suspension bridge.

Ichiriusai Hiroshige, *A Bridge Across the Nishigawa*

A female writer was in the nonhypnosis group. Her agent worked with an art print of *Girls at the Piano*, by Renoir. Her dream diary told of the following dream:

There were many girls about. All seemed to be pretty and there seemed to be some thought of a forthcoming beauty contest . . .

Records were on the phonograph. Light classical music. I was not aware of any particular selection but music was on.

Pierre Auguste Renoir, *Girls at the Piano* (1892).

The provocative data of this study suggest that hypnosis may have speeded up the processing of telepathic material

in the hypnotized subjects, allowing them to incorporate the art prints into their imagery at the laboratory. The non-hypnotized subjects did not perceive the paintings telepathically until they were at home.

In the eight years that we have been working in the Dream Laboratory, eight formal experimental studies have been completed. Of these, five have yielded statistical results supporting the theory of telepathic influences on dream content.

We are convinced that the effect is real, and have been conducting a number of pilot studies to determine new directions for telepathy research and to investigate the influence of many related variables. We want to know, for example, whether telepathic messages are received more easily in one stage of sleep than another. It is known that people awakened from deep sleep often report mental activities—mentation is not the exclusive property of REM sleep—but the deep-sleep mentation often seems to be closer to everyday thought than the symbolic distorted content of REM-dreams.

We conducted a pilot study on a college psychology instructor, waking him from dream periods one night, from deep-sleep periods on others. One of the art prints used was Chagall's *The Fiddler*. The central figure in the painting is a bearded man playing a fiddle. When he was awakened from a REM period the subject reported a dream about Allen Ginsberg, who bears a striking, although somewhat disguised, resemblance to Chagall's bearded Jewish fiddler. On another night, when the agent was concentrating on the same target picture, we woke the subject only during deep sleep, and at times we elicited even more striking correspondences:

All I remember . . . is somebody with long hair, dark hair, and a long beard . . . I don't think it was a real dream either . . . Long beard. Full beard . . . He had a long, full beard and a moustache . . . A very impressive figure in an outdoor scene . . . The guy with the beard . . . was standing . . . with the wind blowing his hair.

Further research is needed to substantiate these findings and to explore other important factors—the personality variables that enter into telepathic influence, the conditions under which telepathy

Marc Chagall, *The Fiddler* (1911-1914).

occurs and the possibility of precognition in dreams. Are the results any different when early and late REM periods are compared? Do the number of REMs in each dreaming episode bear any relation to the incidence of telepathic communications? Are any other stages of sleep favorable to ESP? In anecdotes, spontaneous paranormal experiences are commonest between two people who are emotionally close, which suggests that instead of working with strangers as subject and agent we might find greater incidence of telepathy if we enlisted husbands and wives, friends and lovers. In the meantime, our procedure has been adapted by other dream laboratories; we hope that coordinated explorations can produce additional information concerning telepathic dreams. ♫

Who Believes in Hypnosis?

by Theodore Xenophon Barber

"Keep your eyes on the little light and listen carefully to what I say. If you cooperate and try hard, you can easily learn to fall into a deep hypnotic sleep. Now relax and make yourself entirely comfortable. Relax every muscle in your body. Let yourself be limp. You are completely relaxed. Tired and drowsy. Sleepy, sleepy."

With instructions like these, hypnotists claim to place a subject in a "hypnotic-trance state," a separate state of consciousness considered to be uniquely different from the waking or sleeping state. People are said to be highly suggestible in the hypnotic-trance state, able to do things they could or would not do while awake: they are said to become insensitive to pain, to acquire superhuman strength, and to have complete amnesia regarding the experience when they are returned to the normal state.

Thousands of books, movies and professional articles have woven the concept of "hypnotic trance" into the common knowledge. And yet there is almost no scientific support for it. It has been assumed that the hypnotic-trance state is real—that there is some reliable way to tell whether a person is hypnotized or not, some simple physiological measure—brain waves, eye movements, pulse rate or galvanic skin response, for example—that would clearly distinguish a hypnotized person from a normally awake person. Unfortunately there is no such test.

A basic difficulty is that the notion of "hypnotic state" is used circularly. Theorists say, for example, that a person obeys suggestions because he is in a hypnotic state. But when we ask how they know the person is in a hypnotic state to begin with, they say "because he obeys the suggestions."

Human Plank. But one may reasonably ask how we explain the bizarre things that people can do in hypnotic situations. For instance, how does the stage hypnotist make a man's body so rigid that he can be stretched out like a plank, his head on one chair and his ankles on another?

The problem here is that we are assuming that a person could not perform this feat in an ordinary waking state. But this is not true—the human-plank feat only *looks* hard. The Australian psychologist John Collins found that practically all normally awake persons can remain suspended between two chairs while supported only by the head and ankles. And I find that after I give motivating "you-can-do-it" instructions, almost any male subject can even support another man on his chest; the subject rests his shoulders on one chair and his calves on another, all without hypnosis.

Analgesia. Probably the most dramatic hypnotic feat is the ability to go through an ordinarily painful experience without reporting pain. Some persons even consider suggested analgesia as a test for the presence of hypnosis.

It is true that both the subjective report of pain and the physiological reactions that usually accompany pain can be reduced if a person has gone through a typical hypnotic-induction procedure and has received suggestions for pain insensitivity. Robert Sears, for example, found that under hypnotic analgesia a subject's report of pain could be diminished, and the normal galvanic skin response to a sharp steel point could be reduced by 22 per cent when compared to a waking control condition.

But a simple waking control group is not the best measure of what normal persons can do. When a person goes through a typical hypnotic-induction procedure, he is told to become relaxed, sleepy, and to enter a hypnotic state; he also is given *special suggestions*, such as suggestions intended to reduce pain.

The nonhypnotic group must be treated in the same way as the hypnotic group except, of course, its members are not to be exposed to a hypnotic-induction procedure. That is, in studying analgesia, the nonhyp-

66

notic subjects must also be given suggestions intended to reduce pain.

Pressure Pain. David Calverley and I recently ran the appropriate comparison in a study of analgesia with student nurses. To produce pain we used a heavy weight bearing down on a small area of a finger; this does not produce permanent tissue damage but is reported as very painful. Half of the nurses were exposed to a hypnotic-induction procedure—they were told repeatedly for 10 minutes that they were becoming relaxed, drowsy, sleepy, and were entering a hypnotic state. Then we suggested that if they kept their thoughts on an interesting story that would be played on a tape-recorder during the pain stimulation, they would experience no pain. The rest of the nurses were not exposed to a hypnotic-induction procedure; we simply told them that if they kept thinking about the story on the tape-recorder during the pain stimulation, they would not experience pain.

We found no difference between these groups—both said that they felt less pain and both had fewer physiological reactions to the experience than did student nurses who were simply asked to undergo the pain stimulation without any special instructions or suggestions.

Other researchers have confirmed this finding, often when they didn't expect to. For example, T. E. A. Von Dedenroth has found that suggestions for pain relief are effective in alleviating severe headache and toothache pain in patients who appear to be in deep trances and also in patients who are not hypnotized.

Warts. A few years ago, A. H. C. Sinclair-Gieben and Derek Chalmers, two Scottish investigators, gave a sugges-

"Hypnotists have claimed the ability to improve vision and to change heartbeat rates, blood-glucose levels and stomach-acid secretions."

tion to each of 14 hypnotized patients that his warts would disappear, but only from one side of his body. After three months, nine of the 14 were cured of warts on the "treated" sides. In one case, the warts also disap-

peared from the "untreated" side, six weeks after the "treated" side was cured.

Some warts can be cured by suggestion alone, however. Alois Memmesheimer, Stephanie Dudek and others found that applying an innocuous blue or red dye—and suggesting that this "medicine" would make warts go away—tended to accelerate the cure of warts in schoolchildren.

Hypnotists have claimed the ability to produce and inhibit allergic reactions and labor contractions, to improve vision and to change heartbeat rates, blood-glucose levels and stomach-acid secretions. But in each case there is evidence that the same things can also be obtained by suggestion alone *when no attempt is made to induce hypnosis*, and in about the same proportion of subjects.

Hearing Things. It is true that some persons can be made to hallucinate in hypnosis, but they can also hallucinate without it. In my laboratory at the Medfield Foundation we asked control subjects in two experiments to close their eyes and to hear a phonograph playing *White Christmas*. Later we asked them what they had experienced, and about 50 per cent of the subjects in both experiments said that they heard the music clearly. There was even more report of hallucination when the subjects were given extra motivation—by hypnotic procedures or by task-motivation instructions—though neither type of instruction was better than the other. We got similar results with visual hallucinations—asking each subject to see a cat sitting on his lap.

Deafness. After suggesting to the subject that he is deaf, the hypnotist may ask, "Can you hear me?" Some subjects reply, "No, I can't," thus admitting that they can hear. Or the hypnotist might say, "Now you can hear again," and if the subject then responds normally it is obvious that he could hear all along.

When subjects do not fall for these tricks, there are still ways to tell whether they are really deaf. When a person with normal hearing reads a paragraph aloud and his words are recorded, delayed about half a second and then played back to his ears through headphones, he will show marked speech disruptions—halting, stuttering, and slurring his words. David Calverly and I studied both hypnotic subjects and waking motivated

subjects who, after they received suggestions of deafness, claimed that they were deaf. When exposed to a delayed playback of their voices, they halted, slurred and stuttered, just as if they had normal hearing.

"After suggesting to the subject that he is deaf the hypnotist may ask, 'Can you hear me?' Some subjects reply, 'No, I can't.' "

Regression. Psychotherapists claim that with hypnotic regression their patients can call up long-forgotten memories and actually reexperience events of many years ago. To test this claim objectively, David Calverley and I conducted an experiment with 90 psychology students who had learned a list of nonsense syllables at the beginning of the semester. Toward the middle of the semester, we gave them suggestions to regress to the time they had originally learned the nonsense syllables—"You are going back in time to the beginning of the semester.... You have just learned the nonsense syllables." Some of the subjects were given the regression suggestions after they were exposed to a hypnotic-induction procedure and others were given the regression suggestions under waking conditions. Neither the hypnotic-regressed nor the waking-regressed differed significantly from a control group who were simply asked to recall the syllables without being given any suggestions about regression.

Post-Hypnotic Suggestion. It has been assumed that a hypnotic subject is markedly more responsive than a waking control subject to the suggestion that he will perform a certain act after the experiment. In every study in which this assumption has been put to the test, it has been disconfirmed. Esther Damaser, for example, gave each experimental subject 150 postcards with the suggestion that he would mail the cards back to the experimenter, one card each day. More cards came back from the subjects who were given the suggestion while they were awake than from the ones who were given the suggestion under what was said to be a medium or deep trance.

Amnesia. Many persons assume that on waking from a hypnotic trance subjects are unable to remember what has happened, but the opposite is the case: practically all subjects remember the events of deep trance unless they are specifically told to forget them. And even then the subject may claim to have forgotten, yet show by other measures that he still remembers. Everett Patten, for example, gave selected good hypnotic subjects practice in complex addition problems and then suggested that they forget the practice sessions. All subjects said they had forgotten. He then gave them new addition problems. If they had truly forgotten their practice sessions they would *not* show improvement in performance which typically results from practice. The subjects *did* show improved performance, however, indicating that they had retained the material learned during the practice sessions, even while they claimed they had not.

"Trance." Ernest Hilgard has said that the subject's own report that he "feels hypnotized" should be taken as primary evidence for the presence of hypnotic trance. The problem here is that whether or not a subject reports himself hypnotized depends on many subtle variables such as the wording and tone of the questions that are used to elicit his report. In one study, for example, I interviewed subjects after they had responded to all eight suggestions on a hypnotic suggestibility scale. When they were asked, "Did you feel you *could not* resist the sug-

gestions?," all subjects said yes. But when similar subjects were asked the opposite, "Did you feel you *could* resist the suggestions?," 50 per cent still said yes. Whether or not a person says he has experienced the hypnotic state also depends on what he thinks "hypnosis" is supposed to be. For instance, some subjects believe that "hypnotized" individuals are not

aware of what is going on and are in a zombielike trance. When they find that they do not lose awareness and do not become zombielike when they are exposed to hypnotic-induction procedures, they conclude that they are not "hypnotized" even when they respond to all of the suggestions. Other subjects think that hypnosis is a state of relaxation. If these subjects feel relaxed during the experiment, they report that they feel hypnotized even when they are unresponsive to suggestions. If subjects are told repeatedly that they are becoming relaxed, drowsy and sleepy, they may appear to be in hypnotic trance—they may look passive or lethargic, they may stare blankly when they open their eyes. But if the hypnotist tells them to sit up, be alert, and not look that way, they will appear normal while continuing to respond to suggestions.

The way a person behaves under hypnosis depends in part on what he expects the hypnotic state to be like. Martin Orne once gave a lecture on hypnosis to a class of introductory psychology students. He gave them a list of the typical effects of hypnosis, but he included an extra one: he said that under hypnosis the dominant hand becomes cataleptic—it will stay in whatever position it is placed. When he later put these students under hypnosis, 55 per cent of them went into "trance" with catalepsy of the dominant hand.

Bias. It is difficult to study hypnosis in adults who already have their own ideas of what hypnosis is like. Our conceptions have been shaped by the hand-passes and finger-snaps of stage hypnotists, by books like *Trilby* and *The Search for Bridey Murphy,* by movies like *Manchurian Candidate* and by news stories about Sirhan Sirhan and Charles Manson. We "know" that hypnotized people behave irrationally, with glassy stares, zombielike movements and sluggish, mechanical speech. So when it is suggested that we are under hypnosis, it is no wonder that we tend to behave exactly as expected.

Suggestibility. Simply by telling a subject that he is in a hypnosis experiment rather than in some other kind of experiment one can increase his suggestibility. His suggestibility can also be increased by repeatedly telling the subject that he is becoming relaxed, drowsy and sleepy. But hypnotic procedures are not neces-

sary to produce a high level of suggestibility. If waking control subjects are exposed to task-motivational instructions—if they are exhorted to cooperate and to try to think about and to imagine vividly those things that will be suggested—they show about as high a level of suggestibility as

subjects who are exposed to hypnotic-induction procedure.

Both hypnotic subjects and waking control subjects are responsive to suggestions for analgesia, age-regression, hallucination and amnesia if they have positive attitudes toward the situation and are motivated to respond. They listen to the suggestions without analyzing them critically and they let themselves think about and vividly imagine the things that are suggested—for example, that they are insensitive to pain, that they have returned to childhood or that they hear music playing.

Testimony. We have learned much about hypnosis by interviewing subjects after the experiments. After several suggested analgesia studies we asked both the hypnotic subjects and the motivated waking subjects how they were able to "block out" or ignore the normally painful stimuli. Some said that they tried to imagine or think of themselves as numb and insensitive; others said they tried to think of pleasant events during the experience. We found that one of the most effective techniques was to focus on the sensations and think of them *as sensations* with their own unique and interesting properties. Women are often given instructions similar to these when they are preparing for natural childbirth.

After I learned the technique I was able to produce analgesia in myself without hypnosis. For instance, I found to my surprise that I did not experience my typical anxieties and pains in the dentist's chair when I tried to focus on the sensations—drilling, pricking, pressure—and tried to think of each as unique and interesting.

We interviewed waking motivated subjects and hypnotic subjects who were able to accept suggestions for age-regression. Many subjects said

---

"Since no test has been able to demonstrate the existence of the hypnotic state, there is no reason to assume that there is such a state."

---

that when they were given the suggestions to regress to childhood, they tried to think of their bodies as small and to think of themselves as children in specific situations that they recalled from childhood. They also tried to inhibit contrary or "negative" thoughts—they stopped telling themselves, for example, that they were really adults sitting in a hypnotist's office. My research associates and I find that we too can experience age-regression (with or without "hypnosis") with these techniques—purposely thinking of ourselves as children, vividly imagining situations that had occurred during childhood, and inhibiting all contrary thoughts. We find that we can also accept suggestion to hallucinate by using similar techniques.

Post-experimental interviews have also revealed how some subjects can actually appear to have amnesia. Subjects rarely claim that they simply forgot—they talk about their active attempts to forget and avoid remembering—"I know what it is but I just kind of stop myself before I think of it"; "I put the material out of my mind by thinking of other things."

This is not as difficult as it first appears. For instance, if I tell you emphatically to forget the first part of this article, you will recall the material only if you pause briefly and think back to what you have read. If you prevent yourself from making that brief pause to think back, and keep your attention on the present material, you can truthfully state that at this moment you do not recall what you read earlier.

It is clear that by studying the subjective reports of hypnotized and motivated control subjects we may learn about techniques to help realize some of the unused potential of the human mind.

Concept. I have put the terms "hypnosis" and "hypnotic state" in quotation marks when they were first referred to because I think the terms have no clearly defined referents; they can be used, after the fact, to explain every conceivable finding. For example, in 1964 I reported the finding that people were more suggestible when they were told that it would be easy to respond than when they were told that it would be difficult. The hypnotic-state theory has no difficulty with this finding—it simply assumes that the statement "it will be easy" produces a deeper hypnotic trance than the statement "it will be difficult." But suppose the data had come out the other way—showing that subjects did best when told their task was going to be difficult. The hypnotic-state theory would be unruffled —it would just assume that a deeper trance was produced by the suggestion that the task will be difficult.

When my researches showed that control subjects could exhibit high responses to suggestions of analgesia, hallucinations, amnesia and so forth when given only task-motivating instructions, the hypnotic-state theorists were not impressed. They simply said that my control subjects had spontaneously slipped into hypnosis without my knowing it. And since these theorists assume that the hypnotic state is necessary to produce these effects, the fact that I observed the effects in motivated control subjects meant that the subjects must have really been hypnotized!

Since the concept "hypnosis" can be used to explain every conceivable experimental finding, it is questionable whether it actually explains anything at all. And since no test has been able to demonstrate the existence of the hypnotic state, there is no reason to assume that there *is* such a state.

"Hypnosis" may eventually go the way of "ether" in physics and "phlogiston" in chemistry—concepts that went through brief popularity but have long since been abandoned because they were unnecessary to explain anything in the real world. ♌

PARAPSYCHOLOGY

New Neighbor or Unwelcome Guest

By Gardner Murphy

THE HOUSE OF SCIENCE has many rooms, but it is not yet large enough to accommodate all the children Nature sends to the door. Unwelcome guests are an embarrassment. It is tempting, but also rude and backward, to slam the door in their faces. A stray who is turned away must remain outside the family; those who cannot bear the disorder of construction will never make their house into a mansion.

The aim of parapsychology is to authenticate, assemble, categorize and assimilate certain "absurd" events that Nature sends our way. It does this by examining raw data and then by analyzing the somewhat more systematic data arduously achieved through experiment. A few examples, first, of the "spontaneous cases" that parapsychology confronts. The experiments will follow in due course.

A close friend of mine was driving hard over the rolling land of southwestern Wisconsin, hoping to get home to Cedar Rapids, Iowa, by midnight. About six o'clock an impression began to overwhelm him that something was seriously wrong, and by seven he knew that he must not drive straight on to Cedar Rapids but must stop at Dubuque and call his wife. He argued with himself back and forth, thinking there was absolutely nothing wrong at home, and why should he go to Dubuque—a city he had never visited. Still, he knew the name of a hotel there, and he knew he would have no trouble making a phone call. The impression of foreboding grew upon him alarmingly. There could be nothing wrong. But there was. He got to Dubuque and found a telegram from his wife announcing the death of their infant daughter. The little girl had not been

ill. The message was, in a sense, protective, for the young man found it slightly easier to bear the news on the Western Union form than he would have at home with his wife.

I say nothing about this example except to make two points. First, it is what we call a spontaneous case of telepathy, regardless of what its ultimate meaning may be. Second, I emphasize what we do *not* know. We do not know why the wife thought that the husband could get a message in Dubuque. She had herself perhaps become confused, and there is a possibility here of a two-way distant interaction, as there often seems to be. We do not know whether the wife had previous experiences with "sending" and the husband with "receiving" such messages, and if so, under what conditions. We do not know what state of mind or body the man was in, or how his sense of foreboding fitted into other psychophysiological dispositions. Finally, we know nothing whatever about physical factors in the transmission of this particular message.

These and other questions are usually unanswered in spontaneous cases of telepathy. It is a sad fact that after 75 years of noting these experiences, most psychical researchers are still concerned mainly to get them authenticated and do not go any further. They talk to the people who had the experience, they talk to witnesses, they record dates and if possible they offer diary notes, letters or other independent supports. But suppose we had to build a science of psychology only by carefully authenticated observations. Suppose, worse still, that we based our experimental studies only on events in laboratories, with very little reference to spontaneous situations in

the outside world. More than laboratory work, parapsychology needs enormously better spontaneous cases, especially ones that give us more knowledge of the psychophysiological situation of the persons involved. Well-planned experiments can follow, not precede.

A young man had been teaching an amateur astronomy class at the "Y" in Dallas. When he arrived home, he sat on the edge of his bed before lying down. Suddenly there in the room was his father, wearing a work cap and work clothes, with a caliper rule in his lapel pocket. How could this be? His father was in California. As he greeted his father, the figure disappeared and a messenger from Western Union came up the path with a wire from the mother in California saying that the father had just died. He had been working on the car that day, and beside the bed on a chair were his cap and work clothes, with a caliper rule in the lapel pocket.

Here again, we know very little about the physics, the psychology, the "meaning" of the experience. One person may call this telepathy, another may not. It is not clear that the process of naming it is really helpful in providing a scientific perspective within which the event makes sense.

In an early attempt to "control" events something like these without destroying their spontaneous quality, the French chemical engineer Rene Warcollier organized a group in Paris whose purpose was to "transmit" to a second group in New York. Warcollier, in a dreamy state, was trying *not* to think about the image of a stag's horn that had figured in the experiments earlier that day. He visualized the beakers and cups of his laboratory; in particular, he saw in his mind's eye a glass funnel. One of the people in New York drew, at this moment, a two-handled compote glass [see illustration, below]. She remarked that the handles were "like the horns of a stag." This experiment is characteristic of the way much parapsychological data is studied.

"But let us get on," says the psychologist, "with well-designed experiments, with an emphasis upon quantitative method and adequate statistics." The outstanding experiment of Warcollier's era, just after World War I, was carried out at the University of Groningen in the Netherlands. Experimenters in an upper room looked down through plate-glass sheets into a lower room in which a subject, in a black cage and blindfolded, received randomly selected numbers and letters. The numbers and letters indicated to him which square on a checkerboard, lying just beyond a slit through the black drapes of his cage, he should touch. He did fantastically well over several weeks, each week getting huge "antichance" values. Then, apparently rather suddenly, whatever was happening came to an end. The same effect occurred later in experiments conducted by George H. Estabrooks at Harvard—phenomenal scores at first, followed by a fade-out—and it will certainly continue to occur at long as we do not know what is at work.

One of the primary demands made upon modern experimenters is truly repeatable experiments. An excellent example of what has and has not been achieved is the work of Gertrude R. Schmeidler, beginning with studies at Harvard during World War II and continuing at the City College of New York since that time. Her basic hypothesis was that, when tested under proper experimental conditions, those people who accepted the possibility of success under the conditions of the experiment would score significantly above chance expectation; those rejecting this possibility would not.

Extensive experimentation at Harvard showed that she was right. Schmeidler divided her subjects into two groups, those who accepted the possibility of ESP under the conditions of the experiment and those who did not. When the subjects were placed in a closed room and asked to identify the order of cards in another closed room 40 feet away, the first group scored significantly above chance expectation. The second group scored not at chance, but below chance. As cycle after cycle continued, it became clear that this was a consistent pattern:

those who "believed in" ESP scored well above chance, and those who rejected it scored significantly below.

Schmeidler has duplicated the results of this first study about 20 times now, and most independent investigators who use a similar method have found the same pattern. But her experiment has not been replicated in the full, formal sense. It is not possible to tell with absolute certainty which run of 25 cards will be successful; nor is it possible, within a given successful run, to identify specific scores.

In another group of telepathic experiments, Montague Ullman and Stanley Krippner, working at the Maimonides Medical Center in Brooklyn, have found that pictures shown to "senders" in one room can affect the dreams of sleeping "receivers" in another room, nearly 100 feet away and behind many closed doors. For example, when Ullman and Kripp-

ESP EXPERIMENT. Did thoughts of man in Paris reach woman who drew this in N.Y.?

ner showed Marc Chagall's The Drinker [see illustration, opposite] to a sender in one room, the dreams of the receiver (awakened during periods of rapid eye movement) went like this:

First dream report: No apparent correspondences.

Second dream report: "I don't know whether it's related to the dream that I had, but right now there's a commercial song that's going through my mind—it's about a beer. About Ballantine beer. The words are, 'Why is Ballantine beer like an opening night, a race that finishes neck and neck, or a ride on the toboggan slide?' The commercial is running through my mind, and this song . . . There's this big dinner party . . . A young woman had apparently come to the city with somebody else who had come to this dinner . . . and she was wearing what was supposed to be a cocktail dress, and it was black, and the shape of it was mostly nondescript, but it was studded with rhinestones . . . That table was really empty all the time. All it had on

it was plates, empty white plates . . ."

Third dream report: ". . . I had been in a restaurant next door, eating . . ., and in this restaurant there was a separate section that was a bar, and in the dream I was at this place a number of different nights. The dream seemed to have some sort of time dimension because there was a bartender, a short fellow. There was another guy there, and the first night they sent over a drink for me . . . This girl wanted them to go or something . . . She had loads of make-up on, and lots of black eye shadow, and black eye pencil lining; her eyes and black eyebrows, and her lips were black, too . . . And she wanted to know what I had done with my hair because I had my hair in a pony tail and it was very short in front, and she thought I'd cut it . . . That whole bar business and the restaurant and the booth are like a place that I was at in Massachusetts . . . The most strange thing about the whole dream and all of its complications is the transformation of Carol . . . to this garish, very pasty, very thick make-up base, and this black lipstick and black eye business and black eyebrow stuff. I associate that immediately to that black dress with too many rhinestones on it in the other dream . . . The black business seems to leave the realm of something that I can say is a personal association . . ."

Ullman and Krippner's work with one gifted subject, especially, has been replicated at a very high level of significance. The subject, a male psychotherapist, was paired with a male psychologist for a seven-night series. The psychotherapist was able to match his own dreams against the art prints that had been shown to the psychologist at a statistically significant level of accuracy. Three outside judges matched the dream transcripts and the target pictures even more accurately than did the psychotherapist himself.

Two years later, the same pair took part in an eight-night study. This time, the psychologist-sender used a box of "multisensory" materials as well as a target picture. For example, a picture showing an artist was accompanied by a canvas and water-color paints so that the psychologist could "act out" the role of the artist. When three judges again matched the psychotherapist's dream transcripts and the art prints, the results were highly significant.

The brilliant new experimental work of Thelma Moss and J. A. Gengerelli of UCLA has also been replicated with some success. Moss and Gengerelli, observing that most spontaneous cases of telepathy occur when the sender is under emotional stress, surmised that experiments with cards might not be the best way to test telepathy in the laboratory. So they set out to experiment with the transmission of emotionally charged material.

Senders viewed slides and listened to tapes on various subjects that were likely to arouse emotion of some sort. One slide-tape presentation concerned the assassination of President Kennedy, which had occurred nine months earlier. It included excerpts from the Inaugural Address; the song *In the Summer of His Years;* pictures of the President's arrival in Dallas; the motorcade; Robert Kennedy and Jackie leaving Dallas; the flag-draped bier with Jackie and her children kneeling beside it. The tape concluded with the President's voice: "Ask not what your country can do for you; ask rather what you can do for your country."

At the conclusion of the presentation, each sender and (in another room) each receiver was asked to report his feelings and impressions. One pair's responses went like this:

Sender

This of course was the ex-President Kennedy speaking to the American people, and then following his assassination which was dreadful, with scenes of Jackie trying to protect him, and then later—where I believe she was at the hospital — with the bloodstains on her suit, and then of course the final resting place and the floral bouquet of our President, and his voice again was heard with his famous words.

Receiver

I seem to have the feeling of sadness or sorrow . . . as if I were crying . . . or something tragic has happened and that I was grieving over something . . . much the same as one might feel attending a funeral of a dear friend . . . or a well-known figure in whom one had faith. The feeling is one of grief or sorrow for someone being lost or gone. I feel that I am not alone . . . I'm in a group of people who are similarly either bereaved or grieving over something that is lost irretrievably . . . or someone who has died. I seem to feel that most of these people are sad, or crying, or both. I think that's about all.

When Moss and Gengerelli asked a group of judges to match the responses of 30 senders and 30 receivers to the various slide-tape presentations, seven

"THE DRINKER." This painting by Chagall helped show effect of telepathy on dreams.

out of 12 judges were able to do so significantly more accurately than they would have by chance. Only one of the 12 judges (all professional psychologists and psychiatrists) matched the impressions of 23 control sender-receiver teams at a level significantly above chance.

Of course it would be better if the groups of judges could be eliminated and if the receivers' responses, punched on cards in a pattern, could be objectively matched with a pattern punched on senders' cards. To develop such a procedure will take time. Today, groups of judges are standard practice in many experiments. It can gradually be improved or replaced.

Many psychologists think of psychology as a well-articulated structure of many experiments. Parapsychology has the same goal. The serious parapsychologist tries to investigate the full range of interactions between organisms and their environment through mediating agencies not known to the science of today. He must be ready to investigate lights, sounds and movements of objects, in relation to wishes and fears—clocks that stop at the moment of death or, in a lighter vein, the behavior of "hot dice."

However, the experimental method is only one part of the total field of parapsychology and, because of this, parapsychology bears more resemblance to, say, astronomy or geology than it does to physics. Astronomers use the terrestrial laboratory of physics to deal with such phenomena as ionization, the spectroscopic analysis of stellar chemical elements, and so forth, but this does not

make astronomy, as a whole, an experimental science. Similarly with geology. You may carry a rock into the petrology or mineralogy laboratory and study it experimentally, but this does not make geology an experimental science. Parapsychology—and psychology as well—is much more like geology than it is like physics, because experimentation is only one corner of its methodology. It is the *intelligible system of events,* not the experimental method, that constitutes the science; the experimental method must fit into a cosmic frame.

How does this bear on research strategy in this pioneer field?

Our *first* need, I think, is for better recording and analyses of cases of spontaneous telepathy, working from these to better-planned developmental, cross-cultural and experimental studies.

Our second great need is for persons with broad knowledge of the published literature in the field, because it is among them that we may develop the systematic theoretical model-building that we so badly need.

The third need is to find fellowships and scholarships for people with a sound and broad understanding of science and of scientific method, who know something about the history of the struggle of science against poorly understood phenomena. Most psychologists get their experimental training and their general scientific training in the easy groove prepared for them by an instructor who knows a research specialty, who knows the methods, who knows what is likely to happen in the rather safe little experiments that are acceptable for master's and doctor's degree requirements. But a person has to be able to open the door to the unknown, to let it in and make friends with it, in order to do anything that is likely to be new or valuable in a frontier area.

Fourth, we need people who are philosophically sophisticated and who can think about time, space, motion and energy without becoming frightened. They must not get bogged down in unreal questions as to what could or could not be a chance effect. They must be concerned (as are the astronomer and the geologist) with model-building, and (as is the philosopher) with conceptualization that goes beyond the assumed inevitable operation of the time-space-energy modalities as we know them through 19th Century physics.

Most of all, we need in this field people who understand the concept of replication of experimental findings. We need people to develop repeatable experiments, the corners of solid fact that allow the filling out of a new kind of science, one that deals with parameters of personality of which we are almost wholly ignorant.

I have not spent time on controversies, which spread on and on. The problem is one of clear conceptualization, steadfast derivation of hypotheses, building of research methodology, and systematic replication. Some will go on saying we are credulous, and some of us are. Some will go on saying we are frauds, and some of us are. The problems will continue and the effort to resolve them will continue. The poorly sketched frontier of today will become a more solid frontier, advancing into a definite conquerable territory — if we can have the kinds of people that I have named: the systematic and careful collectors of evidence, the well-trained experimentalists, the historians of the frontier battle of science, the scientific conceptualizers, the philosophers, and above all the systematic replicators.

There may remain some misunderstanding about the relation of replication to the building of a science. For a large number of replicated fragments can still fail to create a satisfying intellectual system. Henry Margenau, professor of physics and natural philosophy at Yale, has cogently developed the concept that science is much more than a system of interrelated experimental findings. It must be woven into a tight structure at the center, with basic concepts clearly and coherently expressed, and with an open fringe permitting new facts to fall into place. But its integrity must be such that each part is consistent with all the rest, and at the same time it must allow from day to day the advent of new observations that are not inconsistent with those already obtained and systematized. This requires much more than "operational" thinking; it involves operations, construct validity, internal coherence and, Margenau believes, an aesthetic satisfaction—a certain elegance—as well.

Parapsychologists expect a bit more than they will get when they ask for careful attention to their successfully replicated experiments. Take, for example, the Schmeidler experiments. Even if every replication, by her and by others, gave data like those already reported, this would still not make the phenomena congruent with our general physical conceptions of the relations of subjects to their environments. Or take Ullman's studies. Regardless of replication, they still will not fall easily into the psychiatric and psychological patterns that characterize the beliefs of most investigators, subjects and the reading public. Experimenters will find it difficult, for example, to get "study sections" and staff support from large Federal granting agencies. And Moss and Gengerelli's findings, which are in some ways a tremendous breakthrough, do not present that internal consistency that makes it likely we have here a highly repeatable and predictable type of performance. Even if we did, it would take more than psychological common sense to generate the principle that emotionally charged target materials are likely to be successfully transmitted to a subject at a distance under conditions of proper shielding and safety against any possibility of sensory communication. Moss and Gengerelli, as well as Ullman and Schmeidler, will have to await the time when their experiments dovetail not only with the psychology but with the physics of today's world view.

I do not quite mean *today's* world view. The quantum-relativity-uncertainty physics of today has, for the most part, no objection to parapsychological phenomena at all. Many modern physicists greet the new experiments with interest and even enthusiasm. It is the physics of the 19th Century, persisting in terms of current space-time patterns, that makes the phenomena "impossible." A cultural lag is common, after all, in science as well as in religion and folklore. Thus the congruence of parapsychological data with physical data depends upon the maturation of psychology and of the communications currently used by psychologists to relate findings to what is conceived to be physical reality. It is too much to expect that the reality of 1968 be studied; that is not the nature of the history of thought.

E. G. Boring has dealt with these issues in a somewhat different way, notably through his repeated expressions of unwillingness to accept parapsychological data that do not fit into the current world view. When you talk about how bats can navigate without hitting wires, Boring is skeptical of the scientific utility of any approach that does not include the wires and the bats' receptors, and the physical relations between them. He is skeptical of all parapsychological findings that do not define the physical relation between stimulus and receptor. This is a perfectly normal and natural point of view to take if one operates within the framework of a psychology based on the essentially Newtonian relation of physical stimulus pattern and organismic response. And I agree with Boring that most scientists will continue to insist upon a physicalist link before they will toy with phenomena that, in their nature, cannot easily provide such a physical modality, especially phenomena that relate to future events not inferable from present knowledge.

However, Boring is not talking about the conditions under which a very new science can win accreditation. Suppose the issue were stated somewhat differently: does science spring full-blown from the folklore that is its ancestor? The answer would appear to be no. There are long periods of "proto-science"—periods of exploratory, adolescent behavior—that sometimes give way to maturity and sometimes do not.

Parapsychologists must expect to be regarded as strange and even antisocial if they persist in investigations that are intrinsically "anti-scientific" and therefore somewhat dangerous to their colleagues. There is no sense, however, in spending time feeling sorry for oneself. The thing to do is to accept criticism with as much grace as possible and get on with the job.

And what can science do for a proto-science that is trying to grow up? Well, it could try opening the door and inviting the young stranger in for a chat. If the gap between the generations is too great for that, perhaps it could at least leave the door unlocked? 𝔔

Big Brother and Psychotechnology

by Stephan L. Chorover   Once again, our urge to invent new technologies is outrunning our wisdom in applying them. We can surgically enter the living brain to permanently alter personality. Behavior modification, psychology's fastest-growing branch, can be defined as the "ability to get someone to do one's bidding." And the use of psychochemicals to control people is now common, notably in our schools.

"I feel very strongly that this country wants and this election will prove that the American people want…a new feeling of responsibility…of self-discipline.…The average American is just like the child in the family. You give him some responsibility and he is going to amount to something.…If, on the other hand, you make him completely dependent and pamper him and cater to him too much you are going to make him soft, spoiled and eventually a very weak individual."—RICHARD M. NIXON, *New York Times*, NOVEMBER 10, 1972.

"There are people in our society who should be separated and discarded. I think it's one of the tendencies of the liberal community to feel that every person in a nation of 200 million people can be made into a productive citizen. I'm realist enough to believe this can't be …we're always going to have our places of preventive detention for psychopaths; and we're always going to have a certain number of people in our community who have no desire to achieve or who have no desire to even fit in an amicable way with the rest of society. And these people should be separated from the community, not in a callous way, but they should be separated as far as any idea that their opinions shall have any effect on the course we follow."—SPIRO T. AGNEW, *Boston Evening Globe*, JULY 1, 1970.

These statements are clear and forceful. They are of special interest because they invoke some popular ideas about human nature and psychology to justify the development and deployment of repressive

I believe that this psychotechnology is being fraudulently advanced as a rational and humane approach to the solution of social conflicts in ways that are essentially totalitarian.

public policies. These ideas assert that the basic causes of our more serious social conflicts lie neither in blocked economic opportunities nor in frustrated human needs, but rather in the prevalence of obnoxious behavioral traits among certain individuals or groups.

This view holds that some people have contemptible moral and psychological defects and that their behavior is ultimately traceable to deeper sources of personal weakness. It claims that permissive parents and lenient public officials spoil people and thereby encourage offensive social behavior. It follows from this view that when we formulate public policies to deal with social conflict, we should focus not on faults in the social system, but rather on disorders of personal adjustment. In other words, we should develop behavioral "remedies" instead of social reforms.

Biological and behavioral technologies such as neurosurgery, drug therapy and behavior modification are being used more and more as "remedies" for socially offensive behavior. I believe that this *psychotechnology* is being fraudulently advanced as a rational and humane approach to the solution of social conflicts, and that it is being abusively deployed to repress social dissidence, deviance and disorder in ways that are essentially totalitarian. I want to describe how psychotechnology is being used to predict, isolate, identify, monitor and control several kinds of individual and social behavior, and show that the entire enterprise is arbitrary, arrogant, irrational and inhumane in both conception and execution.

"Diseases" to Justify Slavery. In 1851 Samuel A. Cartwright, M.D., delivered a detailed lecture to the Louisiana Medical Association on "The Diseases and Physical Peculiarities of the Negro Race." The Cartwright Report was published in the prestigious *New Orleans Medical and Surgical Journal*. It remains a classic contribution to the vast literature of white racism. It attempted to justify the institution of Negro slavery on the basis of "incontrovertible scientific evidence" showing the "unalterable" biological inferiority of blacks.

Cartwright used the language and presumed authority of science to show that "the slothful negro" was biologically destined for bondage by virtue of his "childlike" body and mind. He described a host of peculiarities, stigmata, disorders and diseases from which "indolent Negroes suffer" and which are "the true cause of that debasement of mind which has rendered the people of Africa unable to take care of themselves." He claimed to have discovered anatomical and physiological facts that confirmed the essential justice and humaneness of slavery.

He reported, for example, that he had found clear anatomical confirmation of, "the Creator's will with regard to the Negro." Specifically he found their knees to be "more flexed or bent than any other kind of man," and concluded that this makes the Negro, "the submissive knee-bender which the Almighty declared he should be."

More importantly, we would now call two of the "diseases" he identified "behavior disorders." Cartwright insisted that slaves who ran away from their masters were not willfully disobedient. On the contrary, they were suffering from a disease of the mind. He named this disease *drapetomania* (from the ancient Greek words *drapetes* for *runaway*, and *mania* for *madness*) and suggested that the best remedy is to treat all "Negroes with firmness and kindness, and they are easily governed."

But sometimes the treatment fails, Cartwright said, because of another disease also "peculiar to Negroes." This one he named *dysaesthesia aethiopis*, or "hebetude of mind and obtuse sensibility of body." He described it as one of the more prevalent "maladies of the Negro race" and expressed wonder that it had escaped the attention of his medical colleagues for so long. Afflicted individuals, he said, tended to engage in much mischief, to slight their work, to abuse tools and break them and generally to raise disturbances. Most remarkably, he saw the disease as being accompanied by an "obviously pathological" change in the functioning of the nervous system: an apparent insensibility to "pain when being punished." The treatment Cartwright prescribed included anointing the entire body with oil and, "slapping the oil in with a broad leather strap," and then putting "the

patient to some hard kind of work in the open air and sunshine."

We cannot dismiss Cartwright as a mere crank. He was a distinguished physician and a leading figure in the medical community. Nor can we dismiss his report as a quaint relic of bygone days. The mentality that spawned it lives on in the scandalous racism of contemporary "scholarship" on the genetics of intelligence. It also lives on in the "scholarship" that proclaims social dissent and deviance to be the result of diseased brains, disordered minds or inadequate histories of reinforcement.

The "Insane" Dissenter. The Soviet Union has a notorious reputation for treating political dissidents as if they suffered from mental disorders. Many distinguished writers, scientists and artists have been confined to mental hospitals after speaking out against official policy. Consider the case of Zhores Medvedev. In 1969 the well-known biochemist and gerontologist was dismissed from his scientific post. In 1970 he was forcibly confined to a mental hospital where he underwent various "diagnosis" and "treatment" procedures. His only "disorder" was his insistence on writing and publishing strongly worded critiques of official Soviet policies. Yet psychiatrists diagnosed him schizophrenic, on the grounds that he engaged in two unrelated activities, gerontology and public criticism. Two noted members of the Soviet Academy of Sciences then wryly suggested that the psychiatrist should receive a Lenin Prize for discovering a new psychopathological entity— the Leonardo da Vinci syndrome. But Medvedev, like most of those who come to our attention, has an international reputation and few are ready to consider him really insane. Those who deserve our attention, therefore, are the "common people" who may be psychiatrically labeled and "treated" without provoking world opinion.

Traditionally, political criminals have been taken seriously, dealt with as enemies of the state, and punished with prison, exile or execution. Political conflict, however, involves the clash of ideas and principles—things which cannot easily be destroyed with criminal penalties. In fact, criminal sanctions often serve to empha-

*The political dissident successfully deprived
of his presumed sanity becomes a mere invalid, and
his opposition is thereby invalidated.*

size the importance of outlawed ideas.

More than any other form of public behavior, political activity depends upon
the credibility of the participants. In order
to be credible and have a chance of success, the political individual, especially
the dissident, must be perceived as a
serious source of ideas. Something special
happens, then, when a political dissident
is authoritatively labeled "mentally ill"
by someone who enjoys a position of public power and trust. When psychologists
or psychiatrists "diagnose" dissident behavior as the product of an unbalanced
mind, they declare (on the basis of science no less) that the individual is not to
be considered a serious adversary, but
rather a mere lunatic.

The political dissident successfully
deprived of his presumed sanity becomes
a mere invalid, and his opposition is
thereby invalidated. Unless he is like
Medvedev, with influential friends who
know the truth, the authorities can
hardly lose this game of psychological
power politics. And unless the people at
large stop believing in these absurdities,
the authorities will continue such totalitarian tactics.

Psychiatry and the Pentagon Papers. It
would be a mistake to imagine that the Soviets are alone in the deployment of psychiatric diagnoses and treatments for political purposes. A case in point from our
own country is that of Daniel Ellsberg. It
was clear from the outset that the Government, fearing additional disclosures and
adverse publicity, was reluctant to proceed with the prosecution of the Pentagon
Papers trial. It is against this background
that we may inquire into the reasons for
sending a White House burglary team to
Los Angeles, where on September 3, 1971,
they allegedly broke into the offices of
Ellsberg's psychiatrist, Lewis Fielding.

According to the testimony of E. Howard Hunt (one of the accused leaders of
the break-in who was subsequently tried
and convicted in the Watergate case) the
mission of the burglars was to obtain material for use by the White House in constructing a "psychological profile" of Ellsberg. Why? I believe that what the
Government hoped to find in Fielding's
files was something about Ellsberg that
would suggest that he was "psy-

chologically disturbed" on or about the
time that he released the Pentagon Papers.
If an argument to that effect could have
been successfully advanced, the Government might have used it in at least two
ways. First, it might have been used simply as a publicity device, as a means to dis-
credit the belief that Ellsberg was a man of
principle whose dramatic actions had
been based mainly on political and moral
considerations.

Against Ellsberg's contention that the
Government had consistently lied, and
that the American people were entitled at
last to learn the full, sordid details about
our involvement in the Indochina war,
the White House might have hoped to
show that Ellsberg himself was a disturbed
individual whose private reasons for acting as he did were less wholesome than the
reasons he publicly professed. A second
way in which the Government might
have sought to use psychiatric information about Ellsberg was as a means of
avoiding the trial itself, and its attendant
disclosures and embarrassments. After all,
if a case could be made to the judge that
Ellsberg acted irrationally and was therefore not legally responsible for what he
had done, then the way might have been
opened for a ruling that Ellsberg was not
competent to stand trial and ought to be
committed, instead, to a mental institution, where he would be able to receive appropriate diagnostic and treatment services. While admittedly
speculative, this "scenario" is hardly implausible. It is, on the contrary, consistent
with the prevalent practice of using an os-
tensible humane and enlightened process
to achieve essentially inhumane and repressive ends.

Not every attempt to invalidate dissent
by attributing it to a mental disorder is so
easily recognizable as political repression.
Most are even more dangerous because
they are undertaken in tones of responsible humanitarianism that leave little
room to question the moral convictions
that lie behind them. Cartwright's report,
for example, probably arose from the very
heart of his belief in the rightness of slavery. Similarly, many Soviet psychiatrists
probably believe that their social system
is so manifestly sane that there must be
some form of mental illness lurking in a

mind that would seek to change it. And if
that is the case, isn't it more humane to
"cure" someone than to shoot him?

The origins of this abuse of science lie
partly with behavioral scientists themselves, with the choices they make about
how to study man and society. Whenever
we begin to investigate a social or behavioral problem, how we decide what the
cause and best solution are—in other
words, how we make a diagnosis—depends
on what aspects of the situation we
choose to study. When we decide to study
a problem in a certain way, we are making
a decision that has political impact, for
this choice heavily influences what our
conclusions will be.

A Question of Science. From a scientific
point of view, no single aspect of a phenomenon can be assumed to take precedence over another. All aspects contribute equally to our understanding of it.
The physicist, for example, accepts the
equal validity of one theory that explains
physical systems in terms of waves, and
another that explains the same systems in
terms of particles. But whenever he
chooses to use one, it precludes using the
other. We face a similar situation when
we try to describe the behavior of a human organism. We must decide whether
to focus on molecules and cells, tissues
and organ systems, the individual, interpersonal groups, or social institutions. All
of these levels are equally important. Each
provides information available from none
of the others.

In conventional technological practice
we tend to view "the problem" in only
one way at a time. But if we start with a
predisposition to identify and deal only
with symptoms or disorders of the individual, as many behavioral scientists do,
we adopt an arbitrary and essentially non-
scientific perspective. We inevitably tend
to ignore other possible approaches. Once
we focus our attention on the behavior of
the individual, it becomes highly unlikely
that we will be disposed to deal with the
larger social context in which the behavior occurs.

That context becomes for us what the
physicist calls a *frame of reference*—a set
of objects or events assumed to be unchanging. Thanks largely to the insights of
Einstein, the physicist now knows, in ele-

Many social scientists contend that deviance can help preserve a social group by drawing its nondeviant members together in a posture of solidarity and mutuality.

gant mathematical terms, that he cannot presume to understand the events he observes without taking into account the nature of the frame of reference and his own position in it. Many behavioral scientists and public officials responsible for dealing with social problems have yet to learn that they cannot understand the behavior of individuals without studying the context in which it occurs.

The Systems View of Control. The biologist approaches living organisms with an awareness that each living thing is really a complex system made up of other interacting subsystems and is itself part of larger environmental and social systems. The biologist also knows that the behavior of organisms exhibits a high degree of control, but can rarely point to a single center or controller. The life processes of an organism are controlled in many ways, both by the organization of its internal systems and by its interaction with environmental systems. This general systems view denies the simplistic "law and order" view-that social conflicts are caused by deviant individuals who are unable or unwilling to "fit in."

Persuading people to abandon the "law and order" concept of control is one of the more serious problems facing us in the conduct of our interpersonal and social affairs. If we seriously accept the more sophisticated and scientific concept of system control, we would then think not of the individual in isolation, but as part of the larger context in which he or she behaves.

The family is a good example. It is a typical complex, self-regulating system, each member of which is vulnerable to pressures from other systems. Yet individual members are often treated as if they were not part of the larger systems of control. In many families, for example, a member occasionally begins to exhibit some form of unexpected or deviant behavior. Once the rest of the family see this behavior, they tend to close ranks and agree that the deviant person "is in trouble," "needs help," or, "ought to be taken care of." They may seek the aid of their physician, a policeman, a religious counselor, a psychotherapist, or other available social resources. Generally, the individual who has been "acting up" is duly placed in the hands of a person or agency supposedly competent to help "solve the problem."

Whether or not this brings the disturbing behavior under control is beside the point. The family presumes too much when it places the cause of the difficulty within the deviant individual. They assume that the cause is located where the effect occurs. Such an arbitrary assumption can rarely be justified scientifically when one deals with complex systems.

In asserting itself as the frame of reference, the family ignores the possibility that the problem's cause may be deeply embedded in the family system as a whole. Their group consensus may in fact function as a defense against considering this possibility. The assumption that cause and symptom lie in the same individual may protect the immediate coherence of the group, but at the cost of long-run disaster.

Living Boundary Markers. This same process appears to function in larger social groups. Many social scientists contend that deviance can help preserve a social group by drawing its nondeviant members together in a posture of solidarity and mutuality. Some social systems actually seem to need deviant individuals as living boundary-markers. They help maintain the system by showing its members the limits of acceptable behavior. They also enable people to deny in themselves the bad qualities they attribute (often falsely) to the deviants.

Deviance is thus not a property of behavior itself as much as a value judgment conferred upon it by the group. If we accept this idea, we see that deviance is a pattern of behavior that a group considers so dangerous, embarrassing or irritating that it brings sanctions against it. This is an important point, because it establishes a basis for distinguishing between *deviance* and *disease*. That the definition of deviant behavior is *essentially* social and cultural suggests that it ought to vary with time and circumstance. History testifies to the fact that types of biological disease remain constant (for example, cancer, epilepsy, gout) whereas types of deviance change as society evolves. The deviant in one social context may be the witch, the heretic or the sorcerer, and in others, the runaway slave, the juvenile delinquent, the homosexual, the Jew, or the junkie.

In both families and societies practical and political interests may be served by attributing blame, by identifying symptoms as causes, and by controlling individuals whose behavior is defined to be dangerous or disturbing. But to contend that such practices have a scientific justification denies the insights of science itself and confuses authority with wisdom.

Once deviant behavior has been successfully reduced to the status of a personal affliction it has been taken out of its social context and stripped of its countercultural connotation. This is what the Cartwright Report attempted to do. It is precisely what is happening in Soviet Russia. And it is happening in our own society. Let us examine a few instances in which American psychotechnologists are attempting to "separate and discard" deviant individuals.

Surgery for Social Violence. Soon after the Detroit riots in 1967, an important letter appeared in the *Journal of the American Medical Association*. The authors acknowledged that the social causes of urban rioting are "well known," and that the "urgent needs" of the underprivileged should not be minimized. But they did not propose to deal with these causes or needs. They focused instead on the search for, "the more subtle role of other possible factors, including brain dysfunction in the rioters who engaged in arson, sniping and physical assault."

Just as Cartwright cautioned his readers not to mistake the "misbehavior" of slaves for intentional rebellion, the authors of this letter warned that we shouldn't believe the urgent social and economic needs of the ghetto are solely responsible for urban riots. "If slum conditions alone determined and initiated riots," they asked, "why are the vast majority of slum-dwellers able to resist the temptations of unrestrained violence? Is there something peculiar about the violent slum-dweller that differentiates him from his peaceful neighbor?"

After raising these "scientific" questions, the authors proceeded to cite evidence showing that focal lesions in the brain are capable of spurring "senseless" violent outbursts. Although the available evidence comes from patients with long-standing histories of severe epilepsy, they

It explicitly seeks to justify as "therapeutic" the destruction of brain tissue in people who exhibit allegedly unprovoked, uncontrollable and unreasonable fits of violent behavior.

concluded that violent behavior in general likely has a comparable biological basis. They insisted that, "we need intensive research and clinical studies of the *individuals* committing the violence. The goal of such studies would be to pinpoint, diagnose and treat those people with low violence thresholds before they contribute to further tragedies."

The letter was written by William Sweet, Chief of Neurosurgical Services at Massachusetts General Hospital, Vernon Mark, Director of Neurosurgical Services at Boston City Hospital, and Frank Ervin, then a psychiatrist at Massachusetts General Hospital. Ervin is now at the University of California at Los Angeles Medical School where he is an associate of the recently formed Center for the Prevention of Life-Threatening Behavior. In 1970 Mark and Ervin published *Violence and the Brain*, an account of their methods of identifying and treating people with "poor control of violent impulses."

In their psychotechnological approach to what they term "the dyscontrol syndrome," Mark and Ervin focus on the limbic system of the brain. This complex system plays an important role in the diverse moods and feeling-states we associate with subjective experiences of pleasure, pain, anxiety, sadness, fear and anger. Within the limbic system, a cerebral region called the *amygdala* is a main target for contemporary neurosurgeons interested in "violence and the brain."

Diagnosis by Behavior. Mark and Ervin's book claims to describe their work with patients suffering from "dyscontrol syndromes" due to "limbic brain disease." But as a scientific treatise it has many shortcomings. For example, the authors fail adequately to describe their methods of diagnosis, except to acknowledge that, "since we do not at present have any way to test directly for the presence of limbic brain disease, we must rely on two indirect methods of diagnosis. The first is to see if the violent person has any signs and symptoms of recognizable brain disease . . . ," and if this fails, "to compare their behavior with that of people known to have this sort of disease."

Their book is mainly a promotional treatise. It explicitly seeks to justify as "therapeutic" the destruction of brain tis-

sue in people who exhibit allegedly unprovoked, uncontrollable and unreasonable fits of violent behavior. They do not seriously consider the possibility that the causes of such behavior may lie elsewhere than within the brain of the individuals committing the violence. And they do not give clear and complete accounts of the symptoms that justify the use of radical physical treatments such as injections of various drugs, surgery on the limbic system, and electrical stimulation of the brain with implanted electrodes. Nor do they provide a critical assessment of a number of disastrous outcomes from their "therapeutic interventions."

Mark and Ervin dedicate their book to, "the Neuro-Research Foundation of Boston, whose goals for the early diagnosis and proper treatment of the violent patient parallel our own." They and Sweet established it for that purpose and first planned to locate it at the Massachusetts General Hospital, a prestigious private institution in Boston catering mainly to the needs of middle- and upper-class patients. When scientists, physicians and administrators there raised objections, Mark, Ervin and Sweet moved it to the Boston City Hospital. This ancient, beleaguered public institution caters primarily to black and lower-class patients from the surrounding South End.

Psychosurgery's Friends. The psychosurgical approach to violence may be regarded with disdain by much of the scientific and medical communities and may provoke apprehension among the general public, but certain law-enforcement agencies have greeted it with enthusiasm. During one six-month period, for example, the work of the Neuro-Research Foundation was aided by a grant of $109,000 from the Law Enforcement Assistance Administration of the U.S. Department of Justice. They used the money to develop methods of identifying penitentiary inmates with patterns of habitual violence and evidence of brain damage.

The number of neurobiological projects aimed at controlling the behavior of deviant individuals rather than at understanding the complex causality of social conflict is growing disproportionately. In 1971, for example, R.K. Procunier, Director of Corrections of the State of Califor-

nia outlined a "proposal for the neurosurgical treatment of violent inmates." According to this plan, aggressive inmates would first be taken to medical facilities at Vacaville and then to the University of California at San Francisco Medical Center where, "surgical and diagnostic procedures would be performed to locate centers in the brain which may have been previously damaged and which could serve as the focus for episodes of violent behavior. If these areas were located and verified that they were indeed the source of aggressive behavior, neurosurgery would be performed, directed at the previously found cerebral foci."

Who would be the patients in such a program? Here is part of an official affidavit describing one inmate who was being transferred to Vacaville for psychiatric evaluation:

"_____ was 25, older and more mature than the bulk of the . . . inmates. He was aggressively outspoken, always seeking recruits for his views that the institution and its staff were oppressing all the inmates and particularly the black inmates. He was proficient at karate, and his files showed that he had been observed teaching other inmates karate techniques at another institution . . . [he] had been one of a half-dozen men who led a work-stoppage and attempted general strike which had lasted for several days . . . he was continuously in contact with friends and attorneys on the outside who encouraged his activities and provided him with books attacking society. He set a fire in May as a demonstration of his political views."

Although psychosurgery has been performed on a number of inmates in the California Correctional System, the Director of Corrections' plan was not put into effect. It was stalled by public protests when news of it leaked to the press. But early in 1973, Governor Ronald Reagan announced his support for the formation of the Center for the Reduction of Life-Threatening Behavior at UCLA. This center is attempting to mount a controversial program unmistakably similar to that outlined by Mark and Ervin.

Surgery and Social Reform. The new wave of psychosurgery that threatens to become a political tool has been made possible by important advances in brain-be-

*The use of psychochemicals to control
deviant behavior is more widespread than anytime
in the past, and growing rapidly.*

havior research. While we are still far from a detailed understanding of how brains work, we do know that the continuity, coherence and stability of our life experience depends on the structural and chemical integrity of our brains. We know that when the brain is damaged by injury or disease, behavioral changes are likely to result. From this we have come to view certain behavior disorders as dysfunctions of the brain.

We have developed powerful techniques for treating some of these dysfunctions directly. We can treat epilepsy and Parkinsonism with drugs and sometimes with neurosurgery. We know that certain forms of mental retardation result from hereditary defects in metabolism, and we now can detect and correct some of these in infancy. Perhaps the most dramatic and gratifying examples of brain-behavior relationships are those in which the surgical removal of a brain tumor causes a complete disappearance of the symptoms.

For patients whose behavior problems clearly result from underlying brain disorders, we often have no alternative to using psycho- or neurotechnology. No amount of attention to the social environment, no amount of counseling, psychotherapy, argument, punishment or other indirect approach will suffice. We simply have no more effective or reasonable way of dealing with some disorders than by means of a direct assault on the brain itself.

But few cases are this straightforward. In many instances of interpersonal conflict, the causes are clearly social and the wisest treatment would be social reform rather than biological manipulation. The fact that we *can* alter violent behavior patterns with chemicals and surgery does not mean that a brain dysfunction or "limbic brain disease" causes them. Even if we can discover a difference in a deviant individual's brain, we cannot conclude that this causes his deviant behavior or that it is justifiable to correct his behavior by altering his brain.

Too many contemporary neuro- and behavioral scientists seem committed to a narrow, unrealistic view of human social behavior. They focus mainly on the possibility of controlling behavior. If this trend continues, psychotechnology will in-

creasingly become a favorite tool of social and political repression.

Spare the Speed and Spoil the Child. Psychosurgery is not the only threat in this respect. For instance, no one doubts that we are in the midst of a drug crisis. But in reality it is a crisis of tranquilizers and stimulants much more than of marijuana and LSD. The use of psychochemicals to control deviant behavior is more widespread than any time in the past, and growing rapidly. Not only do doctors and psychiatrists use them to control the mood and behavior of their patients, but most Americans use them to control themselves. Their erroneous assumption is that if an individual can't cope with his social world, the problem lies within himself. The danger is that people are using drugs to overadapt themselves to the pressures of society rather than mobilizing their discontent to make society more humane.

Certainly there are cases in which the use of psychochemicals is appropriate. But to the extent that drugs soothe and eliminate tensions that otherwise would produce beneficial social changes, psychochemicals may also serve as tools of social control. An alarming example is the growing use of chemicals to control children.

Parents and teachers have always had problems controlling children. Traditionally they have used such tools as coercion with punishment or threat, and persuasion with encouragement, love and education. But these do not always work the way they are supposed to, and both families and schools frequently produce "misbehaving" children.

Many authorities focus solely on the children themselves, and fail to consider seriously that the causes of their misbehavior might lie in the social systems of which they are a part. Like Cartwright, they deny that misbehavior may be intentional or socially "meaningful." They prefer, like Cartwright, to use the social status quo as their stable frame of reference and maintain that deviant behavior is a symptom of a disturbance within the child. Some of these authorities thus declare that certain children are victims of a newly discovered disease (known mainly to American psychiatry) called "minimal brain dysfunction" (MBD). According to

Paul Wender's authoritative text on MBD, it "is probably the single most common disorder seen by child psychiatrists. Despite this fact, its existence is often unrecognized and its prevalence is almost always underestimated."

Doctors can find nothing demonstrably "wrong" with the brain biochemistry or physiology of "MBD" children. They do not suffer from epilepsy, postencephalitic mental retardation or other identifiable diseases. They are diagnosed as having MBD on the basis of behavioral criteria that are socially defined. The principle symptom of MBD is "hyperactivity," but by a curious pharmacological process no one really understands, the way to slow down a hyperactive child is with stimulants such as amphetamines or Ritalin (methylphenidate hydrochloride).

Different Environments and Brains. Many scientists are searching for the biochemical, physiological and structural differences in the brains of hyperactive children. I suspect they will eventually find them, and that their discovery will be hailed as evidence that MBD is a truly biological disease. This conclusion then will be used to further justify the use of powerful psychochemical "remedies" for the behavioral "symptoms." But we know from recent experiments that we can induce measurable changes in the anatomy, physiology and biochemistry of the brain by exposing laboratory animals to different experiences. Animals raised in one kind of environment develop brains that are substantially different from those of litter mates raised in radically different environments. This suggests that the diversity of life experiences can induce a diversity of brain characteristics. But it does not imply that such diversity is undesirable, or that certain characteristics are bad or unhealthy. And it certainly does not justify the use of drugs to deal with "problem children."

Even if we knew beyond doubt that the children's symptoms arose independently of environmental influences, resorting to psychotechnological management would remain highly questionable. We should never intervene without the assurance that the child's brain differences pose a larger threat to his health than does the treatment. Today, many MBD

*Heroin use does drain vital human resources
from our communities, but this is not the real cause of
public concern. The real cause is crime.*

children are being treated without either assurance.

I doubt that anyone really knows how many American children are being treated with daily doses of stimulants. One practitioner who uses them estimates that the number exceeds 250,000 nationwide.

Such "treatment" sometimes continues for years, at dose levels that can produce various side effects. Undesirable side effects occur "in an appreciable fraction" of cases, according to Wender, who points out that the long-term (postpuberty) fate of the MBD child "is uncertain and his clinical picture cannot be drawn."

With the "discovery" of the MBD syndrome, the seemingly endless search for biological determinants of social problems appears to have reached a new dimension. Highly potent drugs that act on the brain in unknown ways are being deployed on a large scale to control children with no demonstrable biological disease.

The advocates of drug-management often pay lip service to alternate approaches, but generally fail to explore them. But if we let scientific method rather than technical expediency guide our efforts, we would investigate family systems and school environments as well as individual behaviors. Of course this would require serious scientific research and might involve great complexity and expense. And in the end it might turn out that the most reasonable "treatment" would be more freedom or better schools. But as long as our priority remains behavior management, technological approaches will grow stronger.

We are laying the groundwork in childhood for the psychotechnological control of adults. In my judgment the widespread use of stimulants to control children represents an official form of drug abuse. As the tools grow more powerful, the prospects are vanishing for saving our children and for saving ourselves from this dehumanizing chemical and biological warfare.

The "Bad" Drug. While official forms of drug abuse continue almost unnoticed, our political leaders keep us preoccupied with the "heroin problem." Yet biologically, heroin is actually one of the least threatening drugs. Contrary to popular belief, prolonged heroin use causes no apparent tissue damage, little impairment of judgment or coordination, and no inclination to engage in violent behavior. It is not necessarily addictive; addiction occurs as a result of complex physiological and psychological circumstances that we do not understand well. And it is not a "killer" drug. Nearly all the deaths blamed on it are due either to impurities, to its adverse action with other drugs, or to the criminal and clandestine conditions surrounding its distribution and use.

Heroin use does drain vital human resources from our communities, but this is not the real cause of public concern. The real cause is crime. Our leaders are not particularly concerned with the social conditions that produce drug use, or with the fate of drug users. They encourage us to believe that the "heroin problem" is one of protecting ourselves and our possessions. Toward that end they encourage the use of psychotechnology.

In the 19th century, morphine was proposed as a cure for opium addiction. Soon after Bayer laboratories synthesized heroin, they announced it as a cure for morphine addiction. Now we have Methadone as a cure for heroin addiction, and Methadone itself is addictive. Leaders of communities that experience the most devastating effects of drug abuse know that replacing one form of narcotic with another will not solve the problem. They also know it merely soothes the effects of poverty and discrimination, enabling victimized people to live with conditions that they might otherwise attempt to change.

It is highly doubtful that heroin itself causes crime. But it is fairly certain that its high price does. If we followed Britain's example and legalized it, we could supply it for about 18 cents per prescription and eliminate the motivation for heroin-related crime. We could save billions of dollars each year. Of course, this would not "solve" the problem, but it would be a reasonable first step.

Beyond that, effective treatment programs cannot be based, as they are now, on coercive narcotic maintenance or withdrawal. They must be based on voluntary use, withdrawal and rehabilita-

tion. And they must involve at least equal attention to the systems that produce and maintain illicit drug use. There is no rational basis for concentrating more attention on the junkie than on the systems that control his behavior. The refusal to analyze and change larger social systems is one of the reasons that programs to control individuals (like Methadone-maintenance) do not work.

Past failures have not brought about a reexamination of basic premises, but rather a hardening of hearts. Last January, for example, Governor Nelson Rockefeller called for mandatory life imprisonment of drug sellers and proposed that bounties be offered to those who inform on users or sellers. Jerome Jaffe, formerly the Administration's highest drug-abuse official, proposed that detection, detention and treatment techniques similar to those used by the military might be used in schools and other institutions to break the back of our heroin "epidemic." [*See "As Far As Heroin Is Concerned, the Worst Is Over," PT, August 1973.*]

In spite of the failure of both legal and technological approaches to the drug problem, I see little indication that the Government will change its policy. Until a more rational approach becomes politically feasible, I expect the search for more sophisticated control techniques will continue and I know that there are behavioral scientists eager to participate in the venture.

Psychology With Blinders. Behavior modification also has mushroomed into prominence during the last decade. It is now used with growing confidence in mental institutions, schools, business and individual therapy. Its proponents urge parents and Government authorities to give up their outmoded methods of coercion and punishment in favor of more efficient and "humane" behavior-management techniques. Their promotion has proven effective, and these techniques are catching on.

Proponents of behavior mod often distinguish it from other psychotechnologies. They generally reject the notion that deviance and misbehavior result from mental illnesses or diseases within the individual. They hold instead that behavior patterns are largely conditioned by re-

The problem lies in the social practices that permit and encourage the unbridled pursuit of power. Those who seek and hold power have found that technology can be a valuable ally.

wards and punishments from the environment, and some behavior modifiers seriously seek social reform. But many never attempt to find the causes of the behavior problems they treat. They may even cite this as an advantage. With behavior modification, their argument goes, there's no need to waste time and money hunting for the causes of a problem in order to cure it. Behavioral engineering can "remedy" it directly.

"Behavior control," says Perry London in a book by that title, "is the ability to get someone to do one's bidding." From the viewpoint of someone in a position of power, this definition is as congenial as it is useful. Accordingly, the "behavior-modification remedy" often consists of simply giving those in authority the tools to control others. Rarely does the behavior modifier question the legitimacy of this authority and rarely does he pause to analyze the responses, the systems, and values that the deviant individual is being conditioned to accept.

Behaviorists do change the environments that shape deviant behavior. But this usually means little more than giving increasingly effective means of control to those in power. Their techniques are often based on "positive reinforcement" and thus may not frighten us as much as the manifestly cruel "aversive conditioning" depicted in *A Clockwork Orange*. But it is precisely because they are superficially more acceptable that they may be more dangerous to all of us in the long run.

Behavior modification shares with the other psychotechnologies a narrow problem-solving perspective and a naive "law-and-order" concept of control. Behaviorists often assert that all behavior can be adequately described in terms of stimuli, responses and reinforcements. This view leads to a preoccupation with only those aspects of a problem that can be analyzed in these terms, and permits only a narrow range of possible solutions.

From a scientific point of view, the idea that control involves getting "someone else to do one's bidding," is a woefully impoverished concept. Behavior is regulated in many ways, and people can be controlled by various techniques. The crucial questions, however, concern how, and to

what degree we should endeavor to control each other. If we remain predisposed to study the control that can be exerted over the behavior of isolated individuals and continue to ignore the complexity of underlying systems, we may fail to discover a whole range of possible solutions to our most crucial problems.

Beneath the Rhetoric of Science. Technology seems to carry a halo of sophistication and respectability in our society. We tend to associate technology with efficiency and impartiality, two of the dominant ideals of our culture. But when we look below the superficial phrases used to justify psychotechnology, we see that its deployment is neither scientific nor politically neutral. Our wisdom has fallen far behind our technical ability.

Technology, like every instrument of power, should be applied with sensitivity as well as authority. I believe wisdom is tragically absent from the growing use of psychotechnology to control social deviance and political dissent. In each case I have discussed, a narrow technological definition of "the problem" is being used to justify repressive programs. Neither the appeal to "scientific objectivity" nor the resort to humane-sounding medical terminology should be allowed to obscure their repressive intent.

There are many who would blame this state of affairs on technology itself, or on the scientific knowledge that supports it. I believe, however, that the problem lies in the social practices that permit and encourage the unbridled pursuit of power. Those who seek and hold power have found that technology can be a valuable ally. They have shaped its development and deployed its results to their own advantage.

If we are ever to discover a humane approach to social conflict, we will have to recognize that human behavior is part of a complex sociobiological *system*. If we are ever to end the use of our knowledge about brains and behavior as a tool to repress, separate and discard deviant human beings, we will have to recognize that deviance is mainly an issue of sociology and politics rather than biology and psychology. Deviance reflects a divergence of ideas and a clash of behavior patterns. We must recognize its social meaning and deal with it on this level.

Neuropsychology teaches us that human beings are varied, complex and poorly understood. If we accept this modest insight, we will take an important step away from the arbitrary and rigid technological posture into which we have become frozen. Then we may see that the obsession to control behavior ignores the subjective, sociological and historical context in which all behavior occurs. In spite of its great practical power, the purely technological orientation toward human beings is blind to these important aspects of our existence.

Curiosity and Compassion. Once we recognize that political expediency and not scientific objectivity lies behind the growing use of psychotechnology, we will have begun to move the serious problems of human society into the arena of ideological controversy where they rightfully belong. For too long the "experts" and politicians have been allowed to carry on a mutually self-serving dialogue. They assert that there are certain "basic issues" in every important policy matter that are either too complicated or too sensitive for the average citizen to deal with. This position can never be justified in a society that claims to be democratic. I am something of an expert in neuropsychology myself, and I am certain that every citizen is qualified to pass judgment on the public policy issues of psychotechnology.

If science teaches us anything, it is to believe in doubt, respect complexity, and rigorously search for deeper understanding of the human condition. The basis of science should be curiosity, just as the basis of our relations to each other should be compassion. Curiosity and compassion are two complementary aspects of human existence. They are part of the same system of thought, and there is no reason to drive them apart. We need both if we are to develop a humane science of human behavior.

With courage and insight we may still be able to seize back from technology both our freedom and our dignity. In the words of a poet, *No equation can divine the quality of life, no instrument record, no computer conceive it—only bit by bit can feeling man lovingly retrieve it.* ♫

III. the sensory world

Physical scientists have observed and measured the "real" world with sophisticated instruments. Yet there is a vast difference between the world that is known through physical measurement and the world that is perceived through normal unaided observation. The study of the psychological processes that enable humans and animals to become aware of the world in which they operate is the study of perception. After some 300 years of dispute, many basic problems in the understanding of perception are unresolved and continue to challenge scientists. One dominant question is whether the human ability to perceive is acquired through experience (the viewpoint held by empiricists) or whether some or all of this ability is innate (the position taken by nativists). Related to this question are the problems of how people perceive size, shape, brightness, and color; how people see a three-dimensional world based on a two-dimensional retinal image; and how they perceive complex patterns of motion. While scientists have primarily studied the visual processes, there are equally puzzling problems confronting those who do research on hearing, taste, smell, and the sensitivities of the skin.

Another major question in the study of perception deals with the most appropriate methods for determining the principles by which sensory mechanisms function. Introspection is a mental technique used by nineteenth-century philosophers to discover and describe sensations and the events that give rise to sensation. Donald Hebb argues that the mind cannot observe itself and that the early introspectionists were merely making theoretical inferences. He advances a theory of cell-assembly activity to show how sensation and imagery become direct sources of self-knowledge. This knowledge, however, is not immediate and is based on inference rather than on observation.

Most perceptual research deals with vision. In his study of visual perception, Irvin Rock confronts the heredity-environment controversy. While he does not deny the brain's reliance on past experience in helping people to see the world as they do, he believes that the brain can adapt to only certain kinds of distortions and that the perception of depth and distance is probably innate. Rock and other researchers have made their discoveries by outfitting subjects with a variety of lenses and prisms. Although the images cast on the retinal surface may undergo great transformations, subjects tend to see the size, color, shape, and position of objects as constant.

Some people, called "eidetikers," can look at, say, a page of printed matter and days later scan a precise image of it and produce it from memory. Charles Stromeyer reports on a woman with "photographic memory" and notes that the ability tends to be more prevalent in young children than in adults. It may someday be possible, however, to train adults to become eidetikers and thus increase their ability to store and retrieve tremendous quantities of information. There are a number of tests for eidetic ability, and Stromeyer includes some that the reader can try.

Discussing the sense of touch rather than vision, Ronald Melzack, a recognized expert in the physiology of pain, discusses the analgesic effects of the ancient Chinese art of acupuncture. Acupuncture, like electroconvulsive therapy, seems to work as a medical procedure, but traditional theories of the perception of pain do not explain why it works. The specificity theory of pain perception, which assumes that pain is felt at the precise location of stimulation, seems unable to account for the evidence provided by actual experiences with acupuncture analgesia; Melzack proposes, instead, a gate-control theory of pain that can explain the physiological basis for the success of acupuncture.

Fascinating explorations in comparative and physiological psychology are typified by James Simmons' research on how bats perceive their environment. Bats navigate with a biological sonar system called echolocation. In the process of echolocation, the bat generates a sound and then identifies objects and obstacles by the reflected echoes. Simmons shows how he and his associates use simultaneous discrimination-learning techniques to test the bat's sonar perception of object size, shape, and distance. The bat's auditory mechanisms are being studied in much the same way that visual processes are investigated in other animals, because echolocation seems to substitute for vision in the bat. Research on the perceptual mechanisms of lower animals, including bats, will someday enable scientists and engineers to improve navigation and communication devices, eliminate misperceptions, and increase the sensory powers of those whose mechanisms have been damaged through accident or disease.

THE MIND'S EYE

by Donald O. Hebb

IN OUR CULTURE, we take it for granted that each of us knows his own mind directly and can describe its operations. To doubt this capacity for introspection, this ability of the mind to observe itself, is to invite incredulity. Yet the evidence is clear that this capacity does *not* exist. Our belief in it is of quite recent origin.

Undoubtedly you know much of what goes on in your mind and can report it. Undoubtedly you have private evidence that bears on the current activity of your mind. Thus, in important respects, your knowledge of yourself is more complete and reliable than the knowledge others may have. Yet it is clear that this knowledge must be inferential and theoretical —at least in part. A second person may be better able than you to evaluate your present mental state and predict your behavior. In principle self-knowledge may depend on the same kinds of inference that knowledge of another depends on.

No one has so far considered the nature of such inference, and it should be done. We should look at the idea of the self, the knower and the perceiver. Objectively, of course, the whole man is the self and the perceiver. I do not mean to suggest anything else. But there are some fascinating phenomena concerning the hallucinations of an immaterial self. These phenomena constitute an important psychological problem, and they may help to account for the false conviction that the mind can look at itself. The immaterial self is a myth, but myths are psychological realities. They affect behavior as well as beliefs.

I propose that introspection is an illusion so strongly established that it amounts to hallucination. To hallucinate is not abnormal. It occurs with normal people in normal conditions in the dream. A severe lack of sleep will induce hallucinations, which we may think of as waking dreams. It is not necessary to take drugs, to suffer mental illness, or to have an addled brain in order to see visions. Isolation will do it, together with monotony—the monotony, for example, of seeing nothing but the white lines on a curving modern highway for mile after mile at night.

Apparently visions and gross misperceptions are quite familiar to people who frequently drive long distances in the Western United States. But each driver thinks he is unique and prefers not to talk about what he has seen. This may change when drivers discover that others sometimes see jackrabbits big enough to step over their cars. A. L. Mosely of the Harvard School of Public Health discovered that all of a group of 33 long-distance truckdrivers had experienced hallucinations, some of which led to accidents, as when a driver braked suddenly to avoid a stalled car that wasn't there.

Because people are reluctant to report such visions, we do not know how widespread these phenomena are. Solitary sailors have suffered hallucinations. Charles Lindbergh reported that a spirit or spirits accompanied him in his lonely flight across the Atlantic. Significantly for the idea that monotony is involved, these spirits left as soon as he sighted fishing vessels off the Irish coast.

We do not know how many airplane pilots have seen things — or how many unexplained crashes have resulted—but if truck drivers see imaginary objects, it is not out of the question that a pilot might see another plane on a collision course ahead of him and crash in an attempt to avoid the phantom plane. Solitary pilots at high altitudes may suffer from what Brant Clark and Ashton Graybiel call the *break-off phenomenon*. The pilot feels somehow detached from reality, in a way he finds hard to describe. Clark and Graybiel got no report of hallucinations, but another investigation found a striking one. The pilot reported that he found himself observing his plane from the outside, seeing it like a toy suspended in space with himself placed like a puppet at the controls.

The illusion of introspection may be the same kind of phenomenon. The normal, healthy mind is capable of improbable tricks. And the conviction that we perceive something is not enough to show that we do perceive it. Perception is complex; self-perception may be even more so.

If our minds have the power to observe themselves, they have not had it long. The Greeks did not talk about mind as open to self-inspection, and the Christian philosophy of the Middle Ages, with its demonic conception of mind, is hardly consistent with introspection. Biologists consider that man is still evolving, so it is conceivable that a new mental capacity could have shown up in Western Europe in the late 17th Century. The alternative is that John Locke did not discover a new capacity in 1690, but invented one. Our problem today is to disinvent it. We must learn to rid ourselves of that fantasy of direct self-knowledge.

We can see what happened to Locke. He knew that a man can report quite accurately things that are going on in his mind — as judged by his subsequent behavior. It must have seemed to Locke that if the mind knows its own activity, the mind must somehow *perceive* that activity.

The mechanics of this perception remained a puzzle, but as Gilbert Ryle pointed out, Locke found a saving analogy in looking in a mirror. The mind, he thought, may somehow *reflect* on itself and its content. This figure of speech became common property in the next hundred years, losing all technical flavor. Some more impressive word was needed by the philosopher-psychologist to designate what was still not understood, and in the 19th Century, *introspection* met that need. Introspection, looking inward, is still a figure of speech—if anything, a worse one than *reflection*. It is easier to develop a fantasy of the mind looking inward than a fantasy of the mind using a mirror — and then forget that this *is* fantasy.

The mind does not observe itself. No two trained introspectors could agree in their descriptions of what they found unless they were members of the same school, brought up as supporters of the same theory. This by itself is almost conclusive evidence that they were not observing, but making theoretical inferences. George Humphrey has shown that the trained introspectors of Cornell, dedicated to the proposition that introspection is the description of sensory content, actually described not sensation but the event that gave rise to the sensation. Any conclusions drawn about mental content in such research can only be matters of inference. Clearest of all is the use of inference in the demonstration of *imageless thought* by Oswald Külpe and his colleagues at Würzburg.

The simplest of the Würzburg demonstrations concerns the mental set connected with the performance of simple arithmetical operations. A person is instructed to add pairs of digits briefly projected on a screen, and to observe his own mental processes as he adds them. At another time, he subtracts with similar instructions. After the subject is well into either task, he reports that as he sees the pair of numbers, the answer pops into his mind—nothing more. With the stimulus of **6**

2 he does not find himself saying "add" before saying "eight" or "subtract" before saying "four." He is *set* to add or to subtract, but no evidence of the set is found in introspection. Yet something is there, for the same stimulus produces the response "eight" at one time, "four" at another. The conclusion is inescapable: an active mental process exists whose presence is known to the subject only because it *must* be there to account for the difference in the responses he makes at two different times.

From John Locke onward we find reports that introspection finds nothing but sensory content: actual sensations (due to stimulation) and images (sensation aroused—theoretically—by some associative mechanism). This is a far cry from observation of the mind itself, though if we assume that the sensations are *in* the mind, we could consider the mind to be observing itself. But the mechanism of sensation and of imagery is a mechanism of looking outward. In the light of what we know today about spontaneous activity in the nervous system, there is nothing here to justify the notion of self-observation by the mind.

When I describe the imagery I may have in the course of thinking, it is quite common for me to hear some unregenerate subjectivist say, "Aha, so you do introspect!" It does not follow.

Each of us has private information about the activities within his own skin: imagery, pain from headache, hallucination and so on. But this information—which is indeed private because it is not available to another observer—is nonetheless provided by the mechanism of perceiving the world around us. It is not the result of introspection.

An excellent example is pain from a phantom limb. After an arm or leg has been amputated, there is still the hallucinatory awareness of the part that has been cut off—so convincing that at first the patient, if he does not see the stump, may not realize that the limb is gone. In a few cases, perhaps 10 or 15 per cent, the patient also feels pain in the missing part. Subjectivists might argue: the patient complains of pain in his right hand, but he has no right hand; so the pain is only in his mind; when he describes it, he introspects, describes mental content, not something that really happens to his body. But the argument cannot be sustained. We are still dealing with a sensory mechanism, even if the mechanism has gone awry.

When you burn the skin of your hand, you say "Ouch!" or "My hand hurts!" This is a normal response involving sensory input to the brain, the excitation of the central processes of perception and consciousness, and the motor output determined by the central processes. Human thought processes are never really simple, but in principle we can see this as a typical reaction to the environment. When I burn my hand and say "Ouch!" no question of the mind's looking inward arises and my speech is not dependent on introspection, any more than is a dog's yelp when you tread on his tail.

Now suppose that a man's arm is amputated. The nerve pathway from the hand is of course interrupted. There is no possibility that an excitation will arise in the hand, but the same excitation, in principle, can start higher in the sensory line leading to the brain. Nerve cells are capable of firing spontaneously and do so normally if they are not exposed to external stimulation. If now the man reports that he still feels the presence of the amputated hand, or if he complains of pain from cramped fingers in that hand, we are dealing with the same mechanism that makes us say "Ouch!" when a normal hand is injured.

Consider the memory image. We commonly hear the voice of an absent friend, see a scene from last summer's holiday, or in trying to recall a passage from a book, see where it was on the page. Such experiences can be understood in the same way as the pain from the phantom limb, except that they would not be the product of spontaneous activity of the central circuits. In these cases the circuits may be thought of as excited by associative mechanisms in the brain.

Suppose you stand before the Rockies and say "I can see the mountains." Here we have a visual stimulus, transmission through the brain, and verbal response —all plain sailing for objective psychology. Now we change the conditions a bit. After the vacation trip you are reminded of your experiences (another thought process excites the same central combination of processes that were excited when you actually were looking at the mountains) and you say again, "I can see the mountains." This is visual imagery—called imagery and not perception only because we know that the adequate stimulus is not present. It is the reexcitation of the same or most of the same cell assemblies that were excited during the original perception. No question of introspection arises. In principle the two cases are very similar. In both, a perceptual activity is excited in the absence of the original sensory stimulation.

It is quite respectable for an objective psychologist to have imagery and report it; his virginity is not thereby brought into question. Apart from such mild gibes at us objectivists, there is a point here of some importance, namely that our imagery is a valid and relatively

direct source of knowledge of present brain activity.

Now consider a revealing little experiment devised by Alfred Binet, the inventor of intelligence testing, in an attempt to distinguish between people with visual imagery and those with auditory or tactile imagery. (His attempt failed, because visual imagery is not what you might think.) The subject studies a typical letter square:

```
x e a g
r l i s
o f z g
d y u p
```

When he has a clear image of it, we cover the letters and ask him to *look at* the image he has formed and repeat the letters. He repeats them readily, but going from left to right in each line, in turn from top to bottom. Now we ask him to look again at his image and repeat the right-hand column of letters from bottom to top, or the letters forming the diagonal from lower right to upper left. He finds, usually to his surprise, that he cannot do so nearly as quickly as before, and that he must rehearse the whole line in order to *see* the letter at the end.

Clearly, he has not formed an image at all, in the sense of something he can look at. If he had, he could easily read off the letters in any order. What he does is reinstate the original perceptual process, which—because of his long habit of reading English—runs from left to right. The imagery turns out to be the recurrence of a *sequence* of individual part perceptions (together with a much vaguer concurrent perception of the whole group of letters).

In the same way, a person who remembers verse by reading from an image of the printed poem might be asked to recite the last word of each line of a stanza, from bottom to top. When he first tries this, he will be surprised to find how much rehearsal he needs in order to see the last word of each line.

There is nothing here to suggest an unfettered examination of exhibits in some picture gallery of the soul. What we have instead is a repetition of the same series of perceptual events in their original order — for the image in this case turns out to be a rigidly organized *sequence*.

Our conclusion that reported imagery is not evidence of the mind's self-contemplation applies to other kinds of self-knowledge. Take as example fear and anxiety.

For any person there is a class of situations that can cause fear, with sweating and trembling and interrupted digestion along with strong tendencies to flee. The stimulus situation excites central-nervous-system activity, which in turn produces overt signs of fear. The same central processes are also capable of producing the utterance, "I am afraid." Now suppose we tell our subject that a madman is looking for him with a pistol. Even though the fear-producing situation has not yet occurred, the brain processes are aroused associatively, and the subject sweats and trembles and has an accelerated heart-beat. He may also say "I am afraid," thus reporting on his state of mind, but this is no more evidence of introspection than is his quickened pulse. This mental activity *is* fear and it causes all types of fear behavior, verbal as well as nonverbal.

Now suppose some pathological process causes the brain activity. There is no threat—immediate or remote—but spontaneous firing of disordered neural cells nevertheless results in the words "I am afraid." If we ask "Of what?" the patient with pathological anxiety may have to say "I don't know." Again, the mechanism of response to the environment operates even if the mechanism has gone awry and no longer is adaptive. But it is not an inward-looking mechanism.

There was a time when I could introspect and did so freely, making all sorts of interesting observations. I was well indoctrinated by the common philosophy that said anyone could observe his own mental activities. Later, when I became aware of all the evidence of casting doubt on the existence of introspection,

I began to look more critically at the process itself. I found that introspecting included some imagery of looking into the interior of my skull from a point at the back of my head. Unfortunately, this seemed so ridiculous that I rapidly became unable to introspect any longer.

My former introspection involved seeing the world and at the same time seeing myself see it, or recalling some sensory event and watching myself recall it. I then mistook the properties of the perceived or imagined object for properties of the process of perception.

I was *seeing* the perception or image inside my skull, I thought, and I understood perfectly the objection of those who would say that the perception of the evening sky cannot be simply a barrage of nerve impulses reaching the brain, that it is nothing so mechanical, so aggregational and atomistic. Perceiving the sky itself but looking inward at the same time, I took its unity, extendedness and beauty for properties, not of the sky, but of the *percept* itself, which therefore could not be a flood of individual nerve impulses, no matter how highly organized these impulses might be.

My apparent introspection had two quite unexpected features. There was the hallucinatory element, and there was a doubled mental process, of observing the world from one point in space while simultaneously observing myself from a second point — the back of my head, just inside my skull. I have already made the point that hallucinations can occur in sober, normal people. Now let me go one step farther and show the existence of bicameral thought processes — the capacity to entertain two trains of mental activity at one time. The capacity is quite common and easily demonstrated, but has gone unrecognized in the classical literature.

There is a longstanding dogma to the effect that attention is unitary. The dogma is purely a matter of theory and is plainly contradicted by behavioral evidence.

I propose that thought is the activity of cell assemblies that are excited by sense input, as well as by the activity of other assemblies, in a complex network of neural firing. I use the term *phase sequence* to designate a series of these assembly actions (presumably not a series of single actions, but a complex flow in which five, 10, 20 or more assemblies might be active at any one time). Considering the millions of assemblies of which the brain must be capable, it is conceivable that two or more such phase consequences — trains of thought — might occur at the same time.

Common features of human behavior show that two trains of thought do occur simultaneously, but that this bicameral process may be possible only with highly practiced forms of behavior. In addition, one of the processes may have to be sensorily programmed. I interpret this to mean that at least one and probably both phase sequences must be highly organized if they are to exist side by side without interference.

It is quite possible, for example, to carry on an ordinary conversation while driving a car through normal traffic. Both activities involve complex perceptions constantly giving rise to inference, meaning and adaptive response. Both, that is, require constant, if not elaborate, thought. On the other hand, an unexpected traffic situation abruptly ends the conversation, and it is not possible to adequately argue a difficult point while driving.

On occasion, when reading aloud to a person whose literary tastes were not mine, I have found myself at the bottom of a page with no notion at all of what the heroine had been up to. I had to go back and hastily skim the page in order to keep up with the story. I had thought of something else for the better part of a page, but my audience had not detected any change of pace. Reading aloud requires the mechanisms of verbal thought and here, without question, two trains of thought were running side by side in my head.

The clinical observations of Wilder Penfield and those of Roger Sperry are relevant to the double train of thought. Penfield elicited thought sequences relating to a patient's earlier experiences by stimulating the temporal lobe while performing brain surgery under local anesthesia. Even though the evoked memories seemed very real to the patient, he always was aware that he remained in the operating room. In Sperry's cases, the corpus callosum — that great bridge connecting the right and left halves of the brain — had been cut. The patient now had two sets of perceptions, thoughts and intentions, one set in the left hemisphere and another in the right. Because the left half of the brain handles most verbal behavior and the right half deals better with spatial relations, it is conceivable that the normal car driver who can talk and steer at the same time does one with the left half and the other with the right half of his brain.

Self-knowledge and imagery that has to do with the self may not always depend on the doubled train of thought. The disturbance of self-concept in the airplane pilot, who had the vivid image of looking at himself and his plane from the outside, must have been a case of doubling. Presumably he was at the same time managing the controls and watching the instrument panel. But there may have been no doubled train of thought in my fantasy of introspection, for it seemed a unified process of simultaneously looking into the interior of my skull and looking at objects in the external world.

Grotesque? Implausible? Inconceivable? Not really. The process is inconceivable only if we have fixed ideas about images and imagery, especially if we think of imagery as the reinstatement of actual sensory experiences — as did most of the 19th Century psychologists.

Imagery is a much more complex matter. Obviously there is no difficulty about imagining improbable things like Pegasus, unicorns and thunderbolt-hurling gods. This is creative thought, fantastic or not. But the creativity of memory images may be subtler and unrecognized. Some time ago I discovered to my surprise that my vivid recollection of a certain field, about two acres in extent, involved a visual image of the field as seen from about 30 feet in the air. I had never seen the field from this point. An informal survey of undergraduate students turned up 30 per cent or so who found—also with surprise — that they recalled familiar areas in the same manner.

More to the point, however, are certain forms of imagery relating to our own bodies. It is comprehensible, of course, that we can deliberately imagine what we would look like if seen from a distance, but a less complete imagery of the same kind may occur unintentionally and without recognition in other circumstances.

Recall a time when you stood waist-deep in water and stretched out on your back to float. Now ask yourself whether this memory includes a fleeting sight of a face with water lapping about it. Such a visual component of the memory is, of course, fictitious, and we tend to suppress in recall or not to notice the elements that strike us as improbable. Or recall the last time you left the room you are now in, closing the door behind you. See if you detect in the supposed recall some imagery of the body of a person with a hand on the door. But we must look for this type of imagery, for its existence is not suggested in either technical or popular ideas about memory and self-knowledge, and we are likely to extract from the complex imagery of thought only things we *know* are there.

Such imaginal components of thought remain unidentified in part because they are typically incomplete — at least in my own case. My introspection included only the eyes (and perhaps the upper part of the face) gazing into the cavern of my skull. The imagery of myself leaving the room and closing the door is shadowy at best, except for hand, arm and shoulder.

In these examples of being in one place and seeming to see ourselves in another, the imaginal elements are fleeting and unobtrusive. In some circumstances, however, they may persist and become disturbing because of the inferences we draw from them. If our theory of mind includes a soul that can leave its body, the experience may be acceptable

and we may even seek it as a sign of favor from the gods. But if we conceive of a soul firmly attached to the body and not peripatetic (at least until death), and if we assume that only the insane see visions, the experience will be frightening and the circumstances conducive to it will be avoided.

> "When General X makes a speech... I find my fingertips itching and have imagery of shoving his head in a bucket of water."

We know something about these circumstances and can make some guesses about how they operate. An essential factor appears to be monotony of sense input. College students were put in experimental isolation, seeing only diffuse light (no pattern vision), hearing only a monotonous buzzing sound (no meaningful sound), lying with covered hands (to prevent tactile perceptions) on a comfortable bed. They remained continuously in this condition of minimal sensory variety except for an hour or two each day for eating and going to the toilet.

After two or three days, those who could endure the monotony began to have hallucinations that were chiefly visual, but that, in a few subjects, included disturbances of the self. Sometimes a student felt that he had two bodies, or that his head was detached from his neck, or that his mind was floating in the air above his body. More commonly students reported seeing com-

plex scenes as vivid as motion pictures.

We know that unchanging or monotonously repeated sensory events lose their power to elicit response or to excite the higher centers of the brain, and this is what appears to have happened. Ordinarily sensation provides a constant guiding influence upon the thought process. This modulation of cortical activity helps both to excite cortical neurons and to maintain organization in their firing. When this influence is decreased or abolished, the spontaneous activity of the cortex must be unorganized much of the time. In fact, the students in the experiment frequently were so lethargic that they were unable even to daydream. But suppose the spontaneously firing neurons happen to include enough of a cell-assembly to activate the whole assembly and thus to excite other assemblies, producing an organized pattern of firing. The subject would find himself with vivid imagery: vivid because the sensory output, which we may suppose normally inhibits the processes of imagery, is now decreased or absent. The main content of thought would then consist of imagery, without the usually competitive perceptions of the real environment.

Visual imagery predominated in the isolation experiment, presumably because only vision was completely controlled. And we can understand as primarily of visual origins some of the misperceptions by those students whose minds seemed to leave their bodies. Suppose that as he lay on the bed, the student thought of himself with imagery of his body as seen from above. Because he lacked effective sensation from his body to keep him clearly aware of bodily contact with the bed, he would find himself *looking at,* instead of imagining, his body on the bed.

If you look at something, you must be at a distance from it. The natural inference is that your true self has left your body and is wandering in the void. A person from our culture, not believing in such possibilities, might conclude that he was going mad and leave the situation as quickly as possible. Some experimental subjects did leave the room suddenly and hastily, refusing explanation. Later in the experiment, when it was known that such hallucinations might occur routinely, the students were less disturbed and could report their experiences.

The yogi, however, with his different theory of existence, might infer that he had successfully freed his soul from the husk of his body. He would seek the experience as often as possible by maintained immobility, quiet and fixity of gaze — a procedure that is calculated to minimize sensory input and maximize hallucinatory effects.

According to his critics, the objectivist has self-knowledge and yet cannot admit it or make use of that knowledge in his study of man. Such criticism has confused private evidence, one basis of inferential self-knowledge, with introspective evidence and direct self-observation by the mind. I have tried to show that describing my imagery or reporting endogenous pain or saying that I am afraid does not show the existence of introspection.

We can now see that it takes no extraordinary mental agility, no special technical skill, to think of yourself as you would of another person. If your memory of an action includes a momentary sight of yourself doing it, if the doubled train of thought permits you to see yourself doing something while you

do it, then there can be no essential impossibility of thinking about yourself as you would about another, making inferences and theorizing about your behavior, with the added advantage of private evidence.

It is true that it is difficult to achieve the perspective of another person when your social behavior over periods of time is in question. But this is not a barrier to seeing segments of your own behavior in objective terms. It means in practice that you must test any theory primarily with others as experimental subjects, no matter how you arrive at the theoretical idea.

Self-observation clearly has much to contribute to our understanding of the human animal. A friend asks a question; an indiscreet answer springs to my lips but is not spoken (I have auditory imagery of words to speak, but the speech is inhibited by other mental processes). In such circumstances I may realize for the first time that someone annoys me or looks ridiculous in my eyes.

However, thought is by no means exclusively verbal. When General X makes a speech and I find my fingertips itching and have imagery of shoving his head in a bucket of water, I know what I think of X and of the speech. When on a hot summer day I see a sheet of smooth water and then feel heretofore unnoticed sweat on my face and back and have vis-

ual and somasthetic imagery of immersing myself in the water, I learn something about my previous mental state (unrecognized discomfort). If nothing prevents me from a swim, I can predict my future behavior. But if the imagery of swimming is accompanied by imagery of an impatient wife at the airport, my prediction may take an entirely different shape.

Thought consists of more than imagery as Külpe showed. Our imagery does not actually control our behavior, but imagery may be the basis of inference in self-knowledge. The cell-assembly activity that is perception, when directly excited by sensation or associatively excited by imagery, is *part* of the thought process. Sensation and imagery are thus very direct sources of self-knowledge. The knowledge is still mediate, however, not immediate: inference, not observation.

Inferences derived from imagery supplement those inferences that I as well as others may make from overt actions. Sometimes the conclusion we draw from imagery may be fantastic instead of factual, as when the yogi concludes that his soul travels through space or when I—early in my career—thought I was directly perceiving my mental processes. But imagery is also the basis of sober, reportable everyday knowledge that we have of our own thoughts and attitudes. ∩

Perceptual Adaptation

By Irvin Rock

SUPPOSE YOU WERE FORCED to wear goggles with prisms inserted. Everything would be fringed with color; straight lines would seem curved, and all objects would appear to the side of their actual location. Would objects around you forever appear distorted or would you, in time, begin to see the world as it normally looks? Would you ever adapt to such a world?

To answer this question, let us consider first how we see the world without prisms. We all learned in school that the eye functions like a camera, with an image formed by the lens at the back of the eye and transmitted to the brain. There is much truth in this common explanation. And yet the camera theory cannot fully explain the way we see the world. Think about the problem of the perception of size. It is true that if we look at one cube that is twice as large as a cube beside it, the image of the larger cube on the retina will be twice as big as the image of the smaller,

and we will perceive the large cube as twice as big.

But suppose the large cube is farther away? We know that the more distant an object is, the smaller its image is in the eye. But even if the larger cube is moved so far away that its image on the retina is the smaller, it still will seem larger. Psychologists call this size constancy.

The size of the image cast on the retina does vary with distance, but the perceived size does not change appreciably. And so the size of a retinal image is not the only basis for our perception of size. It would seem that the brain also takes into account the distance of an object before "deciding" on the size to perceive.

Constancy of size is not an exception, but rather a typical example of the way we see the world. When the sun goes behind a cloud, the light reaching our eyes from everything around us diminishes, but white objects continue to look white, gray continues to look gray (achromatic color constancy).

When we see a circle at a slant, the shape of its image becomes elliptical, but the perceived shape changes only slightly, if at all (shape constancy).

When we move, the image of everything in our field of vision shifts across the retina, but the objects do not seem to move (position constancy). Therefore, an explanation based purely on the photographic image cast on the retina does not explain adequately how we see.

You may argue that I have described not the act of seeing, but of knowing. You might well say that we do see the distant object as smaller, but judge it to be larger because we have learned about perspective and the effect of changing distance, or that we do see the world moving when we move, but know that we are moving, not the world.

But your argument is wrong. We do tend to see in terms of these constancies. This point is illustrated by a photograph originally devised by Edwin G.

Boring of Harvard University. In our illustration, the girl seated down the corridor looks much larger than we would predict from the small image she casts. This is borne out when the picture of the girl in the distance is cut out and placed alongside the other, at the same distance from the observer [see illustration, page 92]. In the first picture, you take distance into account in reaching an impression of the girl's size.

Is the fact that the distant girl in the first picture looks larger than the same girl in the second merely a matter of knowing? Such a claim constitutes a forced and false description derived from what we think we ought to see based on our implicit acceptance of the camera model of vision. This model maintains that vision is directly determined by the retinal image and must be constant when the image is the same and change whenever the image changes. Years ago, psychologists such as Edward Titchener were caught up in precisely this tendency of altering the facts to fit their theories of perception.

Recently, T. G. R. Bower of Harvard has shown that two-month-old infants perceive on the basis of constancy, namely that they take distance and slant into account in perceiving size and shape. The behavior of chickens, fish and many other species suggests that they also see in terms of constancies rather than in terms of the physical properties of their retinal images. It is difficult to believe that lower organisms and infants see in terms of the changing image, but behave otherwise because they know better.

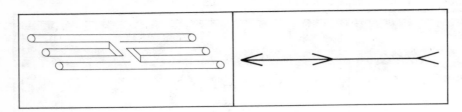

Research like this has led psychologists to claim that there is a separate discipline of perception. They believe that there are laws of perception that must be discovered and that these laws cannot come from the elementary facts of vision, or be understood as factual knowledge gained about the world.

One further argument may be mentioned. Optical illusions cannot be explained on the basis of the retinal image, since the image accurately mirrors the objective state of affairs. Nor can the illusions be based on knowledge; they defy knowledge. For example, we *know* the two line segments in the familiar Müller-Lyer illusion are of equal length, but even after we have confirmed our knowledge with a ruler, one segment still looks longer than the other [*see illustration, above*]. Therefore, all optical illusions attest to the impotence of knowledge about a situation to affect its appearance.

Does this mean that perception is not based on past experience? Not necessarily. I have argued that we cannot reduce perception to *knowing*; we *see* the world on the basis of certain complex central processes that take into account information about things like distance, slant, illumination, or our own movement. We cannot rule out the brain's use of past experience in achieving these perceptual experiences.

The two tablets shown suggest that past experience plays a role in what we see [*see illustrations, below*]. One tablet contains cuneiform writing in *bas-relief;* the other contains the same writing in *intaglio*. Yet the figure on the right is the one on the left turned upside down. The point I wish to emphasize is that we *see* the writing in this way: it looks as if it protrudes in one case and is indented in the other. The knowledge I have just given you—that these are pictures of the same object—has essentially no effect on the way they look. This illusion is based on the position of the shadows (shadow underneath—object protrudes; shadow above—object is indented).

There is reason for believing that this perceptual effect *is* based on past experience. Both sunlight and indoor artificial light typically come from above. Logically, then, a bump on a flat surface usually will be shadowed on the bottom and highlighted on the top. So we could learn—though quite unconsciously—that shadows are associated with protrusion and indentation.

One rather bold experiment supports this theory. E. H. Hess of the University of Chicago reared chickens from the time of hatching in cages where the only light came from below. These chickens, unlike normally reared chickens, pecked more at photographs of grain with the shadow at the top, suggesting that these photographs looked to them like protruding objects—and, therefore, like grain.

But this experiment is the exception. Even after a century of work dominated by psychologists—and before them, philosophers—who believed we *learn* to see the world the way we do, there is little solid evidence to support this belief.

In fact, there now is rather good evidence that form and depth perception are innate, that form and depth are perceptible at birth or soon thereafter. Bower's work shows that even perception in terms of constancy of size and shape is either not learned in humans or learned quickly—soon after birth—in some completely unknown way.

But what about the prismatic spectacles and the like that distort the world by refracting light? It has been known since the days of Herman von Helmholtz and Wilhelm Wundt in the last century that, if you continue to look through the prism, you will adapt to the distortions. Soon things no longer appear either as displaced or as curved as when you first looked through the prism.

This would appear to be a clear case of *learning* to perceive. If so, if we can demonstrate the effects of such experience on seeing in the adult, then perhaps we can conclude that perception in the young infant develops similarly. Study of adaptation to prismatic distortion now takes on real importance. In the laboratory we can produce, in a relatively short time, the effect of experience on perception. The next step would be to investigate the conditions necessary to induce these effects.

Many laboratory attempts have been made to study adaptation to visual distortion. As early as 1896, George Stratton at Berkeley undertook to view the world through an inverting lens system. His retinal image was reinverted—since the normal retinal image is an inverted one—and the world appeared upside

down. He hoped to discover whether, in time, the world would appear normal —or right side up—again. Stratton wore the device continuously for eight days, never permitting himself to see the world except through the lenses. To judge from his day-to-day description of his experiences, the outcome was not altogether clear.

This difficult and trying experiment has been repeated about once every decade since and—in my opinion—the results still are not clear. Stratton claimed he adapted or was well on the way to a complete righting of the scene. Others after him seemed to get no such effect, though T. Erismann and Ivo Kohler of Innsbruck recently claimed their observers did adapt.

There are several difficulties with Stratton's experiment. No objective methods were used to supplement and to clarify the observer's often unclear introspections. The choice of optical distortion—*complete* re-inversion of the retinal image—compounds the difficulty. A less drastic change would have been advisable, because it is difficult to imagine partial adaptation with complete re-inversion. The world will look upside down or right side up, but not tilted by some lesser magnitude. A further difficulty is the confusion between changes in behavior and changes in perception.

In addition to the altered appearance of things, lenses or prisms also lead to incorrect movements at the outset. Stratton reached upward for things that were

actually below the head, and vice-versa. Or he reached leftward for things that were actually to the right, and vice-versa. One may learn to correct these errors and nevertheless continue to *see* the world upside down.

Indeed, everyone who has undertaken this experiment has adapted behaviorally. Incorrect movement tendencies have disappeared and some observers have learned to bicycle and to ski while wearing the inverting lenses. Whether they adapted to the distorted appearance of things is another matter. This is not to deny that these two aspects of adaptation are related.

Except for these sporadic experiments on re-inversion, no systematic work on adaptation to distortion was done until recently. This delay in systematic investigation probably can be traced to the work of J. J. Gibson of Cornell University, who set out in 1933 to study the ability of observers to reestablish sensory-motor coordination when they viewed the world through prisms. However, his observers reported that straight lines that were curved by the prisms later tended to appear less curved. Gibson therefore shifted his focus of interest to this problem. Reasoning that a prism creates a curved retinal image and that this curved image later appears to straighten, he felt that the crucial thing was the curved image. His next—and plausible—move, one that I believe had an important historical impact, was to abandon the prism technique in favor of looking at a truly curved line. Surprisingly enough, he found that if you stare at a curved line for a few minutes, it will look less curved. If a straight line is then introduced, it will look curved in the opposite direction. This is the now well-known Gibson normalization effect. (He made a similar discovery about a tilted line.)

Gibson reasoned that objects tended to approach the norm from which they are departures. Since lines can curve symmetrically in either direction, a straight line is the norm or neutral point. If a curved image tends to lead eventually to an impression of straightness, then we may suppose that the entire coordinate system has shifted to a new neutral point. If this shift occurs, a straight image will no longer appear straight.

Prismatic distortion was no longer the focus of study. The prism seemed irrelevant to Gibson's work; it was only one method of creating a curved image. The normalization effect could not be

adaptation to a distorted world based on learning to see the world more accurately. In this effect the observer came to see *less* accurately, for after a while the truly curved line looked less curved. Therefore, it was not learning in the usual meaning. Interest shifted from prism adaptation to adaptation effects based on fixating curved and tilted lines.

The field of prism adaptation had to be rediscovered. Investigators had to realize that there *is* a class of effects such as Stratton first studied: Perceptual change based on learning to see a distorted world more correctly. The work of Erismann and Kohler played a major role, for when their observers wore the distorting devices over weeks or even months, they encountered dramatic changes and equally impressive after-effects when at last the prisms were removed. Richard Held of M.I.T. gave this work impetus by developing objective techniques for studying change and by showing experimentally that normalization effects of the kind Gibson discovered could not account for the changes that take place in wearing prisms.

A typical modern adaptation study is divided into three parts: pre-test, exposure period, and post-test. In the pre-test, the experimenter establishes just how each observer judges the perceptual property under investigation.

For example, the observer is asked to indicate when a flexible, luminous rod appears straight. Because he is shown the rod in a darkened room, he must respond in terms of the absolute appearance of the rod. He cannot compare it with other contours in his field of vision. Several measures are taken and the average computed. Then the observer puts on the prisms, set in goggles, and his exposure period begins. He performs relevant activities, more often than not merely walking through the laboratory corridors. For the post-test, he is brought back to the darkened room, his goggles are removed, and once more he views the flexible rod. The difference between pre-test and post-test is the measure of adaptation. Any adaptation will be revealed by an after-effect. In this experiment, a curved rod will appear straight, since a curved image has—during exposure to the prisms—come to yield an impression of straightness.

It is also possible to conduct all three stages with the observer wearing prisms. Adaptation in this procedure is revealed by the selection of a curved rod in the pre-test and a straight rod in the post-test. It can be argued that, if the ob-

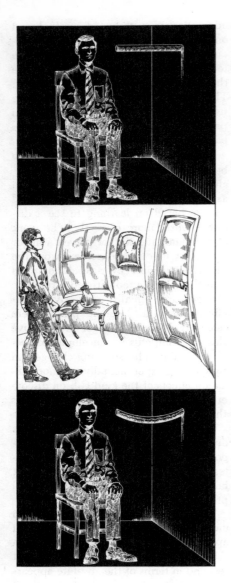

server wears prisms during the testing, he will try to discount the known distortion in order to give the "right" answer. Without prisms, he has no reason to compensate and adaptation will be revealed by an "error." Thus, the aftereffect obtained without prisms gives impressive evidence that a change in the nervous system does take place.

The findings of various adaptation studies indicate that adaptation to *displacement* occurs readily. If the observer is given enough exposure, this adaptation will be more or less complete. When an object straight ahead is prismatically displaced, the observer must turn his eyes to look at it. Many investigators agree that this kind of adaptation is based on the observer's interpretation of the turned position of his eyes as *not* turned. Hence, after exposure, an object fixated with eyes turned appears straight ahead.

There is now fairly good evidence that

observers will adapt to a *tilted image*, a superior procedure to Stratton's 180-degree transformation. In the pre- and post-test, the observer sets a luminous line until it appears vertical. Exposures of a half-hour to an hour induce changes of from three to 10 degrees, providing objective data that an image need not be in its usual position for the observer to see it as upright. Stratton's belief thus appears to be confirmed.

Adaptation to altered curvature exists, but is relatively small. In one study, adaptation was only 30 per cent of the total distortion after observers wore prisms for 42 days. Nevertheless, the adaptation—and this is also true for tilt —is greater than the Gibson normalization effect can explain. Within a very short time, there is also appreciable adaptation to distortions of *size*.

The curve of adaptation levels off after the first day or two of exposure. After that adaptation increases very little. The reason for this is unknown, nor do we know whether adaptation other than that to displacement will be complete if the exposure is continued indefinitely.

Erismann and Kohler reported certain dramatic effects such as simultaneous adaptation to blue filters on the left side of both goggles and to yellow filters on the right; simultaneous adaptation to compression of images on one side and expansion on the other. However, it has not been possible to reproduce the color effect and we still lack adequate confirming evidence about the compression-expansion effect and other effects of this kind.

We must now consider the theoretical problem of adaptation to distortion. Are we to suppose that perception is so malleable that no matter how we distort the retinal image, the observer ultimately will adapt and see the world as we do? If this is true, how can we reconcile it with the findings that many perceptual attributes are present at birth and do not depend on learning? What mechanism underlies such changes in appearance?

I believe the answer is that perception is not completely malleable. We can adapt only to certain kinds of distortion. The information within the retinal image *does* supply us with the necessary core of what we see.

Suppose we hypothesize that the retinal image provides crucial information about *relationships* between objects. Consider the following example. Imagine you are looking at two straight lines, A and B, with line A being vertical and line B tilted, and A being longer than B

[*see illustration below*]. Assume that line A is straight ahead of you. In terms of the *relationship* of the image of A to that of B, we can say that A is longer than B and that A and B diverge, being closer at one end than the other. That is all.

Now if you look at this same configuration through a wedge prism, holding the position of your eyes still, the image will be distorted [*see illustration below*]. The entire pattern will be displaced sideways on the retina, and A and B will be curved. But the basic relationships are preserved: A remains longer than B, and A and B diverge from one another. If you look at the pattern through a lens that magnifies or minifies the lines, then, while the absolute size of the two images will be altered, the relationship of their sizes to one another will not be affected. If you look at the same pattern through an optical device that tilts the entire retinal image, the relationship of tilt of the lines *with respect to one another* will not be altered [*see illustration below*].

Therefore, if the crucial information given by the image is relational, the kinds of distortions that are being studied are not distortions at all! On the other hand, if a more drastic kind of distortion were introduced, such as a random scattering of points on the image [*see illustration below*], I think you will agree it is unlikely that an observer will ever adapt. He would never come to see A and B as we do.

But, if perception depends only on the relationships within the image, why does the world look distorted when *first* we look through prisms? This point has been completely overlooked by investi-

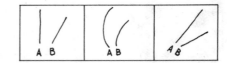

gators, who have assumed that it is intuitively self-evident that the world looks distorted because the image is distorted.

Let us consider this previously ignored problem of the initial distortion. Perhaps the absolute aspects—not the relationships of the two lines—will explain the distortion. Lines A and B produce images of specific size at any specific distance; A's image on the retina is vertical,

B's is tilted; the images of both A and B are straight. Perhaps the visual experience of a lifetime associates these absolute aspects with their corresponding perceptual properties: the size of the image with the perceived size; the orientation of the image with the perceived orientation; the curvature of the image with the perceived degree of curvature. Such associations are preserved in the form of enduring memory traces, and these traces are faithful representations of the absolute features of the retinal image and the associated perceptual properties.

If this is true, A appears tilted when first viewed through a tilting prism, not for any innate reason, but because a

formation of a new association while wearing prisms becomes plausible. Through learning, a curved image is associated with a straight line.

vertical orientation of the retina has become a sign of the perceptual vertical in the neural organization underlying perception. (Orientation here is with respect to the observer. The prism does not change the orientation of A with respect to B.) A appears smaller when viewed through a reducing lens, not because a smaller image innately demands a smaller percept, but because the specific size of the image has become a sign of a specific perceptual size. A and B appear curved when first viewed through a wedge prism, not because a curved image innately suggests a curved line, but because only a straight image has become a sign of a perceptually straight line.

Given this explanation, it is obvious how we adapt to prisms. It is only when the perceptual properties of absolute tilt, size, curvature and the like are *not* linked innately to absolute features of the retinal image that a theory of adaptation makes sense. For it would be hard to understand why, if image curvature innately determines perceived curvature, the perception of curvature is subject to change. But if the relationship of image curvature to perceived curvature is a *learned* one in the first place, then the

We have not yet explained how the observer forms these new associations. It is not enough to say he does so by looking through prisms. To illustrate this point, imagine a stationary observer who looks at A and B through a tilting prism. Suppose that he can see only this pattern; everything else being invisible. A will look tilted and B almost horizontal, and they will continue to do so. Unless information is provided that tilted A is vertical and horizontal B is tilted, no new associations can be formed. The observer would not adapt.

Suppose, however, the observer now can see his own body. The image of his body, seen through the prisms, will un-

dergo the same tilting transformation. It, too, will appear tilted [*see illustration above*]. Consequently, he now can learn that the tilted image of A is actually "vertical," for it is parallel to his body.

Other information than direct sight of the body can lead to adaptation. Movement by the observer could be an important clue. The seated observer who can see only A and B through the prisms has no reason to see the lines as they really are. But suppose he stands up [*see illustration left*]. Since A appears tilted with respect to himself, he would expect to move obliquely away from A. Instead, he finds that he remains directly in front of A; the direction of his movement is clearly in alignment with A. (A is in fact vertical and the observer is in fact moving directly upward.) From his movement, he learns that A is indeed vertical with respect to himself.

The same informative value of movement applies to curvature distortions. Imagine an observer who looks through curving prisms at a horizontal straight line on a wall. If he sits or stands still and sees only the line, there is no reason for its curved appearance to change. But if he walks parallel to the wall, peculiar changes of the line's image will occur [*see illustration below*]. That part of the line that had been in front of him will appear to move upward, and the part he is approaching will move downward. In other words, the lower-

most bulge of the line will always remain directly in front of him. This is because the line *is* straight. Wherever he is, the tendency of the prism will be to displace that part of the line to his side upward to a greater degree than the part straight ahead. These changes in the image of the line inform him that its curvature is parallel to the direction in which he is moving. Because he moves in a straight path, the line must be straight.

We have not yet considered an obvious source of information—what we can find out from our other senses, particularly from touch. Suppose the observer who looks at A through tilting prisms then runs his hand along the line. You would expect that it would be easy for him to tell that the line is actually vertical.

In fact, in both philosophy and psychology there is a long tradition that can be traced to Bishop Berkeley of belief in the educating role of touch in the development of adequate visual perception. We see correctly in spite of the logical limitations of the retinal image as a source of information—for example, the image is two-dimensional, but vision is three-dimensional—so that it has seemed plausible to believe we learn to see by touching things and moving around in the environment.

But running the hand along the tilted line does not lead to visual change. Quite the contrary. The line will *feel* tilted. So dominant is vision that the impression yielded by our sense of touch is distorted to conform with our visual impression, even when it is wrong.

In our laboratory we have presented an observer with a conflict between vision and touch. In a simple experiment, the observer views a square through a lens that reduces the image to half its actual size. A one-inch square appears as a half-inch square. The observer is allowed to grasp the square, but a cloth below the square prevents him from seeing his hand. And he is not told that

he is looking through a reducing lens [*See illustration left.*]

In this conflict between two senses, the observer experiences only what he sees, and the *feel* of the square conforms to the *look* of it. The "feel" is captured by vision. As for adaptation, if the observer is given a prolonged exposure to this contradictory experience, vision does not change at all. Touch changes! The impression of size by touch alone—with the eyes closed—has changed following exposure to the conflict. The one-inch square now feels smaller than it did before the experiment began. It is therefore hard to believe that adaptation to prismatic distortion can be based on touch.

Contrast this failure to adapt visually to a reduced image with a different experiment. The observer is exposed to a reduced image, but he is given visual information. He does not have to rely on his sense of touch. In this experiment, the observer looks through a convex mirror that makes everything appear diminutive. Through this, he sees a good portion of his own body and an array of familiar objects, such as playing cards or checkers and checkerboard [*see illustration below*]. Tests of size perception are conducted before and after exposure to this optically reduced scene.

During the exposure period, which can be as brief as 10 minutes, the observer either remains stationary or plays solitaire or checkers. The reduced images of objects lead increasingly to an impression of normal size. In the test following exposure, the observer judges a luminous line of about 10 inches in length seen in the dark to be about 12 inches long, suggesting that considerable adaptation to the reduced image has taken place.

I believe that the crucial information here consists of sight of the body and the array of familiar objects. If the observer saw only a rectangle through the convex

mirror, it no doubt would continue to look about half its actual size. But when he sees a playing card maintain its normal size in relation to other objects, particularly to his own minified hand, he receives information that the reduced image is of a much larger object than first it seemed to be.

If perceptual adaptation is a fact, and if my suggested hypothesis concerning memory traces is plausible, a difficult question remains. How can memories affect the way things look? I cannot answer this question, but it is interesting to consider other cases where memories probably have such effects.

Consider the familiarity and meaningfulness of objects. Logically, it must be the case that a figure "4" *looks* familiar and meaningful because of memories associated with it. If so, these memories

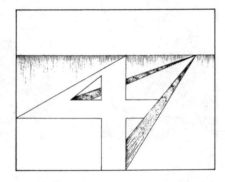

must enter into the neural organization underlying such perceptual experience. Even more to the point, because it involves space perception, is the drawn figure of a cube. The memories of three-dimensional cubes apparently are aroused by the sight of the drawn figure, and these memories then must enter the neural organization that leads to the visual impression that a two-dimensional drawing is three-dimensional. Recall the photographs of the cuneiform carvings. The memories of how shadows fall on three-dimensional objects must play a determining role in the way these photographs appear to us.

These are examples of past experience contributing to present perceptual experience. It is in this way, I would speculate, that adaptation effects can be understood. In our laboratory experiments, memories of how a tilted or curved line "behaves" somehow affect the way these lines look to our observers after prolonged exposure. On the other hand, our perception of the *relationships* between objects in the environment is in all probability innately determined. Not learned, but there all the time. ∩

Eidetikers

by Charles F. Stromeyer III

ELIZABETH IS A YOUNG TEACHER at Harvard, very intelligent, a skilled artist. She has a talent that most painters don't have. At will, she can mentally project an exact image of a picture or scene onto her canvas or onto another surface. This hallucinated image appears to contain all the detailed texture and color of the original. Once the image is formed, it remains still and Elizabeth can move her eyes about to inspect the details.

Elizabeth (not her actual name) says she can project a beard onto a beardless face, for example, or leaves onto a barren tree—additions so strong that they can obscure the true image. However, she never confuses eidetic images with reality, and spontaneous imagery rarely bothers her.

Her ability to recall and visualize images is not limited to pictures or scenes. Years after having read a poem in a foreign language, she can fetch back an image of the printed page and copy the poem from the bottom line to the top line as fast as she can write. She says that she used her eidetic memory for high-school and undergraduate examinations, but found it less useful in graduate school.

Elizabeth is an eidetiker; she has a photographic memory. A person with this ability can briefly examine a picture or a printed page and later (sometimes days later) project onto a neutral surface an image that preserves the color and detail of the original.

Talmud. Other remarkable cases have been reported. The Shass Pollaks, Jewish memory experts described by George Stratton, could tell what word appeared in what position on each page of the 12 volumes of the Babylonian Talmud. Alexander Luria of the University of Moscow describes, in his classic book *The Mind of a Mnemonist,* the eidetic processes of a man with a limitless memory.

The study of eidetic imagery has been renewed recently in America by Ralph Haber, a psychologist at the University of Rochester. Haber screened 500 school children from the second through sixth grades. He selected young children because earlier studies, most of them before 1935, found that eidetic imagery is relatively common in young children, although it is rare in adults.

Each child sat before an easel that held a neutral gray card. The child was shown a picture and asked to look it over carefully for 30 seconds. The picture was taken away and the child told to look at the gray card and describe what he could still see. Each session was tape-recorded.

Stripes. One of the pictures, taken from *Alice in Wonderland,* showed Alice at the base of a large tree talking to the Cheshire cat. One 10-year-old boy said he saw a long-lasting image. "Do you see something?" he was asked. "I see the tree, gray tree with three limbs. I see the cat with stripes around its tail." Asked to count the stripes, the boy paused. "There are about 16," he replied, "and I can see the flowers on the bottom. There's about three stems, but you can see only two pairs of flowers. One on the right has green leaves, red flower on bottom with yellow on top."

The most striking aspect of the eidetic child's report is the vividness and completeness of the image before him. Such a detailed report would be unusual, even if it were based on everyday memory—which it did not appear to be.

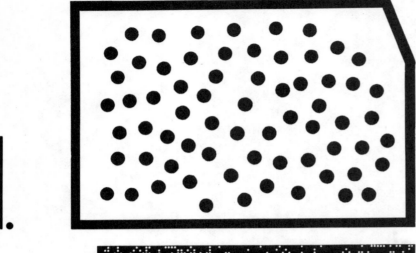

1.

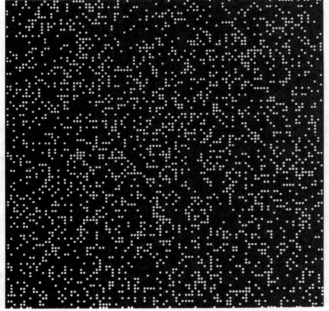

2.

TESTS. Do you have the ability to form an eidetic image? On these pages are two tests. Very few adults can form eidetic images, but the ability is supposed to be fairly common in young children.

The author is looking for eidetikers to help in his research. If you think that you can form an eidetic image and see the hidden figures in these tests, write to his research colleague, J. O. Merritt, Psychology Department, 622 William James Hall, Harvard University, Cambridge, Massachusetts 02138.

TEST 1. Carefully examine the dot pattern for several minutes. Move your gaze about to inspect all details. Do not stare at one point. Shut your eyes and try to recall an image of the pattern. If you can build up a good image, turn to the next page and superimpose your eidetic image on the dot pattern at the top. Make the rectangular borders coincide exactly. Do you see any numbers or letters? Each pattern alone is a random array of dots, but when one is superimposed on the other, very clear figures will appear.

TEST 2. Cover your left eye and with only your right eye carefully examine this 10,000-random-dot pattern. Scan the pattern for a few minutes, then close your eye and try to recall an image of it. At first you may be able to recall only parts of the pattern. If you are able to form an image, keep scanning the pattern for about 10 minutes or until you have a detailed eidetic image. Now close your right eye and open the left. Turn the page and look at the second picture. Keep your right eye closed and try to visualize the image on the previous page. If you are successful, you will see a figure float off the page toward you.

Details. About half of the children tested reported seeing some image of at least one of the pictures. But many of these images were afterimages; they persisted for only a short time and included little detail. However, Haber found 20 children with some eidetic imagery who could describe small details of the pictures. After the image faded, an eidetic child remembered the picture only slightly better than did a child who lacked eidetic memory.

Unfortunately, the test used by Haber cannot distinguish between superior memory and a projected eidetic image. Because of this, the reality of eidetic imagery has been questioned. Two other tests have been proposed. In the composite-picture test, a person must form an eidetic image of one drawing and then superimpose the image on a second drawing. Together the two pictures will produce a third, composite picture. But too often a subject can look at the component drawings and guess the composite picture.

A better test is to show a person a pattern of dots until he can form an eidetic image of it. He then is told to superimpose the image onto a second pattern of dots. The combined dots produce a set of numbers or letters. Non-eidetic persons cannot detect the numbers or letters. The test cannot be faked easily, nor does it depend on memory.

Dots. We used a variation of this test in our experiments with Elizabeth at Harvard. But instead of simple dot patterns, we used the computer-generated stereograms developed by Bela Julesz of Bell Telephone Laboratories.

Each stereogram consists of a pair of random-dot patterns. When a person looks at these patterns through a stereoscope, which presents one pattern to the right eye and the other pattern to the left eye, he sees a figure emerge in depth. When he looks at the random-dot patterns without the stereoscope, he can see neither figures nor depth.

Using only her right eye, Elizabeth viewed a 10,000-dot pattern for one minute. After a 10-second rest, she looked at the other 10,000-dot pattern with her left eye. We asked her to superimpose the eidetic image of the right-eye pattern on the actual left-eye pattern. Without hesitation she reported that she saw the letter T coming toward her.

Next we showed her both patterns through the stereoscope and she said the T was identical to her eidetic image.

Now we inverted the left- and right-eye patterns. When she projected the eidetic image onto the actual pattern, she saw an inverted T behind the surface. The T oscillated in depth, but had sharp outlines.

Float. In the next experiment, Elizabeth looked at another random-dot pattern with her right eye. This time she looked at the pattern in three-minute periods, separated by a minute of rest, until she had looked at it for 12 minutes. Twenty-four hours later she looked at the companion pattern with her left eye and projected the eidetic image of the right-eye pattern onto it. Within 10 seconds she said she saw a square floating above the surface.

These tests provide proof that eidetic imagery exists. Elizabeth had not seen the stereograms before the experiment. It seems impossible that she could memorize the position of 10,000 dots in the brief time we allowed her to look at the patterns. Even if she could, this would not explain the depth she saw. Three-dimensional vision is possible only when each eye sees a different image.

Depth. To demonstrate the extremely detailed information contained in the eidetic image, we tested her with a million-dot random pattern. She formed an eidetic image of the pattern and could retain it for up to four hours. We have not yet tested her for longer periods with the million-dot pattern.

Elizabeth could selectively recall any one of a number of images. In one experiment she formed images of four 10,000-dot patterns presented to her right eye. The next day she viewed a single pattern with her left eye and recalled each of the four eidetic images on request. When the images were superimposed on the left-eye pattern, each created a different figure that was seen in depth.

Since she had claimed that an eidetic image could obscure a real object—for example, that a projected beard could hide a chin—we decided to test whether an eidetic image could suppress an actual pattern.

We devised a stereogram that had two patterns, X and Y, for the left eye and one pattern for the right eye. Elizabeth looked at the pattern X with her left eye until she had formed an eidetic image. Then we presented pattern Y to her left eye and the right-eye pattern to her right eye. After she saw the combined figure in depth, we asked her to call up the eidetic image of the left-eye X pattern. The eidetic X image suppressed the Y pattern before her eye, and she reported seeing a new figure in depth.

Tilt. These experiments show that the eidetic image is eye-specific and strong enough to obscure a real object. Furthermore, the image does not change its orientation in space as the head is tilted. For example, Elizabeth tilted her head 90 degrees to one side and viewed an upright pattern until she formed an eidetic image of it. When she projected the eidetic image, she claimed it always remained upright. She could easily combine the eidetic image with an actual upright pattern and see the resulting figure in depth.

In another set of experiments, we use the Land color phenomenon. Edwin Land, originator of the Polaroid camera, discovered that black-and-white film could produce full-color pictures. Two pictures of the same scene are taken on black-and-white film, one through a red filter and the other through a green filter. The picture taken through the red filter is then projected onto a screen through a red filter, and the picture taken with a green filter is projected through a green filter or without a filter (that is, with white light). When the two images are superimposed, the projected picture has all the colors of the original scene—blues and yellows as well as reds and greens. Full color can be produced with various filter combinations—for example, green and orange or red and blue-green.

Accuracy. For the Land demonstrations, we used two sets of squares. There were nine squares, some light, some dark, in each set. We projected one set through red light onto a screen and Elizabeth gazed at it until she had formed an eidetic image. The next day we projected a different set of squares onto the screen through green light. Elizabeth combined her eidetic image of the red squares with the green and reported the hue, saturation and lightness of each of the nine squares. She saw a full range of colors—red, blue, purple, reddish-brown, gray, yellow and green.

Immediately after her report, both Elizabeth and the experimenter viewed the real image for comparison. The colors produced by her eidetic image proved to be very accurate. There were minor deviations: several of the squares in the eidetic combinations were slightly more saturated than the actual colors.

Elizabeth could combine two eidetic images—one of the red and one of the green squares—and see a colored display. We also tested her with red-and-white light and green-and-orange light, with similar results. The reported colors were exceedingly accurate.

The experiment was repeated in light so dim that the contours of the squares were barely discernible. The green pattern was below the color threshold so it appeared gray. The red pattern was bright enough to be just above the color threshold. Again Elizabeth could use her eidetic image to produce a combined pattern that she saw in full color.

Afterimages. We have conducted a number of other perceptual tests to determine the properties of eidetic images. Some early researchers maintained that the eidetic image produces an effect similar to that of an actual visual stimulus. If this were true, then eidetic images should produce afterimages and movement aftereffects.

To test for afterimages, Elizabeth scanned a green-and-black grating. She reported no afterimage while she formed

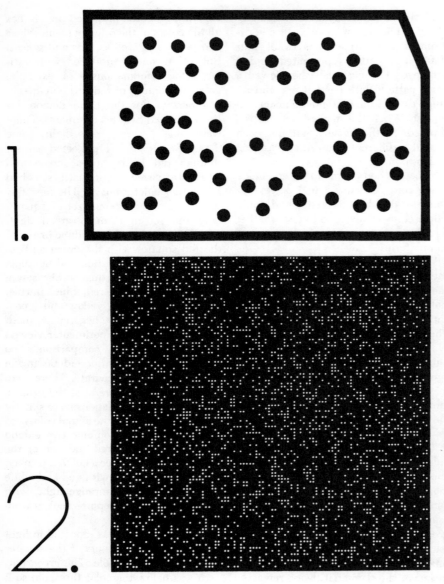

1.

2.

expand. The aftereffect appeared identical to that produced later when she looked at an actual spiral, and the duration of both effects was the same.

Scan. To form an eidetic image of a complex pattern, Elizabeth prefers to scrutinize the pattern part by part, often shutting her eyes to see if she has a good image of that part. She could not form eidetic images without moving her eyes. She had to scan even the simplest shapes to build up the eidetic image.

Simple images can be recalled rapidly, but complicated patterns often do not appear *in toto;* instead, parts may appear successively until the entire image is recalled. For example, it once took Elizabeth about 10 seconds to recall a 10,000-dot eidetic image.

Breakup. The eidetic images are sharp and finely detailed. Elizabeth formed an image of a fine, high-contrast-stripe grating. Two days later the image was as sharp as the original pattern.

When the eidetic image begins to fade, it does not blur as an afterimage does, but dims and breaks apart.

The fact that an eidetic image built up with one eye will combine with a pattern presented to the other eye to form a perception of depth indicates that the eidetic image may be represented quite early in the visual system, before the site of binocular interaction, perhaps beyond the retina in the lateral geniculate nucleus or occipital cortex.

Many intriguing questions remain. Can an eidetiker form an image of a completely imaginary scene? Can eidetic images be altered by removing or introducing new elements? Can one synthesize an image of something not seen before?

Movie. Can an eidetic image be formed of a moving scene? Elizabeth claims once to have seen in full detail an eidetic 10-second episode from a Laurel and Hardy movie that she attended the week before.

Obviously, more research is needed. For the past 35 years psychologists have been skeptical about the existence of eidetic imagery. Few modern theories of memory take into account this type of image retention. We have proved that eidetic imagery exists, but we still have much to discover about its nature. ◘

the eidetic image. But later, when she stared at the projected eidetic image she subsequently saw a magenta-and-blue-striped afterimage. The afterimage appeared identical to one formed by staring at the actual pattern. However, unlike normal afterimages, the eidetic afterimage remained constant in size when it was projected to different distances, and it did not move when Elizabeth moved her eyes.

Spirals. To test motion aftereffect one looks at a rotating-contracting spiral for a few minutes and then stares at the cen-

ter of a stationary spiral. The stationary spiral will seem to expand. If the original spiral rotates in the opposite direction so that the moving spiral appears to expand, the stationary one will seem to contract.

Elizabeth first formed an eidetic image of a stationary black-and-white spiral. She then stared at a rotating-contracting spiral for two minutes. Immediately afterward she shifted her gaze to a black-velvet surface and called up the eidetic image of the stationary spiral. As she stared at its center, the spiral seemed to

How Acupuncture Works

A Sophisticated Western Theory Takes the Mystery Out

By Ronald Melzack

Acupuncture analgesia works in China. That we know from films distributed by the Chinese Medical Association and from reports by American and British doctors who have visited China in recent years. The millennia-old Chinese practice of inserting long fine needles into carefully chosen points on a person's body often does stop pain. In the last decade Chinese physicians have used the technique extensively, freeing surgeons to perform major operations on the abdomen, chest or head of a patient while the patient stays awake and alert. We don't know how acupuncture analgesia works. According to the theory of pain traditionally taught in our medical schools, it shouldn't. When we receive eyewitness accounts like the recent report from British physician P. E. Brown, we are left either to wonder or to scoff. ''My first introduction to this method of anesthesia was during a visit to the Cheng Hwa Hospital in Shanghai,'' writes Brown. ''I was taken into the [operating] theater to see a man in his mid-30s have [part of his lung removed].... He was fully conscious and able to speak to me. There was only one acupuncture point, situated over the right biceps muscle. A needle two inches long was inserted and manually rotated by the 'anesthetist.' She was rapidly rotating the needle for 10 to 15 seconds, at intervals of half a minute.''

During the operation the patient remained totally calm, Brown reported, and his pulse and blood pressure remained normal. ''I was allowed to sit with him,'' Brown continues, ''and ask him questions about the amount of pain or discomfort he might be feeling, but he insisted there was no pain.''

Brown went on to cite some of the advantages of acupuncture analgesia. The surgeon operated as slowly and deliberately as he chose to without worrying about drug levels or side effects. The patient lost only a slight amount of blood. Immediately after the operation, the patient was sitting up in bed. The analgesic effect of acupuncture lasted several hours after the operation.

Needles Are Better Than Drugs. There are additional advantages. Acupuncture holds promise for elderly patients otherwise often endangered by the side effects of anesthesia by drug. It also holds promise for patients suffering pain syndromes difficult to treat, such as the neuralgias, or the phantom-limb pain suffered by amputees [see ''Phantom Limbs,'' by Ronald Melzack, PT, October 1970]. The critical factor in the effectiveness of acupuncture is fairly intense, continuous stimulation of tissues by needles—by twirling the needles or passing an electric current between them. An American physician, E. G. Dimond, observed surgeons in Canton operate on a man who had a nonhealing ulcer. The acupuncturist inserted four needles into each ear. The needles were connected to a battery. Stimulation of the ear tissue set off a chain of neural signals that somehow blocked the pain while the man's abdomen was cut open, and part of the stomach removed. But even though we can follow the crude mechanics of acupuncture, we still don't understand how it works.

Acupuncture analgesia confounds established Western medical doctrine on several major counts. By inserting needles into one part of the body, acupuncture produces an effect in another part of the body. For a thyroid operation in one hospital, an acupuncturist inserted a needle one inch deep into each forearm at a point about four inches above the wrist. For a thyroid operation in a second hospital, an acupuncturist inserted needles in the neck and the back of the wrists.

According to our *specificity theory* of pain, this doesn't make sense. The specificity theory maintains that specific pain receptors in our body relay signals directly to the brain. The transmission line resembles a simple telephone switchboard: dial in a signal at one end and the bell rings at the other. The theory assumes that a person will feel pain precisely where he is stimulated. But this contradicts the observed effect of acupuncture analgesia.

The advocates of specificity theory further assume that the amount of pain felt depends on the intensity of stimulation. But the analgesic effect of carefully placed, rapidly rotating needles shows that this is not always so. Acupuncture needles may initially produce pain, yet they also anesthetize. There is no explanation for the way the needles block nerve impulses, or why pain is relieved for hours after the needles are withdrawn.

Yin and Yang. The traditional Chinese explanation of acupuncture is completely different from the specificity theory. The Chinese theory is that the two universal forces—yin and yang—are biologically present in our bodies in the form of spirits (yin) and blood (yang). The spirits and blood course through the body along a series of separate channels called meridians. Acupuncture points lie on these meridians, or at their intersections. Traditionally, there are 365 acupuncture points along 12 meridians, although in recent years these numbers have changed.

When yin and yang fall into disharmony, according to the theory, disease and pain occur. The insertion of acupuncture needles at specific sites permits the two forces to come into harmony again. Although the history of acupuncture is uncertain, we know that acupuncture points have been determined, to some extent at least, by empirical observation: needles inserted at particular points have produced certain results.

The yin-yang theory is still popular among the ''barefoot doctors'' practicing folk medicine in rural China. But from a Western standpoint the theory is unsatisfactory. It falls too far outside our own scientific approach to medicine.

A second, psychological explanation of acupuncture—that its effects are due to hypnosis—makes sense to the Western mind but fails to hold up. Consider:

• Hypnosis requires prolonged training on the part of the patient. Professional medical hypnotists say that to produce a trance sufficiently deep to allow surgery requires at least four to eight hours of initial training, plus additional time for specific instruction. The sessions normally take place over days or weeks. With acupuncture analgesia, a patient's prior acquaintance with the procedure appears *not* to be essential.

• Professional hypnotists are able to produce surgical analgesia in about 20 percent of their patients. Available evidence suggests that a much higher percentage of patients in China, reportedly as high as 90 percent undergo surgery after acupuncture.

• Subjects in a deep hypnotic trance rarely speak spontaneously or move around. Acupuncture patients talk spontaneously, show interest in their operation, eat oranges and may even look after a baby just delivered by Caesarean section while the doctor is still suturing up the incision.

All this is not to deny that psychological factors play an important role in acupuncture analgesia. But the psychological factors involved are far more subtle than plain hypnosis.

Where does this leave us? Is there then no adequate explanation for how acupuncture works?

Where East and West Meet. I believe the specificity theory of pain is wrong. We can organize our neurological data into another theory of pain that makes sense from a Western standpoint, and can explain acupuncture as well. In fact, evidence in our own medical journals contradicts the specificity theory on the same points acupuncture does.

Acupuncture defies the specificity theory by strongly indicating that there are neurological links between distant body sites. Pain from cardiac disease often shows the same thing. Patients with cardiac disease frequently develop pain, called ''referred pain,'' in the left shoulder, arm and upper chest. The pattern of pain is the same for most of these patients. Brief pressure on trigger areas in the shoulders and chest often produces pain that lasts for hours.

Persons who do not have heart disease sometimes show a similar distribution of trigger zones in the shoulder and chest. Pressure applied at these trigger areas produces marked discomfort that

sometimes lasts for several minutes *after* removal of the stimulus.

There are patterns of referred pain in other parts of the body. These patterns are so consistent from person to person that physicians often diagnose a disease on the basis of the pattern.

Injection of anesthetic drugs like Novocaine in a trigger zone can remove referred pain and, often, the original pain stemming from the disease itself. The frequency of painful attacks may decrease significantly after a single such injection. Sometimes, the pain disappears permanently.

Physicians can also relieve pain by vigorously stimulating trigger areas. They use this method to abolish referred pain in certain muscle groups. Dry needling of the area—simply moving a needle in and out of the area without injecting any substance—is sometimes effective.

Lesions in the central nervous system also reveal neurological interactions between distant body sites. Patients who have had nerves in their spinal cords cut, mostly for the relief of cancer pain, sometimes report that pin pricks applied to the deadened parts of their bodies, say the leg, produce pain at distant sites such as the chest or back. Some patients feel the pricking pain at the points of old injuries.

Why Do Mustard Plasters Work? The specificity theory of pain is at a loss to explain how acupuncturists control pain by intense stimulation of body tissue. But pain relief by cutaneous stimulation, a technique known as counterirritation, is one of our own oldest methods for pain control. Mustard plasters, ice packs, hot-water bottles are all counterirritants. We still use these methods even though the specificity theory fails to account for their effectiveness.

We also know that brief, mildly painful irritation often brings about substantial relief of severe pathological pain. The relief frequently lasts long after the stimulation has stopped. Vigorous massage of the nerves that control feeling in the lower head and jaw, for instance, may permanently abolish the pain of *tic douloureux*, characterized by painful, convulsive spasms of the face and mouth. Similarly, injection of a saline solution into the tissues of the back may produce a sharp, brief pain followed by prolonged relief of phantom-limb pain. Saline injections into an amputee's stump may have the same effect.

We have experimental evidence that one pain may produce a marked decrease in our sensitivity to other types of pain. By applying freezing cold to the shin of either leg, we raise the threshold of pain caused by electrical stimulation of the teeth by 30 percent; the elevated threshold may last for two hours or more.

Another stumbling block to the specificity theory is that acupuncture relieves pain *even after the needles are withdrawn*. This suggests a relationship between stimulus and pain more complex than the one-to-one relationship implied by the specificity theory.

Data from our medical annals corroborates the idea that the one-to-one relationship between stimulus and pain is oversimplified. Teeth drilled and filled without a local anesthetic may hurt when the sinuses are stimulated as long as 70 days later. A single shot of Novocaine to the appropriate jaw nerves ends the pain for good. We might argue that the drilling and filling cause a chronic local irritation. But then why does the single shot of Novocaine end the pain *for good*?

I think the drilling and filling trigger a prolonged change in central nervous activity—a change of neural activity triggered by a brief, painful input, and one that can be nullified by a single total blockade of the input.

From the point of view of specificity theory, this notion is folly. But from the point of view of the *gate-control theory* of pain, it makes sense.

Closing the Gate on Pain. The gate-control theory suggests that the transmission of pain signals from the body to the spinal cord and brain is not a fixed, immutable process but a dynamic one capable of modulation and plasticity. The theory proposes that a gatelike mechanism exists in the pain-signaling system. The gate may be open, partially open, or closed so that in certain circumstances signals from injured tissues may never get to the brain.

This theory offers an explanation for how acupuncture works. Proposed in 1965 by Patrick D. Wall and myself, it suggests that the modulation of pain signals can occur in three ways:

Large fibers in the sensory nerves running from the body's surface to the central nervous system tend to "close the gate" when stimulated, and thereby diminish the level of perceived pain. Small fibers in the same nerves tend to transmit signals that open the gate and produce increased pain. Acupuncture needles, then, may stimulate the large fibers.

This possibility provides a logical explanation for how acupuncture works when the needles are inserted near the site of surgery. In Caesarian surgery, for example, the needles are often inserted on each side of the line of incision. The "large fiber" mechanism is less plausible for explaining acupuncture analgesia when the needles are distant from the surgical site, as is usually the case.

The pain-signaling system can also be modulated by areas in the brainstem. (I call this the *central biasing mechanism*.) Portions of the reticular formation in the brainstem are able to inhibit the perception of pain by sending blocking signals through fibers that descend to the spinal cord, or through fibers that run to other transmission areas in the brain.

The brainstem is neurally connected to a large part of the body. When portions of the brainstem are electrically stimulated, a profound analgesia is produced in a widespread area of the body. Studies with rats indicate that stimulation of these brainstem regions may produce analgesia in a quarter or half of the body, so that when the rats are pinched, pricked, or shocked in these body areas, they fail to respond in any way that indicates pain. The duration of analgesia observed in these experiments often outlasts the period of stimulation. This finding suggests that the neural activities that "close the gate" keep operating for a prolonged period of time once they have been triggered.

The third way our nervous system modulates pain signals, according to the gate-control theory, is by means of fibers that descend from the cortex. The cortex is the brain's center for memories of cultural experiences, expectation, suggestion, anxiety, all psychological

processes known as "higher-central-nervous-system activities."

Psychological processes can have a profound effect on pain. Anxiety and fear, for example, enhance the perception of pain. Experiments show that a person perceives a given intensity of shock or heat to be more painful when he is anxious than when he is not. Furthermore, morphine effectively reduces pain only when the pain is accompanied by high levels of anxiety. Procedures that diminish anxiety, then, also decrease the level of perceived pain. The more explicit the suggestion that a

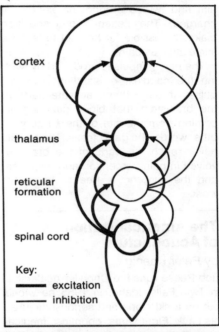

GATES FOR PAIN SIGNALS. Schematic chart shows interactions of pain signal system. Left arrows show path of pain signals, right arrows how brain blocks signals.

procedure will eliminate pain, the greater the likelihood that it will do so.

How Acupuncture Works. Take these three gate-control mechanisms together, and I think we have a plausible explanation of how acupuncture analgesia works. The second mechanism for modulating pain seems to be particularly powerful. Acupuncture stimulation, by activating the brainstem, triggers the nervous system to close the gate to pain signals.

We still have only fragmentary information about acupuncture. Observers who have visited China report that the technique is not used routinely on all patients. Who is selected and who is rejected? Many patients undergoing acupuncture analgesia also get small doses of conventional analgesic drugs. Do these drugs interact with the acupuncture procedure? We should be getting more information from China soon.

In the meantime, let me, by conjecture, construct the way I think acupuncture works step by step:

The patient's faith in the procedure as a result of long cultural experience, together with the explicit suggestion that the patient will feel no pain, greatly diminishes his anxiety. Mild analgesic drugs further relax the patient, who is about to have long needles stuck into him and twirled around, or electrically charged. The patient's predisposition makes it possible for him not to feel the stimulation as pain.

The nerve impulses produced by twirling the needles, or sending electrical pulses through them, activate parts of the brainstem that block pain signals coming from the site of the surgery. In other words, the gate closes. The signals never reach the parts of the brain involved in pain perception and response, and the surgeon is free to begin his work.

The Americanization of Acupuncture

by Peter Koenig

Bob Reese runs the Chrysler dealership in Twin Falls, Idaho. In 1955 he wiped out on a ski slope and seriously injured his back. Eight years, countless medical consultations and two spinal fusions later, he was still in pain. Reese went to the Mayo Clinic in Rochester, Minnesota, to have a nerve in his spine severed. The operation did little good.

In 1970 he flipped a skimobile and broke his back. The pain was debilitating. "For six months I went around to orthopedic specialists," says Reese. "None would operate. My back was so puttied up with ground-up hip bone from the spinal fusions, they said the risk was too great. Therapy didn't help either. Then, two years ago a friend in Dallas sent me a clipping about acupuncture. The article mentioned a fellow named Dr. Liao in Middlebury, Connecticut. I called Dr. Liao, but he was booked up for months. He gave me the name of a

fellow in Laramie, Wyoming, a Dr. Henry, at the university there. Well, I've had two rounds of acupuncture treatments now, and the pain is 90 percent gone. I can stand up straight again. Some of my friends think I've been smoking pot. They say, 'If you *believe* in hypnotism and faith healing and all that, then anything can happen.' I say baloney. I know the pain is gone. And I also know the treatments were cheap, $15 a session."

Wherever the practice of acupuncture has not run afoul of state law there are similar stories. Physicians familiar with acupuncture, and oriental-trained practitioners have surfaced in Washington, D.C., Chicago, Denver, Seattle, as well as in Laramie, Wyoming. Sung Jui Liao, mentioned fleetingly in a national news story last summer, has been swamped by calls from all over the country. Liao, who got his M.D. at the Hsiangya Medical College [sponsored by the Yale-in-China Association] at Changsha, China in 1942, specializes in rehabilitative medicine. "I use acupuncture as one part of my treatment," he emphasizes, "only when indicated."

The handful of other physicians in the U.S. trained to practice acupuncture do the same, combining Western diagnostic skills with the traditional Chinese pain remedy. These physicians have quietly been practicing acupuncture for years, well within the law. The legal problems concerning the practice of acupuncture are recent. They date back only to the summer of 1971—to the news stories following the U.S.-China detente and columnist James Reston's celebrated appendectomy in Peking.

The stories focused an unwelcome spotlight on acupuncturists practicing in herb shops and back rooms without M.D.s. The stories also whetted public curiosity about acupuncture. Americans read of eminent U.S. physicians—Boston heart specialist Paul Dudley White, biologists Arthur Galston of Yale, and Ethan Signer of M.I.T.—going to China and sending back word that yes, there was something to this acupuncture even though it defied standard Western medical tenets. Americans read that Winston Churchill, John F. Kennedy, Marshal Lon Nol of Cambodia, Willie McCovey of the San Francisco Giants, Prince Bernhard of the Netherlands, and Roman Gabriel of the Los Angeles Rams, had all submitted to having needles stuck in their bodies to stop pain. One national news

weekly ran a picture of opera star Anna Moffo after she underwent acupuncture. "Anna Moffo," the caption read, "Needle Relief."

Americans learned that in many Western countries, particularly France, acupuncture is an established medical technique; that at 23 Rue Clapeyron-75, Paris 8, France, there is an International Acupuncture Society. They read eyewitness accounts of complicated surgery in China performed under acupuncture analgesia. One acupuncture story from every journalist to set foot on Chinese soil became almost obligatory.

Americans followed President Nixon's trip to China. Walter Tkach, the President's personal physician, was quoted as saying that the Chinese "have something very superior to our own method of anesthesia." Tkach suggested the Chinese send a delegation to the annual American Medical Association convention to demonstrate acupuncture—a scientific exchange which, incidentally, has yet to take place.

By early 1972, the acupuncture boom in the U.S. was well launched. Entrepreneurs—medical and nonmedical, authorized and unauthorized—had begun to promote, peddle, push and sponsor acupuncture correspondence courses, do-it-yourself acupuncture kits, acupuncture seminars, acupuncture demonstrations, acupuncture books and acupuncture clinics. This, of course, brought on warnings of quackery, or quackupuncture. The American Society of Anesthesiologists, a group that knows a great deal about pain control, and also a group that has a great deal to be concerned about should acupuncture embed itself in American medicine—urged extreme caution in touting the benefits of the technique. State officials responsible for safeguarding the medical consumer went on the alert.

The Chinese-Americans who had practiced acupuncture for decades slipped out of sight. Last September in New York City, police threatened to crack down on practitioners like Huan Lam Ng, working in a small herb shop at 11 Mott Street. But most oriental-trained medical men without M.D.s managed to stay well clear of U.S. officialdom.

"I practiced long before there was a law," says Tomson Liang in Oceanside, California. "Now they say I can only practice under medical supervision in medical schools. So I work with doctors at the University. It's unfair, but what can I do? The thing I don't understand, though, is how can American doctors supervise acupuncture if they know nothing about it?"

The legal battles over acupuncture revolve around the acupuncture clinics opened since the 1971 boom. A year ago, internist Arnold Benson rented office space in a fashionable part of Manhattan and rounded up a staff of Chinese acupuncturists. Last November New York state Supreme Court Judge Thomas C. Chimera ordered the clinic temporarily closed, after the state attorney general called it "a clear and present danger to the health and welfare of the people of the State of New York." The attorney general's position was supported in an affidavit by John J. Morton, chairman of the state board of medicine.

Rather than fight it out in the courts, Benson simply moved his clinic to Washington, D.C. District of Columbia law, unlike New York state law, allows Chinese acupuncturists without credentials to practice under the direct supervision of an M.D. Benson sees about 100 people a day.

Less fortunate is Reuben Amber. A psychologist by academic training, a chiropractor and homeopath later, Amber learned acupuncture at a medical clinic in Cuernavaca, Mexico. He practiced acupuncture in Great Neck, Long Island until last November when he was arrested for practicing medicine without a license. Amber argues that acupuncture is not allopathic medicine. Acupuncturists, he believes, should be licensed the same way chiropractors are. His case is pending.

In Beverly Hills Morton Barke opened the West Coast Medical Group, Inc. last December. The group, Barke, a gynecologist, and three Korean-trained medical men without M.D.s, specializes in acupuncture. Barke and two patients have filed a class-action suit challenging the constitutionality of the 1972 California law that limits the practice of acupuncture to medical schools. Their argument: there isn't enough acupuncture skill at medical schools to go around, which discriminates against the average citizen. "My personal feelings are that oriental-trained acupuncturists should be allowed to

practice on their own," says Barke. His lawsuit, however, passes over this point.

Only in Nevada can acupuncturists without M.D.s legally practice on their own. A bill bringing them up from the underground was signed into law in April. The day the bill passed the state legislature, the AMA expressed deep shock.

As the various acupuncture enterprises multiply, so do the inevitable calls for calm, order and hard facts. Enter the medical research establishment. On February 28, a handful of men from the fancy medical schools across the country convened at the National Institutes of Health in Washington for two days to compare notes, articulate research goals, and map out a coordinated research strategy in regard to acupuncture. John Bonica, chairman of the anesthesiology department at the University of Washington, heads the NIH advisory panel on acupuncture.

With John Bonica in Seattle, experimental psychologist Richard Chapman is working to see precisely what acupuncture can and cannot do. Chapman's interest stems from pain research similar to Ronald Melzack's "We see people at our pain clinic every day who have been poisoned by drugs," he says. "These people go doctor shopping. The first doctor prescribes one drug. The second doctor prescribes another. One woman who came in the other day was psychotic from all the drugs she'd taken." Chapman wistfully hopes that interest in acupuncture will sensitize the U.S. to the Eastern concept of health as balance, in contrast to the Western view that health is the absence of germs.

Pang L. Man, director of research at Northville State Hospital in Michigan, has a research project underway to see how well acupuncture alleviates pain from neuralgias.

Han Twu Chiang, an anesthesiologist at Massachusetts General Hospital in Boston, is studying the skin's peculiar electrical conductivity at acupuncture sites.

Alon P. Winnie at the University of Illinois is experimenting with acupuncture analgesia for childbirth. Other researchers are experimenting with acupuncture for dental surgery.

Meanwhile, the acupuncture boom continues. Last fall, Random House published a revised edition of British acupuncture authority Felix Mann's 1962 book, *Acupuncture: The Ancient Chi-*

nese Art of Healing and How It Works Scientifically. Mann timed a speaking tour in the U.S. to coincide with the book's reappearance. In March the British Book Centre came out with *Chinese Acupuncture* by Taiwanese authority Wu Wei-P'ing. University of California medical historian Ilze Veith is compiling materials from China, which she will translate and organize into a textbook on acupuncture. She earlier translated the *Nei-Ching*, a medical book written in China under the Yellow Emperor 4,000 years ago. The *Nei-Ching* describes the art and some of the uses of acupuncture. Veith's historical outlook somewhat jaundices her view of the current discoveries being made about acupuncture in the U.S.

In February in San Diego the University of California extension program offered "An Evening of Acupuncture." Anesthesiologist James Vanderveen presided over the panel discussion as a favor to a friend, and found himself embroiled in a controversy involving the state medical board. One of the panel participants was not an M.D., and a local physician objected.

The North American College of Acupuncture in Vancouver, Canada, continues to make available a $1,700 two-to-three-year correspondence course. It includes a four-week trip to Hong Kong for clinical practice.

Two insurance companies in Chicago recently announced that they would pay claims for "legitimate" acupuncture. "We have no intention of paying claims for back-alley acupuncture treatments," said Herbert C. Parsons, vice president of Continental Casualty. But, added Irvin K. Silchuck, vice president of Continental Assurance, we assume that the state medical societies are going to develop regulations for acupuncture soon.

"There definitely is a lot of action," says anesthesiologist John W. C. Fox at the Downstate Medical Center in Brooklyn, New York. "The public is interested in pain relief." Fox himself learned acupuncture in France and in England from Felix Mann. "It's going to have great impact on the treatment of pain conditions," he says. "But I don't think it will replace chemical anesthesia. I think acupuncture will become another string in our bow." ∩

The Sonar Sight of Bats

LIVING CREATURES have developed a remarkable variety of ways to obtain information about their environments. An animal's surroundings contain many different forms of energy and a variety of substances. As different animals go about their daily or nightly activities, they sense an impressive number of these energies and substances. Every aspect of behavior in any animal is under direct, immediate control by the information abstracted from the light, the heat, the vibrations, the chemical concentrations, the physical environment.

Nature has been particularly ingenious in providing ways for animals to detect objects without having to move up to them and bump them. Vision serves a wide range of different animals, from the invertebrates to the most elaborate mammal. Airborne and waterborne sound provides many organisms with information about things somewhere in their vicinity. Vibrations of the ground also act as stimuli for terrestrial animals. The sense of smell tells many animals that something is near, and the rattlesnake can even detect heat radiated from a source warmer than the rest of his surroundings.

By James A. Simmons

In a few instances, nature gives animals portable sources of energy with which to explore the environment. Orientation by self-emitted energy is analogous to a man exploring a dark room with a flashlight. Whirligig beetles, insects that live on the surface of water, detect objects by rippling the water and picking up reflections of these ripples. Some species of fish generate electrical fields in the water around their bodies and detect objects by means of the disturbances the objects cause.

The most famous and best-studied type of emitted-energy orientation is found in bats. These little animals, already interesting to zoologists in their means of loco-motion, reproductive processes, and choice of living quarters, find their way around with a full-fledged sonar system. For a number of years research on the hearing and perceptual capabilities of bats has been under way at the Auditory Research Laboratories of Princeton University.

Bats are creatures of the night. They sleep by day in caves, abandoned mines, culverts, attics, old barns, trees and any of a hundred other quiet, sheltered places in which they can hang. In the evening they emerge to seek food and water. Their nocturnal habits have resulted in their inclusion with other beings of darkness and the supernatural in most of our folklore.

The bats owe their enormous biological success to the night and to their peculiar adaptations to life in darkness. With hardly any light with which to see, they fly at daredevil speeds through trees, bushes and jungle thickets, dart about in the air catching small flies and mosquitoes, and fly in and out of deep caves, often through winding passages and in the company of hundreds and hundreds of other bats. Yet a bat rarely bumps a branch or misses a meal.

In geographic range, in numbers of individuals, and in the number and variety of different species bats are indeed flourishing. They have existed in basically the same form for over 50 or 60 million years. Although often regarded as rodents, "mouse-angels," bats are in fact a separate group of mammals, distinct from rats, mice and squirrels. Zoologists classify bats in the order Chiroptera (wing-handed). The order is divided into two groups.

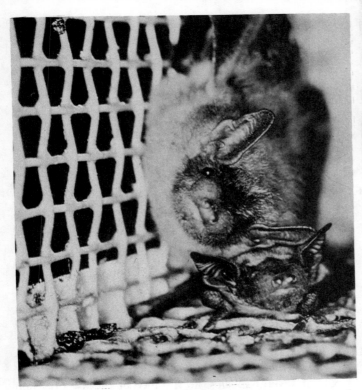

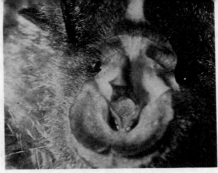

EQUIPPED WITH SONAR. Two specimens of bats are shown, the big brown bat at left with one of her laboratory-born infants, and the greater horseshoe bat, above, who broadcasts its sonar signals through its peculiar nose. These creatures have portable sources of energy with which to explore the environment.

One of the suborders, Megachiroptera, is composed of bats less specialized for flight than the other. Megachiropterans have excellent vision and live on a diet of fruits. Perhaps the best-known of these is the "flying-fox," a large fruit-bat with a wingspread of five feet.

The other suborder, Microchiroptera, consists of bats that are well equipped for life in the air. They have powerful wings, and they also seem to have relatively poor vision and habits that usually keep them well away from light. Microchiropterans differ considerably in their diets. Some eat insects captured in the air or on the ground, some eat fruit or the nectar of flowers, and some capture and eat small birds and mammals, including other bats. The vampire bats are so specialized they eat only the blood of mammals or birds. To get by without being able to see, the various bats of the suborder Microchiroptera have evolved a remarkable way of getting information about objects in the environment.

The Bat Problem

The little, insectivorous bats of North America and Europe have long been zoological curiosities. Their proficiency in moving around at night attracted some attention. In the 18th Century an Italian monk, Spallanzani, and several of his collaborators discovered that blinded bats could live and fly around without any apparent trouble. They found that impairment of hearing was the only way to disorient a bat. The science of the day reacted against the unconventional implication that bats "saw" with their ears, and most of Spallanzani's contemporaries assumed that the bat's skill in flying arose from touch sensitivity to near-by objects.

Little more became of the question of how bats found their way about until the 20th Century, when knowledge in acoustics provided a basis for renewed speculation.

In 1912 the British inventor Hiram Maxim suggested that the bat detects obstacles by feeling echoes of the sounds of its wing beats as they reflect back from objects. Several years later, H. Hartridge, an English physiologist, proposed that bats navigate with a kind of sonar, emitting high-frequency sounds and detecting echoes of these sounds.

In 1938, Donald R. Griffin, a zoologist then working at Harvard University, found that bats do indeed emit extremely high-frequency cries, often much higher in frequency than the upper limit of human hearing (or 20,000 cycles per second). Griffin and Robert Galambos worked together for several years on the discovery and established that the bat's ears can respond to such high-frequency sounds, and that the basis for obstacle avoidance in bats is the detection of echoes of its cries.

Bats navigate with a sophisticated biological sonar, called *echolocation*. They emit a series of short, sharp cries that contain frequencies from 25,000 cycles per second to well over 100,000 cycles per second. Some kinds of bats emit loud sounds, some emit soft sounds, some emit sounds of almost constant frequency, some emit frequency-modulated sounds, and some emit sounds rich in harmonic frequencies. All of the Microchiropteran bats use echoes of their own characteristic cries for sensing objects in the environment [*see illustration, p. 108*].

Echolocation is an active process in which the bat generates a sound and identifies objects and obstacles with the reflected echoes. Although many animals can detect and locate near-by objects by picking up sounds that the objects themselves may emit or by sensing changes in the environmental noise level near the objects, relatively few animals use active sonar. The excitement stirred up by the discovery of the bat's echolocation led to the discovery of the use of sonar by porpoises and to the possibility that other animals, including some birds and terrestrial mammals, might also echolocate. Man himself can echolocate, as has been shown by several experiments on blind persons and on blindfolded subjects. To be sure, man can also echolocate with apparatus built for that purpose, as in the cases of ultrasonic scanning devices in medicine and underwater sonar systems.

We are accustomed to *seeing* objects in our surroundings. It is ordinarily with vision that we locate and iden-

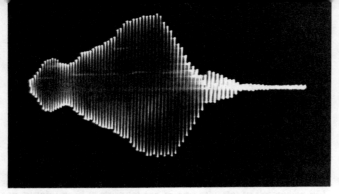

ECHOLOCATION CRY. Photograph of oscilloscope trace of a bat cry, which lasts about 2 milliseconds; is frequency-modulated.

tify objects, navigate from place to place and find our way around obstacles. Qualities such as size, shape, distance and texture have underlying visual cues like relative size, visual angle, perspective, parallax and stereoscopic vision. These visual cues are in turn based on the physical properties of the light that stimulates our eyes.

Hearing is another important human sense, but not in entirely the same way as vision. We use hearing for communication, for detecting, locating and identifying sound sources, and for music.

But bats use hearing in place of vision to gather information about distant objects. Banished for its own good to a life away from light, the bat perceives the important qualities of objects not with the intensity, wave length and distribution of light striking the retina, but rather with the intensity, frequency and time of arrival of sounds at the ears. The bat "sees" near-by objects, in terms of the physical parameters of the echoes of its own cries as they return from the objects. The ears and brain of the bat have become highly specialized for rapidly processing the auditory cues in the echoes so that the essential details about obstacles or targets are detected in time to catch a moth or avoid a branch.

The bat's behavior is exquisitely controlled by the perceptions of the environment it derives from echolocation. We can inquire about the bat's mode of perception in much the same way as we traditionally have investigated vision. What kinds of judgements can a bat make about objects that it perceives with sonar? Animals that use vision easily can perceive object size, shape, location and distance. Can the bat also detect such things? The bat's performance in flight and skill in hunting of course suggest immediately that it readily can perceive size, shape, movement, etc., but can we demonstrate some of these perceptions experimentally?

In an attempt to learn more about the extent to which echolocation can substitute for vision, I have been working on the ability of several species of bats to make judgements of the size of objects, the shape of objects, and the distance to objects. I have found that when examined by the methods normally reserved for visual perception, the bat's sonar is very versatile, every bit as flexible as would be expected from the performance of bats in nature.

The species that I have used for the study of distance, size and shape discrimination is the big brown bat, *Ep-*

tesicus fuscus. This hardy insectivorous bat thrives in captivity, easily adapts to discrimination training, and can echolocate with great skill. It emits sounds that sweep in frequency from just under 50,000 cycles per second down to about 25,000 cycles per second, and its cries easily can be detected, even with crude, homemade condenser microphones (*see illustration, left*).

Since bats are among those mammals that occasionally carry rabies, all our staff members are vaccinated against the disease, and no one handles any bat without protective gloves.

When beginning discrimination studies with bats, there is one important experimental precaution to consider. The visual capabilities of echolocating bats are not well known. Available evidence suggests that bats are probably not very good at visual pattern perception, but no one is certain. To eliminate the possibility that vision may be used in discrimination learning experiments, at least some of the bats must be deprived of sight. For most species, the best way to do this is actually to remove their eyes while they are anesthetized. The operation is safe, and the animals appear to recover completely. In discrimination experiments with dozens of bats of several species, no instance of the use of vision has come up. That is, blinded bats and normal bats do *not* perform differently on discrimination experiments.

Sonar Perception of Object Size

To find out whether an animal's vision is sufficiently acute to perceive the size of a stimulus, you can try to train the animal to distinguish between a large stimulus and a small stimulus. If it can learn to respond to one of the two stimuli, say the larger, but not to the other, then you have demonstrated that in some way the animal is able to perceive the relative size of each stimulus and to identify correctly the larger one. This technique is called *simultaneous discrimination learning,* and it is a basic tool for the study of sensory and perceptual capabilities in animals.

Although size discrimination is a problem usually encountered in connection with visual perception, there is no reason why we cannot try to train echolocating bats to discriminate between objects differing in size. A sim-

BAT RESPONDING TO STIMULI. The mouth is open for emission of sonar cries in experiment for distance-discrimination.

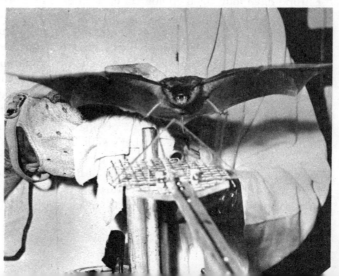

SIZE DISCRIMINATION EXPERIMENTAL SET-UP. Bat sits on the single platform at left and examines the two landing platforms and targets with its sonar. It responds by flying correctly to whichever platform carries larger triangle more than 90 per cent of the time.

ple experimental set-up can be used for training bats to distinguish between a large stimulus and a small one (*see illustration, above*). The bat is taught to sit on the platform at the left and to examine the other two platforms and the triangular shapes mounted on them. The targets are 30 centimeters away from the bat. Notice that one of the triangles is larger than the other.

Each time the bat flies from the starting platform to the landing platform that has the large triangle, he is rewarded with a choice bit of food—a piece of an insect. The positions of the triangles are "randomly" interchanged from right to left and back again to ensure that the bat is responding to the size of each stimulus and not to its position. After a week or two of training the bat can choose the platform with the larger stimulus more than 90 per cent of the time.

Acuity of Size Perception

We used a series of triangles to demonstrate that the big brown bat can distinguish between objects of different sizes with surprising accuracy [*see illustration, top left, p. 110*]. We first showed the bat a pair of triangles that differed greatly in size. Each bat was trained to fly to the large triangle in this pair until it could do so with a minimum of errors for 75 trials. As expected, the bats learned to discriminate between the triangles easily.

Then we transferred the bat to a pair slightly closer in size. We carried out 50 trials on this second pair, rewarding the bat with food for every correct response. Pair by pair, with 50 trials on each pair, the bat moved through a series of six additional pairs of triangles.

As each new pair was shown to the bat, the size difference between the larger and the smaller triangle became a little bit smaller. Finally, the bat came to the seventh pair, in which the size difference was reduced to zero; the triangles were equal in size. As the size difference got progressively smaller, it became harder and harder for the bat to pick correctly the larger of the two triangles. Eventually, the size difference became too small for the bat to choose the larger triangle. The bat responded half of the time to one triangle, and half of the time to the other.

We charted the performance of three bats trained on the entire series of triangles [*see illustration, top right, page 110*].Using an *arbitrary* level of 75 per cent correct responses, we established the threshold of size discrimination for the bats. This threshold is an approximation of the smallest size difference that the bat can detect with any kind of consistency. The light level in the lab was very low for the sessions with sighted bats.

One of the three bats that had been trained was blinded and run on the series of triangles again. The

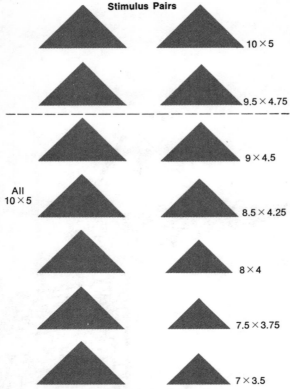

Stimulus Pairs

10 × 5

9.5 × 4.75

All
10 × 5

9 × 4.5

8.5 × 4.25

8 × 4

7.5 × 3.75

7 × 3.5

(Dimensions in centimeters)

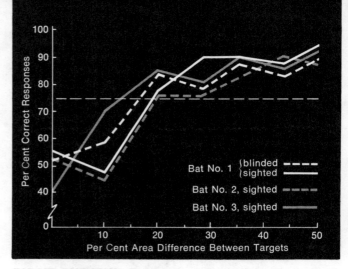

TARGET SELECTION. Bat is trained to respond to the large triangle in the bottom pair (see chart at left) and its ability to correctly pick the larger triangle in each of the other pairs is measured. Chart above clearly shows that the bat does not need to use its vision for these consistent-size discriminations.

blinded bat had a threshold of about 16 per cent difference in stimulus surface area, which was almost the same as the average threshold for the three normal runs.

It is clear that visual cues did not play a decisive part in the discrimination performance of the bats. (Bats that were blinded from the start of training perform the same as these three bats, so it appears that *Eptesicus* simply does not need to use vision at all for these size discriminations.)

The threshold difference for the blinded bat lies between the fifth and sixth pair of triangles shown to the bat (*see illustration top left, above*). By looking at the outlines and dimensions of the stimuli, you can see that the bat's sonar appears to be an adequate substitute for vision as far as size is concerned.

By bouncing artificial sounds off the triangular targets used in the experiment, you can learn something about the auditory cues the bats used to discriminate the triangles. The targets in the pairs turn out to differ in the intensity of the echoes they reflect. The triangles in the most easily discriminated pair differ by about eight decibels in the intensity of their echoes. As the size difference gets smaller, pair by pair, the echo intensity difference gets smaller, too.

Sonar Perception of Shape

As we have seen, an echolocating bat can determine the relative size of one of two stimuli with a good deal of acuity. If the stimuli were the same in size but different in shape, could the bat still learn to choose between them? To see if echolocation can be used to tell something about the shape of an object, I have used triangular stimuli of the same kind used in the size experiments.

One stimulus was an isosceles triangle 10 centimeters wide and five centimeters high, the same size as the largest triangle in the first experiment. The other triangle was five centimeters wide and 10 centimeters high. Both targets had the same surface area, but one was short and wide and the other was tall and thin. These triangles were mounted on landing platforms and used in the same way as before.

Both sighted and blinded bats learned to discriminate between the two different shapes. When the training was carried out exactly as in the size discrimination experiment, the level of performance reached by the bats corresponded to an intermediately difficult size discrimination, something like the fourth pair of triangles in the size experiments.

What about the echoes that the bats use to distinguish the shapes? Over the frequency range used by the big brown bat, the echoes differ somewhat in intensity. The difference is from one to three decibels, depending on the frequency. These intensity differences are about the same as the difference between the members of the fourth pair of triangles in the first experiment. It seems quite possible that the shape difference was detected by means of the echo intensity differences.

Depth Perception by Sonar

Humans find it rather easy to judge the distance to an object with vision, and there exists a large variety of visual depth cues. Can bats use their echolocation to determine how far away an object is? Considering the exceptional ability of many species of bats accurately to track flying insects, one expects them to be able to judge the range of a target. The discrimination procedure used for size and shape perception was adapted to the study of range determination by bats.

Just as before, the bat was placed on a starting platform and confronted with two landing platforms and targets. The triangles on the platforms were identical in size and shape, both were 10 centimeters wide and five centimeters high. The distance to the targets previously was fixed at 30 centimeters. Now it was the distance to the targets that the bat had to discriminate.

The bat was trained to fly to whichever platform was closer. At first, the near target was 20 centimeters away, and the far target was 30 centimeters away. The distances were alternated left and right in the same "random" fashion as were the sizes and the shapes. After the bat learned to discriminate between targets that differed in distance by 10 centimeters, the difference was reduced by moving the nearer target back to 21 centimeters. A number of trials were completed, and then the distance difference was reduced by another centimeter, moving the nearer target to 22 centimeters. In steps of about a centimeter, the difference in distance between the targets was further reduced to seven centimeters, then six centimeters, and so forth until the two

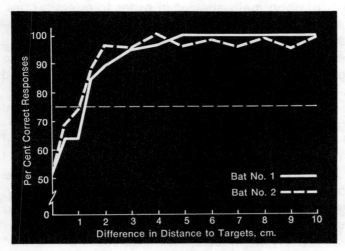

DISTANCE ACCURACY. Two blinded bats were trained on a series of special distance discrimination tests beginning with a difference of 10 cm. and gradually proceeding down to zero.

targets were finally presented to the bat at equal distances. This procedure allowed us to estimate the range difference threshold for two stimuli presented at the same time.

We trained two blinded specimens of the big brown bat on a series of distances beginning with a difference of 10 centimeters and proceeding down to zero (*see illustration, above*). Large differences, between 10 centimeters and three centimeters, were easily discriminated; the bat flew to the closer platform on nearly every trial. When the range difference fell below three centimeters, however, the bat's discrimination performance declined. The average threshold for a large number of specimens of *Eptesicus* is 1.2 centimeters. This threshold, a measure of the accuracy of the bat's determination of distance, is only four per cent of the total distance of 30 centimeters.

The extreme accuracy of the bat's determination of the range of a target is not restricted to *Eptesicus*. In addition to the insect-eating *Eptesicus*, a European insectiv-

orous bat, *Rhinolophus*, and a carnivorous, tropical bat, *Phyllostomus*, have also been studied. These other bats are about as accurate as *Eptesicus* in judging distance.

Besides the great accuracy of the bats' discriminations, there were several other surprises in the range experiment. Suffice it to say that the results of this experiment, together with more recent ones, show that the bat determines which target is closer by the difference in arrival time between echoes from the nearer and farther targets. The signal processing done by the bat on echoes from targets separated by a few centimeters is a complicated matter, and current experiments on sonar ranging by bats are only just beginning to clarify what happens.

Echolocation: A Biological System

As we have seen, echolocation does a creditable job of providing a way for bats to appreciate objects in the environment without vision. Their sonar allows bats to do a lot more than merely to detect the presence or absence of objects "out there." They can make rather fine distinctions between objects both as to the nature of the object and also its location. There are other questions that arise. Can a bat localize an object horizontally and vertically as well as it can in distance? Does a bat get information about the texture of objects? Experiments now in progress are hopefully going to answer such questions.

In addition to the straightforward study of stimulus perception by sonar, there is the problem of the basis for echolocation in the bat's hearing. New techniques for electronically simulating targets by presenting faked echoes to the bat are proving very useful in analyzing the auditory cues used in the exploration of targets. These techniques are designed to study the mechanisms of echolocation, and perhaps they will even tell something of the brain processes of the bat's sonar.

The 20th Century has been a century of surprises for scientists. This is no less true for the student of animal behavior than for the particle physicist, molecular biologist, or neurophysiologist. The unearthing of the means of orientation in bats has been one of the more unexpected events for zoologists and comparative psychologists.

Interest in bat sonar is but an example of a general trend. Scientists have rediscovered biology in a very big way in recent years. The ingenuity in design and function of biological systems has attracted many people to research on living systems. Discoveries in sensory physiology and psychology, in the molecular basis of genetics, and in many other areas of biological activity have highlighted the impression that really challenging problems are to be found in the study of organisms and their workings. The more that we find in the processes of living creatures, the more humble we may feel as fabricators of mechanism and machinery. What man can yet compress a multi-purpose sonar system into the form of a lump of jelly about as big as your thumb, make that system seek out its own operating power, and even more, use such a system to produce others like it as a by-product of its own operation?

iv. learning, memory, and language

The human ability to function successfully in this complex world is largely dependent on the capacity to acquire knowledge and skills, to retain what is important, and to communicate thoughts and feelings to others. Thus, the topics of learning, memory, and language are of central concern in psychology.

Learning has been operationally defined as "a relatively permanent change in a behavioral tendency that occurs as a result of reinforced practice" (Kimble and Garmezy, 1968). For years psychologists have been arguing over such issues in learning as the relative effectiveness of rewards and punishments as reinforcers or modifiers of behavior and over exactly what is learned when learning does occur. Some of the questions that psychologists who study learning must ask are: Is learning a gradual process accomplished through trial and error, or is it suddenly acquired through insight? Is learning possible without reinforcement? Do lower animals learn in the same way that people learn? How many kinds of learning are there?

One of the most prominent contributors to the psychology of learning is B. F. Skinner, the foremost spokesman for behaviorism and its role in education and in the design of societies. Skinner's research on the operant conditioning of behavior through schedules of positive and negative reinforcement has probably sparked more interest and controversy than any other development in experimental psychology to date. In an interview with Mary Harrington Hall, Skinner reviews the essentials of his theory and delineates some areas where practical applications of his conditioning principles have proved successful. He takes issue with those who favor a mentalistic psychology, in particular the cognitive theorists and the psycholinguists who believe in a structural analysis of verbal behavior and innate linguistic capacities. The interview concludes with Skinner's observations on clinical psychology, and he contrasts psychotherapy with operant-conditioning techniques in the treatment of disordered behavior.

Roger McIntire demonstrates Skinnerian principles at work in behavior-modification therapy. He says that when systems of rewards are used to shape the behavior of individuals with psychiatric problems, it is unnecessary to search for the underlying psychological causes of abnormal behavior in order to effect a cure. Examining parent-child interactions in the context of maladaptive learning, McIntire claims that the main business of being a parent is to decide which of a child's behaviors to reward or ignore.

Not all psychologists agree with the general laws of learning that arise from laboratory demonstrations—usually with animals—of classical and operant conditioning. Martin Seligman and Joanne Hager question the efficacy of the equipotentiality premise in learning theory, which says that all species are equally able to learn in the same way. They contend that "universally applicable" laws ignore the fact that there are limits to learning, limits that evolution and natural selection have set for each species. They also point out that the emphasis psychologists have given to the arbitrary examples of conditioning in the laboratory has produced learning principles and theories that are actually specific only to those examples. Seligman and Hager propose a preparedness dimension to describe the limits of learning: The laws of learning vary from one situation to another, depending on the genetic and biological preparedness of the animal to learn the contingency at hand.

Seligman does feel, however, that many events observed in the laboratory can provide society with solutions to some of its most troubling problems, such as chronic depression and feelings of utter helplessness that afflict many individuals. In studying parameters of Pavlovian conditioning procedures, Seligman and his colleagues noticed that dogs who receive inescapable shock while restrained in a harness are likely to learn that responding never pays off in a traumatic situation. In either dogs or people, the helplessness syndrome develops when it seems that the environment cannot be controlled. Seligman found that dogs can be immunized against helplessness by giving them experience with escapable, controllable shock before they encounter inescapable shock; this treatment seems to inoculate the dogs against passivity in future traumatic situations. Seligman suggests that, like his dogs, people can be immunized.

Richard Atkinson applies learning theory to modern educational technology and demonstrates how computer-assisted instruction can provide individualized instruction to fit the requirements of any student. The storage, display, and statistical capabilities of the computer make it possible to analyze each student's mistakes, to deliver appropriate remedial exercises, and to inform the teacher/researcher of the program's effectiveness for the class as a whole. Atkinson's approach to computer-assisted reading instructon can be described as applied psycholinguistics; the results of his pedagogical tactics hold considerable promise for improving the efficiency and effectiveness of learning.

At present little is known about the physiological basis for learning. Psychophysiologist J. Anthony Deutsch provides empirical data to support the theory that physical changes in the brain that accompany learning are somehow related to the increase of transmission efficiency in synaptic structures.

Treating the process of remembering on a more general and applied level, Gordon Bower has been investigating mnemonic strategies, clever techniques that can increase the ability to retain needed information. He describes various systems that serve as memory aids and presents experimental evidence of their effectiveness. Bower once attended a convention of mnemonists, and he reveals the secrets behind the rather spectacular mental gyrations of some of the conferees. He also notes some amusing frailties in their memory systems.

Just as learning and memory seem to rely on specific brain structures and mechanisms, there may be innate properties of linguistic organization and structure in the human mind. The heredity-environment controversy in language acquisition is explored by Noam Chomsky. He takes issue with the classical empiricist view, which describes the child's acquisition of language in terms of experience and control by environmental factors.

On most fields where the heredity-environment battle is fought, there seems to be some middle ground for compromise. Such is the case in the language war. While Chomsky and his disciples put stock in the notion that language is built into the genes and Skinnerians press for an explanation in terms of operant conditioning, there are theorists who feel that learning and heredity are equally important. Donald Hebb, Wallace Lambert, and Richard Tucker develop a model that offers a viable alternative to the extreme positions taken by the nativists and empiricists in the psycholinguistic battle. However, the war continues. . . .

B. F. Skinner

By Mary Harrington Hall

Burrhus Frederic Skinner is very much the man of today. And when history makes its judgment, he may well be known as the major contributor to psychology in this century.

He is the modern spokesman for behaviorism and for behavioral engineering in the design of societies; he brought experimentation in animal behavior to a quantitative scientific level; and he is known as the father of the teaching machine and programmed learning—education's revolutionary wave of the future.

B. F. Skinner has great feeling for the importance of his work. But on the personal level, he doesn't just wear his fame lightly, he seems totally unaware of it. He is casual and modest. At 63, he is relaxed and attractive, his hair is sandy, and he looks a fit and trim 50.

He does value his productive working hours, and he programs his time very carefully indeed. He is Harvard's Edgar Pierce Professor of Psychology, and he has a perfectly good office on campus. However, he claims to be more productive at home. He does his best

thinking (and charts his productive hours) in a remarkable study in his basement. It is a modern, ordered study which is soundproofed, air-filtered, and temperature-controlled. He can turn off the outside world, or turn it back on with an elaborate electronic sound system.

His is a veritable *air crib* of an office. Skinner has always been as imaginative as he is inventive. The Skinners' younger daughter, Deborah, spent most of the first 30 months of her life in the Skinner-designed air crib, a mechanical baby tender. The air crib, a big box with cleanliness and climate controls and a sliding glass door of clear safety glass, has never caught on with the baby-raising public.

His novel, *Walden Two,* certainly has. Published in 1948, this Utopian novel is far more popular now than when it was first published. Skinner is such a stubborn iconoclast that he would be hopelessly out of place in his own *Walden Two,* a society designed so perfectly that even frustrations had to be introduced artificially.

The genial Carl Rogers, father of Rogerian Therapy, once said: "The most awful fate I can imagine for Fred would be to have him constantly 'happy.' It is the fact that he is very unhappy about many things which makes me prize him."

Skinner's scientific contributions and his point of view are based on his principle of operant conditioning—control of behavior through systems of positive and negative

reinforcement. In the course of refining his work, Skinner taught pigeons to play table tennis by reinforcing correct responses with a few grains of corn. His pigeons also have played the piano—just a few simple tunes—and have operated systems for guiding submarines and bombs. Skinner has a raffish sense of humor, and the pigeon-guidance systems began as a gag while he was working with the Office of Scientific Research and Development during World War II.

To observe and measure animal behavior, he developed the famous Skinner Box, which long has been used by good animal researchers everywhere. Actually, the term "Skinner Box" is a public label which Skinner deplores for his "Operant Conditioning Apparatus."

B. F. Skinner started out to be a writer. He majored in English at Hamilton College (Phi Beta Kappa, naturally) and failed at fiction in Greenwich Village before he went to Harvard in 1930 to work on his Ph.D. in psychology. He taught first at Harvard, then went to the University of Minnesota where he delighted in giving a course in the psychology of literature. He was head of the psychology department at the University of Indiana before returning to Harvard 20 years ago.

His best known scientific books include *Science and Human Behavior, The Behavior of Organisms, Verbal Behavior,* and *Schedules of Reinforcement.*

Mary Hall: Would you please explain to me that neat chart above your desk?

B. F. Skinner: I just like to keep some records of what I do. I do my writing and all of my really serious thinking here. And I clock the time. I turn the clock on when I enter and turn it off again when I leave. Whenever the light is burning on the clock up there, that clock is running. When the clock covers twelve hours, I plot a point. I've kept this record for about six or eight years now. I can watch my productivity change during the years. Look at the curve—that flat spot indicates a lecture. My productivity suffers from that, so I avoid lectures. Actually, I'm averaging about three truly productive hours a day. This is my only really creative time. The rest of the day I'm still working, and I don't quit. But I don't do anything very important. I've figured that I average about two minutes of creative time per published word.

Hall: You have certainly caused a lot of discussion about raising children. I understand that your daughter who was the famous Skinner baby now is raising her own "baby in the box."

Skinner: Interestingly, it is the child of our other daughter, the one who was *not* the famous "baby in a box." That phrase still is irksome. It was coined by the *Ladies Home Journal* and could not be less accurate.

I realize in watching my granddaughter how much of the day is given over to contingencies of reinforcement. It is very hard to maintain them, though. How easy it is to do the wrong thing. She starts a little fuss, and you go right over to her. That's the awful thing about raising children. Everything works against you. You are likely to do the wrong thing, especially in an ordinary house. Home is not the place to bring up children; it isn't made for that. You have mighty attractive objects around the house, and then you spank the children for being attracted to them. That's nonsense.

Hall: That's one of the reasons that you designed the air crib, isn't it?

Skinner: Yes, the air crib is nothing but a solution to the problem of physical environment. A child is a very precious possession. What bothers me particularly is that you recognize that when you are talking about whether you are going to use sheets and a blanket or an air crib tonight, but you don't recognize it at all when you ask, what am I doing to this child to create the behavior that is going to be worthwhile in the future.

The principle of the air crib is really very simple; it solves a very simple problem. Diapers have an obvious function, while all the rest, the blankets and sheets, are just to keep the child warm. And they don't do a very good job: The child gets overheated and the blankets get kicked off and it gets cold and all of that. The air crib—heated, ventilated space—is the obvious solution.

Hall: I've always thought that the volume control on an air crib is a good idea. Once you've done what you can to make your baby comfortable, you can turn down the volume if he cries just for exercise.

Skinner: Remember, the air crib is for the baby, not the parents. The whole point is that this clean, glass-enclosed structure is roomier and healthier than a crib. The baby is more comfortable.

Hall: But it meets with lots of resistance?

Skinner: Well, in the first place it is an area where everybody, mothers in particular, feel they know all about everything. I suppose it took a hundred years to get over believing that you had to keep a child rocking all day long. At one time they had dogs walking on treadmills just to keep the cradle rocking. Now that's disappeared, just as the ordinary crib will probably disappear sometime soon. The ordinary crib is a small jail, if you want to put it that way, with bars. You put the child behind bars. The air crib at least has a clear view without bars. You don't have the feeling that you are preparing the child for a life of crime later on.

Hall: Do you really think the air crib solves the problems of bringing up baby?

Skinner: Not really. It solves only a very simple physical problem. I despair of teaching the ordinary parent how to handle his child. I would prefer to turn child-raising over to a specialist. I just can't believe that an ordinary parent can do a good job. What has happened in the past is that a culture has set up a routine way of handling kids. You spank them for what is wrong; you don't spank them for what is good; and so on. Some of those produce a given type of person. Some produce enterprising persons, others seem to produce lazy persons. But the main point is that we don't have stable cultures any more; so the average parent doesn't know what to do. The books on child care are more confusing than any-

thing else because you can't apply what they recommend: "Go and love your child."

That would be all right, but you can't go and buy three ounces of love at the store. And if the child really isn't lovable, you simply have to fake it. Fake love is probably the worst of all commodities. But I don't really know; that's why I tend to be a Utopian dreamer.

Hall: I'm curious. How were you raised, Fred? Were your parents strict?

Skinner: Yes, I don't think my mother and father ever had any doubts about what I was to be punished for or not. But now we really don't have an on-going culture that gives us any guidance on how to handle people. My parents came from a very strictly defined culture. My mother knew exactly what was right. I can't even remember when I learned what was right or not right, or what I should do or shouldn't do. The rules were right there in the culture; there was never any question. Well, now that's all gone; we have thrown that over, but we have to go on designing from moment to moment to produce a better way.

"And if the child really isn't lovable, you simply have to fake it."

Hall: Not even religion provides unquestioned rules today.

Skinner: And I don't know whether I want to improve religion or not. I prefer to get rid of it, but until we can get rid of it safely, it may be well to make sure that it functions.

Hall: Until you have a substitute you'd be in terrible danger. And what are you going to replace a religion with?

Skinner: Yes. Well, the whole thing is not to turn the world over in a day. This applies in international politics, too. When you had strict nationalistic lines, territories to be defended, methods of defending them, nationalism, national honor, it was different. Now we don't know. Should we appease, should we threaten? We're asking our statesmen now to use a more creative application of principles that have not gotten into international culture. That's a good, positive need. We don't have time to build a culture so that nations will begin to behave in a consistent way.

Hall: You do get uncertain in a world where you don't even know what an act of war is.

Skinner: Yes. Well, that is the trouble right now. The whole definition of nationalism. A part of this is the fact that many people do begin to feel themselves citizens of the world. Nationalism isn't as strong as it used to be. You have interest beyond your own nation. That upsets everything. When nations are sharply defined, then whether you are at war or not is perfectly clear.

Hall: Do you think that better ways of handling people might be arranged?

Skinner: Well, positive reinforcement seems to offer most of the answers.

Hall: Are you talking about reward learning? Are those the contingencies that you were talking about earlier?

Skinner: Well, I am talking about operant conditioning. People often confuse that with what they refer to as reward learning. Trouble is that specifications in terms of reward and punishment are incomplete. They don't say enough. It is true that people work for rewards; usually a reward means something agreed upon. You do something and you will be rewarded, and so on.

The rewards of a good life are eternal bliss. Now these are contracted rewards, the nature of the situation is that you do this and you will get the following. That isn't involved at all in operant conditioning. Moreover, the point isn't just that hungry rats will work for food or that a sex-starved man will work for sex, and so on. What's fundamentally important — this is very little understood by people outside the field — is what they are actually doing when a reinforcing stimulus occurs.

The whole study of operant conditioning lies in the tricky relationship between what the rat is doing and the moment of truth when the food appears. Oh, some of it is the study of what events are reinforcing and what kinds of behavior can be reinforced, but most of it is the study of the temporal and spatial relations between behavior and its consequences.

That is the heart of the matter.

The relationships of importance always involve three things: the situation, call it the stimulus if you like; the behavior, call it the response if you like; and the consequences, the reinforcers. We say that the reinforcers are contingent on behavior in a given situation or that a reinforcer is contingent on a response in the presence of a given stimulus. When those contingencies are arranged, the probability of the behavior changes. The behavior becomes more probable in the presence of the stimuli that were present when it was reinforced and less probable when not reinforced, and so on.

Hall: But where exactly does the notion of contingencies come in?

Skinner: That's the whole question of schedules of reinforcement, which is the most important part. You can reinforce every tenth response, every hundredth response, every thousandth response, or you can reinforce a response every minute, every five minutes, and so on. Some of the schedules which are now being studied are extremely complicated and can only be mediated by extremely sensitive apparatus. The most surprising thing is that organisms usually feel these schedules. They respond appropriately to them. That is the heart of the matter. Knowing the contingencies and the history of reinforcement, you can predict the behavior. You can arrange a contingency; you can control the behavior. And of course both prediction and control have widespread implications in human affairs, and in animal affairs, too.

Hall: If you could be remembered for just one contribution to psychology, would that be your analysis of contingencies?

Skinner: Yes, I suppose, if I am limited to just one thing, it would be the whole question of the contingencies of reinforcement arranged by schedules of reinforcement and their role in the analysis of operant behavior. It's a shame. Nobody pays much attention to it at all. It's an extremely interesting and complicated and fascinating field. I think it is my basic scientific contribution.

In fact, I am even now getting a little bit more interested in it, myself, if that is possible. Particularly in the implications of this sort of thing for the design of cultures in general. I have no doubt at all that programmed instruction based on operant principles will take over education. I have no doubt that operant therapy

will be very important in the management of psychotics and also in the treatment of neurotics.

Hall: If we're talking about designing cultures, Fred, let's talk about your novel, *Walden Two*. Two generations now have read it, and it's on the required reading list at most schools. I love that book.

Skinner: I think *Walden Two* has made people stop and look at the culture they have inherited and wonder if it is the last word or whether it can be changed. And even to suggest ways of changing it. I would still put my basic scientific contribution to operant behavior as the analysis of contingencies of reinforcement, but what I really expect to be known for is the application of all this to education, psychotherapy, economics, government, religion, I suppose, and its use in designing a world that will make us into the kind of people we would like to be and give us the things that we could all agree that we want.

Hall: But the society in *Walden Two* is based mainly on positive reinforcement, isn't it? What about punishment, holding down crime, and those strict codes of ethics by which you yourself were brought up?

Skinner: Positive reinforcement, properly used, is extremely powerful. Aversive control (that means punishment mainly and arranging that people do things to get away from or avoid unpleasantness) is immediate and quick and so we use it. But I really think that the use of aversive control has serious, inherent disadvantages. It is used at a terrible cost. That of course doesn't mean that you can change tomorrow.

I always thought, for example, getting back to possible Utopias, that when the Zionist movement took over Israel, it was a terrible mistake for them to emphasize an army. They should have gone in and demonstrated to the world that they could have a culture without any army. What they have got now is just another national culture emerging. Armies compel, they put on pressure, they attempt to control the behavior of other nations with aversive techniques. We say let them do this or that or we will blow you to pieces.

Hall: Now we are talking about the tragedy in international politics. I really don't see acceptance of alternatives to force very soon. Do you?

Skinner: Well it's not only international

issues, it's domestic issues, too—the whole business of how you use power and how you use positive reinforcement. Again, it's a matter of the contingencies. Whether you are going to do something either positive or negative, send in food and medical supplies or drop bombs, for example; the important thing is that the behavior of the other country should be contingent on what you are doing to them, so that the other country will do more or less of something you desire.

But I don't get the impression that anyone is paying any attention to this at all. In Vietnam, for example, certainly the only idea is that somehow or other if you make them suffer, they will give up. Well, if you have to use sources of pain, for heaven's sake use them at the right time and in the right way. It's the behavior that's being neglected. If you ask people what kind of world they want to live in, they will mention all the things that are reinforcing to them, such as food, sex, personal relations, nature, music, art, but they won't say what they are going to be doing to get those things.

The analyst would say love is a terribly important thing. He's likely to overlook what you're doing when you're loved.

"No one has ever portrayed an interesting heaven."

That's the really important thing. That's the whole crucial issue. That's what's wrong with all conceptions of heaven. No one has ever portrayed an interesting heaven. There is music in the streets, gold bricks in the pavement, and what not. But it's a boring existence because nothing is doing. Afterworlds of other cultures are of the same nature. The American Indian isn't much better off. He wants a happy hunting ground, according to song and story. Ridiculous. He doesn't just want food, he wants a happy way to get it.

Well, to get back to the Vietnam business, it isn't really whether you are using money or love or power. It's how you use

it. We're pouring a tremendous amount of power into Vietnam but the contingencies are absolutely lousy. We are simply not doing things at the right time, properly contingent on the behavior, in order to change the behavior of anyone over there. This is the whole problem.

Hall: You mentioned earlier that our domestic policy suffers from an ignorance of these considerations.

Skinner: Yes, certainly. Here we're going to give large sums of money to the poor. If you just give it to them, you aren't strengthening behavior at all. It is true that you are satisfying certain needs, and that is generally good. They will no longer be hungry; they will no longer be living in filth; that's reasonable, and is the kind of thing one does out of compassion.

But all the money that is going to go into this could be so enormously more effective if it were properly contingent on the kinds of behavior that you want these people to engage in. You might ask the question: Why aren't these people enterprising? Why don't they clean up their own apartment houses, and so on? It isn't that they are unable to live in better surroundings, they just don't do whatever it is that makes their surroundings better. And the solution is so very simple: You just have to make what is being done for these people contingent on their doing something.

Hall: Let's get back, if we may, to programmed instruction. This really has taken hold in a big way in education, hasn't it? But are current teaching machines effective? They bore me.

Skinner: You're right to be bored. It certainly is not because there are no good programs. Oh, you can write terrible programs, and they don't do at all what they are intended to do. But many, many good programs are being written, they are being improved all the time, and fantastic things can be done. It's really just the application of what we know about contingencies of reinforcement to a suitable and efficient method of education.

It's really nothing more than arranging for reinforcing consequences immediately following the behavior of the student in the proper context. But you have to bring the educators around to seeing the advantages, and that takes time.

Hall: They are resistant, the people in education? How typical.

Skinner: Yes, a change of this magnitude takes years. It really takes a new gener-

ation—on which we are having quite a considerable impression. I don't think that you can really ever beat down the prejudice of the older generation. I am convinced now that science never progresses by converting.

Among my contemporaries, for example, I can mention only one or two who really very seriously changed their attitudes toward the study of behavior as a result of anything I have ever done or said. That's to be expected, of course. They have invested a great deal in certain lines and you can't expect them to admit that they were wasting their time and have thrown away their lifework.

I would say that, to take a sweeping generalization, almost all the work done with the memory drum is worthless. I mean, they manage to cook up an interesting little problem, but I think in general it's worthless. However, I can't ask people who have worked with memory drums all their lives to admit this or to examine what goes on when somebody looks at a memory drum and tries to memorize something. They just don't want to look too closely at that. They are so afraid that they might find out that they are wrong and not amounting to anything. I suggest that they take a look around and see what is seriously being done in other fields.

Few of the educational psychologists, for example, even know what programming is all about. But the younger people are refreshing: they are looking for what really works, for the wave of the future, the techniques by which you really can manage behavior for the better in a way that actually works. And so when they look at programmed instruction and at the operant treatment of neurotics and psychotics, they see that these things really work, thank goodness.

That's how scientific change comes about, because the young have not been spoiled by miserable histories of reinforcement into running away from possible sources of much greater reinforcement.

Hall: You sound very optimistic about the future of operant conditioning.

Skinner: And justifiably so, I think. You see, as sad as it is to relate, there really isn't very much competition for the allegiance of bright and informed young psychologists. Positive reinforcement really works, and contingencies of reinforcement are really very important, and we are actually very successful in predicting and controlling behavior. These are things you just have to accept.

The young men just entering the field do accept them. They see that this is where the business is going. To paraphrase President Truman after he defeated Dewey, the competition may feel that this is all too bad and sad and cannot quite figure out how it came about, but it is true and so we will just have to make the best of it.

Hall: What about the rival schools of psychology? They object to operant conditioning on the grounds of dehumanization, of mechanization.

Skinner: Well, that's a different issue. I think the main objection to behaviorism is that people are in love with the mental apparatus. If you say that doesn't really exist, that it's a fiction and let's get back to the facts, then they have to give up their first love.

You can't expect a Freudian to say, yes, I will admit that Freud's only contribution was in demonstrating some unusual causal relations between early experience and the present behavior. He loves the superego, the ego, and the id, and the various geographies of the mind and all of that stuff.

I say we can get along without that. In fact, we can get along better without it, because we've misrepresented the facts that Freud discovered.

They won't go along with that. You are asking them to throw away their lifework. Or their only confidence, because they don't really care very much about tracing existence of problems to their environment except to show how the unconscious is causing trouble. They're interested in the mental apparatus. To ask them to give that up would be like asking an engineer to go into sculpture. You may convince him that sculpturing is more important than building bridges, but he's a bridge builder. He wouldn't know how to start something over. This Freudian business is dying out, anyway. As for the cognitive seed, that never was anything. They are not doing anything; they are not getting anywhere; and the operant people are.

Take the issue of language, which has lately become the hunting ground of the cognitive people—not that they have been able to find much. I hear that they have come out with the notion of innate ideas, which takes us right back to the dark, mentalistic ages of the 19th century. That's not progress.

Hall: Did your book, *Verbal Behavior*, gain much acceptance in those quarters?

Skinner: Not really, but I am not unhappy about this, I am willing to wait. Verbal behavior apparently has not been understood by the linguist or the psycholinguist.

They have no conception of what I mean by verbal behavior. They made almost no contribution to it, and they apparently are resolved not to make any if they can help it.

In the famous Noam Chomsky review of my book, I suspect you will find what amounts to a hatchet job, although I have

"This Freudian business is dying out, anyway."

never read the review myself. I did read a couple of pages, saw that he missed the point, and I never read the rest. What the psycholinguists miss is any conception of a functional analysis as opposed to a structural analysis of verbal behavior.

Hall: You do have a sweet, succinct way about you. Keep talking.

Skinner: I mean that they try to make sense out of the dependent variable only. They really don't want to look into the situation in which a person is speaking or listening to speech. That would make them psychologists, and they don't want to do it. And so they argue that you don't need to. And then, of course, they try to argue that verbal behavior isn't real behavior, that it goes back to ideas and cognitive processes. They lean very heavily on the mentalistic psychology, and they are going to be let down because there is no such psychology. But as I said earlier, now they are postulating innate ideas, and that is next to worthless, if not a little bit comical. But I am in no real hurry, I have had my say. I am not interested in arguing with them at all. When all their mythical machinery finally grinds to a halt and is laid aside, discarded, then we will see what is remembered fifty or a hundred years from now, when the truth

will have all been brought out in the open.

Hall: That takes care of mythical machinery. Where is progress, then?

Skinner: Well, certainly not in mentalism or psychophysics; it's a dead end. You see the old idea was, and still is, as a matter of fact, that you could have a science of mental life. Mental events were going to obey mental laws. All you had to do was find out what those laws are, and you had a life of the mind. This could be scientifically analyzed, perhaps. But what actually happened was that people wanted to find out where the mental events came from, and of course they came from the outside world.

So you study sensation and the relation between the psychic and the physical, and the field is still essentially in that condition. The fact is that a hundred and some years ago they decided that this relation was logarithmic and now they are trying to say that it is a power function. But it is basically unproductive: they believe in a world of sensation, the way that things seem to be rather than the way things really are.

Hall: Are you cheerier about clinical psychology and psychotherapy?

Skinner: Well, they won't get anywhere if they don't get results. And you can't get results by sitting around and theorizing about the inner world of the disturbed. I want to say to those people: get down to the facts. But they seem to be threatened by facts. Operant conditioning—the proper arrangement and management of contingencies of reinforcement—has been fantastically successful with a number of problems of disordered behavior.

Take autistic children, for example. Our success in that area is a real threat, you see, to the people who think that the problem is something about the inner life, or the lack of identity, or alienation, or whatever all those things are that these kids are supposed to be suffering from.

What they are suffering from in fact is very bad schedules of reinforcement. That is something you can change for them, but this is not done. And you really can't expect mentalistic psychologists to do things like that; their approach just simply destines them to inadequacy and failure.

Oh, but they are so sincere. They want to understand the boys, to sit and talk and gain their confidence, and all of this stuff. Meanwhile, there is a very simple way in which you can begin to get them to behave in a very respectable way and to learn the kinds of skills that will give them a chance to be effective citizens.

Take the problem in correctional institutions, for example. One of our people recently took over one of the buildings in a training school for boys and organized it on the basis of a point-reinforcement system. The boys were paid for their work, and they had to buy everything except basics. For free they could get the basic diet and a place to sleep in the dormitory, but anything else they had to buy. And the most points were given for learning something interesting with the help of teaching machines, or without. They got points for learning.

Don't you see, that's the *point*. It made them discover for the first time that they could learn something, and that learning something was valuable. This is a very important thing. Most of them had been convinced by our school systems that they were stupid. They discovered that they really weren't. It's remarkable, surprising, it really works! How very different it is from hand-holding and getting to know the boys.

Hall: You can't slough off people like Carl Rogers and Rollo May and Bruno Bettelheim. They're constructive.

Skinner: Oh, certainly, in certain cases. You know Rogers' technique is to agree with everything everybody says—reinforce support. Have you ever heard the story of Carl Rogers and the duck?

Hall: No, please tell me. Carl is the hero, or victim, of more apocryphal stories than is any other leader in psychology. How fortunate that he has a good disposition.

Skinner: Someone took Carl out duck hunting one morning. It was a bad day, cloudy or something, and hunting was very bad. Toward the very end they were about ready to go home. One duck came in. Carl shot at the duck. At the same time somebody else shot it from down along the shore. The duck fell into the shallow water. Carl walked toward the duck, and the other guy emerged and walked out to get it, too. They met at the duck, Carl looked up at the man and said, "You feel this is your duck." Of course the point of the story is that Carl got the duck. His technique does work, you see.

Hall: I'm going to do an interview with Carl. He's entitled, at this point.

Skinner: You see, Rogers' whole approach is based on the notion that the individual somehow or other has his own salvation within him. And this may not be true. Really it's a matter of the history of reinforcement. Someone brought up in a good old Protestant background probably does have enough behavior to save himself in certain circumstances. But cultures change. Rogers' approach is based on a culture which by and large is coming not to exist any more. This means that he really hasn't gotten at the basic processes.

What would he do, for example, if someone came up with the solution that he had better murder his boss? Rogers isn't going to say, "Oh, you should murder your boss!" and let it go at that. No, he couldn't do it. The only way you can be successful with these things is to get at the basic processes and work with them. It's simply too superficial and dangerous to rely on the previous history of reinforcement—the culture—when that is something that is going to change at least every few generations.

Hall: What do you see surfacing in other areas of psychology that may be of interest in the future?

Skinner: Well, I don't see much of anything interesting going on. The study of sensation is of some interest, but I think primarily as the physiology of how the eye works and how the ear works, the field of perception is not yet up to the level

"If I could do it all over again, I'd never teach those pigeons to play Ping-Pong."

it will reach, though it is an interesting business. But there is not much going on there now.

Some people are working on what conditions lead one to learn to see things in different ways, and that could be fun, if done properly. I have no interest in so-called cognitive psychology. I just don't think there is much there.

Psychological testing, I mark all of that off. Verbal learning, I mark all that off. I just wouldn't look at anything that had to do with the memory drum unless someone suddenly convinced me that someone had something new there. I have never been able to read papers dealing with mazes; once you know something about behavior, it is transparently clear that you simply don't know what's going on in a maze or a jump stand at all.

Hall: Obviously you aren't just the creator of operant conditioning. You are a true believer. Of course you are still hard at work. What does the immediate future hold for you?

Skinner: Well, I may not have too much future personally. I keep on saying I've got about five more good years left, but I have been saying that for about three years already, so I don't know how many good years I have. But I keep in good health, take care of myself. I have always had a lot of things I wanted to do, and I have had quite deliberately to rule out some things which I would have enjoyed.

Three or four years ago I gave up my laboratory. I was still getting grants, as I could now. Grants were hard to get in the old days, but I could get them now. I wanted to turn it over to younger people, and so I said to myself that I have had 35 years of laboratory science, so I will quit. I also have withdrawn pretty much from teaching, but I don't mean to stop working. I spend as much time as I can on creative things. I have always wanted to do a little something worthwhile every day, and the rest of the time is thinking and reading. I have several important books which I want to get out. I think we have put our finger on something of extraordinary importance here—and when we get the truth out, everything will follow these operant rules which we have seen and are still discovering. With them one cannot make a very serious mistake. And since this is where the future of psychology lies, it's well worth the telling.

Hall: If you had your life to live over again, if you were just beginning your career, what would you do differently?

Skinner: Just one thing. I performed one experiment that has never ceased to reverberate. I've been laughed at by enemies and kidded by friends. If I could do it all over again, I'd never teach those pigeons to play Ping-Pong. ◙

THEY HAD A BEDTIME PROBLEM in the Thompson household. Douglas Thompson, a strapping 18-year-old, couldn't get to sleep. Twenty-five or 30 times a night he would go to his mother's bedroom to tell her about his worries. Each visit took one or two minutes, and night would slip into morning as the worries went on.

Douglas' worries were small ones—had the downstairs' lights been turned off? Was the TV antenna properly oriented? Mrs. Thompson (the names are pseudonyms) usually reassured Douglas —yes, the lights are off; yes, the antenna is set right. Sometimes she spoke sharply. When Douglas did not talk to his mother it took a long time for him to get to sleep.

This had been going on for two years. Douglas had consulted a psychiatrist, taken sleeping pills and tranquilizers, and consulted a psychologist once a week for six months. Still he had the sleeping problem.

Change. I found all of this, on the whole, unsurprising. It seemed clear that Douglas' behavior persisted for three reasons: 1) the mother's attention and sympathy served as a reward, 2) this rewarding attention was given for the poor behavior, and 3) the behavior itself was easy.

To change the behavior, it was necessary to give the reward at a more appropriate time and for a better behavior, and to make the poor behavior more difficult to perform.

Mrs. Thompson was told not to listen to Douglas' worries after bedtime. Instead she was to set a special time early each evening to talk to Douglas in the living room for 30 minutes. If Douglas visited her bedroom after the discussion, then she was to cancel the next evening's talk in the living room. For his part Douglas was to keep a record, noting each night the time he entered his bedroom and, next morning, the approximate time he fell asleep. Also he was to log every worry as it came to him.

We were embarked on behavior-modification therapy. In the first week Douglas visited his mother's bedroom twice. During the second week he made one visit and after that the bedtime visits ceased altogether.

By the third week the living-room sessions were lasting only 15 minutes, and before the seventh week, Douglas discontinued them.

Douglas' worries also dropped off dramatically. Within three weeks the number of items recorded in his bedroom worry diary dropped to almost none.

Cause. Douglas' behavior had been changed, but what about the underlying psychological cause of the problem? The behavioral approach eliminates long and possibly fruitless searches for underlying psychological causes that may or may not be susceptible to change and therefore may or may not be relevant in therapy.

A person's behavior is consistent with his experiences—his past successes and failures. We learn from practice, from trying certain behaviors and benefiting from the trials. It is a fundamental law of learning that *one learns what one does*. The things we practice are the things we learn best.

An accurate description of behaviors also points the way to alter those behaviors. For Douglas, the crucial procedure was to stop the bestowal of a subtle reward—his mother's concern and attention—for a bad behavior. Douglas had to test the new rules. When the consequences were as consistent as he was told they would be, his behavior changed.

This can be dangerous because one's behavior may become emotional when the usual routine doesn't get the usual results. I call this the vending-machine response. If a Coke machine fails to give you a Coke for your dime, do you thoughtfully and carefully change your behavior? No. You bang on its little buttons, kick it and insult it. So it takes courage and patience to withhold an expected reward as Douglas' mother did.

Praise. An easier and more positive behavioral approach is to look for something to reward. It may be necessary to settle for something less than perfect. For example, when one is teaching table manners to a two-year-old it may be necessary at first to praise any use of the spoon that gets food anywhere near the face. Later, praise may be saved for behavior nearer the target. What seems to elude most of us impatient adults is that we have to start *somewhere* and that the somewhere may have to be very far down indeed when we are dealing with children.

The most common error most of us make is to demand too much for too

SPARE THE ROD USE BEHAVIOR MOD

by Roger W. McIntire

small a reward when we begin to teach something new to a child. The first little steps need big rewards. "But this is bribery," some protest. "Shouldn't a child do most of these things without reward, just for the joy of learning? Some children are good and do what is expected without any reward, don't they?"

First we must realize that good children get many and large social rewards and they snowball. For example, when a child starts off well, he is well-rewarded with praise; when he is well-rewarded, he keeps going; when he keeps going, he is further rewarded, and so on.

Snowballing can work the other way too. Some children are not rewarded for being good or learning. They expect no rewards because they have received none in the past. If a child starts slowly or poorly on something, he gets little encouragement; instead, he is badgered. The lack of reward slows him even more as he gets older. Performance that would have been rewarded is not, because "he should have been doing that years ago, anyway."

Candy. For example, in one study, 12 first- and second-grade children were diagnosed as "predicted reading failures" because they had failed a reading-readiness test. We divided the children into three groups. During the first week we determined their average error in word identification. Each group had an average error of about 40 per cent.

Then one group of children received concrete reinforcement — a raisin or a peanut or candy-coated chocolate—for each correct response. They also began with a very simple task that guaranteed success. We showed each child a picture-word combination and asked him to match it to a duplicate word card and say the word aloud. This technique helped the children fade into a learning task before going on to more difficult tasks. The remaining two groups received neither reinforcement nor the fading procedure.

The average error of the group that experienced reinforcement and fading dropped to five per cent. The other groups continued at a 40 per cent error rate. When we stopped the reinforcement and the fading for members of the first group, their error rate soared to 50 per cent.

We tried the candy reinforcement without the fading technique on one of the groups. The error rate declined, but only by four per cent.

The use of the fading technique alone was more effective than reinforcement alone. Average error dropped from about 40 to eight per cent.

When we used both reinforcement and fading on all three groups, the error rate dropped to less than five per cent. In general we had great success helping children who had been regarded as potential reading failures.

Colors. In another experiment, we demonstrated that we could bring tests and homework under behavioral control. We worked with a class of fifth-graders and a class of sixth-graders. Twice a week, for half an hour at a time, we had the students in a special-project room where there were models, educational games, teaching machines and materials for baking and cooking and ceramics.

We divided the activities into three levels, red, yellow and white. The red level included all activities. There were two ways for a child to get into the red groups: by getting 90 per cent or more in his spelling and math work or by improving his last score by 10 percentage points. Children in this group almost always chose to bake and cook.

The yellow level included games, work on ceramic candy dishes, or work on teaching machines. To be in the yellow level, a child had to remain within 10 percentage points of his previous score, in either direction. The white level was restricted to work with the teaching machines. A child fell into the white level when his score dropped more than 10 percentage points, but he could gain the highest reward and move into the most attractive group by improving his score by 10 percentage points.

Then we told the fifth-graders that their spelling work would no longer count for privileges in the special-project room. At the same time we told the sixth-graders that math would no longer count. Performance dropped immediately in the work that did not count.

Next we reversed the contingencies. We told the fifth-graders that math would no longer count but spelling would, and we told the sixth-graders that spelling would no longer count but math would. Once again performance scores dropped dramatically for the unrewarded work.

The results show that performance in school can be controlled with suitable rewards, and that abrupt withdrawal of rewards can affect performance, at least negatively.

Strike. We all are interested in some return for effort. I recall a father who rejected a reinforcement plan for correcting his son's behavior because he thought the boy should be grown-up enough to do the right thing without a payoff. When the counselor thanked the father for taking time off from work to talk about his son's problem, the father replied, "Oh, that's all right. We're on strike for a raise." Apparently, when his payoff was involved, it was different.

Attention, praise and general encouragement are effective rewards in the home. Of these, attention often has the greatest influence on a child's behavior. Because attention is so influential, a parent must be on guard not to support bad behavior by paying attention to it, as did one mother who turned from a talk with a neighbor to deal with her daughter who was screaming, "Mommy! Mommy!" She yelled back, "What is it?" The daughter yelled "Hi!" and ran away.

The mother unintentionally gave an example of yelling by yelling herself and she reinforced the behavior by paying attention to her daughter when she yelled. Selecting behaviors to be rewarded or ignored is the main business of being a parent.

Nag. Some parents ride their children —*blow your nose, tuck in your shirt, don't touch*. They give the child a great deal of attention but little support and encouragement. Other parents seem to follow a rule: *when in doubt, reward; hardly ever punish*. A complete lack of limits provides no information about right and wrong behaviors. Both children and adults continually explore limits. If there are none, behaviors may get out of hand.

Ideally, as a child grows the limits on his behaviors are lessened gradually; he should experience expanding responsibility and independence. Unfortunately for many children the pattern is a long period of limitations and then an abrupt change into independence.

The typical American teen-ager is thrown out of the nest at about 17, when he goes off to college or to work. He has to achieve instant adulthood and the process can be painful, especially when what he does has severe social consequences. Because the teen-ager must adjust to everything at once, he may find it too much; he may rebel, rejecting the behaviors so valued by the adult world.

Perhaps the commonest cause of this revolt is the failure of parents to let children make some of their own decisions when they are younger and learn to live with the consequences. Teen-agers who are allowed to make decisions and reap consequences experience the success and failure of their decisions. After successes, ideally, parents are encouraging; after failures, parents support youngsters by pointing out and helping with the search for alternate behaviors. A long period of trial and error is possible for a child whose parents are willing to permit it. When the young adult leaves home without this practice, there is no time for discussion, exploration or selection (or for rejection). He is rushing into adulthood and time has run out.

SOME YEARS AGO one of us (Seligman) went out to dinner. He had an excellent *filet mignon* with *sauce Béarnaise*, his favorite, and then he went off with his wife Kerry to see the opera *Tristan und Isolde*. Some hours later he became violently ill with stomach flu and spent most of the night in utter misery. Later, when he attempted to eat *sauce Béarnaise* again, he couldn't bear the taste of it. Just thinking about it nauseated him.

At first glance, his reaction seemed to be a simple case of Pavlovian conditioning: a conditioned stimulus (the sauce) had been paired with an unconditioned stimulus (the illness), which elicited an unconditioned response (throwing up). So future encounters with the sauce caused a conditioned response (nausea). At second glance, however, he realized that the *sauce-Béarnaise* phenomenon had violated all sorts of well-established laws:

1 The interval between tasting the sauce and throwing up was about six hours. The longest interval between two events that produce learning in the laboratory is about 30 seconds.

2 It took only one such experience for him to associate the sauce with sickness; learning rarely occurs in only one trial in the laboratory.

3 Neither the *filet mignon*, nor the white plate on which it was served, nor his wife, became distasteful to him; he associated none of them with the illness, only the *sauce Béarnaise*. But, according to laws of Pavlovian conditioning, all events or objects that occur along with the illness (the unconditioned stimulus) should have become unpleasant.

4 His reaction had no cognitive or "expectational" components, unlike most conditioning phenomena. When he found out that another close colleague got sick the same night, he knew that the sauce hadn't caused the malaise at all—stomach flu had caused it. But knowing that the sauce was not the culprit did not inhibit his aversion to it one bit.

5 Finally, his loathing of *sauce Béarnaise* stayed with him about five years, whereas associations formed by Pavlovian conditioning generally die out in about a dozen trials.

Laws. This experience led us to reconsider the phenomena that pass for conditioning in the laboratory.

Psychologists have long assumed that in the simple, controlled world of the laboratory they would find general laws of behavior. Learning theorists in particular have relied on the deliberately unnatural quality of the experiment: they argued that the arbitrary pairing of any stimulus with any response, or of any response with any reinforcer, would guarantee the generality of the results.

For example, Ivan Pavlov, in his textbook example of classical conditioning, taught dogs to salivate to a clicking sound by giving them meat along with the clicks. When he stopped handing out the meat, the dog eventually stopped salivating to the sound. Pavlov assumed that this illustrated a behavioral law—extinction—that would apply beyond the specific stimulus (the clicks) and response (salivation) of his experiment. Similarly, psychologists have assumed that if they trained a rat to press a lever in order to get pellets of flour—an example of instrumental conditioning—the rules describing the rat's behavior would transcend the particular instance of bar-pressing and flour pellets.

Smile. Learning theorists, whether they study classical conditioning or instrumental conditioning, thus tend to believe that what an animal learns about is relatively unimportant. They believe that virtually all stimuli, responses and reinforcers can be paired equally well, if they but use correct techniques. Moreover, we have general laws that describe the acquisition, inhibition, or extinction of such pairings. We can teach a pigeon to peck for grain as easily as we teach a rat to run for water and as easily as we teach a child to smile for approval. The underlying psychological laws are the same for all three behaviors.

This belief—the *equipotentiality premise*—is the foundation of mainstream learning theory today. Our most eminent learning theorists have shared the premise: Ivan Pavlov, B. F. Skinner, Clark Hull, and William K. Estes. But it is wrong. There are limits to learning, limits that evolution and natural selection have set for each species.

Advantage. Learning theorists may argue that 60 years of research have indeed found certain general laws that hold for a wide range of arbitrarily chosen events. For instance, we know that intermittent reinforcement will keep an animal working longer for a reward than continuous reinforcement will. This is true whether the subjects are rats, pigeons, or human beings, whether the response is running, pecking, or bar-pressing, and whether the reinforcer is food, water, or sex.

Perhaps, we reply, but the activities that we teach animals in the laboratory do not generally occur in the real world. When do rats normally have to press levers in or-

Biological Boundaries of Learning:
The Sauce-Béarnaise Syndrome

You can lead a horse to water but no amount or manner of conditioning will teach it to talk.

by Martin E. P. Seligman and Joanne L. Hager

der to get flour pellets? When do dogs come across little metronomes that signal meat? Learning theorists say that such random associations are intentionally artificial; that way the results are not contaminated by the animal's biology or previous experience.

But biology and experience do make a difference, and the emphasis that psychologists place on arbitrary events does not ensure laws that are general; it produces laws that are specific to arbitrary events, arbitrarily paired. Evolution has not prepared dogs and rats to learn about clicks that predict food or levers that turn off shock when they are pressed. Not so for the *sauce-Béarnaise* phenomenon. In nature, stomach illness frequently follows unusual-tasting food, often with a delay of a few hours. An animal that has been poisoned by a new taste—and lived to tell the tale—would have a selective advantage: if he could learn to stay away from that taste in the future; if he could learn that lesson quickly, preferably with only one experience; if he could avoid being misled by other stimuli surrounding the new taste; and if that knowledge did not disappear (extinguish) rapidly.

From this evolutionary standpoint, mankind has long been prepared for the *sauce-Béarnaise* phenomenon. By contrast, natural selection has not prepared most animals for such typical laboratory experiences as buzzers paired with electric shock.

Readiness. Thus we have come to disagree with the assumption that conditioning has no limits. We propose a *preparedness dimension* to describe and delineate the limits of learning. We suggest that an animal brings to any experiment certain physiological equipment and predispositions, some of which are appropriate to the situation and others that are less so. The animal has a specialized sensory and motor system, we know; but more important, it has an associative apparatus that also has a long evolutionary history. This history will make some lessons easier to learn than others, some lessons more difficult to forget than others, and some more generalizable to other experiences than others.

We think it likely that *the very laws of learning vary from one situation to another, depending on the preparedness of the animal* to learn the contingency at hand. We see this preparedness concept as a continuum. In a given situation, an animal may be *prepared, unprepared,* or *contraprepared* to learn its lesson.

¶ By *prepared* we mean that the biology and genetics of the animal contribute greatly to its ability and readiness to make the association at hand. We can make the parameters of the task difficult, and it will still learn its lesson, and frequently the very first time.

¶ By *unprepared* we mean that nothing in the animal's natural history contributes to its learning the association; it learns after many trials.

¶ By *contraprepared* we mean that the animal is not at all biologically and genetically suited to make the association—dogs, for instance, are contraprepared for learning to yawn to get fed. No matter how easy we make the task, the animal will never learn.

Rock. This approach puts instinct and learning on the same continuum. Instinct, in our formulation, is simply an extreme case of preparedness. Further, we can measure the animal's extent of preparedness by the number of trials it requires to learn the association; it is this simple measure that makes the dimension continuous.

Thus, if we confront an animal with a stimulus, and it makes the response we are looking for the first time, we may say that its behavior is a clear illustration of instinct or a reflex. (A falling rock, for example, will elicit a startle reflex that is instinctive in human beings.) If the animal makes the conditioned response after only a few trials, we may say that it is somewhat prepared. If the animal responds correctly after many trials, it is unprepared. And if it never learns to make the association, or if it does so only after very many trials, we say that the animal is contraprepared.

Rats. Typically ethologists, who in studying wild animals in their natural habitats, have explored events on the prepared end of the scale, such as imprinting; learning theorists have restricted themselves to the unprepared region, teaching rats to associate colors, say, with food. Few researchers have studied the contraprepared end of the continuum. We use this continuum to integrate the evidence that learning is not equipotential.

The same week that Seligman was undergoing the agonies of the stomach flu, John Garcia of the State University of New York at Stony Brook published the first of a series of articles in what were then relatively obscure journals. Though the series had been rejected by the blue-ribbon journals of psychology, they are now recognized as perhaps the most important studies of animal learning of the decade. Among their consequences was that they explained the *sauce-Béarnaise* phenomenon.

Garcia and Robert A. Koelling confronted their rats with a sweet-tasting liquid and a light-sound stimulus, both paired with radiation sickness—a malaise characterized by stomach upset. But only the taste, not the bright light or loud sound, became unpleasant to the rats. In the complementary experiment, they paired the sweet taste and the light-sound stimuli with electric shock. This time, the rats associated the light-sound combination, not the taste, with the shock.

Cuckoo. This one experiment illustrates both ends of the preparedness spectrum. The rats were *prepared* to associate taste with illness, and this association occurred in spite of the hour-long delay between the taste and the illness. But the rats were *unprepared*—perhaps contraprepared—to associate taste with electric shock, to link external events (light and noise) with nausea. The evolutionary advantage is obvious: animals that are poisoned by a distinctively flavored food and survive, do well not to eat that food again.

Garcia's research was not well received in traditional quarters. One psychologist, who had worked for years on delay of reinforcement, remarked publicly, "Those findings are no more likely than bird shit in a cuckoo clock." Nevertheless, researchers have replicated the findings many times since.

Wisdom. Garcia's research helped solve a long-standing problem in physiological psychology: that of specific hungers. We had known that animals deficient in a given nutrient, such as thiamine or riboflavin, seek out substances that contain the missing nutrient. How do they manage this? The wisdom-of-the-body hypothesis proposed that foods containing the needed vitamin somehow taste better; or that the animal's ability to detect foods with the needed nutrient is increased. But such a hypothesis is unparsimonious and inelegant; it requires that there be a separate mechanism to handle each of the dozen or more nutrients for which specific hungers have been identified. When an animal lacks calcium, for example, why should foods with calcium come to taste better, rather than foods with riboflavin?

At the time Garcia was working on stomach poisoning, Paul Rozin and his colleagues Willard Rodgers and James Kalat at the University of Pennsylvania made a breakthrough. Rozin showed that specific hungers and specific aversions are symmetrical: when an animal becomes thiamine-deficient on one diet, he is sick to his stomach, and this in turn makes the animal dislike its deficient diet. Thiamine-deficiency, in short, is a form of food poisoning; and Rozin's rats were biologically prepared to associate the illness with the taste of the deficient diet. This association held over long intervals between the conditioned stimulus (the diet) and the unconditioned stimulus (the illness); and the animals always connected the illness with the food, never with such irrelevant external stimuli as the food container or the location of the food.

In addition, Steven Maier and Donna Zahorik of the University of Illinois found that animals will prefer new tastes that accompany the recovery from their illness.

In sum, one mechanism—biological preparedness to associate tastes with gastrointestinal consequences—replaces the dozen-odd mechanisms that were previously needed to account for specific hungers.

Snake. Garcia's insights are also relevant to psychopathology in man. We can interpret human phobias as prepared classical conditioning. Phobias too are selective: we have phobias about heights, the dark, crowds, animals and insects, but we do not have phobias about pajamas, electric outlets, or trees, even though the latter may accompany trauma as often as the former. Isaacs Marks of London's Maudsley Hospital related a typical case. A seven-year-old girl, playing one day in the park, saw a snake, but she was not particularly alarmed. Several hours later she accidentally smashed her hand in a car door, and soon thereafter developed a fear of snakes that lasted into adulthood. Notice that she did *not* develop a car-door phobia, which would have been more logical. Moreover, considerable time elapsed between her seeing the snake and having the accident.

Phobias are highly resistant to extinction—they last a long time; and, like taste aversions, they are unaffected by cognitive understanding. It does not help a person with a cat phobia to know that cats are harmless, just as it didn't help Seligman to know that the flu, and not *sauce Béarnaise,* caused his sickness.

Cats. The preparedness dimension applies to instrumental learning as well as to Pavlovian (classical) learning. (In instrumental learning the animal finds that its behavior will produce a reward or a punishment—the reward will maintain its response and punishment will diminish it.) We actually had evidence for this 70

years ago, when E. L. Thorndike began his pioneer studies of animal learning.

Thorndike put cats into large puzzle boxes and studied the ways that they learned to escape: in one the cat would have to pull a string to get out, in another it had to find the crucial lever, and so on. The last one, box Z, had only a door, which Thorndike would open for the cat whenever it licked or scratched itself. Each of these actions has an instrumental function: the cat scratches itself when it itches, and licks itself when it is dirty.

Thorndike found that freedom—getting out of the puzzle boxes—was sufficient reward for his cats; their freedom reinforced the behaviors of pulling strings, pushing buttons, or pressing levers. But his cats had a great deal of trouble learning to get out of box Z. They found it exceedingly difficult to associate scratching and licking with the opening of the door. Thorndike himself suggested that there may be some instrumental associations that the nervous system just cannot make; his box-Z cats were demonstrating their contrapreparedness to learn that lesson. But Thorndike's suggestion has been lost on modern-learning theorists.

Key. Similarly, psychologists have long taught pigeons to peck at keys for grain. Key-pecking, they assumed, was an arbitrary behavior that they could reward. But we must note one important difference between a pigeon's pecking and, say, a rat's pressing levers. In nature, lever-pressing has nothing to do with getting food; but pecking has everything to do with the bird's eating. Thus we would infer that birds are more prepared to peck keys than rats are to press levers. Indeed, Paul Brown and Herbert Jenkins of McMaster University in Hamilton, Ontario found that the pigeon will learn to peck keys even when this behavior does not produce grain. They confronted the birds with a lit-up key, then gave them some grain, and this was enough to get them to start pecking. The pigeons even continued to peck when the probability of getting food did not increase—in fact, even when the probability decreased.

Robert Bolles of the University of Washington found that similar considerations hold in avoidance learning—what animals will and will not learn to do to avoid certain painful things. Rats learn to press bars for food pellets, and also readily learn to jump or run from a dangerous place to a safe one to avoid electric shock. From this, equipotentiality theorists would deduce that rats should be able to

learn to press bars to avoid shock. But it isn't so. It is a long and tedious procedure to train a rat to press a bar to avoid shock. Similarly, pigeons will peck keys for grain, but not to avoid shock. They can certainly avoid danger in other ways, however: if we ask pigeons to fly or run from shock, they learn quickly. Bolles concluded that to train an animal to avoid a painful stimulus, we must choose from among its species-specific repertoire of *defensive* actions, not from its appetitive repertoire. Natural selection must have prepared the animal before human beings can train it.

Gulls. As learning theorists encounter more and more experimental anomalies of the kind we have described, they are becoming more open to the importance of ethological findings on prepared behaviors—an area with which comparative psychologists such as Daniel Lehrman, T. C. Schneirla, M. E. Bitterman, and Gilbert Gottlieb have long been familiar.

Beginning with its modern founders, Konrad Lorenz and Nikolaas Tinbergen, ethology has been concerned with the behavior of animals in the wild, scrupulously noting the behaviors specific to each species rather than searching for common laws of learning. Ethologists had therefore known for years that learning is not equipotential.

For instance, Tinbergen found that herring gulls (in their natural environment) learn to recognize their own chicks within hours, but they will not learn to recognize their own eggs even after weeks—though both eggs and chicks are easily distinguishable to the human observer. Lorenz studied imprinting: the fact that ducklings, at a critical period of development, begin to follow whatever object (mother, locomotives, Lorenz himself) is moving in their environment. This following apparently relieves the ducklings' distress, and is highly resistant to change.

Songs. Stephen T. Emlen, a Cornell University ethologist, thinks that genetically prepared learning is relevant in bird migration as well [*"Birds," PT, 4/72*]. His indigo buntings apparently are prepared to learn about the circumpolar constellations, and to use these cues in migration, for they will learn to migrate to and from Orion when they are raised in a planetarium with this constellation at the pole rather than the Little Dipper (the real polar constellation).

Birds also are prepared to learn the songs appropriate for their species and studies of the critical periods in song-learning may illuminate human language learning. Peter Marler of Rockefeller University studied the white-crowned sparrow. In nature, this bird learns its song by listening to adults of the species. If the young bird does not hear the song between 10 and 50 days of age, however, its song is deficient when it is adult. Moreover, its ability to learn during this period is selective: it will not pick up the song of another species, even if this is the only song it hears.

Children. Marler's research meshes with that of Noam Chomsky at M.I.T. and Eric Lenneberg at Cornell, both of whom have studied language learning in children. Their data show that children do not learn to speak and understand language the way rats learn to press levers—contrary to B. F. Skinner's argument that reinforcement shapes both kinds of behavior. In all but the most impoverished linguistic environments, children will speak and understand the language that they hear. We do not need to arrange our words carefully for them to do so, nor need we reward or punish their verbal attempts.

It appears that both young sparrows and young human beings are prepared to focus on the sounds of their own species, and that species only.

Evidence. One might ask what difference it makes if there are strong biological and genetic constraints on what can and cannot be learned. We now have tentative evidence that different laws of learning, different physiological bases, and even different cognitive mechanisms may underlie prepared and unprepared learning.

1 DIFFERENT LAWS OF LEARNING. Unprepared associations disappear readily if they are not continually reinforced. Prepared learning is much more robust. Imprinting, phobias, and taste aversions persist in the absence of reinforcement. They last even when they have lost their purpose; they seem to take on autonomous lives of their own that remain impervious to extinction.

2 DIFFERENT PHYSIOLOGICAL BASES. Prepared associations are neither fragile nor plastic. Taste aversions can be learned under anesthesia, and they are not to be broken down by electroconvulsive shock or by inactivation of the cerebral cortex. Unprepared associations are much more fragile and plastic. We can mold them and shape them and destroy them with reasonable ease.

3 DIFFERENT COGNITIVE MECHANISMS. Finally, unprepared learning is largely cognitive—it involves expectations, selective attention, and intention. Prepared learning, by comparison, seems blind and noncognitive. When unprepared learning occurs, information-seeking is important: stimuli that are redundant do not become conditioned. In contrast, even redundant tastes become aversive when they are paired with nausea.

Evolution has not left the learning of prepared associations to cognitive processes alone. Perhaps this is why love and sexual attachments—to say nothing of phobias—are irrational: they are all survival related. An animal that must act instantaneously cannot take time out to ruminate.

Order. So we must recognize that the learning apparatus of men and animals may be just as evolutionarily specialized as perceptual and motor apparatus. The environmentalist model, which tries so hard to be an uncontaminated situation for the study of behavioral laws, inadvertently may have injected a bias of its own: that because the animals would learn to do most of the odd things the experimenters wanted them to do, there were no biological limits on what animals could learn. We now know that this is not true. Learning theorists played a major part in showing us that biology is not destiny, that the environment can shape and focus behavior. But they went to an unwarranted extreme. A truly general learning theory must take into account the entire spectrum of preparedness. And we hold out some hope that laws of a higher level of generality may emerge.

If, for example, future work supports the existing evidence that ease of extinction varies with preparedness, we would have a truly general law of extinction. We cannot say what will develop in the future as the largely unexplored areas of prepared and contraprepared learning are studied; it may be that any search for general laws will prove to be a will-o'-the-wisp. But we think otherwise; scientists seem to be prepared to create order out of chaos.

The preparedness dimension should generate some important questions and new directions for research. We may learn how prepared man is to learn about aggressive and sexual behaviors in various situations. We can examine the things we do—the things we learn, perceive, remember, understand, fail to understand, believe, disbelieve—and find out whether we do them as we do because we are *Homo sapiens*, animals evolved and still evolving. By finding and probing these biological boundaries, we may open vast dimensions of experience for man. ◪

Can We Immunize the Weak?

by Martin E. P. Seligman

ARCHIE HAS TURNED 15 and is moving toward total drop-out. Soon he will quit school, where he feels increasingly ignorant, useless and helpless, and enter the larger world where he is guaranteed to feel similarly ignorant, useless and helpless, and where the consequences will be more serious.

Archie has been shaped for this from infancy. He never knew his father, his mother was seldom at home, and Archie grew into childhood almost alone in an ugly, monotonous, bullying, nonverbal world. At five-and-a-half he was far behind his schoolmates in handling standard English; he wanted to follow the teacher's instructions but she used too many words he didn't know and he was afraid to ask what she meant. As he dropped farther and farther behind in verbal skills, school became more and more incomprehensible. But every year or so he was pushed on to the next grade.

Archie's vicious circle of failures has begun, and it seems almost inevitable that a series of horrors awaits him in the outside world. The outcome is almost predestined.

A few years ago, Mr. Thompson was a grocer in a small Midwestern town. His business was never very good; despite his frantic efforts, his credit dried up, his debts grew, and his customers went away. His wife of 17 years left him. Soon after this his only son was run over by a truck and his crumbling world at last collapsed. Mr. Thompson lies curled up in his bed in a back ward of a state hospital, staring at a wall. He hasn't spoken for a year and a half. He is not much trouble—it is fairly easy to feed and clean him. He probably will be kept alive for many years.

Archies and Mr. Thompsons are little more than statistics. They are creatures of the welfare roll, the state or federal mental-health budget, the police blotter, the editorial, the casebook in psychopathology. In almost every Archie or Mr. Thompson we can find failure, depression, the feeling of powerlessness, some final giving up that requires institutional notice by society.

What can be done for the Archies and Mr. Thompsons of this life?

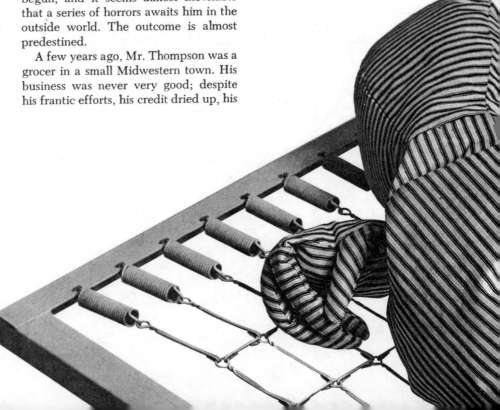

That such patterns of helplessness are today so widespread and recurrent suggests that we know very little about preventing or curing them. One thing that experimental psychologists can do is call attention to the events taking place in their laboratories and suggest functional analogies—or at least intriguing ones—that may be useful when society is ready to be truly serious about cures and prevention of helplessness. A few years ago Bruce Overmier, Steve Maier and I stumbled onto a behavioral phenomenon that suggests such an analogy.

In the laboratory of R. L. Solomon, we had been using dogs and traumatic electric shock to test a particular learning theory. We strapped dogs into a Pavlovian harness and gave them electric shock —traumatic, but not physically damaging. Later the dogs were put into a two-compartment box where they were supposed to learn to escape shock simply by jumping across a barrier from an electri-

fied section into a nonelectrified section. We found that if a harnessed dog first experienced shock over which it had no control (that is, nothing it did affected or related to the shock), something bizarre happened when we put it in the shuttlebox. But first let me tell you what a nonshocked or naive dog does in the shuttlebox.

When a conditioned stimulus (CS) comes on—for example, the lights go dim —the experimentally naive dog looks around. Ten seconds later strong electric shock comes through the floor. The dog howls, runs around frantically, defecates and urinates, and finally throws itself over the barrier. This response gets it out of shock and turns off the conditioned stimulus (the lights come back on). A few minutes later the second trial occurs. When the CS goes on this time, the dog looks afraid. Ten seconds later when the shock comes on again, the dog goes through a shortened and more purposeful or adaptive version of the first howling-running behavior, and jumps over the barrier faster than before. After a few more trials, the dog stands poised at the barrier and leaps over at the instant of shock. Eventually it avoids shock altogether by jumping as soon as the lights dim.

However, if a dog receives inescapable shock in the harness 24 hours before escape training, its behavior is dramatically different. At the onset of the first shock in the box, the dog howls, runs around, defecates and urinates—but only for a few seconds. It then settles down and takes the shock, whining and howling but making few escape movements. Typically, it does not get across the barrier. (We terminate shock after 60 seconds if the dog doesn't jump.) On the second trial, the dog runs around a little, but soon stops; it again stands or sits, howling and whining. After a few more trials, the dog makes virtually no escape movements, and appears to have given up.

Occasionally, one of these passive or helpless dogs, after enduring three or four shocks, will jump over the barrier and escape shock. A naive dog's first escape response reliably predicts that it will continue to escape shock in increasingly adaptive ways. Most helpless dogs, however, do not catch on after one escape; they soon revert to taking shocks.

We have concerned ourselves with three questions about this striking phenomenon: (1) Why does it occur? (2) How can such passivity be cured once it has set in? (3) How can victims of inescapable shock be prevented from passively accepting subsequent trauma?

To find what causes helplessness, we must look closely at what a dog can do during inescapable shocks. It can turn its head, pull on the restraining straps, bark, wag its tail, etc. What these voluntary responses have in common is that they haven't the slightest effect on the shock.

Traditional learning theorists have supposed that animals could learn only two relations between their responses and rewards: either that a certain behavior produced a reward, or that the behavior no longer produced a reward, and was thus extinguished. We now think that animals can also *learn* a third relation—that in certain situations no response makes any difference. It is, we think, this third learning that is behind the seemingly unnatural passivity to trauma that the helpless dogs display.

What might be expected of a dog that learns that its entire response repertoire is irrelevant? Such a dog might simply stop trying to do anything about shock. We think our passive dogs just don't try because they have *learned* that it doesn't pay. Learning that reward and response are unconnected is an *active* form of learning, and as such can interfere with the learning of new relationships. This may account for the fact that when passive dogs do jump the barrier, they do not learn that their response has in fact produced shock termination.

We are suggesting therefore that it is not that trauma *per se* produces helplessness, but rather that helplessness results from a learned relationship to trauma; the animal has learned that trauma is always inescapable and uncontrollable. To test this idea, we worked with two groups of dogs in the harness. For one group, shock was independent of all responses. The other group could turn off shock merely by pressing panels beside their heads. We theorized that if dogs learned to stop shock by turning their heads, they later would escape and avoid shocks in the box. The group undergoing uncontrollable shocks would have learned, conversely, that they were helpless and would be passive or helpless in

the box. This is exactly what happened.

Learning that the environment cannot be controlled is central to developing the helplessness syndrome. This idea suggested to us that canine helplessness could be prevented and, once it happened, broken up.

Suppose a dog sits on one side of a box, session after session, and takes shock without trying to escape. How can you make it begin to respond successfully? Obviously, you must get it to learn that the relationship between its responses and shock termination could be one of control. We dropped meat on the other side of the barrier to encourage helpless dogs to escape shock; we took the barrier out altogether; we called to the dogs from the nonelectric side. Nothing worked. As a last resort, we pulled them back and forth across the box on leashes, forcibly demonstrating to them that movement in a certain direction ended shocks. This did the trick, but only after much dragging. Dogs so treated finally learned to escape shock on their own.

Modern psychotherapy uses retroactive measures almost exclusively; it attempts to cure ills that are well established. This has given the entire therapeutic discipline a pronounced backward-looking character. It's worth pointing out once again that some of the most spectacular successes in medicine have been scored with future-looking or preventive therapy; that is, with immunization. Could we immunize dogs against the effects of inescapable shock? If a dog's first experience with shock is with *controllable* shock, will this exposure in and of itself prevent later inescapable shock from producing helplessness? The answer is yes. If a dog first gets escapable shock in the box, and then gets uncontrollable shock in the harness, it will escape normally when it is returned to the box. Such a dog will also struggle much more in the harness than

naive dogs, trying to gain control over shock that actually is uncontrollable.

In actual or scientific and ethical terms, the distance is vast between the Archies and Mr. Thompsons on one hand and dogs in a box on the other. All such distances must be crossed by speculation or imagination; the most we can ask is that the imagination be educated, and that the speculation touch a few testable signposts.

Take Mr. Thompson. To what extent did his history of failure, of independence between what he did and what happened to him, cause his present state? To what extent would a lifetime of experience controlling his environment have prevented failure from reducing his response repertoire to nil? Could he even yet be cured by a leash-dragging technique similar to ours? Our analogy suggests that he might be. (It says nothing about whether he *ought* to be — whether we should undertake to deny the human mind its last refuge of dissolution or madness.) But the present way of treating patients like Mr. Thompson, with its emphasis on keeping them quiet and docile, only encourages passivity.

And Archie? From the cradle on, if mother (a combination of affection and intelligence) isn't around to feed you and change you when you cry, crying becomes an irrelevant response. (We might consider crying to be a kind of speech.) If affection and intelligence don't respond, whatever you try, then trying becomes irrelevant. Would it be possible to bypass parental neglect, and an entire generation of shamelessly incompetent teaching professionals, and teach the Archies of this world that there are many situations in which response does control the environment? Could we inoculate Archies against helplessness?

Our canine analog suggests very strongly, I think, that such immunization is possible.

The Computer as a Tutor   by Richard C. Atkinson

Last year, for the first time, a sizable number of children received most of their daily reading instruction from a computer. The children were first-grade students at the Brentwood School in East Palo Alto, most of whom came from culturally disadvantaged homes. By the end of the year, they not only had learned to read better than a companion group taught by teachers, but they had shown the project staff a considerable amount about computer-assisted instruction—about how and with what effect computer technology and learning theory can be combined and put into practice.

Concrete research in computer-assisted instruction is badly needed to balance the tremendous number of speculative reports that have appeared over the past few years. The Stanford Project has only begun—it is continuing this year with the new first grade—and much of the initial year must be considered a de-bugging period for both the computer system and the curriculum material. Nevertheless, the experience has provided us with solid data. My claims will be less grand than many that have been made for computer-assisted instruction, but they will be based on a substantial research effort.

Work on the Stanford Project began in 1964 under a grant from the Office of Education. The purpose of the project

was to develop and implement computer-assisted instruction courses in initial reading and mathematics. Because of our individual research interests, my colleague Patrick Suppes has worked on the mathematics curriculum and I have been responsible for the reading course.

When we began, no lesson material suitable for computerized instruction of either mathematics or reading had yet been developed, and an integrated computer system for instruction had not yet been designed and produced by a single manufacturer. Curricula and system have been developed together over the past three years, and each has had a decided influence on the other.

Three levels of computer-assisted in-

struction can be defined. The levels are not based on the type of hardware used, but principally on the complexity and sophistication of the interaction between the student and the system. An advanced student-system interaction may be achieved with a simple teletype terminal, and the most rudimentary interaction may require some highly sophisticated computer programming and elaborate student terminal devices.

At the simplest interactional level are the *drill-and-practice* systems that present a fixed, linear sequence of problems. Student errors may be corrected in a variety of ways, but no real-time decisions are made by the computer for modifying the flow of instructional material according to the student's response history. An example of drill-and-practice systems are the fourth-, fifth-, and sixth-grade programs in arithmetic and language arts that have been developed at Stanford University to supplement classroom instruction. These programs are being used by as many as 2000 students a day in California, Kentucky, and Mississippi; the entire network is controlled by one central computer located at Stanford University. It takes little imagination to see how such a system could be extended to cover the entire country.

At the other end of our scale of student-computer interactions are *dialogue* programs. The goal of the dialogue approach is to provide the richest possible interaction, one in which the student is free to construct natural-language responses, to ask questions in an unrestricted mode, and in general to exercise almost complete control over the sequence of learning events. Such programs are under development at several universities, but progress has been limited.

The third level of computer-assisted instruction lies between the drill-and-practice and the dialogue programs. Called *tutorial* programs, these have the capacity to modify the sequence of instructional material on the basis of a single response or some subset of the student's response history. Such programs allow students to follow separate and diverse learning paths through the curriculum, based on their individual performance records. The probability is high in a tutorial program that no two students will encounter exactly the same sequence of lesson materials. However, student responses still are quite restricted because they must be chosen from a prescribed set of responses or written so that a relatively simple text analysis will be sufficient for their evaluation.

The computer-assisted reading instruction program at Brentwood School is implemented on the Stanford Tutorial System, which was developed under a contract between Stanford University and the IBM Corporation. Subsequent developments by IBM of the basic system have led to what has been designated the IBM-1500 Instructional System, which soon should be commercially available.

The basic system consists of a central process computer with magnetic discs for memory storage, proctor stations for monitoring student performance, and 16 student stations. The central process computer acts as an intermediary between each student and his particular course material, which is stored in one of the memory discs. A student terminal consists of a film screen, a cathode ray display tube, a light-pen, a modified typewriter keyboard, and earphones. [*See illustration above.*]

The cathode ray tube is essentially a television screen on which letters, numbers, and simple line drawings can be generated under computer control. The film screen is a rear-view projection device which permits the display of still pictures in black and white or in color. Each film strip is stored in a self-threading cartridge and contains over 1000 images, any of which the computer may select very quickly for display. The audio

WHAT THE STUDENT SEES, HEARS, AND DOES. Above, a student hears a word pronounced and then sees it, both pictorially and in written form. Below, a student touches her light pen to the screen to tell the computer that she can read the word "cat."

messages are stored in tape cartridges which contain approximately two hours of messages and, like the film cartridge, may be changed very quickly. To gain the student's attention, an arrow can be generated on the cathode ray screen and moved in synchronization with an audio message to emphasize given words or phrases, much like the "bouncing ball" in sing-along films.

The main responding device used in the reading program is the light-pen, which is simply a light-sensitive probe. When the light-pen is placed on the cathode ray screen, the position touched is sensed and recorded by the computer. Responses also may be made on the typewriter keyboard. However, only limited use has been made of the keyboard in the reading program because we have not yet attempted to tackle the problem of teaching first-grade children to use a typewriter.

The sequence of events in the system is roughly as follows. The computer assembles the necessary commands for a

given instructional sequence from a disc-storage unit. The commands include directions to display a given sequence of symbols on the cathode ray screen, to present a particular image on the film screen, and to play a specific audio message. After the appropriate visual and auditory materials have been presented, a "ready" signal tells the student that a response is expected. The response is evaluated and, on the basis of this evaluation and the student's past history, the computer makes a decision as to what materials will be presented next.

The time-sharing feature of the system allows us to handle 16 students simultaneously and to cycle through these evaluative steps so rapidly that from the student's viewpoint it seems that he is getting immediate attention from the computer whenever he makes a response.

Our approach to computer-assisted reading instruction can be described as applied psycholinguistics. We began by formulating hypotheses about the reading process and the nature of learning

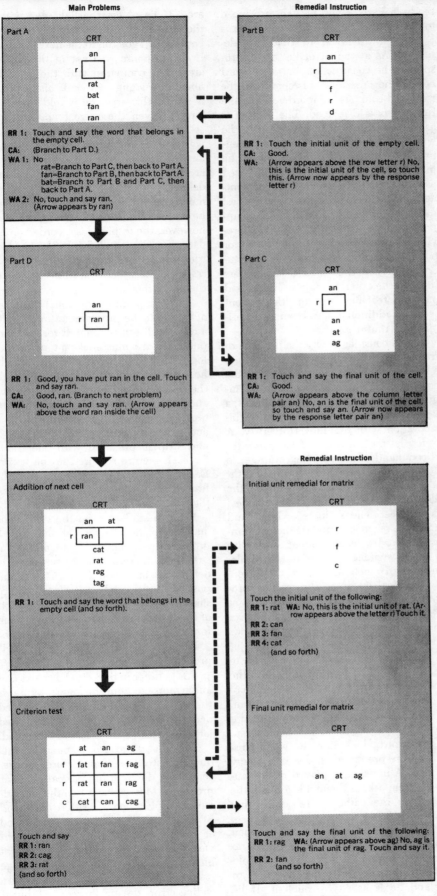

HOW THE STUDENT CONSTRUCTS A MATRIX. Each cell in a matrix is constructed individually by the process shown in Parts A through D. When the nine-cell matrix is complete, the student takes a criterion test (lower left) that covers all nine words.

to read, on the basis of linguistic information, observations of language use, and an analysis of the function of the written code. These hypotheses were tested—and then modified and retested—in a series of studies structured to simulate actual teaching situations. Very little curriculum material ever can be said to be the perfect end-product of rigorous empirical evaluation; however, we would claim that the fundamental tenets of the Stanford reading program are based on considerable empirical evidence, and they will be further modified as more data accumulates.

The instructional materials are divided into eight levels, each composed of about 32 lessons. The lessons are designed so that the average student will complete one in approximately 30 minutes, but this can vary greatly. Some students finish much sooner and others, if they hit most of the remedial material, can take two hours or more. Within a lesson, the various instructional tasks can be divided into three broad areas: decoding, comprehension, and games and other motivational devices.

Decoding involves such tasks as the identification of letters and strings of letters, word-list learning, and phonic drills. *Comprehension* involves such tasks as having the computer read to the child or having the child himself read sentences, paragraphs, or complete stories about which he then is asked a series of questions. The questions deal with the direct recall of facts, with generalizations about the main ideas in the story, and with inferential questions that require the child to relate to his own experience information presented in the story. Finally, many types of *games* are sequenced into the lessons, primarily to maintain the students' interest. The games are similar to those usually played in the classroom, and they are structured to enable the computer to evaluate the developing reading skills of the child.

Let us consider an example of what a student sees, hears, and does on one of the decoding tasks in a lesson [*see illustration at left*]. This task, called "matrix construction," provides practice in learning to associate orthographically similar sequences with appropriate rhyme and alliteration patterns. Rhyming patterns are presented in the columns of the matrix and alliteration patterns are presented in the rows of the matrix. The matrix is constructed one cell at a time. The initial consonant of a consonant-vowel-consonant word is called the initial unit, and the vowel and the final

131

consonant are called the final unit. The intersection of an initial unit row and a final unit column determines the entry in any given cell.

The problem format for the construction of each cell is divided into four parts: Parts A and D are standard instructional sections, and Parts B and C are remedial sections. Parts B and C are branches from Part A, and may be presented independently or in combination.

On the cathode ray screen the student first sees an empty cell with its associated initial and final units and an array of response choices. He hears a message to touch and say the word that belongs in the empty cell. If the student makes the correct response, in this case touches *ran* with his light-pen, he proceeds to Part D, where he sees the word written in the cell and is told "Good, you have put *ran* in the cell. Touch and say *ran.*"

The array of multiple-choice responses in Part A is designed to identify three types of errors: final unit incorrect; initial unit incorrect; both initial and final unit incorrect.

If in Part A the student responds with *fan* instead of *ran,* he is branched to remedial instruction (Part B), where attention is focused on the initial unit of the cell. If a correct response is made in the remedial section, the student is returned to the beginning for a second attempt. If an incorrect response is made in the remedial section, an arrow is displayed on the screen to indicate the correct response, which the student then is asked to touch.

If in Part A the student responds with *rat* instead of *ran,* he is branched to remedial instruction (Part C) on the final unit of the cell. The procedure is similar. However, it should be noted that in the remedial instruction the initial letter never is pronounced by the audio system, whereas the final unit always is pronounced. If the student responds in Part A with *bat* instead of *ran,* then he has made an error on both the initial and the final unit, and he is branched through both sets of remedial instruction.

When the student returns to the beginning after completing a remedial section, a correct response will advance him to Part D. If a wrong response is made on the second attempt, an arrow is placed beside the correct response area and held there until a correct response is made. If the next response is still an error, a message is sent to the proctor terminal and the sequence is repeated from the beginning.

When a student has responded correctly in Parts A and D, he is advanced to the next cell of the matrix, which is a problem identical to that just described. As a student makes correct responses, he constructs a matrix of word cells. When the matrix is complete, the rows and columns are reordered and the full matrix is displayed. The student is asked in a criterion test to identify the words in the cells. He completes the entire test without interruption, even if he makes mistakes. Errors are categorized as initial, final, and other. If the percentage of total errors on the criterion test exceeds a predetermined value, then appropriate remedial exercises are provided. After working through one or both of the remedial sections, the student is branched back for a second pass through the criterion matrix. The second pass is a teaching run, and the student receives additional correction and optimization routines.

Let us consider briefly the problem of translating the curriculum materials into a language that can be understood by the computer. The particular computer language we use is called Coursewriter II, a language developed by IBM in close collaboration with Stanford University. A coded lesson is a series of Coursewriter II commands that cause the computer to display and manipulate text on the cathode ray screen, display images on the film screen, position and play audio messages, accept and evaluate keyboard and light-pen responses, update the performance record of each student, and, with a set of switches and counters, implement the branching logic of the lesson.

A typical lesson in the reading program, which takes the average student about 30 minutes to complete, requires more than 9000 Coursewriter commands for its execution.

An example from a task designed to teach both letter discrimination and the meaning of words will illustrate some of the complexities of the coding problem. A picture illustrating the word being taught is presented on the film screen. Three words, including the word illustrated, are presented on the cathode ray screen. A message is played on the audio system asking the child to touch the word on the cathode ray screen that matches the picture on the film screen. Using the light-pen, the student then can make his response. If he makes no response within 30 seconds, he is told the correct answer, an arrow points to it, and he is asked to touch it. If he makes a response within the time limit, the point that he touches is compared by the computer with the correct-answer

area. If he places the light-pen within the correct area, he is told that he was correct, and goes on to the next problem. If the response was not in the correct area, it is compared with the area defined as a wrong answer. If his response is within this area, he is told that it is wrong, given the correct answer, and asked to touch it. If his initial response was neither in the anticipated wrong-answer area nor in the correct-answer area, then the student has made an undefined answer. He is given the same message that he would have heard had he touched a defined wrong answer; however, the response is recorded on his data record as undefined. The student tries again until he makes the correct response, at which time he goes on to the next problem.

To prepare an instructional sequence of this sort, the programmer must write a detailed list of commands for the computer. He also must make a tape recording of all the messages the student might hear during the lesson in approximately the order in which they will occur. Each audio message has an address on the tape that enables the computer to find and play it when required. Similarly, a film strip is prepared with one frame for each picture required in the lesson. Each frame has an address and the frames can be presented in any order. [See illustrations, page 134.]

While a student is on the system, he may complete as many as five to ten problems per minute. If all of the instructional material had to be coded in detail, the task would be virtually impossible. Fortunately, there are ways of simplifying the coding procedure if parts of the instructional materials are alike in format and differ only in specified ways.

For example, the "bag" and "card" problems [see illustration bottom left, p. 134] differ in the actual displays and audio messages, but the logical format is the same. They therefore can be defined once, given a two-letter name, and used later by giving a brief macro command.

The use of macro commands cuts down greatly the effort required to present many different but basically similar problems. Macros have two distinct advantages over codes written command by command. The first is ease and speed of coding: the call of one macro is obviously easier than writing the comparable string of code. The second advantage is increase in accuracy: not only are coding errors drastically reduced, but if the macro is defective or needs to be changed, every occurrence of it in the lesson can be corrected by modifying

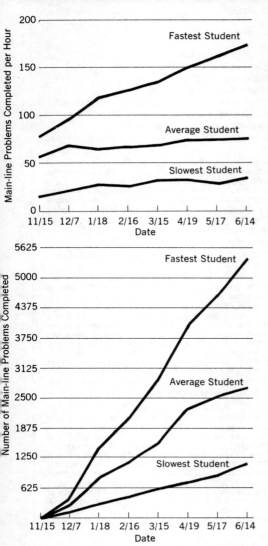

By the end of the year, the fastest students had completed some 4,000 more problems than the slowest students (top), and their speed continued rising steadily (bottom).

the original macro. The more standard the various problem formats, the more valuable the use of macros becomes. Approximately 92 per cent of our reading curriculum has been programmed using about 110 basic macros.

A bank of switches and counters in the computer keeps a running record on each student. Our program includes enough switches and counters to allow some quite sophisticated schemes for optimizing the teaching routines. For instance, we can present a series of words, and require five consecutive correct responses to each of the words. Or we can select for presentation certain phrases which previously have produced the greatest number of errors. As a consequence of decisions like these, each student pursues a fundamentally different path through the reading materials.

Computer-assisted instruction began at the Brentwood School in November of 1966. We selected this school partly be-

cause it was large enough to provide a sample of well over 100 first-grade students, partly because the students were primarily from culturally disadvantaged homes, and partly because the past performance of the school's principal and faculty had demonstrated a willingness to undertake educational innovations. Half the first-grade students received computer-assisted instruction in reading, and the other half, which functioned as a control group, was taught reading by a teacher in the classroom. However, the children in the control group were not left out of the computer project; they received their mathematics instruction from the computer.

Within the lesson material there are a core of problems that we have called main-line problems, meaning problems over which each student must exhibit some form of mastery. Main-line problems may be branched around by passing certain screening tests; they may be met and solved; or they may be met with incorrect responses, in which case the student is branched to remedial material.

At the end of the first year of the project, the fastest student had completed over 4000 more main-line problems than the slowest student. We also found that the rate of progress, as measured by the number of main-line problems solved per hour, was essentially constant for the median and slow students, but showed a steady increase for the fast students [*see illustrations at left*]. Whether this last result is unique to our particular curriculum or is characteristic of computer-assisted instruction needs further investigation.

Differences in rate of progress through the curriculum must not be confused with the rate of response to individual questions. The difference in response rate among students was very small. The average response rate was approximately four per minute and was not correlated with a student's rate of progress through the curriculum. The differences in total number of main-line problems completed can be accounted for by the amount of remedial material, the optimization routines, and the number of accelerations for the different students. From the standpoint of both the rate of progress and the total number of problems completed during the year, the computer curriculum appears to be quite responsive to individual differences.

It has been a common finding that girls generally acquire reading skills more rapidly than boys. The sex differences in reading performance have been attributed, at least in part, to the social

organization of the classroom, and to the value and reward systems of female primary-grade teachers. It also has been argued on developmental grounds that first-grade girls are more facile in visual memorization than boys of the same age, and that this facility aids the girls in the sight-word method commonly used in primary readers.

If these two arguments are correct, then one would expect that placing students in a computer-assisted environment and using a curriculum which emphasizes analytic skills instead of memorization by rote would minimize sex differences in reading. To test this hypothesis, the rate-of-progress scores in our program were evaluated for differences according to sex. The result, which was rather surprising, is that there was no difference between male and female students in rate of progress through the computer curriculum.

We also wanted to see whether sex differences affected accuracy. On four standard types of problems—letter identification, word-list learning, matrix construction, and sentence comprehension—the only difference between boys and girls that was statistically significant was for word-list learning.

These results, while not conclusive, do lend support to the notion that when students are removed from the normal classroom environment and given computer instruction, boys perform as well as girls in overall rate of progress.

The results also suggest that with computer-assisted instruction the sex difference is minimized as the emphasis moves toward analysis and away from rote memorization. The one kind of problem on which the girls achieved significantly higher scores than the boys, word-list learning, is essentially a memorization task.

How did the computer-instructed first-graders compare with the control group? Both groups were tested extensively before the project began and again near the end of the school year. The two groups were not significantly different at the start of the year, but at the end of the year the group that received computer-assisted reading instruction performed significantly better on almost all of the reading achievement tests, including the California Reading Test, the Gates-MacGinitie Test and the Hartley.

The average Stanford-Binet IQ score for the students (both experimental and control) was 89. There was considerable variation, but by and large these were not exceptional or gifted children. Students, teachers, and parents reacted quite favorably to the introduction of computer-assisted instruction into the classroom.

Initially, students were given only a few minutes per day on the teaching machines. The time was increased to 20 minutes after the first six weeks; in the last month we allowed students 30 to 35 minutes. We wanted to determine how well first-grade students would adapt to machine instruction for relatively long periods of time. We found that they adapt quite well, and this year we have been using 30-minute periods for all students. This may see like a long session for a first-grader, but our observations suggest that their span of attention is well over a half-hour if the programming is dynamic and responsive to their inputs.

Various optimization routines were evaluated during the year. These evaluations, in turn, have suggested a number of experiments and analyses that might be profitable. Such analyses, combined with the potential for additional research under the highly controlled conditions offered by computerized instruction, could lay the groundwork for a theory of instruction truly useful to the educator. The theory will have to be based on a highly structured model of the learning process, and it must generate optimization strategies that are compatible with the goals of education. The development of a viable theory of instruction is a major scientific undertaking, and substantial progress in this direction could well be one of psychology's most important contributions to society. ♫

or in macro format . . .

Problem 1	CM PW]F01]bat]bag]rat]A01]
	ABCD1]A04]A02]A03]7]1,7,3,18]C1]
Problem 2	CM PW]F02]card]cart]hard]]
	ABCD2]A07]A05]A06]5]1,5,4,18]C2]

what it is to say and show to the student.

Audio information	
Address	**Message**
A01	Touch and say the word that goes with the picture.
A02	Good. Bag. Do the next one.
A03	No.
A04	The word that goes with the picture is bag. Touch and say bag.
A05	Good. Card. Do the next one.
A06	No.
A07	The word that goes with the picture is card. Touch and say card.
Film Strip	
Address	**Picture**
F01	Picture of a bag.
F02	Picture of a card.

Computer Commands	Explanation
PR	**Problem** Prepares machine for beginning of new problem.
LD 0/S1	**Load** Loads zero into the error switch (S1).
FP F01	**Film Position** Displays frame F01 (picture of a bag):
DT 5,18/bat/	**Display Text** Displays "bat" on line 5 starting in column 18 on the CRT.
DT 7,18/bag/	Displays "bag" on line 7 starting in column 18 on the CRT.
DT 9,18/rat/	Displays "rat" on line 9 starting in column 18 on the CRT.
AUP A01	**Audio Play** Plays audio message A01. "Touch and say the word that goes with the picture."
L1 EP 30/ABCD1	**Enter and Process** Activates the light-pen; specifies the time limit (30 sec.) and the problem identifier (ABCD1) that will be placed in the data record along with all responses to this problem. If a response is made within the time limit the computer skips from this command down to the CA (correct answer comparison) command. If no response is made within the time limit, the commands immediately following the EP command are executed.
AD 1/C4	**Add** Adds one to the overtime counter (C4).
LD 1/S1	Loads one into the error switch (S1).
AUP A04	**Plays message A04** "The word that goes with the picture is bag. Touch and say bag."
DT 7,16/→/	**Displays arrow** on line 7, column 16 (arrow pointing at "bag").
BR L1	**Branch** Branches to command labeled L1. The computer will now do that command and continue from that point.
CA 1,7,3,18/C1	**Correct Answer** Compares student's response with an area one line high starting on line 7 and three columns wide starting in column 18 of the CRT. If his response falls within this area, it will be recorded in the data with the answer identifier C1. When a correct answer has been made, the commands from here down to WA (wrong answer comparison) are executed. Then the program jumps ahead to the next PR. If the response does not fall in the correct area, the machine skips from this command down to the WA command.
BR L2/S1/1	Branches to command labeled L2 if the error switch (S1) is equal to one.
AD 1/C1	Adds one to the initial correct answer counter (C1).
L2 AUP A02	**Plays audio message A02** "Good. Bag. Do the next one."
WA 1,5,3,18/W1	**Wrong Answer** These two commands compare the student response with
WA 1,9,3,18/W2	the areas of the two wrong answers, that is, the area one line high starting on line 5 and three columns wide starting in column 18, and the area one line high starting on line 9 and three columns wide starting in column 18. If the response falls within one of these two areas, it will be recorded with the appropriate identifier (W1 or W2). When a defined wrong answer has been made, the commands from here down to UN (undefined answer) are executed. Then the computer goes back to the EP for this problem. If the response does not fall in one of the defined wrong answer areas, the machine skips from this command down to the UN command.
AD 1/C2	Adds one to the defined wrong answer counter (C2).
L3 LD 1/S1	Loads one into the error switch (S1).
AUP A03	**Plays message A03** "No."
AUP A04	**Plays message A04** "The word that goes with the picture is bag. Touch and say bag."
DT 7,16/→/	**Display arrow** on line 7, column 16.
UN	**Undefined Wrong Answer** If machine reaches this point in the program, the student has made neither a correct nor a defined wrong answer.
AD 1/C3	Adds one to the undefined answer counter (C3).
BR L3	Branches to command labeled L3. (The same thing should be done for both UN and WA answers. This branch saves repeating the commands from L3 down to UN.)
PR	**Prepares the machine for next problem**
LD 0/S1	These commands prepare the display for the second problem. Notice
FP F02	the new film position and new words displayed. The student was told
DT 5,18/card/	to "do the next one" when he finished the last problem so he needs
DT 7,18/cart/	no audio message to begin this.
DT 9,18/hard/	
L4 EP 30/ABCD2	**Light-pen is activated**
AD 1/C4	These commands are done only if no response is made in the time limit
LD 1/S1	of 30 seconds. Otherwise the machine skips to the CA command.
AUP A07	
DT 5,16/→/	
BR L4	
CA 1,5,4,18/C2	**Compares response with correct answer area**
BR L5/S1/1	Adds one to the initial correct answer counter unless the error switch
AD 1/C1	(S1) shows that an error has been made for this problem. The student
L5 AUP A05	is told he is correct and goes on to the next problem. These commands are executed only if a correct answer has been made.
WA 1,7,4,18/W3	**Compares response with defined wrong answer**
WA 1,9,4,18/W4	
AD 1/C2	Adds one to the defined wrong answer area and the error switch (S1) is
L6 LD 1/S1	loaded with one to show that an error has been made on this problem.
AUP A06	The student is told he is wrong and shown the correct answer and
AUP A07	asked to touch it. These commands are executed only if a defined
DT 5,16/→/	wrong answer has been made.
UN	**An undefined response has been made if the machine reaches this command**
AD 1/C3	Adds one to the undefined answer counter and we branch up to give the
BR L6	same audio, etc. as is given for the defined wrong answer.

NEURAL BASIS OF MEMORY

By J. Anthony Deutsch

At present the physiological basis of learning is unknown. We know that time alters the stability of memory, and this alteration presumably reflects in some way the underlying physical process. Many theories have been advanced to explain these changes, but only recently have discoveries been made that permit us to test the validity of the theories.

An old but still influential theory, put forward by an Italian physiologist, E. Tanzi, in 1893, postulates that the passage of nerve impulses causes some kind of physical change in the connections between nerve cells. The connections between the nerve cells, or neurons, are called synapses. While it is possible to show in the laboratory that the *functioning* of synapses can be affected by excessive use or disuse, these experiments do not show that changes occur in actual *learning*. A different kind of evidence is needed to show this, and I shall describe how such evidence has been obtained in some of my recent research.

We know that whatever changes produce the physical basis of memory, at least some of them must occur relatively slowly. Remarkable evidence for this comes from everyday accidents. For example, a person who has struck his head violently in an automobile accident may suffer from retrograde amnesia. He may be unable to remember what happened during the week before the accident, but he is able to remember what happened two weeks, two months or two years before. The gap in memory covers a continuous stretch of time, with one end anchored to the time of the accident. As memories return, those most distant in time always return first.

This indicates that as a memory gets older it becomes more difficult to dislodge. So the physical change that underlies memory must alter slowly with time. If this change is an alteration in the *sensitivity* of a synapse, then it should be possible to show this by the use of drugs.

To understand how this can be done,

we must briefly sketch what happens at a synapse when a message is transmitted from one nerve cell to another. The synapse is a microscopic gap (a few hundred angstroms, or less than a millionth of an inch) between adjacent neurons. Inside the neuron itself, a message is transmitted as an electrical impulse or disturbance. When this traveling electrical impulse reaches the synaptic region, it triggers the release of a chemical substance from vesicles at the end of the nerve cell. This chemical transmitter then travels across the narrow synaptic cleft to the receiving nerve cell. The chemical transmitter fits into certain sites on the second nerve cell as a key fits into a lock, mainly because the transmitter molecules have a specific size and shape.

The transmitter, it is believed, depolarizes the membrane of the receptor cell and initiates a new electrical impulse in the second neuron. The electrical impulse then travels along the neuron to the next synapse, triggering the release of a chemical transmitter, and so on [*see illustrations, page 137*].

There are many different types of synapses in the brain, and they may use different kinds of transmitters, such as acetylcholine or norepinephrine (a chemical related to adrenalin). One of the best understood synapses uses acetylcholine (ACh) as the transmitter. ACh is present in relatively high concentration throughout the central nervous system. One of the strange things about this transmitter is that when too much of it accumulates on the synaptic part of the receptor cell, the transfer of messages across that synapse is blocked. To prevent a breakdown in transmission across the synapse, ACh must be inactivated as soon as it has performed its function. This is accomplished by an enzyme called acetylcholinesterase (AChE), which rapidly destroys ACh after it has been ejected.

There are two classes of drugs that interfere with synaptic activity, each in a distinctive way. One kind acts directly on the receptor nerve cells, while the other interferes with the destruction of the transmitter. The first kind is called

RAT IN A MAZE. In laboratory studies of the learning process, a rat is trained to choose the correct branch of a Y-maze either to escape an electrical shock or reach a reward of some kind. It takes about 30 trials for a rat to make 10 correct decisions in a row.

the anticholinergic drugs, or blocking agents. These drugs fit into the same sites on the receptor nerve cells as does ACh. However, although these blocking agents fit into the same sites, they do not initiate an electrical impulse in the second neuron. In addition, these blocking agents are not rapidly destroyed by the enzyme AChE. This means that the drugs can put parts of receptor cells out of action. The larger the dose of a blocking agent, the more sites are inactivated. The effect of the blocking agent, then, is to subtract from the effectiveness of the transmitter ACh.

A number of blocking agents are found in plants. Scopolamine is found in henbane, whose effects were known to the ancient Greeks. In high doses, scopolamine is a nerve poison: it completely stops transmission across synapses. In lower doses it simply reduces the amount of transmission and can be used medicinally to relieve such disorders as stomach cramps. Atropine, another blocking agent, is found in the deadly nightshade or belladona plant. In low doses, it is used to relieve muscular spasms and to dilate the pupil of the eye.

Drugs of the second kind that affect transmission across the synapse are the anticholinesterases, or inhibitors of the enzyme AChE. Since the function of AChE is to destroy the transmitter chemical ACh, inactivation of AChE will lead to an accumulation of ACh at the receiving sites of the synapse. As indicated previously, accumulation of too much transmitter at the receptor will block the synapse.

Another interesting effect of inhibitor drugs occurs when a neuron ejects too little transmitter to trigger an electrical impulse in the receptor cell. With the addition of the enzyme inhibitor, the transmitter is destroyed less rapidly and the amount of transmitter at the receptor cell builds up until it triggers an electrical impulse in that nerve cell.

This boosting effect is used in the medical treatment of myasthenia gravis, a disorder marked by progressive weakening of the muscles. A patient with this disorder may be unable to move, even though there is nothing physically wrong with his nerves or his muscles. The muscular weakness is caused by the release of too little ACh at the junction between nerve endings and muscles. By inactivating the enzyme that destroys the transmitter, enough of the transmitter can build up at the receptor sites to initiate muscle contraction, and paralysis disap-

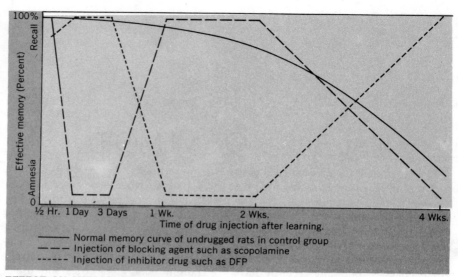

EFFECT ON MEMORY. Results from rat experiments in Y-mazes show how two types of drugs—blocking agents (anticholinergics) and inhibitors (anticholinesterases)—can each produce amnesia or recall, depending upon the time of injection after learning.

pears. However, the dose of the inhibitor drug is critical. If the dose is too large, too much of the transmitter will pile up at the receptor sites, causing a block, and paralysis will return.

We therefore have drugs that enable us to track changes in the efficiency of transmission across a synapse. Blocking agents, or anticholinergics, can completely stop transmission when relatively small amounts of transmitter are released. Yet this same dose of a blocking agent should not interfere with transmission when the amount of transmitter is high. On the other hand, addition of drugs that inhibit the action of the enzyme AChE, which destroys the transmitter, should not hinder transmission when levels of the transmitter are low. In fact, enzyme inhibitors may even improve transmission in this situation. But when the level of transmitter is high, the same dose of inhibitor should block transmission because of the excessive build-up of transmitter at the receptor sites.

Another way of looking at this is to suppose that learning causes changes in the *sensitivity* of the receptor cell rather than changes in the amount of transmitter released. In some respects, this is a more attractive explanation, but we will follow both interpretations in our guided tour of some of my laboratory experiments to discover the physical basis of learning.

In one set of experiments, I studied the effect of drugs on learning in rats: a rat is placed in a maze on a mildly electrified grid. To escape from the electrical shock, the rat must choose whether to run into a lit alley or into a dark alley.

If it runs into the lit alley it escapes the shock. If it runs into the dark alley, the shock continues. It takes about 30 trials for a rat to learn to choose the lit alley. In these studies, learning is defined as the ability to make 10 correct decisions in a row.

After a number of rats have passed the learning test, they are put back into their cages. The rats are divided into several groups. Some are injected with a drug half an hour after the learning trials, others after one day, three days, seven days, or 14 days. A control group does not receive any drugs. Although the rats receive their drug treatment at various times after learning, they all are tested at the same time interval after the drug injection.

It should be noted that the drug doses used in the experiments cause no apparent change in the rats' ability to learn. Groups of rats injected with the drug will later perform as well as untreated rats in learning tests.

When rats are injected with an inhibitor drug, such as diisopropyl fluorophosphate (DFP) or physostigmine, which inactivates the AChE enzyme that destroys the ACh transmitter in synapses, some interesting changes in memory occur.

Rats injected with the drug half an hour after the learning trials forget only a little. They take more trials to relearn the maze than rats from the control group, but require far fewer trials to learn than rats that have never been trained.

When rats are injected with the inhibitor drug one and three days after training, they show perfect retention of learning. But rats treated with the drug seven and 14 days after training lose their memory of the training almost completely. A control group of rats not drug injected, still remembers to choose the lit alley after seven or 14 days.

We might conclude that the inhibitor drug causes premature forgetting. However, this is too hasty a conclusion. If we retest undrugged rats four weeks after they have learned to run the maze, we find that they have forgotten which path to take. But if we then inject them with an inhibitor drug in the same dose as previously caused forgetting, the rats regain their memory almost perfectly. In this case, the injected drug could be called a "memory improver."

We know that the injected drug prevents the enzyme AChE in the synapse from destroying the chemical transmitter after it has been ejected. From these experiments, we can draw the following conclusions. After one day, the amount of transmitter released in the synapse is relatively small (or we could say that the sensitivity of the receptor cell is low). At three days, the amount is still low, since injection of an enzyme inhib-

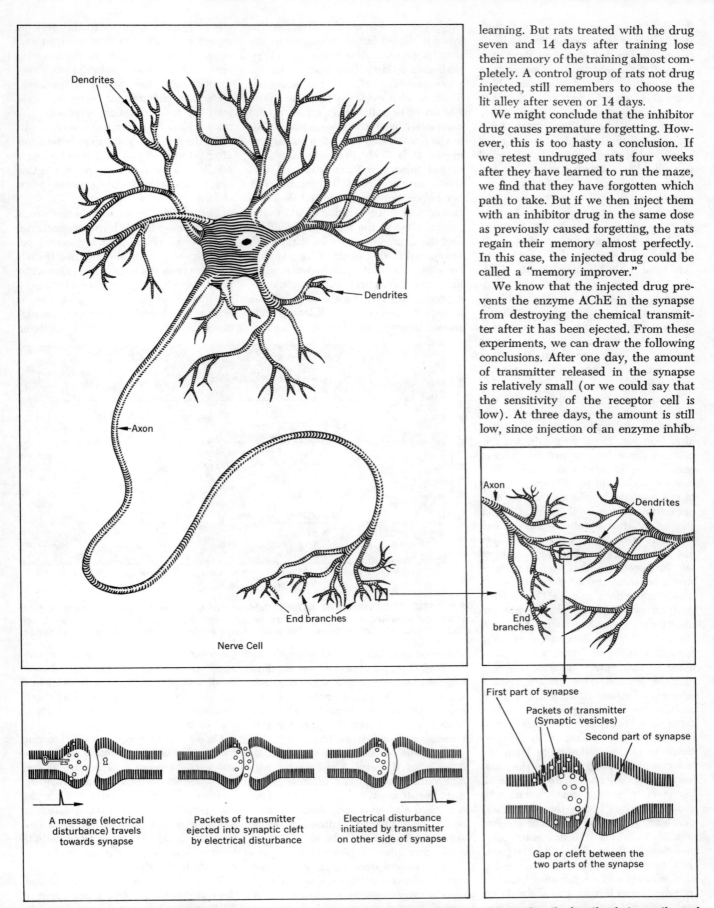

NEURAL PATHWAY. A message travels along a nerve cell (top) as an electrical impulse until it reaches the junction between the end branches of one neuron and dendrites of another. At the synapse, electrical impulse triggers release of a chemical transmitter.

137

itor does not cause a pile-up of enough transmitter at the receptor sites to block the synapse. But at seven days, the amount of transmitter (or sensitivity of the receptor) rises and remains high even at 14 days. Injection of the drug causes a pile-up of transmitter at the receptor and blocks the synapse. After four weeks, the level of transmitter (or sensitivity of the receptor) has dropped to such a low point that the rat has forgotten the learned task. Injection of the drug, however, enables the small amount of transmitter still present to become effective and the rat regains its memory.

These conclusions can be cross-checked by repeating the experiments, this time with blocking agents—drugs that fit into the same sites on the receptor cell as the ACh transmitter. A blocking agent such as scopolamine should abolish memory where we have concluded that synaptic transmission is weak, and leave recall unaffected in cases where we suppose that transmission is high.

In repeating the experiment with scopolamine, we found that memory is unaffected by a drug injection half an hour after learning. But a drug injection one or three days later completely knocks out memory of what was learned. This is what we would predict on the basis of our previous conclusion that the synaptic transmission level is low at one or three days after learning. At seven and 14 days, injection of scopolamine does not affect memory. This also confirms our interpretation that transmission is strong at seven and 14 days.

We can check our conclusion that synaptic transmission gradually improves during the week after learning without the use of drugs. Rats are given only a small number of learning trials in a maze so that correct choices are only partially learned. The rats are divided into several groups. Each group is given a different waiting period—one day, three days, five days, etc.—before it is brought back to the maze. In this session, the rats are allowed to learn the task completely, and we count the number of trials they need to do so. We find, interestingly enough, that the rats who wait seven days before the second session learn with a much smaller number of trials than rats who are tested after one day or three days. This suggests that there is spontaneous strengthening of memory in rats a week after learning.

If our theory is right, one of the things we can expect is that drug-induced disappearance of memory will be tempo-

rary. The action of the drug on the synapse should last only as long as the drug is present. And a number of experiments do show that memory returns when the effect of the drug wears off. There is also evidence that the inhibitor drugs, or anticholinesterases, do not completely inactivate the enzyme AChE in the dose strengths used in our experiments. It is likely that only a portion of the enzyme is inactivated and that the destruction of ACh transmitter is not halted but simply slowed down. If this is so, then the spacing of trials after the injection of the inhibitor should affect the degree of amnesia. If the trials are spaced farther apart, more transmitter should be destroyed between trials. Since too much transmitter at the receptor causes the block in the synapse, increased spacing of a well-learned task should improve recall. And, indeed, it

are millions of neurons in the nervous system and each neuron may have thousands of synapses on it. In the synaptic region, the neurons are intricately intertwined, much like a mass of spaghetti. Detecting changes made by a single learning task is almost impossible. A major difficulty is finding a way to observe the same set of synapses before and after learning—a task similar to finding a needle in a haystack, except that in this case we are trying to find a specific piece of hay.

Fortunately, we can again use drugs to determine whether learning affects the same set of synapses or a different set of synapses on each learning trial. If each trial increases the transmission across the same set of synapses, then the larger the number of learning trials (the more learned the habit), the greater the susceptibility of that learning to inhibitor

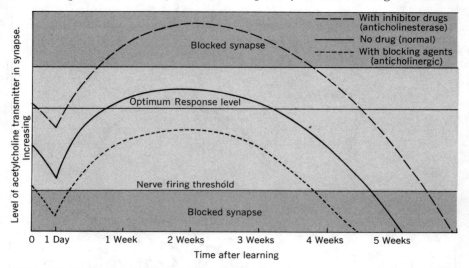

SYNAPTIC TRANSMISSION MODEL. Middle curve shows changes in synapse after learning. Inhibitor drug (*top curve*) or blocking agent (*bottom curve*) can block transmission at certain times. This model helps explain the drugs' paradoxical action.

turns out that this is what happens. In tests of drug-injected rats seven days after the learning session, when the trials are spaced 25 seconds apart, the rats exhibit almost total amnesia. When the trials are set 50 seconds apart, the rats remember their learned task.

From the results of our experiments, it looks as if learning changes a synapse's ability to transmit messages. Our experiments consisted of a large number of trials, and each learning trial could have affected a different set of synapses. On the other hand, each trial could have affected the same set of synapses over and over again. We cannot observe changes in the synapses directly, even with an electron microscope. A typical synapse may measure as little as one millionth of an inch in size. There

blocking. Also, if the same set of synapses is affected by learning, then a small number of learning trials should produce weak transmissions and therefore memory will improve with injection of the inhibitor drugs.

On the other hand, if each learning trial simply changes another set of synapses until enough synapses are altered to ensure correct performance, then the number of trials should not alter the susceptibility of the learned habit to blocking by an inhibitor drug. Each synapse will be altered in an all-or-nothing fashion, and each should be equally susceptible to the drug.

To test these two ideas, we trained three groups of rats. One group received 30 training trials, the second 70 trials, and the third 110 trials. The rats with only 30 trials could be considered undertrained. In their last 10 trials, they chose the correct path only two out of three times. Five days later, half of the rats in each group were given a dose of diisopropyl fluorophosphate, a drug that inhibits the AChE enzyme. The undertrained group injected with the drug performed very much better than their undertrained counterparts who were not given the drug. In their first 10 trials, the drug-treated rats performed almost perfectly. Drugged and undrugged rats from the group with 70 trials performed identically. Overtrained rats (110 trials) injected with the drug, however, performed much worse than their undrugged counterparts, and even worse than the undertrained rats that had been drugged.

In other words, a well-learned habit is blocked by injection of this drug, whereas recall of a poorly learned habit is improved. This indicates that the same set of synapses is stimulated more and more with each learning trial.

To show that the results had nothing to do with the *number* of trials but rather were concerned with the degree of learning, we performed another experiment in which the number of learning trials was the same for all rats. This was done by taking advantage of the rat's propensity to learn more quickly when the light in the safe alley of the maze is very bright. Groups of rats were given the same number of trials, but variations in the brightness of the light in the safe alley led to very different rates of learning. The group with a dim light had learned very little at the end of 30 trials, while a group with a very bright light had learned to make the right choice almost every time. Injection of the inhibitor drug produced the same results: the group with the well-learned habit forgot, the group with the poorly-learned habit performed better.

This seems to confirm that the same set of synapses is affected as learning of the same task progresses. The same synapses are stimulated more and more with each trial. As a result of this stimulation, the synapse becomes gradually more efficient at passing messages. This increase in efficiency occurs without any apparent need for practice or repetition of the learned responses.

Our evidence supports the theory that the physical change underlying learning is the increase of transmission efficiency in a synapse. But our experiments do not provide enough information to decide whether the increased efficiency is caused by increased sensitivity in the receptor or increased amounts of transmitter in the synapse.

We can, however, set up an experiment that will identify the correct explanation. There is a class of drugs that mimics the transmitter action of acetylcholine. One of these drugs is carbachol (carbaminoylcholine), a very close chemical relative of ACh. Carbachol is strongly resistant to destruction by the AChE enzyme. When injected in low doses, carbachol acts together with ACh to excite the receptor nerve. Higher doses of carbachol will block memory. Results of research to date indicate that injections of carbachol will improve new memories but block older ones. When the amount of transmitter is small, the injected carbachol teams up with it to improve memory. When the memory is one week old, if we assume that the amount of transmitter increases, then it is hard to explain why the same dose of carbachol results in a blocked synapse. It is unlikely that the increased amount of transmitter would cause the block, because the transmitter would be destroyed at the normal rate by the AChE enzyme. A more likely explanation is that the receptor becomes more sensitive (requires less transmitter to become activated) and that the carbachol blocks synaptic transmission because it alone can now keep the sensitized receptor nerve cell depolarized, which prevents initiation of new electrical impulses in that neuron.

So, although we have good evidence that learning improves transmission across synapses that use ACh as a transmitter, the evidence that this improvement is caused by an increase in the sensitivity of the receptor is much more tentative.

These findings suggest that some human memory disorders may be due to a lowered efficiency in transmission across synapses, particularly those using ACh as the transmitter. If this proves to be the case, some memory disorders may be improved with relatively simple drugs. But in spite of the effect of our drugs on the memory of rats, we have discovered no memory pill. While one day such a drug might be developed, it is not likely to be one of those used in our research. All these drugs are potent poisons; their effects are mixed—they improve some memories while blocking others—and their effects are transitory. Seekers for a pill to end practice and study forever will have to look elsewhere.

I'll

NEVER FORGET dear old what's his name.

The fact that we forget things important to us is a source of embarrassment and irritation, to say nothing of inefficiency. Forgetting has also been a source of some irritation to psychologists, who are only slowly beginning to understand it.

Hermann Ebbinghaus completed the first studies of forgetting just before the end of the 19th century. Using himself as a subject. Ebbinghaus investigated how much we forget over a period of time. In order to slow down the learning and to avoid unwanted associations with familiar language, Ebbinghaus would learn a series of nonsense syllables (meaningless consonant-vowel-consonant combinations), and then try to recall them after varying periods of time. His famous forgetting curve showed large amounts of forgetting over the first few hours after learning, followed by progressively less loss over ensuing days and weeks.

Ebbinghaus' classic research demonstrated that forgetting occurred in a reliable, orderly fashion. A practical question was how to prevent forgetting, or at least slow it down. Ebbinghaus also had some suggestions there. His main prescription, supported by his evidence, was that forgetting could be reduced by overlearning the material originally, beyond the point of mastery; he also prescribed reviving and rehearsing the material every now and then before its final use. These prescriptions are clearly well taken and underlie most school study guides, which cite the need for periodic reviews for refreshing one's memory.

A second practical question is whether memorizing is a skill that can be improved by special means. Research suggests that the ability to remember is indeed a skill, one on which individuals differ reliably and consistently, and that there are a few clearly specifiable components or subskills to this overall ability. People can be taught some of these skills. As an elementary example, one component of the skill of learning people's names during introductions is that we must first explicitly attend to and register the name clearly as it is told to us. Most of us fail at this initial and most elementary step because we are preoccupied with the other tasks demanded by the occasion—shaking hands, smiling, planning the conversation ahead, or anticipating the next person to be met. In our preoccupation, the name fails to register clearly. So a first prescription would be that if you want to learn names, then you've got to reshuffle your "cognitive priorities" at the time of introduction and attend clearly to the name and repeat it aloud or to yourself. That at least is a beginning. A second component in remembering names, as in remembering many other types of information, is to embellish or elaborate the material to be learned into meaningful terms and then to associate items. Some features suggested by the name would be elaborated into a bizarre association with a distinctive feature of the face or person to the name. Mr. *Carpenter* can be visualized hammering that long spiked nose of his into the wall; Miss *Lockhart* can be visualized with a huge *padlock* going through her *heart* and wrapped around her chest; and so on.

From Olympus to Oculomotor. This second component, of elaboration and visualization to aid in associating materials to be learned, has been investigated recently under the title of "mnemonic strategies" or simply "mnemonics." Most of us already use elementary forms of mnemonics. Our principal is spelled "pal" because he was our pal, but some of us remembered him as the man without princi*ple*. Similarly we spell "conceive" that way because we learned the rule "i before e except after c."

One problem people have is remembering the right *order* of a set of familiar items. Specially coined phrases or coined words are helpful here. Biology students learn the ordering of the 12 cranial nerves by memorizing the lines "On old Olympus' towering top, a fat-assed German vaults and hops." The first letter of each word is also the first letter of one of the major cranial nerves. The "coined-word" procedure consists of taking the first letter of words to be remembered and making a new word from them. Thus the ordering of colors of the spectrum is suggested by the name ROY G. BIV for red, orange, yellow, etc. If we can remember the coined word or phrase, we can order the items correctly. These particular mnemonics fail in the long run because they do not maintain the actual items in memory. Biology students may recall the limerick long after they have forgotten the names of the cranial nerves. A better mnemonic would contain hints for remembering the items themselves as well as their order. For example, using key words that sound like the names of the nerve, they could remember the following story: "At the *oil factory* (olfactory nerve) the *optician* (optic) looked for the *occupant* (oculomotor) of the *truck* (trochlear). He was searching because *three gems* (trigeminal) had been *abducted* (abducents) by a man who was hiding his *face* (facial) and *ears* (acoustic). A *glossy photograph* (glossopharyngeal) had been taken of him, but it was too *vague* (vagus) to use. He appeared to be *spineless* (spinal accessory) and *hypocritical* (hypoglossal)."

One mnemonic technique is particularly useful whenever two or more things are to be associated. Examples include the principal products of a country, foreign-language vocabulary items, and definitions of new concepts. The method consists simply of searching for or elaborating some vivid connection between the two items. One way to establish a connection is to imagine the two elements interacting in some way. To remember the meaning of the word *porte*, one might picture a huge bottle of *port* wine dangling from a *door*. Thus the word's meaning—door—will be called forth by the image.

Consider learning a series of word pairs such as DOG-HAT, MAN-PENCIL, CLOCK-WOMAN, SOFA-FLOOR, and PIPE-CLOWN. People usually learn a list such as this by rapidly repeating each pair as often as possible in the allotted time. The method is reasonably satisfactory for short lists and

by Gordon H. Bower

If we free the mind from rote learning, there's more time for thought. A Stanford psychologist spells out ways to cut the pain of memorization.

HOW TO....UH..REMEMBER!

The value of relating items to each other in a thematic way shows up clearly when one concocts narrative stories as an aid to serial learning.

over short retention intervals. But extend either the length of the list or the retention interval, and the rehearsal method falters seriously. People who have learned to use mental imagery to relate the items of a pair perform much better. They visualize a dog wearing a hat, a man resting a large pencil on his shoulder like a rifle, a woman wearing a clock on a chain around her neck, a section of floor resting on a sofa, and a clown smoking a pipe. When provided with one word of each pair, they can call to mind the interactive image they had formed, and can name the other object in the image. This procedure can improve recall by as much as 100 to 150 percent.

Spinning Stories. The value of relating items to each other in a thematic way shows up clearly when one concocts narrative stories as an aid to serial learning. In one study of this "chaining method," Michal Clark and I instructed college students to make up a story around a list of 10 unrelated nouns which were to be remembered. It usually took a student about one or two minutes to construct his story. Each student studied 12 different lists of words in a period of 30 to 40 minutes. Our control subjects learned the lists using any method they chose; they were allowed to study for a time comparable to that taken by the students composing stories. Following presentation of the last list, we tested retention by giving the first word of each list and asking the student to recall the other items in that list in order.

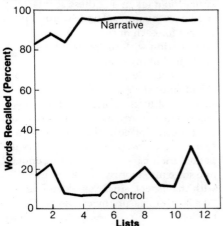

Students who had constructed stories recalled about seven times as many correct items as the control subjects did.

The narrative chaining method is a good mnemonic because the person provides an overall theme by which to organize the critical words. A second mnemonic for learning lists of items is the method of loci ("locations"): it works not by relating the items to be remembered to one another but rather by relating them to a standard list of known locations. One of the first references to this mnemonic system was made by Cicero, who tells the story of a man named Simonides. While attending a large banquet, Simonides was called outside and during his absence the roof of the hall collapsed, killing all of the revelers. The bodies of the victims were so mangled that they could not be identified by their relatives. Simonides, however, was able to identify each of the corpses by recalling where each person sat before the tragedy. He did this by visualizing the room and mentally walking about, "seeing" who had been seated in each chair. This feat so impressed him that he came to believe that all memory worked by placing objects or ideas into definite locations. The mnemonic is known as the method of loci because it depends on pigeon-holing items to be remembered into a series of "locations."

To use the method of loci, you must first establish a list of "memory snapshots" of locations taken from along a familiar route, such as a walk through your house. (A building, campus, or city would serve as well.) You must be able to see clearly and to recite the different distinctive locations on your list. To learn any new list of items you simply take a "mental walk" through your list of loci, placing successive items in your imagination at successive locations along your familiar route. You should connect the items to their locations by visualizing some vivid interaction between the item and the things at a given location. When you need to recall the items, you simply take another mental walk along your familiar route and see what items have been deposited there. For example, suppose

that you need to buy many items at the grocery, including milk, bread, bananas and cigarettes as the first four. The first-four snapshots of your pre-memorized list of locations might be your front hallway closet, the kitchen refrigerator, your favorite easy chair, and the living-room fireplace. To learn the first four items of your shopping list, you should visualize a vivid image of quarts of milk stacked up and bursting in your hallway closet, then

MEMORY FREAKS I HAVE KNOWN

In the popular mind, mnemonic devices are associated with magic, memory tricks, chess wizardry, lightning-fast calculations, and other Olympiad feats of mental gymnastics. Being a naive scientist, I vigorously disbelieved such popular dogma. I pictured instead lawyers, doctors and engineers using mnemonics to lighten the memory load of their jobs. To unmask the poppycock, I went to meet some professional mnemonists in the flesh at the first and only convention of a national mnemonics association in the Spring of 1968 in Hollywood, where else. To my chagrin, I discovered that the popular notion is true. The mnemonists I met were usually entertainers doing shows of magic and trickery. Some were simply zany characters who got their kicks from performing spectacular mental gyrations that leave the rest of us dumfounded and awe-struck. Mnemonists love to entertain and dazzle one another even more than they do a naive audience. Like a reunion of comedians, each mnemonist loves to "top" the other one, with a new trick or new mental skill. They made a charming crowd for a convention: slightly pixilated, wild, madcap, and surprising in their unexpected mental skills.

Arriving at the convention, I saw some 30 people scattered in small conversation a dagger-like loaf of bread piercing the refrigerator door, then large bunches of bananas piled up in your easy chair, and in the fireplace a large pack of cigarettes with several of them sticking out of the pack and smoking. A long list of items to be learned would require a long list of familiar locations in memory. As each object to be learned is studied, it is placed in imagination at the next location on your list of familiar loci. You should try to vis-

ualize a clear mental picture of the object "doing something interesting" at the location where it is placed. Later, in the grocery store, you can recall your shopping list by an imaginary walk through your house, pausing to "look at" what you've placed earlier at the standard locations in your route.

This system provides a series of memory hooks on which you can snag items and keep them from getting away. The

number of loci can be expanded indefinitely according to one's needs. The system does more than just connect an item to something that is already known. It provides a series of permanent hooks or memory pegs to which you already have reliable access. Since the peg-list doesn't change, the pegs provide cues that can stimulate recall of the needed items.

A man who developed the method of loci to a fine art was the subject of Alexan-

---

groups. My first surprise came when I registered and received a *name tag*. The small conversation groups turned out to be mnemonists comparing notes on how best to do some memory trick. One group was discussing several variants of the "perpetual-calendar" system, which enables the user to calculate rapidly, in his head, the day of the week on which any date fell. The system will tell you that February 12, 1809 was a Sunday and July 15, 1922 was a Saturday. Other groups were discussing schemes for fast memorization of the Morse code, or the order of cards in a shuffled deck, or ways to fool an audience into believing you'd memorized a thousand eight-digit numbers or the entire Los Angeles telephone directory. It was amazing guile but trickery nonetheless.

The convention program consisted principally of performances by these talented people. There was a 96-year-old man who memorized 50 three-digit numbers shouted out to him by the audience. Another participant had memorized the powers of 2 up to 2^{100}, which is a very large number indeed. He did it by recalling a key sentence associated with pegword N, the sentence composed of words which were a phonetically coded translation of successive digits in 2 . These coding techniques are explained in my article. The two most spectacular performances were turned in by John Stone, and Willis N. Dysart, whose stage name was Willie the Wizard.

At age 66, Stone had taught himself several complex skills allowing him to carry out nearly simultaneously several activities which, for most people, would interfere with one another. In one of these performances, he would begin with four six-letter words shouted out at random by the audience, from which he proceeded to write rapidly and upside-down a complexly transformed word salad. For instance, given the words GEORGE, STOLEN, MARKER, and ARMPIT, Stone would quickly write a sequence such as:

GИWTEƎVIOꓘ·ꓩꓡOKMGⱢEꓤESꓘA

The pattern of the sequence can be shown by selective erasure or by rearranging letters vertically as follows:

G E O R G E
N Ǝ T O L S
M A Ɐ ꓘ E ꓤ
T I ꟼ M W A

The four words appear on each line, either properly ordered, reversed, upside-down (turn page), or a combination.

The amazing feature was the rapidity with which Stone could reel off these letters, writing them upside-down, all the while reciting "The Shooting of Dan McGrew." He was like a one-man band of mental instruments, a walking counterexample to the "limited channel capacity" hypothesis of cognitive psychologists. Seeking to unlock the secrets of the cognitive universe, I asked Stone what went on in his mind as he did this trick. His answer was totally unrevealing: "I practiced it so long that my hand just automatically knows what to do as my eye looks at successive letters of the key words." Such answers, to the dismay of cognitive psychologists, are also about what we get if we ask a pianist or one-man band to explain how he does his "trick." It's like asking the common man how he can understand rapid speech. He doesn't know; he just can do it.

Willie the Wizard was a lightning-fast mental calculator who could multiply and divide very long numbers at a startling speed. He was led through his paces by his manager, a sort of carnival barker who would announce Willie's next feats, solicit problems from the audience, keep track of problems on a blackboard, and call for applause. The general class of problems Willie liked to work on were freaks of the following form: "If a flea jumps two feet, three inches every hop, how many hops must it take to go around the world, the

circumference being 25,020 miles? Also, how long would it require for the journey if the flea takes one hop per second?" Almost before such questions were finished, Willie would have started rattling off the answer, "It would take 58,713,600 hops, requiring one year, 314 days, 13 hours, and 20 minutes." Like most mental calculators, Willie had memorized a vast array of arithmetic facts (e.g., products of all three-digit numbers); he also used many shortcuts which speed up mental calculations. Such skills are poorly understood. As a person, Willie was shy, with few interests beside arithmetic; higher math like calculus held no interest for him. He was somewhat of an innocent pixie regarding human relations. His business manager helped shield him from people who would exploit that innocence.

The evening following the conference a banquet was held in a private club for magicians, with haunted-house decor straight out of the Adams family. Throughout dinner we were entertained by conferees doing card tricks and memory tricks. I recall one stunt in which the mnemonist looked briefly through a shuffled deck of cards, then recited from memory the order of the 52 cards. As another trick, after shuffling and dealing you one or more cards, he could inspect the remaining deck and tell you which cards you'd taken. For these stunts, he used a prememorized code word (and image) for each of the 52 cards in conjunction with the pegword system explained in my article.

Such tricks kept us entertained throughout the evening. The only memory failures I noticed in the crowd were some late arrivals who had mistaken the time and place of the banquet and two conferees who forgot where they'd parked their cars. As the evening ended, one stage mnemonist shook my hand with that direct, sincere look and said, "It's been a pleasure meeting you, Dr. Flowers."

—Gordon H. Bower

There is also experimental evidence that the method of loci improves memory. Sometimes subjects who use this system are able to recall two to four times as much material as control subjects.

der R. Luria's book, *The Mind of a Mnemonist.* Known simply as *S,* this man performed remarkable feats of memory, recalling long lists of words without effort, and often retaining material many years.

There is also experimental evidence that the method of loci improves memory. Sometimes subjects who use this system are able to recall two to four times as much material as control subjects. In a study by John Ross and Kerry A. Lawrence, students studied a list of 40 nouns using the loci method. Immediately after each student studied the list, he tried to recall it in correct order. The next day the subject returned and again recalled the list before learning a new list of 40 items. Each student learned several lists this way. The average number of words recalled immediately after presentation of the list was 38 out of 40 in correct order. The average recall of words studied a day before was 34 out of 40 in correct order. This performance is vastly superior to that of students who use rote learning techniques.

Shopping With Mnemonics. In a direct comparison of the methods, David Winzenz and I had college students study five successive "shopping lists" of 20 unrelated words. They were allowed five seconds to study each word; they tried to recall each list immediately after studying it, and at the end of the session they tried to recall all five lists (100 items). Some subjects learned using the mnemonic or slight variations on it, while our control subjects were left to learn by their own devices (which typically consisted of rote rehearsal). The subjects using the mnemonic recalled the words far better than the controls on both the immediate test and the end-of-session test. At this end-of-session test, the mnemonic subjects remembered an average of 72 items out of 100, whereas the controls remembered only 28. Furthermore, the items recalled by subjects using the mnemonic were usually assigned to the right position on the right list, whereas the control subjects were very poor at remembering the position and list of the few scattered items they did recall.

A second mnemonic, called the "peg-word system," seems in most respects to be entirely equivalent to the method of loci. Where the method of loci uses mental snapshots of locations as memory pegs, the pegword system uses a familiar list of names of simple, concrete objects. A typical pegword list is one composed of rhymes of the first 20 or so integers. For instance, the pegwords for the first five integers might be 1-bun, 2-shoe, 3-tree, 4-door and 5-hive. The pegs should be names of concrete objects which you can visualize. This pegword list should be well learned so that it can be recited readily (the rhymes help at this stage) before it can be put to use in learning any new set of items.

To memorize a new set of items, you then use the pegwords during study much as you used the locations. You associate each item to be learned with a peg by imagining the two objects interacting in some way. For example, for our earlier grocery list, you would imagine pouring *milk* all over a soggy hamburger *bun,* then a *shoe* kicking and breaking a large stick of French *bread,* then bunches of bananas hanging from a *tree,* then a *door* puffing on a *cigarette* stuck in its keyhole. You can make up any bizarre image you like in order to link the pegword to the item to be learned. When recall is desired, you simply run through your familiar list of pegs and try to call to mind the image you formed earlier associated with each peg.

This system helps whenever the ma-

Item Number	Pegword	Peg Image	Item to Be Recalled	Connecting Image
1	bun		milk	
2	shoe		bread	
3	tree		bananas	
4	door		cigarette	
5	hive		coffee	

Connecting images:
1 *Milk* pouring onto a soggy hamburger *bun*
2 A *shoe* kicking and breaking a brittle loaf of French *bread*
3 Several bunches of *bananas* hanging from a *tree*
4 Keyhole of a *door* smoking a *cigarette*
5 Pouring *coffee* into top of a bee *hive*

Both methods, of course, produced recall far superior to that of control subjects who were not using either mnemonic.

terial to be learned is already familiar, but when the items are relatively unrelated, so that the problem is one of reminding yourself of all of them. Typical applications are to memorizing lists of errands, shopping items, geographical facts (e.g., the principal products of Brazil), unrelated sets of scientific laws, the sequence of points in a speech or sets of arguments you are to deliver, of main events in a play or history or novel you want to remember, and so on.

Since each pegword is attached to a number, you can recall a particular item without running through the entire list as you must do with the method of loci. If asked to recall the ninth item, you simply call to mind your pegword for number nine ("nine is wine") and this will cue recall of the ninth item. Going in the reverse direction, you can also identify the serial position of any item; from knowledge that an *orange* was last visualized drinking a bottle of *wine*, you know that *orange* was the ninth item on your list.

The numerical mnemonic is obviously very similar to the method of loci; the difference is that images of concrete objects rather than images of familiar locations are used as pegs, and that the pegs are numbered. Judith S. Reitman and I compared recall by students using the two mnemonics, and found them to be entirely equivalent so long as the student was asked only to recall the test items in the order he'd studied them. Both methods, of course, produced recall far superior to that of control subjects who were not using either mnemonic. The equivalence of the two methods is understandable if one notes that a "location" (such as my chair, my fireplace) is really nothing more than a coherent collection of "objects," like those prescribed for the numerical pegword system.

The same pegs or loci can be used over and over again to learn new lists of items. No particular difficulty is created by such multiple usages so long as you're interested only in remembering the most recent set of items you've stuck on your peg. Typically we can forget about arbitrary lists once we've used them: shopping

lists are used but once, legal arguments before a jury are gone through but once, and a waitress has to remember only once that the current customer sitting on the left in the third booth gets the ham sandwich on rye. In such cases, the person has no need or desire to retain earlier lists.

Multiple Learning. But problems do crop up whenever the pegword system is used to learn many similar lists in succession, and the person needs to remember all of them later. One example might be learning on Sunday all of your hourly appointments for the coming week; another would be learning multiple shopping lists of things to buy at the grocery, the hardware store, the garden shop, and the drug store. In the experiment Reitman and I did, we simulated this kind of memorizing task by having some subjects use a pegword system and others a loci system to study five lists of 20 words presented once each. They were tested for ordered recall of each list immediately after they'd studied it. They were also tested unexpectedly for recall of all five lists at the end of the hour's session and again seven days later. We told some subjects to learn the items on each new list by calling to mind a separate, distinctly different version (and vision) of the pegword and to link that to the appropriate item. Thus, if the first pegword was 1-*bun*, they should visualize a small cloverleaf dinner roll for associating to the first item in the first list, a large hamburger roll for the first item on the second list, and so on. They were also told not to call to mind earlier images associated to the peg, but to study each list as a distinctly separate set. Other subjects received just the opposite instructions—to use exactly the same image for the pegword and to progressively elaborate grand imaginal scenes in which the peg was interacting in some way with all the prior objects to-be-remembered at that list position. Suppose, for example, that the second words in the first four lists were *dog*, *hat*, *bicycle*, and *cigar*. Then the peg 2-*shoe* would be elaborated successively over lists as follows: a *dog* wearing *shoes*, that *dog* wearing a *top hat* and those *shoes*, that *dog* riding a *bicycle* while

wearing that *top hat* and those *shoes*, and finally that *dog* smoking a *cigar* while riding that *bicycle* and wearing that *top hat* and those *shoes*. Our college students had no difficulty concocting such progressive elaborations, even though they had no more time than those doing the "separate" imagery method.

Although these two conditions gave the same high level of immediate recall after studying each list (86 percent vs. 87 percent), a huge advantage for the progressive-elaboration procedure appeared at the later tests. On the end-of-session test, the progressive elaborators recalled about 70 percent compared to 38 percent for the separate imagers. At the one-week test, the scores were 54 percent versus 12 percent, a fourfold difference.

The problem seemed to be that as the separate imagers learned each new peg-to-item association they tended to *unlearn* the prior associations from that peg. Consequently, on the end-of-session test, these subjects were good at recalling the last list they'd learned, but did progressively worse at recalling the earlier lists of the session. The progressive elaborators, on the other hand, learned each new item by first recalling and rehearsing their "peg scene" containing the prior items and then adding a new elaboration of that scene. By this means, later uses of a peg caused revival and strengthening rather than unlearning of earlier items attached to the peg. As a result, at the one-week test, these subjects did best on the first list they'd learned and worst on their final list.

Overloading the Pegs. The practical prescription is obvious: if many similar lists are to be retained simultaneously using the same pegword list, then you frequently have to revive and rehearse earlier lists as you learn new lists. There are two other obvious ways to avoid the interference and forgetting caused by learning multiple lists. One way is to use a very long list of pegs (say, 100) and segregate items so that List-1 items (e.g., Monday's appointments) go onto pegs 1-20, List-2 items (Tuesday's appointments) go onto pegs 21-40, and so on. A second way to learn multiple lists but still avoid overloading a peg is to have multiple pegword lists at your command. Along with your rhyming pegwords, you might have three lists of 20 loci corresponding to locations along a familiar route inside your house, down the street outside your house, and through the place where you work. Then you can use different peg lists to learn the several similar lists you have to keep in mind. With a little ingenuity, you can

> I once knew a 96-year-old man who could memorize a new list of 50 three-digit numbers shouted out to him by an audience one at a time every five or 10 seconds.

even work out a higher-order peg system to remember which class of items have been associated to which set of pegwords. Man's memory (or mind) seems quite at ease dealing with such superordinate hierarchies of units, since each hierarchy is built up according to a basic principle—namely, that a symbol can stand for an entire set of units but that symbol itself can enter into further associations.

As effective as such pegword systems can be, they are of no value in learning meaningless materials like numbers, which cause one of the biggest memory nuisances. We would like to remember

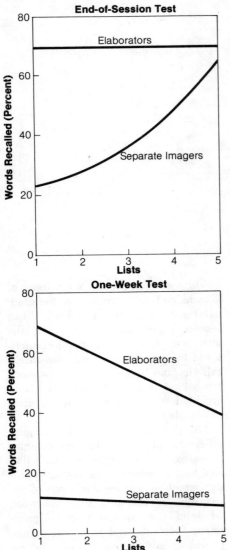

End-of-Session Test

Elaborators

Separate Imagers

Words Recalled (Percent)

Lists

One-Week Test

Elaborators

Separate Imagers

Words Recalled (Percent)

Lists

telephone numbers, social-security numbers, license plates, room or locker numbers; we need to recall birth dates, anniversaries, addresses and ages; students must remember historical dates and the populations of countries; businessmen need to know production figures and budget allotments. A mnemonic system that is particularly helpful with this kind of material is a number-to-sound coding system.

Meet in HAVOK. One first assigns consonant sounds to the numbers zero through nine. For example, the numbers zero through nine might be assigned the letters b, c, n, v, r, h, s, k, l, and t. (More elaborate codings can be used.) Once the code has been learned, then a number can be replaced by its assigned letters. Thus the number 537 becomes HVK. These letters can then be made into a word by adding vowels wherever they are needed, as in HAVOK. And so we recall that we are to meet in HAVOK—that is, in room 537.

Dates, appointment times, and other numbers can be coded and learned in the same fashion. Very long numbers typically have to be broken up into a series of words, to make a phrase. Of course, like learning to play a piano (which requires coding or "translation" from visual score to finger movements), the code needs to be practiced if it is to be effective. You have to become very proficient at rapidly replacing digits by code letters and these by words. However, once the code has been learned, it takes little effort to maintain, much less than the time we ordinarily spend in trying to remember—or look up—important numbers.

Two or more mnemonics can be combined to produce a spectacular performance. I once knew a 96-year-old man who could memorize a new list of 50 three-digit numbers shouted out to him by an audience one at a time every five or 10 seconds. Not only could he recall the list without error, but he could tell you what the 37th item was and that the number 259 was the 18th item. Since he was partly deaf, his main trouble wasn't in remembering the numbers, but in hearing them correctly in the first place. He achieved his mnemonic feat by combining the peg-

word system and the number coding system. He had concrete images as pegs for the first 50 numbers. He also had a coded conversion word with a concrete image for each of the first 1,000 numbers. When given a number, he converted it to its code word and formed an image to connect that code word to the pegword for the first item. For instance, if the third number to be learned was 546, he would convert that to its code word, say, for example, HORSE. If his pegword for the third item was tree, then all he had to do was form an image of a horse leaning up against a tree, or kicking a tree.

Teaching Memory Skills. Most of us feel no compelling urge to learn long lists of three-digit numbers. Such feats make for interesting conversation and may prove entertaining at parties, but are themselves useless. However, the methods underlying such feats can be put to many practical uses. Whether we like it or not, we all have a great many things to remember. We ought then to acquire those skills that would make memorization less painful and more efficient. Our schools should teach memory skills, just as they teach the skills of reading and writing. Although teachers typically describe educational goals in such lofty terms as teaching their students to be critical, insightful, curious, and deeply appreciative of the subject matter, these are usually only extra requirements beyond the learning of basic facts that is demanded as a minimum. Any geography student who thinks Istanbul is in France, or any art-history student who thinks Salvador Dali painted the Sistine Chapel, is going to flunk his exams if he pulls such boners often enough. The point is that we do demand that students learn a lot of facts just as we are constantly required to do in our daily life. You can get a feel for this if you try to carry on an intelligent conversation about some current event, say, the Nixon Administration's war on inflation, without having learned some facts about the topic. But the solution to the problem is probably at hand. By systematically applying the knowledge that we now have about learning, we should be able to improve our skills so that we spend less time memorizing facts. By the strategic use of mnemonics, we might free ourselves for those tasks we consider more important than memorization.

We ought to take advantage of what we know about memory, forgetting, and mnemonics, and we ought to do it soon. You are already beginning to forget the material you just read.

Language

And The Mind

By Noam Chomsky

ow does the mind work? To answer this question we must look at some of the work performed by the mind. One of its main functions is the acquisition of knowledge. The two major factors in acquisition of knowledge, perception and learning, have been the subject of study and speculation for centuries. It would not, I think, be misleading to characterize the major positions that have developed as outgrowths of classical rationalism and empiricism. The rationalist theories are marked by the importance they assign to *intrinsic* structures in mental operations—to central processes and organizing principles in perception, and to innate ideas and principles in learning. The empiricist approach, in contrast, has stressed the role of experience and control by environmental factors.

The classical empiricist view is that sensory images are transmitted to the brain as impressions. They remain as ideas that will be associated in various ways, depending on the fortuitous character of experience. In this view a language is merely a collection of words, phrases, and sentences, a habit system, acquired accidentally and extrinsically. In the formulation of Williard Quine, knowledge of a language (and, in fact, knowledge in general) can be represented as "a fabric of sentences variously associated to one another and to nonverbal stimuli by the mechanism of conditioned response." Acquisition of knowledge is only a matter of the gradual construction of this fabric. When sensory experience is interpreted, the already established network may be activated in some fashion. In its essentials, this view has been predominant in modern behavioral science, and it has been accepted with little question by many philosophers as well.

The classical rationalist view is quite different. In this view the mind contains a system of "common notions" that enable it to interpret the scattered and incoherent data of sense in terms of objects and their relations, cause and effect, whole and part, symmetry, gestalt properties, functions, and so on. Sensation, providing only fleeting and meaningless images, is degenerate and particular. Knowledge, much of it beyond immediate awareness, is rich in structure, involves universals, and is highly organized. The innate general principles that underlie and organize this knowledge, according to Leibniz, "enter into our thoughts, of which they form the soul and the connection . . . although we do not at all think of them."

This "active" rationalist view of the acquisition of knowledge persisted through the romantic period in its essentials. With respect to language, it achieves its most illuminating expression in the profound investigations of Wilhelm von Humboldt. His theory of speech perception supposes a generative system of rules that underlies speech production as well as its interpretation. The system is generative in that it makes infinite use of finite means. He regards a language as a structure of forms and concepts based on a system of rules that determine their interrelations, arrangement, and organization. But these finite materials can be combined to make a never-ending product.

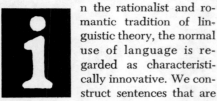

In the rationalist and romantic tradition of linguistic theory, the normal use of language is regarded as characteristically innovative. We construct sentences that are entirely new to us. There is no substantive notion of "analogy" or "generalization" that accounts for this creative aspect of language use. It is equally erroneous to describe language as a "habit structure" or as a network of associated responses. The innovative element in normal use of language quickly exceeds the bounds of such marginal principles as analogy or generalization (under any substantive interpretation of these notions). It is important to emphasize this fact because the insight has been lost under the impact of the behaviorist assumptions that have dominated speculation and research in the twentieth century.

In Humboldt's view, acquisition of language is largely a matter of maturation of an innate language capacity. The maturation is guided by internal factors, by an innate "form of language" that is sharpened, differentiated, and given its specific realization through experience. Language is thus a kind of latent structure in the human mind, developed and fixed by exposure to specific linguistic experience. Humboldt believes that all languages will be found to be very simi-

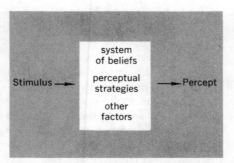

MODEL FOR PERCEPTION. Each physical stimulus, after interpretation by the mental processes, will result in a percept.

lar in their grammatical form, similar not on the surface but in their deeper inner structures. The innate organizing principles severely limit the class of possible languages, and these principles determine the properties of the language that is learned in the normal way.

The active and passive views of perception and learning have elaborated with varying degrees of clarity since the seventeenth century. These views can be confronted with empirical evidence in a variety of ways. Some recent work in psychology and neurophysiology is highly suggestive in this regard. There is evidence for the existence of central processes in perception, specifically for control over the functioning of sensory neurons by the brain-stem reticular system. Behavioral counterparts of this central control have been under investigation for several years. Furthermore, there is evidence for innate organization of the perceptual system of a highly specific sort at every level of biological organization. Studies of the visual system of the frog, the discovery of specialized cells responding to angle and motion in the lower cortical centers of cats and rabbits, and the somewhat comparable investigations of the auditory system of frogs—all are relevant to the classical questions of intrinsic structure mentioned earlier. These studies suggest that there are highly organized, innately determined perceptual systems that are adapted closely to the animal's "life space" and that provide the basis for what we might call "acquisition of knowledge." Also relevant are certain behavioral studies of human infants, for example those showing the preference for faces over other complex stimuli.

These and other studies make it reasonable to inquire into the possibility that complex intellectual structures are determined narrowly by innate mental organization. What is perceived may be determined by mental processes of considerable depth. As far as language

learning is concerned, it seems to me that a rather convincing argument can be made for the view that certain principles intrinsic to the mind provide invariant structures that are a precondition for linguistic experience. In the course of this article I would like to sketch some of the ways such conclusions might be clarified and firmly established.

here are several ways linguistic evidence can be used to reveal properties of human perception and learning. In this section we consider one research strategy that might take us nearer to this goal.

Let us say that in interpreting a certain physical stimulus a person constructs a "percept." This percept represents some of his conclusions (in general, unconscious) about the stimulus. To the extent that we can characterize such percepts, we can go on to investigate the mechanisms that relate stimulus and percept. Imagine a model of perception that takes stimuli as inputs and arrives at percepts as "outputs." The model might contain a system of beliefs, strategies for interpreting stimuli, and other factors, such as the organization of memory. We would then have a perceptual model that might be represented graphically [*see illustration at left, above*].

Consider next the system of beliefs that is a component of the perceptual model. How was this acquired? To study this problem, we must investigate a second model, which takes certain data as input and gives as "output" (again, internally represented) the system of be-

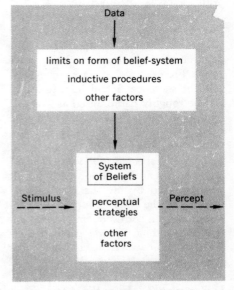

MODEL FOR LEARNING. One's system of beliefs, a part of the perception model, is acquired from data as shown above.

liefs operating in the perceptual model. This second model, a model of learning, would have its own intrinsic structure, as did the first. This structure might consist of conditions on the nature of the system of beliefs that can be acquired, of innate inductive strategies, and again, of other factors such as the organization of memory [*see illustration, 147, bottom*].

Under further conditions, which are interesting but not relevant here, we can take these perceptual and learning models as theories of the acquisition of knowledge, rather than of belief. How then would the models apply to language? The input stimulus to the perceptual model is a speech signal, and the percept is a representation of the utterance that the hearer takes the signal to be and of the interpretation he assigns to it. We can think of the percept as the structural description of a linguistic expression which contains certain phonetic, semantic, and syntactic information. Most interesting is the syntactic information, which best can be discussed by examining a few typical cases.

he three sentences in the example seem to be the same syntactic structure [*see illustration at right*]. Each contains the subject *I*, and the predicate of each consists of a verb (*told, expected, persuaded*), a noun phrase (*John*), and an embedded predicate phrase (*to leave*). This similarity is only superficial, however—a similarity in what we may call the "surface structure" of these sentences, which differ in important ways when we consider them with somewhat greater care.

The differences can be seen when the sentences are paraphrased or subjected to certain grammatical operations, such as the conversion from active to passive forms. For example, in normal conversation the sentence "I told John to leave" can be roughly paraphrased as "What I told John was to leave." But the other two sentences cannot be paraphrased as "What I persuaded John was to leave" or "What I expected John was to leave." Sentence 2 can be paraphrased as: "It was expected by me that John would leave." But the other two sentences cannot undergo a corresponding formal operation, yielding: "It was persuaded by me that John would leave" or "It was told by me that John should leave."

Sentences 2 and 3 differ more subtly. In Sentence 3 *John* is the direct object of *persuade,* but in Sentence 2 *John* is not the direct object of *expect.* We can show this by using these verbs in slightly more complex sentences: "I persuaded the doctor to examine John" and "I expected the doctor to examine John." If we replace the embedded proposition *the doctor to examine John* with its passive form *John to be examined by the doctor,* the change to the passive does not, in itself, change the meaning. We can accept as paraphrases "I expected the doctor to examine John" and "I expected John to be examined by the doctor." But we cannot accept as paraphrases "I persuaded the doctor to examine John" and "I persuaded John to be examined by the doctor."

The parts of these sentences differ in their grammatical functions. In "I persuaded John to leave" *John* is both the object of *persuade* and the subject of *leave.* These facts must be represented

(1)	I told John to leave
(2)	I expected John to leave
(3)	I persuaded John to leave

First Paraphrase:

(1a)	What I told John was to leave (ACCEPTABLE)
(2a)	What I expected John was to leave (UNACCEPTABLE)
(3a)	What I persuaded John was to leave (UNACCEPTABLE)

Second Paraphrase:

(1b)	It was told by me that John would leave (UNACCEPTABLE)
(2b)	It was expected by me that John would leave (ACCEPTABLE)
(3b)	It was persuaded by me that John would leave (UNACCEPTABLE)

(4)	I expected the doctor to examine John
(5)	I persuaded the doctor to examine John

Passive replacement as paraphrase:

(4a)	I expected John to be examined by the doctor (MEANING RETAINED)
(5a)	I persuaded John to be examined by the doctor (MEANING CHANGED)

SUPERFICIAL SIMILARITY. When the sentences above are paraphrased or are converted from active to passive forms, differences in their deep structure appear.

in the percept since they are known, intuitively, to the hearer of the speech signal. No special training or instruction is necessary to enable the native speaker to understand these examples, to know which are "wrong" and which "right," although they may all be quite new to him. They are interpreted by the native speaker instantaneously and uniformly, in accordance with structural principles that are known tacitly, intuitively, and unconsciously.

These examples illustrate two significant points. First, the surface structure of a sentence, its organization into various phrases, may not reveal or immediately reflect its deep syntactic structure. The deep structure is not represented directly in the form of the speech signal; it is abstract. Second, the rules that determine deep and surface structure and

their interrelation in particular cases must themselves be highly abstract. They are surely remote from consciousness, and in all likelihood they cannot be brought to consciousness.

 study of such examples, examples characteristic of all human languages that have been carefully studied, constitutes the first stage of the linguistic investigation outlined above, namely the study of the percept. The percept contains phonetic and semantic information related through the medium of syntactic structure. There are two aspects to this syntactic structure. It consists of a surface directly related to the phonetic form, and a deep structure that underlies the semantic interpretation. The deep structure is represented in the mind and rarely is there a direct indication of it in the physical signal.

A language, then, involves a set of semantic-phonetic percepts, of sound-meaning correlations, the correlations being determined by the kind of intervening syntactic structure just illustrated. The English language correlates sound and meaning in one way, Japanese in another, and so on. But the general properties of percepts, their forms and mechanisms, are remarkably similar for all languages that have been carefully studied.

Returning to our models of perception and learning, we can now take up the problem of formulating the system of beliefs that is a central component in perceptual processes. In the case of language, the "system of beliefs" would now be called the "generative grammar," the system of rules that specifies the sound-meaning correlation and generates the class of structural descriptions (percepts) that constitute the language in question. The generative grammar, then, represents the speaker-hearer's knowledge of his language. We can use the term *grammar of a language* ambiguously, as referring not only to the speaker's internalized, subconscious knowledge but to the professional linguist's representation of this internalized and intuitive system of rules as well.

ow is this generative grammar acquired? Or, using our learning model, what is the internal structure of the device that could develop a generative grammar?

We can think of every normal human's internalized grammar as, in effect, a theory of his language. This theory provides a sound-meaning correlation for an infinite number of sentences. It provides an infinite set of structural descriptions; each contains a surface structure that determines phonetic form and a deep structure that determines semantic content.

In formal terms, then, we can describe the child's acquisition of language as a kind of theory construction. The child discovers the theory of his language with only small amounts of data from that language. Not only does his "theory of the language" have an enormous predictive scope, but it also enables the child to reject a great deal of the very data on which the theory has been constructed. Normal speech consists, in large part, of fragments, false starts, blends, and other distortions of the underlying idealized forms. Nevertheless, as is evident from a study of the mature use of language, what the child learns is the underlying ideal theory. This is a remarkable fact. We must also bear in mind that the child constructs this ideal theory without explicit instruction, that he acquires this knowledge at a time when he is not capable of complex intellectual achievements in many other domains, and that this achievement is relatively independent of intelligence or the particular course of experience. These are facts that a theory of learning must face.

A scientist who approaches phenomena of this sort without prejudice or dogma would conclude that the acquired knowledge must be determined in a rather specific way by intrinsic proper-

ties of mental organization. He would then set himself the task of discovering the innate ideas and principles that make such acquisition of knowledge possible.

It is unimaginable that a highly specific, abstract, and tightly organized language comes by accident into the mind of every four-year-old child. If there were not an innate restriction on the form of grammar, then the child could employ innumerable theories to account for his linguistic experience, and no one system, or even small class of systems, would be found exclusively acceptable or even preferable. The child could not possibly acquire knowledge of a language. This restriction on the form of grammar is a precondition for linguistic experience, and it is surely the critical factor in determining the course and result of language learning. The child cannot know at birth which language he is going to learn. But he must "know" that its grammar must be of a predetermined form that excludes many imaginable languages.

The child's task is to select the appropriate hypothesis from this restricted class. Having selected it, he can confirm his choice with the evidence further available to him. But neither the evidence nor any process of induction (in any well-defined sense) could in themselves have led to this choice. Once the hypothesis is sufficiently well confirmed, the child knows the language defined by this hypothesis; consequently, his knowledge extends vastly beyond his linguistic experience, and he can reject much of this experience as imperfect, as resulting from the interaction of many factors, only one of which is the ideal grammar that determines a sound-meaning connection for an infinite class of linguistic expressions. Along such lines as these one might outline a theory to explain the acquisition of language.

s has been pointed out, both the form and meaning of a sentence are determined by syntactic structures that are not represented directly in the signal and that are related to the signal only at a distance, through a long sequence of interpretive rules. This property of abstractness in grammatical structure is of primary importance, and it is on this property that our inferences about mental processes are based. Let us examine this abstractness a little more closely.

Not many years ago, the process of sentence interpretation might have been described approximately along the fol-

lowing lines. A speech signal is received and segmented into successive units (overlapping at the borders). These units are analyzed in terms of their invariant phonetic properties and assigned to "phonemes." The sequence of phonemes, so constructed, is then segmented into minimal grammatically functioning units (morphemes and words). These are again categorized. Successive operations of segmentation and classification will lead to what I have called "surface structure"—an analysis of a sentence into phrases, which can be represented as a proper bracketing of the sentence, with the bracketed units assigned to various categories [*see illustration, page 148*]. Each segment—phonetic, syntactic or semantic—would be identified in terms of certain invariant properties. This would be an exhaustive analysis of the structure of the sentence.

With such a conception of language structure, it made good sense to look forward hopefully to certain engineering applications of linguistics—for example, to voice-operated typewriters capable of segmenting an expression into its successive phonetic units and identifying these, so that speech could be converted to some form of phonetic writing in a mechanical way; to mechanical analysis of sentence structure by fairly straightforward and well-understood computational techniques; and perhaps even beyond to such projects as machine translation. But these hopes have by now been largely abandoned with the realization that this conception of grammatical structure is inadequate at every level, semantic, phonetic, and syntactic. Most important, at the level of syntactic organization, the surface structure indicates semantically significant relations only in extremely simple cases. In general, the deeper aspects of syntactic organization are representable by labeled bracketing, but of a very different sort from that seen in surface structure.

There is evidence of various sorts, both from phonetics and from experimental psychology, that labeled bracketing is an adequate representation of surface structure. It would go beyond the bounds of this paper to survey the phonetic evidence. A good deal of it is presented in a forthcoming book, *Sound Pattern of English*, by myself and Morris Halle. Similarly, very interesting experimental work by Jerry Fodor and his colleagues, based on earlier observations by D. E. Broadbent and Peter Ladefoged, has shown that the disruption of a speech signal (for example, by a superimposed click) tends to be perceived at the

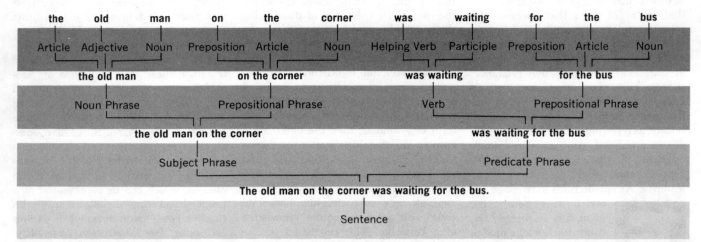

the	old	man	on	the	corner	was	waiting	for	the	bus
Article	Adjective	Noun	Preposition	Article	Noun	Helping Verb	Participle	Preposition	Article	Noun

the old man ——— on the corner ——— was waiting ——— for the bus

| Noun Phrase | Prepositional Phrase | Verb | Prepositional Phrase |

the old man on the corner ——— was waiting for the bus

| Subject Phrase | Predicate Phrase |

The old man on the corner was waiting for the bus.

Sentence

SURFACE STRUCTURE ANALYSIS. A type of sentence analysis now abandoned as inadequate at every level is this labeled bracketing which analyzes the sentence by successive division into larger units with each unit assigned to its own category.

boundaries of phrases rather than at the point where the disruption actually occurred, and that in many cases the bracketing of surface structure can be read directly from the data on perceptual displacement. I think the evidence is rather good that labeled bracketing serves to represent the surface structure that is related to the perceived form of physical signals.

Deep structures are related to surface structures by a sequence of certain formal operations, operations now generally called "grammatical transformations." At the levels of sound, meaning, and syntax, the significant structural features of sentences are highly abstract. For this reason they cannot be recovered by elementary data-processing techniques. This fact lies behind the search for central processes in speech perception and the search for intrinsic, innate structure as the basis for language learning.

ow can we represent deep structure? To answer this question we must consider the grammatical transformations that link surface structure to the underlying deep structure that is not always apparent.

Consider, for example, the operations of passivization and interrogation. In the sentences (1) John was examined by the doctor, and (2) did the doctor examine John, both have a deep structure similar to the paraphrase of Sentence 1, (3) the doctor examined John. The same network of grammatical relations determines the semantic interpretation in each case. Thus two of the grammatical transformations of English must be the operations of passivization and interrogation that form such surface structures as Sentences 1 and 2 from a deeper structure which in its essentials also un-

derlies Sentence 3. Since the transformations ultimately produce surface structures, they must produce labeled bracketings [see illustration above]. But notice that these operations can apply in sequence: we can form the passive question "was John examined by the doctor" by passivization followed by interrogation. Since the result of passivization is a labeled bracketing, it follows that the interrogative transformation operates on a labeled bracketing and forms a new labeled bracketing. Thus a transformation such as interrogation maps a labeled bracketing into a labeled bracketing.

By similar argument, we can show that all grammatical transformations are structure-dependent mappings of this sort and that the deep structures which underlie all sentences must themselves be labeled bracketings. Of course, the labeled bracketing that constitutes deep structure will in general be quite different from that representing the surface structure of a sentence. Our argument is somewhat oversimplified, but it is roughly correct. When made precise and fully accurate it strongly supports the view that deep structures, like surface structures, are formally to be taken as labeled bracketings, and that grammatical transformations are mappings of such structures onto other similar structures.

ecent studies have sought to explore the ways in which grammatical structure of the sort just described enters into mental operations. Much of this work has been based on a proposal formulated by George Miller as a first approximation, namely, that the amount of memory used to store a sentence should reflect the number of transformations used in deriving it. For example, H. B. Savin and E. Perchonock

investigated this assumption in the following way: they presented to subjects a sentence followed by a sequence of unrelated words. They then determined the number of these unrelated words recalled when the subject attempted to repeat the sentence and the sequence of words. The more words recalled, the less memory used to store the sentence. The fewer words recalled, the more memory used to store the sentence. The results showed a remarkable correlation of amount of memory and number of transformations in certain simple cases. In fact, in their experimental material, shorter sentences with more transformations took up more "space in memory" than longer sentences that involved fewer transformations.

Savin has extended this work and has shown that the effects of deep structure and surface structure can be differentiated by a similar technique. He considered paired sentences with approximately the same deep structure but with one of the pair being more complex in surface structure. He showed that, under the experimental conditions just described, the paired sentences were indistinguishable. But if the sequence of unrelated words precedes, rather than follows, the sentence being tested, then the more complex (in surface structure) of the pair is more difficult to repeat correctly than the simpler member. Savin's very plausible inference is that sentences are coded in memory in terms of deep structure. When the unrelated words precede the test sentence, these words use up a certain amount of short-term memory, and the sentence that is more complex in surface structure cannot be analyzed with the amount of memory remaining. But if the test sentence precedes the unrelated words, it is, once understood, stored in terms of deep structure, which is about the same in both cases. Therefore the same amount of memory remains, in the paired cases, for recall of the following words. This is a beautiful example of the way creative experimental studies can interweave with theoretical work in the study of language and of mental processes.

n speaking of mental processes we have returned to our original problem. We can now see why it is reasonable to maintain that the linguistic evidence supports an "active" theory of acquisition of knowledge. The study of sentences and of speech perception, it seems to me, leads to a perceptual theory of a classical rationalist sort. Representative of this school, among others, were the seventeenth-century Cambridge Platonists, who developed the idea that our perception is guided by notions that originate from the mind and that provide the framework for the interpretation of sensory stimuli. It is not sufficient to suggest that this framework is a store of "neural models" or "schemata" which are in some manner applied to perception (as is postulated in some current theories of perception). We must go well beyond this assumption and return to the view of Wilhelm von Humboldt, who attributed to the mind a system of rules that generates such models and schemata under the stimulation of the senses. The system of rules itself determines the content of the percept that is formed.

We can offer more than this vague and metaphoric account. A generative grammar and an associated theory of speech perception provide a concrete example of the rules that operate and of the mental objects that they construct and manipulate. Physiology cannot yet explain the physical mechanisms that affect these abstract functions. But neither physiology nor psychology provides evidence that calls this account into question or that suggests an alternative. As mentioned earlier, the most exciting current work in the physiology of perception shows that even the peripheral systems analyze stimuli into the complex properties of objects, and that central processes may significantly affect the information transmitted by the receptor organs.

The study of language, it seems to me, offers strong empirical evidence that empiricist theories of learning are quite inadequate. Serious efforts have been made in recent years to develop principles of induction, generalization, and data analysis that would account for knowledge of a language. These efforts have been a total failure. The methods and principles fail not for any superficial reason such as lack of time or data. They fail because they are intrinsically incapable of giving rise to the system of rules that underlies the normal use of language. What evidence is now available supports the view that all human languages share deep-seated properties of organization and structure. These properties—these linguistic universals— can be plausibly assumed to be an innate mental endowment rather than the result of learning. If this is true, then the study of language sheds light on certain long-standing issues in the theory of knowledge. Once again, I see little reason to doubt that what is true of language is true of other forms of human knowledge as well.

There is one further question that might be raised at this point. How does the human mind come to have the innate properties that underlie acquisition of knowledge? Here linguistic evidence obviously provides no information at all. The process by which the human mind has achieved its present state of complexity and its particular form of innate organization are a complete mystery, as much of a mystery as the analogous questions that can be asked about the processes leading to the physical and mental organization of any other complex organism. It is perfectly safe to attribute this to evolution, so long as we bear in mind that there is no substance to this assertion—it amounts to nothing more than the belief that there is surely some naturalistic explanation for these phenomena.

There are, however, important aspects of the problem of language and mind that can be studied sensibly within the limitations of present understanding and technique. I think that, for the moment, the most productive investigations are those dealing with the nature of particular grammars and with the universal conditions met by all human languages. I have tried to suggest how one can move, in successive steps of increasing abstractness, from the study of percepts to the study of grammar and perceptual mechanisms, and from the study of grammar to the study of universal grammar and the mechanisms of learning.

In this area of convergence of linguistics, psychology, and philosophy, we can look forward to much exciting work in coming years.

Noam Chomsky
and B. F. Skinner
have divided
psycholinguists into
two warring camps;
here's a model
that defoliates
both sides and clears
a middle ground.

A DMZ in the Language War

by D. O. Hebb, W. E. Lambert, and G. Richard Tucker

AN INDEFENSIBLE NATIVISM is rampant in psycholinguistics today. Most psycholinguists apparently believe that getting grammatical competence does not involve learning; they argue instead that the essential principles of grammar are unlearned—that they, somehow, are transmitted by heredity. We say "somehow," because psycholinguists concern themselves with criticism of learning theory, not with explicating a nativistic mechanism. Their argument rests on two bases: a primitive view of the child's learning, drawn from experiments with rats or pigeons, and an equally primitive view of heredity and environment as alternatives in the explanation of behavior.

Simplistic Ideas. Writers like Noam Chomsky, Roger Brown, Ursula Bellugi, and David McNeill appear to believe that learned behavior is learned only by conditioning and by the reinforcement of overt response. With such simplistic ideas, it is inevitable that a psycholinguist will have difficulty seeing the place that learning occupies in the mastery of grammar. He would agree that a child learns superficial features of language (vocabulary, idiom, accent), but that he can never learn what Chomsky has called *deep structure* because—for one with such views—mastery

of structure is not a matter of conditioning and reinforcement.

Roger Brown and Ursula Bellugi put forth such a view when they compare the development of a noun phrase, with all its complexities, to the growth of an embryo rather than to the growth of a conditioned reflex. The comparison is a good one, but it need not mean that the noun phrase results from neural maturation alone. Other kinds of learning might have effects that resemble embryonic development both in spontaneity and in subtlety of growth. Eric Lenneberg has proposed that the child inherits a "latent language structure"; exposure to the speech of others acts only as a releaser. (In ethology, a releaser is a stimulus that sets off an instinctive activity but has nothing to do with the process of learning.) He stresses the regularity of development in different children, even those from different cultures, implying that the control must be exclusively genetic. But this argument overlooks the great similarity in the early environments of children everywhere. Uniform early experiences can contribute as much to uniform development as a common human heredity.

Chomsky believes that not to know what role learning plays in language de-

velopment is a sufficient reason to suppose that learning does not occur. Speaking of a particular pattern of stress, he says: " . . . It is difficult to imagine how such a principle might be learned, uniformly, by all speakers . . . Consequently, the most reasonable conclusion seems to be that the *principle is not learned at all*, but rather that it is simply part of the conceptual equipment that the learner brings to the task of language acquisition. A *rather* similar argument can be given with respect to other principles of universal grammar."

Heredity as a Ragbag. If it is difficult to show how learning determines universal grammar, it is even more difficult to show how heredity does. But Chomsky does not use heredity and innate ideas to provide an explanation; he uses them to get rid of the problem by removing it from psychological consideration. Dan Slobin has objected to making heredity a ragbag for disposing of difficulties, and George Miller has responded by suggesting that what linguists and psychologists call innate in these discussions must be what is easily learned; to use the term otherwise is to make fun of it.

We agree with Miller. The learner's heredity and his environment are equally important determinants of what learning occurs and how it occurs. We believe that experience has an essential role in the development of any cognitive process, including those processes that control language. This position in no way decreases the overriding importance of hereditary predispositions. The way the human being is built determines that some things will be learned easily—indeed, inevitably, given the opportunity—and that other things will be learned with difficulty; but this still leaves us with the problem of how that learning progresses, and what course it takes.

It is clear that man is born to talk; both capacity and motivation are innate. There is almost a need to learn at least his native language. It is difficult to separate what is innate from what is acquired in

> Psycholinguists generally disregard animal evidence on the ground that no animal has true language.

these circumstances. In behavior like speech, which depends on perception and thought, to ask whether constitution or experience is more important is like asking which contributes more to the area of a field—its length or its breadth. One must understand both to understand either.

The Human Brain. Language learning separates man from all other organisms. Man has a special capacity to develop meaningful patterns of communication, with both gestures and words. This capacity does not depend upon the large size of the human brain; the elephant, with a brain nearly four times as large as man's, has not developed sign language. Something happened in man's development that allocated different functions to different halves of the brain. Speech and most of the control of skilled movement normally reside in the left hemisphere, and perception of nonverbal patterns and spatial relations in the right. This lateralization of function may have made speech pos-

sible. The human infant shows from the first that he is built to speak: he learns speech easily, babbles early, and responds to human vocalization.

Levels of Communication. This comparative picture clarifies the situation, and tells us something specific about the nature of language. There are three levels of communication, broadly speaking:

1 *Reflexive*, characteristic of social insects but also evident in the emotional behavior of higher animals, including man;

2 *Simple purposive gesture*, clearly evident in dog, monkey and ape; and

3 *True language*, a human invention. We can disregard reflexive communication, since the behavior of one ant eliciting supportive behavior from another shows no evidence of purpose or cognition. Similarly, the study of the fascinating "language of the bees" provides no evidence that the wagging dance is more than a reflexively determined pattern of behavior, which may be a stimulus either conditioned or unconditioned to other bees. Recent findings suggest that the dance of the bees does not affect their behavior, and it may not be even a reflexive form of communication.

Gesture is more important and tells us something about man. Psycholinguists generally disregard animal evidence on the ground that no animal has true language. We have clear examples of purposive communication when a chimpanzee begs for food, asks for attention from a human observer, or makes a threatening gesture (unemotionally, with no erection of hair) toward an experimenter who insists on drawing its attention to an unpleasant object. Each is a symbolic action, quite comparable to a human gesture. But the single isolated gesture that makes up the whole communication is about as far as the chimpanzee's capacities normally go, and the two-year-old human child shows something that is qualitatively as well as quantitatively different.

True language is distinctive in its combination of two or more symbolic acts (words or gestures) into one situation and in the ready recombination of the same parts in another situation or for another purpose. This ability to combine and recombine representative actions ("I thirsty," "Mommy thirsty," "no thirsty," "Mommy fix," "Daddy fix") occurs only in man and makes his communications qualitatively distinct from anything seen in the natural development of other animals. This description of language helps us to see what our observations of the human child ordinarily has not made clear,

and it shows how great an achievement Beatrice Gardner and R. Allen Gardner made in teaching sign language to their young chimpanzee, Washoe. By the criteria proposed, Washoe has language: she combines symbolic gestures (from American sign language) in various ways with the intent to communicate. It is evident that this does not make Washoe the equal of the human two-year-old. The chimpanzee generally lacks the responsiveness and capacity for complex auditory discrimination in the vocal range that the child has, and—even more—Washoe learned sign language only after careful planning and intensive training by the human experimenters.

Child and Chimpanzee. It remains to be seen to what extent the symbolic gestures used by Washoe represent separable and independent mediating processes to the same extent that they would for a human child. But the experiment clearly is valuable, for it highlights the nature of the problem of human language. The spontaneity of human language learning, its occurrence despite a complete lack of teaching by the mother, stands out in

> Washoe learned sign language only after careful planning and extensive training by the human experimenters.

clear contrast. Apparently it is the child's innate capacity for auditory analysis that distinguishes him from the chimpanzee. This auditory analysis is as important as skill in the production of speech sounds. In order to produce language, the child also needs the innate capacity to deal simultaneously with distinct representative processes, verbal and nonverbal.

With this hereditary endowment, plus certain capacities for perceptual learning, generalization and abstraction (verbal as well as nonverbal), the child is born into a language-filled environment. This environment has certain verbal uniformities, and is uniform in other ways that sometimes are forgotten. Every normal child, in no matter what culture, hears the sound of the human voice, and whenever he hears his own voice—whether in crying, in coughing or in vocalizing—he feels a sensation in his own throat. Every normal child sees his own hand, at the same time that he moves it; and so on, with respect to his own body and his own activities. All children initially receive care from an older female. They are fed and cleaned and (in most cases, given the species-predictable human weakness for puppies, kittens and infants) exposed to the facial expressions, intonations, and petting that express affection. As the tender nurse also becomes a disciplinarian, all children experience a gradual hardening of this attitude. They sleep in enclosed spaces (whether cave, tepee, house or trailer). They are exposed to the differences between living and nonliving, between human and nonhuman, and between male and female. These examples of predictable features of the environment remind us that children in different families or in different societies have many experiences in common. This common experience must have something to do with the regularity of verbal development.

Goslings and Geese. We used to assume that common heredity must determine any behavior found to be uniform within a species because heredity remains constant while experience varies from animal to animal. This is a fallacy; in some respects animals' environments have as much in common as their genetic constitutions have. Barring human intervention, all goslings are first exposed to adult geese, a fact that is critical in their subsequent "instinctive" social behavior; for if a gosling first sees a member of some other species, imprinting occurs, and—as with the goslings that adopted Konrad Lorenz—normal instinctive adult patterns are disrupted.

Puppies ordinarily grow up in the company of other living organisms, human or canine. They explore a territory that contains some variety of sensory stimulation. Some years ago, Hebb deprived puppies of living company and of territory. These deprived animals, raised in cages, never developed the adult behavior characteristic of the species. Harry Harlow demonstrated the same phenomenon with rhesus monkeys.

Early learning, which arises from exposure to the normal environment of the species, has an essential part to play in the orderly, predictable course of behavior development in these animals. Given

these facts, one hardly can argue that an orderly, predictable development in children's speech means that the development is solely the result of physical maturation. It is true that the learning is not obvious, and the observer may not recognize it if he thinks of learning as synonymous with the strengthening of response tendencies by primary reinforcement. But learning is not obvious in the gosling or the puppy or the monkey, either, and we

can show its existence only with radical experimental procedures.

Latent Learning. The possession of a human brain predisposes one to a kind of learning in which a person makes no apparent response at the time the learning occurs. The learning shows up only in the responses that he makes at some later time. Man's enormous capacity for latent learning is every bit as characteristic of the human species as the reinforcement of response tendencies is.

Latent learning includes perceptual learning and learning that we would call an association of ideas (an old-fashioned term). W. J. Brogden demonstrated it in animals, under the name of sensory-sensory (s-s) association. He exposed a dog or cat to a stimulus combination—a sound followed by a light. After several repetitions, the animal learned to associate the two events—but its learning was latent. To demonstrate it, Brogden had to take a further step. He conditioned the light to an avoidance response, so that the animal attempted to flee when the light went on. Next came the crucial test: the animal hears the *sound* and at once tries to escape, which shows that it did, in fact, associate the sound with the light. This s-s learning has survived all attempts to reduce it to some form of covert stimulus-response learning. Robert Leeper first

demonstrated perceptual learning when he showed that undergraduates who first examined a related figure showed modified perceptions of an ambiguous figure. For example, the wife-and-mother-in-law picture: if they were first shown the young woman only, they saw her in the composite picture; and vice versa if shown the old woman first. This was latent learning with no discernible primary or secondary reinforcement.

Latent perceptual learning, without response reinforcement, also occurs in a mammal as primitive as the rat. Suppose one rears a rat in a wire-mesh cage so small that the animal cannot move about. As it develops, the rat can look through the mesh at the experimental room. At maturity, this rat is decisively better able to solve maze problems than is a rat reared with a similar degree of physical restriction, with light, but who cannot see its surroundings. The perceptual learning of infancy has a lasting effect on the adult rat. It can hardly be less in man.

Cell-Assembly Theory. Let us go beyond the stimulus-response concept of learning. If we view learning as a modification of transmission in the central nervous system (CNS), we can include any change or elaboration within a transmission route, or potential route; and any cross-connection between such routes as learning. Perceptual learning involves potential routes, while sensory-sensory association involves cross-connections between routes. Because the gray matter of the CNS is organized in reentrant paths, a sensory stimulation may initiate a complex central activity, producing changes in cortical transmission paths that do not show up in motor outflow. In such cases, we have latent learning. We have just described the cell-assembly theory. Developed originally to deal with the phenomena of set and attention and with the problem of what constitutes a conceptual activity, the cell-assembly theory is essentially a sophisticated form of connectionism that takes account of phenomena that many learning theorists have ignored resolutely for 50 years in the hope that they would go away.

Tell Me the Time. In addition to perceptual learning and a sensory preconditioning—both repeatedly demonstrated in the laboratory—there is also a form of transient one-trial learning without reinforcement that we can call the acquisition of information. A monkey shows such learning when the experimenter shows it where food is located and only later allows it to go find its dinner.

At the adult-human level one-trial

learning is possibly the commonest, easiest, and most typical form. It goes on constantly during our waking hours. When we hear or see or feel something and remember it—even for a short time and even if we make no immediate response—we are learning. We hear a joke and later object to hearing it again, since we remember the ending; or in passing the clock we notice the time, and if we are asked we can relay the information. In both cases there is learning. At breakfast we hear a forecast of rain and feel no need to talk about it, but our later actions may show that retention has occurred, for we say "No" to having the car washed, tell a child to wear a raincoat to school, or put a cover on the lawn mower. Latent learning without reinforcement is one of the facts of human behavior and it is a normal consequence of perception.

Man also normally associates different percepts of the same familiar object. Lenneberg apparently thinks that two diagrams, such as a profile and a full-face sketch, look similar to a child, implying that this similarity is an innate property of perception. There is no basis for such an improbable idea. The two sketches are associated and represent the same thing—a human being—but this is a quite different proposition. A child repeatedly perceives profile and full face, one after another, in close contiguity. This must produce an association of one percept with the other and with any or all of the other part-perceptions of a human being.

Object and Image. When we perceive a person visually, we have not made a single, unitary percept; we have made a sequence of percepts resulting from changes in visual fixation. Even when we recognize another person at a glance, there is reason to think that we supplement our momentary part-perception with associated imagery, just as the visual imagery of a complex object clearly is composed of a number of associated part-images linked by eye movements and recurring in irregular order. Both perception and imagery are complexes of associated activities.

It seems that there are varying degrees of abstraction and that older ideas have provided for only two levels. We can specify the simple perception and image, and we can specify the concept but we lack the appropriate terminology to indicate the degree of abstraction.

The cell-assembly theory postulates assemblies of the first order (directly related to a specific stimulus), second order (excited by first-order assemblies), third order, and so on. The notion, divorced from its physiological beginnings, implies a hierarchy of representative (or cognitive or mediating) processes. At one extreme is actual perception—a *primary*-level process, vivid and specific but narrow-gauge. For example, we perceive a line of particular slope, or a vowel sound, or a pressure on a particular point on the skin. At the *secondary* level comes our awareness or perception of larger aspects of the object or event, but lacking some of the vividness of actual perception. At a higher level, we have an abstract idea of a class of such objects, or of the same object seen or heard or felt in its different aspects. It is quite clear that these different levels exist, psychologically, and it is also clear that there is an intelligible physiological basis for such a progression. For one thing, it closely parallels the progression of *simple cell*, *complex cell* and *hypercomplex cell*

> It is the child's innate capacity for auditory analysis that distinguishes him from the chimpanzee.

demonstrated physiologically by David Hubel and Torsten Wiesel. Sensory input directly excites the simple cell, which in turn excites the complex cell, which excites hypercomplex cells.

Seeing a Chair. Our perceptions of a complex object include these higher-order cognitions as well as our irregular part-perceptions. A child seeing a chair perceives the seat, the back, and the legs of a chair, and at the same time perceives the chair as a whole (second-order cognition), and perhaps also as a *thing* or object (third— or higher-order cognition)— as an obstacle, as something to lean against or hide behind. The perception of another child throwing a stone includes part-perceptions of the child's movements and the trajectory of the stone, but it also includes the higher-order cognition of *throwing*, as well as possibly the even higher concept of *doing something*.

Both the abstract idea of a thing, an object, a something, and the parallel idea of an action or activity, or something happening, are of first importance for understanding language.

Six Ways to Grammar. The ideas we have discussed clarify a number of problems that arise when we talk about the child's acquisition of speech. We now can propose an intelligible mechanism that helps explain these hitherto unsolved problems. We will deal with six ways that a child learns grammar—1) competence, 2) imitation, 3) plurals, 4) voice, 5) negation, and 6) nouns.

1 Linguists repeatedly refer to a child's "competence," some form of word mastery that the baby possesses before he begins to talk. This unexplained capacity becomes intelligible when it is regarded as the result of early learning.

Saying "doggie" on sight of a dog cannot be a simple matter of connecting a visual stimulus with a motor response. "Doggie" requires the child to connect the cell-assembly complex that is his visual perception of the animal with the parallel complex that is his auditory perception of the word spoken by his mother. This is not stimulus-response learning (connecting a visual stimulus with a vocal response), but a combination of sensory-sensory and perceptual learning; visual-perception learning (from the sight of dogs or similar objects) and auditory perceptual learning as well (probably from repeated hearing of "doggie.")

A Baby's Babble. In his first acquisition of words it is unlikely that a child would ever learn to say the name of an object by hearing it once at the same time that he sees it, though obviously this becomes possible at a later age. It is, however, possible that the child heard the word "dog" repeatedly before he ever saw the live animal. If he hears the familiar word in conjunction with his first sight of a dog—even before the child has begun talking—he may associate it with the sight, and the word will have entered the child's competence. That is, he will perceive, recognize and have associations for it. In addition, the child will build up motor connections at the same time he hears his own vocalizations—at first in the random babbling of infancy but later in more organized combinations of meaningful sounds. The percept, together with the auditory imagery of a word, tends to produce its vocal production.

2 Linguists repeatedly say that children do not learn language by imitation, yet it is evident that imitation plays some part.

The child invariably ends up with the vocabulary, accent and other speech mannerisms of his social group. The apparent contradiction resolves itself when we see that the imitation depends upon prior perceptual learning. The child can imitate only what already is within his competence. In the early stages of language acquisition, his imitation is more a product of learning than a mechanism of learning. Later, as older children and adults sharpen the child's performance, he may use direct imitation as an important means of improving his speech. Imitation occurs in fields other than language, of course, and we must never forget that the acquisition of language is not an isolated aspect of intellectual development but an essential part of the socialization process.

3 If linguists have trouble seeing how mastery of plural forms might be learned, it is because they approach it from a stimulus-response point of view and retreat immediately. With a visual stimulus of one finger, the child learns to say *finger*; with the stimulation of two fingers he learns to add /z/. With stimulus of one toe, he says *toe*, and with stimulus of two, to add /z/. Using the s-r approach, the linguist cannot generalize this learning to qualitatively different stimuli. He cannot explain how the child who learns to say *doggie* on sight of one dog—a new stimulus—says *doggies* on sight of two animals. But forget the s-r strait jacket. On seeing a dog, the child has cognitions at different levels: part-perception; perception of the animal as a distinctive whole; and perception of the animal as a something, a thing. The latter perception occurred with fingers and toes as well, so that when the child associated the /z/ sound with the sight of two fingers, he also associated it with two *things*. When the child encounters two dogs, an already-established association of *things* with /z/ permits him spontaneously to pluralize the form.

A Toe Wiggles. As for the choice between a terminal /z/, /s/ and /iz/, the outcome may result from the mechanics of voiced and unvoiced terminal sounds; or it may be that higher-order verbal cognitions distinguishing voiced from unvoiced sounds are the basis of learning. The fact that the child must choose the appropriate plural ending presents no difficulty for this theory.

The same argument applies to singular and plural verbs. What a child must learn is not so much that *a finger moves* and *fin-gers move*, that *a toe wiggles* and *toes wiggle*, and so on, as that *a thing does* (or acts or changes) and *things do* (or act or change). The abstract idea of an act or change parallels that of a thing or object.

4 Some linguists deny that the passive voice represents a transformation of the active-verb form. Thomas Bever, Jerry Fodor and William Weksel assume that the passive-verb form derives from "an abstract structure never realized in speech." This accords precisely with the ideas we have arrived at independently.

The perception of an event is a sequence of ideas or part-perceptions. This sequence may differ from one observer to another or for the same observer, on different occasions, when perceiving the same event. It is the sequence of ideas in perception that determines the sequence of verbal conceptual processes and thus the subject-predicate relation. Suppose Johnny hits Mary. If we are attending to Johnny, the order of mental events is our percept (of Johnny) (of Johnny's activity) (of impingement on Mary), but if at the time of the event we are attending to Mary instead of Johnny, the order is percept (of Mary) (disturbance of Mary) (arising from Johnny). In the first case the verbal report that results might be Johnny hit Mary, in the second Mary was hit by Johnny.

Faces or Vase? All this may be obvious, but it suggests that the basis of transformation from active to passive (and vice-versa) is not grammatical, but that it depends on the way we perceive, recall, or imagine the event. Just as one may perceive Rubin's reversible figure as either a vase or two human profiles, and just as one may recall a familiar place as approached from different directions, it is clear that one can recall a complex event in a different order from that in which it was originally perceived. One may watch Johnny slug Mary, perceiving the event in that order of ideas; but what one recalls later may be Mary's screams first, followed by the action that gave rise to them. If one was not present, but was just given the sentence "Johnny hit Mary" and asked to put it in the passive, one would reconstruct the scene in imagery and report as if observing it with Mary in the focus of attention. Instead of elaborate formal rules of transformation to encompass all the possible complexities of sentence structure, the relation of active to passive may depend on a nonverbal parallel mechanism, and we propose the normal mechanisms of imagery of a complex event.

5 The child must master three aspects of negation: prohibition of some action by the child himself, absence or nonexistence of something familiar or expected, and denial of something desired. The simplest seems to be prohibition, in which the word *no* becomes a conditioned inhibitor, because the parent follows it with—for example—a slap on the hand. A simple conditioned response explains this learning, not essentially different from a dog's learning to respond to *no*. But something happens at a much higher level when the child plays the adult's role and says *no* to a doll or a pet. This brings up the problem of imitation and the closely related problem of empathy and the partial identification of self with other.

No More Cookie. The use of *no* or *not* to signal the absence of some object means nothing until the child is capable of thought processes representing objects that he does not actually perceive. Something is expected and does not appear. When the child first learns to say *cookie* he is likely to get one; but occasionally the parent responds to the child's word with empty hands and the words "no cookie", or "there are no cookies." The child hears footsteps at the front door and says "Daddy," but the mother says, "No, not Daddy." The essential condition is a contrast between the expectation or request (which involves expectation), and the subsequent perception. The generalized ideas the child handles are the sequence, (something there) (something not there), and on this basis he can derive a concept of negation or absence.

The third form of negation, refusal, may be a combination of the first two. When it is refusal by the mother ("no more cookie") it combines the second form (failure of expectation) with perception of the parent as active frustrator. This combination leads to the temper tantrum that is such a marked characteristic of both human and chimpanzee infants. When at a later stage in development the child says *no* in refusing milk, for example, the refusal may combine the higher-level *no* of prohibition (involving imitation) and the *no* of absence.

6 As a final example of ways children may learn the principles of grammar, we may consider what Slobin has called "nounness." In commenting on David McNeill's radically nativistic position, Slobin says: "It seems to me that the child, to begin with, must know only the criteria of setting up the generic class— for example, nounness—and not all the other criteria of noun subcategories as they are embodied in various languages." Slobin's use of the verb "know" in that statement is too rational and adult in its implications, (we might say that it anthropomorphizes the baby). The child no more has such ideas than a dog that chews a bone knows that it needs calcium in its diet. The brain produces those results as nonlogically and nonformally as the sieve, in a cement-mixing establishment, sorts out gravel into small, medium and large— without knowing a thing.

But with that qualification concerning terminology, we agree with Slobin and believe that the child finds empirical criteria for nounness. Also, we believe that it is possible to indicate what these criteria are.

From Neuron to Noun. In the first stage of language mastery, the child would notice the repeated coincidence of the mother's vocalizations with the appearance of attention-getting activity or a striking or noticeable object—a space-occupying, perceptible and imageable thing. Brown observes that the first nouns that a child masters refer to "concrete, tangible objects," and that the first verbs refer to "observable physical actions." Many neurons are excited when the mother draws a child's attention to some object and at the same time makes a particular sound. Different groupings of neurons are involved from one such occasion to the next, but the same sound will excite the same small sub-group on every occasion, and the organized activity of this sub-group becomes the abstract idea of a name. In this situation, then, the child perceives a particular word (lower-order cognition) but also perceives it as a name

(higher-order, abstract activity accompanying the lower order). In the same way, the child learns to perceive action words as such.

Bobby Kivils. At a later stage, however, the child will use another basis to detect nounness and verbness. He will relate a particular sound to already established nouns and verbs. Thus to take the example of Martin Braine, modified a bit, the child hears "People kivil," "The dog kivils," "Bobby kivils," and categorizes *kivil* as referring to an action, because it occurs in the place of action words he does know, in relation to familiar words. When the child hears a repeatable vocalization following a word he knows as a name (i.e., a noun), the sequence excites both the lower-order cognitions of that vocalization, and also (by association with the higher-order cognition of the preceding noun) the higher-order cognition normally accompanying a familiar verb. The additional element of higher-order

> Latent learning without reinforcement is one of the facts of human behavior and it is a normal consequence of perception.

cognition in our theory removes certain difficulties encountered by Braine's explanation.

A recent set of studies of noun-adjective word order demonstrates the behavioral significance of this general notion. Once a higher-order cognition such as nounness becomes established, it can have a pervasive influence on the processing and assimilation of new verbal inputs. For example, the sequencing of nouns and adjectives plays a substantial role in memorization and recall. A noun-adjective order is a much more useful and efficient schema than the English adjective-noun sequence, even for the English speaker, apparently because the noun serves as a conceptual peg on which one can hang a long and complex series of succeeding adjectives.

The unobtrusiveness and extent of a

child's learning shows up when the French child easily acquires the rules of gender; this aspect of language poses no problem at all for the five-year-old French child, but it creates despair among persons learning French as a second language. Current research reveals that intelligent teachers of French hold interesting views about the problem. The views range from an extreme position— that one really has to be born French to know which words are masculine and which are feminine— to a more reasonable one—that the French child never separates the gender markers from the nouns (e.g., *lamaison, dulait*, not *la maison* or *du lait*) and thus learns each noun in context.

But the French five-year-old knows the gender of nouns he has never before encountered. The mystery of gender dissolves when one points out that there are features of French nouns (especially their endings) that serve as reliable gender markers. The French child undoubtedly uses these markers from infancy, but without awareness. They permit him to know various types of masculine and feminine nouns and to generalize to new nouns with an ability that strikes the non-French student of the language as uncanny.

We have restated and expanded a model of learning that psychologists who study language appear to have neglected. In our attempt to demonstrate the relevance and descriptive power of this approach, we have emphasized the monolingual child learning his first language. Those children who simultaneously acquire two or more languages from the beginning, with no apparent difficulty, provide a more dramatic example of the interplay of human heredity and experience on language development. The ease and thoroughness with which a child acquires two or more languages in infancy highlights the way that the human being builds up extremely abstract higher-order properties of language from primary-order part-perceptions. The bilingual person's knowledge of languages-as-systems exemplifies itself in his capacity to keep two or more systems functionally segregated so that when one is in operation, the other is switched off (or at least nearly so).

Perhaps our model offers a productive alternative to the now-polarized positions taken by the nativists and the empiricists in psycholinguistics. The isolated examples we have chosen are meant to illustrate an approach; they are of course *not* a final answer. Ω

v. psychological development

Developmental psychologists, who focus on aspects of the complex growth of an individual—such as cognitive development and social-emotional development—are currently making fresh attempts to find satisfactory answers to many long-standing controversies in their field. The heredity-environment issue is perhaps the most prominent of these fundamental controversies. Psychologists and the public have recently recognized the crucial importance of an optimal early environment in stimulating intellectual and social growth. However, developmental psychologists have just begun to understand the factors that stimulate the development of socially and intellectually competent human beings.

One of the principal goals of child psychologists is a description of the succession of logical systems that children use to explain their experiences and to structure their knowledge. The seminal theorizing of Jean Piaget—who, with his long-time co-worker, Bärbel Inhelder, is interviewed by Elizabeth Hall—is currently the orientation point for much of this research. According to Piaget, children are born with certain inherited structures and reflexes that, in combination with their inherited tendencies to adapt and organize, make them active seekers of knowledge; children construct an understanding of the world through their own activity rather than through passive response to stimulation. Furthermore, children's thinking undergoes three revolutions between birth and adolescence as they advance from the sensorimotor stage through the preoperational stage to the stages of concrete and formal operations.

By examining children's errors in reasoning, Joachim Wohlwill, working with Piaget and Inhelder, has begun measuring the chasm that separates the intellectual lives of adults and children and that distinguishes between children of different ages. Wohlwill asks if these fundamental shifts in the organization of thought occur purely as a function of maturation or because children will abandon one stage after a sufficient number of conditioned responses. He concludes that counting, matching, and ordering, which constitute a major part of each child's daily play, may stimulate and mold the development of logical facilities.

It is the absence of beneficial everyday learning experiences that may cause some children to lag intellectually, says Sidney Bijou. He argues that "mental retardation" may be more the product of poor behavior shaping than of vague factors, such as defective intelligence, that are often cited. Constitutional abnormalities, inconsistent reinforcement, reinforcement of undesirable behavior, and severe punishment may act singly or in combination to create insurmountable obstacles to further cognitive development.

Many developmental psychologists see intimate links between the development of cognition and other aspects of growth. Like Piaget, Jerome Bruner proposes that the roots of adult intelligence can be seen in the most basic sensorimotor skills. He hypothesizes a feedback system in which cognitive development keeps pace with the child's motor development: Information about the world, which serves as grist for the child's cognitive mill, is acquired at an early stage through his or her physical actions. Conversely, information that is the product of physical interaction is unavailable to the extent that the child is not cognitively sophisticated enough to recognize what he or she can achieve through intentional behavior.

Lawrence Kohlberg uses Piaget's cognitive-developmental approach to analyze the different ways in which children think about their places in the social world. He believes that they pass through as many as six stages of moral development, which are defined by the universality, generality, and impersonality of the children's justifications for a moral action or decision. The order of these stages does not appear to vary across cultures, although the speed with which the stages are reached may vary, as a function of cultural differences.

By studying infant's attentiveness to visual stimuli, Jerome Kagan has demonstrated the effect of early experience on later behavior. It is interesting to note that differences in attentiveness appear during the first year of life and are related to differences in social class. Kagan stresses the importance of enriched environments as early as the first few weeks of life, and he urges an education for mothers that will ensure satisfactory learning conditions for their infants.

Because of the social and political turmoil of the last few years, psychologists are more concerned than ever with determining whether such social phenomena as aggression and sex-role differentiation are rooted ineluctably and immutably in the biological heritage of the human species or whether they are merely the products of social conditioning. The isolation experiments with rhesus monkeys reported by Harry and Margaret Harlow show convincingly that social development, like cognitive development, results from the interaction of biological predispositions to learn certain behavioral sequences and the specific learning opportunities encountered by a young animal. Normally, such social behavior as affection, fear, and mating will blossom with exposure to the experiences that are typical for the young of a species, but this social behavior will be maladaptive in the absence of typical experiences. The Harlows point as well to the importance of early parent-infant or peer-peer interaction in establishing the place of a young monkey in the dominance hierarchy, a natural system that controls the expression of disruptive aggression.

Kagan has investigated the development of sex-role identity and behavior in human beings. He notes the subtle experiential ways in which cultural definitions and expectations of sex-appropriate behavior and attitudes are transmitted to children. While contemporary American society tends to minimize sexual differences where purely social factors are concerned, cross-cultural similarities in sex-role standards and the early age at which both children and monkeys begin to show sex-typed behavior suggest that there is at least some biological justification for retaining male and female roles in matters other than anatomy.

The American style of child-rearing and education is certainly not the only possible one, nor is it necessarily the most successful. Studies of the cultural goals, standards, and educa-tional methods of other countries can provide some perspective on American ways. Leslie and Karen Rabkin, in their discussion of Israeli kibbutzim, examine an aspect of the heredity-environment question that is currently causing bitter debate in this country: Can children develop properly in the absence of a nuclear family that lives together? In kibbutzim, parents see their children for only a few hours a day, yet most evaluations fail to uncover a larger proportion of emotional problems among kibbutzniks than among Israeli children who are not raised on kibbutzim. Perhaps the lesson is that the quality rather than the quantity of parent-child interaction is the most important determinant of children's social-emotional development. However, reports about the performance of kibbutz children as adults and parents are not yet complete. The Israeli experiments could well provide some useful information about the long-range effects of day-care programs, but, as the Rabkins warn, a radical restructuring of American values and goals would be necessary before similar programs could succeed in this country.

The study of Russian nursery schools by Michael and Sheila Cole explodes many of the myths that are believed to characterize Soviet educational philosophy. Rather than promote deindividuation in service to the state, Russian schools recognize and nurture individual differences. Like Piaget and Montessori, Soviet developmentalists consider the roots of adult intelligence to be in early sensorimotor activity, so children are encouraged to play an active role in developing general strategies for gathering and structuring information. However, instead of waiting for children to spontaneously discover logical truths, as Piaget and Montessori would suggest, Russians prefer to make real-world problems the whetstone on which intellectual skills are shaped and honed in preparation for the eventual dedication of these skills to the betterment of Soviet society. National character may dictate to some degree the ways in which a country's children, its greatest natural resource, are brought to a useful maturity.

A Conversation with

Jean Piaget

and Bärbel Inhelder
by Elizabeth Hall

The giant of developmental psychology and his collaborator talk about children — *how* they learn, *when* they learn, *what* they learn.

Jean Piaget: I must warn you that I cannot understand English when it is pronounced properly. If you will say *zis* and *zat* and *zhose,* I will be able to follow you.

Elizabeth Hall: And if you promise to speak French wretchedly, I might understand you. But luckily we have Guy Cellerier here to solve our language problems.

You and Sigmund Freud are regarded as the two giants of 20th-Century philosophy. If Freud has changed our thinking about personality, you have certainly changed our thinking about intelligence, yet a great deal of confusion surrounds your work. Whenever someone tries to explain your theories to the rest of us, he succeeds only in obscuring them.

Piaget: Yes, I've seen that done. Perhaps we will do better today.

Hall: It is interesting that both Fred Skinner and D. O. Hebb intended to become novelists.

Piaget: Is that so?

Hall: I was surprised myself when I first heard it. They regard intelligence empirically, while you began as a natural scientist and look at intelligence philosophically.

Piaget: First we must agree on what you mean by philosophical. All the problems I have attacked are epistemological. All the methods I have used are either experimental or formalizations that Americans would also regard as empirical.

Hall: Psychology was originally a part of philosophy; William James was a philosopher. You have raided the field of philosophy again and captured the area of epistemology.

Piaget: It is true that I have taken epistemology away from philosophy, but I have not taken it only for psychology. It belongs in all the sciences; they are all concerned with the nature and origin of knowledge.

Hall: What caused you to turn from biology and the study of mollusks to epistemology?

Piaget: I began to study mollusks when I was 10. The director of the Museum of Natural History in Neuchâtel, who was a mollusk specialist, invited me to assist him twice a week. I helped him stick labels on his shell collection and he taught me malacology. I began publishing articles about shells when I was 15.

Hall: That's quite young to be publishing scientific papers.

Piaget: Specialists in malacology are rare. Because I was so young, I had to decline invitations from foreign specialists who wanted to meet me. My first paper—a one-page report of a part-albino sparrow I had seen—was published when I was only 10. It was about the time that I began to publish articles on shells that I found a book on philosophy in my father's library. My new passion for philosophy was encouraged when my godfather introduced me to Henri Bergson's creative evolution. Suddenly the problem of knowledge appeared to me in a new light. I became convinced very quickly that most of the problems in philosophy were problems of knowledge, and that most problems of knowledge were problems of biology. You see, the problem of knowledge is the problem of the relation between the subject and the object—how the subject knows the object. If you translate this into biological terms, it is a problem of the organism's adapting to its environment. I decided to consecrate my

160

In somnolent Switzerland lives a gracious giant who has upset the world of developmental psychology. Jean Piaget, born in Neuchâtel on August 9, 1896, has done more to shake psychologists' faith in the stimulus-response approach to child psychology than all the humanistic psychologists of the Third Force put together. Sigmund Freud discovered the unconscious, it is said, and Piaget discovered the conscious.

Piaget believes that reflexes and other automatic patterns of behavior have a minor role in the development of human intelligence. It is only in the first few days of the infant's life that his behavior depends on automatic behavioral reaction. When Piaget first put forth this view of infancy it was radically opposed to accepted theory. Both Freudian psychology and traditional behaviorist theory emphasized that man seeks to escape from stimulation and excitation, while Piaget maintained that the infant often actively seeks stimulation. Some writers claim that the conflict between Piaget's view of intellectual development and modern behavioral theory is more apparent than real and they point to a compatibility between Piaget's system and D. O. Hebb's neurological theory.

In Piaget's view of intellectual development the child passes through four major periods: sensori-motor (birth to two years); pre-operational (two to seven years); concrete operational (seven to 11 years); and formal operational

(above 11 years). It is not until the growing child reaches the two operational stages that he begins to acquire the various concepts of conservation. When Piaget speaks of conservation, he refers to the idea that the mass of an object remains constant no matter how much the form changes. For example, if you give a five-year-old two tumblers, each half-full of orangeade, he will agree that there is the same amount of orangeade in each. But if, before his eyes, you pour the orangeade from one glass into a tall, narrow container, he will say that there is more orangeade in the new glass than in the old one. The five-year-old has no concept of the conservation of substance. A child who does not understand the conservation of length will maintain that a necklace laid out in a straight line is longer than an identical necklace that lies in a circle. The average child acquires both these concepts by the time he is eight. Other important conservations that the child must learn are the conservation of number, of area, of weight and of volume.

Piaget tested many of his ideas on his own three children, watching hour after patient hour as Lucienne, Laurent and Jacqueline developed through infancy and childhood.

Although his theories have received increasingly wide attention, Piaget remains a modest man. He rarely grants interviews and for 10 years he has, with some effort, avoided Swiss television cameras. He feels that time

spent talking with reporters is time stolen from his work.

It is said that he speaks no English, and it was with some trepidation that we scheduled a bilingual interview. But there was no need for concern. Piaget perhaps does not speak English, but he understands it. Frequently he answered questions before the translator could say a word. On one occasion he interrupted the translation to say that his reply had been expanded but that he agreed with the addition.

At 73, Piaget follows a full schedule. He teaches four hours a week, supervises doctoral candidates, directs both the Institute for Psychology and the International Center of Genetic Epistemology, and edits the Archives de Psychologie. And he writes. Each morning he produces his daily quota of manuscript before most people are awake. In the summer he retreats to the Swiss Alps where he writes in an abandoned farmhouse. During the year he writes in the airports of the world. Always at least two hours early for his plane—and sometimes as much as five—he settles down to work, meerschaum clenched in his teeth, unaware of the bustle about him. Thirty books and more than a hundred articles now bear his name. But he is being surpassed by his admirers—at the current rate of publication there soon will be many more volumes about Jean Piaget than by Jean Piaget.

—Elizabeth Hall

life to this biological explanation of knowledge.

Hall: With your interest in the relation between the subject and the object, I am surprised that you did not become a Gestalt psychologist.

Piaget: If I had come across the writings of Max Wertheimer and of Wolfgang Köhler when I was 18, I would have. But I was reading psychology only in French, so I was unacquainted with their work.

Hall: In your autobiography, you said that your natural-history background provided protection against the demon of philosophy.

Piaget: The demon of philosophy is taking the easy way out. You believe that you can solve problems by sitting in your office and reasoning them out. Because I was a biologist, I knew that deductions must be made from facts.

Hall: But after you establish the facts, then you go back to your office and work out the problem.

Piaget: Yes. Now, if you don't have a philosophical outlook, you probably won't be a good scientist. Abstract reflection is fundamental to seeing problems clearly. But the error of philosophy—its demon—is to believe that you can go ahead and solve the problem you formulated in the office without going into the field and establishing the facts.

Hall: You once wrote that you detested any departure from reality.

Piaget: That was because of my mother's poor mental health. At the beginning of my studies in psychology, I was interested in psychoanalysis and pathological psychology because of her. But I always preferred the workings of the intellect to the tricks of the unconscious.

Hall: Does your dislike of unreality extend to literature?

Piaget: Oh, no. I read many novels—and I even wrote a philosophical novel many years ago. Novels are not pathological.

Hall: I understand that your study of intelligence came about when you tried to standardize reasoning tests at Alfred Binet's laboratory school in Paris.

Piaget: It was Binet's school, but I was not working on Binet's test. My task was to standardize Cyril Burt's tests on the children of Paris. I never actually did it. Standardization was not at all interesting; I preferred to study the errors on the test. I became interested in the reasoning process behind the children's wrong answers.

Hall: Has anyone tried to develop an intelligence test based on your research?

Piaget: That kind of research is going on in two places right now. Here at the University of Geneva, Vinh Bang—a Vietnamese psychologist—is working on a test. And Monique Laurendeau and Adrien Pinard, two psychologists at the University of Montreal, have been using my experimental methods and giving all the various tests to a single child. Just now they are back-checking to see if their experiments and mine produce similar results, and they are publishing volumes on different aspects of the experiments.

Hall: Would such a test have to be an individual test, or could it be given to a group of children at one time?

Piaget: The hope is that we will have a battery of tests that can be given to a group of children together. The risk is that we will get deformed answers.

Hall: Isn't a group test more likely to run aground on the same shoals that wreck the standard tests—a reliance on the answer instead of the method of reasoning?

Piaget: The difference will be that the clinical method will already have been used in studying the reasoning of children at each stage of development. We will have a background to help interpret the answers. It will have advantages that the I. Q. test lacks because the method of reasoning is unknown.

Hall: Your research — especially in conservation—revealed that children did not understand things that adults assumed they knew.

Piaget: It's just that no adult ever had the idea of asking children about conservation. It was so obvious that if you change the shape of an object, the quantity will be conserved. Why ask a child? The novelty lay in asking the question.

I first discovered the problem of conservation when I worked with young epileptics from 10 to 15. I wanted to find some empirical way of distinguishing them from normal children. I went around with four coins and four beads, and I would put the coins and beads in one-to-one correspondence and then hide one of the coins. If the three remaining coins were then stretched out into a longer line, the epileptic children said they had more coins than beads. No con-

"I always preferred the workings of the intellect to the tricks of the unconscious."

servation at all. I thought I had discovered a method to distinguish normal from abnormal children. Then I went on to work with normal children and discovered that all children lack conservation.

Hall: Isn't it fortunate that you checked?

Piaget: A biologist would have to verify; a philosopher would not have checked.

Hall: When you say that the young child is egocentric, just what do you mean?

Piaget: That term has had the worst interpretations of any word I have used.

Hall: That's why I asked the question.

Piaget: When I refer to the child, I use the term egocentric in an epistemological sense, not in an affective or a moral one. This is why it has been misinterpreted. The egocentric child—and all children are egocentric—considers his own point of view as the only possible one. He is incapable of putting himself in someone else's place, because he is unaware that the other person has a point of view.

Hall: Would this be analogous to man's original belief that the universe revolved around the earth?

Piaget: That is precisely the example I was going to give. It is a natural tendency of the intelligence and it becomes corrected very slowly as the child matures. Many children, you know, believe that the sun and the moon follow them as they walk. A

more prosaic example is the way a young child makes up a new word and assumes that everyone knows exactly what he means by it.

Hall: Then morality doesn't enter the picture until the child is aware of other viewpoints and disregards them. At one time you did extensive work on the way children develop a sense of right and wrong.

Piaget: That was 40 years ago and I haven't gone back to it. But we can talk about it if you like.

Hall: I believe you said that the child's sense of moral judgment is largely independent of adult influence.

Piaget: You must distinguish between two periods in the development of moral judgment. In the first period, a child accepts his rules from authority and the ideas of adults are impor-

tant to him. In the second period, he is independent of adults. Solidarity grows between children and a morality develops, based on cooperation.

Hall: As more mothers work, children are placed in nursery schools at earlier ages, and communal methods of life, like those in the kibbutz, are becoming more common. Suppose adults did not impose standards of right and wrong upon children who were reared in a kibbutz. Would the children develop this sense of moral justice and cooperation anyway?

Piaget: It would happen even earlier. And if the adults are ready to discuss matters seriously with the children they will form a system of cooperation with the adults.

Hall: Would the morality that developed under this cooperative system

163

be likely to lessen the conflict between the generations?

Piaget: I would think so. Children often must discover the idea of justice at the expense of their parents. From about the age of seven or eight, justice prevails over obedience. But this theory should be studied experimentally.

Hall: You would have to go out into the field and test it.

Piaget: I have other pies in the oven.

Hall: I'm interested in the implications for education of the pies you've already baked. In the United States we have a concept called reading readiness. Some educators say that a child cannot learn to read until he has reached a mental age of six years and six months.

Piaget: The idea of reading readiness corresponds to the idea of competence in embryology. If a specific chemical inductor hits the developing embryo, it will produce an effect if the competence is there, and if it is not, the effect will not occur. So the concept of readiness is not bad but I am not sure that it can be applied to reading. Reading aptitude may not be related to mental age. There could easily be a difference of aptitude between children independent of mental age. But I cannot state that as a fact because I have not studied it closely.

Hall: In recent years the new mathematics has come into American schools. Along with a new vocabulary we introduced new concepts like set theory.

Piaget: Seven years would be perfectly all right for most operations of set theory because children have their own spontaneous operations that are very akin to those concepts. But when you teach set theory you should use the child's actual vocabulary along with activity — make the child do natural things. The important thing is not to teach modern mathematics with ancient methods.

As for teaching children concepts that they have not attained in their spontaneous development, it is completely useless. A British mathematician attempted to teach his five-year-old daughter the rudiments of set theory and conservation. He did the typical experiments of conservation with numbers. Then he gave the child two collections and the five-year-old immediately said those are two sets. But she couldn't count and she had no idea of conservation.

Hall: But she had the vocabulary.

Piaget: That's the point. You cannot teach concepts verbally; you must use a method founded on activity.

Hall: If you had the power in your hands, would you make any changes in the school curriculum?

Piaget: We spend so much time teaching things that don't have to be taught. Spelling is a good example. One learns to spell much better just by reading; teaching spelling is a waste of time. And history. We should reduce the amount of time we spend making people disgusted with history. We should concentrate on giving them a taste for reading history—which is not the same thing at all.

There is one addition I would like to make to the curriculum. So far as I know the experimental method is not taught in any school and it is a way of checking your hypotheses. If we can teach this method to children they will learn that it is possible to check their thoughts.

Hall: How would you go about teaching this?

Piaget: In the experimental method you have the problem of what causes a given effect. A certain number of factors intervene and—in order to discover the cause—you must keep all factors constant except one.

Hall: As when you gave the children five flasks of colorless liquid and asked them to produce yellow.

Piaget: That's right. One of the flasks contained only water, another flask contained bleach, and the other three liquids that when mixed together turned yellow. We showed the child the color but not how to make it. The child also had to determine just what sort of liquid was in the flasks that held bleach and water. Not until a child reaches the age of 12 does he test all possible combinations of fluids and solve the problem.

Hall: What if the teacher were to demonstrate this experiment to the class?

Piaget: It would be completely useless. The child must discover the method for himself through his own activity.

Hall: That sounds very much like John Dewey's concept of learning by doing.

Piaget: Indeed it does; John Dewey was a great man.

Hall: Now that we've mentioned an American educator, may I ask what you have called "the American question"? Is it possible to speed up the learning of conservation concepts?

"John Dewey was a great man."

Piaget: In turn may I ask the counterquestion? Is it a good thing to accelerate the learning of these concepts? Acceleration is certainly possible but first we must find out whether it is desirable or harmful. Take the concept of object permanency—the realization that a ball, a rattle or a person continues to exist when it no longer can be seen. A kitten develops this concept at four months, a human baby at nine months; but the kitten stops right there while the baby goes on to learn more advanced concepts. Perhaps a certain slowness is useful in developing the capacity to assimilate new concepts.

We also know that the ease of learning varies with the developmental level of the child. In the same number of learning sessions children who have reached an advanced stage make marked progress over younger children. It appears that there is an optimum speed of development. If you write a book too slowly it won't be a good book; if you write it too fast it won't be a good book either. No one has made studies to determine the optimum speed.

Hall: But wouldn't the optimum speed vary with the person? Some people naturally write faster than others—and write just as well.

Piaget: That's highly possible. We know the average speed of the children we have studied in our Swiss culture but there is nothing that says that the average speed is the optimum. But blindly to accelerate the learning of conservation concepts could be even worse than doing nothing.

Hall: I think we ask the American question because the ever-increasing length of education troubles us. Many of us would like to find some way to shorten those years that go into professional preparation.

Piaget: It is difficult to decide just how to shorten studies. If you spend one year studying something verbally that requires two years of active study, then you have actually lost a year. If we were willing to lose a bit more time and let the children be active, let them use trial and error on different things, then the time we seem to have lost we may have actually gained. Children may develop a general method that they can use on other subjects.

Hall: And we come back to learning by doing. Some of your experiments

"Blindly to accelerate the learning of conservation concepts could be even worse than doing nothing."

with the child's concept of space indicate that children come to a Euclidean world view very slowly. Does this same conception of space evolve in all peoples, or is it a feature of Western culture?

Piaget: I wouldn't say that Euclidean geometry is cultural. You know, historically scientific geometry began with Euclidean metric geometry. Projective geometry followed and only later did we develop topology. But so far as theory goes, both projective and metric geometry can be derived from topology. Now if you examine the way a child develops his idea of space, you will see that he first develops topological intuitions, so that the child's ideas are closer to mathematical theory than to history. To get back to your question, any group—if they develop that far—would certainly acquire a Euclidean geometry, because once you have the topological intuitions and actual measurement, it is the simplest geometry.

Hall: Then you do not believe that our language determines the way we see the world?

Piaget: There is a very close relationship between language and thought, but language does not govern thoughts or form operations. It is lan-

guage that is influenced by operations and not our operations that are influenced by language.

Dr. H. Sinclair has made some interesting experiments along this line. She had two groups of children; one group had conservation, the other group did not. She took the group of children that did not understand conservation and taught them the language used by the children who understood the concept. They learned to use "long" and "short" and "wide" and "narrow" in a consistent way. She wanted to see if the concepts would come once the language was learned. They did not. If a ball of clay was pulled into a sausage, the children could describe it as "long" and "thin." But they did not understand that the clay was longer but thinner than the ball and therefore the same quantity.

Hall: What if the language does not express a concept?

Piaget: The thing that changes with different languages is the way we partition reality—the way we break the world into composing parts. But this translation of concepts into their parts is not essential to thought.

Hall: Jerome Bruner has studied child development extensively and he is one of your respectful critics. Could you explain to me the difference between your theoretical approach and that of Bruner's?

Piaget: It is very difficult to explain the difference between Bruner and me. Bruner is a mobile and active man and has held a sequence of different points of view. Essentially Bruner does not believe in mental operations while I do. Bruner replaces operations with factors that have varied through his different stages—Bruner's stages, not the child's. Bruner uses things like language, like image. When Bruner was at the stage of strategies he used to say that his strategies were more or less Piaget's operations. At that time our theories were closest. Since then he has changed his point of view.

Hall: Might we say that one day Bruner may reach the operational stage?

Piaget: The answer to your question is that Bruner is an unpredictable man—this is what makes his charm.

Hall: Can we learn about man only by studying man? Or can we go into the laboratory and study rats and primates?

Piaget: Comparative studies are necessary but one must not make the mistake of believing that a rat is sufficient. Many theories of some schools that I will not name are based on the rat. It is not enough for me.

Hall: But I can mention a school of psychology. Could you describe your differences with behaviorism?

Piaget: That's too broad a term. Let's talk instead about behaviorist empiricism; I think that's what you're really asking about. Empiricism implies that reality can be reduced to observable features and that knowledge must limit itself to those features. Biologists have shown that the organism constantly interacts with its environment; the view that it submits passively to the environment has become untenable. How then can man be simply a recorder of outside events? When he transforms his environment by acting upon it he gains a deeper knowledge of the world than any copy of reality ever could provide. What is more empiricism cannot explain the existence of mathematics which deals with unobservable features and with cognitive constructions.

In biology the exact counterpart of behaviorist empiricism is the Lamarckian theory of variation and evolution—a long-abandoned doctrine. When we look at the famous stimulus-response schema we find that behaviorist psychologists have retained a strictly Lamarckian outlook. The contemporary biological revolution has passed them by. If we are to get a tenable stimulus-response theory we must completely modify its classical meaning. Before a stimulus can set off a response the organism must be capable of providing it. We talked earlier about the idea of competence in embryology. If this concept applies in learning—and my research indicates that it does—then learning will be different at different developmental levels. It would depend upon the evolution of competences. The classical concept of learning suddenly becomes inadequate.

Hall: Does this mean that individual development is all innate?

Piaget: Not at all. Each man is the product of interaction between heredity and environment. It is virtually impossible to draw a clear line between innate and acquired behavior patterns.

Hall: Are there any pitfalls to trap the unwary psychologist?

Piaget: The danger to psychologists lies in practical applications. Too often psychologists make practical applications before they know what they are applying. We must always keep a place for fundamental research and beware of practical applications when we do not know the foundation of our theories.

Hall: How do you see the future of psychology?

Piaget: With optimism. We see new problems every day.

*A*cross the Rhone River from the University of Geneva, on the other side of the lake, the Palais Wilson stands in a wide lawn. Pansies bloom along the tree-lined quay and down the street Charles II, Duke of Bismarck, rests in his elaborate sepulcher, guarded by his equestrian statue and a flock of pigeons. On the wall that surrounds the palace, a plaque honors the memory of Woodrow Wilson, President of the United States and founder of the League of Nations.

The Palais Wilson houses the Jean Jacques Rousseau Institute, a part of the University devoted to psychology and education. Just next to the Institute, beside the ultra-modern, tourist-filled Hotel President, is a

"Many theories of some schools that I will not name are based on the rat. It is not enough for me."

kindergarten where students from all over the world study the unfolding of the child mind.

Bärbel Inhelder works in a narrow, book-lined office in the Palais Wilson. She is a professor of developmental psychology, and she began her collaboration with Piaget while she was an undergraduate. Together they have written more than nine books, and she is the author of more than 50 articles. She is President of the Association de Psychologie Scientifique de Langue Française and a past president of the Swiss Psychological Society. In 1968, with Piaget, she received the Award of the American Educational Research Association. She has been a Harvard research fellow and a Rockefeller fellow and has lectured at M.I.T., Princeton, Berkeley, Stanford, Temple and Penn State. (Her English, which has a slight German accent, is fluent.)

The primitive life holds great attraction for Inhelder. She spends her summers in a remote cabin in the Alps "far away from everything." There she depends on candlelight and draws her own water, and there—like Piaget—she writes.

Hall: Did you always plan to become a psychologist?

Bärbel Inhelder: It is mostly a matter of chance. I was born in Saint Gall, in the German part of Switzerland. Originally I came to Geneva for a summer course at the University. I wanted to learn some French. I had some background in biology and in education, and then I discovered psychology and Edouard Claparède and Piaget here at the University. Originally I thought I would study psychology for a few years. Then I liked it so much that I stayed on to take my doctorate.

After I had been at the University for a few weeks, first Claparède and then Piaget asked me to do some research.

Hall: In the United States it is highly unusual for a first-year student to be asked to do research.

Inhelder: It is not so very unusual here. During my first year of training, Piaget asked me to put some sugar in water and study children's reactions to what they saw. This led to our work on conservation concepts. My first publication was on conservation. I still remember the day when Piaget said: "Now look. I have some ideas on this. Let's write a book together." So I wrote my first book with Piaget before I delivered my thesis.

Hall: That's exciting.

Inhelder: I was just lucky.

Hall: That was more than chance. What happened after you finished your doctoral?

Inhelder: I went back to Saint Gall, where the cantonal authorities asked me to create a school psychology service. There I began to study the reasoning processes of mentally retarded children and in 1943 I delivered my thesis based on this work. It was not published in English until many years later. (*The Diagnosis of Reasoning in the Mentally Retarded*, John Day, 1968.)

Hall: Did you do any research into the causes of retardation?

Inhelder: I was more concerned with diagnosing the retardation than determining its cause. To start with, my job was to go from one village to the next and examine the children and find out the best way of diagnosing retardation.

Hall: Did you find that mentally retarded children develop conservation theories?

Inhelder: They develop them much later but they go through exactly the same steps normal children do. Using this developmental approach, it was relatively easy to distinguish between pseudodefective children and the truly retarded.

Hall: What caused the pseudodefective children to be labeled as feebleminded?

Inhelder: Often the children were socially deprived. Sometimes they would have specific defects like dyslexia or aphasia. Under the global approach, they had all been considered retarded. We found that such defects would respond to a specific kind of help.

Hall: Have you reached any conclusions as to the causes of mental retardation?

Inhelder: No, I have not. I am a psychologist. We would need a whole team of psychologists, biochemists, geneticists and sociologists to even try to determine *some* of the causes of mental retardation.

Hall: Do you think we will ever be able to determine what is environmental and what is hereditary?

Inhelder: I'm not sure if that is the right way to ask the question. I know the whole problem of heredity and environment has been given renewed attention. In fact, it's experimentally impossible to separate the two factors in human beings.

Hall: There seems to be no way to construct a study that would eliminate environmental influences.

Inhelder: No way at all. If one succeeds in training our young patients to overcome their specific difficulty then it is likely that their potential was more or less normal. From the psychological point of view that's about the only thing we can do. In fact we did all kinds of training studies with a group of children with different difficulties who weren't able to go through normal school training. As a result of our training method— which is an application of our fundamental studies in growth and development—they were able to gain a lot. But one or two of them did not gain at all, so it is highly probable that their potential was not high enough. You have to take each case individually and devote a lot of time to it.

Hall: So there is no easy way out. I was greatly interested in the paper you gave me yesterday. The results you got on the memory studies were remarkable.

Inhelder: The results were in accord

Bärbel Inhelder

with our theories on the development of thought. We showed the children 10 sticks that varied in length and then asked them to draw the sticks from memory. The children under four drew a line of roughly equal sticks; those under five drew groups of paired, unequal sticks. At about five they often drew three groups of sticks—small, medium size and large ones. A month or two later they began to draw a series in ascending length but it was not complete. It's only at about six that the children's drawing became correct evocations of what they had seen.

Hall: It was their recall after six months that was so interesting.

Inhelder: Yes. We asked the same children to reproduce the line of sticks again. But we did not show them sticks. After six to eight months a majority of the children remembered the arrangement better than they had just after they had seen the sticks; that is to say their recall was one "stage" better.

Hall: Just how does this support your theories?

Inhelder: Classical associationist empiricism considers the image to be the residual product of perception—and a fundamental element of thought. We, however, believe that children progressively structure reality by means of operations which gradually increase in complexity. According to this theory, the memory code itself depends on the subject's

operations and the code will be modified during development.

Hall: That means that the memory of things for which children are developing concepts will improve as their concepts improve.

Inhelder: You might put it that way. It indicates that memory images do not stem from perception; they are linked to operational schemes. These schemes control the images and are dominant over the model that has been seen.

Hall: That is impressive. You have been studying children with Professor Piaget for 33 years. What changes would you make in the school curriculum?

Inhelder: There is quite a lot to do in this field. We must first determine more of the developmental laws; we must find out how the child is able to assimilate through his own schemes the knowledge we try to pass on to him. I think it is also very important to know the most fundamental structures of the sciences, grammar and mathematics we want to teach. For this we need the help of good mathematicians, good physicists and good linguists.

Hall: You're not talking about the elementary teachers, but about the teachers of teachers?

Inhelder: I'm really talking about the people who can best help in this research. Here in our center of epistemology we bring together the scientists in the different disciplines —linguistics, logic, mathematics, physics and developmental psychology. The scientists give us a heuristic for our research and we can pass on what we learn about developmental laws to the teachers.

Hall: So your changes would be more in the education of teachers than in the curriculum?

Inhelder: We can train the teachers to make curriculum studies and we can give them advice based on our studies, but I think that the educators themselves must work out their own curriculum.

Hall: What kind of advice might you give them?

Inhelder: The order of the introduction of the fundamental mathematical concepts might be changed to conform to the developmental laws of the child. We could give training in topology very early because it is based on much more elementary structures than is Euclidean geometry. But even Euclidean geometry should not be delayed until the child reaches secondary school. Basic concepts in mathematics and in science can be introduced to children from seven to 10, if these are divorced from their traditional mathematical context.

Hall: Would you have the children do more things themselves instead of just sitting and reading and being lectured to?

Inhelder: Oh, sure. The other essential for introducing basic scientific ideas early is that they be studied through materials that the child can handle himself. Through games for example we can teach probabilistic reasoning long before the child can learn the techniques of the calculus of probabilities or the formal expressions of probability theory. In a science-and-mathematics pre-curriculum, we can establish an intuitive and inductive understanding that will give the child a much firmer foundation on which to build his later formal studies.

Hall: You sound optimistic; how do you feel about the future of psychology?

Inhelder: Quite hopeful.

Hall: So is Professor Piaget.

Inhelder: He likes the profession, as I do.

Hall: There are so many schools of psychology today—analytic and humanist and behaviorist and pseudobehaviorist and neobehaviorist . . .

Inhelder: And even neo-neo-neo behaviorist.

Hall: You use empirical methods in your work, but your theoretical approach is not that of the behaviorist.

Inhelder: George Miller once called himself a subjective behaviorist. If we must be labeled, you could say the same thing about us. We have a much more relativistic approach in regard to what is innate and what is acquired than do the behaviorists, and we hold a constructivist position on development and on the constructions that are going on inside the black box.

Hall: Will we ever get inside the black box?

Inhelder: We can study the input to the box and see how the output changes with age. We can infer some rules, then do more experiments and make new inferences. These are the only things we can do. ∩

"George Miller once called himself a subjective behaviorist. If we must be labeled, you could say the same thing about us."

THE MYSTERY OF THE PRE-LOGICAL CHILD

A five-year-old girl, Mary,
has been taken out of her kindergarten class to participate
in a psychological experiment. She is seated in front of
a table on which two brightly colored necklaces lie side
by side; they are of equal length, and their ends are neatly aligned.
"Let's pretend that the blue one is yours," the psychologist tells her,
"and the red one is mine. Who do you think has the longer necklace,
you or me?" Mary slightly puzzled, replies with conviction, "We
both do!"—her way of asserting that the two lengths are equal.
"That's right, but watch carefully," says the experimenter as she picks
up her own necklace and forms a circle out of it. "Now tell me, Mary,
whose necklace is longer, or is mine still just as long as yours?"
Mary stretches out her arms to illustrate length, and beams:
"Mine is longest! You made yours into a ring, and mine is all *this* long."

By Joachim F. Wohlwill

In schools, psychological laboratories, and child-study centers across the country and throughout the world, children are participating in such experiments in our attempts to answer one of the most difficult and puzzling questions about child development: How does the uniquely human capacity for logical thought develop? How does the child's thinking evolve from a pre-logical stage to one defined by the rules of adult logic? Children are being asked questions about lengths, weights, amounts, and numbers, and about space, time, and probability to see if they use a qualitatively different type of reasoning from that used by adults, or if children—naive realists that they are—place undue trust in appearances.

By the time she is six or seven, Mary will know that the length of a string of beads is conserved—that is, its length will not change even if its longness disappears when both ends are joined in a circle. How does she gain the concept of length as a dimension so that she ignores the perceptual cues presented by changes in shape? Does understanding of dimension, class, probability, and the like come from a natural process of maturation or from extensive teaching and experience? A generation ago the child-mind was pictured either as an empty shell that gradually fills with knowledge picked up piece by piece from the environment, or as an adult-mind-in-miniature which grows to its full size as the child develops. Today, many psychologists believe that neither view is correct. Instead, they see a structured mind, internally consistent yet externally illogical—a kind of Alice-in-Wonderland world where lengths, weights, and distances have as much constancy as the shape of "silly putty."

This new picture has aroused widespread and vigorous debate, not only among child psychologists, but also among educators because it raises a host of questions about our understanding of mental processes in general and about child development in particular. Do we develop in specific stages on our way to adult reasoning? Is this development "pre-set" as is a child's physical growth, or can it be speeded up by teaching and experience? If so, by what methods of teaching and by what kinds of experiences? Since what we call intelligence involves to a large extent conceptual thinking, our inquiry holds important

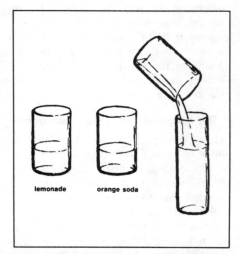

lemonade   orange soda

In an experiment which Jean Piaget made famous, children of different ages are shown two identical glasses, each containing an equal amount of lemonade or orange soda. When the lemonade is poured into a tall thin container, the average five-year-old insists there is more lemonade than orange soda; the six-year-old becomes confused; and the seven-year-old knows the meaning of conservation of liquid.

implications for our understanding of this much-debated subject.

Jean Piaget— Explorer of a New World

The current concern with the conceptual world of childhood and with the child's mode of reasoning has been inspired very largely by the work of Jean Piaget at the Institute Jean-Jacques Rousseau in Geneva, Switzerland. During the past 30 years, Piaget and his collaborators have mapped out, step by step and book by book, the dimensions of the curious and fascinating world which exists in the child's mind.

Let us sit in on one of Piaget's experiments. On the table in front of Johnny, a typical five-year-old, are two glasses identical in size and shape. Piaget's glass is half full of orange soda and Johnny's glass is half full of lemonade. Piaget puts a tall, thin glass on the table and pours Johnny's lemonade into it [see illustration, above.] "Now who has more to drink, you or me?" the famous experimenter asks the five-year-old. "I have," Johnny says. "There's more lemonade in mine because it's higher in the glass." The five-year-old is convinced 'that he has more lemonade in his new glass even when he is asked: "Are you sure it just doesn't look as though there is more?" Piaget points out that his own glass is wider than Johnny's new glass,

but the child replies, "Yes, but this one goes way up to *here*, so there's more." Pointing to the original lemonade container, the experimenter then asks: "Suppose we pour your lemonade back into the glass it came from—then what?" Johnny remains firm: "There would still be more lemonade."

The responses of Lonny, a typical six-year-old, are interestingly different. When the lemonade is poured into the taller, narrower glass and Piaget asks, "Do we both have the same amount to drink?" Lonny, on thinking it over, says, "Well, no." Asked to explain why, he says, "Your glass is bigger." But he becomes confused when the experimenter points out that the new glass is taller: "I guess there's more lemonade in the tall glass." Piaget asks, "Suppose we poured your lemonade back into the glass it came from?" Shades of Alice-in-Wonderland, the answer is, "Then we'd have the same amount to drink."

But now here is Ronny, a year older than Lonny. When the lemonade is poured into the narrow glass, Ronny is sure that there is still the same amount of lemonade as there was before. The conversation goes this way:

"How do you know it is still the same?"

"Well, it was the same before."

"But isn't this new glass higher?"

"Yes, but the old glass is wider."

What do these three tests tell us? Five-year-old Johnny's insistence that there is more to drink in the tall, narrow glass comes from his preoccupation with the most salient fact about the liquids—the difference in their heights. He blithely ignores the difference in the widths of the two glasses. Six-year-old Lonny shows some confusion. He seems to recognize that both the height of the liquid and the width of the glasses must be taken into account, but he can focus only on one aspect of the situation at a time. He recognizes, however, that if the lemonade is poured back into its original container, equality will be restored. But seven-year-old Ronny has no doubts. He *knows* the amount of liquid remains the same because he understands the compensatory relationship between height and width; he understands the concept of conservation of amount.

The Idea of Logical Necessity

Ronny's *understanding* is the critical point for Piaget. It is not merely that

Ronny, at seven, can simultaneously perceive both the height and the width of the containers, but also that he can understand the inverse relationship between the two dimensions and can thus recognize that conservation of amount is a logical necessity. Some children may express this recognition without referring to dimensions at all: "You only poured my lemonade into that glass; it's still just as much." Or, "Well, it's the same as it was before; you haven't given me any more lemonade."

The conservation of amount—which Ronny understands at seven—is but one of a set of dimensions for which children acquire the concept of conservation at different ages. The more important of the "conservations" and the ages at which children, on the average, first show understanding of them, are the following:

Conservation of number (6-7 years): The number of elements in a collection remains unchanged, regardless of how the elements are displaced or spatially rearranged.
Conservation of substance (7-8 years): The amount of a deformable substance such as dough, soft clay, or liquid remains unchanged, regardless of how its shape is altered (as in transforming a ball of clay into a long, narrow snake).
Conservation of length (7-8 years): The length of a line or an object remains unchanged, regardless of how it is displaced in space or its shape altered.
Conservation of area (8-9 years): The total amount of surface covered by a set of plane figures (such as small squares) remains unchanged, in spite of rearranging positions of the figures.
Conservation of weight (9-10 years): The weight of an object remains unchanged, regardless of how its shape is altered.
Conservation of volume (14-15 years): The volume of an object (in terms of the water it displaces) remains unchanged, regardless of changes in its shape.

It must be emphasized that the ages given above are only gross averages; first, because children vary considerably in the rate at which their thinking develops, and second, because their recognition of the concept depends to a certain extent on the way the problem is presented. For example, children may recognize that the number of checkers in a row remains unchanged when the length of the row is expanded, but fail to recognize it when the checkers are stacked in a pile.

The Stage of Concrete Operations

The responses of young children to tests such as those I have described give us a fascinating glimpse into processes which we, as adults, take so much for granted that they scarcely seem to involve thinking at all. But what is the significance of the conservation problem for an understanding of mental development? Piaget holds that the attainment of conservation points to the formation of a new stage in the child's mental development, the stage of concrete operations. This stage is manifested by conservation, and in a variety of other ways which attest to a new mode of reasoning.

For example, if children who have not yet reached the stage of concrete operations are presented with a set of pictures [*see illustration, right*] comprised of seven dogs and three horses, and are asked, "How many animals are there?" they will readily answer, "Ten." They are quite able to recognize that both the subsets—dogs and horses—are part of a total set—animals. But if asked, "Are there more dogs or more animals?" these "pre-operational" children will maintain there are more dogs. They translate the question into one involving a comparison of majority to minority subsets and have difficulty in comparing the elements of a single subset with those of the total set.

For Piaget this indicates that these children as yet lack mental structure corresponding to the logical operation of adding classes—or to use modern jargon, they are not "programmed" to carry out this operation.

The various manifestations of the stage of concrete operations do not necessarily appear at the same time. As we saw, concepts of conservation are attained for various dimensions at different age levels, and one concept may consistently lag behind another closely related concept. Suppose we present a child with two balls of modeling clay, identical in appearance and weight. Let us flatten one of the balls and roll it out into the form of a sausage. Now we will ask the conservation question for two different dimensions, *substance*—"Is there still as much clay in the ball as in the sausage?"—and *weight*—"Does the ball still weigh as much as the sausage?" The same child often will give opposite answers to these questions, and in such cases the child almost invariably asserts conservation for substance while denying it for weight. Thus it appears that the mode of reasoning involved in recognizing conservation of substance precedes that for weight.

The Young Child: Pre-Logical or Merely Naive?

Piaget holds, first, that these phenomena represent qualitative developmental changes in the child's mode of thinking; and second, that they are largely spontaneous and occur independently of teaching or of specific experiences. His views have aroused controversy as vigorous and at times as heated as did the views of Freud. Piaget's descriptions of the phenomena themselves—the diverse ways in which children respond to conceptual tasks—have been on the whole verified and accepted as essentially correct. The controversy rages over the explanation for them. Can the young child's lack of conservation be explained as resulting from a qualitatively different mode of reasoning, characteristic of the pre-operational stage? Or is it merely the result of a naive trust in perceptual cues, combined with a strong tendency to respond to the most obvious, or perceptually salient, aspect of a situation?

For example, the sight of liquid rising in a narrow glass to a height well above that of the shorter, wider glass from which it came conveys a compelling impression of difference in quantity. It is easy to lose sight of the compensating difference in the width of the two glasses. Moreover, in the child's everyday life, glasses tend to be fairly similar in size; thus the height of liquid in a glass is a reasonably reliable index to its amount. There is indeed some evidence to support "naiveté" as an explanation. Studies carried out at Harvard suggest that children who initially lack the notion of conservation can recognize it if the misleading perceptual cues are screened out—that is, if the child cannot see the level of liquid as it is poured into the new container. It must be said, however, that other investigators who replicated this experiment did not obtain similar results.

Martin Braine of Walter Reed Medical Center conducted experiments using the ring-segmented illusion [*see illustration, right*] which showed that children can learn to resist perceptual cues when they are induced to differentiate between appearance and fact. Two shapes, A and B, are first superimposed so that the child can see that B is bigger. A is then placed above B; the child now will assert that A both looks bigger and really is bigger. As a result of a series of such problems in which the experimenter corrects all erroneous responses, the child will learn to pick B as really bigger than A, in the face of the contrary evidence of the senses.

These experiments suggest that the child is inclined to respond naively to perceptual clues, but is this really the whole truth? In collaboration with a student, Michael Katz, I recently carried out the following experiment on the class-inclusion (set-subset) problem described earlier. Instead of presenting pictures of animals, we asked five- and six-year-old children, "Suppose that on a farm there are seven dogs and three horses. Are there more dogs or more animals?" Lo and behold, when the problem was presented in purely verbal form, avoiding perceptual cues, many of the children did consistently better than they did when asked to solve the problem on the basis of pictures [*see illustration, right*].

On the face of it, this finding is the reverse of what might be expected. It is generally considered that at this age children's thinking is highly concrete, making it difficult for them to deal with purely hypothetical situations. However, it may be that the children did better when the problem was presented verbally because the pictures offered perceptual cues which strongly impelled the children to compare the two subsets. This explanation is in line with the view that children have difficulty with such tasks not because their reasoning is faulty but simply because they focus on the compelling aspects of appearance.

Nevertheless, further data uncovered in our studies seem to show that the interpretation is at best a gross oversimplification of the situation. When we tabulated the results for each child and compared scores on the verbal and the picture tests, we found the following: Among the large number of children who did not give any correct answers

Top illustration: When children are shown a picture containing seven dogs and three horses and then asked whether there are more dogs or animals, "pre-operational" children maintain there are more dogs. However, when asked the same question in purely verbal form—without visual "aids"— many of these same children do considerably better. Bottom illustration: In the ring-segmented illusion—in which segment B is really larger than segment A—children gradually learn to resist perceptual cues when they are induced to differentiate between appearance and fact.

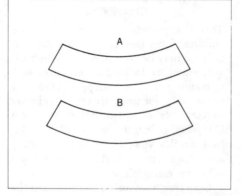

at all on the picture test, almost half also failed to give any correct answers in the verbal test. But of those who did give at least one correct answer to the picture test, 90 percent scored higher on the verbal test.

Eliminating the perceptual factor did *not* guarantee that a child could relate the subsets to the total set. These children seemed quite incapable of recognizing that an object can belong to two classes at once. Improved performance on the verbal test seems to indicate that there is an intermediary phase in the establishment of the class-inclusion concept. During this phase the perceptual cues are still dominant enough to bias the child's recognition of the concept.

Moreover, it is difficult to interpret the results of Piaget's experiment with the two balls of clay on the basis of

perceptual cues alone. Why should the change in shape from sphere to sausage, with length becoming salient, bias the child toward thinking that the *weight* has changed and yet not bias the same child with respect to the *amount of substance*? The question becomes even more significant when we ask ourselves why one concept precedes another.

If we assume that conservation concepts are acquired primarily through experience, we would be led to the conclusion that weight-conservation should be acquired first. The weight of an object, or more particularly the difference in weight between two objects, can be verified directly by weighing an object in one's hand; experiencing differences in the weight of objects begins in infancy. On the other hand, how does one *know* that amount-of-substance is conserved with change in shape? Yet the child recognizes that this "unexperienced" abstraction, "amount of clay," is conserved and does so well before he agrees that the readily-defined, often-experienced entity, *weight*, is conserved.

Conceptual Development— Taught or Spontaneous?

The problems just discussed raise a more general question. Let us return to the types of reasoning displayed by Johnny, Lonny, and Ronny. I did not choose these names just to create a nursery-rhyme effect; I intended to suggest that the three boys could very well have been the same child at five, six, and seven years old. For, in the normal course of events, we expect Johnny to come to think as Lonny did, and Lonny, as he matures, to reason as Ronny did. Yet these changes usually occur spontaneously. In the course of play activities and everyday experience, children pour liquid from one container to another, roll balls of modeling clay into snakes, form rings with strings of beads. But five- and six-year-olds rarely ask themselves questions—or are asked questions by others— which lead them to ponder about things like the conservation of length. They are even less likely to be given direct information about such questions involving conservation.

Somehow, therefore, these logical notions must be acquired indirectly, by the back door, as it were. The question is, where *is* the back door? If we assume that these seemingly spontaneous changes in mode of thinking do not occur in a vacuum, what sorts of experiences or activities can we postulate that may mediate them? What facets of his experience play a role in the child's acquisition of logical principles? It is this question which has been the subject of a great deal of concentrated discussion and research the world over.

Can such rules be taught before the child has discovered them for himself? A great deal of ingenuity has been expended to devise approaches aimed at teaching children "the logical facts of life," especially the conservations. Many such attempts have met with indifferent success, although recent studies have been more encouraging. Nevertheless, even where the zealous psychologist has succeeded in demonstrating the beneficial effect of this or that type of training, the results have been quite limited. That is, the learning has rarely been shown to have much transfer, even to similar concepts or tasks.

There is a real question, then, whether such restricted, short-term training offers sufficient conditions for establishing the basic rules of thought which, according to Piaget, are "of the essence" in the child's mental development. At least equally important, however, is the question—do such experiences represent *necessary* conditions for the development of logical thought?

If we look at what children actually do during the years in which changes in their mode of thinking take place, the answers to our questions may not be quite so difficult to find. For example, children do gain considerable experience in counting objects and so it does not seem unreasonable to suggest that the child comes to realize—quite implicitly—that *number* is a dimension, totally independent of the perceptual aspects of a situation. But doesn't this directly contradict the suggestion that such concepts are not established through knowledge gained from experience? What I am suggesting is this: Through his experience in measuring, counting, and the like, the child may develop a *conceptual attitude* toward dimension in general. Then, confronted with a conservation-type question, he is able to ignore the perceptual cues which had previously been predominant, and can respond only to those aspects which, as a result of his experience, have now become dominant. Thus for Johnny, at five, the situation was dominated by a single percep-

tual cue—height of liquid in the glass. By the time he is seven, Ronny has, one might say, become an operationist; his concept of quantity is determined by the criteria he utilizes in measuring—for instance, as with the number of glasses of equal size that could be filled with the contents of a jar.

Ronny has developed a concept of quantity, furthermore, which may be of sufficient generality to encompass related dimensions that cannot be directly measured. This is particularly true if the dimension that is difficult to measure—for example, amount-of-substance—is assimilated to one that is easily measured—for example, quantity-of-liquid. Indeed, conservation for substance and liquid do appear at about the same time! It is interesting to note that the conservation-promoting attitude can go astray by dint of overgeneralization—a square and a circle made from the same piece of string do not have the same areas, counter to what even many adults assume.

Counting, Measuring, Ordering, Classifying

This interpretation of the way young children form logical concepts suggests that we may better understand their development by looking at activities such as counting and measuring and ordering or seriating, for these are clearly relevant to concepts of quantitative attributes like weight, length, area, and the like. In a similar vein, classifying or sorting are relevant to understanding class and subclass relationships.

Counting, measuring, sorting, and the like are usually part of children's spontaneous, unprogrammed, everyday experience along with the more formal instruction they may receive in school. In research currently under way at Clark University, we are focusing on an intensive study of these activities and on their possible relationships to concepts like conservation and class-inclusion.

For instance, we want to see the extent to which children will arrange spontaneously a set of stimuli according to some plan or order. Children are offered a set of nine blocks with different pictures on each face representing six classes of pictured objects—houses, birds, flowers, vehicles, stars, and dolls. Each class is subdivided according to size, color, and type; for example, there are three kinds of flowers, each pictured in one of three colors. The child is given

a board divided into nine compartments, in a 3×3 layout, into which he can place the blocks in whatever way he thinks they should go, though he is asked to do so in successively different ways. [*See illustration, opposite.*]

We are interested in seeing how many categories the child constructs and how much internal order is displayed in each arrangement. In addition, we want to see how actively and systematically he handles the blocks (for example, in searching for a particular face). Not surprisingly, there is a close relationship between the two aspects of a child's performance: Children who receive high scores for recognition of categories and internal order generally go about their task in a much more systematic manner and manipulate the blocks more actively than the low scorers.

A perfectly consistent arrangement, showing three rows and three columns filled with pictures belonging to the same category, would earn a score of six. The five- to seven-year-olds we have studied thus far tend to be relatively unsystematic in their handling of the blocks, and lacking in consistency and order. On any one trial the median number of rows or columns filled with pictures in the same category is only 0.6. In one study carried out with a group of lower-class children from a day-care center, we found, however, that their scores could be substantially raised by intensive experience in responding to dimensions of order and to relationships of identity and difference in a set of stimuli.

Thus far, we have not found an unequivocal correlation between these measures of block-sorting behavior and conservation. However, we did find that of those children who were very poor in ordering the blocks, only 25 percent showed number conservation. Whereas among the children who did somewhat better at ordering the blocks, 64 percent did show number conservation. The relation between block-sorting scores and performance on the class-inclusion task is much closer, as would be expected, since the two tasks are similar.

In other experiments we looked at children's approach to comparing and measuring lengths, heights, and distances. In general, almost no kindergartners and few first-graders showed awareness of the function of a unit of distance or a reference object. They failed to make use of a plastic ruler to measure distance.

In this experiment the child's ability to recognize and order categories is tested by having him place nine blocks—with different pictures on each face representing six classes of pictured objects—into a 3 X 3 layout of compartments. One interesting finding was that the performance of a group of lower-class children was greatly improved by providing them with extensive experience in responding to dimensions of order.

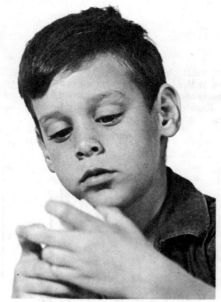

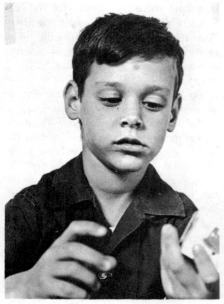
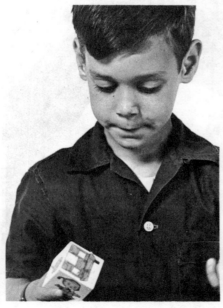

When faced with the set of dowels at the left, most children place the dowels of varying lengths into the constant-size holes in the base—and form an ordered pattern of decreasing heights. However, when faced with the set of dowels on the right in which both the lengths of the dowels and the depths of the holes vary, most children become confused—and cannot produce either of the two ordered arrangements shown.

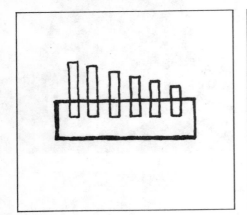
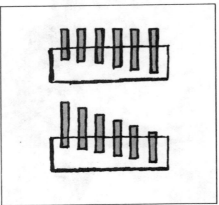

In many instances they did not even think of placing two objects side by side to see which was longer. In other words, since they had as yet no real understanding of length as a dimension, it is not surprising that many lacked conservation.

Other interesting insights were provided by experiments with the dowelboard [see illustration, at left]. When children are given a set of red dowels of different lengths and asked to put them any way they like into the holes of the accompanying wooden base, a majority come up with an ordered series. They are then given an identical set of blue dowels, but the holes in the accompanying base vary in depth, matching the variations in the lengths of the dowels. Thus, if they like, the children can arrange the blue dowels in a series identical to that of the red dowels or, by matching the lengths of the dowels with the depth of the holes, they can produce a series of equal height. Many children find this "problem" highly puzzling. Their behavior often becomes so disorganized and erratic that they produce no sort of order whatsoever. Of the 35 children we tested, 25 were unsuccessful. Again, comparing this kind of ordering ability with conservation-of-number ability, we found that, of the 25 unsuccessful children, 16 lacked number conservation, whereas among the 10 successful children, only 2 lacked conservation of number.

Though our research is still in its early stages, the results thus far obtained encourage us to believe that our approach may help solve the mystery of the prelogical child, and tell us something about how the conservations and other concepts manifested in the stage of concrete operations come into existence.

Our finding that children's scores could be raised by intensive experience suggests a profitable focus for instruction in the primary grades, where little attention is generally given to cultivating the child's measuring and classifying skills. Our guess is that concerted efforts to encourage and guide children's activities in this area might well pay handsome dividends. Beyond merely speeding the development of the skills themselves, an imaginative approach should provide children with a sounder, more broadly based foundation on which subsequent learning of mathematical and scientific concepts can be built.

By Sidney W. Bijou

The Mentally Retarded Child

TRADITION HAS IT that mental retardation is a symptom of something deeper—of something called "defective intelligence," "clinically inferred brain damage" or "familial factors." This view has lost ground in recent years. The more modern one that is replacing it regards retardation not as a symptom but as a form of behavior: limited behavior that has been shaped by past events in a person's life. The new method does not assume that we can know what goes on inside a person. Instead, it concentrates on what can be scientifically observed.

No special theory is necessary to analyze the behavior of a mentally retarded person. The same principles apply to the development of all people—retarded, normal and accelerated. Psychological development, according to behavior theory, consists of interactions between the behavior of the individual as a total functioning biological system and environmental events. It follows then that retardation is the result of conditions that prevent, reduce or delay the development of effective ways of interacting with the environment.

In addition to being a total functioning biological system, an individual is a complex behaving system that changes his environment, and also a source of stimuli that affect his own behavior and the behavior of others toward him. The second characteristic suggests that a person carries around with him part of his environment. This is indeed the case, as we shall see.

When I refer to environmental events, I mean the specific events that are actually related to a person's behavior. This is not the usual definition of environment. The dictionary defines environment as "an aggregate of surrounding things and influences," or as "external conditions." In this analysis, the environment, and synonymously, environmental events, refer only to those stimuli *that can be linked with the behavior of an individual*.

There is one other critical difference in the way behavior theory uses the term. Environment usually refers to the social, cultural and physical conditions that influence a person's life. These conditions are part of the word *environment* as it is used in behavior theory, but so is another category—the biological. This biological environment, the one that a person carries with him all the time, is made up of stimuli that emanate from one's own anatomical structure and physiological functioning.

As the so-called normal individual develops, opportunities become available to him for contact with a succession of environmental events. The rate at which the normal person takes advantage of these opportunities, and to what extent, is more or less typical of his culture. In addition, the normal person's biological structure and physiological functioning are adequate, and they mature at the usual rates. For the retarded person, on the other hand, the pace of successive social, physical and biological conditions is slowed down, and the effectiveness of many contacts is almost nil.

It is the quantity and quality of opportunities for contacts that determine a person's rate of development. The more extreme the restrictions on opportunities, the more extreme the retardation. The factors that contribute to delays and failures in development are therefore a major concern of scientists who hold the behavioral theory of retardation. I shall discuss these factors here in terms of (1) abnormal anatomical structure and physiological functioning, (2) insufficient reinforcement and discrimination histories, (3) the disadvantageous reinforcement of "undesirable" behavior, and (4) severe aversive stimulation.

The four categories will be presented separately for the sake of clarity; in reality, they interact with each other constantly, and in many complicated ways.

Anatomy and Physiology

A person who is biologically abnormal may well have altered response capabilities that affect the nature and progression of stimulating conditions. Since biological anomalies range from mild to severe, their effect on psychological development extends in turn from inconsequential to devastating.

Obviously, responses to stimuli are likely to be affected by impairments of the responding parts of the body and of internal coordinating systems such as the central nervous system. A child cannot possibly learn a response if it requires an anatomical part that the child does not possess or a physiological function of which he is incapable. A child with impaired vocal cords cannot be trained to make all the sounds necessary for normal speech. (He may, of course, be able to learn different responses that will serve the same purpose in the sense that they will affect the environment in the same way.)

Not so obviously, the stimulus that precedes a response may also be affected adversely by biological impairment. When skills in body management and locomotion are inadequately developed, the number and type of physical and social stimuli available for contacts are limited. Restricted mobility generates fixed behavioral repertoires. A child limited to lying on his back can only experience stimuli that are above his body or brought into his line of vision, while a child who can roll from side to side and sit up can interact with stimuli over a greatly extended range. Similarly, a child who can reach, grasp and retrieve an object can have infinitely more experiences than a child who has yet to develop manual coordination and skill. The child who can move about can become involved in a great many novel situations compared to a physically handicapped child who must depend upon the good will of others for his locomotion. The biological impairment of some children makes certain stimuli forever inaccessible to them; for others, the stimuli will become available on a delayed time-schedule.

The stimulation of the physically impaired child may also be restricted because of the way the child *looks* to others —because of his social stimulational characteristics. If the child's physical appearance is repugnant or unappealing, people may avoid him, leave him as quickly as possible, or ignore him. As Donald Zimmerman has commented, "These results superimpose social deprivation upon physical defect."

Because our society likes to think it demonstrates concern for the physically impaired, aloof behavior is often made to appear unavoidable. For example, a physically disabled youngster can be without positive social interactions for long periods because his parents are too "busy" looking after the other children and his siblings are too "bogged down" with homework to engage in extended play with him. The children in the neighborhood exclude him from their games because he cannot "keep up with them." And the school principal bars him from school because he is not "ready."

Avoidant, abbreviated and dutiful social relationships deprive any child, physically impaired or not, of the basic intellectual and social interactions that only people can provide. For example, complex behavior, such as thinking in abstract terms or solving problems, develops in later childhood and beyond only if people are available to arrange and rearrange stimuli (set up problems, bring dissimilar things together and point out similarities and differences), to stimulate responses (ask questions, offer hints and prompts), and to react appropriately to the responses given (confirm correct responses, assist in changing incorrect responses). Innumerable interactions of this sort, some very subtle, occur every day in the life of a normal child in the home, neighborhood and preschool. For example, a mother on her way to the store may see a cow grazing in the pasture and say to her preschooler, "What is that over there?" To the response, "Doggie," she may say, "No, that's a cow," and describe the differences between the two animals. Similarly, the development of appropriate emotional behavior patterns seems to require, among other things, repeated experience with social contingencies such as attention, praise, approval and affection for desirable behavior; with social support following adverse events, such as consolation after injury or frustration; and with corrective procedures that do not generate new emotional problems.

Structural and functional biological impairment is a fact of life, and many of the children it affects will always have limited behavioral repertoires: They will always be developmentally retarded.

The important thing is that their development should progress as far as possible, and behavioral scientists will always be interested in ways of helping them accomplish this objective.

Reinforcement and Discrimination

Reinforcement is a difficult word to define to everyone's satisfaction. It is roughly synonymous with "reward," but only very roughly. As used here, reinforcement refers to a stimulus environmental event following a response that increases the probability of a similar response in a similar situation in the future. Behavior that is sensitive to such consequent stimulus events is called *operant behavior*. It includes verbal, motor, social and intellectual responses as well as much emotional behavior.

The stimulus following operant behavior is called a *stimulus event*, to emphasize that some identifiable change has occurred. The change may add something to the situation (giving a glass of orange juice to a child following his request, "Mother, may I have a glass of juice?") or removing something from it (taking off a child's sweater in response to, "My sweater itches"). Stimulus events that strengthen operant behavior are called *reinforcing stimuli*, and they are said to have a reinforcing function.

Reinforcement does not take place in isolation. Other events occur at the same time, creating conditions that increase or decrease the probability that operant behavior will occur. Of particular interest here are stimulus events that occur immediately before the response that is likely to be reinforced. They are called *discriminative stimuli* (or cues) and are said to have a discriminative function, because they provide the signal for behaving in a way that will probably produce reinforcement. Reinforcing stimuli and discriminative stimuli are therefore interdependent.

One stimulus can serve *both* functions: it can be both a discriminative and a reinforcing stimulus. A smile from a parent in response to a child's good table manners may increase the probability of good table manners in the future (a reinforcing stimulus). A smile from the same parent in the living room may serve as a cue for the same child to climb onto the parent's lap (a discriminative stimulus). In the same way, receiving a sweet may be a reinforcing stimulus that strengthens the preceding behavior, which was the statement, "I want a cookie." The same cookie on a plate may be a discriminative stimulus

for reaching, grasping and bringing to the mouth. Because of the interlocking relationship between discriminating and reinforcing stimulus functions, we consider them together as conditions that retard or promote development.

In general, a child's progress in building a repertory of discriminations (as well as one of motor skills) depends on four things: the number and kind of opportunities made available to the child by the action of people (particularly parents); the properties of available physical objects; the characteristics of the child's structure and physiological functioning; and his maturational and health condition. On the one hand, interactions that reinforce, discriminate and interrelate culturally serviceable behavior are expected to produce people with large repertories of socially, intellectually and vocationally valuable (highly reinforceable) behavior. Reports by Lewis Terman and his co-workers on the background and achievements of high I.Q. children and their offspring support this contention. On the other hand, environments with meager opportunities for reinforcement, discrimination, and the development of complex motor and verbal behavior are expected to produce children with limited repertories of socially serviceable behavior. With respect to the role of meager opportunities, Charles Ferster says:

"Under this category belong individuals who are not making contact with important parts of their environment simply because their history did not include a set of experiences (educational) which could develop these performances during the normal maturation of the individual. Especially in the area of everyday social contacts, considerable skill is necessary for producing social reinforcements, and the absence of this skill either results in an individual without a social repertoire or one who achieves effects on his social environment by indirect means, as, for example, using aversive stimulation to gain attention."

On the basis of inferences from behavioral principles, there are at least three sets of circumstances under which inadequate behavior of this type may evolve: when reinforcements, particularly social reinforcements, are infrequent and weak; when reinforcements are lacking (extinction) or given indiscriminately; and when programs for the development of essential discrimination and skills are lacking or ineptly arranged.

Infrequent and Weak Reinforcements.

Under-staffed child-care institutions may be responsible for one set of circumstances in which reinforcements are infrequent and given in small amounts. For example, Wayne Dennis and Pergouchi Najarian observed children one to four years old in three Iranian institutions, each of which used different child-rearing practices. In two of the institutions, the children were markedly retarded in motor skills; in the other there was little evidence of such retardation. The investigators summarized their findings as follows:

"The extreme retardation in Institutions I and II was probably due to the paucity of handling, including the failure of attendants to place the children in the sitting position and the prone position. The absence of experience in these positions is believed to have retarded the children in regard to sitting alone and also in regard to the onset of locomotion. The lack of experience in the prone position seems in most cases to have prevented children from learning to creep; instead of creeping, the majority of the children in Institutions I and II, prior to walking, locomoted by scooting. In Institution III, in which children were frequently handled, propped in the sitting position and placed prone, motor development resembled that of most home-reared children. The retardation of subjects in Institutions I and II is believed to be due to the restriction of specific kinds of learning opportunities."

In a later study of a similar institution in Beirut, Lebanon, Yvonne Sayegh and Wayne Dennis reported that additional stimulation given to infants could accelerate development. In their words, "appropriate supplementary experience can result in rapid increases in behavioral development on the part of environmentally retarded infants."

Inadequate reinforcement—and the retardation that it leads to—may also occur in a home where, except for basic biological care, the child is left to his own resources because his parents are preoccupied with outside activities or with serious physical or mental health problems. Ferster has discussed how such child-rearing practices contribute to behavioral deficits in the early development of a severely disturbed child:

"The most fundamental way to eliminate a kind of behavior from an organism's repertoire is to discontinue the effect the behavior has on the environment (extinction). A performance may also be weakened if its maintaining effect on the environment occurs intermittently (intermittent reinforcement). Behaviors occurring because of their effects on the parent are especially likely to be weakened by intermittent reinforcement and extinction, because the parental reinforcements are a function of other variables and behavioral processes usually not directly under the control of the child."

He went on to point out that speech and social behaviors are those most likely to be adversely affected by extinction (non-reinforcement) and intermittent reinforcement, because at this early stage of a child's life the parents are the most important source of reinforcers for the development of those behaviors.

Note that I referred to parent-child interactions that create behavior deficits in severely *disturbed* young children. How does this relate to the task of analyzing retarded development? Simply this: there is good evidence that the conditions and processes contributing to severe behavioral disturbances in children also slow down development. Failure to perpetuate a behavior eliminates that particular behavior—one that the child has already established for dealing with current situations—from the child's repertory. It also puts him at a disadvantage in learning new behavior that requires a foundation of responses of the sort lost. Verbal development is a case in point. Because it is basic to so much other behavior, inadequate reinforcement of early verbal behavior can result in deficits in intellectual, social, emotional and even motor development.

Many retarded children are also behaviorally disturbed, and practically all severely maladjusted children are also developmentally retarded. We distinguish between the behaviorally disturbed and the developmentally retarded only for practical purposes in grouping children for residential care and for educational and training programs.

There is another condition that may produce weak social reinforcement on a sparse schedule: the physical appearance of a child considered repulsive by the social community. As I mentioned earlier, an atypical biological makeup can result in a shortage of adequate social contacts and experiences with physical objects. As a result, the markedly unattractive child does not have adequate opportunities to develop relationships with new reinforcing and discriminative stimuli.

Indiscriminate Reinforcement, or None.

One of the ways behavior (particularly that supported by weak social and sensory stimulation) is eliminated is by withholding reinforcement. This process is called *extinction*. One might say that the extreme case of intermittent reinforcement is extinction.

There is a wide variety of behavior supported by scattered social interactions (a nod, a smile, a pat for showing commendable perseverance) and by the stimulation of physical things made available in interesting ways. When a family must struggle with poor health, adjustment difficulties, drug addiction, alcoholism and the like, it may not provide the social interactions or physical objects necessary to reinforce behavior.

Behaviors may also be weakened or remain undeveloped if reinforcements are delivered indiscriminately, with no relevance to the response the parent wishes the child to learn. An example with which we are all familiar is the child who is chronically sick, disabled or incapacitated. The parents, understandably concerned, react by maintaining close supervision and responding almost continuously, and without question, to each and every one of the child's needs or demands, reasonable or unreasonable. If the child screams for no obvious reason, the parent comes running, thus reinforcing the screaming; if the child spews out his food, the parent coaxes him to eat another mouthful; if the child demands constant companion-

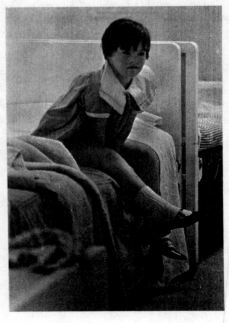

ship, someone is stationed nearby. This situation also tends to reduce the child's exploratory behavior, with consequences that will be discussed below.

Poor Development of Skills.

If there are few or no occasions for the child to interact with responsive people and interesting things, then there are few opportunities for him to acquire and retain serviceable behavior supported by reinforcement processes. Serviceable behavior includes skills in body management, manual dexterity, crawling, walking, running, jumping, skipping, climbing and skating; the transformation of sounds into words, phrases and sentences; and the relating of words, spoken or written, to things, symbols and other words.

In a number of situations, severe restrictions on a child may retard his development. Here are a few.

(1) *When a child is treated as though he were abnormal or chronically ill.* A study of a four-year-old girl in a laboratory nursery school showed that the infantilization practices of the parents resulted in the complete absence of speech, and in gross motor incoordination to the point where she was unable to move about without stumbling and falling.

(2) *When the parent engages in abnormal or idiosyncratic practices.* In a classic case, Kingsley Davis described an example of a deaf-mute mother who kept her illegitimate child in isolation. Mother and child spent most of the time together in a dark room, shut off from the rest of the family. The situation was discovered when the child was six and a half years old. She communicated with her mother by gestures and made only "strange croaking sounds." Efforts to determine whether the child could hear were at first inconclusive; later it was established that her hearing was normal. She displayed fear and hostility toward others, particularly men. As one might expect, reactions to objects were unusual: when presented with a ball, she used it to stroke the interviewer's face. Psychological testing yielded a mental age on the Stanford-Binet of one year and seven months, and a social age on the Vineland Social Maturity Scale of two and a half years.

(3) *When the environment is thinly populated with stimulating people and intriguing things.* A sparse social environment not only reduces the frequency of social reinforcing stimuli, it limits the opportunities for a child to engage in programmed activities that result in discriminations normally expected in his particular culture. People are necessary to arrange the environment so that the child can learn intellectual skills and develop a store of knowledge. People are necessary to create opportunities for the development of manners and morals. People are necessary to provide circumstances that establish values, interests and attitudes appropriate for community life.

(4) *When the necessary physical and cultural components of the environment are absent because of economic and social circumstances.* The detrimental effects on development of economic and cultural deprivation have now been recognized and are being stressed in programs designed to help children from underdeveloped areas and disadvantaged surroundings.

Reinforcement of 'Undesirable' Behavior

In some situations, retardation may develop because "undesirable" behavior has been reinforced. Presumably no parent would *want* to develop "bad" behavior in a child, but it may evolve precisely because the parent dislikes it and finds that attending to it reduces or eliminates it. In the long run, though, this type of interaction strengthens both the "bad" behavior of the child and the attending behavior of the parent. The child is positively reinforced by the parent's action, and the parent is negatively reinforced by the action that has terminated the child's "bad" behavior. A familiar example is the child who gets what he wants by having a temper tantrum. Chances are that tantrum behavior was strengthened by the parents' compliance with the condition that instigated the tantrum. Chances are, also, that the parent "gave in" to terminate the distasteful or even alarming behavior displayed by the child. So the parent's response to the tantrum strengthened tantruming on the part of the child, and the child's termination of the current tantrum strengthened "giving in" on the part of the parent.

This may be a plausible technical account of how a parent can strengthen undesirable behavior, but how does it relate to retarding development? First, undesirable behavior may become the child's main way of responding. If a child is constantly screaming or having tantrums, his learning of new socially and educationally desirable behavior will be slow or even static. Furthermore, the results of formal and informal tutorial interactions will be reduced; effective attention and work spans will be relatively short, and even minor nonreinforcement episodes such as correcting a color-naming error may set off strong and prolonged aversive behavior. A report by Montrose Wolf and his colleagues on the behavioral treatment and rehabilitation of a preschool boy diagnosed as autistic, retarded and brain-injured described many instances in which strong aversive behavior had to be weakened considerably, or even totally eliminated, before the boy could be retrained. Second, unpleasant behavior may well make the child socially repugnant and so discourage people from approaching and participating in prolonged educational and social interactions with him. This, in turn, will limit his repertoire of behavior. Children who display obnoxious behavior are often considered unteachable, or nearly so. They find themselves in a situation similar to that of a child who is avoided because he is physically repellent.

Severe Aversive Stimulation

Another kind of interaction that may retard development is called *contingent aversive stimulation.* This refers both to the practice of administering strong punishment to stop a particular behavior and to hurts and injuries that may occur, for example, during medical treatment or in a serious accident.

Aversive stimulation can have several consequences. First, aversive stimulation can stop ongoing behavior—it may suppress the behavior that preceded it. If the stimulation is moderate, the suppressed behavior is likely to reappear. A skinned knee slows down an active youngster only for minutes. If the stimulation is severe, however, suppressive effects may remain for some time. More than one clinical account has been given of a young child who stopped talking for weeks, months or years following severe punishment by an intoxicated or disturbed parent.

Second, the setting in which aversive stimulation occurs may become aversive in itself: formerly neutral or positive situations can become distasteful or frightening. (After being thrown from his favorite horse, the youngster now reacts to the animal with fear.) The removal of such stimuli is negatively reinforcing. It strengthens the tendency to get away from the aversive situation or thing, to avoid it, or to become immobile when it arises. (If attempts to put the child back on the horse are discontinued because the youngster cries and hollers, then crying and hollering behavior is strengthened and fear of the horse and of things associated with it remain.)

One cannot predict which classes of behavior will be strengthened by negative reinforcement, but it is certainly clear that excessive avoidant behavior can restrict the range of interactions available to a child. In many instances the interactions that are terminated may be needed for further development (speaking, for example), and the situations that are avoided may be critical to a normal child-rearing environment (such as those involving the father) and may affect other similar aspects of the environment (all male adults). Thus, stimuli and responses that were not directly involved in the aversive interaction may come to have aversive properties in themselves.

Third, aversive stimuli may evoke physiological responses (such as gastric reactions to a fear-producing event) that affect biological functioning of the child and thereby reduce his potential for serviceable interactions.

While the consequences of strong aversive stimulation are most frequently discussed in the literature of child psychopathology under the heading of severe emotional disturbances (referred to as psychoneurotic, psychotic and autistic), they are discussed here because aversive stimulation also retards development. Just as biological anomalies and social insufficiencies limit opportunities for development, so do strong avoidant reactions. All three foreclose many occasions for a child to make new adjustments.

I have singled out for discussion here the retarding effects of abnormal ana-tomical structure and functioning, inadequate reinforcement and discrimination histories, reinforcement of undesirable behavior, and severe aversive stimulation. There are, however, other processes. For example, there is the possibility that the termination (say, through death) of interactions with a mother-figure after a strong affection bond has been established can have strong retarding effects. It can weaken or even eliminate well-established behavior by removing the cues on which the behavior depended. It should be emphasized, however, that these other processes do *not* include assumed conditions such as "defective intelligence," "clinically inferred brain damage" and "familial factors."

Up from Helplessness

by Jerome Bruner

IT IS A WORKING PREMISE of mine that infant development cannot be understood without considering what it proceeds from and what it moves toward. The human infant has behind him a long process of primate evolution, which has endowed him with certain biological capacities. In front of him, in adulthood, lie not only the behavior man shares with other primates but the use of a culture that is uniquely human. Human culture, as Claude Levi-Strauss pointed out, is based on three types of exchange, carried out through language, kinship arrangements and economies. They are used by all men and by men alone.

From his evolutionary inheritance, then, the newborn child develops the capacity to use a culture that is exclusively human. This is not to say that evolution or culture *causes* infants to develop as they do, but merely to point out the central position that the infant in fact occupies.

It may seem that this view of infant development places a large burden on a very small pair of shoulders. The equipment and the actions at a child's disposal when he begins his enormous task look, at first glance, rudimentary. To illustrate, the research I am about to describe focuses on sucking and looking, reaching and grasping, and prelinguistic communication—little acorns indeed.

Through these activities, however, the infant develops four abilities that are crucial to the use of human culture. He develops, first, voluntary control of his behavior, a highly complex matter that requires the anticipation of an outcome, the choice of a means to achieve it, and the ability to start and sustain a chosen series of acts. Second, he gains internal control of his attention, so that he can direct it toward solutions to problems instead of following the dictates of external stimuli. Third, he learns to carry out several lines of action simultaneously. Fourth, he establishes reciprocal codes that pave the way for speech and other forms of human exchange.

Before I discuss how these abilities develop, I should point out that there are certain inequities in the young child's situation. For example, the infant's sensory equipment provides him with more information than his motor system can use: he can look at a toy well before he can reach out his hand to take it. Similarly, his motor system has more slack, more degrees of freedom for movement, than he can control. He begins to learn by cutting down drastically on his available neuromuscular freedom, developing that form of clumsiness so characteristic of human infancy. Initial learning, then, may be learning to reduce the complexity of response in order to gain control.

Sucking and Looking

The human infant is notorious for his helplessness, but one thing he can do from birth is suck. Sucking begins as a reflex action, and the infant uses it for several functions apparently preordained by evolution: nutrition, discomfort reduction and exploration. Even on the first day of life, however, the child has some control over his sucking and can adapt it to changes in the environment. If milk is delivered to a day-old child in response to only a little pressure on the nipple, the baby will almost immediately reduce the amount of pressure he exerts.

Another thing the child can do almost as soon as he is born is look, but he cannot look and suck at the same time. The newborn infant sucks with his eyes tight shut. If he begins to look at something, he stops sucking. By two or three months of age, when a burst-and-pause sucking pattern has become established, the baby will suck in bursts and look during the pauses between. At four months, he seems able to suck and look simultaneously, but this turns out to be not quite true. Though suctioning stops when the baby looks, a mouthing of the nipple continues. This phenomenon is called place-holding. By maintaining one feature of an ongoing activity, the infant seems to remind himself to resume that activity after he has carried out a different one. His ability to suck-(look)-suck is probably part of a general decrease in the extent to which one activity pre-empts all others.

One way to test an infant's voluntary control is to see whether he will use an action as a means to some new end. Infants as young as one or two months old show considerable ability to use sucking for a novel purpose. They can learn to suck on pacifiers in order to bring about visual clarity—to increase the illumination of a picture in a darkened room (as in E. R. Siqueland's experiment at Brown University), or to bring the picture into focus (as in one by Kalnins in our laboratory at Harvard).

Watching infants do this has taught us something about how they learn to coordinate the two ordinarily independent activities, sucking and looking. A six-week-old baby will suck the picture into focus, but then he starts looking and stops sucking, so that the picture drifts back out of focus again. He may try to resolve this dilemma by sucking without looking until the picture is in focus and then looking and sucking together for a brief period. As soon as he stops sucking, and the picture starts to blur, he averts his gaze. Gradually, the amount of time he can spend both sucking and looking increases. What the child seems to be learning here is not so much a specific response as a sequentially organized, adaptive *strategy* of responses.

Grasping, like sucking, is one of the infant's very early reflexes. By the time he is four weeks old, he automatically catches and holds an object that touches his hand. What role this reflex plays in the development of *voluntary* grasping is a matter of considerable controversy. Some psychologists see a very close relation between the two: they say that voluntary grasping develops from reflexive grasping through a purely internal process of maturational unfolding. Others see little or no relation; they say that a voluntary grasp develops only through interaction with the environment.

In my opinion, both views are false. The existence of prepared reflex machinery clearly facilitates the acquisition of voluntary motor control. For one thing, as T. E. Twitchell of Tufts Medical School has observed, voluntary control often starts with the self-evocation of a reflex, much as in the recovery pattern of hemiplegics. But to leave the matter at that ignores one crucial aspect of voluntary control: intention. Much of the infant's earliest voluntary activity is characterized by the *absence* of aid from prepared reflex mechanisms. Instead, it begins with diffuse activity that bears less resemblance to organized reflex responses than to athetoid behavior (the wormlike movements of fingers, toes, hands and feet seen in certain brain-damaged children). Even when a reflex pattern does precede voluntary control, there is a period of diffuse, athetoid activity before voluntary control begins.

Once it has begun, how does it proceed? As I mentioned earlier, the infant has much more freedom of movement than he can control. His strategy for increasing his control is to impose severe restrictions on his freedom—to keep his elbow locked as he reaches for something, for instance—and to reduce the restrictions as he consolidates his skill within them.

The child uses this strategy as he learns to reach. If an object crosses the visual field of a month-old child, he will move his head in pursuit. As the object approaches him, he changes his level of activity, becoming quieter if he was active or more active if quiet before. Tension in the child's trunk increases. In a six-week-old, this tension takes the form of an attempt to lift the shoulders and arms, even though the child has had no experience reaching for or retrieving objects. By 10 or 12 weeks, the approach of the object makes the infant pump his arms, shoulders and head, staring at the object and working his mouth at the same time. From this position, he may launch swiping movements toward the object, keeping his hand clenched in a fist. I have seen babies blink in surprise as they execute the swipe, as if the "connection" between intention and act were unexpected, that is, as if a "reafference copy" of the act had not been widely distributed to supporting sensory and motor systems.

At about four months, the child has enough control to execute a less explosive, slow reach. He extends his arm toward the object, hand wide open now. His mouth and tongue are working, and his intention is clearly to put the object in his mouth. Indeed, a slow reach always follows the same sequence: activation, reach, capture, retrieval to the mouth and mouthing. If you insert a finger for him to close on, you will bring the action to a stop.

The open mouth and wide-open hand serve a place-holding function similar to that of the rhythmic mouthing of the nipple which reminded the younger infant to resume sucking when he had finished looking. The open mouth keeps the terminus of the act in evidence during the execution of its components; the rigidly opened hand, which is a step forward from the more primitive closed fist, maintains in exaggerated form an intention whose fulfillment has been delayed. As with so much early development, processes that later become internal, such as intention and attention, have external motor representations at first.

A word here about reaching and looking. A seven-month-old may begin a reach with visual guidance, but he is likely to execute the reach without it. When one of our seven-month-olds, Kathy, is in the midst of reaching for a cup, her eyes are closed. If a reach involves some conflict between the line of vision and the course the hand must follow (detour-reaching), the child is especially likely to look away or close his eyes as he reaches. Also, when Kathy tries to get both hands around a cup already held with one hand, she reduced degrees of freedom drastically by the simple expedient of shutting her eyes.

The Use of Tools

Kathy and her cup can show us a little about how the infant begins to develop an ability to use tools. When a seven-month-old starts to use a cup, he has no appreciation of the problem of holding the cup level as he lifts it to his mouth. By 14 months, he solves this problem by making four to six jerky adjustments of his hands and arms as he raises the cup. By 27 months, the choppiness is gone, and the child keeps the rim of the cup horizontal in a smooth movement all the way up.

This is "tool-use" of a sort, but it is quite crude. Several preliminary skills are still missing. An experiment with two-year-olds, performed at Harvard by A. R. Jonckheere, suggests what they might be. We wanted to see whether two-year-olds would use strings as tools to get prizes, a task that required them to pull strings with prizes at the ends toward them in preference to other unbaited strings. They would not. They either pulled in all the strings, or they pulled just the one closest to them.

Three things seemed to make it difficult for the children to maintain problem-solving behavior long enough to retrieve their prizes. First, they tended to play with the strings, the edge of the playpen, and so forth: they altered their goals to suit the means at hand, instead of altering means to meet the requirements of a fixed goal as problem-solving requires. The situation reminded us of the lobotomized cook who could never get to the center of the city to shop because of all the tempting things she encountered en route. Second, the children preferred to use adults as "tools" instead of the strings. They would plead for help, stretching their arms toward the prizes and crying, rather than pull in the strings by themselves. Third, the problem seemed to include too many features for the children to handle. They would look at the prizes, the strings, the bars of the playpen, and seem to be overwhelmed.

Before a child can learn to use tools, then, he must be able to adapt means to ends instead of ends to means; he must do this in preference to asking for help; and he must have enough control of his attention to keep a goal in mind while he decides how to reach it and carries through his plan. We are now at work on several studies dealing with these capacities and will be ready to report on them soon.

Codes and Language

We come now to the acquisition of codes that precede the rules of syntax. There is a sharp distinction, in the first year or so of life, between "doing" behavior and "communicating" behavior—between behavior addressed to things and behavior addressed to persons. For instance, eye contact, which is a major link between parent and child, has no counterpart in "doing" behavior, and neither do smiling, crying and vocalization.

Either the infant has an innate predisposition to expect reciprocation of some kind to these gestures, or he acquires that expectation very quickly. When the expectation is fulfilled by an adult's response to the child's initiative, that seems to convert the child's behavior into a signal, and he proceeds to conventionalize it by stripping it down to its essential elements. For example, the quality of his crying changes, becoming less intense, once it has started to serve as an effective signal.

It is easy to fool oneself into seeing a connection between prelinguistic and linguistic behavior. What an infant does before he can speak may be quite different from what he does when he begins to speak, even within the category of verbalization itself. When a baby starts to babble, for example, he acquires front vowels and back consonants first, and back vowels and front consonants last. But when he learns to speak, the reverse is true. In speech, vowels come in from back to front, starting with /a/, and consonants from front to back, starting with /p/. As David McNeill has said, the baby completes his vocabulary of phonemes by filling in the space between the two.

It is almost surely true, however, that early interaction codes are the basis for some aspects of later communication and language. The channel for any kind of signal system, prelinguistic or linguistic, must derive from the enrichment of these interaction codes.

But the *form* the signal system takes must come from elsewhere. I believe that it constitutes a refinement of human sensorimotor skill. Indeed, the growth of phonology itself requires the refinement of a neuromuscular skill: the ability to delineate the sounds between those produced by the mouth as a funnel opened outward (the voiced /a/) and as a funnel opened inward (the unvoiced /p/).

I would even suggest that the modularization present in phonology, which can be described as the formation of binary oppositions, can be seen in cruder form in the development of other human skills. The way the infant moves his hands progresses from the "babble" of athetoid movement of the fingers to the sharply contrasting tight-fisted and then wide-open hand during reaching. Also, the infant's early attempts to combine syntactic structures are reminiscent of the choppy movements of his arm and hand as he first tries to keep his cup level. In both cases, there is a division of part acts into roughly equal time segments, and then the coordination of part acts into a smooth sequence.

It is even possible to conceive of a nonlinguistic origin for so essential a rule of language as predication. All languages, without exception, employ this principle, which involves dividing an event into a topic and a comment. For instance, in the statement "John is a boy," John is the topic and his boyhood is the comment on the topic.

There are two homologues in human nonlinguistic behavior that might predispose us toward language that uses predication. One of them concerns information processing; the other has to do with manipulative skill.

Many cognitive theorists distinguish between focal attention and a more diffuse sort of sensing. They postulate that we organize events by synthesizing successive focal attendings. Each instance of focal attention requires the extraction of one or a few features from a more general sensory input and is, therefore, a "comment" on a "topic." Other theorists say that, when we direct our attention toward something, we do so because we have noted a deviation from a "neural model" of some steady state. When deviation reaches some critical level, we attend or orient. The deviation, then, is a "comment" on the neurally represented steady state, or "topic."

The parallel between predication and the use of the hands is based on the distinction between a power or holding grip and a precision or operating grip. Many primates have no precision grip at all, though it is well developed in the great apes. But only man is predisposed to use one hand (usually the right) for the precision grip and the other for the power grip. Once specialization has begun, which is not until the infant is about a year old, the child works out many routines for holding an object with one hand and working on it with the other. This is a predicative procedure, and it probably has a profound effect on tool-use and tool-making.

Let me risk the speculation that the differentiation between holding and operating on what is held may follow the same rule as the differentiation between focal and diffuse attention, and that both may presage the use of topic and comment in language. The same rule may also undergird the other two systems of exchange that are unique with man, kinship and economy.

This examination of infant development has shown, I hope, that the infant's behavior is intelligent, adaptive and flexible from the outset. The degrees of freedom the child can control at first may be few, but the strategies he devises for working within his limitations are typical of a species that plainly is different from other primates. Infancy may be a limited enterprise, but it already has within it the pattern that makes possible man's growth as a user of culture.

You're a good man, Charlie Brown!
You have humility, nobility and a
sense of honor that is very rare indeed.
You are kind to all the
animals and every little bird.
With a heart of gold, you believe
what you're told, every single
solitary word. You bravely face
adversity; you're cheerful through
the day; you're thoughtful, brave
and courteous. You're a good man
Charlie Brown! You're a prince, and
a prince could be a king.
With a heart such as yours
you could open any door—
if only you weren't so wishy-washy.

The Child as a Moral Philosopher

By Lawrence Kohlberg

How can one study morality? Current trends in the fields of ethics, linguistics, anthropology and cognitive psychology have suggested a new approach which seems to avoid the morass of semantical confusions, value-bias and cultural relativity in which the psychoanalytic and semantic approaches to morality have foundered. New scholarship in all these fields is now focusing upon structures, forms and relationships that seem to be common to all societies and all languages rather than upon the features that make particular languages or cultures different.

For 12 years, my colleagues and I studied the same group of 75 boys, following their development at three-year intervals from early adolescence through young manhood. At the start of the study, the boys were aged 10 to 16. We have now followed them through to ages 22 to 28. In addition, I have explored moral development in other cultures — Great Britain, Canada, Taiwan, Mexico and Turkey.

Inspired by Jean Piaget's pioneering effort to apply a structural approach to moral development, I have gradually elaborated over the years of my study a typological scheme describing general structures and forms of moral thought which can be defined independently of the specific content of particular moral decisions or actions.

The typology contains three distinct levels of moral thinking, and within each of these levels distinguishes two related stages. These levels and stages may be considered separate moral philosophies, distinct views of the socio-moral world.

We can speak of the child as having his own morality or series of moralities.

Adults seldom listen to children's moralizing. If a child throws back a few adult cliches and behaves himself, most parents—and many anthropologists and psychologists as well—think that the child has adopted or internalized the appropriate parental standards.

Actually, as soon as we talk with children about morality, we find that they have many ways of making judgments which are not "internalized" from the outside, and which do not come in any direct and obvious way from parents, teachers or even peers.

Moral Levels

The *preconventional* level is the first of three levels of moral thinking; the second level is *conventional*, and the third *postconventional* or autonomous. While the preconventional child is often "well-behaved" and is responsive to cultural labels of good and bad, he interprets these labels in terms of their physical consequences (punishment, reward, exchange of favors) or in terms of the physical power of those who enunciate the rules and labels of good and bad.

This level is usually occupied by children aged four to 10, a fact long known to sensitive observers of children. The capacity of "properly behaved" children of this age to engage in cruel behavior when there are holes in the power structure is sometimes noted as tragic (*Lord of the Flies, High Wind in Jamaica*), sometimes as comic (Lucy in *Peanuts*).

The second or *conventional* level also can be described as conformist, but that is perhaps too smug a term. Maintaining the expectations and rules of the individual's family, group or nation is perceived as valuable in its own right. There is a concern not only with *conforming* to the individual's social order but in *maintaining*, supporting and justifying this order.

The *postconventional* level is characterized by a major thrust toward autonomous moral principles which have validity and application apart from authority of the groups or persons who hold them and apart from the individual's identification with those persons or groups.

Moral Stages

Within each of these three levels there are two discernable stages. At the preconventional level we have:

Stage 1: Orientation toward punishment and unquestioning deference to superior power. The physical consequences of action regardless of their human meaning or value determine its goodness or badness.

Stage 2: Right action consists of that which instrumentally satisfies one's own needs and occasionally the needs of others. Human relations are viewed in terms like those of the marketplace. Elements of fairness, of reciprocity and equal sharing are present, but they are always interpreted in a physical, pragmatic way. Reciprocity is a matter of "you scratch my back and I'll scratch yours" not of loyalty, gratitude or justice.

And at the conventional level we have:

Stage 3: Good-boy—good-girl orientation. Good behavior is that which pleases or helps others and is approved by them. There is much conformity to stereotypical images of what is majority or "natural" behavior. Behavior is often judged by intention —"he means well" becomes important for the first time, and is overused, as by Charlie Brown in *Peanuts*. One seeks approval by being "nice."

Stage 4: Orientation toward authority, fixed rules and the maintenance of the social order. Right behavior consists of doing one's duty, showing respect for authority and maintaining the given social order for its own sake. One earns respect by performing dutifully.

At the postconventional level, we have:

Stage 5: A social-contract orientation, generally with legalistic and utilitarian overtones. Right action tends to be defined in terms of general rights and in terms of standards which have been critically examined and agreed upon by the whole society. There is a clear awareness of the relativism of personal values and opinions and a corresponding emphasis upon procedural rules for reaching consensus. Aside from what is constitutionally and democratically agreed upon, right or wrong is a matter of personal "values" and "opinion." The result is an emphasis upon the "legal point of view," but with an emphasis upon the possi-

bility of *changing* law in terms of rational considerations of social utility, rather than freezing it in the terms of Stage 4 "law and order." Outside the legal realm, free agreement and contract are the binding elements of obligation. This is the "official" morality of American government, and finds its ground in the thought of the writers of the Constitution.

Stage 6: Orientation toward the decisions of conscience and toward self-chosen *ethical principles* appealing to logical comprehensiveness, universality and consistency. These principles are abstract and ethical (the Golden Rule, the categorical imperative); they are not concrete moral rules like the Ten Commandments. Instead, they are universal principles of *justice*, of the *reciprocity* and *equality* of human rights, and of respect for the dignity of human beings as *individual persons*.

Up to Now

In the past, when psychologists tried to answer the question asked of Socrates by Meno "Is virtue something that can be taught (by rational discussion), or does it come by practice, or is it a natural inborn attitude?" their answers usually have been dictated, not by research findings on children's moral character, but by their general theoretical convictions.

Behavior theorists have said that virtue is behavior acquired according to their favorite general principles of learning. Freudians have claimed that virtue is superego-identification with parents generated by a proper balance of love and authority in family relations.

The American psychologists who have actually studied children's morality have tried to start with a set of labels—the "virtues" and "vices," the "traits" of good and bad character found in ordinary language. The earliest major psychological study of moral character, that of Hugh Hartshorne and Mark May in 1928-1930, focused on a bag of virtues including honesty, service (altruism or generosity), and self-control. To their dismay, they found that there were *no* character traits, psychological dispositions or entities which corresponded to words like honesty, service or self-control.

Regarding honesty, for instance, they found that almost everyone cheats some of the time, and that if a person cheats in one situation, it doesn't mean that he *will* or *won't* in another. In other words, it is not an identifiable character trait, *dis*honesty, that makes a child cheat in

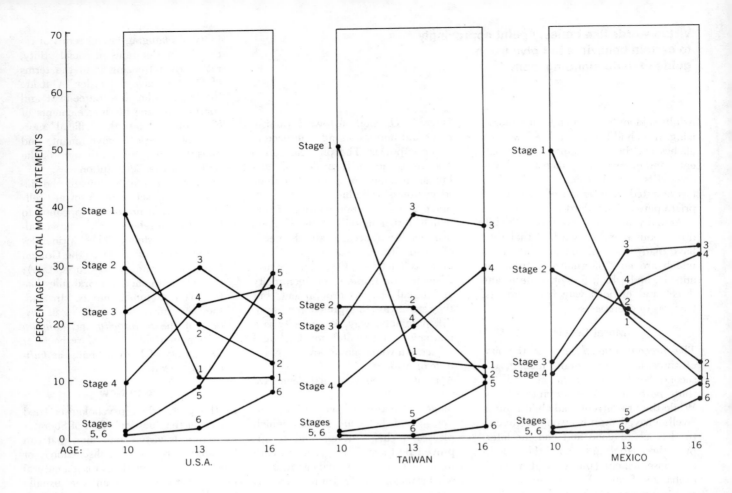

1. Middle-class urban boys in the U.S., Taiwan and Mexico (*above*). At age 10 the stages are used according to difficulty. At age 13, Stage 3 is most used by all three groups. At age 16 U.S. boys have reversed the order of age 10 stages (with the exception of 6). In Taiwan and Mexico, conventional (3-4) stages prevail at age 16, with Stage 5 also little used.

2. Two isolated villages, one in Turkey, the other in Yucatan, show similar patterns in moral thinking. There is no reversal of order, and preconventional (1-2) thought does does not gain a clear ascendancy over conventional stages at age 16.

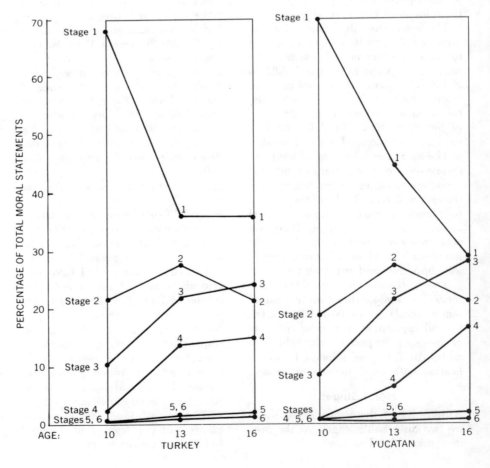

a given situation. These early researchers also found that people who cheat express as much or even more moral disapproval of cheating as those who do not cheat.

What Hartshorne and May found out about their bag of virtues is equally upsetting to the somewhat more psychological-sounding names introduced by psychoanalytic psychology: "superego-strength," "resistance to temptation," "strength of conscience," and the like. When recent researchers attempt to measure such traits in individuals, they have been forced to use Hartshorne and May's old tests of honesty and self-control and they get exactly the same results —"superego strength" in one situation predicts little to "superego strength" in another. That is, virtue-words like honesty (or superego-strength) point to certain behaviors with approval, but give us no guide to understanding them.

So far as one can extract some generalized personality factor from children's performance on tests of honesty or resistance to temptation, it is a factor of ego-strength or ego-control, which always involves non-moral capacities like the capacity to maintain attention, intelligent-task performance, and the ability to delay response. "Ego-strength" (called "will" in earlier days) has something to do with moral action, but it does not take us to the core of morality or to the definition of virtue. Obviously enough, many of the greatest evil-doers in history have been men of strong wills, men strongly pursuing immoral goals.

Moral Reasons

In our research, we have found definite and universal levels of development in moral thought. In our study of 75 American boys from early adolescence on, these youths were presented with hypothetical moral dilemmas, all deliberately philosophical, some of them found in medieval works of casuistry.

On the basis of their reasoning about these dilemmas at a given age, each boy's stage of thought could be determined for each of 25 basic moral concepts or aspects. One such aspect, for instance, is "Motive Given for Rule Obedience or Moral Action." In this instance, the six stages look like this:

1. Obey rules to avoid punishment.
2. Conform to obtain rewards, have favors returned, and so on.
3. Conform to avoid disapproval, dislike by others.
4. Conform to avoid censure by legitimate authorities and resultant guilt.

5. Conform to maintain the respect of the impartial spectator judging in terms of community welfare.
6. Conform to avoid self-condemnation.

In another of these 25 moral aspects, the value of human life, the six stages can be defined thus:

1. The value of a human life is confused with the value of physical objects and is based on the social status or physical attributes of its possessor.
2. The value of a human life is seen as instrumental to the satisfaction of the needs of its possessor or of other persons.
3. The value of a human life is based on the empathy and affection of family members and others toward its possessor.
4. Life is conceived as sacred in terms of its place in a categorical moral or religious order of rights and duties.
5. Life is valued both in terms of its relation to community welfare and in terms of life being a universal human right.
6. Belief in the sacredness of human life as representing a universal human value of respect for the individual.

I have called this scheme a typology. This is because about 50 per cent of most people's thinking will be at a single stage, regardless of the moral dilemma involved. We call our types *stages* because they seem to represent an *invariant developmental sequence*. "True" stages come one at a time and always in the same order.

All movement is forward in sequence, and does not skip steps. Children may move through these stages at varying speeds, of course, and may be found half in and half out of a particular stage. An individual may stop at any given stage and at any age, but if he continues to move, he must move in accord with these steps. Moral reasoning of the con-

ventional or Stage 3-4 kind never occurs before the preconventional Stage-1 and Stage-2 thought has taken place. No adult in Stage 4 has gone through Stage 6, but all Stage-6 adults have gone at least through 4.

While the evidence is not complete, my study strongly suggests that moral change fits the stage pattern just described. (The major uncertainty is whether all Stage 6s go through Stage 5 or whether these are two alternate mature orientations.)

How Values Change

As a single example of our findings of stage-sequence, take the progress of two boys on the aspect "The Value of Human Life." The first boy Tommy, is asked "Is it better to save the life of one important person or a lot of unimportant people?" At age 10, he answers "all the people that aren't important because one man just has one house, maybe a lot of furniture, but a whole bunch of people have an awful lot of furniture and some of these poor people might have a lot of money and it doesn't look it."

Clearly Tommy is Stage 1: he confuses the value of a human being with the value of the property he possesses. Three years later (age 13) Tommy's conceptions of life's value are most clearly elicited by the question, "Should the doctor 'mercy kill' a fatally ill woman requesting death because of her pain?". He answers, "Maybe it would be good to put her out of her pain, she'd be better off that way. But the husband wouldn't want it, it's not like an animal. If a pet dies you can get along without it—it isn't something you really need. Well, you can get a new wife, but it's not really the same."

Here his answer is Stage 2: the value of the woman's life is partly contingent on its hedonistic value to the wife herself but even more contingent on its instrumental value to her husband, who can't replace her as easily as he can a pet.

Three years later still (age 16) Tommy's conception of life's value is elicited by the same question, to which he replies: "It might be best for her, but her husband—it's a human life—not like an animal; it just doesn't have the same relationship that a human being does to a family. You can become attached to a dog, but nothing like a human you know."

Now Tommy has moved from a Stage 2 instrumental view of the woman's value to a Stage-3 view based on the husband's distinctively human empathy and love for someone in his family. Equally clearly, it lacks any basis for a universal human value of the woman's life, which would hold if she had no husband or if her husband didn't love her. Tommy, then, has moved step by step through three stages during the age 10-16. Tommy, though bright (I.Q. 120), is a slow developer in moral judgment. Let us take another boy, Richard, to show us sequential movement through the remaining three steps.

At age 13, Richard said about the mercy-killing, "If she requests it, it's really up to her. She is in such terrible pain, just the same as people are always putting animals out of their pain," and in general showed a mixture of Stage-2 and Stage-3 responses concerning the value of life. At 16, he said, "I don't know. In one way, it's murder, it's not a right or privilege of man to decide who shall live and who should die. God put life into everybody on earth and you're taking away something from that person that came directly from God, and you're destroying something that is very sacred, it's in a way part of God and it's almost destroying a part of God when you kill a person. There's something of God in everyone."

Here Richard clearly displays a Stage-4 concept of life as sacred in terms of its place in a categorical moral or religious order. The value of human life is univer-

sal, it is true for all humans. It is still, however, dependent on something else, upon respect for God and God's authority; it is not an autonomous human value. Presumably if God told Richard to murder, as God commanded Abraham to murder Isaac, he would do so.

At age 20, Richard said to the same question: "There are more and more people in the medical profession who think it is a hardship on everyone, the person, the family, when you know they are going to die. When a person is kept alive by an artificial lung or kidney it's more like being a vegetable than being a human. If it's her own choice, I think there are certain rights and privileges that go along with being a human being. I am a human being and have certain desires for life and I think everybody else does too. You have a world of which you are the center, and everybody else does too and in that sense we're all equal."

Richard's response is clearly Stage 5, in that the value of life is defined in terms of equal and universal human rights in a context of relativity ("You have a world of which you are the center and in that sense we're all equal"), and of concern for utility or welfare consequences.

The Final Step

At 24, Richard says: "A human life takes precedence over any other moral or legal value, whoever it is. A human life has inherent value whether or not it is valued by a particular individual. The worth of the individual human being is central where the principles of justice and love are normative for all human relationships."

This young man is at Stage 6 in seeing the value of human life as absolute in representing a universal and equal respect for the human as an individual. He has moved step by step through a sequence culminating in a definition of human life as centrally valuable rather than derived from or dependent on social or divine authority.

In a genuine and culturally universal sense, these steps lead toward an increased *morality* of value judgment, where morality is considered as a form of judging, as it has been in a philosophic tradition running from the analyses of Kant to those of the modern analytic or

"ordinary language" philosophers. The person at Stage 6 has disentangled his judgments of—or language about—human life from status and property values (Stage 1), from its uses to others (Stage 2), from interpersonal affection (Stage 3), and so on; he has a means of moral judgment that is universal and impersonal. The Stage-6 person's answers use moral words like "duty" or "morally right," and he uses them in a way implying universality, ideals, impersonality: He thinks and speaks in phrases like "regardless of who it was," or ". . . I would do it in spite of punishment."

Across Cultures

When I first decided to explore moral development in other cultures, I was told by anthropologist friends that I would have to throw away my culture-bound moral concepts and stories and start from scratch learning a whole new set of values for each new culture. My first try consisted of a brace of villages, one Atayal (Malaysian aboriginal) and the other Taiwanese.

My guide was a young Chinese ethnographer who had written an account of the moral and religious patterns of the Atayal and Taiwanese villages. Taiwanese boys in the 10-13 age group were asked about a story involving theft of food. A man's wife is starving to death but the store owner won't give the man any food unless he can pay, which he can't. Should he break in and steal some food? Why? Many of the boys said, "He should steal the food for his wife because if she dies he'll have to pay for her funeral and that costs a lot."

My guide was amused by these responses, but I was relieved: they were of course "classic" Stage-2 responses. In the Atayal village, funerals weren't such a big thing, so the Stage 2-boys would say, "He should steal the food because he needs his wife to cook for him."

This means that we need to consult our anthropologists to know what content a Stage-2 child will include in his instrumental exchange calculations, or what a Stage-4 adult will identify as the proper social order. But one certainly doesn't have to start from scratch. What made my guide laugh was the difference in form between the children's Stage-2 thought and his own, a difference definable independently of particular cultures.

Illustrations number 1 and number 2 indicate the cultural universality of the sequence of stages which we have found. Illustration number 1 presents the age trends for middle-class urban boys in the

**"Socrates, Lincoln, Thoreau
and Martin Luther King tend to speak
without confusion of tongues."**

U.S., Taiwan and Mexico. At age 10 in each country, the order of use of each stage is the same as the order of its difficulty or maturity.

In the United States, by age 16 the order is the reverse, from the highest to the lowest, except that Stage 6 is still little-used. At age 13, the good-boy, middle stage (Stage 3), is not used.

The results in Mexico and Taiwan are the same, except that development is a little slower. The most conspicuous feature is that at the age of 16, Stage-5 thinking is much more salient in the United States than in Mexico or Taiwan. Nevertheless, it *is* present in the other countries, so we know that this is not purely an American democratic construct.

Illustration 2 shows strikingly similar results from two isolated villages, one in Yucatan, one in Turkey. While conventional moral thought increases steadily from ages 10 to 16 it still has not achieved a clear ascendency over pre-conventional thought.

Trends for lower-class urban groups are intermediate in the rate of development between those for the middle-class and for the village boys. In the three divergent cultures that I studied, middle-class children were found to be more advanced in moral judgment than matched lower-class children. This was not due to the fact that the middle-class children heavily favored some one type of thought which could be seen as corresponding to the prevailing middle-class pattern. Instead, middle-class and working-class children move through the same sequences, but the middle-class children move faster and farther.

This sequence is not dependent upon a particular religion, or any religion at all in the usual sense. I found no important differences in the development of moral thinking among Catholics, Protestants, Jews, Buddhists, Moslems and atheists. Religious values seem to go through the same stages as all other values.

Trading Up

In summary, the nature of our sequence is not significantly affected by widely varying social, cultural or religious conditions. The only thing that is affected is the *rate* at which individuals progress through this sequence.

Why should there be such a universal invariant sequence of development? In answering this question, we need first to analyze these developing social concepts in terms of their internal logical structure. At each stage, the same basic moral concept or aspect is defined, but at each higher stage this definition is more differentiated, more integrated and more general or universal. When one's concept of human life moves from Stage 1 to Stage 2 the value of life becomes more differentiated from the value of property, more integrated (the value of life enters an organizational hierarchy where it is "higher" than property so that one steals property in order to save life) and more universalized (the life of any sentient being is valuable regardless of status or property). The same advance is true at each stage in the hierarchy. Each step of development then is a better cognitive organization than the one before it, one which takes account of everything present in the previous stage, but making new distinctions and organizing them into a more comprehensive or more equilibrated structure. The fact that this is the case has been demonstrated by a series of studies indicating that children and adolescents comprehend all stages up to their own, but not more than one stage beyond their own. And importantly, *they prefer this next stage.*

We have conducted experimental moral discussion classes which show that the child at an earlier stage of development tends to move forward when confronted by the views of a child one stage further along. In an argument between a Stage-3 and Stage-4 child, the child in the third stage tends to move toward or into Stage 4, while the Stage-4 child understands but does not accept the arguments of the Stage-3 child.

Moral thought, then, seems to behave like all other kinds of thought. Progress through the moral levels and stages is characterized by increasing differentiation and increasing integration, and hence is the same kind of progress that scientific theory represents. Like acceptable scientific theory—or like *any* theory or structure of knowledge—moral thought may be considered partially to generate its own data as it goes along, or at least to expand so as to contain in a balanced, self-consistent way a wider and wider experiential field. The raw data in the case of our ethical philosophies may be considered as conflicts between roles, or values, or as the social order in which men live.

The Role of Society

The social worlds of all men seem to contain the same basic structures. All the societies we have studied have the same basic institutions—family, economy, law, government. In addition, however, all societies are alike because they *are* societies—systems of defined complementary roles. In order to *play* a social role in the family, school or society, the child must implicitly take the role of others toward himself and toward others in the group. These role-taking tendencies form the basis of all social institutions. They represent various patternings of shared or complementary expectations.

In the preconventional and conventional levels (Stages 1-4), moral content or value is largely accidental or culture-bound. Anything from "honesty" to "courage in battle" can be the central value. But in the higher postconventional levels, Socrates, Lincoln, Thoreau and Martin Luther King tend to speak without confusion of tongues, as it were. This is because the ideal principles of any social structure are basically alike, if only because there simply aren't that many principles which are articulate, comprehensive and integrated enough to be satisfying to the human intellect. And most of these principles have gone by the name of justice.

Behavioristic psychology and psychoanalysis have always upheld the Philistine view that fine moral words are one thing and moral deeds another. Morally mature reasoning is quite a different matter, and does not really depend on "fine words." The man who understands justice is more likely to practice it.

In our studies, we have found that youths who understand justice act more justly, and the man who understands justice helps create a moral climate which goes far beyond his immediate and personal acts. The universal society is the beneficiary. ∩

The Many Faces of Response

By Jerome Kagan

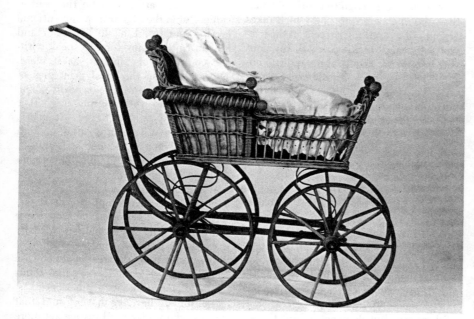

Each generation of psychologists seems to discover a fresh set of phenomena and a sparkling new object to study. The favorite of the academic psychologist during the opening years of this century was the adult trained to report sensations of color, lightness, and weight. Then, as psychology decided that learned habits and biological drives were more critical than feelings and sensations —and easier to objectify—the white rat captured the stage. The current star is the human infant, and the theme centers on his emerging mental life.

The human child has become a favorite subject for many reasons. Historical explanation always has been basic to American psychology. The belief that early learning governs later behavior stems in part from our recently strong commitment to behaviorism, and from our hope that bad habits which are learned early in life can be unlearned, or at least that good habits can be taught to the next generation.

The work of Harry Harlow and his colleagues with monkeys and terrycloth mothers has intensified psychologists' concern with the effects of early experience on later behavior, as has the heavy stress that psychoanalytic theory places on the first five years of life.

Interest in the young child clearly rests on more than one base. But a major catalyst for experimentation with the infant was the work of Robert Fantz of Western Reserve University, which showed that by remarkably simple methods one could determine what a baby was looking at. To everyone's surprise, the infant turned out not to be perceptually innocent. The hope that we might be able to determine what a baby perceives led us to believe that we might begin to probe his mind.

Moreover, some psychologists believe that the infant provides a simple prototype of adult processes. After all, important discoveries about heredity in man were made by biologists who studied generations of fruit flies. The maxim that the easiest way to discover basic principles is through the study of simple forms has become a part of scientific catechism. Thus many hope that the infant will yield some of nature's basic truths about psychological functioning.

Three primary questions currently motivate infant-watching. Observation of the baby may lead to a better under-

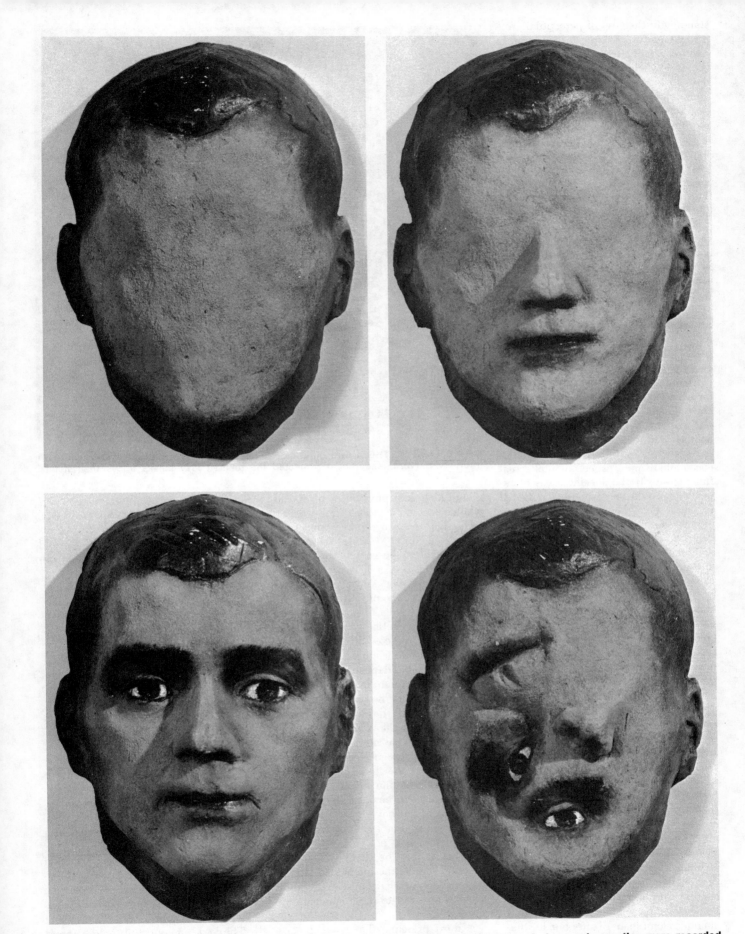

ATTENTION, PLEASE. These painted clay masks were shown to infants of varying ages and changes in reaction were recorded.

standing of the laws of perceptual processing and the principles of learning. In addition, the belief—which derives from the overwhelming differences among day-old babies — that variations among young infants preview the psychological structure and behavior in the older child requires validation.

Finally, there is the "early learning" hypothesis. How early during the first year of a child's life do different experiences begin to influence later behavior? This question was the main impetus for the research project that I shall describe.

There are many possible approaches to the problem. The one we chose was to study infants of divergent social classes in order to determine how early and in what form the lower-class child begins to behave differently from the middle-class child, and perhaps to detect the experiences that produced the differences. It already is known that by the time children are five years old differences from class to class are enormous.

Membership in a social class stands for a varied and complex set of experiences. One of its most predictable consequences is differences in the quality of mental performance. The lower-class child is likely to differ from the middle-class child in many aspects of intellectual functioning. If the specific areas of retardation could be diagnosed, remedial procedures could be suggested.

Our research group at Harvard has been attacking this problem through a longitudinal study of infants from lower-middle-, middle-, and upper-middle-class families. The major focus of the study was mental development. Specifically, the study was directed at differences in the rate and quality of the development of schema. (A schema can be defined as a kind of mental image or memory of an event. It is not a photographic copy, but a caricature of an event—a partial representation. It is somewhat like a diagram that represents only the essential aspects of an object.)

We presented the infants in our study with facsimiles of human faces and human forms. Then we recorded how long they looked, how much they babbled, how frequently they smiled, and how their hearts reacted to these stimuli. In essence, the focus of inquiry was the attentional behavior of the infant.

Several forces control the duration of an infant's attention to a visual event, and the relative importance of each force changes during the first two years of life. For the first six to nine weeks, the infant maintains long spans of attention to stimuli that move and to stimuli that contain

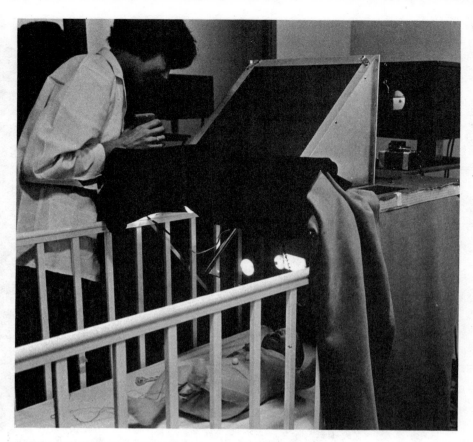

MASKS ABOVE THE CRIB. Four-month-old infants lay on their backs while at intervals Harvard researchers projected the painted clay masks above their heads.

a high degree of physical or black-and-white contrast. New-born infants tend to focus their eyes on the apex of a black triangle against a white background rather than on the center; that is, they focus on the border between the black triangle and the white background, which is where the physical contrast between light and dark is greatest.

The infant's initial study of the environment is directed by an unlearned preference, but this force soon gives way to a second that is dependent upon learning. Before the infant is four months old, the length of time he watches an object is governed by the degree to which what he is watching differs from an internal schema that he has now acquired.

Stimuli that resemble or are not very different from the infant's schema will attract and maintain his attention with the greatest intensity. Stimuli that closely match or have no relation to his schema will hold his attention for a much shorter time. It is not clear why this is true, but it may be that the sustained attention reflects the infant's attempt to match the somewhat novel event to his schema—an effort to assimilate or to understand it.

A third principle that governs early attention involves the nests of associa-

tions to particular objects and events built up during the child's first two years. During this period, he learns collections of reactions to objects. A two-year-old often labels and describes familiar objects in his environment. "Look at the cat," he says. "Look at the doggie eating," or "Baby is crawling out the door."

The child's attention often remains riveted on an event while a chain of associations is expressed. Since the child does not learn complex nests of symbolic associations until the second year, this factor would not be expected to exert a strong influence on attention until that time.

Each of these three processes—physical contrast, discrepancy between event and schema, and rehearsal of acquired associations—emerges at different times in the child's development, but each is always operative at least to some extent. It is reasonable to assume that these factors join together to affect attention. An event that presents high physical contrast, that differs from the infant's schema, and that elicits long nests of associations will hold his attention longest. Perhaps this is why the television commercial can capture the child's attention so effectively.

The data from our study lends support to this assumption. We studied 160 first-born Caucasian infants, from families with different social-class backgrounds. In the lower-middle-class group, one or both parents had failed to finish high school, and the fathers were employed as unskilled laborers. In the middle-class families both parents had finished high school and some had attended college, and the fathers were either white-collar workers or skilled laborers. In the upper-middle-class group, both parents were college graduates and some had graduate training, and the fathers were employed in professional or executive jobs.

We observed the infants in the laboratory at 4, 8, 13, and 27 months of age. To date, all of them have been studied at 4, 8, and 13 months. Half have been assessed at 27 months. Mothers and children also were observed at home when the children were 4 and 27 months old.

Each time the infants came to the laboratory, we showed them a set of three-dimensional, flesh-colored clay faces [see illustration, page 193]. The four-month-old infants were placed on their backs in cribs, and the masks were presented above them [see illustration, page 194]. The older babies sat in highchairs that faced a screen, while their mothers sat beside them. Each face was displayed on the screen for 30 seconds at a time; then the field was blank for 15 seconds before the next face appeared. The child saw each mask on four separate occasions, and the four masks were presented in random order. During each episode we recorded the length of the child's fixation on the face, his vocalizations, smiling, fretting or crying, and changes in his heart rate.

One index of attention is the duration of an infant's fixation on the mask. The fixation times were highest at 4 months, dropped dramatically at 8 and 13 months, and then began to rise again at 27 months, a pattern consistent with the varying influences on early attention already discussed. Contrast and discrepancy are the two major factors governing attention at 4 and 8 months. At 4 months, the masks are very different from the child's schema of a human face, while at 8 months and 13 months his schema of a face is so well formed that discrepancy is not so great.

Two of the masks had eyes. Since the eyes provided physical contrast, four-month-old infants watched these masks longer than they did the two masks without eyes. But contrast is subordinate to discrepancy at 8 and 13 months of age. Thus the presence of eyes becomes less important at the older ages; by the time the child is 13 months old, the presence of eyes has no effect at all.

The richness of associations affects the length of time a child will study objects when he is 27 months old, but its effect is weaker at the younger ages. At 27 months, fixations were longest to the disarranged face; the richness of associations acted together with schema discrepancy to lengthen the attentional span.

Support for this conclusion comes from a related investigation. Gordon Finley, now at the University of British Columbia, has shown chromatic paintings of facial stimuli to one-, two-, and three-year-old middle-class children in Cambridge and to peasant Mayan Indian children living in the Yucatan Peninsula of southeastern Mexico [see illustration, top of page 196]. At all three ages, the American children showed longer fixation times than the Mayan children, and at two and three years of age the disarranged face elicited longer fixation times for both groups of children than did the regular faces [see illustration, bottom of page 196].

At both two and three years of age the American children vocalized much more to the masks than the Mayan children did. The American three-year-olds talked to the faces for an average of ten seconds; the Mayan children talked for only three seconds. This suggests that the longer fixation times of the American children were accompanied by rehearsal of associations to the faces.

Social-class differences in attentiveness emerge clearly during the first year of life, but the time at which they appear depends on the particular response studied. With infants of 4, 8, and 13 months, the association between social class and fixation times became stronger with age, and it was always higher for girls than for boys. One group of infants was tested at 4, 8, and 13 months. The stimuli seen first at 4 and 8 months were four human faces. At 13 months, the first stimuli seen were four human forms. [See illustrations, below.] The relation to social class was low at 4 months, moderate at 8 months for girls but low for boys, and high for both sexes at 13 months but higher for girls than boys.

The stronger association between social class and duration of fixation for girls has two possible interpretations. Perhaps girls are biologically more homogeneous at birth than boys are, and perhaps this means that differential experience in the world is more faithfully reflected in the behavior of girls. That is, if girls differ less than boys at birth, we might expect a more consistent relation in girls be-

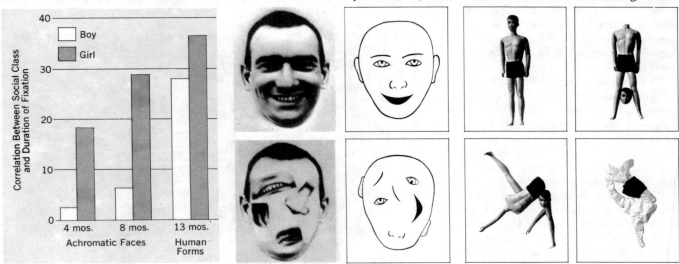

SOCIAL CLASS DIFFERENCE. Attentiveness to visual stimuli is affected by social class. When infants of four and eight months were shown these faces and 13-month-old infants were shown these human forms, the association was clearly stronger for girls.

tween specific experiences that are presumed to promote attention and subsequent attentive behavior.

Consider the following analogy: Two hands are placed separately on two pieces of clay, each piece of clay representing an infant. One piece of clay is of uniform softness and pliability; the other is lumpy, and varies in pliability. If the two hands come down on the two pieces of clay with the same force, each makes a different impression. The homogeneous clay reflects more faithfully the force that was imposed on it than does the clay with variable pliability.

An alternative interpretation is not inconsistent with the first, but it requires no biological assumptions. It assumes instead that social class has a stronger influence on the way mothers treat their daughters than on the way they treat their sons. Observation of some of our four-month-old children in their homes supports this idea. Middle-class mothers talked substantially more to their daughters than lower-class mothers did; this difference was not present in lower- and middle-class mothers of sons. The longer fixation times at 8 and 13 months by the daughters of well-educated mothers may be a function, in part, of the greater face-to-face stimulation that the child may receive. Longer face-to-face contact may cause the child to show longer fixation times not only to interesting facial stimuli, but perhaps to all classes of interesting events.

A study by Judith Rubenstein, of the National Institute of Mental Health, supports this argument. On two occasions she visited the homes of 44 Caucasian babies five months old and observed the behavior of their mothers. The mothers were classified as high-attentive, medium-attentive, or low-attentive, depending upon the number of times they looked at, touched, held, or talked to their babies.

The babies with highly attentive mothers spent longer times studying and manipulating a novel stimulus than did babies of low-attentive mothers. It was as if the close reciprocal play experienced by the babies with highly attentive mothers established their interest in long explorations of interesting events.

The use of a decrease in heart rate to assess processes related to attention has a short but interesting history. One reason cardiac deceleration was not used earlier to measure attentional reactions can be traced to general arousal theory. This theory implies that when an organism is "tense" about anything—fear, sexual pas-

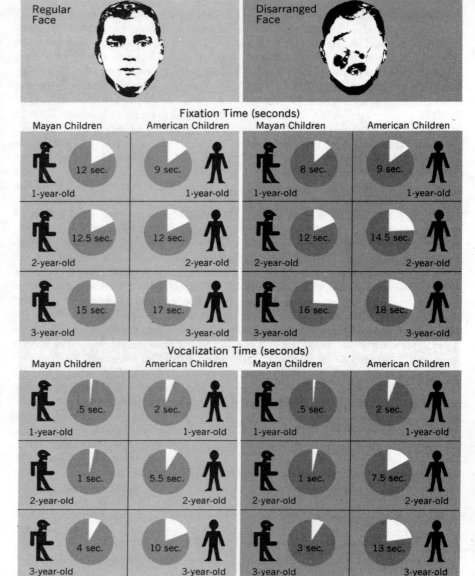

CULTURAL DIFFERENCES. American and Mayan children of the same ages, when shown paintings of human faces, showed consistent variations in reaction times.

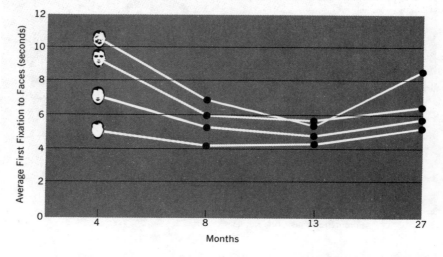

FIXATION TO FACES. The pattern of fixation times to the four masks shown by infants of varying ages corresponded to the known influences on early attention.

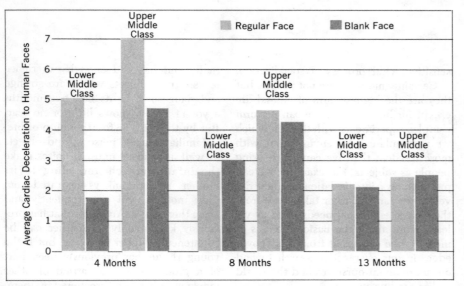

CARDIAC DECELERATION. Heart rate corresponded to social class at four months.

sion, or intense attention—it will show autonomic reaction patterns which reflect internal arousal. That is, among other things, it should show an increase in heart rate. Thus investigators did not search for *decreases* in heart rate in response to episodes that involved attention, and they often did not know how to interpret them when such did appear.

Then John and Beatrice Lacey of the Fels Research Institute demonstrated clearly that cardiac deceleration was a dominant reaction when an organism attended to external events. Once a relation between cardiac deceleration and attention to external events had been established in adults, it became useful with young children, who cannot tell you what they perceive.

In a recent study, Robert McCall of the University of North Carolina and I showed that an infant was likely to show a cardiac deceleration when the stimulus was moderately discrepant from an existing schema—when the event surprised the child, but not too much.

Bearing this hypothesis in mind, let us turn to the social-class differences noted in our study. The differences in cardiac deceleration between the lower- and upper-middle-class children in response to the clay faces were largest at 4 months, and statistically significant. The differences were smaller at 8 months and minimal at 13 months [*see illustration above*]. Thus the relation between social class and an attentive reaction to the faces increased with age for fixation time, but it diminished with age for cardiac deceleration.

The relatively large difference between classes on cardiac deceleration at 4 months is to be expected if we view

cardiac deceleration as most likely to occur when the infant is surprised by a stimulus that is a bit discrepant from his schema. If the lower-class child had a poorer schema for a human face, then these three-dimensional clay faces, particularly the blank faces, would bear minimal resemblance to his schema. A related point here is that, at 4 months of age, not one lower-class boy smiled at the blank face, whereas 22 per cent of the middle-class boys did. The smiles can be interpreted as signs of recognition, indicating some perception of similarity between the blank face and the child's schema for a face.

The absence of large cardiac decelerations at 13 months suggests that the faces were not surprising to these infants. However, neither large decelerations nor class differences in deceleration should be expected at that age. The long fixation times shown by upper-middle-class

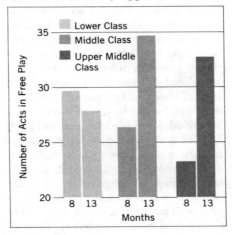

FREE PLAY. Social class affects activity in free play, so that the lower-class infants' responses decrease at a time of increased responses among higher social classes.

children at 13 months are a result of rich nests of associations. The less rich associations of the lower-class child lead to shorter fixation times.

Class differences in infant behavior show up not only in the laboratory, but in the playroom as well. At 8 and 13 months, the children were brought with mothers into a small room containing a variety of toys—a brightly colored wooden bug, a red plastic dog, a pail, a set of wooden blocks, a wooden mallet, a pegboard, a shaft of plastic quoits, a toy lawn mower, and a furry dog.

We recorded the number of changes of activities that each child made within the free-play period—that is, the number of times the child changed his active attention from one toy to another. The number of changes decreased in lower-class children between 8 and 13 months, but it increased in middle- and upper-middle-class infants [*see illustration, bottom of this page*].

These differences are interpreted to mean that the upper-middle-class children had a richer response repertoire at 13 months and thus did not tire of the toys as quickly as the lower-middle-class children did. This interpretation is congruent with the longer fixation times displayed in the laboratory by upper-middle-class children at 13 months. As with fixation time, the increase in the number of activity changes during play between 8 and 13 months was more striking for girls than for boys, paralleling the greater effect of social class on fixation time for girls.

Differences in the behavior of infants from divergent classes appear to emerge as early as the first year of life and in an expected direction. By the time the child is three years old, the differences are even more obvious. Lower-class children have a limited vocabulary, they speak less intelligibly, and they seem to be less involved in problem solving.

Our data suggest that these later differences may have their roots in the first-year period. It seems reasonable to begin educational procedures with lower-class mothers at this time in order to persuade them that the child learns schema for his environment from the first weeks on. The effect of educating mothers at a time when their children are experiencing rapid mental growth might help the infant, and it also might increase the emotional involvement of the mother with her child. Ultimately, it might facilitate the child's formation of those motives and standards during the preschool years that have such an important bearing on later development. ◯

The Young Monkeys

By Harry and Margaret Harlow

When we watch a newborn rhesus monkey with its mother, the infant seems to display signs of affection almost at once, clinging to the mother's body and climbing into her arms. The slightly older infant cries piteously when separated from its mother. Still later, as the maternal bond weakens, the young monkey reaches out to others its own age for companionship and, finally, for sexual satisfaction.

These examples illustrate the three basic social responses of primates — affection, fear, and social aggression. In fact, the responses usually emerge in that order as the infant monkey matures.

Affection, the reaction to cuddling, warmth, and food, comes first in these broadly based and sometimes even overlapping categories. Then comes fear, as the infant begins to explore a sometimes dangerous world. And finally, there is social aggression when the monkey is older, more exploratory, and better able to handle itself.

These responses obviously are not the simple component behavior patterns which B. F. Skinner has described, nor are they like Pavlovian reflex reactions. Rather, they are highly complicated and built-in patterns of behavior which can be modified by learning. Under certain circumstances, normal development can be blocked, and the patterns disrupted. When this is done under experimental conditions, we can learn more about the sensitive, vital process of socialization.

Certainly monkeys are not people, but they are the highest form of animal life except for humans, and we can perform complex experiments with them in which we manipulate their environment with more freedom than we can when using people as subjects. For example, we can put monkeys into isolation as they develop, we can add to or take away from their basic emotional needs. And as we learn more about the basic emotions of monkeys we can profit from this knowledge, in our ever-active search to find out more about ourselves and the world of life we live in.

The Beginnings of Affection

The first sign of affection by the newborn rhesus monkey is a reflex action which facilitates nursing. The infant grasps its mother's fur and moves upward on her body until restrained by her arms. This brings the baby monkey's face close to the mother's breast, and the infant begins to nurse. Throughout the first two or three weeks of life, the response of infant to mother continues to be based on reflexes, although the baby gradually gains voluntary control of its motor behavior. But even after the young monkey is skilled enough to walk, run, and climb by itself, it continues to cling to its mother. The bond of affection between infant and mother continues to grow stronger instead of weaker during the next few months.

The mother monkey warmly returns her infant's affection, and this reciprocal affection operates in a way that helps prepare the young monkey for participation in a more complex social environment. The mother shows her fondness by cradling, grooming, caressing, and protecting her baby. At first, this affection is primarily reflex behavior and is stimulated by the touch, sound, and sight of the baby. Interestingly, the baby need not be the female monkey's own, for pre-adolescent, adolescent, and adult females are attracted to all the infants in their group. Given the opportunity, even females who have not recently borne young will adopt infants, and this indicates that hormonal changes associated with parturition are not essential to the establishment of maternal affection.

Fear

Fear responses show themselves after the young rhesus has matured intellectually and has had enough experience to recognize objects which are strange and dangerous. In its first two months a young rhesus shows little or no fear. But by the third or fourth month of life, unfamiliar places, persons, and objects as well as loud or unusual noises make the infant screech and cling to its mother. Young monkeys separated from their mothers will cry frequently and clasp themselves. An infant that has previously known only its mother can be frightened by other monkeys, but if the young rhesus has previously been part of a group, it will be afraid of other monkeys only when threatened by them, or actually hurt.

Making Friends

By the time they are two months old, young monkeys that have been allowed to live in groups show an interest in other monkeys, especially infants. First contacts are usually brief, beginning with physical exploration which can be one-sided or mutual. From these early experiences come more complex play behavior and the development of affection for other young monkeys. Emotional attachment to monkeys of the same age usually appears before the emergence of fear. However, if such attachments are not permitted to develop — if, for instance, the young monkey is kept apart from his peers—there is some possibility that this friendly emotion will not emerge at all. Nevertheless, the infant that has received a good deal of maternal affection can sometimes make friends even when the normal age for doing so has passed.

Emotional bonds among those of the same age usually grow stronger as the maternal relationship begins to ebb. The infant's first emotional experience, the attachment to its mother, is quite distinct from later emotional ties. For example, the peer relationship originates in and develops through play. Young monkeys that have not been permitted to establish relationships with other infants are wary of their playmates when finally allowed to be with them, and these deprived monkeys often fail to develop strong bonds of affection. Yet monkeys that have been deprived of mother love but provided with early contacts *can* develop ties with their peers which seem comparable to the bonds formed by mother-reared infants.

Affection of age mates for one another

is universal within the entire primate kingdom. It starts early in all species of monkeys and apes, and it is evident throughout the life span. The beginnings of human sociability, however, are more variable because children's opportunities to contact their age mates differ from family to family and from culture to culture. Four decades ago, research by Charlotte Buhler and her associates in Vienna showed that human infants in their first year of life generally are responsive to one another. This can be confirmed informally by anyone who looks in on a pediatrician's waiting room where healthy young children contact one another quickly. If held, they strain toward one another, and if close together, they reach out to one another. They smile at each other, and they laugh together.

Sex Roles

In early infancy, the child's sex is relatively unimportant in social interactions: Human boys and girls, like male and female monkeys, play together indiscriminately at first. But though this continues for several years in humans, behavioral differences begin to appear in monkeys by the third or fourth month and increase steadily until the animal is mature.

Male monkeys become increasingly forceful, while the females become progressively more passive. A male will threaten other males and females alike, whereas females rarely are aggressive toward males. During periods of play males are the pursuers, and the females retreat. As they grow older, increasing separation of the sexes becomes evident in friendship and in play.

During their juvenile period, one to two years of age, and even after, rhesus monkeys as a rule form pairs and clusters of friends of the same sex. Only in maturity when the female is in heat does the pattern change, and then only temporarily. Male-female pairs dominate until the mating period ends. And then the partners return to their own sex groups. With humans, too, friendships with those of the same sex predominate in childhood, adolescence, and maturity. Even when men and women attend the same social event, men often cluster together with other men, while women form groups by themselves. Clubs for men only, or for women only, further demonstrate this sexual split.

At both the human and subhuman levels, this separation is undoubtedly based on common interests which in turn are based on anatomical and physical differences between the sexes. For example, male primates of most species are larger and stronger than the females and better-equipped physiologically for feats of strength and physical endurance. This probably leads the male to more large-muscle activities. Culture influences do not create differences in behavior between the sexes, but they do mold, maintain, and exaggerate the natural differences. Thus boys, not girls, are encouraged to become athletes, and women boxers and shot-putters are generally regarded as oddities.

The importance of peer relationships in monkeys cannot be overemphasized. All primates that live in groups achieve much of their communal cohesiveness and adult sexual social behavior through affectionate relationships with others of the same age. Monkeys learn their sex roles through play. By the third or fourth month of life, male and female sexual behavior is beginning to be different. By the time they are a year old, most monkeys who have been reared in groups display mature and specialized sexual behavior, except that male intromission and ejaculation do not occur until puberty, at about four years of age.

Social Aggression

Sexual differentiation usually is learned by monkeys before social aggression appears. After numerous and varied studies at the University of Wisconsin, we have concluded that unless peer affection pre-

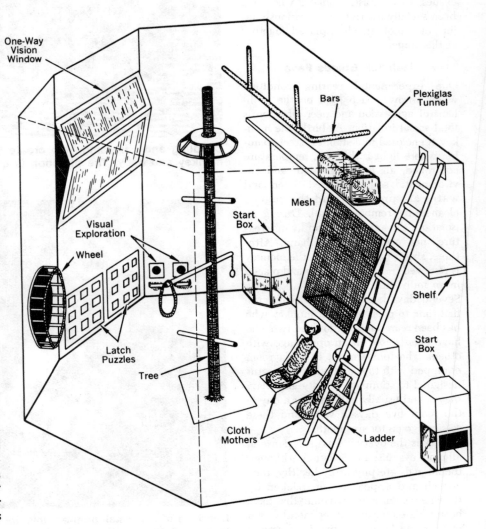

Social playroom for the young monkeys.

199

cedes social aggression, monkeys do not adjust; either they become unreasonably aggressive or they develop into passive scapegoats for their group.

Rhesus monkeys begin to make playful attacks on one another almost as soon as they are old enough for actual contact, and their aggression increases steadily throughout the first year of life. The young monkeys wrestle and roll, pretend to bite one another, and make threatening gestures. But they do not hurt each other, even though their teeth are sharp enough to pierce a playmate's skin.

If the young rhesus has had normal group contact during infancy, it will show restraint toward both friends and strangers. Only if threatened or to protect weaker members of its group will it fight.

While in the group the young try to find a place in the hierarchy, and as dominance is established a relative peace ensues. In contrast, monkeys who have been socially deprived may seriously injure one another when placed together at this stage.

Isolation Breeds Fear

One experimental rearing condition which throws much light on the problems of aggression and peer affection is total social isolation. At birth, the monkey is enclosed in a stainless steel chamber where light is diffused, temperature controlled, air flow regulated, and environmental sounds filtered. Food and water are provided and the cage is cleaned by remote control. During its isolation, the animal sees no living creature, not even a human hand. After three, six, or twelve months, the monkey is removed from the chamber and placed in an individual cage in the laboratory. Several days later it is exposed for the first time to peers—another monkey who has been reared in isolation and two who have been raised in an open cage with others. The four are put in a playroom equipped with toys and other apparatus designed to stimulate activity and play; they spend usually half an hour a day in the room five days a week and these sessions go on for six months.

Fear is the overwhelming response in all monkeys raised in isolation. Although the animals are physically healthy, they crouch and appear terror-stricken by their new environment. Young that have been isolated for only three months soon recover and become active in playroom life; by the end of a month they are al-

Cuddling and caressing help create the maternal bond between mother monkey and baby. The affection is quite mutual.

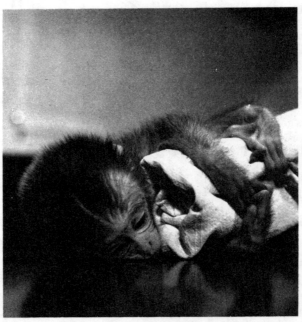

Deprived of a normal mother, this infant monkey forms a strong emotional attachment to an artifical, cloth mother.

When a six-month-old monkey, raised in total isolation from birth, is finally put together with other normal monkeys his own age, the infant cowers in fear and never learns to play.

By the time they are two months old, young monkeys begin to explore the world—and each other. They make friends and play. The maternal bond weakens.

Two baby monkeys, raised from birth together, become like Siamese twins; they cling together chest to chest. If artificially separated from each other, they clamor to resume clinging.

When several baby monkeys are raised together from birth, they often cling together in a choo-choo line. They tend to play together a great deal and to develop sexually at an early age.

most indistinguishable from their control age mates. But the young monkeys that had been isolated for six months adapt poorly to each other and to the control animals. They cringe when approached and fail at first to join in any of the play. During six months of play sessions, they never progress beyond minimal play behavior, such as playing by themselves with toys. What little social activity they do have is exclusively with the other *isolate* in the group. When the other animals become aggressive, the isolates accept their abuse without making any effort to defend themselves. For these animals, social opportunities have come too late. Fear prevents them from engaging in social interaction and consequently from developing ties of affection.

Monkeys that have been isolated for twelve months are very seriously affected. Although they have reached the age at which true aggression is normally present, and they can observe it in their playmates, they show no signs of aggression themselves. Even primitive and simple play activity is almost nonexistent. With these isolated animals, no social play is observed and aggressive behavior is never demonstrated. Their behavior is a pitiful combination of apathy and terror as they crouch at the sides of the room, meekly accepting the attacks of the more healthy control monkeys. We have been unable to test them in the playroom beyond a ten-week period because they are in danger of being seriously injured or even killed by the others.

Our tests have indicated that this social failure is not a consequence of intellectual arrest. In the course of thirty-five years of experimentation with and observation of monkeys, we have developed tests of learning which successfully discriminate between species, between ages within species, and between monkeys with surgically-produced brain damage and their normal peers. The tests have demonstrated that the isolated animals are as intellectually able as are monkeys of the same age raised in open cages. The only difference is that the isolates require more time to adjust to the learning apparatus. All monkeys must be adapted to testing, but those coming from total isolation are more fearful and so it takes longer for them to adjust to the situation.

And Aggression

We continued the testing of the same six-

and twelve-month isolates for a period of several years. The results were startling. The monkeys raised in isolation now began to attack the other monkeys viciously, whereas before they had cowered in fright. We tested the isolates with three types of strangers: large and powerful adults, normal monkeys of their age, and normal-one-year olds. The monkeys which had been raised in the steel isolation cages for their first six months now were three years old. They were still terrified by all strangers, even the physically helpless juveniles. But in spite of their terror, they engaged in uncontrolled aggression, often launching suicidal attacks upon the large adult males and even attacking the juveniles —an act almost never seen in normal monkeys of their age. The passage of time had only exaggerated their asocial and antisocial behavior.

In those monkeys, positive social action was not initiated, play was nonexistent, grooming did not occur, and sexual behavior either was not present at all or was totally inadequate. In human terms, these monkeys which had lived unloved and in isolation were totally unloving, distressed, disturbed, and delinquent.

And Sexual Inadequacy

We have found that social deprivation has another long-term effect which is particularly destructive—inadequate sexual behavior. This is found in all males and most females reared in total or semi-isolation. Whereas some of the females that have been in semi-isolation still show a certain amount of sexual responsiveness, this is probably due to their easier role in copulation. The separate actions required for copulation begin to appear in young infants, but these actions are not organized into effective patterns unless early social play—particularly of a heterosexual nature—is allowed. Monkeys that fail to develop adult sexual patterns by the time they are 12 to 18 months old are poor risks for breeding when they are mature.

For example, we found in one study that semi-isolated females that are placed with breeding males avoid social proximity and do not groom themselves. They often engage in threats, aggression, and autistic behavior such as clutching and biting themselves, and they frequently fail to support the male when mounting occurs. In contrast, normal females seldom threaten males, are

not aggressive, and do not engage in autistic behavior; they maintain social proximity, groom themselves, and provide adequate support for the mounting male.

Parallel tests with males show that socially deprived males are even more inadequate than their female counterparts. Compared to the normal males, they groomed less, threatened more, were more aggressive, rarely initiated any sexual contact, engaged in unusual and abnormal sexual responses, and—with one exception—never achieved intromission.

The sexual inadequacies of the socially deprived monkeys did not come from a loss of biological sex drive. High arousal was often seen, but it led to inappropriate responses—autistic behavior, masturbation, and violent aggression—all in a frenetic sequence lasting only a few seconds.

Monkeys Without Mothers

In another series of experiments on the emotional bases of social development in monkeys, we raised some infants with continuous peer experience and no mothers. Two, four, and six monkeys were reared together in groups. The groups of two tended to cling together in the first few weeks, chest to chest, and this behavior persisted long after normally raised infants would have stopped clinging to their mothers. The two young monkeys moved about like Siamese twins joined at the chest. When some external force turned up to break the two apart or one rhesus attempted to explore an object, the other quickly tried to resume the clinging posture. This immature behavior continued until the animals were put in separate cages, although we found that it could be drastically reduced if the pairs were reared together for a fixed period of time, separated for another specified time, and then subjected to alternate togetherness and separation.

We also found that four or six infant monkeys living together in one cage tend very soon to form a line in which one rhesus leans forward and the others get behind him in a single file, each clinging to the back of the animal in front of him. If the first monkey moves without breaking loose, the whole group usually moves in unison with it, but if the lead rhesus frees itself, the pattern breaks up, to be re-formed shortly.

While monkeys reared in pairs play very infrequently—the tight clasp they have on one another restricts movement —the infants raised in larger groups play extensively. In one respect, the monkeys which have been raised in the larger groups are quite precocious: Their sexual behavior is perfected at an early age and as adults they breed readily. This is in sharp contrast with the absence or insufficiency of sexual activity in male and female isolates.

Throughout our studies, we have been increasingly impressed by the alternative routes monkeys may take to reach adequate social behavior, which by our criteria includes affection toward peers, controlled fear and aggression, and normal sexual behavior. In protected laboratory conditions, social interaction between peers and between mother and child appears to be in large part interchangeable in their effect on the infant's development. A rhesus can surmount the absence of its mother if it can associate with its peers, and it can surmount a lack of socialization with peers if its mother provides affection. Being raised with several age mates appears to com-

pensate adequately for a lack of mothering, although it is likely that animals reared in this way would be at a disadvantage if confronted by monkeys that had had a mother and early experience with others their age as well.

From an evolutionary point of view, there is an advantage to the animal in having two independent sources of affection—mother and peers. Each in part compensates for the deficiencies of the other. Mothers vary considerably in the depth and type of their attachment to their children. A rhesus mother denied normal affection in her early life may be so detached from her infant and, in many cases, may be so brutal that the effects could be devastating for her infant unless there were companions available for play. Human mothers may also exhibit detachment and physical abuse, which pediatricians refer to as the "battered baby" syndrome—a much more prevalent phenomenon than police and court records indicate.

Isolation studies which begin at birth and continue until some specified age

provide a powerful technique for the analysis of maturational processes without interference from an overlay of learning. Indeed, the isolation experiment is one of the few methods by which it is possible to measure the development of complex behavior patterns in any pure or relatively pure form. While it is commonly thought that learning shapes preestablished, unlearned response patterns, this is barely half of the picture, at least as far as social learning is concerned.

One of the most important functions of social learning in primates—and perhaps in all mammals and many other classes of animals as well—is the development of social patterns that will restrain and check potentially asocial behavior. These positive, learned social patterns must be established before negative, unlearned patterns emerge. In this sense, social learning is an anticipation of later learning: The inappropriate exercise of negative behavior can be checked within the social group while the same behavior is permitted toward intruders threatening from without. ⏎

Check one: □Male □Female

by Jerome Kagan

Every person wants to know how good, how talented and how masculine or feminine he or she is. Of the many attributes that go into the concept of self, sex-role identity is one of the most important.

It may seem odd that anyone should be unsure of his sex-role identity. A five-foot, 11-inch, 18-year-old human with X and Y chromosomes, testes, penis and body hair is, by definition, a male. It would seem that all such men should regard themselves as equally masculine. But the human mind, in its perversity, does not completely trust anatomical characteristics and insists upon including psychological factors in the final judgment. Man is as foolish as the cowardly lion who had to be reassured of his courage by the Wizard of Oz.

A sex-role identity is a person's belief about how well his biological and psychological characteristics correspond to his or her concept of the ideal male or female. The definition of the ideal—the sex-role standard—is influenced by the values of his particular culture. A Kyoto girl is taught that gentleness is the most important feminine quality; a Los Angeles girl learns that physical beauty is an essential quality.

A person is said to have a strong or firm sex-role identity when his subjective judgment of himself comes up to the standards of the ideal. If there are major discrepancies between the ideal and a person's view of himself, he has a weak or fragile sex-role identity.

To get at the dynamic significance of a person's sex-role identity, we must confront four questions: (1) How does a person initially learn sex-role standards? (2) Just what is the content of the standards? (3) Are some sex-role standards generalized across cultures? (4) What are the implications of a firm sex-role identity and a fragile one?

A child learns sex-role standards the way he learns many other concepts. He learns that an object that is round, made of rubber, and bounces is called a ball. He learns more about the definition of a ball by watching how it is used, by listening to people talk about it, and by playing with one himself. By the age of two he has learned that certain objects are called boys and men; others, girls and women. He learns the definition by noting what they do, how they look, and what they wear, and by listening and watching as others discuss the sexes. The categorization of human beings into the two sexes, usually in place by two and a half years, is one of the earliest conceptual classifications a child makes.

Sex roles are defined not only by physical attributes and behavior, but also by opinions, feelings and motives. Most American girls regard an attractive face, a hairless body, a small frame and moderate-sized breasts as ideal physical characteristics. American boys regard height, large muscles, and facial and body hair as ideal.

Some psychological traits that differentiate males from females are changing in American life. Aggression is one of the primary sex-typed behaviors. The traditional sex-role standard inhibits aggression in females, but licenses and encourages it in boys and men. It is difficult to find a psychological study of Americans that fails to note more aggressive behavior among males than among females.

Young children agree that males are more dangerous and punishing than females. This view also persists at a symbolic level: Six-year-olds believe that a tiger is a masculine animal, and that a rabbit is feminine. In one experiment, pairs of pictures were shown to young children. On the first run, the child selected from each pair the picture that was most like his father. The second time, the child selected the picture that was more like his mother. In the third run, he picked the one more like himself. Boys and girls alike classified the father as darker, larger, more dangerous and more angular than the mother. The boys classified themselves as darker, larger, more dangerous and more angular than the girls.

These perceptions are not limited to

our culture. Charles Osgood of the University of Illinois showed similar pairs of abstract designs or pictures to adults from four different language groups: American, Japanese, Navajo and Mexican-Spanish. He asked each adult to indicate which picture of the pair best fitted the concept of man and which fitted the concept of woman. As the children had done, the adults from all four cultures classified men as large, angular and dark and women as small, round and light.

Dependency, passivity and conformity are also part of the traditional sex-role standard. Females in America and in most European countries are permitted these qualities; boys and men are pressured to *inhibit* them. Thus men experience greater conflict over being passive; females experience greater conflict over being aggressive.

These differences over aggressive and dependent behavior are reflected in a person's action, and in a reluctance to perceive these qualities in others. As part of an extensive personality assessment, 71 typical, middle-class American adults watched while some pictures depicting aggression, and some depicting dependency were flashed onto a screen at great speed. Each person was asked to describe each picture after it was flashed seven times. The women had greater difficulty than the men in recognizing the aggressive scenes; the men had greater difficulty in recognizing the dependency scenes.

Sex-role standards dictate that the female must feel needed and desired by a man. She must believe that she can arouse a male sexually, experience deep emotion and heal the psychological wounds of those she loves. The standards for males also stress the ability to arouse and to gratify a love object, but they also include a desire to be independent in action and to dominate others and to be able to control the expression of strong emotions, especially fear and helplessness.

The American male traditionally has been driven to prove that he was strong and powerful; the female to prove that she was capable of forming a deeply emotional relationship that brought satisfaction and growth to the partner—sweetheart or child.

These values are reflected in the behavior of young children from diverse cultures. John and Beatrice Whiting of Harvard University observed children from six cultures and found that the boys were more aggressive and dominant than the girls. The girls were more likely than boys to offer help and support to other children.

In one study, my colleagues and I observed two-year-old boys and girls in a large living room. The girls were more likely than boys to stay in close physical contact with their mothers during the first five minutes. Then a set of toys was brought into the room and the children were allowed to play for a half hour. Most children left their mothers immediately and began to play. However, after 15 or 20 minutes many became bored and restless. The girls tended to drift back to their mothers, while the boys preferred to wander around the room. Michael Lewis of Educational Testing Services has reported similar differences in children only one year old. Linda Shapiro of Harvard has studied pairs of two-year-olds (two boys or two girls) in a natural setting and found the girls more trusting, more cooperative, more nurturing and less fearful of each other than the boys.

It is interesting to note that the rhesus monkey and the baboon, who are not taught sex-role standards, display behavioral differences that resemble those observed in young children. Harry Harlow and his colleagues at the University of Wisconsin have found that threatening gestures and rough-and-tumble contact play are more frequent among young male than among young female monkeys, whereas passivity in stress is more frequent among the females.

Some of the differences between males and females seem to stretch across cultures and species, suggesting that sex-role standards are neither arbitrary nor completely determined by the social groups. Each culture, in its wisdom, seems to promote those behaviors and values that are biologically easiest to establish in each of the two sexes.

The individual's sex-role identity, as noted, is his opinion of his maleness or femaleness, not a summary of his physical attributes. In one study, Edward Bennett and Larry Cohen of Tufts University asked American adults to select from a list of adjectives those that best described their personalities. The women described themselves as weak, fearful, capable of warmth and desirous of friendly and harmonious relationships with others. The men described themselves as competent, intelligent and motivated by power and personal accomplishment.

Sex-role identity differences among children arise from three sources:

First, a family-reared child is predisposed to assume that he or she is more like his or her parent of the same sex than like any other adult, and is inclined to imitate that parent. If a father is bold and athletic, his son is more likely to believe he possesses these masculine attributes than is a boy whose father is not athletic.

Second, the child is vulnerable to the special definition of sex roles shared by his peer group. A boy who is clumsy on the playing field is more likely to question his sex-role identity if he lives in a neighborhood devoted to athletics than he is if he lives in a community that values intellectual prowess.

Third, sex-role identity depends heavily on the quality of sexual interaction in adolescence. The sex-role identity has two important six-year periods of growth: one prior to puberty when acquisition of peer valued sex-role characteristics is primary, and one during adolescence, when success in heterosexual encounters is crucial. If the adolescent is unable to establish successful heterosexual relationships, he will begin to question his sex-role identity. To the adult, the potential for attracting the affection of another and entering into a satisfactory sexual union is the essence of the sex-role standard.

Let us consider the implications of a firm sex-role identity and a fragile one. Each of us tries all the time to match his traits to his notion of the ideal sex role. This is but one facet of the human desire to gain as much information about the self as possible. When one feels close to his ideal standard, his spirits are buoyed. He is confident he can come even closer, and he makes the attempt. If he feels he is far from his standard, he may turn away from it and accept the role of a feminine man (or a masculine woman). Acceptance of a culturally inappropriate role reduces the terrible anxiety that comes from recognizing in one's self a serious deviation from an ideal that cannot be obtained. The only possible defense is to redefine the ideal in attainable terms.

The continuing attempt to match one's attributes to the sex-role ideal allows men to display a more intense involvement than women in difficult intellectual problems. Males are supposed to be more competent in science and mathematics; as academic excellence is necessary for vocational success, it, therefore, is an essential component of a man's sex-role identity.

Adolescent girls view intellectual striving as a form of aggressive behavior because it involves competition with a peer. Since many females believe they should not be overly competitive, they inhibit intense intellectual striving. A visit to college dining halls often reveals males arguing so intensely that the air crackles with hostility. Intense debate in the female dining hall is less frequent because it threatens the girl's sex-role identity. Men seem to be better able to argue about an issue because they do not always take an attack on an opinion as an attack on the person.

Although intense intellectual striving is more characteristic of adult men than it is of women, this is not the case among young children. In the primary grades, girls outperform boys in all areas. The ratio of boys to girls with reading problems ranges as high as six to one. One reason for this difference is that the average American six- or seven-year-old boy sees school as a feminine place. On entering school he meets female teachers who monitor painting, coloring and singing, and put a premium on obedience, suppression of aggression and restlessness. These values are clearly more appropriate for girls than for boys. Studies of children affirm that they see school as feminine and seven-year-old boys naturally resist the complete submission it demands. If this is true, a community with a large proportion of male teachers should have a smaller proportion of boys with serious reading retardation. Some American communities, such as Akron, Ohio, are testing the hypothesis.

Depression and anxiety affect the sexes differently. Women are likely to suffer psychological stress when it is suggested that they are not attractive, loving or emotional. Some women experience serious depression after giving birth because they do not feel strong love for the infant and they question their femininity. Men become anxious at suggestions that they are impotent or not competent, successful or dominant. Depression is likely to follow a man's career failure.

The sex-role standards of a society are not static, and changes in the standards that surround sexuality and dependence are just becoming evident. The American woman has begun to assume a more active role in sexual behavior; her mother and grandmother assumed passive postures. This reach for independence has extensive social implications. Some college-educated women feel that dependence, especially on men, is an undesirable feminine trait. They want to prove that they can function as competently and autonomously as men and this pushes them to develop academic and career skills.

Why? The intense effort spent on getting into and staying in college has persuaded the young woman that she should use her hard-won intellectual skills in a job. And technology has made it less necessary for a woman to do routine housework and forced her to look outside the home for proof of her usefulness.

Most human beings seek the joy of accomplishment. A man tries to gratify this need in his job and he has something concrete with which to prove his effectiveness—an invention, a manuscript, a salary check. Woman once met her need to be useful by believing that her sweetheart, husband or children required her wisdom, skill and personal affection. Instant dinners, permissive sexual mores, and freedom for children have undermined this role. It is too early to predict the effect of this female unrest. It should lead to a more egalitarian relation between the sexes. It could make each partner so reluctant to submerge his individual autonomy and admit his need for the other, that each walks a lonely, and emotionally insulated path. Let us hope it does not.

O but what about love? I forget love
not that I am incapable of love
it's just that I see love as odd as wearing shoes—
I never wanted to marry a girl who was like my mother
And Ingrid Bergman was always impossible
And there's maybe a girl now but she's already married
And I don't like men and—
but there's got to be somebody!

Gregory Corso

Children of the Kibbutz

by Leslie Y. and Karen Rabkin

What is believed to be essential for mental health is that the infant and young child should experience a warm, intimate and continuous relationship with his mother (or permanent mother-substitute—one person who steadily mothers him), in which both find satisfaction and enjoyment."

Very few professionals in child development, or parents, disagree with the mothering concept that John Bowlby expresses. Precisely for this reason, it is valuable to examine a society in which a different image of child rearing prevails. That society is the kibbutz—in Israel—where the child is entrusted to more than one mothering figure.

The remarkable and revolutionary living experiment that is the kibbutz has been in existence in Israel for more than 60 years—and more and more, kibbutz values are cited in debate about the American system of child-rearing. Current concern over the needs of disadvantaged children, particularly poor blacks from broken families, makes us wonder whether collective child-rearing could be a part of the solution. George Albee and others who theorize about new community models say we need group socialization for disadvantaged children.

More than 200 kibbutzim dot Israel. Although their total membership of about 80,000 is only three per cent of the country's population, the kibbutzim have contributed a disproportionate share of the nation's military and political leaders. One-third of the officers in Tzahal (Israel's army) are kibbutzniks and nearly 60 per cent of a recent class of air-force pilots were kibbutz-born. Most well-known Israeli figures live in or were born or reared in kibbutzim. Among them are former Prime Minister David Ben-Gurion, the late Levi Eshkol and General Moshe Dayan, who was born in the first kibbutz, Deganyah Aleph, on the bank of the Jordan River. (Dayan's parents left the kibbutz, however, joined the more family-centered *moshav* movement, and reared him there.)

The kibbutz is a voluntary, predominantly agricultural collective settlement of community-owned property (except for a few personal belongings) and of collective economic production and child care. The kibbutz motto is: from each according to his abilities, to each according to his needs. The emphasis on cooperation means, of course, that kibbutz ideology rejects certain basic ideas of our own social system—the importance of private property, private enterprise and family child-rearing.

The kibbutz grew out of the desire of a group of young, turn-of-the-Century,

Eastern European Jewish intellectuals to found a new and democratic society in what was then Palestine. They had experienced the dying years of the Russian Czarist regime, with its brutal anti-Semitism, and were fired by the Zionist dream for Israel; they wanted a society free of the prejudice that closed the world they had left behind, dedicated to full social and political equality. The promise of the Russian Revolution that a decadent society would be remade inspired the kibbutz founders and strengthened their Utopian ideals.

Kibbutz founders rebelled against the double standard for men and women and the traditional structure of the Jewish family. Wife and child had been subservient to the husband and father, and the division of labor confined the woman to the home, excluding her from the community's social, cultural and economic life.

To counter the double standard, kibbutz founders took dramatic steps: they based their marriage relationships on consent instead of on legal contract; they established communal kitchens, dining rooms and laundries to free the women from household chores and give them full roles in the economic and social life of the kibbutz. Kibbutz founders also created a system of collective education to free the mother from the responsibilities of child-rearing and to tie the child more closely to the group.

For 18 months, in 1967 and 1968, we lived in a kibbutz and studied child development. Our kibbutz (we'll call it Kiryat Yedidim) is like many others in this small country. It nestles in a valley at the foot of a mountain range in northeastern Israel, reclaimed by its founders from swamp water and Bedouins.

About 400 adults—the number includes those who are away for army service—and 250 children make up the Kiryat Yedidim community. Our kibbutz, which spreads over 2,500 acres, produces cotton, citrus, olives, carrots, onions, potatoes and several types of fodder. The farming is highly mechanized. A dairy flourishes, thanks to an especially productive cross-breed of Dutch and Arab cattle; poultry thrives on a large scale; fish ponds specialize in carp, an Israeli favorite; and flowers flourish in hothouses.

The village radiates from a communal dining hall, which also shelters weekly movies, community meetings and celebrations. Stretching out in front of the dining hall is a well-landscaped lawn, the work of four full-time gardeners and a source of great community pride. Children's houses stretch out to the west of the dining room. To the south and east are the fields. Behind the dining hall is a handsome new social club and library where people drink coffee, talk and read the papers.

Houses vary from one-room units with community bathrooms—used only by unmarried persons—to new two-room apartments, each with bathroom and kitchen, which house nearly all members over 30. Also, there is a variety of older housing with private baths, kitchens and porches. Usually four living units make up a building, the newest being two-storied. The rooms are pleasantly furnished. Paths connect all the houses and living areas. Many people use bicycles to get around, but most move about on foot. Jeeps and tractors transport nearly everyone to work.

The children of Kiryat Yedidim live and take their meals in their own quarters, sleeping from earliest infancy without adults. Two night watchmen circulate from one of the children's houses; a switchboard hooked to microphones in each house alerts the watchmen when a child is in distress. Specially trained female kibbutz members (metapelet; plural, metaplot) provide care, socialization and education. The metaplot are mostly young women, 21 to 35. A few older women work with school children; all of the married metaplot have children of their own. Several hours a day and on most holidays the child visits his parents, who become friends and companions.

When the newborn baby arrives from the hospital, usually after three days, he is placed in a nursery with five other infants. The old but freshly painted nursery building is divided into three wings, each containing entry hall, kitchen and two rooms. Outside is a porch where cribs sit during mild weather. Beyond that is a lawn where mothers play with their infants during visits. Inside, a few pictures decorate the bright, airy rooms; rattles, teething rings, brightly colored decorations are attached to the cribs; mobiles hang overhead. (There are no pacifiers; the belief is that infants should be self-reliant—in this case on their own thumbs—as early as possible.) The open structure permits visual and verbal interaction among the babies.

The mother, who is relieved of work for six weeks, visits as often as necessary to feed her baby. Israelis prefer breast-feeding but do not pressure mothers about it. As the baby is weaned, the mother resumes her work halftime, adding an hour a month, and the metapelet takes over part of the solid feeding.

By about nine months, the mother is making only short visits. Until the infant is 18 months old, mothers get daily half-hour work breaks for visits. The infant house, always open and flexible, can meet special needs of mother and child. A woman who has severe anxiety over separation from her baby is allowed to sleep in the infant house. The metapelet and the woman in charge of the education program counsel the mother in this crisis. While the metaplot are responsible for satisfying the infants' needs, parents spend several hours daily with their children; these are periods of affectionate interplay—parents generally avoid disciplinary or other training situations. Children quickly begin to anticipate these evening parental visits, and the visiting remains a source of gratification long beyond childhood. (One recent kibbutz graduate, commenting on the psychological distance between parents and children during high-school years, told us, "No, you don't go to see your parents so much—you're busy with your group, studies, activities—but they are always good for chocolate.")

After a year, the child joins five of his peers in a toddlers' house. Usually two groups of six live in a building. Nurses prepare breakfast and snacks in the buildings but bring hot things for lunch and dinner from a central children's kitchen. The children play with clay, blocks, toy cars and tractors, balls, rattles, picture books, cans for sand and water, wagons and doll furniture. Outside are a sandpit, swings, slide, and crawl-through barrels.

In the toddlers' house the child encounters a new metapelet and new physical surroundings. The socialization process begins in earnest. He learns to interact with peers, to dress and feed

> *"a sense of __we__ and __they__ emerges very early. Children support their group against others, exclude out-group members from play, and show concern when a member is absent"*

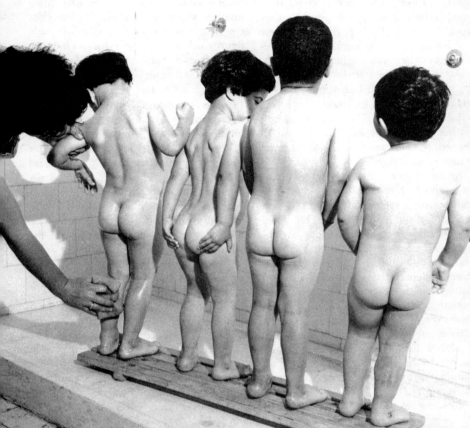

himself and starts toilet training (between the 15th and 18th month; it usually ends by age three). Warmth, affection and permissiveness characterize the care in these sensitive areas. Nurses stress independence and praise those who eat with spoons and dress themselves. The child, of course, learns a number of routines, dictated by group needs, that will be expected of him all his life—meals at certain times, designated play periods and places, and a definite bedtime—but an effort is made to balance the need for order with the child's individual needs.

Kibbutz education is designed to lay the foundations for group identification. As Shmuel Golan, the late theoretician of collective education, wrote: "[a] ... feature of collective education that represents a positive value from the child's earliest years is the feeling of belongingness that it fosters—a feeling of being an essential part of, and rooted in, a society of his peers."

We noticed that a sense of *we* and *they* emerges very early. Children support their group against others, exclude out-group members from play, and show concern when a member is absent. The group expects him to share objects in the children's house, but not something he brings from his parents. The child who shares is praised lavishly.

When the children are between the ages of three and four, a nursery teacher —*ganenet*—takes charge of their social and intellectual development. A group of six moves to a new building—the kindergarten—and joins two other six-member groups. The enlarged group—a *kvutza*—remains the nexus of the child's life until high school.

At this stage, the *ganenet* prepares the ground for real intellectual training. She divides playtime into free and structured sessions, the latter sometimes referred to as work. As one *ganenet* explained, "What the children do freely, that's play, but anything I give them to do—that is, anything organized—is work." The *ganenet* places special emphasis on sensory training—the aim is to enhance the child's ability to use his senses to explore the world. Sheila and Michael Cole (he's on the faculty of University of California, Irvine) noted a similar emphasis in Russian nursery schools [*see their article on page 212*], though the kibbutz approach is less formal. Kibbutzniks

spend many kindergarten hours building things, painting, dancing and playing games. They also grow their own flowers and vegetables and tend animals. From the time they can walk, the children visit the various work settings—the kitchen, fields, gardens, the garage, where they smell, touch, hear and taste the adult world, and equally important, see their parents at work—closing the gap, somewhat, between adult and child worlds.

After a year or two in kindergarten, the children reach a transitional class in which they embark on basic intellectual training—word-recognition, reading and mathematical concepts. Akin to our kindergarten, the transitional class stresses readiness activity.

At about seven, the child enters grammar school. Here he commences full-scale learning and encounters youngsters both older and younger than he. They devote an hour a day to work assignments, all age groups working together. They clean tables in the dining room, arrange their rooms and cultivate a vegetable garden. The teachers are well-trained graduates of the kibbutz movement's own teacher's college. Classroom instruction, based on the project method, is highly informal. Children call the teacher by her first name; there are no examinations or grade marks and passing is automatic.

The project method, kibbutz educators believe, permits a deep, integrated approach to learning. We watched children in a project study transportation development, build models and ride a variety of vehicles. In the process, they learned some history, economics, geography and some elementary mechanics. At the end of the study period, they made exhibits.

Kibbutz education integrates the child's learning with his surroundings, through nature studies and projects that focus on animals, weather and the kibbutz itself. The children camp out and hike to mountains and fields. Kibbutz founders come to tell tales of the pioneer days. Kibbutz children develop a sense of belonging that deeply impressed us, the kind of involvement in their world wanted in American schools by such social critics as Paul Goodman.

In the spring of his last year in grammar school, the child enters the youth movement with which the kibbutz is affiliated—an important and symbolic move

that locks the child more securely into the kibbutz. At about 12, when he has finished the sixth grade, the young kibbutznik enters the combined junior-senior high school (*mosad*). This wider society—composed of 300 children from several kibbutzim and the nearby city—involves significant change for him. For the first time he meets important male figures other than his father. They are teachers and youth group leaders (*madrichim*) who guide his moral and ideological growth. His group, after being together for seven years, breaks apart; members go into new groups that include children from outside the kibbutz.

Now the student experiences a greater physical separation from parents and kibbutz, along with a new, strange freedom—institutional patterns are much less rigid. He begins to work in the kibbutz economy—one and a half to three hours a day, depending on age—alongside the adults. By the time he graduates from high school, he will have had enough work experience to choose work that most interests him.

Through sustained, all-encompassing contact in the peer group, the children identify with and depend on the group. Until the age of 18, life varies only slightly for both sexes. Boys and girls sleep in the same room and until the end of grammar school shower together and use the same toilets. (In the beginning they showered together until age 18, but not now.) Not surprisingly, youngsters brought up in close proximity feel like siblings and rarely intermarry. As the kibbutzniks put it: "How can you marry someone you sat next to on the potty?"

Until the end of high school, children are not kibbutz members; they belong to the children's society, which is a microcosm of the regulatory and social agencies of the kibbutz. The children's society elects a student council, plans social programs, punishes troublemakers and helps plan curriculum. After high school, students are elected to kibbutz membership, then leave to serve their compulsory army duty.

Behavioral scientists and educators are interested in kibbutz life because it is a way of life purposely, totally and willingly built around the principles of community and cooperation. And infant care, socialization and the education of children all reflect a determination to abolish family-centeredness and create an atmosphere in which parents and children can maximize love and affection.

Kibbutz educators believe that collective education reduces parent-child conflict for several reasons: (1) the child, supported by the kibbutz, is economically independent of his parents; (2) equality of the sexes eliminates the patriarchal family system; (3) the importance of the nurse allows the child to love someone other than his parents; (4) because nurses handle the primary discipline, the daily visits of parents and children can take place under ideal conditions; (5) jealousy and anger that have to be repressed in the family can be expressed in the kibbutz because the child can find more legitimate objects of aggression among peers; and (6) the collective framework shields the child from overprotective or domineering parents who might block his efforts to become independent.

The results of planned socialization are not easy to evaluate but many professionals, influenced by Bowlby, believe that multiple mothering creates many emotional problems among children. Children raised in institutions often lack stimulation and maternal warmth. These professionals fear that this may also be true of kibbutzniks.

Albert Rabin, of Michigan State University, did a study comparing kibbutz infants and infants reared in the *moshav*, the Israeli communal settlement that retains a private family structure. His results with the Griffiths Infant Scale suggest that kibbutz infants are somewhat less socially responsive than *moshav* infants, but he felt it was due more to the comparatively large number of infants who are under a single nurse's care than to the mother's limited contact with the child. Nevertheless, Rabin's findings support the idea that kibbutzniks are emotionally deprived.

In a more recent and larger study, however, Reuven Kohen-Raz, of Jerusalem's Hebrew University, who used the more carefully constructed Bayley Infant Scales of Mental and Motor Development, found that kibbutz infants at one, six and 12 months show higher overall achievements than Bayley's U.S. sample. Even when they were compared with infants of highly educated parents in private Israeli homes, kibbutz babies consistently performed better. At the

least, this should quiet pessimists who claim that collective child-rearing retards the intellectual development of infants.

Interestingly, when Rabin compared 10-year-olds, older adolescents and young army men from the kibbutz with a *moshav* group, he found indications of higher intellectual achievement and personal adjustment among the kibbutzniks. Rabin concluded: "The facts are that kibbutz child-rearing was designed to raise new kibbutz members, and is quite effective in doing so."

Anthropologist Melford Spiro, of the University of California at San Diego, studied Kiryat Yedidim a generation ago. We followed up his work because the stability of the kibbutz population and Spiro's unpublished data lend dimension to our study. When Spiro studied the kibbutz in 1951, the oldest kibbutz-born child was 28 and only about a dozen were over 21, but he concluded that the individual reared through collective education is "an efficient, productive and functioning adult. He is an adult with a sense of values and a conscience that assures the implementation of these values. He is motivated to carry on the basic features of kibbutz culture—its collective ownership, distribution according to need, agricultural work, collective child-rearing and its devotion to esthetic and intellectual values."

We have only begun to analyze the result of our study but they already confirm Spiro's impressions. One must, as David Rapaport noted, "pay a price . . . in the coin of developmental crises and pathology" for any system of socialization. And, despite the fact that kibbutzniks call childhood a "Garden of Eden," there *are* crises in collective education. For example, moving a child from one dormitory to another often creates insecurity. Also, kibbutzniks undergo stress when they try to balance their need to be individuals with the need to conform to the group. We hope our study results will illuminate the meaning of these crises in personality development.

Meanwhile, we can sum up the kibbutznik: he is a healthy, intelligent, generous, somewhat shy but warm human being, rooted in his community and in the larger Israeli society. He shows no sign of the emotional disturbance we would expect from a violation of our ideal mother-child relationship.

What can we learn from the kibbutz

experience? Can we integrate collective education into our social and economic structure? Is it a panacea for educating the poor? We think not. We cannot translate this socialization system into American terms. To do so we would need a basic overhaul of the goals of our society. To release children into our individualistic, competitive society after rearing them collectively, emphasizing cooperation and responsibility for one's group, would be too much of a psychological jolt. Nor is kibbutz education based on cutting parental ties, a notion implicit in many proposals for using the kibbutz model with poor children. The child may suffer painful and destructive conflicts unless he sees the family and the collective as allies and collaborators.

But we see other possibilities. Bruno Bettelheim once asked: "Is it possible that the privatization of so much of modern middle-class life is not the consequence but rather the cause of human isolation from which modern man suffers and which the kibbutz way of life has tried to counteract?" The kibbutznik has a deep sense of belonging to his kibbutz and his country. The privatization of our family life may counter this belongingness. We may find that if we expose our children to meaningful group experiences in early life, we will give them a sense of integration in something beyond their family, enabling them to identify with the community and the nation.

The need for an exclusive mother-child relationship overconcerns so many mothers who need to work or to study that no matter how competent the substitute caretaker, they feel that the child inevitably suffers psychologically from these separations. Alberta Siegel, "The Working Mother: A Review of Research," suggests that a mother's employment can have a positive, stimulating effect on a child's development. Knowledge that the multiple-mothering of the kibbutz has no long-range ill effects should enable us to see the problem from another angle. Incidentally, the fact that the father is at home and with the child a great deal in the kibbutz is another matter for our matricentric society to reflect upon.

But these are *our* problems. Meanwhile, the kibbutz continues to develop and refine its ways of life, and incidentally to provide a fascinating counterpoint to the family life and education that we so completely take for granted.

Russian Nursery Schools

By Michael and Sheila Cole

IT WAS FREE-PLAY PERIOD at Preschool 67 in the northwest suburbs of Moscow, and it was early summer. Two three-year-old boys were building a castle in the sandbox, occasionally getting in the way of a little girl who was tunneling. A red-faced youngster was hard at work hauling pails of water for the boys from a nearby pond. In a far corner of the yard, two little girls were playing with dolls. Sitting under an arbor in another corner, alone, was a three-year-old girl with short, dark hair, singing softly to herself.

We had seen the girl spend the play period that way for several days, and we mentioned her to the teacher, a young woman who had been trained at one of the Soviet Union's pedagogical institutes. "Oh, that's Irichka," she replied. "Irichka is happy to be alone. She's that kind of child—quiet and able to amuse herself."

To us, it seemed odd that a woman who was supposed to be raising children in a collective should show such an easy acceptance of individualism. But the more we learned about Soviet nursery schools, the more apparent it became that we had brought with us from the United States a full bag of misconceptions.

We spent the summer of 1966 in the Soviet Union, chiefly to help with preparations for the 18th International Congress of Psychologists. In the United States at the time, Head Start programs were springing up all over, and the newspapers were full of heartwarming accounts of children listening to stories and receiving medical check-ups for the first time in their lives. A heated debate was also underway among teachers and psychologists about what kinds of program would best prepare these children for the public schools, whose task in turn would be to make them productive and socially useful members of our society.

Especially because of this situation at home, we were eager to find out all we could about Soviet nursery schools. We spent almost a week at Preschool 67, talking to the children, teachers and principal. Later, we visited the Institute of Preschool Education in Moscow and interviewed its director, A. V. Zaporozhets. The Institute is responsible for recommending a nursery-school program to the Soviet Union's Ministry of Education, and its psychologists perform the research on which the recommendations are based. Once the program has been adopted by the Ministry, it is used throughout the country.

Nursery schools have been part of the system of universal education in the Soviet Union since the time of the Bolshevik Revolution. Although they are not compulsory, preschools are the first link in the Soviet educational system. The Communist Party assigns to nursery schools the task of insuring the normal development of all children—preparing them for school and teaching them proper work habits, so that they, like their American counterparts, will grow into productive and socially useful members of their society.

Preschool 67 is just like thousands of nursery schools in the Soviet Union. Its drab, two-story building comes from a blueprint in use throughout the country for almost 10 years, and its educational program and goals are also identical to those in effect elsewhere.

The pupils range in age from two to seven; there are 150 of them, all from homes in the neighborhood of the school. One group of 25 lives in the school's small dormitory, going home only on weekends and holidays. The others arrive between eight and nine in the morning and leave between four and six in the afternoon.

There is a long waiting list at Preschool 67, as there is at most nursery schools, and admission is based on need. Priority is given to children who have two working parents and no grandmother or other baby-sitter, to orphans, and to children from very large families or from homes where there is sickness or some other problem. Payment, which is determined by the parents' income, ranges from $2.20 to $13.00 a month.

When we arrived at Preschool 67, the children were eating breakfast on one side of a large, airy, toy-cluttered room. The older children used cloth napkins and sat at tables covered with white cloths. These amenities, we were told by Sofia Shvedova, the warm, grandmotherly director of the preschool, were both a reward for good table manners and an incentive to improve. "We ask the children to see how clean they can keep the tablecloth," she said. "But we never shame them when they have an accident."

"We know that some children eat less than others, but we give them all the same amount anyway," Mrs. Shvedova went on. "We let them eat as much as they can. We occasionally feed the little ones. But we don't force a child to love all food. We try to teach him little by little."

"In nursery school, children should grow to be healthy, alert, life-loving, playful, agile individuals with good bearing."

FROM *PROGRAM OF EDUCATION IN THE NURSERY SCHOOL* (Ministry of Education, 1962)

At nursery school, the children receive three substantial meals a day—they are not supposed to eat at home on school days except for an occasional snack—and they take their naps there as well.

In other words, the nursery school is responsible for the health and physical development of the child. This lessens the burden on the working mother, and it also reflects the Soviets' very different view from ours of the relation between children and society. The Soviets believe that children are a natural resource, perhaps the most valuable resource a society has. Although the raising of the child is entrusted to the family, the ultimate responsibility for the child's development belongs to the State itself.

As the children finished their breakfast, they wiped their mouths on their napkins, asked the nanny if they could be excused, thanked her, and went to the other side of the room to play. A few children stayed behind; it was their turn to help clear the table.

Teaching the children to take care of their own needs, and to help with the chores and with the younger children, is an important part of the "work training" portion of the nursery-school program. The children do not receive concrete rewards for their "work," but they are profusely praised when they do a good job.

"They should all work well," Mrs. Shvedova said. "But we know that there are individual differences and that one child is not as capable as another. We try to measure them all against their own achievement. We can't give a

child a gold star when he breaks a plate, but we can say, 'Tolia did a very good job today. He tried very hard. He broke a dish, but he did it because he was trying so hard.'"

Surprising as it might seem to many Americans, Mrs. Shvedova's insistence on acknowledging individual differences and on judging the child against his own abilities is based on official ideology. The government-distributed manual for preschool teachers says that nursery schools should teach friendship and cooperation and also form individuality: the school's program of physical, intellectual, moral, work and esthetic training should take into account the age and individual characteristics of each child.

Later in the morning, a teacher took Preschool 67's three- and four-year-olds aside to read them a story. The

children listened intently. When the teacher had finished, she asked them to retell parts of the story and to answer questions about it, gently correcting their mistakes and insisting on answers that were complete, grammatical sentences. One little girl was over-eager: she shouted the right answer before a slower and shyer child could finish. The teacher restrained her gently and then encouraged the other child to answer by himself.

Teaching the children to speak Russian correctly and to express themselves fully is one of the major aims of the preschool program. Language training is a continuous process, carried on throughout the day by means of books, stories and direct contact with adults.

In another room, the older children followed their teacher's story in books of their own. Before the teacher began to read, she asked the children several questions about books and how they are used. During the story, she stopped often to ask what letter or sound a word began or ended with. Later, she requested summaries of the plot and descriptions of the characters.

For five- and six-year-olds, who will soon start school, there is great emphasis on skills like these. The preschool is in close touch with the grade-schools that the children will attend, and it teaches them the work habits and procedures that are used there. Reading and writing as such are not formally taught in nursery school, but reading and writing readiness are. The children learn to analyze the sounds they hear in the spoken language and to write the elements used in the letters of the Russian alphabet.

Elementary mathematical concepts are introduced gradually, through the use of concrete materials. The children learn to count to 10 by eye, ear, touch and movement; to answer questions of number, size and position in space; and to subtract or add one or two to any number up to 10. It is only in the last year of nursery school, when the children are six years old, that they begin to work with written numbers and with the symbols $+$, $-$ and $=$.

After lunch, we stood at the door of a dormitory crowded with high, white iron bedsteads and watched the children take their usual two-hour rest. They were supposed to be asleep, but they seemed determined not to succumb. Stripped to their underwear and covered with sheets, they tossed, turned, whispered, sucked their thumbs, asked the nanny for glasses of water, and requested permission to go to the potty—or reported that it was too late.

The nanny treated the bed-wetters and thumb-suckers matter-of-factly. If a child wet his bed, she changed his sheets and underwear with little fuss and no reprimands. She privately asked a few older children to take their thumbs out of their mouths, but when the thumbs were put back in a few moments she seemed not to notice.

After their naps, the children went outside to play. The yard was provided with swings, sandboxes and little pools of water; there were also gazebos and arbors, tables and chairs, and bookcases full of games, toys, books and arts-and-crafts materials.

One two-year-old boy, ignoring these enticements, began to wander off the nursery-school grounds. The nanny in charge, a motherly middle-aged woman, ran after him and brought him back. She scolded him affectionately, threatening to punish him by making him sit still.

"He's such a little one," she said. "He really doesn't understand. It's impossible to really punish him."

Mrs. Shvedova told us later that punishment is meted out only if the children hurt someone or are very disobedient. "The first time a child is bad, we don't do anything. We try to understand. But after a while we must punish, because of the other children. We try to suit the punishment to the child and the situation. We know the children well, and we know what each one will consider a punishment." Corporal punishment is frowned on in the Soviet Union, and the usual method of discipline is the temporary withdrawal of affection and praise.

During the play period, one group of girls five or six years old went to an arts-and-crafts area to color. They

were eager to please and to show us their work, which was very neat. When one girl offered to draw us a picture to take home to our daughter, we requested a dog. "I can't," she said. "No one has taught me how."

In Soviet nursery schools, drawing is a lesson—something to be learned. There are exercises on how to draw straight lines, circles and other forms, and simple figures. These exercises are not considered play, and the teacher

"Teachers should teach the children to respect people and work, and to be interested in work, community life and nature." FROM *PROGRAM OF EDUCATION IN THE NURSERY SCHOOL*

keeps a little folder of each child's work to encourage a serious attitude toward it.

Looking through these folders, we found that the children's drawings were all the same. The teacher had shown them how to draw a house, a person, or whatever, and they had done it. Unlike most Americans, who believe that a child will be creative "naturally" if he is given the chance, the Soviets believe creativity is more than a matter of opportunity. It requires training. But they are quick to point out that the object of training is not stilted, narrow drawings like those in the folders at Preschool 67. How to teach creativity properly is a problem now being studied at the laboratory of esthetic education of the Institute of Preschool Education.

However, the development of creativity does not seem to be very high on Soviet preschools' list of priorities. When we asked Mrs. Shvedova what goals Preschool 67 had for its children, she replied, "We want them to be

smart and honest. If they are honest, they will be fair. We want them to love beauty, to be real people. We don't want them to be all alike, but originality and creativity are not that important."

One thing that *is* important is sensory training, which the Soviets define rather more broadly than we would. At the preschool one morning we watched a row of three-year-olds, seated on small benches under an arbor, receive a lesson in sensory training that was also a lesson in language. The teacher showed the children five vegetables and named them: an onion, a beet, a carrot, a cabbage and a potato. Then she put the vegetables in a cloth sack and asked a child to draw one out and name it.

When each child and the teacher had named the vegetables several times and repeated the names in unison, the teacher told the children that the five objects together were called vegetables. The class said the word "vegetable" several times and was dismissed.

The four- and five-year-olds had a harder task. After they chose a vegetable from the sack they were asked, without looking at it, to name it and tell everything they knew about it—its color, its shape, how it grows and how it is eaten. The rest of the children in the group corrected and helped them.

According to the Russians, perception is more than the physical reception of energy by the sense organs. It also involves the organization of perceptual signals—the way a person selects and systematizes certain characteristics of perceptible reality so that he can use them in such activities as speech, music, art and work. For the Soviets, then, perception means not only "perception" as we usually think of it; it includes a number of cognitive functions as well. When a child learns to perceive, he learns to orient himself in the world of the senses.

The Russians will allow that this can occur spontaneously, as a by-product of normal activity. But they do not believe that spontaneous development is very efficient or very effective. As A. V. Zaporozhets, director of the Institute of Preschool Education, explained when we talked with him, "Our nursery schools differ from most of those in the West, where there is no special program of education and it is believed that, given the chance, a child will ask questions and learn through his own initiative."

Soviet psychologists, Zaporozhets continued, disagree with both Jean Piaget and Maria Montessori. According to Piaget, the kind of thinking a child is capable of depends on his age. If beans are poured from a short, fat jar into a tall, thin one, a child of four is likely to think the tall jar contains more beans, while a child of six or seven will not be fooled. Piaget attributes this to the fact that the older child understands the principle of conservation.

The Russians, Zaporozhets said, do not agree "that a child cannot do such and such until a certain age. We think that teaching plays a decisive role in learning, and that a child can do quite a bit more than we previously imagined he was capable of."

They do think it is *easier* to develop certain abilities at certain ages, although they are not sure which abilities are easiest to develop at which age. As a working policy, they try to develop intuition and sensory abilities in early childhood, leaving abstract thought for later on. "We believe that thought is a hierarchical structure. For a complete intellect, the entire system, from the most concrete

perception the Soviets are talking about, is to teach the child to use his sensory apparatus to the fullest.

The teacher gives the child two cardboard circles (or triangles, or squares) that are the same size but different colors. She asks the child to put one circle on top of the other so that the edges are even, and to run his finger along the edges of the figures so that he can tell whether he has aligned them correctly or not. Then she gives the child a circle and a square of the same color—say, blue—and shows him a *red* square. His task is find which of his figures has the same *shape* as hers. The child makes his choice and verifies it by placing it on the teacher's model. If it fits, the child is praised; if not, the teacher suggests he try the other figure.

As *Sensory Training* points out, the object of perceptual training is to prepare the child for future activity. In short, the Russian approach is highly pragmatic and task-oriented. Perhaps for this reason, the schools make considerable use of construction exercises. Like drawing, building requires the child to perform a detailed visual examination of the form, size, and spatial arrangement of an object, but *Sensory Training* warns that there is an important distinction between construction and pictorial tasks. A picture always reflects the exterior characteristics of an object as it is visually perceived; construction serves a practical purpose. "Garages are built for cars, barns for animals, houses for dolls. Constructions are made by children to be used—acted with."

to the most abstract, must exist. You don't have to rush to the third stage when you haven't gotten through the first."

Like Montessori, Zaporozhets said, the Soviets think sensory abilities should be developed during early childhood. But "Montessori believed that the child is born with all his sensory abilities and that training will simply strengthen them. We think this is incorrect."

As the handbook for nursery-school teachers written by Institute psychologists, *Sensory Training*, explains, the Russians find the Montessorian system of training too formal, too "pure," too far removed from the everyday world in which the child must use his senses. They believe it is not enough to acquaint the child with an endless variety of sensory data. He must be taught a generalized method of orientation and investigation—an approach to the world of the senses—which will efficiently give him the information he needs. This is best done informally, within the context of regular nursery-school activities such as making models, drawing, constructing things with sand or blocks, singing, dancing and storytelling.

Abstract exercises in which the child discriminates triangles from circles in an unanalyzed way are thought to teach him very little. In the Russian nursery school, a child is taught not only that red is different from blue but that red is the color of apples and, indeed, that red apples are ripe apples and ripe apples are edible apples.

The child is taught to use his senses, and he is also taught what the things he perceives mean and what words he can use to describe his sensory experiences precisely. At the same time, he is encouraged to generalize and categorize on the basis of his immediate sensory experience—he is taught, for instance, that onion-beet-carrot-cabbage-potato equals vegetable.

Here is a typical elementary exercise in sensory training, used with two- and three-year-olds. The object of the exercise, which is preliminary to developing the kind of

"Children's moral traits and the character of their personality should be formed while they are in nursery school." FROM *PROGRAM OF EDUCATION IN THE NURSERY SCHOOL*

Thus a teacher might provide the children with bricks, have the children pile them up in different ways and test the stability of the piles, and then suggest the construction of a road. Or she might give the children beams of different lengths and ask them to build a corral. She would point out the various factors the children should consider if the corral is to serve its purpose—that it must be high enough to prevent the animals from jumping out, that the beams must be close enough together to keep the animals from squeezing through, and so forth.

Although the stress in exercises like these is on purpose and practicality, note that it is also on *activity*, and particularly on physical activity as an important way to develop perceptual skills. The child is an active agent in his own development. *He* places the geometric figures together and runs his fingers around the edges; *he* piles the bricks and builds the corral.

This emphasis on the role of active experience in the child's development has its counterpart in contemporary American developmental theory. Richard Held of M.I.T., for example, has shown that there is a close relation between motor experience and visual perception, especially when one must coordinate what one sees with what one does. In one well-known experiment, Held provided a man and a woman with special glasses that shifted their visual fields to the right. Then he had the woman sit in a wheelchair while the man pushed the chair around the

campus. When the two were tested later, the man—who had had motor experience with the visual shift—was much better than the woman at correcting for the distortion that the glasses created.

In a similar experiment, Held placed two kittens in a circular box whose walls were painted with vertical stripes. One kitten sat in a cart; the other wore a yoke and walked around the box rather in the manner of a water buffalo, moving the cart around as he did so. Although the kitten who got the free ride saw the same things as the walking kitten, the walking kitten seemed to learn more. When the two were tested later, the kitten that had the motor experience showed superior ability to perform a number of tasks that required visual-motor coordination.

The notion of the child as an active agent in his own development also occurs in the work of Jerome Bruner of Harvard. Just telling the child a set of facts, Bruner says, does not produce real learning. The child must operate on his environment in such a way that he discovers solutions to the problems it poses. As the child searches for solutions, his approach becomes more sophisticated and also more effective. For example, young children who have not learned how to gather information efficiently play 20 Questions by asking about specific items: "Is it the dog?" "Is it Mommy?" Older children try to structure their questions so that each yields a maximum amount of information: "Is it a living American man?" Through a process of active searching, the older children have learned generalized techniques for gathering information.

Much of the research now being done by Zaporozhets and his colleagues at the Institute is based on this general premise that activity leads to learning. There are experiments, for example, on teaching cooperation and consideration of others through role-playing. Several children who are not friendly with each other are asked to perform a joint task—to tell a story together, or to put on a puppet show—in the hope that they will be friendlier after than they were before.

We arrived in the Soviet Union with a mental image of a monolithic preschool system, chiefly Pavlovian in theory and rigid, regimented and stifling in practice. Soviet psychology does include some Pavlovian concepts, and Soviet preschool programs do follow a common outline, but these are a much smaller part of the whole picture than we had supposed. In fact, the theoretical and empirical research conducted at the Institute would command the respect of developmental psychologists in Geneva or New York, and the care given the children of Preschool 67 could serve as a model anywhere—anywhere, that is, where children are treated as one of society's most valuable resources.

VI. individual differences and personality

One major approach in psychology is to search for general principles, or laws, of behavior that account for the actions of most people. Another approach is to measure and assess the individual traits that determine a given person's ability to manipulate and cope with the environment. Both approaches are a part of the study of individual differences, which grew from the theoretical assumptions of pioneer neurologists who attempted to correlate personality and intelligence with the individual's particular brain characteristics.

Phrenologists felt that personality and intellectual traits are innately determined, and, because there are personality and intellectual differences among individuals, areas of the brain that are responsible for these differences must have developed idiosyncratically. David Bakan reviews the doctrine that specific regions of the brain are responsible for specific mental functions (a doctrine of cortical localization of function). He shows how phrenologists based their empirical work on this belief and how many made life-long searches for the areas of the brain that would account for differences in ability. Although the phrenologists' method of measuring personality by noting the shape of the skull was unscientific by contemporary standards, their investigations did start American psychology toward a serious investigation of individual abilities and personality characteristics.

The most controversial topic in the area of individual differences is that of intelligence. How many kinds of intelligence are there? What constitutes a fair measure of intellectual ability? Noting the flaws and discrepancies in intelligence testing, Raymond Cattell has suggested that there are two kinds of intelligence, which he labels "fluid" and "crystallized." Fluid ability includes those skills that have little relation to a well-stocked memory or to cultural experiences, such as perceptual or performance skills. Crystallized ability, on the other hand, is based on judgmental skills that have been acquired by cultural interaction. Intelligence tests generally measure crystallized ability; Cattell argues that greater use of culture-fair tests of fluid ability would provide a basis for equal opportunity in education and in the world of work.

John Garcia is one of a growing number of concerned psychologists who doubt that existing standardized intelligence tests are a real measure of human abilities. As Garcia points out, several intrinsic assumptions of IQ tests make them useless for comparing the intelligence of biosocial groups. Their main weakness is the narrow, biased collection of items used to sample the characteristics that are thought to be the basis of intelligence.

Focusing on the heredity-environment controversy, Theodosius Dobzhansky outlines the possible determinants of intellectual ability. Confronting the controversy over racial and social aspects of intelligence, he finds the evidence for the heritability of intelligence ambiguous at best and shows how manipulation of the environment can improve intellectual ability. He also argues for appreciation of abilities other than intellectual ones.

Assuming that intelligence tests and personality tests are a valid predictor of one's success in school or in an occupation, are such measures an invasion of privacy? Floyd Ruch finds that much of the disagreement over the use of psychological tests is an outgrowth of confusion over definitions of privacy and over methods of reporting test scores. He feels that tests, used properly and legally, can help match people to jobs on an objective basis that is superior to any other known procedure.

Personality testing often relies on the subjective interpretations of the clinicians who decipher the results. Frank McMahon presents evidence that the interpretation of tests can be strongly influenced by a psychologist's biases and preconceptions. He proposes a new type of test containing items that are perfectly transparent to test takers; he also prescribes a discussion between clinician and test takers of any significant problems raised by the test itself.

Loren and Jean Chapman focus their criticism of psychological testing on the use of projective tests in particular. They have conducted research that shows how clinicians who interpret such tests project their own personalities and assumptions onto descriptions of their patients' personalities.

Personality theorists often construct self-report questionnaires to assess general differences in attitudes and styles of behavior. On the basis of one such test, Julian Rotter distinguishes between individuals who feel that they control their destinies and those who feel that they are the pawns of fate. Rotter's system of classifying external and internal control helps to explain attitudinal differences among social classes and individual modes of responding to critical issues.

Not far removed from the concept of external and internal control is Matina Horner's explanation of why bright women sometimes fail. For women, the desire to achieve is often contaminated by a motive to avoid success, which is brought about by social rules dictating "proper" feminine behavior. Horner's research clearly indicates that achievement motivation in women is much more complex than the same drive in men. She points to the dangers of using psychological studies of males as the basis for universal laws of human behavior.

Personality theory and research often shed light on important social problems; for example, ethologists and psychologists have long sought to understand the triggers and mechanisms of aggression so that human violence can be reduced. In a series of experimental laboratory studies, Leonard Berkowitz demonstrates the potential effects of observing violence on a person's own aggressive impulses. His research has direct implications for gun-control legislation and television programing. In investigations of personality traits like these, the interaction between the individual and society is apparent; both the individual and society must be considered in any complete statement about behavior.

Phrenology IS FOOLISH?

By David Bakan

THERE IS A SHOP like it everywhere. It's a narrow dim little thing, crammed with the oddments of half a dozen times and cultures. It looks dusty but really isn't; it should contain valuable "curiosities," but one is at a loss to say what their value might be. For the most part, the contents of such a shop are unintelligible. Those square brown bottles look as if they once were used; there is a painted cast-iron dog that clearly was a toy; there are tons of old prints, swords and walking sticks. That's an astrolabe, perhaps, and that the visor from a suit of armor. The rest is yesterday's nameless junk become today's *bizarrerie*. Sometimes a passerby may glimpse, through a ship's wheel or behind a row of campy Perseuses, a smallish porcelain bust.

This bust usually has thin, sensitive, slightly smirking lips and a high, poetic-looking forehead. Beginning under the eyes is a network of lines that wriggle up over the brow and spread out over the skull, forming a series of contiguous patches reminiscent of a picture puzzle, or of a well-cracked hardboiled egg. In each patch or puzzle-piece there is a neatly lettered word: Combativeness, Ideality, Reverence, Self-Esteem, Language and some 30 more, all nouns and all capitalized, abstract, and long—the lexicon of some stone-dead philosophy.

"What's *that*, for heaven's sake?"

"Oh, that's something they used in phrenology," a friend might chuckle. "You know, that thing about reading the bumps on your head? Some sort of parlor game, like table-tipping, automatic writing, palm reading and that kind of thing."

The bemused citizen won't get much more from a good desk dictionary, where he will find something like this:

The doctrine or belief that the outer configurations of the skull indicate the position and the strength or intensity of various mental faculties and characteristics. [From Greek *phren, phrenos,* mind + -logy, science or study of]—

phren. o.log'ic or i.cal *adj*—phre.nol'o. gist *n*-

In other words, there is little readily available within the store of popular or current academic knowledge that would connect our porcelain bust with some of the most prestigious names in early 19th Century American culture, and nothing to suggest that "phrenology" may have had an important influence on the development of 20th Century American psychology.

Well, what was "phrenology"? (Since those smug quotation marks are altogether too eager to pounce on yesteryear's science and are already reaching for much of today's science, let's dispense with them.) Examined historically, phrenology appears to have two parts: the *-logy* or science part, and the hooplah or country-fair part, each of which has made its contribution to 19th Century American culture — that same culture within which 20th Century psychology developed certain peculiarly "American" features.

Phrenology As Science

The *-logy* part of phrenology was, at least in terms of the *theory* of scientific inquiry, neither "pre-science" nor "pseudo-science"; it was science pure and simple, indeed the better of its day. The science part of phrenology grew from the researches of two men, Franz Joseph Gall (1758-1828) and Johann Kaspar Spurzheim (1776-1832). Both men were Germans and physicians, and both are accorded respect by the historians of science as pioneer neurologists. Spurzheim modified Gall's theories in certain particulars, but together they laid down and publicized the three broad hypotheses within which phrenology conducted itself.

If I say that phrenology, as it was understood by Gall and Spurzheim, postulated and studied *the influence of physiological and anatomical characteristics upon mental behavior,* and, in particular, asserted and studied *the cortical localization of function,* it doesn't sound too terribly quaint or "pre-scientific," and that is precisely the larger framework in which phren-

ology should be viewed. In accordance with these two overarching hypotheses ("laws" or "facts" we are perhaps unwisely tempted to call them now), the phrenologists conceived of a human brain having some 37 independent powers or functions.

About 14 of these functions were considered "intellective" and the remainder were "affective," like Amativeness (the various sexual urges or "passions"), Adhesiveness (the ability to form and maintain attachments to persons), Ideality (the power or faculty of imagination), Self-Esteem (a favorable term meaning "self-respect" or even "self-understanding"), Reverence, Benevolence and so on. These powers were located in different regions or "organs" of the brain, the organs or physical sites being named after their respective powers or functions.

Deriving from the relationship of function and cerebral region was the famous "doctrine of the skull," now the only feature by which phrenology is remembered. The doctrine of the skull held that *the development of the cerebral regions affected the size and contour of the cranium,* so that a well-developed part of the skull would indicate a correspondingly well-developed organ or mental faculty.

These three hypotheses formed a lamp of theory under which Gall and Spurzheim proceeded with painstaking caution. Their labors may be described in terms such as "empiricism," "observation" and "testing of propositions." The phrenologists were extremely and scientifically self-conscious, and particularly crusty about what they called "metaphysical authors and mystical psychologists." The latter speculated in their armchairs, and did not go out and observe as Lord Bacon had advised. By metaphysical authors they meant, for example, John Locke, an ancestor in the direct line of Titchener and the structuralists, whom American functionalists were later to attack so keenly. The early phrenologists used the word "metaphysical" as a term of utter opprobrium; indeed, their tone on the whole subject of armchair speculation and untestable propositions reminds one of the behaviorist

Max Meyer, who posted a sign over the entrance to the laboratory of the University of Missouri that said "No metaphysicians or dogs allowed," or of John B. Watson, who snapped at misty-eyed souls that there was no such thing as mind. In an address to the Boston Phrenological Society in 1832, a speaker delivered the following positivistic blast:

"Enemies [of phrenology] have said that it is an *irreligious* science—that it leads to *materialism.* My objection to this argument is, that it is entirely senseless. My allegation is, not that it is false, but unintelligible. The question, *whether the brain thinks,* is merely logomachy; the words, however correct in grammatical construction, have not any correspondent ideas, and cannot have . . ."

Shades of Ludwig Wittgenstein, and words that should delight anyone favorable to modern positivistic thought. James Shannon, president of Bacon College in Kentucky, an advocate of phrenology, put the *-logy* part of phrenology quite unexceptionably:

"Whoever maintains that the brain is the organ by which the mind acts, and that the mind performs different functions by different parts of the brain, is a phrenologist. This is the broad basis upon which the science of phrenology rests. All beyond this are merely the details of the science, and subjects of enquiry and observation."

What caused difficulties for scientific phrenology were the limitations of the means of inquiry and the emergence of data that was less than wholly confirmatory. Gall, Spurzheim and other phrenologists were attempting to account for the obvious fact that some men had mental gifts or powers that enabled them or compelled them to perform in ways different from others. They succeeded in approaching this scientifically, in the sense that they imposed a reasonably comprehensive, reasonably noncontradictory organization or order upon the data *available to them.* Prior to the advent of phrenology there was a relative chaos of unconnected observations: some men clearly had a capacity for friendship, others equally clearly had not; some had lofty or fertile imaginations; some had great gifts of logical analysis; some had an intense interest in sex, while others were more sluggish.

The aim of the phrenologists in assigning human functioning to these particular 37-odd categories was in no way

FRANZ JOSEPH GALL

JOHANN KASPAR SPURZHEIM

different from the aim of modern psychologists interested in assessing human functioning. It was to find variables on which people differed from each other, of such a nature that manifestations of the variables would correlate highly among themselves, but the correlations among the variables would be low.

It will be noted that I have just formulated the problem of the categories for human assessment in terms of correlation. Indeed, it was the absence of appropriate correlational devices, including techniques of factor analysis, that turned out to be a major reason for the failure of scientific phrenology to thrive.

What the early phrenologists needed was a statistical tool enabling them to study relatively large samples in terms of correlation among personality and intellectual manifestations in behavior. Such a tool hadn't been invented yet, and so they applied instead cruder sorts of correlational analyses. Yet their efforts at collecting data, tabulating them and categorizing measurements by types of personality as they could assess them are very obvious harbingers of the methods of personality assessment in use today.

Even an experimental orientation is distinctly evident in Pierre Flourens' experiments with pigeons' brains, in the course of which the French physiologist demonstrated (in 1845) that the excision of the cerebellum—the phrenologists' organ of Amativeness—did *not* impair the urge or ability to reproduce. In 1861 the French surgeon and anthropologist Paul Broca demonstrated that the faculty of speech was *not* seated behind the eyes, but in another part of the brain entirely. Although these two experiments were plainly "sponsored" by the

phrenological movement, they constituted a double-barreled *coup de grâce* in the eyes of an already highly skeptical scientific community.

The empirical orientation of the phrenological movement was itself associated with the movement's becoming the object of skepticism. The empirical conscience of Spurzheim and other responsible phrenologists was expressing grave doubts about the so-called doctrine of the skull, which was giving way under the weight of observations that skull characteristics and behavioral manifestations were not as highly correlated as had been believed (even without the help of correlation coefficients). By the mid-1830s serious phrenologists were at pains to dissociate themselves from it.

Yet by this time the word phrenology was so firmly bonded to the doctrine of the skull, which was always conceived of as only a part of phrenology, that the refutation of that doctrine could only be interpreted as the failure of the whole movement. Meanwhile another kind of phrenology, more popular but much less scientifically meticulous, had seized upon the doctrine of the skull and made it its central feature. By the late 1840s the scientific and intellectual community had accepted the identification of phrenology with its vulgar expression and

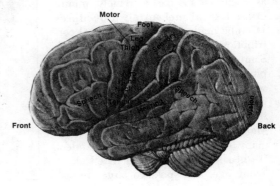

GEORGE COMBE

shrank from the slightest contact with it, to the extent of "repressing" its connection with the scientific research that continued to be done in both Europe and America.

Phrenology As Hooplah

Johann Spurzheim arrived in Boston on August 24, 1832. He gave many lectures and demonstrations, including a series of lectures at Harvard, with a special series for the medical faculty. As one contemporary observer put it, "the professors were in love with him." Some six frenzied weeks after his arrival Spurzheim died, mostly it would seem of exhaustion, his brains having been thoroughly picked by the Brahminical professors. There was a widely attended funeral, with most of intellectual Boston in attendance. A specially formed committee, headed by Josiah Quincy, the president of Harvard, expressed "a sense of the public loss sustained by the death of this distinguished man," and the Boston Phrenological Society was formed as a memorial to him.

In September of 1832, George Combe, a Scottish lawyer, came to America. Combe, though not a physician, had thoroughly studied the work of Gall and Spurzheim, and he could demonstrate Spurzheim's new dissecting techniques as well as all the extremely minute craniological measuring procedures. (Combe made important technical contributions to the methodology of Dr. Samuel G. Morton, whose works in physical anthropology are considered seminal.) This polished and witty man very favorably impressed Daniel Webster, William Emery Channing, Horace Mann, Dr. Samuel Gridley Howe, and many other leading New Englanders. He became the darling of that lecture-loving age, and spoke to large enthusi-

astic audiences in Boston, New York, Albany, Philadelphia, Baltimore, Washington and other eastern cities.

The initial enthusiasm for phrenological lectures was the property of that same fairly large, relatively homogeneous class of cultivated persons who were responsible for the burst of intellectual activity often referred to as the New England Renaissance, and having Boston-Cambridge-Concord as its hub. As this first vociferous enthusiasm on the part of the lyceum crowd began to wane —partly because phrenology ceased to be as novel as, say, mesmerism—the popularists saw a good thing and moved in.

The belief that science was a particularly direct and efficacious instrument for improving human life had been expressed and put into practice by Franklin and Jefferson; this belief had spread rapidly and taken deep roots, nurtured by the ripples of material prosperity resulting from the nation's first major industrial expansion. The ordinary citizen became increasingly receptive to anything that was "scientific." Phrenology was touted as scientific, promising to analyze a person thoroughly, quickly and sympathetically (that is, "democratically"). It guaranteed to show him, scientifically, the way to personal improvement and personal happiness.

The energetic tutelage to the nation of the firm of Fowler and Wells spread phrenology and enriched them. The huckstering mind is essentially the same in all times and climates, whether speak-

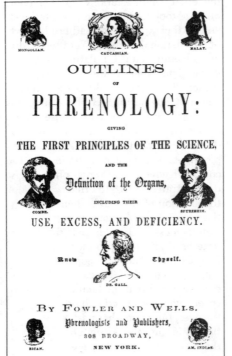

ing from the back of a painted wagon or in front of a TV camera. And the vast majority of men have always wondered with varying degrees of intensity who they are and who their neighbors are, and how they can "perfect" themselves; just as surely they have welcomed anyone or anything that promises unambiguously to tell them. Thus phrenology came to enjoy an extraordinary popularity in mid-19th Century America. Fowler and Wells turned it into a national industry. They had "parlors" in New York, Boston and Philadelphia. They booked lecture tours for traveling phrenologists in every corner of the nation. The list of their publications on phrenology was virtually endless. They published all the classical literature, and they themselves were tremendously prolific; their *Phrenological Self-Instructor* was a best-seller. They sold all sorts of paraphernalia to be used in connection with examinations and demonstration:

busts, pointers, charts, skulls, casts of famous heads. As the vogue spread from the salons of the East, popular phrenology became increasingly cluttered with these paraphernalia, each itinerant phrenologist adding, according to his genius, some additional gimmick. In the space of a few decades, popular phrenology became a rural entertainment whose quack-ridden charlatanry was a source of embarrassment to any thoughtful man.

But before popular phrenology got quite out of hand, it put into wide circulation one of the major devices associated with all psychometric movements, the printed rating-scale specifying clear alternatives. On each of these rating-scales or "test forms" the phrenologist would indicate the magnitude of each of the 37-odd functions or organs. The ratings varied from "small-medium-large" to nine-point values, sometimes further

222

qualified by pluses and minuses. The scales were accompanied by complete explanations, so that the person phrenologized could read about himself in detail and gain a clear "mental daguerreotype," as a Fowler and Wells advertisement put it, of himself. It was a fundamental assumption of popular phrenology that one could infer the nature of mental functioning on the basis of information collected in an hour or so. This assumption met almost no resistance and is still retained in most modern psychometric methods.

The Cultural Interweave

The science of any period is a rich source of what are essentially images or metaphors that illustrate, if not shape, that period's view of itself. After a certain time-lag, these images or metaphors become the skeleton on which the articulate members of a culture unwittingly drape their various arguments and propositions. The influence of evolution and natural selection as Victorian metaphors has been widely discussed; "relativity," however vaguely understood, has impressed itself deeply on 20th Century culture as a metaphorical equivalent of "discontinuity," "isolation," or "loneliness." (It is only a short symbolic step from trains passing each other in the daylight to ships passing in the night.) As the most widely discussed science of its period, phrenology also provided a set of images or metaphors or formulaic ideas that could be applied to widely varying problems and situations.

The wide acceptance of phrenology as a valid science and as an exciting entertainment meant that its assumptions were assimilated on a large scale. You simply couldn't talk about phrenology intelligently and sympathetically unless you first accepted its fundamental premise that man himself could be studied scientifically and that the phenomena of mind could be studied objectively and explained in terms of natural causes. On a less articulate level, millions of people absorbed such a premise as they lined up to have the bumps on their skulls read.

From its beginnings in Gall and Spurzheim to its brassiest moments in the sideshow, phrenology expressed the notion that the different parts of the brain could be altered, trained or flexed

as the different parts of the body or musculature could be. Perceived as a sort of mental flash or headline — THE MIND IS A SET OF MUSCLES — this notion became a metaphor that was of immense practical use to all sorts of people.

Humane men and women were, for instance, desperately concerned with the plight of the insane. So long as the mind or brain was conceived of as a unitary, non-material entity—a disembodied bit of the Godhead—treatment of the insane could only take the form of horrified neglect or active punishment. The mind of the lunatic had been "taken back," divinely withdrawn in retribution for some secret sin or crime, and the devil(s) had moved into the vacuum. It was very difficult to square this idea with alternations of lunacy and lucidity without raising theological questions about a divine Indian-giving; treatment sometimes consisted in quite literally beating the devil out of the temporarily afflicted. Phre-

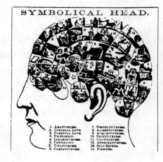

SYMBOLICAL HEAD.

nology's simple assertion that only part of the brain was afflicted was accepted *because it worked;* it enabled people to argue quite sensibly for conditions in which a particular weakened faculty could in some way be modified by "exercise." You could no longer exile or punish people for insanity any more than you could punish them for more physical forms of weakness.

This image or metaphor of brain exercise applied equally well to criminals. Reformers armed with phrenological arguments objected to capital punishment or physical punishment of any sort, and advocated instead proper conditions for exercise and thus, interestingly enough, for the indeterminate sentence. In all cases they urged the modification of treatment with respect to the phrenological or mental characteristics of the individual criminal.

A more specific though less significant event might be chosen to illustrate the genuine *practicality* of phrenology in its time. Blind deaf-mutes were considered utterly beyond the reach of human aid. Dr. Samuel Gridley Howe, who became the head of the Perkins School for the Blind in Boston, had Laura Bridgman examined phrenologically. The analysis of her skull "proved" that she had an active, intelligent brain. Work was then begun that enabled Laura Bridgman to become the first systematically educated blind deaf-mute, work that continued long after the doctrine of the skull had dropped into the scientific limbo.

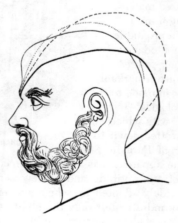

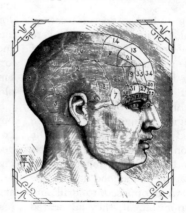

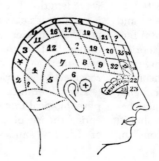

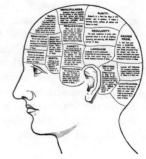

EDGAR ALLEN POE

WALT WHITMAN

Phrenologists took a deep interest in the psychology of learning and were well represented in the avant-garde of educational reformers. Horace Mann, who as the first secretary of the Massachusetts Board of Education revolutionized public instruction, was steeped in phrenological thought. (He had been so impressed by George Combe that he named a son after him.) Phrenologists urged a short school day, together with physical training and a good deal of free play; they were opposed to drill and the use of punishment; they advocated "learning by doing"; they objected to training in the classics exclusively and urged the training of all the mental faculties — always with the metaphorical model before them that learning was simply the proper exercise of the muscles. (In connection with their belief that environment influenced mental behavior, they argued that infants should be exposed to as many "sensations" or stimuli as possible. Recent studies in the cheerless wards of municipal hospitals have drawn much the same conclusions.)

In its role as a vehicle for cultural values, popular phrenology was intensely democratic, in the Jefferson-Jackson tradition. It confirmed every man's notion that he had individual talents that needed only to be discovered and exploited. These talents could be scientifically identified and a vocation chosen —they (and not, for example, social background) constituted a sufficient and legitimate entree to whatever career was indicated. That individual potential could be identified speedily and scientifically became an acceptable *fact*. Horace Greeley advocated editorially that phrenology be used in the selection of trainmen, as a way of reducing accidents. Want ads like this one, which appeared in the *New York Sun,* became fairly common:

"Apprentice wanted.—A stout boy not over 15 years of age, of German or Scotch parents, to learn a good but difficult trade. N.B.—it will be necessary to bring a recommendation to his abilities from Messrs. Fowler and Wells, Phrenologists, Nassau Street. Apply corner of West and Franklin Streets."

Fowler and Wells did a booming business in such recommendations, and it is difficult to dismiss them as just another exhibit in the vast museum of suckerdom. Computerized matchmaking firms are doing a profitable business today, and their printed forms are remarkably similar in mode to the phrenological "test forms" with which stout boys trotted down to the corner of Franklin Street. It has become apparent that a goodly percentage of the aptitude and achievement tests widely adopted by school systems and by industry test only the ability to read or verbalize on certain middle-class wave lengths. The interesting thing here is not that it's easy to sling phrenological mud at modern psychometrics, but rather that *all* forms of psychometric assessment have been very generously received by American culture.

Even literature was informed by the phrenological movement. Poe based his entire theory of poetry on the faculty of Ideality, and his Roderick Usher types are cast in phrenological molds. Whitman salted his poetry and prose with phrenological names. He particularly loved Adhesiveness, because he was told that he had a large dose of that "comradely" virtue, and was so taken by the rating scale done for him by Fowler and Wells that he had it bound into the early editions of *Leaves of Grass.*

In its role as a discipline, phrenology performed importantly in the front lines of the virulent war between science and religion. Phrenology was bitterly attacked by conservative church groups for its radical implications for the life of society. It was regarded as inevitably leading to atheism and, because it made moral or immoral behavior dependent on the nature of the body, to immorality. Some observed with considerable outrage that things like soul, spirit and faith had to be squeezed into the organ of Reverence, just one among 37, and rather smaller than that of Amativeness, for instance. In short, there was a good deal of preliminary skirmishing, to be followed by the great battles between religion and science which were to be occasioned by the publication of *On the Origin of Species* in 1859.

In his introduction to that work, Darwin mentions a book called *Vestiges of the Natural History of Creation.* The *Vestiges* was published (anonymously) in 1844 and had gone through 10 editions and revisions by 1853. It had caused a frightful stink, having advanced a theory of the evolution of species which, however, lacked the theory of natural selection to be added by Darwin. The author of the *Vestiges* was Robert Chambers, a Scotsman

CHARLES DARWIN

and close friend of George Combe and his brother Andrew, physician to Queen Victoria and also a leading spokesman of the phrenological movement. Darwin praised the *Vestiges* in the following terms:

"In my opinion it has done excellent service in this country in calling attention to the subject [evolution], in removing prejudice, and in thus preparing the ground for the reception of analogous views."

Cannot the same thing be said for phrenology as a whole? That it prepared the ground by introducing into the arena of public discussion many of the same issues and in many of the same terms? The phrenological movement displayed a perhaps inordinate optimism about the possibilities of change through education and modification of the environment, an optimism very like John B. Watson's. To mention an even more striking parallel, the "atmosphere" of phrenology is most congenial to many of the social and scientific assumptions that stand behind B. F. Skinner's *Walden Two* utopianism.

Man, and man's mind, could be studied objectively. Radical changes could be effected in the mind by altering the relationships among the various cerebral functions and by modifying the environment in which those relationships are formed. These radical changes in mental behavior were, for the most part, necessary and desirable. These are the conclusions that American functionalists drew from the Darwinian theories. And they are for the most part central to phrenological thought. The *Vestiges* drew heavily upon phrenological thought; phrenological thought got a thorough airing in the United States in the 1830s and '40s; and Darwin drew heavily on the *Vestiges*. That is to say, there seems to be a discernible underlying continuity or "tradition" of psychological theory and practice stretching from the early 1830s into the 20th Century, and it seems reasonable to suggest that the general terms in which phrenologists articulated their optimistic science sank into American culture and remained there, to be rearoused with the advent of the self-consciously scientific psychology of the late 19th and 20th Centuries.

ROBERT CHAMBERS

WILLIAM JAMES

JOHN DEWEY

Now is perhaps the time to underscore a point that must seem obvious; namely, that phrenology was a science of *individual differences*. It was grounded in the belief that every man had a different "cerebral musculature," and that conditions could and should be individually tailored to innate differences and with respect to the flexibility allowed by the analogy to the musculature. Gall and Spurzheim wanted to know *why* some men made good bankers or poets or murderers, and phrenology was the system they constructed as an "answer." Popular phrenology quickly appropriated this system and bent it to intensely practical uses—aptitude testing, vocational guidance, marriage counseling and patching up the sore spots of a man's life wherever they might lie.

'Ganz Amerikanisch'

Within psychology as a whole, there are two major approaches to psychological phenomena. One is the effort to obtain general propositions that hold for the generalized human organism. The other is a study of individual differences, the measurement and assessment of those individual capacities that enable a given person to adjust to and manipulate his environment. The study of individual differences lies at the cen-

ter of the functionalism that began with William James and with John Dewey and J. R. Angell. Historically, such functionalism exists in a prior or telegonic relationship with industrial psychology, with the social psychology of William McDougall, and with certain applications of behaviorist doctrines, all of which form a strand or cluster of emphasis felt to be characteristically American.

Psychology is usually considered to have been born as an independent discipline in the last quarter of the 19th Century. At this time, young American scholars went to Germany to learn the "new" psychology, largely from Wilhelm Wundt, who in 1879 had set up the first important laboratory for experimental psychology. His laboratory was designed to generate and test propositions that would be true for all persons, for a human mind assumed for the purposes of research to be generalized and nonunique. The American students returned to their colleges and universities to set up laboratories, do research and teach in the new ways they had acquired in Germany. However, almost immediately they began to use their new methods to study individual differences. They seemed to consider this radical change of target hardly worthy of comment, but Wundt referred to it as *ganz amerikanisch*—entirely and typically American.

Historians of psychology account for this seemingly instinctive shift of emphasis by speaking of pressures soundlessly exerted by the cultural environment, and they point to the confluence of Darwinian theories and the general competitiveness of American society as major sources of those pressures. But a case can be made, perhaps, for the following plot summary: the widespread familiarity with phrenological theories; the "repression" of these theories on the part of the scientific community both because of the failure of the doctrine of the skull and because of the excesses of popular vulgarized phrenology; the advent of the Darwinian argument, informed by many of the same theories; the enthusiastic and perhaps even uncritical reception by the scientific community of Darwin's theories; the ready seizure by American functionalists of certain Darwinian motifs, especially those relating to organic structure and function as the products of successful adaptation; the remarriage of these motifs with a bias toward individual differences that had been lurking in the context of scientific psychology since Spurzheim talked to the Boston doctors.

Are I.Q. TESTS Intelligent?

By Raymond Bernard Cattell

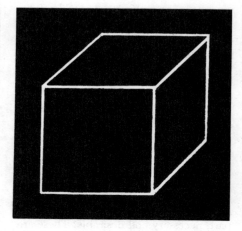

THE DILEMMA OF THE MENSA SOCIETY dramatizes the current upheaval in intelligence testing. Roughly three out of four of the prospective members selected on one kind of intelligence test failed to be selected by a second test, and three out of four of those chosen by the second type could not meet the standards of the first test. This international society, which limits entry to those at the 98th percentile or above in intelligence, was forced to make a policy decision on *which* kind of intelligence the society would consider.

Present controversy on the meaning of intelligence and of intelligence testing has erupted only in the past decade. It centers on whether there is a single factor of general intelligence and on the adequacy of present tests to measure it. My research indicates that there are two kinds of intelligence, fluid and crystallized, and that the former, which is independent of culture, can be measured as accurately as the latter.

To grasp what we now know of intelligence and the devices which attempt to measure it, one first must understand the background of the current dispute. In the first decade of this century, Charles Spearman brought to a field crowded with untutored, arbitrary, and generally naive definitions of intelligence, the theory of the "g" factor, a unitary, objectively defined, general-intelligence factor. For 50 years, Spearman's g factor has remained the only firm basis for the objective determination and measurement of intelligence.

This factor was defined by weights applied to different kinds of intellec-

tual performances, and its existence was proved by the peculiar form of correlation coefficients that appeared in correlations of ability measurement. If correlation coefficients show that four abilities, a, c, e, and g, are mutually positively related when measured over a group of 300 people, whereas the correlations are essentially zero on the abilities b, d, and f, we can assume some underlying unity behind a, c, e, and g.

There is no reason that there could not be two, three, or more such correlation clusters in a large group of abilities. But Spearman argued that the squared table of all possible correlations among a widely sampled set of abilities had a uniform slope which pointed to the existence of only one factor. To support this argument, he went beyond correlation clusters and developed factor analysis—a means of discovering the influences behind clusters.

Factor analysis is a method of calculating—from the various correlation coefficients of measured individual performances—the number and the general natures of the influences that account for observed relations. Through such an analysis, Spearman found the tests that bore most heavily on his general intelligence factor were those that had to do with reasoning and judgment. He therefore defined this factor as the capacity to educe relations and correlates.

Factor analysis also tells us how much of the individual variation in some particular performance is accounted for by each of the several factors that combine to produce that kind of behavior. Spearman concluded that g had about

a 9:1 ratio to special abilities in determining mathematical learning rate; about 7:1 in accounting for the size of one's properly used vocabulary; about 2:1 in determining musical ability; and about 1:4 in judging drawing ability.

Decades later, Louis Thurstone developed a multiple-factor analysis. This improvement over Spearman's methods led to Thurstone's discovery and definition of a dozen primary abilities, among them verbal comprehension, word fluency, number, space, and reasoning. Neither g nor the I.Q. were invalidated by Thurstone's work. On the contrary, advances in factor analysis rectified the only known statistical and structural flaw in Spearman's work. General intelligence now emerged from multiple-factor analysis as a single *second-order factor,* based on the intercorrelation among primary factors. The general intelligence concept was strengthened, for the pyramids of primary factors provided a far more reliable base than did the grains of innumerable small variables.

The question of how Thurstone's primary abilities grew out of Spearman's general ability remained unanswered, but researchers tended to neglect its importance. Instead of investigating the natural structure of abilities, the experts devised tests to fill the holes in a subjective framework. And so, for 30 years, there has been only trivial consolidation in this field, with a consequent hardening of attitudes and custom among professional intelligence testers.

As one who investigated with both Spearman and Thurstone, I at first was as much disturbed as intrigued when I thought I saw flaws in their monolithic structure. The first signs appeared in data on the second-order analysis of primary abilities. There was evidence that *two* general factors rather than one were involved. On rather slender evidence, I put forward in 1940 the theory of two g's. Those original disquieting conceptions since have been strengthened by the accumulation of evidence.

The breadth of a factor and the number of factors depend upon what tests an experimenter uses to gather his data. From the 20 primary abilities surveyed by John French, John Horn obtained some four or five broad abilities, such as fluid intelligence, crystallized intelligence, speed, and visualization. But the broadest of all such abilities, and the ones with a semantic claim to the label "intelligence," are fluid and crystallized.

Crystallized general ability, "g_c," shows itself in judgmental skills that have been acquired by cultural experience: vocabulary, good use of synonyms, numerical skills, mechanical knowledge, a well-stocked memory, and even habits of logical reasoning. G_c is high on the subtests that traditionally have been built into intelligence tests: vocabulary size, analogies, and classifications involving cultural knowledge of objects in the problem. Crystallized ability stretches across the whole range of cultural acquisitions. Mechanical knowledge—which is negligible or even negative on fluid ability—has a measurable effect on crystallized ability.

Tests of fluid ability, "g_f," have little relation to a well-stocked memory. They are culture fair perceptual and performance tests and those specially developed tests of judgment and reasoning which have been considered relatively culture free. They involve solutions to tests of classifications, analogies, matrices, topology, and problems that do not involve much educational acquisition. Fluid ability does have a role in numerical reasoning and even in verbal skills. It is fairly powerful in spatial reasoning and very powerful in inductive reasoning. [See illustration, upper right.]

The difference between fluid and crystallized general abilities becomes apparent when the intellectual responses of two persons who contrast in them are described. To find a person high in fluid ability but low in crystallized, we should have to take someone who accidentally has missed schooling. I have measured deck-hands and farmers who scored much higher than average professors in fluid ability but who acquired no com-

Primary Abilities of Specific Batteries	Research I: Boys (57) and Girls (5) of 6½ Years Old		Research II: Boys (151) and Girls (154) of 9, 10, & 11 Years Old		Research III: Boys and Girls (277) of 12 & 13 Years Old		Research IV: Men and Women (297) Adult Range	
	g_f	g_c	g_f	g_c	g_f	g_c	g_f	g_c
Verbal	−17	74	22	63	15	46	10	69
Spatial			73	03	32	14	30	−07
Reasoning	10	72			08	50	23	30
Number	43	49	47	35	05	59	24	29
Fluency					07	10	−03	25
Series: Culture Fair					35	23		
Classification; Culture Fair	58*	−11*	78*	09*	63	−02	48*	−08*
Matrices: Culture Fair					50	10		
Topology: Culture Fair					51	09		
Perceptual Speed							20	06
Flexibility							−03	03
Induction							55	12
Intellectual Speed							51	10
Mechanical Information							−15	48
Ego Strength	−07	−09					01	43
Self Sentiment							01	43
Super Ego								
Surgency								
Anxiety	10	−33	04	−04			−05	−26

Fluid and Crystallized General Ability Factors at Various Ages. Crystallized general ability shows itself in those judgmental skills dependent upon cultural experience, while fluid ability affects tests unrelated to well-stocked memory. Flexibility is distinct from either g_c or g_f. Note the consistent level of g_f scores throughout all age groups.
*Combined score on four subtests of culture-fair test.

parable level of crystallized ability because they had not systematically applied their fluid intelligence to what is usually called culture. Such men will astonish you in a game of chess, or by solving a wire puzzle with which you have struggled in vain, or in swift insights into men and motives. But their

vocabularies may be arrested at a colloquial level, their knowledge of history negligible, and they never may have encountered algebra or geometry. These men often excel at the strategy of games, and one suspects they are naturally good soldiers. Lord Fisher, who designed the Dreadnought battleship, said, "In war

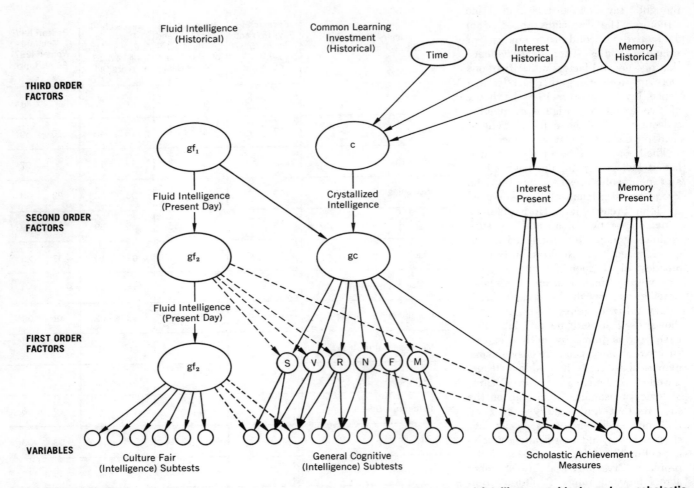

Causal Relations Between Fluid and Crystallized Ability Factors. Scores on the general intelligence subtests and on scholastic achievement measures are the result of time, interest, memory and both fluid and crystallized intelligence. Arrows indicate the direction of influence and solid arrows show major lines of influence. Note the lack of other influence on culture fair subtests.

you need surprise." Surprise bursts from situations in which crystallized intelligence is useless. Napoleon claimed that he would make his despairing opponents "burn their books on tactics." The characteristic of fluid intelligence is that it leads to perception of complex relationships in new environments.

The individual with a high level of crystallized intelligence has different capacities. He will have learned many intelligent responses to problem situations. He will recognize an engineering problem as requiring solution by differential calculus, and he will diagnose a defective sentence by pointing to a dangling participle. He could not have acquired these skills, however, unless he had the fluid ability to see them.

To illustrate a case where crystallized ability is clearly higher than fluid ability, we must take either a person in whom there has been some recession of fluid ability, as through aging or brain damage, or a person who has been over-educated for his ability—say, someone like Sheridan's Mrs. Malaprop, taught

a bigger vocabulary than natural judgment permits handling.

Crystallized and fluid intelligence abilities could not be isolated until technical progress in factor analytic experiments made their recognition possible. These two structures have been confirmed repeatedly by researchers over the whole age range, from five to 50.

Fluid and crystallized ability factors are positively correlated. According to the theory of two broad intelligences, fluid intelligence is a general relation-perceiving capacity, independent of sensory area, and it is determined by the individual's endowment in cortical, neurological-connection count development. It is a broad factor because such integrating power can be brought to bear in almost any perceptual or reasoning area. Crystallized ability, on the other hand, appears as a related circle of abilities—verbal, numerical, reasoning—that normally are taught at school. The extent to which an individual takes or leaves what he is taught depends on his fluid ability, on his years of formal education,

and on his motivation to learn. Thus, crystallized general ability reflects both the neurological integrative potential of the individual and his fortune in cultural experience.

Crystallized ability is not identical with scholastic achievement. Many scholastic skills depend largely on rote memory, whereas what factor analysis shows is crystallized ability in that section of school learning involving complex judgmental skills that have been acquired by the application of fluid ability. [*See illustration above.*]

Once these two general abilities are located and independently measured, further distinguishing characteristics appear. The age curve of growth for the two abilities turns out to be quite different. Fluid ability follows a biological growth curve and approaches a plateau at about 14 years, whereas crystallized ability shows an increase to 16, 18, and beyond. The evidence points to some steady decline in fluid intelligence after about 22 years of age, but crystallized intelligence keeps its level as far into later years as adequate samples have been taken. [*See illustration, right.*]

The standard deviation of the calculated I.Q.—mental age divided by actual age—is almost exactly 50 per cent greater for fluid than for crystallized ability, 24 points instead of 16 points. Socio-educational research might determine whether arranging brighter and duller streams of classroom instruction would permit more divergence of crystallized I.Q.

There are substantial indications that fluid and crystallized intelligence respond differently to brain damage. Localized injury may produce localized loss of skills, while leaving other abilities untouched. By the nature of fluid ability, an impairment in any cortical locality should produce some loss of general fluid-ability performance.

A pilot study on nature-nuture ratios suggests that heredity bears a greater relation to fluid than to crystallized intelligence. Tentative estimates of relative variance are 90 per cent for g_f and 70 per cent for g_c. An independent demonstration of the higher hereditary influence of fluid-ability levels has been given by John Loehlin, who compared the primary factor within pairs of both fraternal and identical twins. Verbal ability, fluency, and reasoning primaries naturally showed environmental influence, but a general genetic factor corresponding to fluid ability was apparent.

My own research and that of others indicates that day-to-day changes do occur in intelligence. Our subjective conviction that we are brighter on some days than we are on others is borne out by measures of g_f variability over time, as might be expected from the closer dependence of fluid intelligence upon total physiological efficiency.

Many of the puzzling phenomena in intelligence testing are explained if we consider that the traditional intelligence test actually is a mixture of fluid and crystallized factors. Discoveries of different ages for the end of intelligence growth, significant differences in the standard deviation of I.Q.'s, and different ratios of the weight of heredity and environment on the I.Q. all result from a confusion of the two factors in the usual intelligence test.

When I first called attention to the flaws in the general intelligence theory, I at once proceeded to investigate the correlations with the general fluid ability factor of a variety of "perceptual" tests. From my research came the culture fair intelligence test associated with present uses in cross-cultural studies and Head-

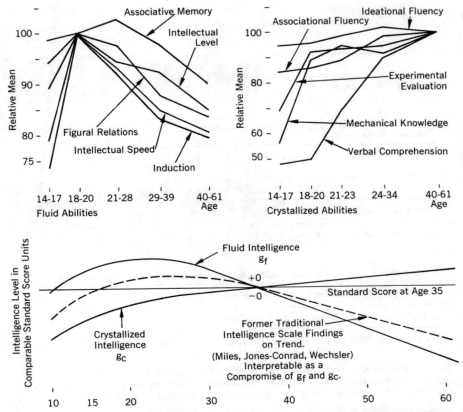

Age Curves Compared for Fluid and Crystallized General Ability and Traditional Tests.

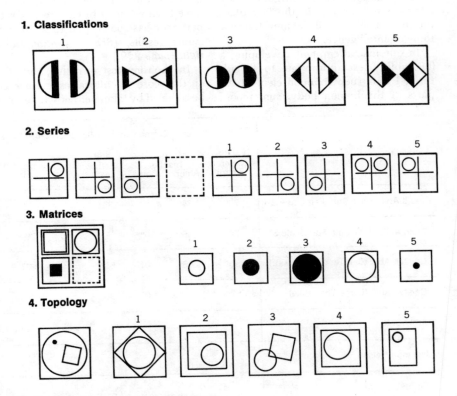

Sample Items from a Culture Fair Test.

1 Which one of these is different from the remaining four? (No. 3)
2 Which of 5 figures on right would properly continue 3 on left, i.e., fill blank? (No. 5)
3 Which of figures on right should go into square on left to make it look right? (No. 2)
4 At left, dot is outside the square and inside the circle. In which of the figures on the right could you put a dot outside the square and inside the circle? (No. 3)

1. Comparison of American and Chinese Children, 10 Years of Age, by IPAT Culture Fair Scale 2 (Rodd, 1960).

	American (1007)		Chinese (Hong Kong) (1007)	
	Mean	Stand. Dev.	Mean	Stand. Dev.
Culture Fair Form 2A	24.10	6.66	24.04	5.70

2. Comparison of American and Chinese College Students (Mean Age 18 yrs.) by IPAT Culture Fair Scale 3 (Rodd, 1960).

	American (1100)		Taiwanese (765)		Chinese Mainland Chinese (525)	
	Mean	Stand. Dev.	Mean	Stand. Dev.	Mean	Stand. Dev.
Culture Fair Form 3A	21.99	4.50	21.99	4.50	22.88	4.47
Culture Fair Form 3B	26.90	4.50	26.95	4.47	27.23	4.53

3. Correlation of Culture Fair and Traditional Tests with Social Status (McArthur and Elley, 1964).

1. Traditional Test (California Test of Mental Maturity)	+0.38
2. Traditional Test (Modified) (Lorge-Thorndike)	+0.27
3. Fluid Ability (IPAT Culture Fair) (On 271 12-and 13-Year-Olds)	+0.24

Cultural Differences and Culture Fair Scores. That culture is no barrier when a culture fair test is used shows in American and Chinese scores on the same test. The correlation between c_f and social status measures the relation of real ability to the status.

start programs. But whatever its present practical importance, the origin of these culture fair tests was in the first place the theoretical goal of defining the new form of intelligence.

In our first attempt at developing a fluid-ability test appropriate to all cultures, I took such common elements as parts of the human body, sun, moon, rain, and stars, as well as random blotches. But only the perceptual forms have been retained in later tests, for experiment has shown that these give accurate results. [See illustration, lower right, page 229.]

In choosing test elements, the effect on the score of cultural experience can be reduced by taking either what is over-learned in all cultures or what is absolutely strange to all. Anything in between these extremes is bound to show the influence of the culture in the test scores. To take overlearned items is more practicable, because valuable test time is wasted in getting responses on completely strange items.

To avoid pointless sociological arguments, we called fluid-ability measures culture *fair* rather than culture *free*. Objection from teachers to a culture-free concept arises from confusion between the cultural familiarity and test sophistication effects on test scores. *All* tests, culture fair tests included, are susceptible to test sophistication, and scores may continue to improve for some four to six retests. Scores increase due to familiarity with instructions, with layout, with timing, and with the tricks any good person being tested can learn. Studies by Sarason, Feingold, and me have shown that practice in the culture-fair type of spatial and analogies perception produced no real gain, unlike training in the verbal and numerical fields that dominate the traditional intelligence test. But with subjects unused to paper-and-pencil tests, and with subjects from other cultures, it would be ideal always to repeat testing several times and to throw away the results of the first three or four encounters.

The culture fair concept does not imply that no significant differences ever should be found between different populations living in different cultures or

		Correlation with School Total Achievement								Other Intelligence Tests		
	Validity General Factor	Marks by Teacher Amer.	Chin.	Stand. Ach. Test	English Amer.	Chin.	Read-ing	Math Amer.	Chin.	Calif. Test of Mental Maturity Verb.	Numer.	Wisc. I.Q.
Fluid Abil. (IPAT Cult. Fair Scale 2)	.79*	.34*		.35*			.52++					.72++
Fluid Abil. (IPAT Cult. Fair Scale 3)	.78°	.35**	.35**	.59 .49	40	30+		64	47+	42	56	
Crystal. Abil. (Cal. Test Ment. Mat.)	.58*	.66*	0?	.65*		0?			0?			
Crystal. Abil. (Lorge-Thorndike)	.52*	.43*	0?	.35*		0?			0?			
Army Beta					25			34		27	58	
Henmon Nelson				.81								
Pintuer							.85++					.80++

* McArthur & Elley, 271, 12 and 13 year olds   + Rodd & Goodman (Atten. corrected on school test)   ° Bajard
** Domino, 94 college students   ++ 79 children in Bridge Project School

Correlations of Fluid and Crystallized Intelligence Tests with other Measures. The validity in terms of general ability saturation is highest for the culture fair scales, but correlation with school grades is higher when the traditional intelligence test is used.

subcultures or social classes. The bright people in most societies tend to migrate to higher socio-economic levels. The correlation of .20 to .25 between fluid ability measures and social status presumably is a measure of the relation of real ability to status, but the correlation of .38 found with traditional intelligence tests represents also the scholastic gain of those with the luck to be born into more-educated families.

Where ulterior evidence suggests that peoples *are* equally gifted, a culture fair test must show absolutely no difference of score despite profound differences of culture. No differences have been demonstrated on the culture fair scales among American, British, German, French, and Italian samples. A more severe test was made by William Rodd, who compared Chinese (Taiwanese) and American school children and university students on identically printed culture fair tests. The raw scores are identical to three significant figures for Midwestern American and Taiwanese school children. American college students do not differ from the Taiwanese, but there is a significant difference between Taiwanese and mainland Chinese, which could be the result of differences in methods of student selection. [*See illustration, upper left, opposite.*]

But testing does suggest that significant mean population differences *can* exist. Samples have shown higher means in the south than in the north of Japan, in the north than in the south of Italy, and in New Zealand migrants as compared with unselected British Isles stock. Further research might develop a world map of intelligence resources.

For school-age children, when intelligence tests are most used, the correlation between g_f and g_c scores is positive and substantial. It will probably become even higher if regular school attendance becomes universal and methods used in more efficient school systems become uniform. From this high correlation, casual administrators may argue that one kind of test—the old kind, of course —is enough. Indeed, hard-headed realism may assert that the traditional I.Q. test is preferable, because the g_c test predicts this or next year's scholastic performance slightly but systematically better than does the g_f test. [*See illustration, bottom, opposite page.*]

But if a maximum prediction of next year's academic achievement were all that one desired, one would not use an intelligence test at all! For a higher correlation can be obtained from *this* year's grades, or from a proper combination of intelligence, personality, and motivation measures, as our research has shown.

The purpose of an intelligence test is different. It should help us to understand the causes of a given person's good or poor grades or to predict what he will do in the future in radically changed circumstances. Over an interval of a year or so we can expect habits and situations and the momentum of interest to make scholastic performance *now* the best predictor of grades in the future. But when a person's life turns a corner, as when he goes from liberal education in the school to technical education in a career, the crystallized-ability measure may be quite misleading. A fluid-ability I.Q. from a culture fair test is likely to be a better predictor of performance.

The same principle holds if we compare children of fundamentally different backgrounds. The Binet in French, administered to a mixed group of 100 French, 100 American, and 100 Chinese children, would show a correlation of I.Q. with French language skills, but the Binet score would be no general predictor of language ability among the Americans and Chinese. In the same situation, a culture fair test would correlate with the native-language performance about equally in each of the three language groups.

During the school years, culture fair tests are both theoretically and practically useful, especially in localities with language or cultural differences. But the dual I.Q. becomes indispensable almost anywhere when testing adults. The two I.Q. values for a given person may be very different, and the kinds of prediction made from each will differ. Crystallized ability may remain steady or even climb, for it increases with age and experience, but fluid ability falls after age 22. A middle-aged man handles most situations in our culture more intelligently than he would have when he was 20, but if a younger and an older man were transferred to an absolutely new society, the probably higher fluid-intelligence level of the younger man would be likely to show itself. Where performance in radically different situations is involved, the man of 50 will perform very differently from what would be predicted for him on the basis of his g_c mental age. The g_f mental age would have predicted this difference.

Despite the tremendous accumulation of experience concerning intelligence testing between 10 and 20 years of age, there has been comparatively little over the 20- to 70-year range, and we know little about what happens to age trends, distribution, or sex differences of intelligence in that period.

Our society, which values high intelligence, must make some kind of policy decision on *which* kind of intelligence should be given emphasis in this period. A decision on culture fair and traditional test usage becomes even more imperative for the psychologist whose testing helps determine jobs and clinical outcomes. As men leave school and go into their special occupational fields, the statistical general factor begins to disintegrate, or to persist only as an historical relic. Vocabulary tests for the average man reveal a distinct falling off in ability after school. And if women in middle age are tested by intelligence tests (at least as mostly designed by men), they undergo an apparent drop in crystallized ability not shown by men.

To continue to regard the traditional intelligence tests as a general intelligence measure when applied after the age of 20 is pure illusion. If a g_c score predicts relation-perceiving capacity in new fields, it does so indirectly by harking back to the fact that scholastic ability at 18 was a measure of g_f intelligence. If that happens not to be true for a person, or if such things as brain damage have occurred since, the g_c prediction can be badly in error.

The need for a dual I.Q. score is rooted not only in what happens to the man but in what happens to the culture. A comparison that I made of all 11-year-olds in a city of 300,000 before World War II with 11-year-olds in the same city after the war and 13 years later showed no trace of any significant difference on a culture fair test. Yet Godfrey Thomson's comparisons on the British Binet at about the same period showed a very significant upward shift. Results in America by Frank Finch with various traditional crystallized-ability tests showed an even greater upward shift. The standardization of a traditional test becomes unanchored from the moment it is made, and it drifts in whatever direction the tide of educational investment happens to take. In this more prosperous age, the direction is upward. Since no such drift is demonstrable with culture fair, fluid-ability measures, error of prediction is less flagrant.

New answers to educational, political, and social questions may be reached through culture fair intelligence testing. Culture fair tests are not toys for anthropologists to take to remote cultures. They need to be used here and now to open equal educational opportunity to all our subcultures of class and race. ∎

by John Garcia

THE ONLY THING that a race-horse owner likes better than a fast horse is a faster horse. To get a faster horse requires systematic breeding of fast horses to fast horses. Any selective breeding program requires a test for the trait that the breeder chooses to improve. The horse breeder uses the race-track record as an objective test for speed; his system appears to be remarkably successful, since track speeds continue to improve.

Because they choose track records as the main breeding criterion, horse breeders have produced lines of animals deficient in other respects; their specialized breeding (and specialized training) frequently make thoroughbreds unsuitable for trail riding, obedience training, or, for that matter, anything other than carrying a 100-pound jockey around a flat, dry, ovoid track for one mile—in the counterclockwise direction. In fact, it is incorrect to say that thoroughbreds are the fastest horses: if it rains on race day, the favorite loses; change the race to a quarter mile, or 100 miles, hold it on rocky terrain, or spread it out over a two-week pack trip, and the track record—and generations of breeding for speed—become worthless as predictors. The hereditary speed of the thoroughbred horse, and the meaning of the track-record speed test, are tied to the fixed environment of the race track.

Rats. In 1929 at the University of California at Berkeley Robert C. Tryon set out to breed a race of intelligent rats. Like the horse breeder, he needed a measure of the trait with which he was concerned. The rat crawled through a large automatic maze, hurried along by gates clicking closed behind it. Pressure plates on the maze floor made a record of the corridors it passed through. While all of Tryon's rats eventually found their way to the feeding pen at the exit, some consistently made more blind side excursions than others. Tryon bred his "bright" rats—the ones that went directly

to the food—to each other, and did the same with his "dull" rats. About seven generations later Tryon was the owner of one thoroughbred line of bright rats, and one equally thoroughbred line of dull rats. But their brightness and dullness didn't mean much outside of Tryon's particular type of maze; the bright animals often did no better than the dull ones in tests in other learning situations. Tryon and other researchers began to suspect that the bright rats had scored high on Tryon's test because they were insensitive, undisturbed by clanking doors and switches. Other evidence suggested that the bright rats took the direct route because they were extremely food-oriented. Moreover, it appeared that the dull rats showed more caution and a more general tendency to explore than the bright rats. Both of these traits would be considered admirable and intelligent in other environments. To get a rat with a full spectrum of adaptive talents one probably should go to the city dump and trap one—the one that is hardest to catch.

Conspiracy. The story of Tryon's rat race ends in vindicated truth; even a scientifically controlled breeding program based on an objectively measured test did not yield a rat general intelligence test or show the heritability of general intelligence.

Horse breeders still use race-track records as the main criterion in breeding thoroughbred track horses, but horse men understand that the thoroughbred is a special-purpose horse for a special environment. A person who used only race-track records as guides in buying or breeding fast trail horses would be considered naive indeed, yet an exactly analogous situation exists today in human-intelligence testing and research.

The I.Q., or "intelligence" is a sort of social contract between educators and mental testers. The recent controversy on the relative intelligence of biosocial groups has given I.Q. a meaning and existence that ignore the very real limits on mental-measurement techniques: the designers of I.Q. tests built into them some intrinsic assumptions that make them useless for comparing the intelligence of biosocial groups. The use of I.Q. data for group comparisons changes the social contract into a social conspiracy to label particular groups inferior and to propagate the status quo. If we study the evolution of the I.Q. test, these intrinsic assumptions—biases and limitations—become vividly apparent.

Choice. Our culture's most accepted, used, and standardized measure of "general intelligence" is the Stanford-Binet I.Q. test; Alfred Binet initiated the design in France between 1905 and 1911; Lewis Terman imported the project into the United States at Stanford University in 1916.

Robert Tryon was aware of some of the limitations of this testing. In 1935 he pointed out that the idea of a single "general" intelligence depended on arbitrary assumptions made in the statistical procedures used to define intelligence factors. Different schools of psychometry can, and do, analyze the same test results into one, two, seven, or a virtually infinite number of more-or-less independent ability factors [*"Are I.Q. Tests Intelligent?" by Raymond B. Cattell, p. 226*]. The number of intelligences emerging is a result of an arbitrary choice between viewing "more-or-less" independent abilities as "more" independent (treating them as distinct mental attributes), or as "less" independent (lumping them together).

Binet built the test on the assumption of a single "general-intelligence" factor, this immediately affected the choice of individual items used for questions. Terman didn't want questions that would emphasize the more independent aspect of abilities; he did not want clusters of items—groups of questions in which getting one answer right would predict success on the other items of that group. He

IQ: THE CONSPIRACY

I.Q. measures everyone by an Anglo yardstick. It was not designed to be used in this manner. "Jensen, Shockley and Herrnstein confirm that there is a conspiracy to make a narrow, biased collection of items the 'real measure' of all persons."

threw out items that formed clusters and kept questions that seemed to be independent of each other but that correlated well with the total score.

Picasso. Except for this internal restriction, the designers were free to select questions from a myriad of types and sources. Terman restricted his choice to items from the school curriculum—worse yet, he picked only from those parts of the curriculum that school authorities deemed important: reading, writing, arithmetic. The traits manifested in Picasso's art, or those separating a master mechanic from a 10-thumbed apprentice, were pushed aside into the "specialized-abilities" category. If Terman had taken items from the machine shop, music class, art class, and other areas, concepts about what and whom to regard as intelligent might be broader than they are. Stanford-Binet I.Q. tests score "scholastic-performance intelligence," not "general intelligence."

Anglo. The question of item sources was only the first of several problems that the testers handled with such pragmatic ingenuity. For the test to be useful, it had to have a standardization group—a reference group to determine what score is "normal," "high," or "low." The designers understood that the American school population at the turn of the century was a motley group, immigrants with a bewildering variety of ethnic, social and language backgrounds. But to insure validity in the standardization, it was necessary that the student understand the language and forms of the test questions. Accordingly, the testers included in the group only the children of white, English-speaking parents. The Stanford-Binet became an Anglo I.Q. test; it is hardly surprising that items based on common English usage are the most reliable subtest in it.

The psychometrists reached a third strategic landmark as they anticipated, detected, and resolutely suppressed the inelegant effects of the maturing of intellect: if older children are more successful than younger children on each test item, the raw score (number of correct answers) will show a nice, smooth increase with age. But many items do not behave this well. *A table is a thing. True or false?* might be a difficult question for a very young child. Children well into the school system would tend to get it right. A college philosophy student (or a precocious child) might consider a table to be a "concept" and mark the item false. The test designers eliminated any item that did not show a simple age-dependent performance improvement. Each time they narrowed the range of acceptable questions the concept of intelligence got smaller.

Age-change perturbations exist, in part because preschool children, schoolchildren, and postschool adults come from different biosocial strata. Five-year-old, 12-year-old, and 19-year-old girls are very different in biological attributes, and the cultural environments they live in change radically as they change in age.

Toys. The psychometrists were in some ways extremely perceptive investigators. They understood that items drawn from the core curriculum of the school would be inappropriate for testing preschoolers, so they included items that tested ability to recognize toys—items from the home environment—to enable themselves to measure a child's "general intelligence" even before he entered school. In theory, preschool items and core-curriculum items could be installed in any proportion; in practice, the designers blended the items until they wiped out any abrupt change in score in the population at the point of entering school. Although this technique hides the discontinuity on the score graph, the perturbation persists in the rest of the universe. The I.Q. score of a child in the early grades of school can predict fairly well his I.Q. in his later school career. In contrast, a child's preschool I.Q. is a very poor predictor of what his I.Q. will be after he gets into the school system.

A young person's raw score increases until he is about 17, then it begins to decline slowly. Unhappily, researchers sometimes present this phenomenon as a true record of the rise and fall of intelligence. The only real meaning is that a person who is out of school is not quite as adept at school items as he was when he was in school. The I.Q.s of persons who make a life work of going to school continue to increase well past their 17th years, as long as they stay in school.

While a person's ability to handle school items declines after he leaves school, his ability to deal with the rest of the world often improves. Most automobile-insurance companies reduce a driver's insurance premium when he reaches his 25th birthday; they have determined empirically that a person's ability to deal with problems of highway survival usually does not develop fully before that time. If we search for other items that reflect greater capacity for dealing with the postschool environments and blend these items with the school and preschool items, we will discover that intelligence continues to grow beyond the high-school years.

Lumberjack. It might be possible to incorporate good postschool items into an I.Q. test, but it would not be easy. It may be possible now, with test questions, to sample some of the abilities needed by an accountant or a computer programmer, or a professor. But how do you find items reflecting the mental abilities of a good quarterback, composer, therapist, or lumberjack that will fit into a brief (two-hour-limit) test with readily reckoned pencil-mark answers? You don't.

Academicians sense no dissonance in this gross limitation. It confirms their subculture's view that they are, and are trainers of, the generally intelligent.

Sixteen. The I.Q. test fails to measure general human intelligence for exactly the same reason that the thoroughbred track record cannot reflect general horse

---

"Male and female I.Q.s are equal because the equality is designed into the test."

speed and the Tryon maze cannot measure general rat intelligence. The test environment is far too narrow to emulate more than a sliver of the possible environments in which men and women find themselves.

Although the test designers ironed out the abrupt age-change in raw score and made it follow school progress, it still changed with age. The testers wanted a "general intelligence" that would be reasonably constant throughout life so they invented the Intelligence Quotient (I.Q.), obtained by dividing the subject's mental age (M.A.) by his chronological age (C.A.). Mental age comes from his raw score in a manner deliberately adjusted to assure that the mean I.Q. for any standard (Anglo) age group is 100 points. A child who gets a raw score above the average for his age group gets an I.Q. score higher than 100; a child who gets less than the mean raw score gets an I.Q. of less than 100.

The device seems fairly legitimate until the population reaches age 16, at which point the increase in mental age tapers off while chronological age continues to increase at the rate of one year per year. If the designers keep the mental-age/chronological-age ratio intact, the I.Q. of a person declines rapidly after this age. The psychometrists prevented this by simply freezing chronological age at 16. This technique was not completely successful; persons grew older and still produced somewhat lower I.Q.s as they aged. The testers handled this depressing development with a more sophisticated device: they replaced the mental-age/chronological-age ratio with the "deviation I.Q." They set the mean I.Q. of each age group at 100 points and also arbitrarily declared that the intelligence of persons within every age group is distributed symmetrically (with a standard deviation of exactly 16 I.Q. points). If there are any changes of intelligence with age, or any changes in the parceling of intelligence among the members of an aging

group, these changes will never be visible in the I.Q. scores.

These ingenious efforts stabilize the I.Q. of the population, but the I.Q. scores of individuals still fluctuate widely. An estimated 60 percent of persons may change I.Q. more than 15 points between their sixth and 18th birthdays. In this same period an estimated 10 percent of persons may change I.Q. scores more than 30 points. This is enough to move a child from "normal" either up to "genius" or down to "moron."

Gender. Male/female differences also are revealing. Males, as a group, surpass females on subtests of speed and coordination of gross motor activities, spatial-quantitative problems, mechanical tasks, and on some types of quantitative reasoning; females surpass males in fine motor skills, perceptual skills, memory, numerical computation, and verbal skills.

These findings form a battleground for a classic nature-nurture argument. The biologically inclined can point to well-documented differences on several levels—they invoke chromosomal, anatomical and physiological sex differences. They explain the evolution of these differences in terms of selective pressures of the child-bearing role which restricted women to the protected center of the primitive village while men, placed on the perimeter of the tribal territory—hunting, defending, detecting threats—were under influences that put a premium on different abilities.

A sociologist, preferring to believe that social environment is the great determinant, can point to impressive obvious differences between men and women in social training and value systems. We reward women for accepting the complex of inclinations labeled "feminine," and ridicule them for acquiring mechanical or mathematical—"male"—skills.

Design. Although this debate is still in full swing, by 1937 the Stanford-Binet architects had opted out of the dispute

with a characteristically practical device. They disregarded items that strongly favored either men or women. By blending items that slightly favored females with just enough "male" items, they perfectly equalized the I.Q.s of male and female.

Whether they are social or biological or important or insignificant, the sex differences are real; they reemerge in the results of the Graduate Record Examinations, in which men are better on the "quantitative" subtest, and women dominate the "verbal-aptitude" subtest. Here the testers use a different device to avoid confronting the contrast: the subtest percentile score for each person is generated against the raw scores of that person's own sex group. Male and female I.Q.s are equal because the equality is designed into the test.

We could easily treat other biosocial subgroups in the same way. When Chicano children score lower than Anglos on a test made of Anglo items there's no need for debate about hereditary and environmental factors. All we need to do is write some items that favor Chicanos and blend them properly with Anglo items. Alternatively, we could make a separate Chicano test and standardize it for a Chicano reference group with a mean of 100 and a standard deviation of 16. Presto, Chicanos are as "intelligent" as Anglos.

Break. Some advocates of intelligence testing express a pious concern that including "Chicano items" or "black items" will attenuate the predictive power of the I.Q. The I.Q. test lost discrimination power when the architects made male I.Q. equal to female I.Q.: moreover, when they discarded some of their good items (on grounds of sexual discrimination) they undoubtedly sacrificed a bit of test-retest reliability. No one complained about this. Using minority items might indeed reduce the predictive value of I.Q. under the status quo. It is equally conceivable that including non-Anglo items will increase the prog-

"When Chicano children score lower than Anglos on a test made of Anglo items there's no need for debate about hereditary and environmental factors."

nostic value of I.Q. when equal opportunity for minorities is a social reality. If a man gets an even break on the test, but nowhere else, the test will surely be a poor predictor.

Equalized male-female norms also highlight the bias against women in the universities: girls dramatically surpass boys in grade-school performance, yet men are accepted into graduate university programs almost to the exclusion of women. Once again we can choose among biological or social arguments explaining either why this is so, or why it should be—none of this concerned the I.Q. designers: they assigned intellectual equality to boys and girls, men and women, although retaining an excess of male items would have made the test a better prediction of university success.

It seems that the predictive power of the I.Q. test is sacrosanct only when the predictions are culturally convenient.

When a social psychologist attempts to use the I.Q. to examine questions of cultural subgroup difference, or of the relative importance of heredity versus environment, he encounters two dilemmas and one puzzle. The first dilemma is the illusion of the ''culture-free'' I.Q. test; the second is the inseparability of environmental and hereditary effects. The puzzle is that some I.Q. pushers refuse to see these dilemmas.

The common method of designing a ''culture-free'' I.Q. consists of standardizing and selecting items against reference groups from at least two different subcultures. When a researcher finds an item that favors one group he may conclude that the item is ''culturally biased'' and eliminate it. If he uses this approach, the test preordains equal intelligence. Of course, alternatively, he could keep the items that discriminate, and accept them as reflecting real and significant cultural difference. Unfortunately, he must decide whether he believes the cultural differences are meaningful at the same time that he is creating the test that he hopes will answer that question.

Psychophysiologists are in the race to produce a culture-free I.Q. test. Although their work is not widely known or used, there is something especially seductive about an I.Q. score produced from brain-wave records (with oscillograph and computer readouts) that makes it necessary to mention these tests. The physiologically prone psychometrist works with such items as brain-wave changes which he measures while he projects patterns into the subject's eyes. He claims, correctly, that his items are objective, automatic, and not directly dependent on linguistic or other skills. But he still has the old questions of which items to keep, who should be in the standardization group, etc. The psychophysiologist usually validates and designs his test against the individual's Stanford-Binet score; if his test reproduces the Stanford-Binet I.Q. score for a person he is pleased and deems the test valid. When the instrumentalist takes this route he inherits virtually every bias built into the Stanford-Binet—but buries them yet one level deeper.

Twins. The attempt to assess the influence of heredity on intelligence is an equally quixotic undertaking. The classic work in this area compares I.Q. difference within pairs of children; identical-twin pairs, fraternal-twin pairs, sibling pairs, and unrelated pairs. In essence this study showed that mean I.Q. differences within pairs depended more on degree of kinship than on whether the pairs were reared together or apart.

The problem of this approach is that the experimenter assumes that pairs reared together are in identical environments and he also assumes that pairs reared apart are in dissimilar environments. Both assumptions are off base.

First of all, foster brothers reared together are not in identical environments during their prenatal development and conditions in the mother's womb can in turn be affected by her environment. We know something about the more dramatic environmental influences (such as that of drugs like Thalidomide) during pregnancy. But nutritional, disease, and

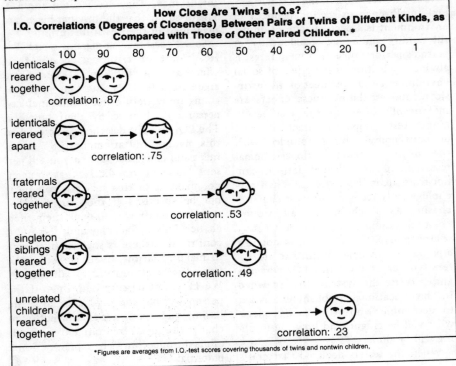

How Close Are Twins's I.Q.s?
I.Q. Correlations (Degrees of Closeness) Between Pairs of Twins of Different Kinds, as Compared with Those of Other Paired Children. *

Identicals reared together — correlation: .87

identicals reared apart — correlation: .75

fraternals reared together — correlation: .53

singleton siblings reared together — correlation: .49

unrelated children reared together — correlation: .23

*Figures are averages from I.Q.-test scores covering thousands of twins and nontwin children.

''The very notion that a single general intelligence exists independent of environment is a peculiar one of doubtful validity and of no social utility.''

psychosocial factors are less known and, no doubt, much more subtle. Yet the developing fetus' brain is a likely place for subtle influences to leave long-term marks—the pairs reared apart are still subject to the early effects of their original parents' environments.

Second, when a pair is separated and reared apart there is not enough difference between their new environments to produce a significant environmental effect on their I.Q. Adoption agencies have overt and covert policies designed to place a child in a social environment quite similar to the one he was born into. To vary the environment the researcher should place the foster child by drawing lots from a pool of all the parents in the world. In twin studies the environmental variable is inadvertently held constant so the hereditary effects seem to be big. The results are meaningful only under the particular social constraints present in the society during the study. This research tells us nothing about what may happen if we lift all constraints on social mobility.

Jews. The egalitarian structure of the Israeli kibbutz and the diversity of cultural background among members permit us to see what can happen to I.Q. if social factors are equalized. Outside the kibbutz in Israel, Jewish children of European parents have a mean I.Q. of 105, while a mean I.Q. of children of first-generation Oriental Jews is only 85. Some would suspect that the difference is genetic. When children of both groups grow up in the kibbutz nursery, after four years, they achieve exactly the same mean I.Q. scores—115 points. This does show us how labile I.Q. can be, but we should not conclude that the Oriental home inhibits intellect, or that the kibbutz environment stimulates it. It is far likelier that the Oriental home develops facets of intellect that are invisible to I.Q. tests, while the kibbutz makes a child test-wise.

A black child in a Northern city is not nearly as integrated into the test culture as the Oriental child in a kibbutz. He spends eight hours each day in a de-facto-segregated school and 16 hours in the black section of the city. An Oriental child in the kibbutz spends 22 hours a day in the nursery. The I.Q. of the black child usually does not reach the level of his Anglo urban counterpart. Chinese-Americans and Japanese-Americans score higher than Anglos do. None of this means much about inheritance of I.Q. Anglo scholastic I.Q. measured in a member of non-Anglo biosocial group is a semimythical property. While I.Q. is only a tiny mental facet of the Anglo culture, it does have some biological reality if we use it only on Anglos. The heritability of I.Q. is higher in white persons than it is in black persons. This is not very odd: an Anglo I.Q. measured on a black person exists more on the psychometrist's score record than it does in the mind or brain of the black. Although the mind and brain will always manifest some effects of heredity, the psychometrist's score records are totally outside of genetic control.

Tail. The very notion that a single general intelligence exists independent of environment is a peculiar one of doubtful validity and of no social utility. A person's performance on a mental test is always a reflection of the effect of social environment and the effect of his intrinsic mental attributes; these effects are inextricably fused in the test result. Mental tests sample the effects of social domains completely confounded with the effects of mental attributes. Social research and sophisticated statistics cannot tease apart these effects. When psychology fully recognizes this it can stop chasing its psychometric tail around empty questions and loaded answers.

Unhappily, the I.Q. game is not just a parochial squabble confined to an esoteric corner of ivy halls. I.Q. pervades and perverts the systems that spawned it. The educational establishment uses it to determine who will reach college, what will be taught, and how the teaching will be done.

When the testers declared that crafts and esthetics did not manifest intelligence, they gave us English departments that produce critics, but not authors, and art departments more appropriate for art historians than for artists.

We have a university that is not universal at all.

Mirror. The I.Q. malady does not even respect campus boundaries. It has been a long time since the testers and educators made their covert contract to define core-curriculum scholastic ability and ruling-class culture as "general intelligence." During all this time the intricacies and minutiae of I.Q.-test design and the noncommital posture of the testers have made the conspiracy invisible to its victims. Recently Arthur Jensen, William Shockley, and Richard Herrnstein have put forth claims that they have, with I.Q. tests, found genetic deficiencies of "intelligence" in minority groups. They write as if these deficiencies were real manifestations of the biological world; they present I.Q. data as if it were an unbiased measure of a real general intelligence. They have tilted the I.Q. mirror so far that the original biases are magnified in their own distortions.

Social-assistance programs such as Head Start are criticized because their effects are not visible in I.Q. data. Some argue from Jensen's data that such programs are wasteful since disenfranchised persons are limited by their heredity. The I.Q. was not designed to be used in this manner and attempts to do so are inept and dangerous. When you tell persons "your genetics dictate that you cannot make it in this society" you must not be surprised if they suspect that there is a conspiracy to deny them their chance. Jensen, Shockley and Herrnstein confirm that there is such a conspiracy to make a narrow, biased collection of items the "real measure" of all persons. We must not be surprised, then, if the person pursues the only alternative he has, by violence if need be, which is to change the social environment so that it offers the opportunity to express personal potential.

"When you tell persons 'your genetics dictate
that you cannot make it in this society'
you must not be surprised if they suspect that
there is a conspiracy to deny them their chance."

DIFFERENCES ARE NOT DEFICITS

by Theodosius Dobzhansky

A distinguished geneticist pores over the evidence
for the heritability of intelligence, finds it
ambiguous, and is not convinced by Jensen's argument.

THE DOCTRINE that all men are created equal is widespread in much of the modern world. We take equality for granted in American tradition, spell it out in the Declaration of Independence, but the idea frequently bogs down in misunderstanding and apparent contradictions. Equality is often confused with identity, and diversity with inequality.

Even some reputable scientists claim biology demonstrates that people are born unequal. This is sheer confusion; biology proves nothing of the sort. Every person is indeed biologically and genetically different from every other. Even identical twins are not really identical; they are recognizably separate persons who may engage in different occupations and achieve unequal socioeconomic status. But this phenomenon is biological diversity, which has nothing to do with human inequality.

Human equality and inequality are sociological designs, not biological phenomena. Human equality consists of equality before the law, political equality and equality of opportunity. These are human rights that come from religious, ethical or philosophical premises, not from genes. The United Nations recognized this fact in its 1952 UNESCO statement on race: "Equality of opportunity and equality in law in no way depend, as ethical principles, upon the assertion that human beings are in fact equal in endowment."

We may grant equality to all members of the human species or to only a small segment of the population, but we cannot brush away genetic diversity; it is an observable fact. And later in this article I will indicate how a society of equality of opportunity is most propitious for human self-fulfillment.

The reader may question whether genetic diversity has a social significance. At first thought, the answer seems to be no. With the exception of some pathological variants, one's form of enzyme or blood group seems to make no difference socially but genes may have effects that modify several characteristics. One cannot rule out the possibility that apparently neutral genetic variants may produce physiological or mental changes. For example, some scientists claim that B, A and O blood groups have something to do with resistance to plague, smallpox and syphilis respectively. The validity of this claim is still under scrutiny.

It has been established, however, with varying degrees of certainty, that many human traits which unquestionably matter to their possessors and to society, are genetically conditioned. Intelligence, personality, and special abilities are all susceptible to modification by genetic as well as environmental factors. And recent sensational and inflammatory pronouncements about the genetic basis for racial and socioeconomic differences in IQ make mandatory a critical consideration of the subject.

The Blank Slate. The underpinnings of human intelligence are still somewhat unclear. The most extreme environmentalists say we enter the world with a blank slate upon which circumstance writes a script. Strict hereditarians, on the other hand, believe that parental genes dictate our abilities.

A moderate form of the blank-slate doctrine appeals to many social scientists, who believe we are born with essentially equal potentialities, and become different primarily through upbringing, training and social position. They say that cultural and socioeconomic differences can explain the disparity in intelligence scores between races and classes.

Even a tempered view of genetic predisposition is distasteful in a competitive society. It seems hardly fair that some persons should start life with an advantage over others, and particularly repugnant to think that one race or class is superior to another. But dislike of a theory does not prove or disprove anything.

A third, and more likely, explanation exists for individual and group differences in IQ. Both environment and genetic conditioning may be at work. In this explanation, the bone of contention is not environment versus heredity, but how much environment and how much heredity.

For a clear understanding of the matter, we must define what we mean by IQ. An intelligence quotient is not a measure of the overall quality or worth of an individual. Someone with a high IQ may be vicious, selfish, lazy and slovenly, while someone with a lower score may be kind, helpful, hard-working and responsible. Even psychologists disagree about the mental and psychophysical traits an IQ test measures. Sir Cyril Burt was one of those who claimed that "we may safely assert that the innate amount of potential ability with which a child is endowed at birth sets an upper limit to what he can possibly achieve at school or in afterlife." He believed IQ measures this supposedly innate ability. Others deny that intelligence testing provides any valid information, and see it merely as a device that the privileged use to maintain their status over the less advantaged. Further, there is always the danger that IQ tests are biased in favor of the race, social class, or culture of those who devised the tests. Certainly all existing intelligence tests fall short of being culture-free or culture-fair [see "I.Q.: The Conspiracy" by John Garcia, on page 232].

The Unknown Heritability Factor. It is undeniable, however, that there are significant statistical correlations between IQ scores and success in schooling, advances in the existing occupational structure, and prestige in Western societies.

Researchers have also securely established that individual differences in scores are genetically as well as environmentally conditioned. The evidence comes from more than 50 independent studies in eight countries. But how much of this variation is due to genetics, or heritability as scientists call it, is unknown. The best estimates come from studies on twins and other close relatives reared together and apart. Arthur Jensen has carefully reviewed these data, and his analysis has indicated that approximately 80 percent of individual differences in IQ are inherited. This degree of heritability is high compared to the genetic components of other traits in different organisms. It is much higher than that of egg production in poultry or yield in corn, yet animal and plant breeders have substantially im-

Because people misunderstand the significance of the high heritability of IQ, we should clarify what it does and does not mean. To begin with, it does not mean that genes alone condition IQ.

proved these characteristics through genetic selection. In insects, artificial selection has induced spectacular changes for traits that are only half as genetically conditioned as human IQ.

Because people misunderstand the significance of the high heritability of IQ, we should clarify what it does and does not mean. To begin with, it does not mean that genes alone condition IQ. A possessor of certain genes will not necessarily have a certain IQ. The same gene constellation can result in a higher or lower score in different circumstances. Genes *determine* the intelligence (or stature or weight) of a person only in his particular environment. The trait that actually develops is *conditioned* by the interplay of the genes with the environment. Every person is unique and nonrecurrent, and no two individuals, except identical twins, have the same genes.

Studies of Twins. Marie Skodak and Harold M. Skeels showed the influence of environment on IQ in their study of identical twins raised together and apart. They found a consistently lower IQ correlation between twins raised apart compared to that between twins reared together. Because identical twins have identical genes, the greater IQ differences in twins raised apart, compared to those reared together, must be due to their different environments.

Now let us consider people in general rather than a particular person. Genes really determine reaction ranges for individuals with more or less similar genes. Genetic traits emerge in the process of development as one's genetic potential is realized. Similar genes may have different effects in unlike environments, and dissimilar genes may have similar effects in like environments.

But it is not useful to say that genes determine the upper and lower limits of intelligence, since existing environments are endlessly variable and we constantly add new ones. To test the reactions of a given gene constellation in all environments is obviously impossible. For example, how could one discover the greatest height I could become in some very propitious environment, or the shortest stature I could have in another environment and still remain alive? It is even more far-fetched to forecast stature in environments that may be engineered in the future, perhaps with the aid of some new growth hormone.

More importantly, heritability is not an intrinsic property of IQ, but of the population in which it occurs. Consideration of limiting cases makes this obvious. If we had a population of genetically identical persons, all individual differences in IQ would be environmentally determined. There would be *no* genetic influence affecting the *differences* in IQ that developed among them. Alternately, if all members of the population lived in the same environment, all IQ differences would be genetic. Therefore, we must confine our estimates of the heritability of IQ to the population under study and to the time we collected the data.

Research Across Race and Class. When we look at estimates of heritability, we must keep in mind the genetic and environmental uniformity or heterogeneity of the population studied. Most of the information on IQ comes from studies on white, middle-class populations. The most abundant data pertain to research on twins and siblings raised together. Children in the same family do not grow up in identical environments, but their surroundings are certainly more alike on the average than those across socioeconomic classes or races. Estimating heritability of IQ differences in one population is beset with pitfalls. Crossracial and crossclass research is even more difficult.

Scientists have documented differences in average IQ for various socioeconomic classes. This is neither surprising nor unexpected, since we know that educational and other opportunities are unequal for members of different social classes. Burt summarized data on 40,000 parents and their children in England. He gathered information on higher professional, lower professional, clerical, skilled, semiskilled and unskilled workers. Fathers in the higher professional category had an average IQ of about 140. This score was about 85 for the unskilled laborers. Children's average IQs ranged from about 121 for the higher professional group to about 93 in the unskilled sample. The children of the high professionals scored lower than their fathers while the children of the unskilled workers scored higher than their fathers. This is the well-known phenomenon called regression toward the mean. Regardless of whether the IQ differences between occupational classes are mainly genetic or environmental, children do not fully inherit the superior or inferior performance of their parents.

The Jensen Research. The situation is analogous with human races. Researchers have found a consistent 10 to 20 point disparity in average IQ scores between blacks and whites in the U. S. And because races, unlike socioeconomic groups, are usually physically recognizable, this disparity is often blamed on inferior black genes. But persons who belong to different races, whether they live in different countries or side by side, do not always have equal opportunities for mental development. Nobody, not even racists, can deny that living conditions and educational opportunities are disparate in races and classes.

After psychologist Arthur Jensen explicitly recognizes that heritability of individual differences in IQ cannot be used as a measure of average heritability across populations, he tries to do just that. In fairness to Jensen, he presents a detailed analysis of the environmental factors that could account for the discrepancy, but

Dobzhansky

It is accurate to say that whenever a variable human trait, even an apparently learned habit such as smoking, has been studied genetically, some genetic conditioning has come to light.

then he concludes that none of these factors or their combinations can explain the difference in average black and white IQ scores. He appeals to studies which try to equate black and white environments by comparing populations of equal socioeconomic status. This diminishes the IQ difference between the two races, but it does not erase the difference. Jensen takes this as evidence that a strong genetic component is operating. I remain unconvinced.

W. F. Bodmer and L. L. Cavalli-Sforza have pointed out the inadequacies of equating similar socioeconomic status with similar total environment. In their words: "It is difficult to see, however, how the status of blacks and whites can be compared. The very existence of a racial stratification correlated with a relative socioeconomic deprivation makes this comparison suspect. Black schools are well known to be generally less adequate than white schools, so that equal number of years of schooling certainly do not mean equal educational attainments. Wide variation in the level of occupation must exist within each occupational class. Thus one would certainly expect, even for equivalent occupational classes, that the black level is on the average lower than the white. No amount of money can buy a black person's way into a privileged upper-class white community, or buy off more than 200 years of accumulated racial prejudice on the part of the whites . . . It is impossible to accept the idea that matching for status provides an adequate, or even substantial, control over most important environmental differences between blacks and whites."

Average Vs. Individual. The controversy over the relative influence of nature and nurture on racial differences in IQ has grown hotter since scientists documented the high heritability of *individual* IQ. Racists try to gain maximum propaganda mileage from this fact, but the different

race and class *averages* may be less genetically conditioned than individual variations in IQ.

Sandra Scarr-Salapatek shows evidence of this proposition in her study of twins in Philadelphia schools. She attacks the presumption that the influence of genetics and environment is simply additive, and suggests that the two factors may operate dependently and in different ways. She hypothesizes that genetic differences show up more in persons who mature in favorable surroundings, but remain hidden or unused in individuals from adverse or suppressive environments. If her assertion is correct, the heritability of IQ should be lower among disadvantaged groups (both social and racial) than among privileged classes. On the other hand, if genetic and environmental influences simply add together, heritability should be uniform in all groups.

Scarr-Salapatek tested the two hypotheses in her study of intelligence and scholastic-aptitude test data on 1,521 pairs of twins attending public schools in Philadelphia. She compared test scores across races and across socioeconomic levels and found that differences between upper and lower class blacks were much smaller (5.3 points) than those between whites of similar classes (16.1 points). More importantly, for both blacks and whites, test scores varied more among advantaged than among disadvantaged children. She concludes: "From studies of middle-class white populations, investigators have reached the conclusion that genetic variability accounts for about 75 percent of the total variance in IQ scores of whites. A closer look at children reared under different conditions shows that the percentage of genetic variance and the mean scores are very much a function of the rearing conditions of the population. A first look at the black population suggests that genetic variability is important in advantaged groups, but much less important

in the disadvantaged. Since most blacks are socially disadvantaged, the proportion of genetic variance in the aptitude scores of black children is considerably less than that of white children . . ."

Scarr-Salapatek's work lends further support to the possibility that we can explain at least a part of racial and socioeconomic differences in IQ with environmental reasons. But nothing I have said excludes the possibility that there is also a genetic component in such differences. We simply don't know. The available data are inadequate to settle the question.

Care and Tutoring. Suppose, for the sake of argument, that the average intelligence of some class or race is lower than the average for other classes or races in the environments that now exist. This still would not justify race and class prejudice since one could still induce important changes in manifested intelligence by intensive care and tutoring of children. Perhaps it may even be possible to nullify or to reverse the disparity of group averages by altering environments and practices of child rearing.

We have seen that individual variability within classes and races is both genetically and environmentally conditioned. This is true of IQ as well as scholastic aptitude and achievement. We should keep in mind that IQ is not a unitary trait determined by a single gene, but rather it is a composite of numerous genetic components. IQ surely is not the only genetically conditioned trait. Less detailed but still substantial evidence suggests that many personality characteristics and special abilities, from mathematics to music, have genetic components. It is accurate to say that whenever a variable human trait, even an apparently learned habit such as smoking, has been studied genetically, some genetic conditioning has come to light. In any case, genetic conditioning, no matter how strong, does not preclude improvement by manipulation of the envi-

Dobzhansky
Additional readings on this
controversy by Jensen, Gans,
and Nisbet appear in *PT*,
December 1973.

ronment, as we have shown in our discussion of race, class and IQ.

Let us return to my original thesis that we can maximize the benefits of human diversity in a society where all individuals have truly equal opportunities. It is utterly unlikely that the incidence of all genetically conditioned traits will remain uniform throughout all socioeconomic classes. While genes for a particular trait, such as IQ, eyesight or stature, may be more common in class A than in class B, this does not mean that all A persons and no B individuals will possess these genes. Since only gene frequencies are involved, an individual's potentialities are determined by his own genetic endowment, not by his class or race. So only in a society of equal opportunity for all, regardless of race or class, will every individual have a chance to use his fullest potential.

Scholastic ability and achievement are important determinants of social mobility in a society with equality of opportunity. Schools and universities are principal ladders for socioeconomic rise. Insofar as achievement is genetically conditioned, social mobility is in part a genetic process. In "Genetics and Sociology," Bruce K. Eckland writes " . . . talented adults rise to the top of the social hierarchy and the dull fall or remain on the bottom. Therefore, as the system strives to achieve full equality of opportunity, the observed within-class variance among children tends to diminish while the between-class variance tends to increase on selective traits associated with genetic differences." Some may be chagrined to learn that increasing equality of opportunity *increases*, rather than decreases, genetic differences between socioeconomic classes. But I intend to show that if we had true equality of opportunity, the classes as we know them now would no longer exist.

The Benefits of Diversity. We can maximize the benefits of human diversity without creating a meritocracy in which

the genetic elite concentrate in the upper socioeconomic classes. With anything approaching full equality, those most genetically and environmentally fit for each trade, craft or profession will gravitate to that occupation. But these aggregations of genetic aptitudes will not result in socioeconomic classes or castes. I believe they will develop into new social phenomena, barely foreshadowed at present.

These aptitude aggregations will differ from our present socioeconomic classes primarily by their fluidity. Aggregations will gain new members who are not descended from old members. These gains will be offset by losses of some of the progeny of old members who will join other occupational groups. Some gains and losses may come to pass when individual occupations become more or less attractive or socially important. Others will be genetically conditioned and hence genetically significant. They result from the segregation of trait genes and must not be frustrated by the impulses of parents either to make their offspring follow in their own occupational footsteps, or to propel them to more privileged job categories.

But it is unlikely that every member of, say, the musicians aggregation, would have the gene for music, even if such a gene really existed. More likely the genetic basis of musical talent is a constellation of several genes, and possibly of different genes in different persons. Some children in the group will lack this genetic predisposition toward musical talent, and move on to other aggregations. Conversely, some talented musicians will be born in other aggregations, and will pass into the aggregation of musicians. This is to some extent analogous to present social-class mobility, but it is more closely tied to human genetics. While socioeconomic mobility is only vertical, aggregate mobility is horizontal and vertical.

Genes for various aptitudes exist in all social strata and professional aggregations,

but propinquity and assortive mating will greatly increase the number of marriages between individuals who carry genes for similar aptitudes. This will not necessarily yield a bumper crop of geniuses, but it enhances the possibility.

Differences, Not Deficits. It is not surprising that not everybody welcomes the prospect of equality. Even a few biologists have concocted horrendous tales of its genetic consequences. They say equality has drained the lower classes of genetic talents, and only worthless dregs remain. We can dispel this fantasy by pointing out that a former untouchable is a cabinet minister in India's government, and that after most of the aristocracy was destroyed during the Russian revolution, able individuals from the former lower classes took over the functions of government.

On the other hand, it may not seem realistic to envisage an entire society consisting of elite aggregations. Maybe one large aggregate will be left with no particular aptitudes. To this I can only say that I agree with Scarr-Salapatek. Differences between humans "can simply be accepted as differences and not as deficits. If there are alternate ways of being successful within the society, then differences can be valued variations on the human theme regardless of their environment or genetic origins." We must not brand people or professions as elite or common. To compliment equality of opportunity we need equality of status. Manual labor is not intrinsically inferior to intellectual labor, even though more of us may be more adept at the former than at the latter. The presence of rare abilities need not detract from appreciation of more common ones. Though this may be hard to accept for individuals who grew up in a class society, I feel it is ethically desirable. Moreover, history is moving in this direction. Ω

PERSONALITY
Public or Private

by Floyd L. Ruch

At a time when even the olive in a man's martini may be
bugged, invasion of privacy is indeed a crucial issue.
The era of the miniature microphone, the test
that tells all, and the electronic eye that sees too
much brings with it the threat of Big Brother
watching for his chance to snip away at the
tenuous threads of freedom. And so we react.

Thus the legal pendulum is about to swing
so hard that it may well strike down real
advances which behavioral scientists
have made toward putting the right
people in the right jobs. Hot headlines
shape extreme action, and Congress
now is considering Senate Bill 1035,
which would bar the use of both
personality and polygraph tests
in selecting government
employees, except for

PERSONALITY TEST

those in the FBI, the CIA, and the National Security Administration. Naturally, government contractors with an eye to their economic future would follow governmental hiring procedures, so this bill would reach far beyond the ranks of federal employees.

Obviously the personality test, which is aimed at predicting future performance and action, is not even related to the lie-detector test, which records fact, is exceedingly difficult to administer scientifically, and carries with it tremendous legal implications. They should not be considered together.

Why are they being considered in the same bill? What has led the American people and Congress to so fearful a view of personality testing? In part, it is a reaction against science. Medical research has developed truth serums and behavior-controlling drugs; advancing technology has brought infrared photography, the one-way mirror, the miniaturized tape recorder, the polygraph, and the directional microphone—plus the giant computer, with its almost limitless capacity for data storage and retrieval. These are appallingly efficient instruments to obtain information the individual might prefer to keep to himself.

Even in the use of the microphone and tape recorder, where the devices are tangible and the information obtained is clear-cut, there has been confusion and controversy about what constitutes an invasion of privacy. How much more fiercely the battle rages around something so intangible as personality tests, the results of which must be interpreted rather than quoted! The furor invades the nation's newspapers, and columnist George Dixon has remarked of the tests, "The questions are the kind you would ask the girl next door—if you wanted her to move."

Personality testing has been under fire for a decade, but the use of psychological testing in employee selection nonetheless has increased at a rapid pace. A recent study conducted among personnel directors indicated that psychological tests of all kinds showed a steady increase within a five-year period. [*See illustrations, this page*.]

Don't Say I'm Unsociable

When they apply for jobs, people willingly admit that they are poor spellers or inaccurate typists, but they do resent tests which may "accuse" them of being unsociable, and applicants who accept tests of skill and aptitude very often resent answering questions about their attitudes and feelings. Yet the introvert who feels it is his own business that he doesn't much enjoy the company of others is far less likely to enjoy his work and to succeed in a sales job than is the man who genuinely likes the aggressive role in social contacts.

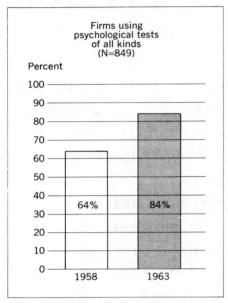

Growth in use of personality tests for employment selection, 1958-1963.

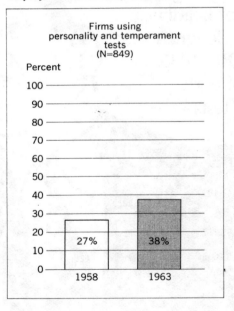

To what lengths should a company go in evaluating the personality qualifications of applicants without violating privacy? Are such tests really a threat? Let us look at what they are all about.

Applicants may deliberately lie to get a job, but lies are no defense for the applicant who feels that a test invades his privacy. Actually, the extent and quality of lying, as revealed by ingenious "lie detector" scales built into many tests,

itself is often an indication of the individual's fitness for a given job. This concept of *sensible deception* is an elaboration of the fact that everyone must engage in a certain amount of concealment and polite white lies to smooth social relations. Simulation in personality tests shows whether a person is sensibly realistic, overly candid (and hence naive), or so clumsy that he portrays himself as perfect.

Our study of the widely used, highly investigated, and well-respected Minnesota Multiphasic Personality Inventory (MMPI), which has a built-in correction for faking, shows that faked scores actually may have greater value in predicting success, particularly of salesmen, than those which have been corrected for faking.

The MMPI was given to 182 sales representatives from nine companies, ranging from beverage sales to business forms. Within each sample, the subjects were divided into an upper- and a lower-criterion group, based upon sales managers' ratings. The five MMPI scales which are normally corrected for faking differentiated significantly between the two groups when *not* corrected. The use of the corrective factor, the K scale, *decreased* validity. Persons who score high on the K scale are highly poised and easily hide feelings of social insecurity under a smooth facade—a characteristic of good salesmen. These results indicate that making acceptable scores on a test of this kind is in part a matter of learning how to answer in the way that impresses the employer most favorably.

Other studies using firemen, nurses, Air Force officers, and dental students have shown that frank instructions to answer questions as the subjects think they should be answered for job qualification produces answers which predict success more reliably than those obtained with the standard instructions to tell the truth. Certainly scores obtained in this way are a test of social skills, not an invasion of privacy!

The testing-privacy issue has festered for years, and it finally achieved front-page importance in 1965 when Congress conducted hearings on whether the use of psychological tests in the selection of government employees constituted an invasion of privacy. Many members of both houses felt that tests should not inquire about sex practices or religious beliefs. Psychological testing in depth was regarded by Congressmen as tantamount to peering into an employee's bedroom window. Rep. Cornelius Gallagher (D), N.J., charged: "...the Federal Government has been...searching the minds of Federal employees and job applicants through personality testing."

Personality testing is a natural for humorists. Columnist Art Hoppe once cited five MMPI test questions: (1) "I love my mother"; (2) "I am contented with my sex life"; (3) "Flirting is often a lot of fun"; (4) "I feel very guilty about my sins"; and (5) "I like westerns on television." Hoppe explained that a bright job applicant knows the psychologist thinks he should love his mother, have a satisfactory sex life, be unrepressed enough to flirt, and never feel "very" guilty. "A popular transvestite who had learned to live with his Oedipus complex would be contented, flirtatious, and free of guilt about loving his mother," he wrote. "But he would be unlikely to enjoy Westerns on television." Hoppe added: "...but I shudder to think of this country run by a bunch of transvestites with Oedipus complexes who happen to like Westerns on television. Honest though they may be."

Psychologists, who maintain that psychological testing helps a democratic society function effectively by discovering and evaluating scientifically the true potentialities of its citizens, have defended testing in and out of Congress. Good testing, the professionals argue, minimizes the factor of human error in the judgment of individuals and provides objective standards of comparison.

In the hearings, the experts emphasized the need for certain precautions in the use of tests to prevent their abuse. Psychologists presented to the Senate Committee two basic conditions essential to useful and legal psychological testing in employee selection. First, valid testing must be supervised by a psychologist who is qualified to administer and to interpret the particular test being used. (A specialist in the use of tests in the area of vocational counseling or clinical psychodiagnosis is not automatically an expert in the personnel field.) Second, the test data must constitute only a *part* of the information used in hiring. When these conditions are met, psychological tests can be of value in identifying those in any occupational group who have a great potential for success.

The American Psychological Association maintained that psychological instruments should not be used carelessly or unjustly against human privacy, and that psychologists are not competent to make a final judgment on the legality of a given personnel procedure. Arthur Brayfield, the APA spokesman, stated: "The right of a person to be fairly judged

in employment is surely a basic right. The right of the Federal Government to know a reasonable amount about employees or prospective employees is surely also an important matter, and ultimately is crucial to maintaining our democratic existence."

APA recommendations for proper psychological testing in Government assessment procedures include: assurance that all non-research testing which is not directly under the Civil Service Commission be placed under the direction of qualified psychologists; the right to review and appeal, upon request of an individual, those personnel decisions in which test data play an important part; creation of an advisory panel of non-government psychologists to review all agency evaluation procedures; and establishment of a National Academy of Sciences-National Research Council consulting group to survey and evaluate current assessment procedures and to make recommendations for the future. (The American Psychiatric Association presented similar recommendations.)

Other testimony, however, was less favorable to personality testing. Dr. Karl Menninger disapproved of paper-and-pencil tests. Rorschach ink-blot tests are more effective, he said.

Among the heads of Federal Agencies using personality and temperament tests, there was a disagreement about their value. John W. Macy, Jr., Chairman of the Civil Service Commission, insisted that personality tests then being given were practically useless in employee selection. (The University of California's Mason Haire long has insisted that even under the best of conditions testing for routine jobs will result in only a 4 per cent improvement over random selection, while testing for executive jobs can be improved by 15 per cent.)

Sargent Shriver, then the Peace Corps director, was enthusiastic about the value of personality testing. Based on previous experience with similar programs, a 50 per cent dropout rate for psychological reasons had been predicted for the Peace Corps. Instead, only 8 per cent of Peace Corps members dropped out for psychological reasons during a four-and-a-half year period and of these, only .7 per cent left for psychiatric or neurotic reasons, Shriver said. Shriver was borne out by Dr. Abraham Carp, of Air Force Aeronautical Systems personnel laboratory, who said MMPI effectively aided in weeding out applicants with actual or potential personality disorders. He defended the charged invasion of the applicant's re-

ligious and sex life on grounds that responses to particular items are not used; evaluation of personality traits is based on aggregate scores on MMPI scales. Moreover, all MMPI test answers and other personality test data are destroyed at the end of the training period. The MMPI, with certain modifications, is still used by the Peace Corps.

The hearings settled nothing, but they did air an important issue. No widespread misuse of the MMPI or any other test was discovered, nor was any major injustice revealed. However, the hearings were more than a tempest in a teapot, because they touched on such broad principles. Although some misconceptions about testing may have been fostered, a clear case for the selective value of psychological tests in Government employment was also presented.

Then, a year-and-a-half ago, the Johnson administration asked Government contractors to use personality tests in hiring only to the extent of Civil Service Commission use. This rocked supporters of psychological testing in employment, and I am one of them, because the Commission uses testing solely in connection with medical evaluation, or for professional clinical diagnosis and counseling.

A Test Catalogue

Private industry recognizes the nature of the right of privacy and safeguards it when tests are used as a part of the selection process. An outstanding example is Sears, Roebuck, and Company, which has an extensive testing program including personality testing.

V. J. Bentz, Director of Psychological Research and Services at Sears, has outlined the company's ground rules for obtaining the necessary information for hiring without violating individual privacy. It involves the concept of mutual commitment. The corporation seeks to find out as much as possible about an applicant's job fitness. And the applicant in turn seeks a job where his unique abilities and attributes can be used to best advantage.

In any test, relevance should be another key concept, Bentz says, and tests should remain pertinent to the position sought. In a recent survey on family birth-control techniques, over 90 per cent of a large sample of housewives readily divulged the most intimate details of their birth-control practices. However, when asked about family income, a large percentage of the women refused to answer. The question was not relevant. It *was* an unwarranted invasion of their privacy. Personality variables may be irrelevant to performance on an assembly line, and such testing be unwarranted; but these variables are crucial in high-level executive positions.

The Bentz testing program at Sears also includes a depth concept. Inventories or questionnaires which ask straightforward questions may provide generalized behavior descriptions. They may show that a job applicant prefers working alone to working with others and thus would do better as a bookkeeper or a draftsman than in sales. That makes sense, but to try to determine by projective techniques *why* the person is so unsocial would be an unjustified invasion of privacy. Certainly a man's sex life, for instance, is his own business, except where sexual aberrations could leave him wide-open to business blackmail.

The use of projective techniques involves an element of deception and interferes with mutual trust, Bentz's fourth dimension. This includes informed consent on the part of the applicant and rules out any intent to deceive, either on his part or on the part of the company. "Thus," said Bentz, summarizing the Sears program, "the corporation and the applicant make a search toward mutually desirable ends—to wed job requirements to an individual who (by virtue of his skills, abilities, aptitudes, and characteristics) can perform effectively in that position."

Outgrowth of Confusion

In general, it appears that much of the disagreement about the invasion of privacy is an outgrowth of confusion—either confusion about what constitutes privacy or confusion about what constitutes psychological testing, or both. We all agree that protection from unwarranted invasion of privacy is essential in our society. The questions are: What exactly is privacy? How can it best be protected?

If privacy is defined to include every area bearing on job success, then personality tests clearly invade privacy. So do all other methods of investigation, and the employer should make a decision based on the bare facts of work history. Clearly, efficient business operation demands more than that. However, tests which delve into matters unrelated to job success are unnecessary and should by all means be prohibited.

Another source of confusion about the nature of testing arises from failure to distinguish between individual *test questions* and *summarized test findings*, which are reported to employers by reputable consulting firms. In ethical companies with ethical staff psychologists

or reputable consulting firms, employers are not told specific answers of job applicants. Thus an employer never would know how an employee answered the question: "Do you like to attend parties once a week or oftener?" But from this and a number of similar questions dealing with social activities, the psychologist obtains a composite picture that enables him to rate the applicant on sociability. This general sociability level, relevant to success on the job where meeting the public is essential, is passed on to the employer.

It is also important to avoid confusion between the two types of personality tests. One test is the objectively scored *self-inventory* in which the person answers questions about his own behavior and conscious feelings, these answers being subject to the person's own "Fifth Amendment." In fact, the bright person taking such a test well may modify his answers to make what he thinks is a good impression through *sensible deception*. In contrast are the subjectively scored *projective techniques* which allegedly reveal the applicant's unconscious psychodynamics. The well-known Rorschach test is the best example of this second type.

We have found that summary scores from various self-inventory tests are job-related and reliable for use in employee selection. Their use is defensible in that it works for the common good of the employer and the applicant. It reduces the chance of the employer hiring a person who will prove incompetent on the job and at the same time protects the applicant from accepting a job on which he is likely to fail.

Not The Rorschach

The use of the Rorschach is quite a different matter. There *is* no published evidence that its findings are in any way job-related, and therefore there is no practical justification for its use in predicting success on the job. If the claim could be proven that the Rorschach penetrates the person's conscious defenses to tap the lower layers of the unconscious, this would be an unwarranted invasion of privacy because it is accomplished by denying him his right *not* to incriminate himself, as well as because the findings through this method are not job-related.

When the nature of privacy and the nature of testing are clearly understood, many points of controversy are automatically resolved. Moreover, psychologists themselves *do* exert controls over testing, Government users of tests *do* safeguard individual rights, and private employers

do attempt to preserve the right to privacy as they seek essential information for selection or promotion. Unless these trends should be reversed—and this is exceedingly unlikely, especially in view of the wide publicity the issue has received—it appears that psychological testing, far from constituting a threat to privacy, increasingly will provide a means for the individual, through the controlled sharing of information unique to himself, to find the best avenues for realizing his potential.

But Do People Like Tests?

Where employees have been widely exposed to testing of all kinds, reactions have been favorable. A recent study elicited the attitude of employees toward specific personality-test items. Only two employees of the manufacturing company polled declined to take the test. The 77 males and 75 females who participated were identified only by age, education, and sex.

Two of the most unpopular questions were: "Do you cry rather easily?" and "Do odors of perspiration disgust you?" but the item which aroused the greatest opposition was: "Do you feel strongly against kissing a friend of your own sex and age?" Females under 25 years of age were most offended by the items, males over 25 least offended. A majority of the large group studied said that less than one per cent of 361 test questions were personally offensive. Some 30 per cent of those polled found no annoying questions at all.

Tests, used properly and legally, help match people to their jobs on a more objective basis than is otherwise possible. But even under ideal conditions of self-regulation, there will be exceptional cases in which it will be necessary to weigh dispassionately and objectively the degree of invasion of privacy against the good to the individual and the organization resulting from this invasion.

I firmly believe the merits of questionable cases should be decided through judicial process, rather than through hasty and emotional legislative action. In an issue so complex that even psychologists and psychiatrists are unable to agree, the leisurely and scholarly approach of the courts is more likely to strike an equitable balance than is a vote cast during an emotional upheaval. The proposed legislation would label personality testing officially as a bad device, and thus would set back the real progress which has been made in this field. Why toss away one of society's useful modern tools?

Personality Testing –
A Smoke Screen Against Logic

by Frank B. McMahon Jr.

MANY YEARS AGO—but not long enough—I took Psychological Testing I and II, Projective Testing I and II and a couple of Advanced Testings I and II. I shall never forget the day the class was analyzing the results of a Rorschach ink-blot test and the professor became extremely excited over a response to one of the cards: ". . . and here," the patient had said, "I see a church steeple, over here a church, and down here is the grass."

"You see," the professor explained, "the church steeple represents a phallus; the grass, pubic hair; and we are dealing with a conflict between religious restriction and sexual desire."

And in another class, we discussed a sentence-completion item from another personality test: *"One night I . . . awakened and went to the refrigerator to get something to eat, a hot dog, I think."* Well, this was written by a young woman, and its interpretation I shall leave to the reader, whose wildest fantasies could not outdo those of the psychologists.

Or the objective test item: "I'm not as healthy as I used to be." (Checked true.) That one sent us scurrying through the other tests for indications of abnormal anxieties or mental disorders, never once giving even passing thought to the possibility that on that day the test taker may have needed an Alka-Seltzer.

One of the great geniuses of the psychological movement was Sigmund Freud. Freud helped everyone but the psychologist. To the psychologist Freud gave the psychoanalytic method, in which the analyst is free to roam the patient's subconscious without fear of successful contradiction. The Freudian method was a handle that the psychologist could grasp in all emergencies, a method that allows contradictory diagnoses and deceives the psychologist and alienates the patient. In interpreting a patient's subconscious, it is axiomatic that what is sought is unknown both to the patient *and to the psychologist.*

Granted, remarkable strides have been made as a result of Freud's work. We have, for example, pretty clear evidence that people are not always what they seem to be on the surface. The possibility that sexuality is a childhood trait as well as an adult preoccupation seems clearly established. But one of the leaders in current dream research, Calvin Hall of the University of California, Santa Cruz, made a list of sexual symbolism found in various psychology books and articles. There were 102 such objects, including anything resembling a gun or stick, and actions such as ploughing and flogging. Like cars, sexual symbols have suddenly become too numerous. What started as a good idea has suddenly swamped us in an asphyxiating smog. Sexual symbols and their inter-

pretation have almost supplanted the patient himself.

On the other hand, the late Gordon Allport, Harvard professor and former president of the American Psychological Association, suggested that if we wanted to know about a person, the first step was to ask him directly. Unfortunately, his suggestion has gone by the wayside. We psychologists are afraid to relinquish our position of omnipotence in relation to the patient and to elicit his aid in understanding man.

Today, a mixture of fear and desire for power grips clinical psychology. The desire for power indirectly manifests itself in the American Psychological Association's valid attempts to have clinicians as expert witnesses at trials. A recent court victory has validated these attempts, solidifying clinical psychology's growing power base. On the other hand, fear indirectly manifests itself, making it seem clinicians have something to hide, in the restrictions against undergraduates purchasing Rorschach cards and in the incomprehensible jargon that has been set up to explain and understand psychological disturbances.

Psychologists have had a long and difficult struggle in gaining recognition. Unfortunately, the price of this recognition has been to obscure understanding and diagnosis by double talk or even triple talk. If this results in the patient being kept in the dark, it is immaterial

"We interpret elaborate
psychological tests in the same
[old] way…searching most
of all for hidden symbols…"

because few psychologists feel the patient should have any say. Witness the common phenomenon at a hospital "staff" conference: heads nodding, slight smiles, everything short of cheering at a say-nothing statement such as, "He's fixated at this level because during these early years his father was stern, lenient, hostile, neutral, castrating, overprotective." Choose any of the above. They all work!

With psychology now strong enough as a science, the sad part is that we do not go back and pick up the pieces. Are we really testing what we think we are testing?

Psychology has had a strange developmental pattern. In order to get rid of the idea that man is a completely rational animal, we stressed his inability to understand himself. We stressed that the fountain pen represented something other than itself—it represented a penis. Now that we have proved our point (that man is not always rational), psychologists are caught in an equally extreme myth that man is a spidery maze of disguised sickness.

We must go back and talk with the patient—if need be, about something as insignificant as the pen. "Tell me, Mr. Patient, what does this pen mean in your dream (or your Rorschach card)?" The patient may say it means that he wants to be a writer, that he feels his imagination and its expression are constricted.

Rather than loosen the hold on the past, however, we interpret elaborate psychological tests in the same way, over and over, searching most of all for hidden symbols, deep meanings. The patient knows this. That there is trickery involved is most obvious to him. The patient is on guard and legitimately so. The psychologist is on guard, and legitimately so. We have, then, a contest of who can outfox whom. The psychologist has the upper hand, of course, because he can interpret anything he finds in the tests any way he wants.

Another problem, repeatedly pointed out by men like Lee Cronbach, Hans Eysenck, Gordon Allport and Carl Rogers, is that we are playing roulette odds

when we predict anything of substance via psychological tests as they now stand. For example, roughly half of the studies on the validity of Rorschach tests are positive, half are negative. Take your pick.

In any case, validity studies (which tell whether a test measures what it is supposed to measure) show personality tests to be of such low validity that the issue is often sidestepped. A validity of 1.00 is perfect and in the personality testing field a validity of .25 is often considered pretty good. Lee Cronbach, however, in *Essentials of Psychological Testing*, says a validity of .25 is poor. Depending on how a validity study is performed, who the test takers are, what their backgrounds and intelligence are, a validity of .25 can mean a personality test has little better than fifty-fifty accuracy. Reliability, which is closely related to validity, tells how *consistent* a test is in measuring what it is supposed to measure. The Minnesota Multiphasic Personality Inventory, which is considered the king of self-report tests, has reliability coefficients that begin as low as .50. [Self-report tests are ones where the patient reports on himself, by himself, via written answers to true-false questions like: I am contented with my sex life.]

Dr. Anne Anastasi, a prominent psychologist in the testing field, reports one reliability study (to note the extreme) on the MMPI Paranoia scale that was a minus quantity, −.05. She then explains that the scales don't mean what they say, anyway.

"For example, we cannot assume a high score on the Schizophrenia scale indicates the presence of schizophrenia . . . moreover, such a score may appear in a normal person."

In the face of such evidence, I think there are two major reasons for the continued ingrowth of the psychological testing movement. First, in order to maintain a mythical sense of professionalism, we are overinterpreting, being overerudite and succumbing to a fear of *not* seeing something in a test. Second, and running counter to the first reason, to

understand the infinitely complex human mind we would have to ask some the patient for assistance and take some of what he says at face value, integrating his material with our testing. Unfortunately, some psychologists think this is like the surgeon asking the patient where to cut.

Basically, there are three types of psychological tests: objective, semi-projective and projective (true-false, sentence completion and ink-blot).

Examining these three types in 1959, K. B. Little of the University of Denver and Edwin Schneidman of the National Institute of Mental Health had 48 clinical psychologists assess the tests of persons already interviewed and tested by other clinicians who had diagnosed these persons as ranging from psychotic to normal. These 48 investigators found that the clinicians tended to "overinterpret" the tests of the normal group. The clinicians assigned to normal persons the diagnostic label of "neurotic."

Subsequently, I decided to do an experiment of my own to test further the hypothesis that clinicians "overinterpret." I ran a study comparing psychology graduate students as raters of test results with raters from outside psychology. Objective, semi-projective and projective material was abstracted from the tests of 36 individuals receiving psychotherapy and 27 who said they had never received psychological treatment. The 27 responded to a questionnaire, on which they did not have to put their name, to the effect that they had never felt the need of, or sought, treatment. Of course, statistically, there would be more "disturbed" persons among those who were receiving treatment. I selected replies of the 63 persons to each type of test, avoiding replies that appear infrequently in response to a given test stimulus. I gave the replies to 16 clinical psychology graduate students, all of whom had completed their course work in psychological testing and were within a semester of receiving their Ph.D.s. I selected 16 business-administration majors at a comparable level of graduate

"The patient is on guard...
The psychologist is on guard...
We have a contest of
who can outfox whom."

study as the second group of raters.

The two sets of graduate students evaluated the replies of the "neurotic" and the "normal" groups according to whether they thought the test takers were "normal" or "neurotic."

Our finding was that in an overall evaluation of the replies to the Minnesota Multiphasic Personality Inventory and the sentence-completion test the business-administration students were able to differentiate "normal" from "neurotic" replies with approximately as much accuracy as were the students in psychology. What is possibly more interesting is that in differentiating between "normal" and "neurotic" on the Rorschach tests the business students outdid their counterparts in psychology.

Detailed examination showed that the psychology students interpreted the Rorschach replies of more intelligent test takers as being more disturbed; they overinterpreted the symbolic content given by the brighter persons.

Considerable evidence from other studies shows that more intelligent people produce more symbols. If symbolic interpretation is indeed the primary factor in overinterpreting, then normal persons of higher intelligence are likely to receive abnormal ratings.

This is not meant to suggest that laymen are necessarily better at test interpretation than psychologists, but that psychologists are evolving ever more elaborate test interpretations that remove the clinician further and further from the reality of the patient.

One could go to the extreme of saying that in the case just cited clinical training was of no benefit to diagnosis. My contention, however, is that training has been aimed in the wrong direction. It encourages a preoccupation with digging out what may not even be in a person's psyche: elaborate and secret unconscious meanings. Instead, clinical training should be used in conjunction with both common sense and what the patient says of himself. In place of the tricky diagnosis, we should focus on what the patient is saying, in most cases taking

his word for it (statistically better than roulette) and trying to integrate both sources into a comprehensible whole.

Oddly enough, although both groups of raters were able to distinguish "normal" from "neurotic" replies on the MMPI and the sentence-completion tests, the content of the test items themselves did not seem to be critical in the rating procedure. That is, if certain test items consistently meant disturbance, these items should have been consistently rated as such. This was not the case. There were only 22 out of 376 test items that 75 per cent of the raters rated the same way.

This suggests that the content of the test items themselves is not being accurately interpreted. The traditional psychological test may not be pinpointing the content that is most meaningful to the patient and most enlightening to the psychologist.

In 1963, I published a new personality test designed to be administered on a "man-to-man" basis. Each and every question was completely transparent, or face-valid. The test taker could easily tell that a certain response would count "against" him. A face-valid item looks to the test taker to be what it is. An example of an item that is *not* face-valid is, "I used to like to play drop the handkerchief."

For this "man-to-man" technique to work, I had to avoid the ambiguity of the typical test. Therefore, after each traditional psychological test item I inserted a qualifier that the test taker could use to keep from feeling (and being) shoved behind the eight ball. For example, "Some people have it in for me," True or False, followed by: If true, "I can't seem to get them off my mind," True or False.

This couplet type of questioning means that if the individual checks both parts "true," he is acknowledging a problem in his life that is important enough to admit to twice. Obviously, the couplet does not make clear the deeper meaning of the item, nor can the meaning really be made clear by any self-report test.

6. a. I do not think there is a God. T F
   b. IF TRUE: My life seems empty because there seems to be no purpose to i

7. a. I am not an important person— at least to those around me. T F
   b. IF TRUE: I feel I am just about worthless.

8. a. I sometimes work so long at something until others lose their patience with me.
   b. IF TRUE: I often lose patience with myself over my persistence. T F

9. a. I have made a satisfactory adjustment in my sex life. T F
   b. IF FALSE: I feel capable of making such an adjustment in the near future. ⁊

10. a. I have periods of such great restlessness that I can't sit still. T F
    b. IF TRUE: Most of the time I feel like a rubber-band stretched tight. T F

11. a. I often worry about religious problems. T
    b. IF TRUE: I feel depressed and confused about religion. T F

12. a. In my family there is not much love and companionship. T F
    b. IF TRUE: I get enough love and companionship from others (friends, other relatives, etc.). T F

13. a. When I go to a party, I generally find myself either alone or with just one other person. T F
    b. IF TRUE: Because of this, I feel "ill-at-ease" at most parties. T F

14. a. The world seems more like a jungle than "civilization." T F
    b. IF TRUE: I don't feel very safe or secure in my everyday life. T F

COUPLET QUESTIONS. Above are samples of author McMahon's bold innovation, which was designed to combat trickiness and inaccuracy in psychological tests.

"In place of the tricky diagnosis, we should focus on what the patient is saying."

The couplet does signal areas in which the patient desires further discussion. More important, the couplet relies heavily on the patient himself.

The test is then scored, but instead of writing a report that is known only to the psychologist, as is customary, we return the test to the test taker for discussion. To discuss each item on a standard objective psychological test would be a big job considering the large (more than 500 on the MMPI) number of items. But by using the couplet method, we can construct an effective test with just under 50 items. The psychologist may point out that certain of the test taker's replies to the test suggest problem areas. The discussion should further clarify the meaning and purpose of any test item and the extent to which an item, in the opinion of the psychologist or the test taker, should be further explored. I consider this discussion an essential ingredient of the testing process.

Psychologists using the test quickly found that it helped place the patient-doctor relationship on an above-board basis. The meaning behind the items and the methods of coping with the problems the items suggested could be explored with mutual confidence.

We further analyzed the test structure to determine what meaning was inherent in the single test item versus the couplet. For example, the traditional test item, "Some people have it in for me," was rated by a group of psychologists. Interpretations of its meaning ranged from "indicates an aggressive individual" to "he's got paranoid traits."

A second group of psychologists rated the same item, except that we added the couplet or qualifier, "I can't seem to get them off my mind," and marked it *false*. Interpretations changed considerably. Many fewer psychologists now thought that the statement, "Some people have it in for me," indicated severe disturbance. Their interpretations, however, still varied widely.

At this point, I performed an informal validity study of my test. Patients who had discussed the test items with the therapists were asked, after three sessions, to list important problems not covered so far in the therapeutic relationship. Only one of 32 persons indicated he had failed to touch on his major problems.

In numerous other validity studies, the couplet test has been compared with the longer and less face-valid type of objective tests. The results of these other tests were the same as those obtained with the couplet test in enough cases to yield correlations of between .80 and .95 (and none below .80), which are high. Other studies of the couplet test yielded validities in the .70 and .80 range. In these studies, therapists who were unaware of the results obtained with couplet tests rated patients with other diagnostic tools. Comparison of their results with the couplet test results showed the high validities.

Therapy with regressed patients has been most effective when the therapist takes the time to learn the specific language of the patient himself. [See "The Shattered Language of Schizophrenia," on page 270.] He might have to learn, for instance, that the patient conceives of God as a Chinese four feet tall, with a mustache. This can take a great deal of time and effort and only a few therapists have been heroic enough to bother.

Similarly, most of us are not now allowing for the meaning that patients attach to their symbols when they take tests. I do not intend to imply that symbolism or hidden meaning is not of the utmost value. It seems only logical, however, that the patient should help us to understand the symbols. I think the reason for the high validities of the couplet test is that the test is neither clever nor tricky. It says to the patient, "You help me to understand you." Why not try him out?

Test Results Are What You Think They Are

by Loren J. and Jean Chapman

Every day psychiatrists and clinical psychologists must make vital decisions:

What is his problem? Should he be committed to a mental hospital? Is he a suicide-risk or a homicide-risk? Is this patient well enough to be discharged from the hospital, or should he stay?

For help with their decisions the clinicians almost always use psychological tests.

According to a survey by Norman Sundberg, the two most widely used tests of any kind are the Rorschach inkblot test and the Draw-a-Person test (DAP). Both are projective tests, based on the premise that a person projects part of his personality when he responds to an ambiguous, unstructured situation. For example, since there are no objective shapes in an inkblot, anything a person sees in one presumably reflects his own drives, conflicts and personality. Similarly, when one draws a picture of a person on a blank sheet of paper, he is thought to project a bit of himself into his creation.

Self. But our recent research suggests that the Rorschach and DAP may be projective tests in more ways than one. In interpreting the results of these tests, the average clinician may project his own preconceptions and assumptions into his description of the patient.

Our first studies in this area were with the Draw-a-Person test, in which a clinician gives the subject a pencil and a blank sheet of paper and asks him to draw a person. Karen Machover published the test in 1949. She described the pictures typically drawn by persons with various emotional problems and explained how to interpret several picture characteristics as keys to personality. She said, for example, that "the paranoid individual gives much graphic emphasis to the eyes," and "the sex given the proportionately larger head is the sex that is accorded more intellectual and social authority."

Machover's test manual is filled with far-reaching generalizations about what kinds of persons draw what kinds of pictures, but she presents very little supporting data.

Parts. Some clinicians have been unwilling to take Machover's word for it; they have tested her assertions experimentally. Jules Holzberg and Murray Wexler, for example, tried to determine whether paranoid persons really do draw elaborate eyes. They compared the drawings of 18 paranoid schizophrenic patients and 76 student nurses, but they found no difference in the way the two groups drew eyes.

Dozens of similar studies have tested Machover's predictions about other picture characteristics—head, ears, lips, hair, clothing, mouths, etc.—but again and again the DAP signs have failed to hold up. A few experimenters have found that better-adjusted subjects tend to produce better overall drawings, but the overwhelming conclusion from the research evidence is that the specific content of a drawing is not a valid indicator of personality characteristics.

Sign. It should be pointed out that this type of research does not demand perfect discrimination. If 50 per cent of homosexual persons draw figures in a certain way, and only 25 per cent of other persons draw figures that way, the drawing characteristic may still be considered a valid diagnostic sign, since in the long run it may contribute information toward a diagnosis of homosexuality.

Most clinicians know about the research showing that the DAP signs are invalid, yet many thousands continue to use the test regularly because they claim they have seen the signs work in their own clinical practice. "I'll trust my own senses before I trust some journal article," said one clinical psychologist. "I know that paranoids don't seem to draw big eyes in the research labs," said another, "but they sure do in my office."

Illusion. Some critics say that clinicians are so wrapped up in their theories and traditions that they are not influenced by the facts. We think there is another explanation, however. The clinician who continues to trust DAP signs in the face of negative evidence

249

may be experiencing an *illusory correlation,* a phenomenon we discovered several years ago in research on word associations.

We found that words that are highly associated with each other tend to be seen as occurring together more often than they really do. In these experiments a subject sat in a comfortable chair as we projected various word-pairs (e.g., *bacon—tiger*) onto a large screen in front of him. The word pairs changed every two seconds. The word on the left side of a pair was always one of four possible words: *bacon, lion, blossoms,* or *boat.* Each word appeared as often as any other (25 per cent of the time), but it appeared always on the left side of the screen. The word on the right side of a pair was either *eggs, tiger,* or *notebook,* with equal probabilities.

We arranged the word-pairs systematically so that each left-side word appeared an equal number of times with each right-side word. For example, when *bacon* appeared on the left side, *eggs* was paired with it on a third of the trials, *tiger* on another third of the trials, and *notebook* on the remaining third. But when we asked the subjects later about the word-pairs, they said that when *bacon* appeared on the left, *eggs* was paired with it 47 per cent of the time, and that when *lion* was on the left, *tiger* was the word that most often appeared on the right. Even though every word-pair appeared as often as every other, the subjects claimed that the pairs with strong verbal association occurred more often than the others.

The tendency to see two things as occurring together more often than they actually do we called illusory correlation.

There seemed to be an essential similarity between students who claim that certain words occur together more often than they actually do and clinical psychologists who claim to see validity in the DAP test signs when the research says there is none.

Tell. The DAP signs and interpretations may be different today from what they were when Machover introduced the test over 20 years ago, of course, so we asked modern professionals how they used the test. We sent questionnaires to 110 clinicians who were active in diagnostic testing. We wrote brief descriptions of six types of patients and asked each clinician to tell us what characteristics he had seen in the drawings of each. The six descriptions were 1) "He is worried about how manly he is," 2) "He is suspicious of other people," 3) "He is worried about how intelligent he is," 4) "He is concerned with being fed and taken care of by other people," 5) "He has had problems of sexual impotence," and 6) "He is very worried that people are saying bad things about him." We told the clinicians to assume in each case that the patient was a man who drew a picture of a man.

We received 44 completed questionnaires, and it was clear that the clinicians generally agreed with each other as to the drawing characteristics they had seen in each case. For example, most clinicians (91 per cent) said that the suspicious patient would draw large or atypical eyes. Eighty-two per cent said that a person worried about his intelligence would tend to draw a large or emphasized head.

The agreement was not perfect, but it was impressive. In general, the clinicians agreed on two or three drawing characteristics that they would expect from each type of patient.

Pairs. Most of the clinicians had Ph.D.s and they averaged 8.4 years' experience in psychodiagnostics. We wondered what sort of DAP signs observers would find when they had almost no experience at all.

To find out, we gathered 45 drawings of male figures—35 by psychotic patients at a nearby state hospital and 10 by graduate students in clinical psychology. We measured each picture for head size, eye size, etc., and had independent judges rate the drawings on the more subjective characteristics, such as muscularity and femininity.

To each picture we attached two of the six diagnostic statements we had sent out to clinicians—for example, "The man who drew this 1) is suspicious of other people, and 2) has

SYMPTOMS OF PATIENT

Characteristics of drawings	Worried about manliness		Suspicious of others		Worry about intelligence		Need to be fed and cared for		Sexual Impotence		People saying bad things	
C Clinician S Student	C	S	C	S	C	S	C	S	C	S	C	S
1 broad shoulders, muscular	**80%**	**76%**		6%		8%		12%	**25%**	**31%**		6%
2 eyes atypical			**91%**	**58%**		6%		3%	2%	2%	**43%**	**26%**
3 head large or emphasized		5%		13%	**82%**	**55%**	2%	7%		3%	9%	10%
4 mouth emphasized			7%	5%		1%	**68%**	8%	2%	1%	5%	5%
5 sexual area elaborated	14%	5%							**55%**	8%		
6 ears atypical			**55%**	6%		3%			2%		**64%**	7%
7 facial expression atypical		**17%**	**18%**	**44%**	2%	**21%**	2%	**21%**	2%	**14%**	**18%**	**52%**
8 feminine, childlike	**23%**	**22%**	7%	12%	2%	11%	**32%**	**39%**	**23%**	**25%**	11%	13%
9 hair distinctive	**23%**	13%	2%	2%	2%	8%		1%	11%	6%		3%
10 detailed drawing	**20%**	8%	2%	6%	**34%**	13%		3%	7%	3%	2%	6%
11 passive posture	5%	4%	2%	8%		2%	**36%**	**21%**	2%	2%		8%
12 buttons on clothes							**23%**	1%				
13 sexual area deemphasized									**18%**	**27%**		
14 phallic nose, limbs	9%								**23%**	2%		
15 fat		2%		1%			7%	**16%**		4%		1%

PICTURE CHARACTERISTICS. Pictures drawn by men with various types of problems, as seen by experienced clinicians and naive students. The characteristics listed are those mentioned by at least 15 per cent of the clinicians or the students for at least one symptom. [Ratings over 15 per cent appear in bold type.] For nearly every drawing characteristic, the symptom most often associated with it by the clinicians is the same symptom most often associated with it by the students.

had problems of sexual impotence." There were 15 distinct pairs that could be made from the six statements, so we used each pair on three different pictures.

We assigned the statements systematically to all types of pictures. For example, "He is worried about how intelligent he is" appeared just as often on pictures with small heads as on pictures with large heads.

We then screened a group of college students and selected 108 who claimed they had never heard of the Draw-a-Person test and knew nothing about how it was interpreted.

We tested the students in groups. Before each testing we briefly explained the rationale of the DAP test. We said the student would see a series of drawings, along with brief statements about the men who drew them. We said that many of the men had the same problems, and that the students should examine the pictures carefully and look for common characteristics in the drawings by men with each type of problem. The students then looked at the pictures in a prearranged random order, with 30 seconds allowed for each picture.

Proof. Though we had carefully counterbalanced the pictures and the statements so that there were no objective relationships between them, nearly every subject reported that he *saw* relationships. And the relationships that students found were remarkably similar to the relationships that clinicians reported seeing in everyday practice. There were some differences, of course, but the students tended to describe the typical drawing of each type of patient in the same terms that the clinicians had used. And in the students' case, we know the signs were illusions, because they were not in the data.

Our previous research on word-pairs suggests an explanation: recall that we found that words with strong associative connections tend to be seen as occurring together. Perhaps the same mechanism was behind the DAP signs. We made a word-association questionnaire to determine how closely the symptom areas (suspiciousness, intelligence, impotence, etc.) are associated with various parts of the body (eyes, head, sexual organs, muscles, etc.). Questions took the following form: "The tendency for SUSPICIOUSNESS to call to mind HEAD is

1) very strong, 2) strong, 3) moderate, 4) slight, 5) very slight, 6) no tendency at all."

We gave the questionnaire to 45 students who had not participated in the other parts of the experiment. The verbal associations they reported neatly paralleled the illusory correlations that naive students had seen between symptoms and drawing characteristics. And the verbal associations were an even closer match with the correlations reported by practicing clinicians.

Pay. In our next experiment we tested 56 subjects on three successive days to see whether they would realize that there was no true correlation between symptoms and pictures if they had a chance to look at the test materials more than once. The correlations were seen as strongly on the third day as on the first. We began to realize how strong an illusory correlation can

---

"Most clinicians know about the research showing that the DAP signs are invalid, yet many thousands continue to use the test regularly."

---

be and we wondered what conditions, if any, would allow one to overcome it.

We tested a series of 41 new subjects individually, and let each look at each picture as long as he wanted to. To encourage them to study the pictures carefully, we offered 20 dollars to the student whose judgments were most accurate.

It didn't work. The students saw the illusory correlations just as strongly as ever.

Finally we pulled all the stops and gave the subjects every opportunity we could think of to check their own perceptions. We gave each subject the full stack of drawings to study by himself; we told him he could look at them in any order for as long as he wanted. He could sort the pictures into piles and make direct comparisons. He could put all the drawings by suspicious men in one pile and study them for similarities. We gave every subject scratch paper, a pencil and a ruler; we again offered 20 dollars to the person whose judgments were most accurate, and we gave each subject a copy of the final questionnaire

so he could see what questions he would have to answer.

Manly. In these generous conditions the illusory correlation did drop significantly for most of the symptoms, but it didn't disappear. For example, in normal conditions 76 per cent of students saw a relationship between worrying about one's manliness and the tendency to draw muscular figures; in the new conditions, 45 per cent still claimed to see the relationship that wasn't there. The illusory correlation is powerful, and remarkably resistant to any attempts to change it.

Students even claim to see the typical correlations when the cards are stacked in the opposite direction. In one study, for example, we placed the statement, "He is worried about his intelligence" only on pictures with *small* heads; the statement about suspiciousness appeared exclusively on drawings with *small* eyes, etc. This reduced the illusory correlation somewhat, but didn't eliminate it. Sixteen per cent still said that patients who worried about intelligence drew big-headed figures and 50 per cent still saw a relationship between worrying about one's manliness and the tendency to draw muscular figures—even though the true relationships were in the opposite direction.

It is clear from our research that clinical interpretations of the DAP test likely have a strong component of illusory correlation. And the decisions that clinicians make about their patients may be projections of the clinicians' own preconceptions.

Blots. We wondered whether there were illusory correlations in the most popular test of all—the Rorschach inkblots—and if so, whether they would be seen as clearly as real correlations, the few Rorschach signs that have been found to be valid indicators of certain personality characteristics.

In the Rorschach's 50-year history, many clinicians have reported, for example, that certain responses are given more often by homosexuals than by others. In 1949, William Wheeler summarized 20 Rorschach signs of homosexuality. Other researchers have tested the Wheeler signs, but only two of the 20 signs have been found valid by more than one investigator. One of these (number seven) is a response to the fourth inkblot of "a human or animal—contorted, monstrous, or threatening." The other valid sign is Wheeler's number eight, the report of an ambiguous animal-human figure on the fifth card.

Signs. To find how clinicians actually use the Rorschach to diagnose homosexuality, we sent questionnaires to 76 clinicians, asking them to describe two percepts that homosexual patients typically see in the 10 Rorschach inkblots. Of the clinicians who returned completed questionnaires, 32 said they had seen the Rorschach protocols of a number of homosexuals. These 32 clinicians described several Rorschach signs, but the ones they mentioned most often were 1) buttocks or anus, 2) genitals, 3) feminine clothing, 4) human figures of indeterminate sex, with no clear male or female features, and 5) human figures with both male and female features. All of these are Wheeler signs that have not been supported by research. On the other hand, only two clinicians mentioned valid sign number seven—a contorted, monstrous figure, and none mentioned the other valid sign, number eight—a part-human-part-animal figure.

Some clinicians, it would appear, see signs in the Rorschach that aren't there, and fail to see the signs that are there. Again our work with word-associations suggests a reason. The two valid signs are not intuitive: homosexuality does not easily bring to mind either snarling beasts or human-animal crossbreeds. But homosexuality does have a high verbal association with the five signs clinicians reported most often. Somehow it is intuitively reasonable to expect that homosexuals might tend to see buttocks, feminine clothing, or mixed-sex figures in inkblots.

Ideas. We tested these notions objectively by asking 34 independent student judges to rate how strongly the word "homosexuality" tended to call to mind various ideas. Their ratings agreed—the popular but invalid signs have a stronger verbal association with homosexuality than do the two unpopular but valid signs. This suggests that the signs of homosexuality that clinicians claim to see in the Rorschach may simply reflect their own assumptions and expectations.

We tested this contention with a design similar to the one we used to study the Draw-a-Person test. We obtained several Rorschach cards, and on each we attached a response—some perception that a person had supposedly seen on the card. There was a circle around the area of the card that the response referred to.

On some inkblots the response was a valid homosexuality sign (e.g., "a giant with shrunken arms"), on others the response was a nonvalid sign (e.g., "a woman's laced corset"), and on others it was a neutral sign (e.g., "a map of Spain"). Below the response were two descriptions of the person who had made the response. We selected these descriptions in all possible pairs from a group of four: 1) "He has sexual feelings toward other men," 2) "He believes other people are plotting against him," 3) "He feels sad and depressed much of the time," and 4) "He has strong feelings of inferiority." We, of course, were most interested in the first statement.

Mix. As in the DAP studies, we systematically assigned the symptom

---

"It seems likely that the illusory correlations that a clinician observes are reinforced by the reports of his fellow clinicians."

---

statements to the cards so that there was no consistent relationship between any of the statements and any of the signs.

After the students looked at a series of cards, we asked them what kind of Rorschach images had been reported by patients with each of the four types of symptoms. The homosexual men, the students reported, more often saw buttocks, genitals, etc.—in short, the same five nonvalid signs that clinicians had reported. None of the students saw a relationship between homosexuality and the two valid signs.

In a later variation we purposely introduced a negative correlation into the test materials, so that the statement "He has sexual feelings toward other men" *never* appeared on a card that had been perceived as feminine clothing, buttocks, etc. This did not reduce the illusory correlation—the students saw it just as strongly as before.

Tie. These studies show how easy it is to believe that two independent events are connected, especially when there is some subjective verbal associ-

ation between the events. Our subjects saw massive illusory correlations between symptoms and projective test signs on a brief, structured task. The clinician's task is much more complex, of course. A real patient's problems are numerous and vague—rarely does a patient have only two clearly defined symptoms. And real patients make many different responses on projective tests, not just one. It also seems likely that in actual practice the illusory correlations that a clinician observes are reinforced by the reports of his fellow clinicians who themselves are subject to the same illusions. The consensus would make everyone's illusions stronger. Our students, on the other hand, were not allowed to speak to one another during the test, so each had to find the illusory correlations on his own. For all of these reasons it seems likely that practicing clinicians deal with illusory correlations that are even stronger than the ones our subjects reported.

Hard. We do not mean to imply that clinical psychologists are incompetent or unresponsive to the facts, as some might be quick to conclude. Our data point not to the incompetence of the clinician, but to the extreme difficulty of his task. Clinicians are subject to the same illusions as everyone else. By analogy, nearly everyone says that two horizontal lines have different lengths when they appear in the Müller-Lyer illusion—

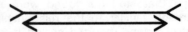

but no one would call a carpenter an incompetent judge of distances simply because he too sees the illusion.

Clinicians must be made aware of illusory correlations if they are to compensate for them. Ideally, the clinician should experience such illusions firsthand. It may be sound training policy to require each graduate student in clinical psychology to serve as an observer in tasks like the ones we have described. He could then examine closely the size and source of the illusory correlations he experiences and thereby, one hopes, learn to guard against such errors in his clinical practice.

The experience would also remind him that his senses are fallible, that his clinical judgments must be checked continually against objective measures, and that his professional task is one of the most difficult and complex in all of psychology. ◘

SOME SOCIAL SCIENTISTS BELIEVE that the impetus behind campus unrest is youth's impatient conviction that they can control their own destinies, that they can change society for the better.

My research over the past 12 years has led me to suspect that much of the protest, outcry and agitation occurs for the opposite reason—because students feel they *cannot* change the world, that the system is too complicated and too much controlled by powerful others to be changed through the students' efforts. They feel more powerless and alienated today than they did 10 years ago, and rioting may be an expression of their hostility and resentment.

Dog. One of the most pervasive laws of animal learning is that a behavior followed by a reward tends to be repeated, and a behavior followed by a punishment tends not to be repeated. This seems to imply that reward and punishment act directly on behavior, but I think this formulation is too simplistic to account for many types of human behavior.

For example, if a dog lifts its leg at the exact moment that someone throws a bone over a fence, the dog may begin to lift its leg more often than usual when it is in the same situation—whether or not anyone is heaving a bone. Adult human beings are usually not so superstitious—a person who finds a dollar bill on the sidewalk immediately after stroking his hair is not likely to stroke his hair when he returns to the same spot.

It seemed to me that, at least with human beings who have begun to form concepts, the important factors in learning were not only the strength and frequency of rewards and punishments but also whether or not the person believed his behavior produced the reward or punishment.

According to the social-learning theory that I developed several years ago with my colleagues and students, rewarding a behavior strengthens an *expectancy* that the behavior will produce future rewards.

In animals, the expectation of reward is primarily a function of the strength and frequency of rewards. In human beings, there are other things that can influence the expectation of reward—the information others give us, our knowledge generalized from a variety of experiences, and our perceptions of causality in the situation.

Consider the ancient shell game. Suppose I place

... Whether
'tis nobler
in the mind
to suffer
the slings
and arrows
of outrageous
fortune,
Or
to take arms
against a sea
of troubles,
and by
opposing
end them?

External Control and Internal Control

by Julian B. Rotter

a pea under one of three shells and quickly shuffle the shells around the table. A player watches my movements carefully and then, thinking that he is using his fine perceptual skills, he tells me which shell the pea is under. If his choice is correct, he will likely choose the same shell again the next time he sees me make those particular hand movements. It looks like a simple case of rewarding a response.

But suppose I ask the subject to turn his back while I shuffle the shells. This time, even if his choice is rewarded by being correct, he is not so likely to select the same shell again, because the outcome seems to be beyond his control—just a lucky guess.

Chips. In 1957, E. Jerry Phares tried to find out if these intuitive differences between chance-learning and skill-learning would hold up in the laboratory. Phares would give each subject a small gray-colored chip and ask him to select one of 10 standard chips that had exactly the same shade of gray. The standards were all different but so similar in value that discrimination among them was very difficult. Phares told half of his subjects that matching the shades required great skill and that some persons were very good at it. He told the rest that the task was so difficult that success was a matter of luck. Before the experiment began, Phares arbitrarily decided which trials would be "right" and which would be "wrong"; the schedule was the same for everyone. He found that because of the difficulty of the task all subjects accepted his statements of right and wrong without question.

Phares gave each subject a stack of poker chips and asked him to bet on his accuracy before each trial as a measure of each subject's expectancy of success.

The subjects who thought that success depended on their own skills shifted and changed frequently—their bets would rise after success and drop after failure, just as reinforcement-learning theory would predict. But subjects who thought that a correct match was a matter of luck reacted differently. In fact, many of them raised their bets after failure and lowered them after success—the "gambler's fallacy." Thus, it appeared that traditional laws of learning could not explain some types of human behavior.

Guess. Another well-established law of learning states that behavior learned by partial reinforcement takes longer to extinguish than behavior learned by constant reinforcement. In other words, when rewards cease, a behavior becomes weaker and eventually stops—but it takes longer for a behavior to die out if it was learned with intermittent rewards than if it had been rewarded every time it occurred.

William H. James and I tested this proposition. We told some subjects that an ESP guessing task was a matter of skill; we told other subjects that the same task was purely chance. We told some subjects they were correct on half their guesses. At a predetermined point we began to call all guesses incorrect. The subjects who believed they were in a skill task lowered their expectancy of success sooner than the subjects who thought that successful guesses were a matter of luck. Other subjects had been told they were correct on every trial. In this condition it was the chance subjects who lost their expectancy of success soonest.

In these early studies we gave one task to all subjects and told some that it was a skill task and others it was a chance task. To discover how subjects behaved when no such instructions were given, Douglas Crowne, Shephard Liverant and I repeated the study using two different tasks and no special instructions. We found that the "law" of partial reinforcement held true only when subjects thought their successes were the result of chance. Subjects who thought their rewards were due to skill actually took longer to extinguish their responses after constant (100 per cent) reinforcement than after partial (50 per cent) reinforcement. This is the opposite of what one would expect from the laws of animal learning. In this experiment half of the subjects guessed at hidden cards in an ESP test in which cultural expectancies led most of them to assume that success was primarily a matter of luck. The other subjects tried, by pulling a string, to raise a platform with a ball balanced on it—a task that is easily assumed to be a skill.

Actually, the experimenter could control the ball—keep it on the platform or let it fall off—so that both chance and skill subjects had the same sequence of success and failure.

Several other experiments have confirmed that, under skill conditions, constant-reward learning may take longer to extinguish than partial-reward learning. It has become increasingly clear that in chance situations other laws as well are quantitatively and qualitatively different from the laws that apply to skill learning.

I decided to study internal and external control (I-E), the beliefs that rewards come from one's own behavior or from external sources. The initial impetus to study internal-external control came both from an interest in individual differences and from an interest in explaining the way human beings learn complex social situations. There seemed to be a number of attitudes that would lead a person to feel that a reward was not contingent upon his own behavior, and we tried to build all of these attitudes into a measure of individual differences. A person might feel that luck or chance controlled what happened to him. He might feel that fate had preordained what would happen to him. He might feel that powerful others controlled what happened to him or he might feel that he simply could not predict the effects of this behavior because the world was too complex and confusing.

Scale. Phares first developed a test of internal-external control as part of his doctoral dissertation, and James enlarged and improved on Phares' scale as part of his doctoral dissertation. Later scales were constructed with the important help of several of my colleagues including Liverant, Melvin Seeman and Crowne. In 1962 I developed a final 29-item version of the I-E scale and published it in *Psychological Monographs* in 1966. This is a forced-choice scale in which the subject reads a pair of statements and then indicates with which of the two statements he more strongly agrees. The scores range from zero (the consistent belief that individuals can influence the environment—that rewards come from *internal* forces) to 23 (the belief that all rewards come from *external* forces).

A recent bibliography of studies of internal versus external control contains over 300 references. Most of these that deal with high-school or college students or adults use the 29-item scale. This test has also been translated into at least six other languages. Other successful methods of measuring I-E control have been devised and there are now four children's scales in use.

Degree. One conclusion is clear from I-E studies: people differ in the tendency to attribute satisfactions

Internal Control—External Control
A Sampler

Julian B. Rotter is the developer of a forced-choice 29-item scale for measuring an individual's degree of internal control and external control. This I-E test is widely used. The following are sample items taken from an earlier version of the test, but not, of course, in use in the final version. The reader can readily find for himself whether he is inclined toward internal control or toward external control, simply by adding up the choices he makes on each side.

I more strongly believe that:	OR
Promotions are earned through hard work and persistence.	Making a lot of money is largely a matter of getting the right breaks.
In my experience I have noticed that there is usually a direct connection between how hard I study and the grades I get.	Many times the reactions of teachers seem haphazard to me.
The number of divorces indicates that more and more people are not trying to make their marriages work.	Marriage is largely a gamble.
When I am right I can convince others.	It is silly to think that one can really change another person's basic attitudes.
In our society a man's future earning power is dependent upon his ability.	Getting promoted is really a matter of being a little luckier than the next guy.
If one knows how to deal with people they are really quite easily led.	I have little influence over the way other people behave.
In my case the grades I make are the results of my own efforts; luck has little or nothing to do with it.	Sometimes I feel that I have little to do with the grades I get.
People like me can change the course of world affairs if we make ourselves heard.	It is only wishful thinking to believe that one can really influence what happens in society at large.
I am the master of my fate.	A great deal that happens to me is probably a matter of chance.
Getting along with people is a skill that must be practiced.	It is almost impossible to figure out how to please some people.

and failures to themselves rather than to external causes, and these differences are relatively stable. For the sake of convenience most investigators divide their subjects into two groups—internals and externals—depending on which half of the distribution a subject's score falls into. This is not meant to imply that there are two personality types and that everyone can be classified as one or the other, but that there is a continuum, and that persons have varying degrees of internality or externality.

Many studies have investigated the differences between internals and externals. For example, it has been found that lower-class children tend to be external; children from richer, better-educated families tend to have more belief in their own potential to deter-

"Lower-class children tend to be external; children from richer, better-educated families tend to have more belief in their own potential to determine what happens to them."

mine what happens to them. The scores do not seem to be related to intelligence, but young children tend to become more internal as they get older.

Esther Battle and I examined the attitudes of black and white children in an industrialized Ohio city. The scale we used consisted of five comic-strip cartoons; the subjects told us what they thought one of the children in the cartoon would say. We found that middle-class blacks were only slightly more external in their beliefs than middle-class whites but that among children from lower socioeconomic levels blacks were significantly more external than whites. Herbert Lefcourt and Gordon Ladwig also found that among

young prisoners in a Federal reformatory, blacks were more external than whites.

Ute. It does not seem to be socioeconomic level alone that produces externality, however. Theodore Graves, working with Richard and Shirley L. Jessor, found that Ute Indians were more external than a group of Spanish-Americans, even though the Indians had higher average living standards than the Spanish-Americans. Since Ute tradition puts great emphasis on fate and unpredictable external forces, Graves concluded that internality and externality resulted from cultural training. A group of white subjects in the same community were more internal than either the Indians or the Spanish-Americans.

A measure of internal-external control was used in the well-known Coleman Report on Equality of Educational Opportunity. The experimenters found that among disadvantaged children in the sixth, ninth and 12th grades, the students with high scores on an achievement test had more internal attitudes than did children with low achievement scores.

One might expect that internals would make active attempts to learn about their life situations. To check on this, Seeman and John Evans gave the I-E scale to patients in a tuberculosis hospital. The internal patients knew more details about their medical conditions and they questioned doctors and nurses for medical feedback more often than did the external patients. The experimenters made sure that in their study there were no differences between the internals and externals in education, occupational status or ward placement.

Rules. In another study, Seeman found that internal inmates in a reformatory learned more than external inmates did about the reformatory rules, parole laws, and the long-range eco-

nomic facts that would help one get along in the outside world. These subjects did not differ from one another in intelligence—only in the degree of belief in internal or external control.

At a Negro college in Florida, Pearl Mayo Gore and I found that students who made civil-rights commitments to march on the state capitol during a vacation or to join a Freedom-Riders group were clearly and significantly more internal than the students who would only attend a rally or who were not interested at all. The willingness to be an activist seems to be related to previous experiences and the generalized expectation that one can influence his environment.

Studying a Negro church group in Georgia, Bonnie Strickland found that activists were significantly more internal than were nonactivists of similar educational and socioeconomic status.

Smoke. Phares wanted to see if internals really were more effective than externals in influencing their environments. He instructed his subjects to act as experimenters and try to change other college students' attitudes toward fraternities and sororities. Using a before-and-after questionnaire to assess

"Middle-class blacks were only slightly more external in their beliefs than middle-class whites but among children from lower socioeconomic levels blacks were significantly more external than whites."

these attitudes, Phares found that the internal subjects were much more successful than the external subjects in persuading students to change their minds.

It is not surprising that persons who believe that they can control their environments also believe that they can control themselves. Two studies have shown that nonsmokers are significantly more internal than smokers. After the Surgeon General's report, one study showed that male smokers who successfully quit smoking were more internal than other male smokers who believed the report but did not quit smoking. The difference was not significant with females, who apparently were motivated by other variables including, for example, one's tendency to gain weight after quitting.

Bet. Highly external persons feel that they are at the mercy of the environment, that they are being manipulated by outside forces. When they *are* manipulated, externals seem to take it in stride. Internals are not so docile. For example, Crowne and Liverant set up an experiment to see how readily their subjects would go along with a crowd. In a simple Asch-type conformity experiment in which there is one true subject plus several stooges posing as subjects, Crowne and Liverant found that neither internals nor externals were more likely to yield to an incorrect majority judgment. But when the experimenters gave money to the subjects and allowed them to bet on their own judgments, the externals yielded to the majority much more often than did the internals. When externals did vote against the majority they weren't confident about their independence—they bet less money on being right than they did when they voted along with the crowd.

Strickland also studied the way people react to being manipulated. In a verbal-conditioning experiment, she handed each subject a series of cards. On each card were four words—two nouns, a verb and an adjective. The subject simply picked one of the words. Strickland would say "good" whenever a subject picked the verb, for example, which was intended as a subtle social reward to get the subjects to pick more verbs.

In a thorough postexperiment interview she found out which subjects had caught on to the fact that she was dispensing praise ("good") systematically. There were no important differences among subjects who said they did not notice her system. But among subjects who were aware of her attempt to manipulate them, those who actually chose the verbs more often tended to be external—the internal subjects actively resisted being conditioned.

TATs. But internals are negative only when they think they are victims of hidden manipulation. If a manipulative system is out in the open—as in a typical student-teacher relationship—internals may choose to go along readily. Gore clarified this issue in a study in which she asked subjects to tell stories about TAT cards. She told them she was trying to test her theory about which cards produced the longest stories. In one group she told each subject which card she thought was best, and in this case there was no significant difference between the stories of internals and those of externals—the stories all tended to be a little longer than those of a control group that was not given biasing instructions.

But with another group she indicated her favorite picture more subtly—when she presented it to a subject she would smile and say, "Now let's see what you do with *this* one." In this condition, the internals made up much shorter stories than did either externals or control subjects who got no special suggestions. Internals actively resist subtle pressure.

Suspicion. Some externals, who feel they are being manipulated by the outside world, may be highly suspicious of authorities. With Herbert Hamsher and Jesse Geller, I found that male subjects who believed that the Warren Commission Report was deliberately covering up a conspiracy were significantly more external than male subjects who accepted the report.

To some degree externality may be a defense against expected failure but internals also have their defenses. In investigating failure defenses, Jay Efran studied high-school students' memories for tasks they had completed or failed. He found that the tendency to forget failures was more common in internal subjects than in external ones. This suggests that external subjects have less need to repress past failures because they have already resigned themselves to the defensive position that failures are not their responsibility. Internals, however, are more likely to forget or repress their failures.

Today's activist student groups might lead one to assume that our universities are filled with internals— people with strong belief in their ability to improve conditions and to control their own destinies. But scores on the same I-E test involving large numbers of college students in many localities show that between 1962 and 1971 there was a large increase in externality on college campuses. Today the average score on the I-E scale is about 11. In 1962 about 80 per cent of college students had more internal scores than this. The increase in externality has been somewhat less in Midwest colleges than in universities on the coasts, but there is little doubt that, overall, college students feel more powerless to change the world and control their own destinies now than they did 10 years ago.

Clearly, we need continuing study of methods to reverse this trend. Our society has so many critical problems that it desperately needs as many active, participating internal-minded members as possible. If feelings of external control, alienation and powerlessness continue to grow, we may be heading for a society of dropouts— each person sitting back, watching the world go by.

FAIL: Bright Women

A bright woman is caught in a double bind. In achievement-oriented situations she worries not only about failure but also about success.

by Matina Horner

This article, condensed from material in *Feminine Personality*, by Bardwick, Douvan, Guttman, and Horner, is printed with permission of Brooks-Cole Division of Wadsworth Publishing Company.

Consider Phil, a bright young college sophomore. He has always done well in school, he is in the honors program, he has wanted to be a doctor as long as he can remember. We ask him to tell us a story based on one clue: *After first-term finals, John finds himself at the top of his medical-school class.* Phil writes:

John is a conscientious young man who worked hard. He is pleased with himself. John has always wanted to go into medicine and is very dedicated...John continues working hard and eventually graduates at the top of his class.

Now consider Monica, another honors student. She too has always done well and she too has visions of a flourishing career. We give her the same clue, but with "Anne" as the successful student—*after first-term finals, Anne finds herself at the top of her medical-school class.* Instead of identifying with Anne's triumph, Monica tells a bizarre tale:

Anne starts proclaiming her surprise and joy. Her fellow classmates are so disgusted with her behavior that they jump on her in a body and beat her. She is maimed for life.

Next we ask Monica and Phil to work on a series of achievement tests by themselves. Monica scores higher than Phil.

Finally we get them together, competing against each other on the same kind of tests. Phil performs magnificently, but Monica dissolves into a bundle of nerves.

The glaring contrast between the two stories and the dramatic changes in performance in competitive situations illustrate important differences between men and women in reacting to achievement.

In 1953, David McClelland, John Atkinson and colleagues published the first major work on the "achievement motive." Through the use of the Thematic Apperception Test (TAT), they were able to isolate the psychological characteristic of a *need to achieve.* This seemed to be an internalized standard of excellence, motivating the individual to do well in any achievement-oriented situation involving intelligence and leadership ability. Subsequent investigators studied innumerable facets of achievement motivation: how it is instilled in children, how it is expressed, how it relates to social class, even how it is connected to the rise and fall of civilizations. The result of all this research is an impressive and a theoretically consistent body of data about the achievement motive—in men.

Women, however, are conspicuously absent from almost all of the studies.

In the few cases where the ladies were included, the results were contradictory or confusing. So women were eventually left out altogether. The predominantly male researchers apparently decided, as Freud had before them, that the only way to understand woman was to turn to the poets. Atkinson's 1958 book, *Motives in Fantasy, Action and Society,* is an 800-page compilation of all of the theories and facts on achievement motivation in men. Women got a footnote, reflecting the state of the science.

To help remedy this lopsided state of affairs, I undertook to explore the basis for sex differences in achievement motivation. But where to begin?

My first clue came from the one consistent finding on the women: they get higher test-anxiety scores than do the men. Eleanor Maccoby has suggested that the girl who is motivated to achieve is defying conventions of what girls "should" do. As a result, the intellectual woman pays a price in anxiety. Margaret Mead concurs, noting that intense intellectual striving can be viewed as "competitively aggressive behavior." And of course Freud thought that the whole essence of femininity lay in repressing aggressiveness (and hence intellectuality).

Thus consciously or unconsciously the

"The girls . . . showed anxiety about becoming unpopular, unmarriageable and lonely."

girl equates intellectual achievement with loss of femininity. A bright woman is caught in a double bind. In testing and other achievement-oriented situations she worries not only about failure, but also about success. If she fails, she is not living up to her own standards of performance; if she succeeds she is not living up to societal expectations about the female role. Men in our society do not experience this kind of ambivalence, because they are not only permitted but actively encouraged to do well.

For women, then, the desire to achieve is often contaminated by what I call the *motive to avoid success*. I define it as the fear that success in competitive achievement situations will lead to negative consequences, such as unpopularity and loss of femininity. This motive, like the achievement motive itself, is a stable disposition within the person, acquired early in life along with other sex-role standards. When fear of success conflicts with a desire to be successful, the result is an inhibition of achievement motivation.

I began my study with several hypotheses about the motive to avoid success:

1) Of course, it would be far more characteristic of women than of men.

2) It would be more characteristic of women who are capable of success and who are career-oriented than of women not so motivated. Women who are not seeking success should not, after all, be threatened by it.

3) I anticipated that the anxiety over success would be greater in competitive situations (when one's intellectual performance is evaluated against someone else's) than in noncompetitive ones (when one works alone). The aggressive, masculine aspects of achievement striving are certainly more pronounced in competitive settings, particularly when the opponent is male. Women's anxiety should therefore be greatest when they compete with men.

I administered the standard TAT achievement motivation measures to a sample of 90 girls and 88 boys, all undergraduates at the University of Michigan. In addition, I asked each to tell a story based on the clue described before: *After first-term finals, John (Anne) finds himself (herself) at the top of his (her) medical-school class.* The girls wrote about Anne, the boys about John.

Their stories were scored for "motive to avoid success" if they expressed any negative imagery that reflected concern about doing well. Generally, such imagery fell into three categories:

1) The most frequent Anne story reflected strong fears of social rejection as a result of success. The girls in this group showed anxiety about becoming unpopular, unmarriageable and lonely.

Anne is an acne-faced bookworm. She runs to the bulletin board and finds she's at the top. As usual she smarts off. A chorus of groans is the rest of the class's reply. . . . She studies 12 hours a day, and lives at home to save money. "Well it certainly paid off. All the Friday and Saturday nights without dates, fun—I'll be the best woman doctor alive." And yet a twinge of sadness comes thru—she wonders what she really has . . .

Although Anne is happy with her success she fears what will happen to her social life. The male med. students don't seem to think very highly of a female who has beaten them in their field . . . She will be a proud and successful but alas a very *lonely* doctor.

Anne doesn't want to be number one in her class . . . she feels she shouldn't rank so high because of social reasons. She drops down to ninth in the class and then marries the boy who graduates number one.

Anne is pretty darn proud of herself, but everyone hates and envies her.

2) Girls in the second category were less concerned with issues of social approval or disapproval; they were more worried about definitions of womanhood. Their stories expressed guilt and despair over success, and doubts about their femininity or normality.

Unfortunately Anne no longer feels so certain that she really wants to be a doctor. She is worried about herself and wonders if perhaps she isn't normal . . . Anne decides not to continue with her medical work but to take courses that have a deeper personal meaning for her.

Anne feels guilty . . . She will finally have a nervous breakdown and quit medical school and marry a successful young doctor.

Anne is pleased. She had worked extraordinarily hard and her grades showed it. "It is not enough," Anne thinks. "I am not happy." She didn't even want to be a doctor. She is not sure what she wants. Anne says to hell with the whole business and goes into social work—not hardly as glamorous, prestigious or lucrative; but she is happy.

3) The third group of stories did not even try to confront the ambivalence about doing well. Girls in this category simply denied the possibility that any mere woman could be so successful. Some of them completely changed the content of the clue, or distorted it, or refused to believe it, or absolved Anne of responsibility for her success. These stories were remarkable for their psychological ingenuity:

Anne is a *code name* for a nonexistent person created by a group of med. students. They take turns writing exams for Anne . . .

Anne is really happy she's on top, though *Tom is higher than she*—though that's as it should be . . . Anne doesn't mind Tom winning.

Anne is talking to her counselor. Counselor says she will make a fine *nurse*.

It was *luck* that Anne came out on top because she didn't want to go to medical school anyway.

Fifty-nine girls—over 65 per cent—told stories that fell into one or another of the above categories. But only eight boys, fewer than 10 per cent, showed evidence of the motive to avoid success. (These differences are significant at better than the .0005 level.) In fact, sometimes I think that most of the young men in the sample were incipient Horatio Algers. They expressed unequivocal delight at John's success (clearly John had worked hard for it), and projected a grand and glorious future for him. There was none of the hostility, bitterness and ambivalence that the girls felt for Anne. In short, the differences between male and female stories based on essentially the same clue were enormous.

Two of the stories are particularly revealing examples of this male-female contrast. The girls insisted that Anne give up her career for marriage:

Anne has a boyfriend, Carl, in the same class and they are quite serious . . . She wants him to be scholastically higher than she is. Anne will deliberately lower her academic standing the next term, while she does all she subtly can to help Carl. His grades come up and Anne soon drops out of medical school. They marry and he goes on in school while she raises their family.

But of course the boys would ask John to do no such thing:

John has worked very hard and his long hours of study have paid off . . . He is thinking about his girl, Cheri, whom he will marry at the end of med. school. He realizes he can give her all the things she desires after he becomes established. He will go on in med. school and be successful in the long run.

Success inhibits social life for the girls; it enhances social life for the boys.

Earlier I suggested that the motive to avoid success is especially aroused in competitive situations. In the second part of this study I wanted to see whether the aggressive overtones of competition against men scared the girls away. Would competition raise their anxiety about success and thus lower their performance?

First I put all of the students together in a large competitive group, and gave them a series of achievement tests (verbal and arithmetic). I then assigned them randomly to one of three other experimental conditions. One-third worked on a similar set of tests, each in competition with a member of the same sex. One-third competed against a member of the opposite sex. The last third worked by themselves, a non-competitive condition.

Ability is an important factor in achievement motivation research. If you want to compare two persons on the strength of their *motivation* to succeed, how do you know that any differences

"a woman learns that it really isn't ladylike to be too intellectual."

in performance are not due to initial differences in *ability* to succeed? One way of avoiding this problem is to use each subject as his own control; that is, the performance of an individual working alone can be compared with his score in competition. Ability thus remains constant; any change in score must be due to motivational factors. This control over ability was, of course, possible only for the last third of my subjects: the 30 girls and 30 boys who had worked alone *and* in the large group competition. I decided to look at their scores first.

Performance changed dramatically over the two situations. A large number of the men did far better when they were in competition than when they worked alone. For the women the reverse was true. Fewer than one-third of the women, but more than two-thirds of the men, got significantly higher scores in competition.

When we looked at just the girls in terms of the motive to avoid success, the comparisons were even more striking. As predicted, the students who felt ambivalent or anxious about doing well turned in their best scores when they worked by themselves. Seventy-seven per cent of the girls who feared success did better alone than in competition. Women who were low on the motive, however, behaved more like the men: 93 per cent of them got higher scores in competition. (Results significant at the .005.)

Female Fear of Success & Performance

	perform better working alone	perform better in competition
high fear of success	13	4
low fear of success	1	12

As a final test of motivational differences, I asked the students to indicate on a scale from 1 to 100 "How important was it for you to do well in this situation?" The high-fear-of-success girls said that it was much more important for them to do well when they worked alone than when they worked in either kind of competition. For the low-fear girls, such differences were not statistically significant. Their test scores were higher in competition, as we saw, and they thought that it was important to succeed no matter what the setting. And in all experimental conditions—working alone, or in competition against males or females—high-fear women consistently lagged behind their fearless comrades on the importance of doing well.

These findings suggest that most women will fully explore their intellectual potential only when they do not need to compete—and least of all when they are competing with men. This was most true of women with a strong anxiety about success. Unfortunately, these are often the same women who could be very successful if they were free from that anxiety. The girls in my sample who feared success also tended to have high intellectual ability and histories of academic success. (It is interesting to note that all but two of these girls were majoring in the humanities and in spite of very high grade points aspired to traditional female careers: housewife, mother, nurse, schoolteacher. Girls who did not fear success, however, were aspiring to graduate degrees and careers in such scientific areas as math, physics and chemistry.)

We can see from this small study that achievement motivation in women is much more complex than the same drive in men. Most men do not find many inhibiting forces in their path if they are able and motivated to succeed. As a result, they are not threatened by competition; in fact, surpassing an opponent is a source of pride and enhanced masculinity.

If a woman sets out to do well, however, she bumps into a number of obstacles. She learns that it really isn't ladylike to be too intellectual. She is warned that men will treat her with distrustful tolerance at best, and outright prejudice at worst, if she pursues a career. She learns the truth of Samuel Johnson's comment, "A man is in general better pleased when he has a good dinner upon his table, than when his wife talks Greek." So she doesn't learn Greek, and the motive to avoid success is born.

In recent years many legal and educational barriers to female achievement have been removed; but it is clear that a psychological barrier remains. The motive to avoid success has an all-too-important influence on the intellectual and professional lives of women in our society. But perhaps there is cause for optimism. Monica may have seen Anne maimed for life, but a few of the girls forecast a happier future for our medical student. Said one:

Anne is quite a lady—not only is she tops academically, but she is liked and admired by her fellow students—quite a trick in a man-dominated field. She is brilliant—but she is also a woman. She will continue to be at or near the top. And . . . always a lady.

Impulse, Aggression and the Gun

By Leonard Berkowitz

In November of 1966, Robert Benjamin Smith, then 18 years old, entered a beauty shop in Mesa, Arizona, and shot seven strangers, killing five of them. He said he had been planning the murder for three months, ever since his parents gave him a 22-caliber pistol for target practice. His original inspiration, he went on, was the preceding summer's mass killings in Chicago and Austin, Texas.

Almost everyone in the United States read about the murder of the eight Chicago nurses and about the massacre from the University of Texas tower, and millions of Americans own guns. But we cannot disregard Smith's remarks simply because they do not completely explain his behavior.

Now, more than ever before, there is need to answer the question: what effect *do* available weapons and vicarious experience with violence have on a person who is "ready" to commit an aggressive act?

Two series of experiments that my colleagues and I have performed on impulsive aggression bear directly on these questions. The first series indicates that even so small a matter as the casual sight of a gun can sometimes stimulate aggressive behavior. The second suggests that, contrary to what the so-called catharsis theory predicts, the sight of violence can increase the chance that a viewer will express aggression himself.

In experiments to test the effect of the presence of guns on aggressiveness, we observed the behavior of 100 students at the University of Wisconsin under different sets of circumstances. Some students were angry and some were not, some saw the guns and some did not. (We did not reveal the study's real purpose, claiming instead to be measuring the students' physiological reaction to stress.)

The stress, we informed them, would be a series of one or more mild electric shocks. We asked each student to make a list of ideas a publicity agent could use to improve the record sales and public image of a popular singer. Then we gave each student a "partner," ostensibly another experimental subject but actually an ally of the experimenter. The pretend partner's task was to evaluate the student's publicity ideas. If the partner thought the student's ideas were very good, he would give him one electric shock; if he thought the student's work was bad, he would administer up to 10 shocks. Later, the student would be asked to evaluate a similar task of his partner's, and to convey his judgment in the same way.

By prearrangement with the experimenter, the partners gave one shock to half the students and seven shocks to the other half, regardless of the quality of the students' ideas. We assumed that the seven-shock students would feel physically uncomfortable and that they would feel humiliated as well. They were our angry group.

After each student had received the number of shocks allotted to him, the experimenter invited him to trade places with his partner and led him into the room containing the shock machine. The telegraph key that would send the shocks lay on a table at one end of the room. Sometimes the table was empty except for the key; at other times, badminton racquets and shuttlecocks (neutral objects) lay near the key. At still other times, the table held a 12-gauge shotgun and a snub-nosed .38 revolver.

The experimenter acted surprised at the sight of the guns and the racquets and explained that they had been "left over from another experiment." Matter-of-factly, he moved them aside. The students seemed to pay little or no attention to them. Later on, after the experiment was over, the experimenter asked each student what, if any, suspicions the student had felt. No doubts were voiced about the presence of the weapons.

Next, the experimenter showed the student his partner's "work" (actually prepared in advance and uniform for all partners). He reminded the student that he should use shocks to indicate his evaluation of his partner's work and he told the student that this was the last time shocks would be administered in the study.

As we suspected, the presence of the guns affected both the number of shocks the students gave their partners and how long they held the key down for each shock. Some differences between groups were less clear-cut than others; from a statistical point of view, our most significant finding was that the angry men who saw the guns gave more shocks than any other group.

Both common sense and personality theory tend to neglect the "weapons effect" that this study demonstrates. Instead, they stress motives and, perhaps, psychological and social dislocations. What is often overlooked, perhaps because it is a frightening idea, is that much violence is *impulsive*. It is not primarily planned, purposeful activity; neither is it the "inevitable" result of internal drives or maladjustments. These things set the stage and help carry the action forward, but in many cases it is also important that there be a stimulus or immediate cue to trigger aggression.

It is quite conceivable that many hostile acts which supposedly stem from unconscious motivation really arise because of the operation of aggressive cues. The aggression can even be thought of as a conditioned response to the stimulus. If a gun can be that stimulus, then it is a double-barreled threat—an immediate cue that also presents the aggressor with a deadly *means* of aggression.

With our subjects, the guns did not enhance aggression unless the students were angry to begin with. But studies conducted at the University of Indiana show that, at least with young children, anger is not necessarily a factor. In these experiments, youngsters played with an older child whom the psychologist in charge had asked to behave in a friendly, neutral way. There was no quarreling. Then some of the children were given toy guns to play with while others chatted quietly with adults conducting the experiment.

After this preparation, each child was told that the older youngster he had played with earlier had built a structure of blocks on a play table in another room. "If you push this button on my desk, you'll shake the table and his blocks will fall down," the experimenter said. *More of the children who had played with guns pushed the button.*

Neither group of children was angry, but the guns had an effect. Guns did more than lower the children's restraints against aggression; they seemed to pull out aggressive reactions that would not otherwise have occurred. Anger may not always be *necessary* in aggressive behavior, but it certainly facilitates it. And our society offers its citizens a wide array of anger-producing frustrations. It is not necessary to detail them here. It should be mentioned, though, that aggression is more likely to result from unrealized hopes than from deprivation alone. The deprived person who has no hope cannot really be said to be frustrated, because he does not really have a goal he is trying to move toward. A person works harder to get something—whether it is food, a sexual object, or a new car—if he thinks he has a chance. Similarly, his frustration is most severe when he is blocked from a satisfaction he thinks should and could be his.

In social terms, this concept of frustration reveals itself in "revolutions of rising expectations." Poverty-stricken groups are not frustrated merely because they have suffered severe deprivations; they are frustrated when they begin to hope. Privation is far less likely to cause violence than is the dashing of hopes. [*See "Conflict, Crisis and Collision" by Ivo and Rosalind Feierabend, PT, May 68*]. Even given high frustration and an immediate cue, violence will not erupt unless there is a third factor as well: low inhibitions. The "normal" level of inhibitions to violence in our society is not particularly high. We take a lenient attitude toward what is sometimes called defensive aggression. It is quite permissible, even admirable, for a man to defend with vigor not only himself but his family, his home and his country, and not only his physical safety but his principles of honor, law and democracy. Even defensive aggression that is quite violent and smacks more of revenge than defense tends to be seen as an act of courage, a mark of manhood.

The air that hovers over Hollywood and New York (not to mention Washington) smells of the frontier, and one can detect a breeze from the Crusades as well. Nowhere is violence in the cause of good more consistently and more enthusiastically touted than in movies and on TV. Fictional representations of violence are often defended, by people in the industries that sell them and also by many consumers, on the grounds that they serve a cathartic purpose. The theory, loosely derived from Aristotle's view of the function of tragedy, contends that violence which is indulged in vicariously drains a reservoir of accumulated hostility and releases tensions that might otherwise explode into actual violent behavior.

This theory receives additional support from the ideas and writings of the eminent ethologist, Konrad Lorenz. Lorenz stresses the physiological rather than the psychological as a source of behavior: behavior results, he says, from the spontaneous accumulation of some excitation or substance in neural centers. He believes that "present-day civilized man suffers from insufficient discharge of his aggressive drive," and he recommends that society provide people with "safe" ways of venting their aggressive urge.

The question is, do vicarious or real-but-innocuous "outlets" in fact reduce the chances that aggressive behavior will occur? Although many psychologists continue to subscribe to the catharsis theory in some form, many others believe (and have demonstrated in experiments) that witnessed violence can stimulate actual violence and that a little aggression, like a snowball, can gather momentum and grow.

Let us examine the results of another series of studies. In this series, a group of students was made angry by ridicule and electric shock. Then, just before it was *their* turn to administer shocks, they were shown one of two movies. One was an exciting but nonviolent foot race between the first two men to run the mile in less than four minutes. The other was a violent scene from *Champion*, the Kirk Douglas movie in which the prize fighter played by Douglas absorbs a brutal beating in the ring.

The students who saw this movie had been given two different plot summaries to prepare them for the scene. Half were led to regard the beating as justified: Douglas was a heel who had it coming. The other half heard a summary that was much more sympathetic to Douglas: it was clear that he did not deserve what he got.

The filmed violence was not cathartic; in fact, it had an opposite effect, at least on the students who thought the beating was justified. When given a chance to administer shocks to the partners who earlier had delivered shocks to them, these students responded with more aggression than any other group. Rather than feeling purged of their hostility, the students seemed to feel freer to express it. It was as if the justified aggression on the screen justified as well their own aggression against their tormenters.

These findings have been confirmed in five independent experiments, the most recent of which was conducted by James Hoyt and Percy Tannenbaum, now at the University of Pennsylvania. Hoyt and Tannenbaum presented the prize fight to some of the angry students as a grudge-match. Douglas had behaved badly to his opponent, and now the opponent wanted revenge. These students gave more intense shocks than the other angry students, who had simply been reminded that violence was an inevitable part of prize fights.

Results like this present an awkward problem to TV and movie censorship agencies, and to producers who want to make violent films without encouraging real violence. The modern censorship agencies generally insist that crime and violence be used not just to entertain but to teach a lesson—"crime does not pay," for example. How the lesson should be taught is left vague; scriptwriters usually follow the maxim of "an eye for an eye."

But justified aggression is precisely the kind that seems likeliest to encourage the expression of aggression by members of the audience.

The effect is different if violence, though justified, seems excessive. If the punishment is badly out of proportion with the victim's crime, all aggression becomes less acceptable to the viewer, and his inhibitions rise. When some of the angry students who saw the boxing film were told that the fight had very serious results—Douglas was carried unconscious to his dressing room and died there—the scales that had been unbalanced by Douglas' villainy tipped the other way. These students gave fewer shocks to their experimental partners than those who were told the beating merely taught Douglas a lesson and induced him to reform.

In some ways, this is an encouraging finding. It means that viewed violence does not *necessarily* encourage actual violence. It can either lower inhibitions or raise them, depending on the viewer's interpretation of what he sees. Horror is an inhibiting emotion, and violence that strikes the viewer as disproportionate—as "too much" or "too real" —is likely to arouse horror. Many people who enjoyed *Champion* would not enjoy a front-row seat at a real prize fight in Madison Square Garden; many people who like war movies are extremely disturbed by photographs and news clips of the actual fighting in Vietnam.

However, the line between violence that is justified and unjustified, fictional and real, uninhibiting and inhibiting, is anything but clear. To take just one example, the television screen itself puts distance between the viewer and what he sees. Watching a riot on television may be horrifying, but it is less horrifying than being there. The emotional effect of a 90-minute documentary on riots is not so very different from the effect of a documentary-type movie about riots; the effect of a documentary-type movie is not so different from that of a "realistic drama"; and so it goes.

At some point on the continuum, viewed violence *stops* horrifying and *starts* exciting. Once this point has been reached, vicarious experience with aggressiveness begins to lower restraints against the real thing.

And it may begin to do something else as well. Like the guns in the experiment described earlier, witnessed violence can serve as a stimulus for the viewer, especially if he encounters someone he associates with the deserving victim in what he has just seen. At the beginning of the boxing film study, the partners of half the students were introduced as "Kirk" and the partners of the rest were called "Bob." The students who were led to believe that Kirk Douglas' beating was *justified* later gave more shocks to the "Kirks" than to the "Bobs."

In another experiment on this kind of mental association, students lost a chance to win a cash prize because (they thought) their partners had made a mistake. Soon afterwards, the students were asked to evaluate two job applicants, one of whom had the same first name as the partner. The students consistently saw more bad qualities in the applicant who bore the partner's name.

Thus associations help determine the target of an aggressive attack—or, to put it another way, the stimulus properties of a possible target can affect the probability that an attack will occur.

In some cases, however, stimulus and target are not related—all that is required is that both be present. In a study conducted at the University of Iowa, C. A. Loew had college students speak either aggressive or neutral words aloud in what the students thought was the first step of a learning task. Later, when these students were given an opportunity to shock their partners for errors, the ones who had said the aggressive words gave stronger shocks than the others.

As for the snowball effect, when experimental subjects are given a number of opportunities to attack, the intensity of their attacks more often than not builds up. By their own actions, the subjects—even if they are not emotionally aroused to begin with—provide their own aggressive stimuli and pull out further aggressive responses. Aggression stimulates more aggression.

The social implications of the research I have described are clear, though they are much easier to recite than to act on. A society that wants fewer violent outbursts should reduce frustration, leave inhibitions intact and remove immediate cues that can set off aggressive acts.

Reducing frustration in the United States, especially the frustration of social groups, is a long-term project that is receiving considerable attention. I will do no more here than recall the phrase "revolution of rising expectations" and mention that, for many people, expectations are likely to outstrip reality for a long time to come.

Leaving more of people's inhibitions against aggressiveness intact is, I think, a slightly less difficult matter. Is it really necessary to use violence as a major source of entertainment? The catharsis theory does not hold up very well, and the frontier tradition may not be as strong as we think. Perhaps people enjoy violent books and movies more because they are absorbing than because they are violent. Books and movies in which violence plays a small part, or no part at all, are also absorbing; we might be able to arrange to have more of these.

The third possibility, reducing the number of aggressive stimuli people encounter from day to day, is probably the easiest one to effect, and the fastest. This may seem a surprising statement—deciding to remove aggressive stimuli from American life is a little like setting out to clean the Augean stable. But the task seems more manageable when one realizes that most aggressive stimuli fall into only a few large categories, one of the largest of which bears the label "Guns." Guns not only permit violence, they can stimulate it as well. The finger pulls the trigger, but the trigger may also be pulling the finger.

VII. disorders and therapy

Mental disorder is not a new problem, brought about by the stress of living in an overcrowded, technologically oriented world. Almost every culture has had to deal with madness. The earliest documentation of mental disorder was found on a fragment of an Egyptian tomb carving from 5000 B.C. that describes the demonic possession of a princess. In ancient Greece, priests firmly believed that madness was brought about by the will of the gods, whereas people like Hippocrates searched for a physiological basis. In early Rome, there was a more descriptive and empirical approach to psychopathology, and medical malpractice and inhumane treatment of the mentally ill ceased. The Roman approach did not last long, however; medicine went downhill and demonology returned once the Dark Ages began. In the Dark Ages, the devil was seen to be the cause of all madness, and it was a long time before mental disorder was again treated with understanding. The progenitor of modern psychiatry was undoubtedly Sigmund Freud. It was Freud's theorizing that enabled psychoanalytic theory and psychotherapy to achieve so noteworthy a place in contemporary society. But Freud's approach merely provided the spark for an explosion of techniques developed to assist the troubled mind.

Today mental illness is considered the nation's number-one health problem. About twenty million Americans (one out of every ten people in the United States) are said to suffer from one form or another of mental disorder. Half of the hospital beds in the United States are occupied by patients with psychiatric problems. The problems faced by psychologists and psychotherapists are not only problems of the best methods of treatment; the definition of mental disorder—of what abnormality consists of—is still unresolved. Although many different kinds of psychotherapy—from psychoanalysis to group therapy to transactional analysis—have been developed, psychologists and psy-

chotherapists argue the relative effectiveness of each. And some psychologists strongly challenge the notion of "mental illness," suggesting that the troubled person may only be maladjusted to an ill society.

One of the most severe forms of abnormal behavior is infantile autism. As C. B. Ferster states, case histories indicate that autistic children have faced severely damaging situations more often than other children have. Ferster wants to determine more precisely the causes of autism, be they the environment, predisposing biological factors, or an interaction of both. Although there is no effective cure for autism as yet, parallels between autism and adult schizophrenia may provide clues for cures to both types of disorder. One method of treating autism is demonstrated by a clinical psychologist that Ferster has worked with.

In treating schizophrenics, psychiatrists and psychologists often have to deal with their patients' jumbled utterances. Brendan Maher seeks an answer to the most vexing problem in deciphering schizophrenic language: determining the system by which patients choose words when they try to communicate with others. Even if the patients are not trying to communicate at all, the language pattern may hint at what is troubling them. Breaking the code of schizophrenic language could significantly improve the effectiveness of therapy by enabling therapists to better understand and communicate with schizophrenic patients.

Many psychologists search for causes of abnormal behavior in physiological abnormalities. Ashley Montagu, for example, suggests that a specific genetic aberration is the cause of certain types of criminal insanity. He cites several studies that show a significantly higher percentage of males with the XYY chromosomal constitution in prisons and prison hospitals than in the general population. However, Montagu also mentions the ethical and social implications of categorizing a person on the basis of a certain genetic make-up.

Therapy for the mentally ill may take a variety of forms. In an interview with Mary Harrington Hall, Carl Rogers, the father of client-centered therapy, discusses the usefulness and legitimacy of the group-therapy experience. Rogers gives valuable insights into what constitutes effective therapy and why the group experience should be regarded as a major force and potent phenomenon.

David Orlinsky and Kenneth Howard describe the "typical" therapeutic session and then compare it with the patient's ideal session. Their research provides insight into the nature of the actual psychotherapeutic experience, as seen through the eyes of both the therapist and the patient.

Fanita English describes the principles of another form of therapy, transactional analysis. To show how the transactional analyst's role differs from that of a traditional psychoanalyst, English describes the therapeutic treatment of a woman patient in detail. She traces the development of the patient's greater awareness of feelings and shows how the patient acquires more successful ways of dealing with her feelings.

Learning theory can also contribute to the therapeutic process. Operant conditioning, based on the principle that a response or behavior that is reinforced is likely to occur again, is the method that Irene Kassorla and her associates used to train a mute catatonic schizophrenic to speak. Kassorla's study suggests that many psychotics regress once they are admitted to mental hospitals because they lack a reliable schedule of positive reinforcements for desired behavior. It may be possible to help disturbed people by transferring the control of behavior to natural reinforcers such as the opportunity to play, she says.

Everything has its pitfalls, including treatment. This is Everett Shostrom's assumption as he provides a type of "consumer's guide" to group therapy. He explores the guidelines for choosing an encounter group and presents some valuable hints on which groups not to choose and why. Shostrom also recognizes the importance of group therapy and the need to form effective groups to meet the great demand. He discusses why individuals might need group therapy and the kinds of benefits that they can derive from it.

Behavior therapy, says Hans Eysenck, is a more scientific way of treating mental disorder than is psychotherapy. In fact, he says that the recovery rate of untreated neurotics and those who undergo long-term psychotherapy is about the same. Behavior therapy, on the other hand, has provided concrete, measurable results through the use of "treatment" machines, aversion therapy, and other operant-conditioning techniques.

Julian Meltzoff and Melvin Kornreich argue against Eysenck's position; they believe that psychotherapy does bring about positive changes. They urge psychotherapists to welcome the investigations of researchers, because only through research can the effectiveness of psychotherapy be accurately measured and the most effective therapeutic techniques for certain types of people and problems be determined.

Thomas Szasz questions the whole concept of mental illness and the laws that permit involuntary incarceration for mental disorder. A person may claim to be perfectly well, but if that person's friends and a group of psychiatrists say he is sick, he can be committed to an institution against his will. Szasz, concerned with the legal rights of mental patients, wonders if it is proper to commit them for the protection of society when they have done nothing wrong. He insists that committing people to mental institutions to keep them from potentially disturbing others is a form of social control and, like slavery, an unjustifiable crime.

By C. B. Ferster

the autistic child

There are children who live in a world no one can enter. Is there any way to reach them?

THE AUTISTIC CHILD lives in a cage of unbreakable glass. He cannot reach out, and no one can reach in. A good part of the time the child does nothing but sit quietly in a chair, or sleep, or lie huddled in a corner. At other times he is active, sometimes violently so, but his activity affects only himself. He may spend hours compulsively rubbing a rough spot on the floor, moving his fingers in front of his face, babbling to himself, licking his body like a cat, or flipping sand to produce a visual pattern. He may beat his head against the wall, hit himself until he is covered with bruises, or use his fingernails and teeth to tear his own flesh.

Some autistic children are mute. Others make inarticulate sounds or echo bits of the speech they hear around them. But they do not talk to or with other people. When an autistic child does try to communicate, it is by biting, kicking, screaming, having tantrums—primitive forms of behavior, called *atavisms,* which create a situation others will go to almost any lengths to eliminate.

If one were to watch an autistic child for a day and then watch a normal child for a month, one would see much of the autistic child's behavior reproduced by the normal child. Almost any child, on occasion, will gaze out the window for an hour or more, make bizarre faces or have severe tantrums. Any child may run sticks over picket fences, step on (or over) all the cracks in the sidewalk, or chew a piece of rubber balloon to shreds.

But normal children are only out of touch with their surroundings once in a while, and primitivisms are not their only form of behavior. They interact with their physical and social environment in many different ways. The autistic child's behavior is far more restricted. He has very few ways of changing and being changed by the world around him.

Since his behavioral repertoire is so small, what there is of it is used over and over again. It is the *frequency* of withdrawn, self-stimulatory or atavistic behavior, not simply the fact that it occurs, which distinguishes the autistic child from the normal one.

Autism is a very rare disorder, affecting only one child out of 50,000 or 100,000. We need to know how autism comes about and how it may be treated not only because these few children desperately need help but because the study of autism contributes to our understanding of other forms of behavior. There are parallels, for example, between the development of autism in young children and the development of schizophrenia in adolescents. In addition, the past experiences of the autistic child, like his present behavior, differ from those of the normal child not so much in *kind* as in *intensity* and *frequency.*

We do not know yet whether the causes of autism are biological or environmental, or both. Parents of autistic children sometimes report that the child seemed "different" from birth, that he stiffened each time he was picked up. Some autistic children have shown neurological anomalies such as abnormal EEG patterns. So far, however, the evidence for an inborn biological deficiency is meager.

A child's environment can have very dramatic effects on his behavioral development. This has been shown repeatedly. There have been infants who spent most of their early lives locked in closets and became primitive, animal-like children. There also have been primitive, animal-like children who have learned new forms of behavior when a new environment was arranged for them. Thus it makes sense to examine the surroundings of the autistic child for circumstances that might explain the gross deficiencies in his behavior.

The major processes by which behavior is acquired and lost are *reinforcement* and *extinction.* If a rat receives a pellet of food when it presses a bar, the rat will press the bar more and more often. When the pellets are no longer delivered, bar-pressing decreases in frequency and finally stops. Similarly, a person's ordinary speech usually is reinforced by the reply it gets, and a speaker who gets no reply soon stops talking. Behavioral processes are harder to observe in a natural social environment than in an experimental laboratory, but they operate similarly.

The very limited repertoire of the autistic child may come about because his behavior is not successful. Ted is an example of an autistic child whose behavioral development was thwarted because little of his behavior was reinforced. At first this was hard to see, because Ted's mother did not seem unresponsive. She was a very active woman who moved busily around the house, accomplishing many tasks and talking a great deal.

The child, however, was prevented from completing any action he happened to begin. When he reached for a lamp, his mother appeared as if by magic to seize his hand and hold it back. When he reached for the doorknob, again she intercepted him. When he approached his brothers and sisters, his mother separated them. When he held out a receipt he had gotten from the newsboy, she walked past and left him standing with the slip of paper in his hand.

Even the mother's speech did not make contact with the boy. While the boy was in the living room, his mother called him from the kitchen. "Ted, come over here," she said. "I want to read you a story. Ted, Ted, don't you want to read a story? Ted, come over here and read a story. TED, where are you?"

Ted paid no attention. After five minutes of calling, the mother came into the living room and picked up the book. She continued to call, "TED, TED, TED. . . . Come on and read your book." When he happened to wander near enough, she took hold of him, sat him down next to her, and began to read.

The boy did not object and seemed happy to sit with his head against his mother's shoulder. But it was obvious that the physical contact was what kept him there. The reading was irrelevant, as was most of the mother's speech.

In short, only a tiny part of the mother's behavior had a reinforcing effect on the child. Furthermore, by interrupting or ignoring his attempts to do things for himself she was preventing him from successfully completing an action—any action—of his own.

Sometimes a child's behavior succeeds only under very specific conditions—with one particular person, for example. If the circumstances suddenly change, a great deal of behavior can be lost. This happened to a little girl of four, who spent a year in the care of a teen-age baby-sitter.

The girl's mother was a very disturbed, nearly psychotic, woman. She remained in the home while the baby-sitter was there, but she had nothing whatever to do with the child. If the child said "Mom, can I have a cookie?" there was no answer. If she said "Janet, can I have a cookie?" Janet said yes and gave her a cookie. If the girl said "Let's go out," the mother did not answer. Janet might reply and take the child outside.

This situation might be compared to that of a laboratory pigeon being trained to peck a green key instead of a red key. If the pigeon pecks the green key, a piece of grain appears, but if it pecks the red key, nothing happens. After a while the pigeon doesn't bother pecking the red key at all.

When the baby-sitter left at the end of the year, this child lost almost her whole behavioral repertoire. She became incontinent, she talked less and less, she could not be kept in nursery school. Eventually she needed chronic care at a state home for the retarded. The reason for this massive loss of behavior was not just the sudden switch in caretakers but the fact that the mother had been present the *same time* as the baby-sitter. If the mother had been away for the year and had been able to respond normally to the child when she returned, there probably would have been only a slight, temporary break in behavior. If the mother had been away but had *not* been able to treat the child normally when she came back, the same severe loss probably would have occurred, much more slowly.

Parents and children constantly influence each other's behavior. Even punishment is usually more productive than no reaction to the child at all.

This is not to say that punishment is a desirable form of behavioral control. Although its main effect is to *strengthen* behavior that avoids or ends the punishment, punishment can weaken behavior if all positive reinforcement is withdrawn. If a parent not only spanks a child but refuses to speak to him for the rest of the day, he may reduce the frequency of parts of the child's repertoire that he did not intend to affect.

In addition, punishment can promote less advanced forms of behavior. Punishment is most likely to be dispensed when a child is doing something fairly active, such as finger painting on the wall or trying to drive his parents' car. A child who sits on the kitchen floor studying his fingers will probably be left alone. If a child is consistently punished when he tries to have a strong effect on the environment, such attempts will begin to produce considerable anxiety. So the child may substitute simpler activities, such as rubbing a spot on the floor.

He may also resort to primitive controlling behavior, like screaming and tantrums. If he finds that he *can* affect his environment in this way, he is likely to keep on using atavisms in preference to other behavior.

When one sees the amount of control some autistic children exert over their parents by means of tantrums and other atavisms, it is hardly surprising that the behavior is so durable. One child's parents told us that they took turns standing guard all night at the door of his room because a tantrum started if

they left and ceased only when they moved back. Another mother slept with her arm over her child every night for five months, so that she could stop him when he woke and clawed at his face.

Everything described so far—lack of reinforcement, sudden changes in its source, the withdrawal of approval, and practices that encourage primitive behavior—also occurs in the lives of children who do not become autistic. Accounting for the autistic child's massive failure of development therefore presents a problem. The explanation seems to be that the autistic child has faced more severely damaging situations more often than the normal or nearly normal child. Most of the evidence that this is true is anecdotal, but compelling.

One often finds, for instance, that autistic children have parents who are completely unable to respond to the child's behavior. A parent who is a drug addict, an alcoholic, chronically ill or severely depressed may not even acknowledge the child's existence for days on end. One also finds parents who have beaten, tortured, starved or incarcerated their children for long periods of time. One woman kept her child in a dog run.

When we look at the child rather than the parents, we often discover a history of serious or chronic illness during infancy. In such cases, the child's standard way of communicating with the parents usually has been to cry and fret. After the child recovers, the crying may persist, and the parents may very well keep on reacting. So the child deals with the parents through primitive behavior, and the parent responds in order to end the behavior. The child's development, already retarded by his illness, may progress no farther.

A child is not usually identified as autistic until some complex form of behavior (such as speech) fails to develop —that is, until the child is two, three or even four years old. Although this does not prove that autism was not present earlier (indeed, parents occasionally report deviant behavior in very young infants), it does suggest a careful examination of that period in the child's life when the disorder may express itself.

A two-year-old is at a stage of development when his behavior is especially vulnerable to disruption. For one thing, he is more likely than a younger child to provoke a negative reaction from his parents. The activities of a baby are simple and relatively unobtrusive. But when a child begins to crawl, walk, reach for ashtrays and lamps, and cry loudly when crossed, he may also begin to frighten and upset his parents and thus to invite the kind of treatment that weakens behavior.

Furthermore, the child's new behavior is not at all firmly established. New behavior develops fastest when it has a consistent, reliable effect on the environment. Since the child can only approximate what he is trying to do at first, his

efforts succeed only part of the time. If an enthusiastic parental response is lacking too, the child may very well abandon the behavior.

Sometimes a parent will praise the child's first nonsense syllables but become angry a month later when the child still cannot speak in complete, intelligible sentences. This sudden shift in the performance required for reinforcement can have the same effect on the child as suddenly requiring a laboratory pigeon to peck 300 times instead of 25

for a piece of grain: the behavior stops.

However, sudden changes in the kind and amount of behavior required for reinforcement are more likely to occur in adolescence than in early childhood. A 10-year-old may need do no more than hold out his hand for his allowance or run next door to find a playmate. A 16-year-old is expected to work for his money and to master an elaborate courtship ritual. At school, where assignments

used to be frequent and short, the teenage student may have to work for weeks or months before he finds out from the teacher how he is doing. In general, the adolescent must perform a substantial number of specific acts before his behavior is reinforced, often without benefit of a complete series of intermediate, transitional experiences.

If the change in kind or amount of behavior an adolescent must deliver is too sudden or too large, the effect on his development can be disastrous. One can-

not build the Empire State Building if there is only a toothpick holding up the 20th floor. One schizophrenic boy had a job as a truck driver before he was hospitalized; he would not stop at the restaurant where the other drivers ate because he did not know how to order food from the waitress. Another young man in the ward had frequent and violent temper tantrums; their source turned out to be his inability to tie his shoelaces.

Autistic children are very difficult to treat. Until recently, they were considered virtually hopeless. So much of the normal repertoire is missing; a long history of experiences must be recreated; dealing with a six-year-old child as if he were one or two years old presents innumerable problems. Some therapists have succeeded with prolonged residential treatment. In addition, recent experimental attempts have sometimes produced dramatic changes in the children's behavior. Even when these experiments are not entirely successful from a therapeutic point of view—when, for example, the changes do not last—they represent progress, because they show the child's potential for development.

One promising approach to rehabilitation is illustrated by a project that I am participating in at the Linwood Children's Center for autistic children, located between Washington, D.C. and Baltimore. The Director of the Center, Jeanne Simons, is chiefly a clinician, and I am chiefly an experimentalist. What we are trying to do is produce a kind of model for cooperative work between the two fields.

During our collaboration we found that our methods are a great deal alike. I tend to approach an experiment, even in the animal laboratory, from a clinical point of view; Miss Simons manipulates the environment in her clinic much as I do in the laboratory. I might be called a sheep in wolf's clothing, and she a wolf in sheep's clothing.

Miss Simons is an unusually gifted therapist. Like many gifted therapists, she has trouble explaining to other workers how she gets her results. Her metaphors—"Walk behind the child so that you can see where he is going"—describe the principles of operant reinforcement very well, but they helped the staff little in everyday dealings with the children.

Here was an area where an experimentalist could help. A functional analysis of Miss Simons' methods, in objective language, would make it easier for the staff to understand and evaluate them. It would also give Miss Simons a new perspective on her own work.

As I watched Miss Simons deal with the children, I saw the application of every principle of behavior that I know. But I did not always recognize them at first. There was one boy who teased Miss Simons by pulling her hair. When she continued to give him her full attention, I wondered why. It seemed clear that her attention was reinforcing the annoying behavior. But when I looked more closely, I saw that Miss Simons was holding the boy's wrist close to her hair so that he couldn't pull it. She released her grip only when he made a move toward some more desirable kind of behavior.

To illustrate the kind of thing Miss Simons does (and the way behavioral language can clarify it), I will describe an encounter she had with an autistic girl named Karen.

Karen was mute and she had very little contact with her environment. She would cry continuously and softly, and she had a doll that she always carried with her.

The encounter took place only a short time after Karen arrived at Linwood, and it was the child's first sustained interaction with another person. It lasted for about half an hour. During that time, there were perhaps 200 instances in which Miss Simons' behavior was clearly contingent on that of the child. The general therapeutic goals were to diminish Karen's crying, weaken the compulsive control of the doll, and begin developing more constructive forms of behavior that Karen could use to manipulate the environment herself. The third goal was the most important, and during the encounter it became clear that the extinction of the crying and the weakened control of the doll were by-products of the reinforcement of other behavior.

Miss Simons placed Karen on a rocking horse in the playroom and began to rock her and sing to her. The rocking and singing stopped the child's crying. Then, for brief periods, Miss Simons kept on singing but stopped rocking. She sensed very accurately how long the pause could be without the child's beginning to cry again.

After a few minutes of this, the therapist took the doll from the child and placed it on a table. But she moved the table very close to Karen so that the child could easily take the doll back again. When she leaned over to do so,

Karen rocked *herself* slightly. From then on, Miss Simons sang only when Karen rocked herself, which Karen did more and more frequently.

Miss Simons placed the doll on the table several times and the child calmly took it back. Then Karen *herself* put the doll on the table. Miss Simons began to rock the horse vigorously. The intensity of her voice as she sang kept pace with the rocking.

Up to this time, Miss Simons sang whenever the child rocked herself, but now she occasionally did not sing even though the child rocked. As this new situation began, Karen took the doll back off the table—having been without it for more than a full minute for the first time since her arrival at Linwood.

As she picked up the doll, it accidentally dropped to the floor. Karen began

to cry. "Do you want to pick it up?" Miss Simons asked. "I'll help you." She lifted Karen off the horse and the *child* picked up the doll. When Miss Simons asked if she wanted to get up again, Karen raised her hands and Miss Simons helped her climb back into the saddle.

Karen dropped the doll again, and again Miss Simons helped her pick it up and get back on the horse. This time Karen came closer to mounting by herself, though Miss Simons still provided some support. The therapist rocked the horse vigorously and moved the doll to a couch, not far away but out of reach, and she stopped the rocking for a moment. Karen glanced at the doll and then withdrew her attention. Miss Simons picked up the doll and tapped it rhythmically; Karen looked at her, made a sound, and began to rock in time with the tapping. Miss Simons gave her the doll.

The next time the therapist took the doll away, Karen cried but kept on rock-

ing. Miss Simons began to sing, which stopped the crying. Then she took the child off the horse so that Karen could get the doll from the couch. They sat together on the couch for a few moments, the child on the therapist's lap. When Karen tried to persuade Miss Simons to go back to the horse by pulling her arm in that direction, Miss Simons smiled and picked the child up but carried her in another direction.

Here there seemed to be a deliberate switch in contingencies. Miss Simons had developed a repertoire of performances in Karen that involved the rocking horse. Now she had shifted to a new set of reinforcers, picking Karen up and interacting with her through body contact and singing. She did not reinforce any attempts to go back to the horse. I don't know what Miss Simons would have done if Karen had struggled in her arms and continued gesturing toward the horse, but I suspect she knew this was improbable before she made the shift.

Even though the behavioral processes that operated here were the same ones I knew from laboratory experience, I would not have been able to put them into practice as Miss Simons did. For example, I might have kept Karen on the horse, without the doll, until her crying stopped. What Miss Simons did instead was wait until Karen's behavior was strongly controlled by rocking and singing before she took the doll away. Later, when Karen dropped the doll and began to cry, Miss Simons reacted at once and used the doll itself to reward the girl for picking it up.

Observation of Jeanne Simons' therapy has taught me many new ways in which the behavior of autistic children can be developed. As for her, she says she is more aware of her own actions. She sees more clearly the individual elements in her complex interchange with a child and has a better understanding of the specific effect of each small act. This helps her refine and modify her procedures and also allows her to describe them more clearly for the staff.

"I think I can explain little step-by-step procedures now so that people don't just look blindly at me with awe," she says. "I'm not even sure intuition is so mysterious. I think it's having eyes all over the place and seeing the tiny little things that children are doing. . . . And I am able to see the tiny little steps and explain much better what I am doing with the children. So the magic is out of Linwood—which I think is wonderful!" ∩

the Shattered Language of Schizophrenia

By Brendan A. Maher

SOMEWHERE IN A HOSPITAL WARD a patient writes: "The subterfuge and the mistaken planned substitutions for that demanded American action can produce nothing but the general results of negative contention and the impractical results of careless applications, the natural results of misplacement, of mistaken purpose and unrighteous position, the impractical serviceabilities of unnecessary contradictions. For answers to this dilemma, consult Webster." The document is never sent to anyone; it is addressed to no one; and perhaps intended for no reader.

Another patient, miles away, writes: "I am of I-Building in B..State Hospital. With my nostrils clogged and Winter here, I chanced to be reading the magazine that Mentholatum advertised from. Kindly send it to me at the hospital. Send it to me Joseph Nemo in care of Joseph Nemo and me who answers by the name of Joseph Nemo and will care for it myself. Thanks everlasting and Merry New Year to Mentholatum Company for my nose for my nose for my nose for my nose for my nose."

A British patient writes: "I hope to be home soon, very soon. I fancy chocolate eclairs, chocolate eclairs, Doenuts. I want some doenuts, I do want some golden syrup, a tin of golden syrup or treacle, jam . . . See the Committee about me coming home for Easter my twenty-fourth birthday. I hope all is well at home, how is Father getting on. Never mind there is hope, heaven will come, time heals all wounds, Rise again Glorious Greece and come to Hindoo Heavens, the Indian Heavens, The Dear old times will come back. We shall see Heaven and Glory yet, come everlasting life. I want a new writing pad of note paper . . ." *

Yet another writes: "Now to eat if one cannot the other can — and if we cant the girseau Q.C. Washpots prize-bloom capacities — turning out — replaced by the head patterns my own capacities — I was not very kind to them. Q.C. Washpots under-patterned against — bred to pattern. Animal sequestration capacities and animal sequestired capacities under leash — and animal secretions . . ."*

Experienced clinicians, when called upon to diagnose the writers of language like this, agree closely with each other (80 per cent of the time or more). The diagnosis: schizophrenia. Nearly every textbook on psychopathology presents similar examples, and nobody seems to have much difficulty in finding appropriate samples. It would seem obvious that there must be a well-established and explicit definition of what characteristics language must possess to be called schizophrenic. But when we ask clinicians to tell us exactly what specific features of an individual language sample led them to decide that the writer was schizophrenic, it turns out that they aren't exactly sure. Instead of explicit description, the expert comment is likely to be: "It has that schizophrenic flavor" or "It is the confusion of thought that convinces me."

Impressionistic descriptions abound. The language is described as *circumlocutious, repetitive, incoherent,* suffering from an *interpenetration of ideas, excessively concrete, regressed,* and the like. Doubtless, all of these descriptions have merit as clinical characterizations of the language. Unfortunately, they are quite imprecise, and they give us no adequate basis for developing theoretical accounts of the origin of schizophrenic language. This is, of course, hardly surprising. Quantitative studies of language have been notoriously laborious to undertake. However, two recent developments in behavioral sciences have combined to change the situation quite significantly. The first of these is the development of language-analysis programs for computer use, and the second is the increasing sophistication of psycholinguistics as a framework for the study of applied problems in the psychology of language.

Before turning to look at the consequences of these developments, we should glance at the kinds of hypotheses that have already been advanced to account for schizophrenic language. The first of these might be termed the *Cipher Hypothesis.* In its simplest form this says that the patient is trying to communicate something to a listener (actual or potential) but is afraid to say what he means in plain language. He is somewhat in the same straits as the normal individual faced with the problem of conveying, let us say, some very bad news to a listener. Rather than come right out and tell someone directly that a family member

*These quotations are taken from "The Neurology of Psychotic Speech" by McDonald Critchley

is dying, the informant may become circumlocutious and perhaps so oblique that his message simply does not make sense at all.

In the case of the schizophrenic patient, however, it is assumed that the motives which drive him to disguise his message may be largely unconscious—that he could not put the message into plain language if he tried. Where the normal person is trying to spare the feelings of the listener by his distortions and evasions, the patient purportedly is sparing his own feelings by the use of similar techniques. This analogy can be stretched a little further. Just as the normal speaker is caught in a dilemma —the necessity to convey the message and the pressure to avoid conveying it too roughly—so the patient is caught in a conflict between the necessity of expressing himself on important personal topics and the imperative need to avoid being aware of his own real meanings. Thus, so the Cipher Hypothesis maintains, it is possible in principle to decipher the patient's message—provided one can crack the code. This hypothesis assumes, of course, that there really is a message.

Obviously, the Cipher Hypothesis owes its genesis to psychoanalytic theory. In essence, it is identical with Freud's interpretation of the relationship between manifest and latent dream content. Unfortunately, from a research point of view, this hypothesis suffers from the weakness of being very hard to disprove. No two patients are assumed to have the same code, and so the translation of schizophrenic language into a normal communication requires a detailed analysis of the case history of the individual writer. As the code that is discovered for any one case cannot be validated against any other case, the hypothesis rests its claim to acceptance upon its intrinsic plausibility *vis-à-vis* the facts of the life history of the patient. But plausible interpretations of a patient's language may reflect the creative (or empathetic) imagination of the clinician, rather than a valid discovery of an underlying process governing the patient's utterances.

One more or less necessary deduction from the Cipher Hypothesis is that language should become most disorganized when the topic under discussion is one of personal significance, and less disorganized when the topic is neutral. To date, no adequate test of this deduction has been reported. In the absence of this or other independent tests of the Cipher Hypothesis, it must be regarded for the time being as, at best, an interesting speculation.

A second explanation has been that the patient's communications are confusing and garbled precisely because he wishes to *avoid* communicating with other people. This hypothesis, which we shall call the *Avoidance Hypothesis,* interprets the disordered language as a response that is maintained and strengthened by its effectiveness in keeping other people away. Presumably, the normal listener becomes frustrated or bored with such a speaker and simply goes away, leaving the schizophrenic in the solitude he seeks. This theory rests, in turn, upon the assumption that the patient finds personal interactions threatening. We might expect that casual interactions—such as chatting about the weather—are relatively unthreatening and do not provoke avoidant disorder in language. The language disturbance should become more evident when the threat of personal involvement arises.

At this level, the Avoidance Hypothesis cannot be distinguished from the Cipher Hypothesis. The main difference between the two is that the Avoidance Hypothesis is concerned with a *dimension* of incomprehensibility and does not imply that the incomprehensible can be unscrambled. Both of these hypotheses have their attractions.

"For answers to this dilemma, consult Webster," wrote the first patient we have quoted. Is he just playing a word game with an imaginary reader or is there a meaning to his message? We might remark on the similarity of the prefix in many of the words he uses: *subterfuge, substitution; unrighteous, unnecessary; mistaken, misplacement; contention, contradiction.* His message might, indeed, sound like a random sampling from a dictionary.

Or did the dictionarylike nature of the "message" only occur to the patient himself toward the end—and hence the closing remark? In any event, the sample seems to fit plausibly into the notion that some kind of enciphering was going on between the patient's basic "message" and the language that he wrote.

Our fourth sample of schizophrenic language, on the other hand, seems to be absolutely incomprehensible. Fragments of phrases, neologisms ("girseau") and repetitions—*sequestration* and *sequestired*—combine into a jumble that seems to defy understanding. It is hard to believe that there might be a message in disguise here, or even that the language was uttered with any wish to communicate.

Although both hypotheses can be made to seem plausible, they are intrinsically unsatisfying to the psychopathologist. They do not deal with the most fascinating problem of schizophrenic language: why does a particular patient utter the particular words that he does, rather than some other jumbled-up sequence?

ome beginnings of an answer to this question have begun to emerge. Years ago, Eugen Bleuler commented on the presence of *interfering associations* in schizophrenic language. He suggested that the difficulty for the patient was that ideas associated with the content of his message somehow intruded into the message and thus distorted it. A patient of his, whom he had seen walking around the hospital grounds with her father and son, was asked who her visitors were. "The father, son and Holy Ghost," she replied. These words have a strong mutual association as a single phrase and although the last item, "Holy Ghost," was probably not meant as part of her message, it intruded because of its strong associative links with other units in the message.

Bleuler also noticed the difficulty that patients seemed to have in *understanding* a pun, despite their tendency to talk in punning fashion. A patient asked about her relationships with people at home says, "I have many ties with my home! My father wears them around his collar." The pun on the word *tie* was unintentional, hence humorless.

Against the background of this general hypothesis of interfering associations, my students and I began investigations of schizophrenic language some years ago in Harvard's Laboratory of Social Relations. Our first concern was with the original question of definition. What must language contain to be labeled schizophrenic? Our work began with a plea to over 200 hospitals for examples of patients' writings—whether the patients were schizophrenic or not. Colleaguial response was rather overwhelming, and we amassed a very large number of letters, documents, diaries and simple messages written in almost every state of the Union. (Many of these were inappropriate to our purposes. A carton load of documents in

Planned sentence: I have pains in my chest and wonder if there is something wrong

Associations:

aches	**(weak)**	**(strong)**
doctor	ribs	BOX
	lungs	TRUNK
	body	HOPE

right
bad
failure

Utterance: "Doctor, I have pains in my chest and hope and wonder if my box

---

Spanish from a Texas hospital, some brief obscenities scribbled on match-covers and dropped daily onto the desk of a colleague in a St. Louis hospital and other similar items were eliminated, of course.)

From this mass, we selected a set of documents that were legible, long enough to include several consecutive sentences—and written in English. These texts were then read by a panel of clinicians. Each text was judged independently, and then was classified as *schizophrenic language* or *normal language*. (We obtained typical interjudge agreements of around 80 per cent.) At this juncture we did not know whether the writers of the letters had been diagnosed as schizophrenic or not. Our concern was with the characteristics of the language—and with the clinicians' reactions to it.

Our two sets of texts then were submitted for computer analysis with the aid of the *General Inquirer* program. This program codes and categorizes language in terms of content, and also provides a summary of grammatical features of the language. Out of this analysis, we developed some empirical rules (or a guide on how to write a document that a clinician will judge schizophrenic). Two of the most reliable rules were:

1. Write about politics, religion or science. Letters dealing with global social issues of this kind are highly likely to be regarded as schizophrenic by clinicians.

2. Write more *objects* than *subjects* in sentences. Typical sentences consist of enumerations of classes of objects in a form illustrated in our second and third examples above: "send it to me, Joseph Nemo, in care of Joseph Nemo and

me who answers by the name of Joseph Nemo"; or "I fancy chocolate eclairs, chocolate eclairs, doenuts." Or in chains of associations at the end of a sentence. When, for example, a woman patient writes: "I like coffee, cream, cows, Elizabeth Taylor," the associational links between each word and the one following seem obvious.

This kind of associative chaining already had been described clinically by Bleuler; hence it was hardly surprising that the computer should find it to be a reliable discriminator in our document samples. What began to interest us, however, was the fact that these associations interfere most readily at the end of a sentence. Why not chains of subjects or chains of verbs, and why not at the beginning or middle of a sentence? Furthermore, why is this kind of interference found clearly in some schizophrenic patients and yet never occurs at all in others?

For some time it has become increasingly apparent that, in schizophrenia, *attention* is greatly disrupted. It is hard for a patient to remain focused on any one stimulus for any length of time. He is unable to "tune out" or ignore other surrounding stimuli. These distract him; they enter consciousness at full strength and not in an attenuated fashion as they do with the normal person. Reports by the patients themselves make the point dramatically:

"Things are coming in too fast. I lose my grip of it and get lost. I am attending to everything at once and as a result I do not really attend to anything."[*]

"Everything seems to grip my attention, although I am not particularly interested in anything. I am speaking to you just now but I can hear noises going

on next door and in the corridor. I find it difficult to concentrate on what I am saying to you."[*]

"I cannot seem to think or even put any plans together. I cannot see the picture. I get the book out and read the story but the activities and the story all just do not jar me into action."[*]

xperimental tasks that require close attention, tasks that call for fast reactions to sudden stimuli, or any continuous monitoring of a changing stimulus field are almost invariably done poorly by schizophrenics. Sorting tasks, where the subject must organize objects or words into conceptual groups, are progressively more difficult for the schizophrenic if irrelevant or puzzling factors appear in the material.

We may regard the focusing of attention as a process whereby we effectively inhibit attention to everything but certain relevant stimuli in the environment. As attention lapses, we find ourselves being aware of various irrelevant stimuli —the inhibitory mechanism has failed temporarily.

It is possible that an analogous set of events takes place when we produce a complex sequence of language. Attention may be greater or lesser at some points in a language sequence than at others. The end of a sentence—the period point—may be particularly vulnerable to momentary attentional lapses: one thought has been successfully completed, but the next one may not yet have been formed into utterable shape. Within a single sentence itself, there may be other points of comparative vulnerability, though not perhaps as marked as at the sentence ending.

Uttering a sentence without disrup-

[*] *These quotations are taken from McGhie & Chapman's "Disorders of Attention in Schizophrenia"*

beat
soul → save → heaven
broken

s broken and heart is beaten for my soul and salvation and heaven, Amen.”

tion is an extremely skilled performance, but one that most of us acquire so early in life that we are unaware of its remarkable complexity. (However, we become more aware of how difficult it is to "make sense" when we are extremely tired, or ripped out of sleep by the telephone, or distraught, or drunk.)

Single words have strong associational bonds with other words—as the classic technique of word association indicates. We know that the word "black" will elicit the response "white" almost instantaneously from the majority of people. The associational bond between black and white is clearly very strong. Strong as it is, it will not be allowed to dominate consciousness·when one is uttering a sentence such as "I am thinking about buying a black car." Our successful sentences come from the successful, sequential inhibition of all interfering associations that individual words in the sentence might generate. Just as successful visual attention involves tuning out irrelevant visual material, so successful utterance may involve tuning out irrelevant verbal static.

By the same token, disordered attention should lead to an increasing likelihood that this kind of interference will not be inhibited, but will actually intrude into language utterance. Its most probable point of intrusion is wherever attention is normally lowest.

"Portmanteau" words or puns provide unusually good occasions for disruptive intrusions. Consider, for example, the word "stock." This word has several possible meanings, each of them with its own set of associations. Financial associations might be *Wall Street, bonds, dividend,* etc. Agricultural associations might include *cattle, barn* and *farm;* theatrical associations might be *summer, company*

and the like. Webster's Third International Dictionary gives 42 different definitions of the word *stock*, many of them archaic or unusual, but many of them common. If one set of meanings intrudes into a sentence that is clearly built around another set of meanings, the effect is a pun, and an accompanying digression or cross-current in surface content. The sentences—"I have many ties with my home. My father wears them around his collar,"—seem to skip, like a stone on a lake, from *ties* (bonds) to *home* to *father* to *ties* (neckties). On the surface, this is a witty statement, but the speaker had no idea of what was really going on inside or underneath the form of words. The statement was therefore unwitting and hence unwitty.

Loren Chapman and his associates, in work at Southern Illinois University, demonstrated that schizophrenics as a group are more open to interference from the most common meaning of a punning word. When we use a word like *stock* as a stimulus for word association, we discover that most normal respondents give financial associations first, and may find it difficult to respond when asked to "give associations to another meaning." Associations to the other meaning are weaker or less prepotent, and only emerge under special instructional sets. Chapman's work suggests that if the plan of a sentence calls for the use of a weaker meaning, the schizophrenic runs some risk that associational intrusions will interfere and actually produce a punning effect.

On the other hand, if the plan of a sentence involves the stronger meaning, then there may be no intrusion of associations. And if associations do intrude,

these intrusions will appear relevant to the sentence and will not strike the listener as strange. Which meanings will be strong or weak will depend to some extent upon the culture from which the patient comes. (Personal experience may of course produce uniquely strong or weak associations in individual cases.) However, Chapman was able to predict correctly the direction of errors for schizophrenic patients as a group on the basis of estimates of strength obtained from normal respondents. Thus, some patients may have personal idiosyncracies, but the associations that interrupt the schizophrenic are generally the same as those that are strong for the population at large.

A parallel investigation I conducted at the University of Copenhagen included a study of the language of Danish schizophrenics. I observed the same general effect: patients were liable to interference from strong meanings of double-meaning words. English is a language, of course, that is unusually rich in puns, homonyms, cognates and indeed a whole lexicon of verbal trickery. But it seems plausible to suppose that in any language in which double-meaning words are to be found, this kind of schizophrenic disturbance may be found.

From these observations we can begin to piece together a picture of what happens when schizophrenic intrusions occur in a sentence that started out more or less normally. Where a punning word occurs at a vulnerable point, the sequence becomes disrupted and rapidly disintegrates into associative chaining until it terminates. [*See illustration, above.*]

We may look at schizophrenic utterances as the end result of a combination of two factors: the vulnerability of sentence structure to attentional lapses, and the inability of patients to inhibit associational intrusions, particularly at these lapse points. From this point of view, the problem of language is directly related to the other attentional difficulties which the schizophrenic has; he is handicapped in making language work clearly, just as he is at any other task that requires sustained attention. The emotional significance of what the schizophrenic plans to say may have little or no bearing on when an intrusion occurs, or what it seems to mean. Any sentence with vulnerable points in its syntactic or semantic structure may result in confusion, whether the topic is of great psychological importance or has to do with a patient's harmless liking for chocolate eclairs and doughnuts.

Serious and sustained difficulties in the maintenance of attention suggest a biological defect. Peter Venables at the University of London has suggested swimming or unfocusable attention in schizophrenia may be connected with low thresholds of physiological arousal—stimuli can be very weak and yet trigger strong physiological reactions. This low arousal threshold is found mostly in acute, rather than chronic, schizophrenia.

Evidence from studies of a variety of attentional tasks supports this interpretation. Additional and intriguing evidence was obtained by one of my students, Dr. Joy Rice at the University of Wisconsin. Using electrochemical (galvanic) changes in the skin as a measure, she found that schizophrenic patients who were most responsive to noise stimulation were also the patients who showed the most difficulty in dealing with the meaning of punning sentences. The magnitude of galvanic skin response to external stimulation is presumably greatest in patients with low initial arousal levels (and hence the most receptivity to external stimulation). Rice's data may therefore support the notion that verbal associational interference is part and parcel of a total syndrome of which biological control of attention is a crucial central focus.

recent research into the effects of LSD has shown that it is people with low initial arousal systems who have the "good trips"; the most cursory glance at literary biography will reveal an extraordinary number of poets and writers who were "sensitive," "neurasthenic," and so on. Which leads me to a sort of Parthian speculation.

Look again at the four samples quoted in the beginning of this article. What you see there, I think, is the literary imagination gone mad, if I may use so unclinical a term here. The first sample, had it come from the pen of someone whose brain we trusted, might almost be a crude parody of ponderous political tracts or socio-economo-political gobble-dygook of one sort or another. In the second, the fragment, "With my nostrils clogged and Winter here," is really not bad, and one wouldn't be terribly surprised to find it occurring in, say, the *Cantos* of Ezra Pound. In the third quotation, there are unmistakable echoes from the New Testament, Lord Byron, and Ralph Waldo Emerson, or rather echoes from an entire chamber of the literary heritage. The kind of wordplay indulged in throughout the fourth quote is not essentially different technically from that employed by the later James Joyce, or by the John Lennon of *In his own write*.

What is lacking from these samples, so far as we can tell, is context and control and the critical, or pattern-imposing, intelligence. It would seem, therefore, that the mental substrata in which certain kinds of poetry are born probably are associative in a more or less schizophrenic way. (In the case of poets like Dylan Thomas or Hart Crane, of course, these substrata had to be blasted open by liquor.) The intelligence that shapes, cuts, edits, revises and erases is fed by many conscious sources, most of them cultural; but the wellsprings seem to be, as poets have been telling us for centuries, sort of divine and sort of mad. ♋

Chromosomes and Crime

By Ashley Montagu

Are some men "born criminals"? Is there a genetic basis for criminal behavior? The idea that criminals are degenerates because of "bad genes" has had wide appeal.

Johann Kaspar Spurzheim and Franz Joseph Gall, the inventors of phrenology early in the 19th Century, associated crime with various bumps on the head, reflecting the alleged structure of the particular region of the brain within. Later in the last century, Cesare Lombroso, an Italian criminologist, listed physical stigmata by which criminals might be recognized. Lombroso's marks of degeneration included lobeless and small ears, receding chins, low foreheads and crooked noses. These traits supposedly foretold of a biological predisposition to commit crimes.

In more recent years, Earnest A. Hooton of Harvard and William H. Sheldon of New York claimed to have found an association between body type and delinquent behavior. These claims, however, were shown to be quite unsound.

Of all the tales of "bad blood" and "bad genes," perhaps the two most famous are those of the "Jukes" and the "Kallikaks." The tale of the Jukes was first published in 1875 by Richard L. Dugdale, a New York prison inspector. In his report, "The Jukes: A Study in Crime, Pauperism, Disease, and Heredity," Dugdale covers seven generations, 540 blood relatives and 169 related by marriage or cohabitation. Although Dugdale did not invent the Jukes, he often fell back upon his imagination to bolster his theory of the hereditary causes of crime when the facts failed. When information about individuals was hard to come by, Dugdale resorted to such characterizations as "supposed to have attempted rape," "reputed sheep-stealer, but never caught," "hardened character" and the like.

The Kallikaks were studied by Henry H. Goddard, director of a school for the mentally retarded in New Jersey. In his report, published in 1912, he followed the fortunes and misfortunes of two clans of Kallikaks. Both were descended from the same Revolutionary War

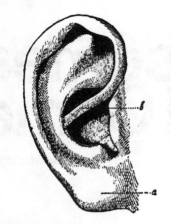

Criminal ear—one of Lombroso's marks of degeneration, from *Criminal Man* by Gina Lombroso Ferrero, Putnam's, 1911

soldier. The bad Kallikaks sprang from this soldier's union with a feeble-minded girl, who spawned a male so bad that he became known as "Old Horror."

"Old Horror" fathered 10 other horrors and they in turn became responsible for the hundreds of other horrible Kallikaks traced by Dr. Goddard. All of the good Kallikaks were descendants, of course, from the Revolutionary War soldier's marriage with a Quaker woman of good blood. Since none of the good Kallikaks seems to have inherited any "bad genes," something rather strange must have occurred in the lineage, for we know that a certain number of the good offspring should have shown some "degenerate" traits.

The Jukes and the Kallikaks are sometimes quoted as examples of what "good" and "bad" genes can do to human beings. While it is possible that a genetic defect may have been involved in some of these pedigrees, the disregard by the investigators of environmental effects renders their work valueless except for their quaint, anecdotal style of reporting.

The question of whether a man's genetic make-up may be responsible for his committing acts of violence has again come forward in the courts.

In France this year, Daniel Hugon was charged with the murder of a prostitute. Following his attempted suicide, he was found to be of XYY chromosomal constitution. Filled with remorse, Hugon had voluntarily surrendered to the police. His lawyers contended that he was unfit to stand trial because of his abnormality.

Richard Speck, the convicted murderer of eight nurses in Chicago in 1966, also is reported to be an XYY.

Tall, mentally dull, with an acne-marked face and a record of 40 arrests, Speck presents a characteristic example, both genotypically and phenotypically, of the XYY type. Whether he was "born to raise hell" as a consequence of his chromosomal constitution, or whether his impoverished social environment would have been a sufficient condition, or whether both were necessary for his fateful development, no one at the moment is in a position to say.

The possible link between an XYY chromosomal constitution and criminals first came to light three years ago in a study of prison hospital inmates. In December 1965, Patricia A. Jacobs and her colleagues at Western General Hospital in Edinburgh published their findings on 197 mentally abnormal inmates undergoing treatment in a special security institution in Scotland. All had dangerous, violent or criminal propensities.

Seven of these males were found to be of XYY chromosomal constitution, one was an XXYY, and another an XY/XXY mosaic. Since on theoretical grounds the occurrence of XYY males in the general population should be less frequent than the XXY type (the latter type occurs in some 1.3 out of 1,000 live births), the 3.5 per cent incidence of XYY males in a prison population was a highly significant finding.

There is still too little information available concerning the frequency of XYY males among the newly born or adults, but there is little doubt that the frequency found by Jacobs and her colleagues is substantially higher than that in the general population. Few laboratories yet are able to do chromosome studies on a large scale, so information available is based on limited population samples from small areas. Current estimate of the frequency of XYY males at birth range from 0.5 to 3.5 per 1,000.

Jacobs also found that the XYY inmates were unusually tall, with a mean height of 6 feet 1.1 inches. Males in the institution with normal XY chromosomal constitution had a mean height of 5 feet 7 inches.

Since publication of the paper by Jacobs and her co-workers, about a dozen other reports have been published on XYY individuals, and all the reports confirm and enlarge upon the original findings. [*See illustration opposite*.] However, in many of these cases only inmates 6 feet or more in height were selected for study, so care must be taken in interpreting the findings.

In a sample of 3,395 prison and hospital inmates, 56 individuals were XYY, nine others had supernumerary Ys in one combination or another. Only eight of the inmates were XXY. Supernumerary Y chromosomes in any other combination are only one-fifth as frequent as the XYY—a significant fact that suggests it is the YY complement in the presence of a *single* X chromosome that constitutes the most frequent anomaly.

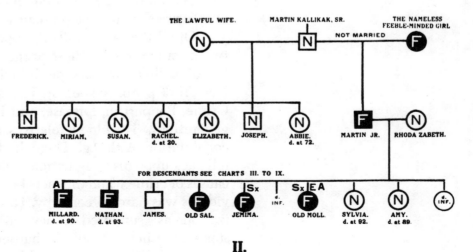

II.

CHART II.

N = Normal   F = Feeble-minded.   Sx = Sexually immoral   A = Alcoholic.   I = Insane.   Sy = Syphilitic.   C = Criminalistic.   D = Deaf.
d. inf. = died in infancy.   T = Tuberculous.

The good and the bad Kallikaks, from *The Kallikak Family* by Henry H. Goddard,
© Macmillan, 1912 (copyright renewed 1940 by Henry H. Goddard)

No.	Population	Status	Height Inches	Intelligence	Traits	XYY	XXYY	XY/XXY	XXY	XYY/XYYY	XYYY	Investigator
10,725	Maternity	Newborn				—	1	5	12	—	—	Maclean, N. et al. *Lancet*, i: 286-290, 1964.
2,607	Ordinary			Subnormal		—	2	—	—	—	—	Maclean, N. et al. *Lancet*, i: 293, 1962.
197	Security	Criminal	73.1	Subnormal		7	1	1	—	—	—	Jacobs, P. et al. *Nature*, Vol. 208: 1351, 1352, 1965.
942	Institutional	Criminal		Subnormal		12	7	2	—	—	—	Casey, M. et al. *Nature*, Vol. 209: 641, 642, 1966.
50	Institutional Mentally ill	Non-criminal				4	—	—	—	—	—	Casey, M. et al. *Lancet*, i: 859, 860, 1966.
24	Institutional	Criminal				2	—	—	—	—	—	Casey, M. et al. *Lancet*, i: 859, 860, 1966.
315	Security	Criminal	6 over 72	8 Subnormal 1 Schizophrenic		9	—	—	—	—	—	Price, W. et al. *Lancet*, i: 565, 566, 1966.
464	Institutional	Delinquent		Subnormal	Aggressive Grand mal	1	—	—	—	—	—	Welch, J. et al. *Nature*, Vol. 214: 500, 501, 1967.
19	Detention center	Criminal Sex crimes	74.1	I.Q. 83	Negro Acne	1	—	—	—	—	—	Telfer, M. et al. *Lancet*, i: 95, 1968.
129	Institutional	Criminal	+72			5	—	—	7	—	—	Telfer, M. et al. *Science*, Vol. 159: 1249, 1250, 1968.
34	Prison	Criminal	69-82½	2 Subnormal	Psychopathic	3	—	—	—	1	—	Wiener, S. et al. *Lancet*, i: 159, 1968.
1,021	Institutional Boys	Delinquent	Tall	I.Q. s 77, 78, 91	Property offenses	3	—	—	1	—	—	Hunter, H. *Lancet*, i: 816, 1968.
200	Institutional	Criminal	+72		Aggressive Sex offenders	9	—	—	—	—	—	Vanasek, F. et al., Atascadero State Hospital, Calif. (in press), 1968.
1	Ordinary	Embezzlement	78	I.Q. 118	Not overtly aggressive Depressed	1	—	—	—	—	—	Leff, J. and Scott, P. *Lancet*, i: 645, 1968.
1	Ordinary	8 yrs. 7 mo.	57	I.Q. 95	Aggressive	1	—	—	—	—	—	Cowie, J. and Kahn, J. *British Medical Journal*, Vol. 1: 748, 749, 1968.
1	Ordinary	5 yrs. 6 mo.		I.Q. 85	Undescended testes Simian creases	—	—	—	—	—	1	Townes, P. *Lancet*, i: 1041-1043, 1965.
1	Ordinary	44 yrs.	72	Average	Trouble keeping jobs	1	—	—	—	—	—	Hauschka, T. et al. *American Journal of Human Genetics*, Vol. 14: 22-30, 1962.
1	Ordinary	12 yrs.		Average	Undescended testes	1	—	—	—	—	—	Sandberg, A. et al. *New England Journal of Medicine*, Vol. 268: 585-589, 1963.

However, the presence of an extra Y chromosome, in any combination, appears to increase the chances of trouble. It also seems that the presence of an extra X chromosome, no matter what the number of extra Y chromosomes may be, in no way reduces the chance of trouble.

The Y chromosome, so to speak, seems to possess an elevated aggressiveness potential, whereas the X chromosome seems to possess a high gentleness component.

It appears probable that the ordinary quantum of aggressiveness of a normal XY male is derived from his Y chromosome, and that the addition of another Y chromosome presents a double dose of those potencies that may under certain conditions facilitate the development of aggressive behavior.

Of course, as with any chromosome, this does not mean that the genes are directly responsible for the end-effect. Rather, the genes on the sex chromosomes exercise their effects through a long chain of metabolic pathways. The final physiological or functional expression results from the interaction of the genes with their environments.

Genes do not determine anything. They simply influence the morphological and physiological expression of traits. Heredity, then, is the expression, not of what is given in one's genes at conception, but of the reciprocal interaction between the inherited genes and the environments to which they've been exposed.

Genes, chromosomes, or heredity are not to be interpreted, as so many people mistakenly do, as equivalent to fate or predestination. On the contrary, the genetic constitution, the genotype, is a labile system, capable of being influenced and changed to varying degrees.

Unchangeability and immutability are not characteristics of the genetic system. The genetic code for any trait contains a set of specific instructions. The manner in which those instructions will be carried out depends not only on those instructions but also upon the nature of their interaction with other sets of instructions as well as with their environments.

The phenotype, that is the visible product of the joint action of genes and the environment, is variable. The idea of genetic or hereditary preformation is as incorrect and unsound as is the doctrine of hereditary predestination. In discussing the behavioral traits so frequently associated with the XYY type, these facts must be especially borne in mind.

How does the XYY chromosomal aberration originate? Most probably the double Y complement is produced during formation of the sperm. During the process of meiosis, in which chromosomes divide and duplicate themselves, normal separation of the sex chromosomes leads to two kinds of sperm—those with an X chromosome, and those with a Y chromosome. If an X sperm fertilizes a normal X ovum, an XX individual (normal female) will result. If the Y sperm fertilizes the ovum, a normal XY male will result.

Failure of the sex chromosomes to separate normally is called nondisjunction. There are two divisions during meiosis. If nondisjunction occurs during the first meiotic division in the production of sperm, this leads to two kinds of sperm cells—those with both the X and Y chromosomes, and those with no sex chromosomes. If an XY sperm fertilizes a normal ovum, an XXY individual will be the result. The XXY individual is a male (Klinefelter's Syndrome), but is usually sterile, lacking functional testes. About 80 per cent of these males develop small breasts and at least 25 per cent are of limited intelligence.

If nondisjunction occurs at the second meiotic division of the paternal germ cells, three types of sperm are produced: XX, YY, and those containing no sex chromosomes. Offspring resulting from fertilization of a normal ovum will be, respectively, XXX, XYY, and XO.

An XYY individual also could be produced if the sex chromosomes fail to separate normally in the early stages of division (mitosis) of a normal, fertilized XY-ovum. However, in such an event, an individual with some type of mosaicism is more likely to occur.

Mosaicism refers to the existence of a different number of sex chromosomes in different tissues or parts of the body. For example, an individual may have only one X chromosome in some of his cells, and three chromosomes (XYY) in other cells. Such a mosaic would be designated XO/XYY. The O refers to the missing X or Y chromosome. If the single X chromosome is coupled with an isochromosome (I)—a chromosome with two identical arms—then the mosaic would be XI/XYY. Of course, other mosaics such as XY/XYY or XYY/XYYY occur.

Major physical abnormalities do not occur in XYY individuals for the reason that the Y chromosome carries relatively few genes. However, the physical abnormalities that do occur are interesting. As in most cases in which an extra sex chromosome is present, there is a high incidence of abnormal internal and external genitalia. Even in childhood, XYY individuals are usually strikingly tall, and as adults usually exceed six feet in height. Facial acne appears to be frequent in adolescence. Mentally, these individuals are usually rather dull, with I.Q.s between 80 and 95. Abnormal electroencephalographic recordings, and a relatively high incidence of epileptic and epileptiform conditions, suggest a wide spectrum of brain dysfunction. Disorders of the

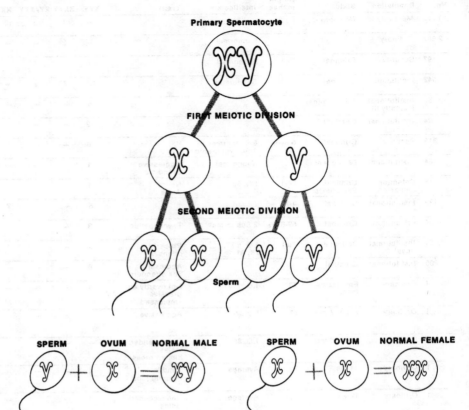

NORMAL MALE MEIOSIS
(Formation of the sperm)

NONDISJUNCTION OF SEX CHROMOSOMES IN MALE MEIOSIS

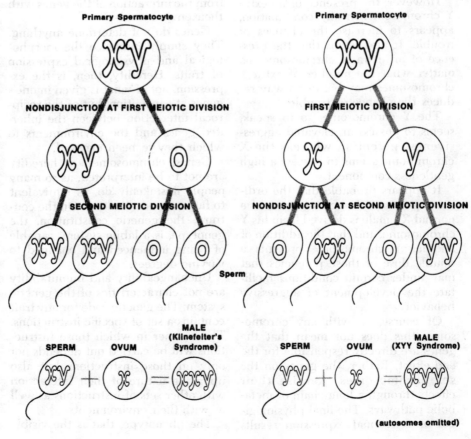

(autosomes omitted)

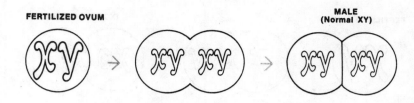

FERTILIZED OVUM

MALE
(Normal XY)

teeth, such as discolored enamel, mal-occlusion and arrested development, also have been noted.

Allowing for the fact that in many cases tall prison inmates were selected for study of the XYY syndrome, and while a number of known XYY individuals fall several inches short of 6 feet, it is nonetheless clear that tallness usually characterizes the XYY individual.

This may be a significant factor in influencing the individual's behavioral development. Among children his own age, an XYY boy may be teased and taunted because of his height, and impelled either to withdrawal or aggression. As a juvenile, adolescent or adult, he may find himself nurtured in environments that encourage physical aggression as a means of adaptation.

This should not be interpreted to mean that all tall men have an XYY constitution. Recently, Richard Goodman and his colleagues at Ohio State University examined the chromosomes of 36 basketball players ranging in height from 5 feet, 11 inches to 6 feet, 10 inches, and found no chromosomal abnormalities.

The resort to brawn rather than brain is not limited to individuals endowed with an extra Y chromosome. Most violent crimes are committed by chromosomally normal individuals. However, the high frequency with which individuals with XYY chromosomes commit crimes of violence leaves little doubt that in some cases the additional Y chromosome exerts a preponderantly powerful influence in the genesis of aggressive behavior.

In a maximum security prison in Melbourne, Australia, Saul Wiener and his colleagues found four XYY-type males in a study of 34 tall prisoners, all between 5 feet 9 inches and 6

feet 10.5 inches in height. A striking frequency of 11.8 per cent! Three of the inmates were XYY, one of whom was charged with attempted murder, the second had committed murder, and the third larceny. The fourth was an XYY/XYYY mosaic, and had committed murder.

An interesting fact is that the tallest of the XYY murderers, 6 feet 10.5 inches tall, had a sister who was even taller. The tallness of the sister indicates that even though the X chromosome is not usually associated with excessive height in families where the males are extremely tall, a trait for tallness may be also carried in the X chromosome.

As a consequence of the discovery of what may be called the XYY syndrome, there now can be very little doubt that genes do influence, to some extent, the development of behavior.

It also appears clear, that, with all other factors constant, genes of the same kind situated at the same locus on the chromosomes of different people may vary greatly both in their penetrance and their expressivity.

Penetrance refers to the regularity with which a gene produces its effect. When a gene regularly produces the same effect, it is said to have complete penetrance. When the trait is not manifested in some cases, the gene is said to have reduced penetrance.

Expressivity refers to the manifestation of a trait produced by a gene. When the manifestation differs from individual to individual, the gene is said to have variable expressivity. For example, the dominant gene for allergy may express itself as asthma, eczema, hay fever, urticarial rash, or angioneurotic edema.

Hence, it would be an error to identify the XYY constitution as *predisposed* to aggressive behavior.

Whatever genes are involved, they often fail to produce aggressive behavior, and even more often may be expressed in many different ways. In fact, the XYY phenotype, the product of the joint action of genes and environment, does vary from normal to various degrees of abnormality.

Some individuals, however, seem to be driven to their aggressive behavior as if they are possessed by a demon. The demon, it would seem, lies in the peculiar nature of the double-Y chromosome complement. That the combined power of several Y chromosomes can be so great, in some cases, as to cause a man to become unrestrainedly aggressive is dramatically borne out by a case reported by John Cowie and Jacob Kahn of East Ham Child Clinic, London, in March 1968.

The first-born, wanted child of a mother aged 23 and a father aged 25 was referred at the age of four and a half years to a psychiatrist because he was unmanageable at home, destructive, mischievous and defiant. He would smash his toys, rip the curtains, set fire to the room in his mother's absence, kick the cat and hit his eight-month-old brother. He was overadventurous and without fear. At two years of age, he began wandering away from home, and was brought back by the police on five occasions. He started school at five years and at once developed an interest in sharp-pointed objects. He would shoot drawing compasses across the schoolroom from an elastic band, and injured several children. In one incident, he rammed a screwdriver into a little girl's stomach.

At the age of eight years, seven months, he was 4 feet 9 inches tall, handsome, athletically proportioned, and of normal appearance. He is of

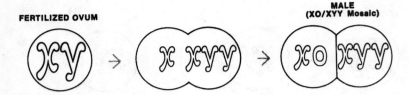

MITOTIC NONDISJUNCTION

FERTILIZED OVUM

MALE
(XO/XYY Mosaic)

(autosomes omitted)

average intelligence, and often considerate and happy. His electroencephalogram is mildly abnormal. Both his parents and his brother have normal chromosomal complements, but the boy is of XYY constitution. His brother is a normally behaving child, and the parents are concerned, loving people.

As illustrated by this case, there is now an increasing amount of evidence that XYY individuals commence their aggressive and social behavior in early prepubertal years. In many cases, the offenses committed are against property rather than against persons. The XYY anomaly, therefore, should not be associated with one particular behavioral trait, but rather regarded as an aberration characterized by a wide spectrum of behavioral possibilities ranging from totally normal to persistent antisocial behavior. The degree of aggressiveness varies, and is only one component of the highly variable spectrum of behavioral contingencies.

We have shown how the XYY chromosomal aberration can originate in nondisjunction during meiosis or during mitosis. But does an XYY male transmit the abnormality to his offspring? To this question the answer is: probably not. One report on an Oregon XYY man indicates the double-Y chromosome complement may not be transmitted. The man has six sons, and all are of normal XY chromosomal constitution.

On the other hand, T. S. Hauschka of Roswell Park Memorial Institute and the Medical Foundation of Buffalo, and his colleagues, who discovered one of the first XYY individuals in 1961, suggest that there may be a hereditary predisposition to nondisjunction. The XYY individual they identified was a normal male who came to their attention because he had a daughter who suffered from Down's syndrome (mongolism). Since Down's syndrome, in most cases, also arises as a result of nondisjunction, this, coupled with other abnormalities in his offspring, suggested that he might be transmitting a hereditary tendency to nondisjunction.

The fact that the XYY complement is now known to be associated with persistent antisocial behavior in a large number of individuals raises a number of questions that the reasonable society, if not the Great Society, must consider seriously.

A first question, if not a first priority, is whether it would not now be desirable to type chromosomally all infants at birth or shortly after. At least one per cent of all babies born have a chromosomal abnormality of some sort, and about one-quarter of these involve sex chromosome abnormalities. Some of these will be XYY. Forearmed with such information, it might be possible to institute the proper preventive and other measures at an early age. These measures would be designed to help the individuals with the XYY chromosomal constitution to follow a less stormy development than they otherwise might.

A second question is how society should deal with individuals known to be of XYY constitution. Such individuals are genetically abnormal. They are not normal and, therefore, should not be treated as if they were.

If the individual has the misfortune to have been endowed with an extra chromosome Number 21, he would have suffered from Down's syndrome (mongolism). He would not have been expected to behave as a normal individual. And why should the XYY individual be held any more responsible for his behavior than a mongo-loid? Mongoloids are usually likeable, unaggressive individuals, and most sociable. The aggressive XYY individual is often the very opposite. Yet the unaggressive behavior of mongoloids is as much due to their genetic constitution as is the aggressive and antisocial behavior of the XYY individual.

Recognizing this fact, it becomes very necessary for us to consider how society and the law should deal with such individuals. We have learned how to identify and treat the hereditary defect of PKU (phenylketonuria), which can result in idiocy if not treated. Cannot we also develop measures to treat the XYY syndrome? Surgical intervention, such as sterilization, is totally inappropriate since it will not "cure" or alleviate the condition, nor will it reduce the frequency of XYY individuals in the general population. The XYY aberration, as far as we know, is not directly inherited, and quite probably arises primarily from nondisjunction of the sex chromosomes in completely normal parents.

Although we are in no position to control the genetic inheritance of an individual, we can do a great deal to change certain environmental conditions that may encourage the XYY individual to commit criminal acts.

A society does not properly acquit itself of its responsibilities if it places the entire burden of caring for abnormal individuals upon the parents. What we are talking about here is not a program of eugenic control, but a program of social therapy. There is every reason to believe that if we can successfully develop effective methods to help the aggressive XYY individual, then we will be moving in the right direction to control those social conditions that drive men to crime—regardless of their genotype.∎

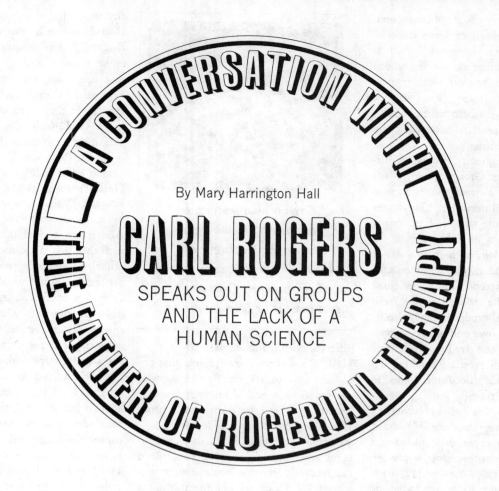

A CONVERSATION WITH
THE FATHER OF ROGERIAN THERAPY

By Mary Harrington Hall

CARL ROGERS
SPEAKS OUT ON GROUPS AND THE LACK OF A HUMAN SCIENCE

Mary Harrington Hall: Shall we talk about groups—encounter groups, T-groups, sensitivity-training groups, group therapy? The group phenomenon demands exploration and explanation. And I've wondered . . . are people drawn toward this intense group experience because they feel loneliness and alienation in our strange society?

Carl Rogers: Of course that's a major reason. Out of the increasing loneliness of modern culture, we have in some social sense been forced to develop a way of getting closer to one another. I think encounter groups probably bring people closer together than has ever been true in history except with groups of people together during crisis. You put men together during war, for instance, and they really know each other to the depths, and so it is in groups. So often someone will say at the end of a group experience: "I just can't believe that I have known

you people here better than I know members of my own family, and you know me better than my family knows me."

We have found a way for closeness to develop with amazing rapidity. I think

that group work is a far more important social phenomenon than most people realize. Group encounters, by whatever name you call them, are becoming a major force.

Hall: A lot of people in and out of psychology question the useful purpose

of such closeness with groups of people who have an experience together for a week or for a weekend, get to know each other's problems and dreams, and then may never see each other again, Carl. Perhaps you're one of the best people in the country to answer this argument. You developed the form of therapy in which the therapist permits himself to become involved with his patient, in a frankly caring relationship with the therapist both permissive and involved. And Rogerian therapy certainly is based on interaction.

Rogers: You're actually putting two questions in a polite way, Mary. What you're questioning is the *usefulness* and the *legitimacy* of the group experience. There is a good deal of argument and furor about the intensive group experience. There have been vituperative articles about how terrible group encounters are, how they take on the Communist brainwashing technique, and such nonsense. You get even more people who think the group experience is simply great. This is a very potent phenomenon. One can't just take it or leave it alone. You either become involved, in which case group encounter does bring about changes in you, or you can resist it completely. The group experience is not something people remain neutral about.

Hall: Let's differentiate between group therapy and encounter groups.

Rogers: They are really two rather different dimensions. Group therapy is for the person who is already hurting, who has problems, and needs help. Encounter groups are for those who are functioning normally but want to improve their capacity for living within their own sets of relationships. And the leader role is, of course, quite different. One leader must be therapeutic, the other more of a facilitator. Traditional group therapy, with its weekly meetings over a long period, well may be replaced one day by an intensive week or month, or even weekend experience. The intense encounter seems to work wonders in therapy, too.

Hall: You know that I always have been somewhat of a skeptic, or possibly afraid, about the group experience, and thus a questioner of the purpose for people getting together to talk a lot—and cry a lot. But I really want to know: what do people bring home to their daily lives from group encounters?

Rogers: There are so many hundreds and thousands of examples to give. The most common report is that people behave differently with their families and with their colleagues. A school administrator (in a workshop we ran for a California school system not long ago) is typical. She said she *felt* different but was unprepared for how quick her family's response would be. She wrote that her daughters sensed a change in her immediately. Before she had been home a day, she and her daughters had talked over a whole list of things—God, death and hell, menstruation, nightmares, a whole range of things.

Both her 14-year-old and her ten-year-old daughter wanted to be bathed by her, the first time in years they had been so intimate. Finally, the young one said: "What did they teach you at that meeting—how to be nice to kids?" The woman wrote that she replied: "No, I learned how to be myself and found out that was pretty nice." Now, this woman is a teacher. I think she is going to be

"Group encounters, by whatever name you call them, are becoming a major force. This is a very potent phenomenon. One can't just take it or leave it alone."

different with her students, too.

Hall: What about the argument that encounter groups are fine for those who are emotionally stable but may be very upsetting indeed for those with problems—and our number is legion?

Rogers: The possibility of damage concerns me, too, but I think the risk is much, much less than is ordinarily presumed. I did a questionnaire study, a six months' follow-up, of more than 500 people involved in groups which I either led or in which I was responsible. Out of 481 people who responded, only two felt the experience had been more hurtful than helpful. You know, a deep relationship is a very rare experience for

"It troubles me, and troubles me deeply, whether we really do know how to have a human science . . ."

anyone, and it always means change.

Hall: How much change and what kind?

Rogers: I think encounter groups help make people more open to experiences that are going on within them, more expressive of their feelings, more spontaneous in their reactions, more flexible, more vulnerable, and probably more genuinely intimate in their interpersonal relationships. Now, I value this type of person, don't you?

Hall: That sounds like the ideal man.

Rogers: Well, there are whole cultures built on exactly the opposite ideal. And many people in our own culture feel also that a person should be contained, disciplined, preferably unaware of his feelings, and should live in terms of a firm set of disciplines that are handed down by someone—God, or someone up there—whomever he looks to as an authority. The person who emerges from encounter groups is likely to be more self-directed and not so easily persuaded by others. I think the absence of open debate about what is the desirable sort of personal development has stirred up misunderstanding and public reaction against the intense-encounter technique.

Hall: But, Carl, you can measure attitude change and you can do empirical studies of behavior change, yet you can't measure the essential experience in groups that brings those changes, can you? How can you explain the phenomenon so people will understand?

Rogers: It troubles me, and troubles me deeply, whether we really do know how to have a human science, Mary. Groups are potent, and something very significant is going on. I have gotten increasingly restive about the point you raise, that we can't measure the essential experience that brings about those changes. I feel very perplexed. A lot of my life has been devoted to measuring; I keep being sure it can be done with the group experience, and then failing.

Last year Michael Polanyi, the British philosopher of science, said something I really didn't like at the time, but he may be right. He said we should lay aside the word *science* for the next decade or two and give people the freedom to find out that we need more *knowledge*. He said the word *science* is so wrapped up with the machinery of science that it was stifling rather than helping us at this point, at least in the behavioral sciences.

"One of the unfortunate things about psychology is that it has tried to make one great leap and become a science like physics . . ."

. . . We may have to go back and do much more naturalistic observation. Out of that might grow a real psychological science, not an imitation of physics."

I know that many of us in psychology have gotten so wound up with methodology that we forget to be curious, really. With today's knowledge, we don't know how to study what happened to a businessman for whom the encounter experience had an on-going effect for sixteen years. I don't know how to study that. Or why was an intense-encounter experience something a high-school girl told me she had found to be the most important and beautiful experience in her relatively short life?

Hall: You seem to be saying that psychology is groping now toward being a more human science. If that is so, what will happen when you break through?

Rogers: I don't know. The closer one gets to trying to assess the intangible things which probably are most important in personality change, the less are customary instruments being used, and the more suspect are the only instruments that seem to me to make any sense. I think that in those intangibles the only person who can help us out is the person to whom something has happened. We need to get more pictures of what it seems like to the person *inside,* who has experienced the change.

If we adapted Polanyi's suggestion and just said: "Well, science or no science

I'm trying to find out something about this," we might have taken a valuable and freeing step. One of the unfortunate things about psychology is that it has tried to make one great leap and become a science like physics. I think we will have to recognize the fact that people observed things, and thought about things, and fiddled around with things a long time before they came up with any of the precise observations which made a science out of physics.

We may have to go back and do much more naturalistic observation, make more of an attempt to understand people, behavior, and the dynamics of things.

Then, perhaps someday, out of that might grow a real psychological science, not an imitation of physics, a human science that should have as its appropriate subject, man. I think the reason so much psychological experimentation is done on rats and cats, and such, is that we realize perfectly that we don't have the tools for understanding human beings.

Hall: But, after all, we do *learn* about humans by animal study. Do you think psychologists have been defensive because psychology is sometimes seen as a stepchild of science?

Rogers: I guess psychologists are about the most defensive professional people around today. We have this terrific fear of looking unscientific. A terrific fear of spinning out wild theories to see how they sound, and a fear of trying them out. We think we must do everything from a *known* base with *known* instruments. Actually, this is *not* the way in which creative scientists, even in the hard sciences, operate. For instance, I think one of the real tragedies of graduate education in psychology is that graduate students in many, many institutions become less and less willing to spout original ideas for fear they will be shot down by their colleagues, and by their professors. This is *not* the way to do things.

Hall: The great intuitive chemists and physicists certainly aren't afraid. They spend a lifetime on hunches, don't they? I'm thinking particularly of one of our mutual close friends, Harold Urey.

Rogers: That's it! They aren't afraid. What psychology needs are ideas that someone dreams up on the basis of hunches and intuition, from experience, or to try to make sense out of some complex set of phenomena. It may take a

lifetime to find out if it was a worthless dream or a really significant pattern of thought. We need that kind of dreaming in psychology, and graduate departments of psychology have no time for dreams. I think they are definitely fearful.

Hall: And maybe it takes someone like you—a former president of the American Psychological Association, a man with every honor his profession and the academic world can bestow—to be so fearlessly critical of his own profession. Or maybe you're impatient to have psychology take that major leap forward to answer your own questions about *why* group encounters do seem to affect people so deeply?

Rogers: Or maybe I'm just used to being involved in controversy? Perhaps all three, Mary. But still, psychology is a defensive profession. I'll give you an example. At a conference last year on "Man and the Science of Man," all the discus-

"Group encounters can help end the tragedy of two races which meet fearfully and don't know what to do. What we need is an enormous effort of the scope of the Manhattan Project. We should call in everyone who has any theoretical contribution to make, everyone who has tried out practical things. We should round up interdisciplinary knowledge that would focus on how tensions can be reduced."

a little counseling. I probably did say that. I'm more optimistic than Rollo. He is an existentialist—so am I, but my philosophy has more room for hope.

Hall: Your background and Rollo May's are quite similar, though, aren't they?

Rogers: We're both from the rural Midwest. I was a farm boy, he from a small town. This is a good, strong background, you know. He graduated from the Union Theological Seminary. After I graduated in history from the University of Wisconsin, I studied there, and then I went across the street to get my Ph.D. in psychology from Columbia. In 1926, the Seminary was a freewheeling, stimulating place to be. Arthur McGifford, a real scholar, was president. A group of us students decided we didn't have enough chance to talk about issues that really concerned us, so we asked for a seminar which we would run ourselves and for which we would receive credit. Any institution today would drop dead if you made such a suggestion. The Seminary agreed and in many ways it well may have been the very first encounter group, although it was a little more intellectual than most encounter groups as we know them today. Many of us left the Seminary and went into allied fields. I still was very much interested in working with people but I didn't want to tie myself to some particular creed.

I worked for the New York Institute for Child Guidance, and for the Rochester Society for the Prevention of Cruelty to Children before getting into the University life, you know. I earned the glorious sum of $2,900 a year on my first job, with a wife and child to support.

Then, of course, I went to Ohio, to the University of Chicago and to Wisconsin, before I got fed up finally with the restrictions of the academic life, particularly with the frustrations for graduate students, and became a fellow of the Western Behavioral Sciences Institute in Southern California.

Hall: Your book, *Counseling and Psychotherapy,* was published in 1942, Carl, but didn't your major impact come about after *Client-Centered Therapy* was published in 1951?

Rogers: I think so, really. Acceptance came very slowly.

Hall: When did you become interested in groups?

Rogers: My first gropings toward using

"The East Coast shows signs of being an older culture. Their procedures are more rigid, with too much stress on paper credentials."

the intensive-group experience in a constructive way came in 1946, when I was in charge of the University of Chicago's Counseling Center. We had a Veterans Administration contract for training all personal counsellors for returning servicemen and we had to make them into effective counsellors within six-week training programs. They all had Master's degrees, but none of them had done much counseling. We couldn't give them individual counseling, which we thought would be the best way for them to learn, so we put them together in small groups. It worked very well.

Hall: There was no such thing as encounter groups then, but was there any group therapy?

Rogers: There was some group therapy just beginning. I remember that in about 1945 I told a group of my students that I would be glad to try to conduct a group-therapy program for them, but it would be my first experience. Now, the National Training Laboratories in Bethel, Maine, started at about this time, but I was unaware of that.

My groups of personal counsellors and students at Chicago became more and more personal in their discussions and revealed more and more of what was going on within them. It was similar to what goes on in an encounter group

---

sions were taped. These were all top scholars. Only three participants refused permission to trust editors to put their taped remarks in shape for future listeners. Two of those three were psychologists. Another example was the dialogue I had in Duluth with B. F. Skinner, the father of operant conditioning, the creator of the modern study of behaviorism. He was unwilling to have the tape of our dialogue transcribed. I thought it was understood in advance that it *would* be transcribed. I call that needlessly fearful.

Hall: By the way, Fred told on interesting anecdote about you in his interview with us in September, Carl.

Rogers: Yes, the ducks. Funny story, but he knows that it's not true. He said I was duck hunting and used the art of gentle agreement to get for myself the duck another man shot. Actually, my brother and I were hunting, we shot at the same time, and tossed a coin to see who got the duck. And I've told Fred I lost the toss. Fred and I actually are friends, you know. He's a marvelous mind. Another friend, Rollo May, whom you rightly labeled in your wonderful interview as "Mr. Humanist," told the story that I once questioned the existence of tragedy by saying that Romeo and Juliet might have been all right with just

today. However, I didn't carry on in this field, partly because I didn't think that group work was a good field for research. I thought that there were enough complexities with the one-to-one-relationship so that we couldn't possibly study a group situation.

Hall: You certainly have changed your mind since that time.

Rogers: Oh, yes, I have certainly revised my opinion. The next time I was closely involved in a group experience was in the autumn of 1950 when I conducted a postgraduate seminar type of therapy held just before the A.P.A. meetings. I remember that for one hour each day I counseled a client in front of a group of twelve. It started off on a somewhat academic basis, but as we got into it, sharing more and more deeply of our personal experiences, our failures, and our difficulties, it became a moving personal experience. All of us left there feeling we had gained deeply. What amazed me was the long, lasting effect from the experience. It was then that I began to realize the potency of group experience.

Hall: Didn't the National Training Laboratories, in Bethel, Maine, begin the sensitivity-training programs for executives, the famous T-Groups, at about the same time you did your first group work at Chicago?

Rogers: At just the time I began putting on summer workshops organized by the Counseling Service Center, I heard that something was going on in the East. Then, one of our members took part in one of the N.T.L. groups, and came back rather unimpressed. We were following different patterns; our groups focused more on the interpersonal relationship and on building a climate where people could express or withhold as much as they wished.

Over the years there has been cross-fertilization, and it is no longer accurate to say we are working two different ways. I conduct N.T.L. workshops every year — the Presidents' Lab program for top executives.

Hall: Where does the term T-Group come from, Carl?

Rogers: T-Groups originally were thought of as *Training* groups. I don't think we are in the business of *training*. The term is misleading. I think there still is a different flavor between N.T.L. workshops—and all Eastern approaches

"At Cal Tech, in the Honker Group, we began to take up issues of deep concern, and since they didn't have to arrive at any motions, and pass them, they discussed frankly."

—and what is going on in the West.

N.T.L. did the real pioneering in the encounter-group movement, and really have been the prime moving force in the whole thing. They have put on thousands of groups, and they are responsible for getting the business community involved to the point where the top men in the country attend N.T.L. Presidents' Labs. All groups start from there. What a great thing they did, and yet the West Coast is far more active than is the East, the home of groups.

Hall: Someone once said—me, I think —that the West is on a great group binge. Why is it that groups are more popular on the West Coast? Do you agree with May, who says it's because the West is anti-intellectual?

Rogers: Actually, I think the East Coast shows signs of being an older culture. Their procedures are more rigid, with too much stress on paper credentials. On the West Coast, partly because it is a newer part of the country, partly because the California psychological climate, in particular, is freer, there is more regard for essentials of the work. We've used nonprofessional leaders in groups. N.T.L. would frown on anyone without the proper paper credentials.

Hall: Do you find the West more experimental in its approach to psychology?

Rogers: I certainly do, and I approve. It will be sad if the West settles into a fixed mold. I believe every organization and every profession ought to be upset— put through the mixer—every decade or so, and start again fresh and flexible.

Hall: What makes California especially so different? Is it the fluid population?

Rogers: I cannot account for it. What gives the particularly loose, freewheeling character to the California psychological climate, I don't know. I just know that you can *feel* it.

Ann Roe, a research psychologist, did an extensive study some years ago on 100 creative physical and social scientists who were most highly regarded. Fifteen years later she said that out of the 100, some 70 now live in California — and they aren't retired for the most part—they're still swingers. The great universities are only part of the answer, I think, but an important part.

Hall: Tell me about your Honker group at Cal Tech, Carl. I know that elimination of the grading system for Cal Tech freshmen and sophomores came out of those sessions.

Rogers: I was surprised to be asked by Cal Tech to serve as a consultant on human and educational problems, and I decided that if I worked with students, it might cause a student rebellion—so I chose faculty.

We weren't a committee or a group with any legal authority. I didn't want that. We put together top faculty and administration people and I think I was able to develop a freer discussion climate than they ever had. We began to take up issues of deep concern, and since they didn't have to arrive at any motions and pass them, they discussed frankly.

Hall: Did the name Honker come from the gabbling of the group?

Rogers: We met first at the Honker Restaurant. The original group met for two years, and finally we had faculty-student groups, and new faculty groups.

We had to break up the original Honkers because the faculty began to fear them as an elite power group. And the new groups were just as effective.

The grading system and a number of good new things just naturally evolved. Most faculty members, incidentally, have never been willing to get off the intellectual level and into the intensive experimental encounter. But there is quite an encounter program now among students.

Hall: You have a grant to do research in the effect of encounter experiences in an educational system, haven't you?

Rogers: We have a two-year Babcock Foundation Grant of $80,000 a year, with an additional $30,000 personal gift from Charles Kettering to see whether the basic encounter group can be an instrument for self-directed change in school systems. Many school systems were interested but I selected the Immaculate Heart College in Los Angeles. It's a marvelous school, and it also certifies about 70 teachers a year, and staffs and supervises eight high schools and 50 elementary schools.

Mary: Carl, I was terribly excited when you told me a year ago that you hoped to do a vertical thing in a school system, starting with administrators in groups, then teachers, parents, and students—and then putting them together. This might end the crashing boredom of most school systems.

Rogers: Well, we've begun now. We've held six weekend workshops, for college faculty, for high-school faculty and student leaders, and for elementary-school principals and teachers. I am hopeful. We'll know in three years.

Hall: What has happened? Are people getting involved?

Rogers: The student councils have asked if our program leaders can meet on a weekly basis to help them iron out interpersonal problems. Lay faculty members have asked for a weekend encounter group for themselves and their spouses. Various departments are asking for encounter groups. Everyone is excited. (Sister Mary Corita, the artist and the most joyous soul anywhere, is in the Immaculate Heart Art Department, you know. So you can imagine what a grand place this college is.)

And just as in all school systems, faculty members resisted group encounters with students, but that is working out.

We meet for solid weekends. Groups may meet Friday evening and all day Saturday, then again until Sunday noon. Or perhaps for a very long Saturday till midnight, and then again for a long Sunday.

Hall: All right, let's say I'm a school principal in an encounter group. What is this going to do for the school system?

Rogers: It will affect the system because you are going to be more demo-

"Many of us live in a precarious balance . . . almost invariably in groups every person finds the balance is disturbed."

cratic and more willing to take feedback from your staff, Mary. The teacher I told you about who suddenly was closer to her own daughters had attended one of our Immaculate Heart workshops.

Some people say, "Well, this approach can't change a system." I say it will make systems more open to innovations.

Hall: What do you think frightens people about intense encounter groups?

Rogers: I think many of us live in kind of a precarious balance. We have learned to get along with ourselves and our world in some way, and the possibility that this balance might be upset is always a frightening one. Almost invariably in groups, every person finds the balance is disturbed, or possibly upset, but finds that in a climate of trust he is enormously supported in being *more* himself.

Hall: As you were talking, I thought of the last lines of *Cyrano de Bergerac*. Dying, he reaches for his gaudy hat and says: "My plume, my sacred plume. My pride, my pose, my lifelong masquerade."

Rogers: That moves me. In an encounter group, people learn they really do not need to keep that masquerade. In our last workshop, there was a man who

came across as being very competent, very efficient, very self-sufficient. You just felt, here's a guy who really has it made. He has an important job and everything is rosy. It turned out that he is *so* hungry for appreciation and love; he feels he lets other people know that he appreciates them but who in the hell listens to him, or cares about him—nobody. I am thinking of one Navy commander, who appeared to be a complete martinet. We weren't very many days into the workshop before he was telling us some of the personal tragedies that he had in his life, particularly of his son—he felt terrible about what he had helped to do to his son. Then he got to telling about how he was known as a disciplinarian, but that when he was the commander of a ship during the war he got himself in trouble with his officers because of one enlisted man who was always in trouble. This officer felt he was really so much like the bad guy that he couldn't punish him. Others would come up with minor offenses and they got so much time in the brig, and this guy would do horrible things and the officer couldn't bear to punish him because the sailor did things he himself never dared to do. Among the many things that happened during his group experience, he decided to go back and try to rebuild his marriage—I don't know how much success he had in that. When he got back he was going to tell his top staff about the real softy he was inside, and try to loosen up his organization. This is the sort of thing where you see that people *can* change and *do* change and *do* become more human.

Hall: This interview with you leads off a special section on the group phenomenon, Carl. The article following this interview is by a very bright young Harvard psychologist, Tom Cottle, who has experimented with self-analytic groups of Negro and white high-school students just *before* their school integration. He thinks such encounters can greatly ease racial tensions. [*See PT, Dec. 1967.*]

Rogers: I'm sure he's right. Group encounters can help end the tragedy of two races which meet fearfully and don't know what to do.

What we need is an enormous effort of the scope of the Manhattan Project. We should call in everyone who has any theoretical contribution to make, everyone who has tried out practical things such as you are describing and such as I have done. We should round up interdisciplinary knowledge that would focus on how tensions can be reduced. Such a project could contribute enormously in the resolving of racial tensions. This approach also could contribute to the resolution of labor and management tensions. I believe it could contribute to the terrifying problems of international tensions, too.

I would not be in the least afraid to be a facilitator for a massive group program in Watts. I know the tensions and bitterness would be terrific, but the people would be speaking for themselves. And I'm sure we could come to a more harmonious understanding than is possible any other way.

Hall: Fred Stoller, who with George Boch invented the marathon group you have said *is* effective, has an article in this group section. So does Mike Murphy, president of Esalen Institute. I know you've led workshops there. What do you think of Esalen, Carl? Murphy says he doesn't think you're sold on it.

Rogers: I admire the nerve Mike has. His basic idea is very good. Living in California has made me realize that there is no sharp dividing line between the cutting edge in psychology and the too-far-out hogwash.

Mike is covering the whole spectrum in his Esalen seminars and workshops. We'll look back in ten years and find that some of the things he has sponsored helped start an important trend.

I'm pleased that he has set up a San Francisco headquarters, because I think that his Big Sur place is a little too involved with the sort of hippie culture that has tended to limit the kind of people who participate in seminars there.

Hall: How do you assess your own contributions to psychology?

Rogers: If I have made a contribution it is around the central theme that the potential of the individual—and I would even add, the potential of the group—can be released providing a proper psychological climate is created. And that is an optimistic point of view!

If I, the therapist, can come through to my client as a person who cares about him and understands what he is struggling to express, he gradually will begin to choose healthier directions for himself.

Hall: Your work certainly has emphasized the importance of interpersonal relationships.

Rogers: That is another aspect of whatever contribution I have made. Instead of focusing on the diagnostic or causative elements of behavior. I always have been more concerned with the dynamics of interaction. Not about how a person became what he is, but about how does he change from what he is.

I always have felt psychologically nourished by deep communication with people with whom I was working. I think sometimes people in clinical work apologize if they feel they are getting something out of it. I believe that if a therapist doesn't find particularly deep relationships with people he works with, he shouldn't be either a therapist or working with groups.

This involvement was very true for me when I was doing individual therapy. When I had to give that up because my life was just too hectic, I wondered what would take its place. And soon I found that working intensively with groups—and with individuals in those groups—provided me with the same kind of psychological nourishment.

Hall: For people who criticize the permissiveness of your approach, the way your son and daughter turned out is an answer which must make you and Helen very proud.

Rogers: Well, they have nice families of their own now. Our son, David, is chairman of the Department of Medicine at Vanderbilt University. He was chosen one of the ten outstanding young men in the country for *Life* magazine's issue on the "take-over" generation. He has two daughters and a son.

Our daughter is Mrs. Lawrence Fuchs. Her husband is Professor of American Civilization at Brandeis University and they have three daughters. He organized the Peace Corps in the Philippines. Natalie took her M.A. in psychology with Abe Maslow (present APA president). She's very interested in counseling work. She's *good,* too.

Hall: You said you were used to being somewhat controversial, Carl. Where have your battles been?

Rogers: Of course I was very much involved in the battles during the 1930's and '40's in which there were many attempts to stop psychologists from prac-

"My therapeutic point of view threatens many therapists. It is far more satisfying to be the man pulling the strings than to be the man (like me) who provides a climate in which another person can do something."

ticing psychotherapy. The last go-around on that was during the 1950's. It's a dead issue now.

Another controversy that somehow hit the clinicians' value system—and threatened many therapists—was my confidence in the potentiality of the individual.

It was my publications, based on my conviction and research, which upset many psychologists and psychiatrists. I said the individual can discover his own patterns of capabilities and his maladjustments, and that he can find insight *on his own* and take action to help solve his own problems.

The point of view threatens people who like to be experts. It is far more satisfying to be the man pulling the strings than to be the man who provides a climate in which another person can *do* something. So, there were attacks— there were famous jokes that about how all I did was agree with people.

Hall: That brings up a question. There is a classic Rogers joke . . . a man in therapy with you is depressed. He says so. You say: "You're *depressed,* aren't you?" He says he feels like jumping out the window in your office, and you say—

Rogers: I *know* the story. My answer, for once and for all time, is that I would not have let him jump out the window.

287

Inside Psychotherapy

By David E. Orlinsky & Kenneth I. Howard

PSYCHOTHERAPY has been described by some as the confessional of the secular man, and as the weekday solace of the overeducated and underemployed suburban housewife. It has also been presented as the individual's best hope for attaining self-knowledge and personal authenticity in a confused and troubled society.

Because of its important place in our culture, psychotherapy has been put on frequent display in novels, films and plays—sometimes humorously and sometimes with serious intent. Yet with all this publicity, what do we actually know about psychotherapy? What takes place after patient and therapist disappear behind the closed office door? What is the experience of psychotherapy really like?

The theories and case histories of psychotherapists offer some answers, and so do the observations and evaluations of scientific researchers. But each of these sources has limitations. The clinical literature, though often suggestive and sometimes brilliant, is almost always impressionistic and purely qualitative. The research literature, though more systematic and quantitative, comprises chiefly objective observations by non-participants and after-the-fact evaluations. Such studies provide valuable knowl-edge, but they give no information about what the patients and therapists see, hear and feel during their sessions; about what they want from therapy, or about what they think of their psychotherapy.

Our desire to obtain reliable, precise information about psychotherapy as a subjective experience—to find out, in a precise, systematic and quantitative way, how the people who participate in psychotherapy see and feel it—led us to develop the Psychotherapy Session Project, based on reports from patients and therapists themselves.

For subjects, we turned to a group of patients and therapists at the Katharine Wright Mental Health Clinic in Chicago. During the first six months of the study, 60 patients filled out reports on a total of 890 sessions, and 17 therapists completed questionnaires on a total of 470 sessions. All patients were being seen in individual outpatient psychotherapy, and almost all had sessions once a week. All the patients were women between 20 and 60 years of age, but most were on the younger side—their average age was 28. In general, the patients were well educated: 90 per cent had finished high school, and a third had completed college or graduate studies. More than 80 per cent were employed, and 25 per cent were currently married.

The therapists who participated were both men and women. They had been trained in psychiatry, clinical psychology or psychiatric social work, with an average of six years' experience in the practice of psychotherapy. Most of them acknowledged some influence of Freud on their thinking and practice, but few would consider themselves psychoanalytically oriented in a strict sense. Like most clinicians, they draw upon a variety of approaches.

The reports were made independently by each patient and therapist as soon as possible after the session was over, while the experience was still fresh in their minds. We used two parallel questionnaires, one for patients and one for therapists, to survey various aspects of the therapy experience [see illustration, next page].

The questionnaires took only 10 or 15 minutes to complete, because they called for simple descriptions and evaluations rather than lengthy analyses. Before the first study, the questionnaires were trial-tested with a substantial number of therapists and patients, and modified where necessary. We tried to avoid the terminology of any special theoretical school or orientation but to include issues that are meaningful to most of them. The confidentiality of each person's answers was strictly assured so he could feel free to give his honest reactions to the questions.

The Typical Session

To gain a composite picture of the typical therapy experience, we tabulated the most frequently endorsed responses of patients and therapists to the items on the questionnaires [see illustration, page 291]. What patients seemed to want most in coming to therapy was to deepen their understanding of personal problems that they have difficulty talking about and, presumably, difficulty dealing with. This deepened understanding might be expected to alleviate the problems, or at least to help the patient deal with them more comfortably and more effectively. As they tried to move toward these goals, patients talked most frequently about themselves as they are in their present intimate social relations and vocational settings.

This contradicts the expectations based on clinical theory, which call for talk about relations with parents or siblings, memories of childhood experiences, and dreams or fantasies.

Though patients might find their sessions helpful, they did not, as a rule, find them pleasant. They tended to feel anxious and tense during interviews—understandably, perhaps, since they were trying to discuss and work out their most difficult personal problems. However, patients did appear to be actively and positively involved in the therapy relationship. This contrasts somewhat with their problematic concerns and felt distress. Patients come to a therapist for help but do not seem particularly helpless, at least in relating to him.

Inspection of the therapists' responses showed that patient and therapist generally worked toward the same goals, with some difference in nuance and detail. Patients, for example, were inclined to seek advice about their problems; therapists were less inclined to offer advice and wanted their patients to experience feelings rather than merely talk about them.

As one might expect, therapists generally felt comfortable with and positively responsive to their patients. (The joke that is told to beginning therapists, optimistically describing a therapist as the less anxious of the two persons in the room, seems to be borne out by the facts.) Our research showed that the popular image of the therapist as a reserved, neutral, unresponsive person seems to be a mistaken view. Therapists related to their patients the same way patients related to them: collaboratively, positively and feelingly.

Returning to the patients, what benefits did they find in their sessions? The most frequently reported satisfactions were a sense of honestly working together with the therapist, help in talking about important troubling matters, and better self-understanding. Thus patients typically did find what they sought in coming to therapy, and what their therapists hoped to give them. The process was often emotionally trying but, with their therapists' active support, the patients seemed to achieve helpful self-understanding.

The Ideal Session

Psychotherapy as it occurs in the typical session is undoubtedly a mixture of better and worse experiences. In order to deepen our understanding of essential therapeutic processes and to develop more effective practices, we felt it was desirable to isolate the better elements of the experience—to portray psychotherapy at its best [see illustration, page 291].A composite picture of the "ideal" experience—the aims, feelings and so forth that distinguish the ideal session—

was drawn from our data by noting the responses that correlated most highly with patients' and therapists' evaluations of the overall quality of their sessions.

Both the ideal and the average therapy experience included a desire on the patient's part for self-understanding and collaborative involvement with the therapist. The wish for insight and collaboration, present in the typical experience, was simply more intense in the ideal experience. And in the ideal experience, patients wanted to display their gains and successes to the therapist rather than to present their problems or solicit help and advice. The accent was on the positive, perhaps because some real gains were being made.

The better the session, the less emphasis patients placed on discussing immediate feelings about themselves. Instead, they stressed dreams or fantasies and memories of childhood experiences with family members, subjects that theoretically reflect underlying or unconscious patterns of motivation. The ideal session came closer than the typical one to clinical expectations of what it is most profitable to discuss in therapy.

The patients' feelings during the ideal session were quite different from those reported for the typical session. Instead of feeling anxious and tense, patients felt confident and pleased. On the other hand, the way patients acted towards their therapists was essentially the same in the ideal and the typical experiences. They were, presumably, more friendly, more interactive, and so forth in the ideal case than in the typical one. As might be expected, in the ideal session patients reported getting all the satisfactions listed on the questionnaire. This finding strengthens our confidence in the validity of their overall evaluations.

Therapists' goals in the ideal and typical sessions were essentially the same. These goals corresponded, in general, to what is prescribed by theories of psychotherapy. However, in the ideal session the therapists' goals also included support for the self-esteem of their patients. (The tendency to be rewarding or encouraging, like the patients' concern to show improvement, may be greater once real gains are at hand.)

In the ideal session, therapists felt more alert and effective, but also warmer and more personally involved, than in the typical session. Their way of relating to patients was essentially the same in the ideal as in the typical session, only more so. Patients and therapists approached each other in much the same

1. How do you feel about the therapy session which you have just completed? [*Alternatives from "one of the best" to "really poor session"*]

2. What did you talk about during this session? [*Checklist of 18 topics representing basic areas of life concerns*]

3. What did you want or hope to get out of this therapy session? [*Checklist of 20 potential patient goals*]

4. How did you act towards your therapist during this session? [*Checklist of 16 types of interpersonal behavior*]

5. How did you feel during this session? [*Checklist of 45 feelings*]

6. To what extent were you looking forward to coming to this session? [*Alternatives from "could hardly wait" to "had to make myself come"*]

7. How freely were you able to talk with your therapist during this session? [*Alternatives from "a great deal of difficulty" to "didn't have any difficulty in talking"*]

8. How clearly did you know what you wanted to talk about during this session? [*Alternatives from "knew clearly" to "my mind was blank"*]

9. How well did your therapist seem to understand how you were feeling and what was really on your mind during this session? [*Alternatives from "understood very well" to "misunderstood"*]

10. Do you feel that what your therapist said and did this session was helpful to you? [*Alternatives from "very helpful" to "made me worse off than I was"*]

11. Do you feel that you made progress in this session in dealing with the problems for which you are in therapy? [*Alternatives from "considerable progress" to "my problems got worse"*]

12. How well do you feel that you are getting along, emotionally and psychologically, at this time? [*Alternatives from "the way I would like" to "I can barely manage"*]

13. What do you feel that you got out of this session? [*Checklist of nine possible satisfactions*]

14. To what extent are you looking forward to your next session? [*Alternatives from "wish it were sooner" to "not so sure I will want to come"*]

15. How did your therapist act towards you during this session? [*Checklist of 16 types of interpersonal behavior*]

16. How did your therapist seem to feel during this session? [*Checklist of 34 feelings*]

A very similar revised version of this questionnaire is now in use with other patients and therapists.

WHAT THEY WERE ASKED. The only major difference between patient and therapist questionnaires was question 13. Therapists were asked "In what direction were you working with your patient during this session?" and chose from checklist of goals.

way, except that patients generally took more initiative in determining what was discussed in the session.

The typical session and the ideal session have many features in common, suggesting that by and large the average experience is a good one—or at least that the typical experience is considerably closer to the best than it is to the worst. But we must remember, too, that the ideal therapy experience is an abstraction, a composite of positive tendencies within the many real experiences of different patients and different therapists. It is not safe to assume that there is only one type of good therapy experience, or only one way to achieve it.

Indeed, we are warned against any such conclusion by other analyses of the questionnaires, which revealed at least three distinct positive patterns in the relationship between patient and therapist. Because these patterns emerge, independently or together, in any relationship, we have called them "therapeutic potentials." A brief description of what they are and how they were found should help illuminate the more complex connections between the typical and ideal patterns of therapy experience.

In the Psychotherapy Session Project,

we have been interested in how the experiences of individual patients and therapists differed from one another, as well as in average or composite patterns. To study these differences, and to define empirically the dimensions along which individual variation occurs, we applied the statistical technique of factor analysis. We analyzed the experiences of patients and of therapists separately, and then combined the results of these and analyzed the experiences of patient-therapist pairs together in order to determine the patterns of "conjoint experience" within the relationship. Three therapeutic potentials — "collaborative analytic progress," "healing magic," and "mutual personal openness" — emerged from this analysis.

"Collaborative analytic progress" is the type of good therapy relationship described in the psychoanalytic literature. It is marked by an effective "therapeutic alliance," or task-oriented collaboration, between patient and therapist; by an emotionally involving but basically cognitive ("analytic") exploration of the patient's significant problems and relationships; and by a sense of forward movement or progress in understanding. The role of the therapist in this pattern

of good therapy experience is that of a "head shrinker," or as younger and more hip patients sometimes say with affection, a "shrink." The image of head shrinking appears to refer both to the characteristic *reduction* of emotional problems through their verbal intellectual formulation, and to the *deflating* effect that recognition of one's less attractive unconscious desires has on the patient's ego.

"Healing magic," on the other hand, is marked by a very positive, enthusiastic, happy response on the part of the patient, who feels greatly helped by the effective power and benevolent acceptance of the therapist. In this type of good therapy experience it seems that it is not so much what the therapist does that counts as it is the personal qualities that the patient perceives in him. The therapist appears to enter the patient's experience as a "good parent" whose concern and acceptance are a balm to hurt feelings. This pattern, known in the psychoanalytic literature as "positive transference," has been likened to a kind of therapeutic honeymoon. Patients sometimes refer to their therapists in this type of positive experience as the "Wizard" (or simply as "Wiz") because of the power he seems to have to make them feel better.(Both the Wizard of Oz and Gandalf, the good wizard in Tolkien's *Lord of the Rings,* come to mind as possible prototypes.) One's tendency in this rationalistic age is to disbelieve in the potency of magic. But only those who have never experienced charismatic influence (or who have never been in love) can doubt that it has real effects in the realm of interpersonal relations.

"Mutual personal openness" is the type of good therapy experience that has been most fully described and advocated in existential, experiential, and recent client-centered writings on psychotherapy. In our sampling this pattern was marked by a sense of equality, trust and personal openness between patient and therapist. The therapist did not appear as a superior or as an impersonal being whose private reactions are hidden from view. Each participant had confidence in himself and confidence in the other, which permitted mutual sharing of "confidences" in a more intimate manner than had been the custom in a "professional" relationship. Mutual personal openness included, on the therapist's part, a willingness to be frankly evaluative and confronting with the patient: to let the patient know what was on his mind. This honest availability of the therapist's personal reactions to the patient was matched, on the patient's part, by a greater willingness or capacity to make inner feelings and fantasies known to the therapist. The patient and therapist appeared to esteem and to treat each other as adult persons who can "take it." Because of the personal nature of the encounter, the patient is frequently on a first-name basis with the therapist: the patient calls the therapist "Carl," for example, rather than "Doctor So-and-so."

Each of the three therapeutic potentials was reflected in the composite ideal therapy experience. The influence of "collaborative analytic progress" is seen from our research in the desire of both patient and therapist to work together to deepen the patient's insight and self-understanding. It can also be seen in the topical focus on dreams, and on memories of childhood experiences with important family members.

The influence of "healing magic," on the other hand, is found in the euphoric quality of the patients' feelings and in their reports that, in the ideal therapy experience, they received all the satisfactions listed on the questionnaire.

The effect of "mutual personal openness" can be traced in the sharing, give-and-take, emotionally responsive manner in which both patients and therapists related to each other, and in the heightened personal involvement shown in the therapists' reports of their own feelings.

Thus the evidence now available indicates at least three paths toward an experience that has therapeutic value. And this evidence may suggest a "three-factor theory" of therapeutic efficacy. The three types of experience are independent but not mutually exclusive, and they seem to be rooted in the potentials of the psychotherapy relationship as a helping and helpful experience. Further exploration along these lines may resolve some of the current differences between the various theoretical orientations to psychotherapy, each of which appears to stress one or another of these therapeutic potentials and to neglect the rest of them.

What we have learned from the Psychotherapy Session Project thus far is particularly exciting to us because it is based on a scientific analysis of the subjective experience of psychotherapy. It has given us an important glimpse "inside psychotherapy." As results come in from other studies now in progress, we hope this glimpse will become a much broader view.

THE TYPICAL THERAPY EXPERIENCE

Patient wants to:	Get a better understanding of my feelings and behavior.
	Get help in talking about what is really troubling me.
	Work out a problem that I have.
	Work together with my therapist on a person-to-person basis.
	Get advice on how to deal with my life and with other people.
Patient talks about:	Feelings and attitudes toward myself.
	Social activities and relationships, friends and acquaintances.
	Relationship with spouse, boyfriend or girlfriend.
Patient feels:	Anxious
	Tense
Patient relates by:	Initiating topics.
	Engaging in a give-and-take relationship.
	Being friendly.
	Being emotional or stirred up.

Therapist tries to:	Increase my patient's insight and self-understanding.
	Move my patient closer to experiencing her real feelings, what she really is.
	Engage my patient in an honest person-to-person relationship, work together authentically.
Therapist feels:	Interested
	Calm
	Involved
	Alert
	Confident
	Sympathetic
Therapist relates by:	Interacting, working together.
	Engaging in give-and-take relationship.
	Being friendly.
	Being emotionally responsive, stirred.

Patient gets:	A sense of having an honest person-to-person relationship with my therapist, of working together.
	Help in being able to talk about what was troubling to me and really important.
	Better insight and self-understanding.

THE USUAL. Patient wants understanding and help, talks mostly about current feelings and activities, often feels anxious and tense; therapist tends to feel interested and calm.

THE IDEAL THERAPY EXPERIENCE

Patient wants to:	Get a better understanding of my feelings and behavior.
	Let my therapist see how I've improved.
	Work together with my therapist on a person-to-person basis.
Patient talks about:	Relationship with spouse, boyfriend or girlfriend.
	Dreams, fantasies.
	Social activities and relationships, friends and acquaintances.
	Childhood experiences with family members and feelings about them.

Patient feels:		
Relieved	Interested	Confident
Trusting	Likeable	Satisfied
Accepted	Calm	Effective
Optimistic	Relaxed	Energetic
Alert	Secure	

Patient relates by:	Initiating topics.
	Interacting, working together.
	Engaging in give-and-take relationship.
	Being friendly.
	Being emotional.

Therapist tries to:	Increase my patient's insight and self-understanding.
	Move my patient closer to experiencing her real feelings, what she really is.
	Support my patient's self-esteem.

Therapist feels:		
Optimistic	Alert	Confident
Satisfied	Pleased	Intimate
Close	Interested	Tender
Involved	Sympathetic	Attracted
Effective		

Therapist relates by:	Interacting, working together.
	Engaging in give-and-take relationship.
	Being emotionally responsive, stirred.

Patient gets:	All listed satisfactions.

THE BEST. Now patient wants to demonstrate gains, talks more about fantasies and the past, usually feels relieved and trusting; therapist feels optimistic and satisfied.

TA: A Populist Movement

The TA movement grew out of a nucleus of therapists who met weekly with Eric Berne during the '50s and '60s. They rejected the elitism of psychoanalysis, which demanded years of expensive therapy made mystifying to the patient by impregnable jargon. From the first, TA was to be a therapy for the people.

Its principles are stated in common language; its group setting keeps the price tag low. There is an extensive training program for TA professionals, but there also is an expanding network of teaching groups that train people to use TA in their own lives and work.

Berne was clearly the pioneer and leader of the movement, but others made important contributions. David Kupfer, the first president of the International Transactional Analysis Association (ITAA), with headquarters in Berkeley, developed many of TA's clinical techniques and helped organize TA's teaching program. Claude Steiner and Fanita English have done important work on Script Analysis, and Kenneth V. Everts, the current ITAA president, has continued the organization's growth. ITAA membership now numbers over 2,400.

Like any movement, TA has its internal differences. Steiner has broken away to form the Berkeley Radical Psychiatry Center; others would like to see the California-based ITAA decentralized. Most TA leaders believe that the diversity of thought brought by growth is providing vitality. The movement has so far not split into factions as did Freud's circle, but the next few years will be crucial.

S O, DAVID HAS JUST BEEN FIRED and he can't marry me," Stella said as the group treatment session began. "I had such high hopes, but—I got stuck with a bum!"

"That's too bad about David's job," said Bill. "But surely—it was not long after your disappointment with John that you said you were crazy about David . . ."

"Don't remind me about that rat," said Stella. "I was so happy with him after Victor left for Europe! Maybe I shouldn't, but I've got to give up on men!" She waited.

"Look," Bill continued, "there *are* some good guys around, you know, like . . ."

"No!" said Stella. She turned away and began to cry.

"There you go again on your crybaby racket!" said George. "You shouldn't be bothering us with all this nonsense!"

"Sure, you can attack *me*, George," said Stella with sudden angry dignity, "but you're not so hot with your boss!"

"You're being unfair to Stella, George," said Gina. "Let's all try to be kind to one another."

"Thank you, Gina," said Stella. "You at least understand . . ."

Before others in the eight-patient group could add their opinions, the therapist intervened by pointing to the circles and lines she had drawn on a large pad of paper.

A group therapist who *interrupts* group process?

Yes. Transactional Analysts actively enter their groups to identify transactions among the members.

Eric Berne developed Transactional Analysis as a method that each patient—not just the therapist—can use to understand the pattern of his transactions with others. Usually when a patient sees exactly how archaic childhood needs determine his current transactions, he can make appropriate changes.

Transactions take place between the separate Ego-States of persons rather than between their total personalities. An Ego-State is a coherent system of feelings and thoughts from which a person operates at any given moment. The first step in TA treatment is practice in differentiating Ego-States as they operate in the here-and-now. There are three of these states, which Berne called PARENT, ADULT and CHILD.

Three Ego States. Each of us starts out with the Child, who incorporates messages from the environment into his own particular system of thought and feeling. As we grow, we each develop the Parent Ego-State, into which we integrate parental instructions and examples. Lastly, usually after the age of 12, the Adult-Ego State becomes functional, for we have acquired the capacity for logical thought and can process reality objectively.

The Adult Ego-State operates like a computer; though it has no feelings of its own, feelings in the Child or Parent can activate it to consider the variables of a situation and to promote or defer action.

By the time a person is grown, all three systems operate interchangeably, often in rapid succession. Internal dialogues, transactions with others, and the events of daily life can trigger switches from

by Fanita English

TRANSACTIONAL & SCRIPT ANALYSIS TODAY

one Ego-State to another. People actually *choose* to operate out of a particular Ego-State, although many persons avoid recognizing this. The choice may come from past conditioning and archaic fears, but it is not necessarily "unconscious." An autonomous person can determine his appropriate Ego-State at any time without being stifled or driven by anachronistic needs. Tone of voice, gesture, facial expression, body posture, and syntax are the keys to identifying which Ego-State is operating at a particular moment, and from them, one can diagram any transaction. In the above fragmentary TA session, for instance, Stella began in a Child Ego-State, then briefly switched to a "Critical Parent" when replying to George. This can be illustrated thus:

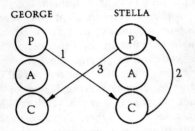

GEORGE   STELLA

1) GEORGE (Critical Parent addressing Child) "There you go again!"
2) STELLA Switches from Child to Critical Parent.
3) "You're not so hot either!"
The diagram shows that Stella's switch of Ego-States crossed the transactional vectors between her and George. When vectors cross, communication between the two persons halts abruptly. In contrast, when Gina spoke out of her Parent Ego-

State Stella reentered her own earlier "Adapted Child" Ego-State; thereupon Gina and Stella started on a complementary transaction:

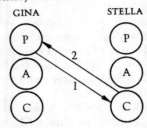

GINA   STELLA

1) GINA (Parent) "Let's be kind" (implied "poor you" to Stella).
2) STELLA (Child to Parent) "You at least understand."

In this transaction the vectors are parallel, showing that the transactional exchange can proceed indefinitely.

Complementary transactions maintain open channels of communication and can be gratifying. However, sometimes they represent the beginning of a "Racket," i.e., a series of complementary transactions in which one or both partners artificially reproduce old patterns, in order to avoid awareness of other, more pertinent, thoughts or feelings. The therapist intervened before Gina and Stella could continue their "poor you" and "I'm unhappy" transactions. These would simply maintain a chronic, unproductive "Racket."

Folks Need Strokes. According to Berne, people transact to exchange "strokes." A stroke is a unit of recognition; the term reminds us that the infant derives his primary vital recognition through physical handling and stroking.

Once past infancy, we symbolize. We register strokes from smiles, frowns, voice quality and, finally, from words. Eventually we "store" strokes and replay them for ourselves at future times. This is an advantage in times of stress or scarcity but not when a person depends on stored strokes in preference to genuine, live strokes that come from honest interchange with others. Such a person remains emotionally withdrawn and comes to depend on contrived strokes like the ones Stella extracted from Gina.

"Positive" strokes can be physical caresses, smiles or words of acceptance. Blows, frowns or verbal criticisms give us "negative" strokes. A person might also send "crooked" strokes, which convey contradictory messages: one from his Parent Ego-State and an opposite one from his Child Ego-State. For example, a suffocating hug might be thought to convey parental love to a baby, but the covert Child message that accompanies the "love" is: "Lose your breath!" "Die!" "Don't be!"

Young children need many strokes for sheer survival. They lap up whatever kinds they get—positive, negative or crooked—and they become conditioned to that mix. Their Child Ego-State concludes that the particular diet of strokes they were raised on is the only kind worth getting. Thus, people who grow up on a diet consisting mainly of negative strokes continue to crave them. Often they become delinquent or addicted to drugs in order to keep receiving the negative strokes they mistakenly believe they need.

Of crooked strokes and troll messages, rackets and games, fairy godmothers and the tense collaboration between Sleepy, Sparky and Spunky. "I'm OK (sober)—you're OK." The whimsical vocabulary of Transactional Analysis demystifies the patient.

In the case of crooked strokes, the covert Child messages that come with parental strokes make a greater impact than the overt ones do, because a young child is particularly attuned to emotional, nonverbal behavior. If a child receives sustained, malevolent, covert messages, he becomes confused and concludes that such strokes are necessary for survival. He adapts to them. Some babies become passive (lifeless); others learn to cry and scream, and others respond in whatever somatic ways bring them extra strokes.

These conclusions remain as magical formulas that continue to operate in the Child Ego-State of a grown person although they become transformed into new symbols, images and words, and they spill over into additional feelings. They determine important aspects of a person's life.

For instance, when Stella was born, her mother felt stuck with a baby. She had an alcoholic, unemployed husband. As a conscientious mother, she stroked Stella, particularly when Stella was crying and making noises that the neighbors could hear, but her Child Ego-State simultaneously sent out "I wish you were dead!" messages. So Stella learned that stroking depended on being unhappy, crying and screaming. Stella's father also stroked her, but his presence was erratic. Even as a toddler, Stella sensed that her angry mother, on whom she depended, resented closeness between Stella and her father and liked it when Stella rejected him. When Stella was five the mother evicted the father from home. Stella, with Child-logic, concluded: to survive I must be unhappy, cry, and reject men, particularly any who might love me; they endanger me and then disappear.

Now Stella, at age 30, operated in the group according to her early conclusions. Her Child sought strokes for unhappiness from Gina's Parent, but rejected strokes from Bill. Her Parent (internal mother) attacked George the way her mother had attacked her father.

TA is contractual. However "sick" the patient, his Adult can be reached for a realistic treatment contract. In many cases, contract negotiations about a treatment goal become crucial first steps in confronting unrealistic fantasies in the Child, or perfectionistic standards in the Parent. As he implements his contract, the patient usually becomes aware of feelings and intuitions operating in his natural Child. (This term is used in contrast to the "Adapted Child" Ego-State, in which a person operates in relation to a real or imagined Parent.)

The group provides opportunities for patients to distinguish among their varied Child Ego-States, their Parent and their Adult. They discover what kinds of strokes and transactions each member seeks and how their own Adult, rather than their Parent, can bridge the gap between reality and the needs of their natural Child.

Usually such insights will free people from anachronistic conclusions; they learn how they can relate to others with more inner freedom. But in some cases intensified Rackets and accelerated Games warn of a dangerous process that requires Script Analysis to offset it. This was true in Stella's case. She was actively implementing a tragic "loneliness script" that doomed her to a hateful and unhappy ending.

A Script for Life. The principles of Script Analysis have evolved out of the accumulated clinical experience of Transactional Analysts. We have evidence that, between the ages of three and seven, a child develops a "script" for his future—i.e., a story-line blueprint that determines how he will live the rest of his life—particularly his important relationships, his feelings about himself and his achievements, and the outcome that he will experience as "success," "failure," "I almost made it," or "at least I tried." The Child Ego-State of the grown person maintains the script and, unexamined by Adult knowledge and logic, it pervades the significant patterns of the person's life. When a person feels "lucky" his script probably calls for good relationships and successful outcomes; there is no need for Script Analysis, except perhaps for improving creativity and flexibility. But in cases like Stella's, nothing short of skillful specific intervention will modify the dangerous and irrational aspects of a script that relentlessly proceeds like a Greek tragedy.

A child develops his script on the basis of his "existential position"—i.e., the way he feels about himself and others. This position is established at about the age of three.

Berne listed four such positions:
I'm OK. You're OK.
I'm not OK. You're not OK.
I'm not OK. You're OK.
I'm OK. You're not OK.
To these I have added a fifth:
I'm OK—SOBER—and—you're OK. This position describes a person who has confronted and accepted human imperfection, yet enjoys being human.

Although Berne claimed that everyone is born a prince or princess, it is impossible to maintain utter innocence. Even a well-cared-for infant inevitably experiences helplessness and rage, so all children experience varying degrees of "I'm not OK, you're not OK" feelings about themselves and their caretakers. Some unfortunate persons remain stuck in this position the rest of their lives, on a behavioral spectrum that ranges all the way from autism to scripts that call for suicide or homicide. In contrast, some lucky persons achieve the position I'm OK—SOBER—and you're OK, because they have been given loving acceptance and safe boundaries for the expression of fear and primary rage.

In many cases people establish a halfway position to ward off primary feelings, expecially when these were condemned or denied by their parents. Either they take the Not OK burden onto themselves and maintain hope in salvation (I'm not OK but you are, so help!) or they project the Not OK outwards (I'm OK but you're not; all would go well if people would do it my way).

Either one of these lopsided positions is a tenuous defense against the terror of an I'm not OK, you're not OK position, and the individual is vulnerable to panic or severe anxiety if his position is shaken, as happens during Script Analy-

Although Berne claimed that everyone is born a prince or princess, it is impossible to maintain utter innocence.

sis. Only well-trained therapists should attempt such work.

Sleepy, Spunky, Spooky. At the time he forms his script, each child has three different coexisting tendencies. He can be: 1) regressive (a curled up child sucking his thumb); 2) explorative (a toddler crawling forth to grab an ashtray); and, 3) adaptive (a child checking mother's facial expression before he moves). These characteristic aspects are personified as Sleepy, Spunky and Spooky in order to identify their separate influences in script formation and in the Child Ego-State of a grown person.

Sleepy represents the most primitive part of the child, with a basic pull to inertia. He depends on parental strokes for survival, lest he sink into autism or death. If the Child of the caretaking parent sent too few strokes or covert "Die!" or "Don't be!" messages, Sleepy keeps a tendency to regressive death and a recurring, desperate hunger for strokes of any kind.

Spunky is the lively part of the "natural" child. He offsets the inertia of Sleepy with his active curiosity, intuition, and eager zest for life. He represents the adventuresome, creative aspect of the individual, but he lacks an instinct for self-preservation and needs protection lest he destroy himself by some unguided action.

Spooky serves to restrain Spunky's thrusts, because he is the one who responds to and assimilates lifesaving "do's" and "don'ts" from his caretakers. He is the part of the child that experiences fear, and he can be controlled by shame. His protective function compensates for the human child's lack of precise instincts, but he is incapable of evaluating the quality of the "protective" messages he takes in. He is the one who draws conclusions about "conditions for survival" and he is dedicated to implementing them, even if his conclusions turn out to be irrational and downright destructive.

We call harmful assimilated messages "injunctions" or "witch" or "troll" messages (good ones are called "fairy godmother" or "kindly wizard" permissions)

because fairy tales depict the emotional experience of children in the incomprehensible gargantuan realm of grownups.

The impetus for a script comes from Spunky, to meet his zest for life and his "time-structure hunger"—i.e., a human yearning to organize the future. However, Spooky participates actively in script formation to make sure that the "conditions for survival" are observed.

In uneasy alliance, Sleepy, Spunky and Spooky struggle to develop a pattern for the future that will accommodate the divergent forces they each represent. These divergent pulls do not cancel each other, because they are not processed logically. The young child's mental system is very different from the adult's, as Piaget has demonstrated. It can maintain, side by side, contradictory combinations of feelings, goals and beliefs. The child thinks syncretically, pulling together incidental analogies, coincidental juxtapositions and approximations of imagery. This process serves him well, because it leads to Spunky's creative combinations and quick flashes of intuition unhampered by ponderous deductive logic. But it also maintains Spooky's magical beliefs and his archaic cause-and-effect conclusions that may some day steer the whole person to disaster.

The Equilibrating Child. At about the age of five or six the child actively seeks verbal content and imagery for the inchoate images, ideas, goals, messages and conclusions he has collected. Many are attached to undigested scraps from fairy tales, cartoons, animal stories, Bible stories, TV shows and stray remarks that he overheard. Reality and fantasy are interwoven. Witches, fiery dragons, genies, curses, magic pitfalls and escapes are as believable as the magical appearance of water from a faucet, fire from a match, or a picture on a TV screen. By means of a complex, back-and-forth mental process of equilibration, such as Piaget describes, the child projects more and more of his view of the future onto a mental screen. One day, a particular fairy tale or animal story turns him on. With a few changes here and there, perhaps some

omissions, this story accommodates all the scraps he was trying to fit together. It offers a plot, and a cast of characters. Now he knows what to look for in his life, and, in varying proportions, he can play hero, villain, rescuer and victim.

As the child grows up, he appears to have forgotten his chosen tale, but the basic plot remains in his Child Ego-State. Later, as an adolescent or an adult, he might suddenly vibrate to a more complex story—a myth or a novel or a biography or a movie. Once again there's the feeling: yes, somehow, that's mine. The person may never realize that there, couched in new, more verbal symbols, is the theme he selected long, long ago, in another, magic realm.

Yet the marvelous, imaginative, but sometimes terrified little girl or boy of five or so who established the original story is not relegated to dusty photo-albums or to the "unconscious" of dreams. That child, complete with magic thinking, lives, breathes, feels and thinks in the guise of the Child Ego-State, actively steering the grown person through the chosen script. Often the tale is exciting, with adventures, thrills, and imaginative solutions; sometimes it is drab or sad or tragic.

The Dismal Script. In treatment it is not necessary to get a detailed view of a person's script. This is often impossible, for the more imaginative the individual, the more complex the script. But each script has clearly recognizable basic themes and patterns which, when grasped, predict the person's future relationships, his adventures, his life course, and even his ending.

The Script Analyst tries to identify and offset dangerous or stultifying patterns or tragic script directions; these are always based on malevolent ("witch") messages from the Child Ego-State of one or both parents, and on archaic, irrational conclusions by Spooky.

A patient's particular combination of Rackets and Games, as they surface in the microcosm of the treatment situation, represent his archaic conclusions.

To get a broad view of his script, we sometimes use a "script matrix"—a dia-

As the child grows up, he appears to have forgotten his chosen tale but the plot remains in his Child Ego-State.

"Therapy should be like a poker game," Eric Berne liked to say, "the result is what counts." He was skilled at getting results with both his poker hands and his patients. He believed therapists should cure or they shouldn't be therapists. In one of his last lectures, he charged that many psychiatrists are losers who simply cultivate the losing habits of their patients. Berne's own success came after a bitter disappointment and years of tireless work. In the middle of his career, he turned away from the psychoanalytic establishment he had long respected, and began to work out the principles of a new therapy that dealt with here-and-now social interaction in layman's language. The result was Transactional Analysis, the best-selling books: *Games People Play* and *What Do You Say After You Say Hello?*, and unofficial status as the public's first analyst-laureate.

Berne was born Eric Lennard Bernstein in 1910, and grew up in a poor Jewish section of Montreal, Canada. His father and his grandfather were physicians, and Eric was always close to the practice of healing. His father's office was on the first floor of their home. Eric often made house calls with him, riding along in a horse-drawn sleigh. Eric was only 10 when his father died, but had already decided to follow him into medicine.

Berne's mother was a poet who worked as a writer and editor for local newspapers to support Eric and his younger sister. She encouraged him in his plans to become a doctor, but by the time he went to college he had caught her interest in writing as well. He studied English, psychology and pre-med at McGill University, and received a B.A. in 1931. In 1935, McGill awarded him an M.D. and a Master of Surgery degree.

He came to the United States to take his internship at Englewood Hospital in New Jersey and then a psychiatric residency at the Yale University Medical School. Faced with the anti-Semitism of America's prewar years, he changed his name to Berne and began a private psychiatric practice in Norwalk, Connecticut. He soon married, and joined the staff of Mt. Zion Hospital in New York. In 1941 he began training at the New York Psychoanalytic Institute, and went through analysis under Paul Federn, a former colleague of Freud.

Two years later Berne was in the Army Medical Corps, making 30-second diagnoses and experimenting with group-therapy techniques. He found that his split-second judgments often were more accurate than those made from careful examination, and began to observe his own intuition as he worked. His early ideas about nonverbal communication and intuition laid the groundwork for his research on Child Ego-states and the birth of Transactional Analysis.

When he left the military in 1946, he was again a bachelor and half-way through his first book. He settled in Carmel, California, and finished *The Mind In Action*, an introduction to psychology and psychiatry now revised and in print as *A Layman's Guide to Psychiatry and Psychoanalysis*.

He also resumed his own education at the San Francisco Psychoanalytic Institute and began a training analysis with Erik Erikson. He met Dorothy De Mass Way and almost immediately wanted to marry her, but Erikson told them to wait until he finished analysis. They took his advice, and were married in 1949. The next year, he took a position with San Francisco's Mt. Zion Hospital, and reopened a private practice.

Throughout the '50s he worked seven days a week, commuting 125 miles between Carmel and San Francisco. He taught, wrote, conducted therapy groups, saw private patients, consulted with the Army, and held seminars each Tuesday night with several younger therapists. In his groups and seminars he tested and discussed the ideas that were to become central to TA. He had always

ERIC BERNE:

aspired to become a member of the Psychoanalytic Institute, the bastion of traditional psychoanalysis. He continued to work toward that goal until 1956, when his application for membership was denied (Erik Erikson has also never been admitted). By then, Berne had 15 years of training and experience behind him, and he suspected it was his unwillingness to give up some unorthodox ideas and techniques that lay behind the Institute's refusal to admit him. He was hurt that he had been unable to get his ideas across to the men he respected, and their rejection doubled his resolve to make his own contribution to psychiatry.

In the next two years, he wrote a series of papers that developed and explained the basic principles of Transactional Analysis. His Tuesday evening seminars became the San Francisco Social Psychiatry Seminars, Inc. The incorporation allowed Berne to publish and edit the *Transactional Analysis Bulletin*. He went to the South Pacific three summers in a row to study socialization and mental illness in various island cultures. And with his typewriter continuously fed from a huge roll of paper, he began to present TA to the public.

Transactional Analysis in Psychotherapy appeared in 1961 and was soon followed by *The Structure and Dynamics of Organizations and Groups*, and *Games People Play*. *Games* appeared without fanfare, but slowly rose to the best-seller lists and brought Berne popular recognition. In that book, Berne labeled and displayed his collection of over a hundred maneuvers people use with each other to win hidden payoffs. His readers found themselves on every page, their games described in simple language and given earthy titles like "Rapo," "Ain't It Awful," and "Gee You're Wonderful,Mr. Murgatroyd."

Berne soon found himself on the pages of *Life* and *Newsweek*, and further estranged from many fellow psychiatrists who charged that he oversimplified. He charged back that they overcomplicated, and argued that psychiatry needed a language that both therapist and patient could understand. He continued to set high standards for himself, and grew quicker to anger at psychiatrists who moaned in staff conferences about why they couldn't cure their patients. "I think Freud would consider most analysts today nothing but picture hangers," he said. And when the Psychoanalytic Institute offered him the membership he had long sought, he declined with thanks.

He followed *Games* with *Principles of Group Treatment*, *Sex in Human Loving*, a children's book called *The Happy Valley*, and *What Do You Say After You Say Hello?* But Berne's strenuous schedule took a heavy toll on his personal life and his health. He and Dorothy were divorced in 1964, and he began to work even longer hours. He still sought female companionship, however, and married Torri Rosecrans in 1967. He gave up none of his writing commitments, and at one time was working on six books. Early in 1970 he and Torri were divorced, and he died of a heart attack in July of that year.

He had finished the manuscript of *What Do You Say After You Say Hello?* just before he died, but it was not published until early in 1972. In it, he breaks new ground with a discussion of script, a notion he and his collegues were drawn to from their study of games. They found that the pattern each person plays out during his life is often set in the first few years of childhood, and began to call this pattern a life script.

Berne came to believe that every script is recorded in the world's mythology. "The life of every human being," he said, "is already charted in Bulfinch or Graves." He called people with winning scripts "princes" and those stuck with losers, "frogs." "My business," he said, "is turning frogs into princes."

—Gary Gregg

A DRIVE TO SIMPLIFY & MAKE IT

gramed outline of the patient's childhood messages as we reconstruct them from his current transactions.

Sometimes we use modified psychodrama or Gestalt techniques, or specially guided imagery or art. Frequently we ask the patient to tell us his version of a childhood story that impressed him, and sometimes we ask him about a later favorite tale, or a particularly upsetting one.

Stella told us what she remembered of her favorite childhood tale: Rapunzel was a beautiful girl who was locked up in a witch's tower. To bring food, the witch would climb up the tower on Rapunzel's long golden braids. One day, after the witch left, a prince climbed up Rapunzel's braids and asked her to run away with him. Before he could bring a ladder to get her down, the witch returned and took Rapunzel away into the wilderness where the poor girl had to remain, crying and unhappy.

This story ties in with Stella's early childhood experience. She had to cry and be unhappy in order to be fed by her mother/witch. Her prince/father liked her, but he could not save her and disappeared, leaving Rapunzel worse off than before.

Stella recalled that in college she had been intrigued by the myth of Scylla, which she summarized for us:

Glaucus, the handsome sea-god, half man, half fish, fell in love with the lovely nymph Scylla when he saw her bathing, but she rejected him, so Glaucus asked Circe, the enchantress, to give Scylla a love potion. Instead, Circe poisoned the water in which Scylla bathed and turned her into a frightful monster. Scylla remained rooted to a rock in howling misery, hating and destroying all sailors who passed.

By comparing these two stories with each other and with Stella's transactions in the group and in her daily life, we can identify a basic theme of Stella's script and predict its frightening direction. Stella's Spunky Child starts out beautiful and attractive to a prince/god (presumably Stella got some good strokes from her father though he was "half fish"—alcoholic?) but his love only endangers her with the witch who provides her with food (strokes), for which she pays with tears and loneliness. Even this does not placate the witch. In the second story, Circe feeds her poison instead of food and sets even sterner "conditions for survival": howl with misery; alienate all men by becoming monstrous, hateful and destructive.

Stella's Spooky Child increasingly implemented these directions. In the session we described, Gina was cast as the mother/witch who gave strokes for unhappiness. Partners such as Gina, chosen principally for their response to unhappiness, eventually become critical (partly through exasperation at the persistent whining of an unhappiness Racket). Their strokes then become "poisonous"—i.e., more ritualized and crooked, or negative. Meanwhile, Stella's Spooky Child deliberately turned away genuine strokes from men like Bill, whom she cast as stand-ins for the ineffective prince. Angry payoffs from "Blemish Games" such as the one Stella played with George offered temporary relief by discharging her accumulated frustration from stroke-deprivation. But Stella's investment in such Game payoffs cut her off from good strokes and threatened to turn her into a lonely howling monster who would attack all "sailors who passed by."

Once the irrational Spooky conclusions are spelled out, many patients can make effective "redecisions" about their lives and can redirect otherwise creative scripts by testing new ways of relating to others. But when Stella made such tries, she experienced severe anxiety and an increase in the migraine headaches that had originally brought her into treatment.

Stella's script was a valiant attempt to overcome severe "Die!" messages she long ago received from her mother's Child and perhaps even from her father's. Beneath the pathetic script lay the dread of an even worse fate (death) if she dared transgress its compromise. Stella did not dare test this compromise for fear of death. She already received the warnings of anxiety and headaches from her Spooky Child whenever she accepted and enjoyed positive strokes from men. Stella was filled with a sense of doom and despair that she could not put into words. She needed permission to live, a permission Stella had never received

In Stella's stories, neither heroine took any initiative. Each remained passive, run by others. Even in fantasy, Stella's Spooky Child did not allow the spontaneous expression of feelings; she could not even enjoy the admiration of the prince/Glaucus. She had received no continuing response or protection from her father. It did not pay to have positive feelings for him; he had been thrown out. Were Stella to express honest emotions and have straight transactions, her Spooky Child believed that she would die. She was enjoined, nonverbally and verbally, against expressing frustration or anger at her mother, on whom she depended for nurture (even though it was witch food).

Even within the protected boundaries of the group, Stella consistently refused to acknowledge any feelings of annoyance at the (female) therapist. She had to please the witch. Yet in accordance with her script, she was systematically rejecting all positive strokes from men, and attacking them more frequently.

Healing Magic? The feeling of being "cursed," which surfaces in patients with "die" messages when their script conclusions are challenged, is not to be taken lightly. It can trigger dangerous action at the very period when the patient seems to be overcoming harmful script injunctions by taking new risks in relationships. This is why some persons have psychotic breaks or car accidents or attempt suicide after peak experiences with charismatic leaders who promote risk-taking without recognizing when a constricting, irrational script is warding off even worse outcomes.

It may sound incredible that an educated professional young woman in 20th-century America could be as deeply under the sway of a curse as the most primitive aborigine, but this is exactly what we discover over and over again in our clinical practice. Even though the same person sounds rational while in the Adult (or even the Parent) Ego-States, his existential convictions about life, death, afterlife and the future remain influential through his Child. And, if there have been doom and death messages, the Sleepy and the Spooky parts of the Child take over power when the person confronts his script conclusions.

A person experiences a "curse" as a flooding of "I'm not OK, You're not OK" feelings, with despair, desolation, hopelessness and total lack of trust. Irrational, magical thinking takes over. Sometimes, in trying to propitiate his unknown ghosts he precipitates the very calamities he dreads.

In such cases, magic must be countered with magic. Nothing short of exorcism will do, to be followed by new fairy-godmother permissions. To exorcise the curse, the therapist puts on a "Merlin;" i.e., she takes on a magical, all-powerful Parental role to deal with the patient's Spooky Child. She indicates that she (the therapist) is more powerful than the old witch, who is way back in the six-year-old realm. The therapist reminds the Child that she has a new guardian of her own—her grown-up self that enables her to use physical mobility and elementary know-how to survive. The therapist bestows permissions: Permission to feel what you feel! Permission to *know* how you feel! Permission to seek out and recognize real strokes! Permission to enjoy! Permission to *live*! And permission to *not hurt yourself*! This last permission must be given with the most force—for in cases like Stella's the other permissions might otherwise be taken as licenses to "go ahead and get into trouble," thereby implementing the curse.

The therapist must also protect the patient's scared Child. The protection must be stronger than the witch's perverse and dangerous racket—"protection" which would compel Stella to do herself in for transgressing the old messages. Before she begins, the therapist's Adult must have computed the precise purpose of the intervention, so there will be no contamination of motive and so the therapist can maintain confidence in her professional potency throughout the process.

The therapist must remember that the process shakes the patient's defensive existential position. Primitive "I'm not OK, you're not OK" feelings revive, and the patient experiences rage and despair. These feelings must be acknowledged and worked with empathetically. They are genuine and far different from previous phony "unhappiness." Paradoxically, such a crisis is the forerunner of success; the patient fights acknowledging it, but he has the tools he lacked

as an infant to deal with the frustrations of reality. He has an *Adult*.

Then the therapist can transfer the temporary power she established over the Child to the patient's Adult. Following "exorcisms," the therapist must openly check any hazards in the patient's life before relinquishing her temporary parental role. The energetic, emphatic permission to not hurt yourself is often spelled out by discussing with the patient's Adult necessary elementary rules about car-driving, alcohol, or other hazards. Together they establish various subcontracts about such matters. As the patient fulfills these subcontracts, her Spunky Child recognizes that it is her *own* Adult that offers her protection, not the therapist's Parent. The patient can afford to drop her active belief in magic, be it in the sorcery of the therapist, or in that of her own archaic witch messages.

The Altered Script? Stella's treatment crisis was terrifying to her but short-lived. It included violent rage at the therapist, but she emerged with the position I'm OK—SOBER—you're OK. She developed more awareness of her feelings and learned to deal with them in the here-and-now, by having more "straight" transactions and good-stroke exchanges with women *and* men. Her headaches disappeared, and it became clear from her transactions in the group and from her friendships outside, that she had stopped implementing her tragic script. Stella's Spunky Child was growing creatively, along with her ability to develop intimate relationships.

Script Analysis is still a new discipline that requires careful training and supervision. Berne began to elaborate Script Analysis only a few years before his death; he, like his followers, felt that there is much clinical research yet to do. Even so, Script Analysis opens the way for accurate predictive work with patients—and one's own self—such as could not be contemplated before.

Behind Script Analysis lie the profound existential dilemmas of human beings: the nature of destiny, of freedom, of social control through fear and shame, and of autonomy. Script Analysis limits itself to dealing with those aspects of a person's fate that he can determine for himself; we are finding that there are many more such aspects than we formerly believed.

It is a heady experience for many persons simply to discover that they can *choose* the Ego-State they will operate in, at a given moment, instead of feeling compelled to respond in accordance with old patterns.

As therapeutic methods, Transactional and Script Analysis include both rational and emotional approaches. We delve into deep feelings, use fantasy techniques at selected points and we even go so far as to use "magic" to frighten off ancient ghosts. However, we maintain the TA principle that, sooner or later, the patient must have the opportunity to understand *with his Adult* what his script messages involve. This means translating preverbal material into comprehensible language and diagrams. It is the patient's Adult, not the therapist and not his Parent, who must determine his choices, preferably in the service of his own blossoming Child.

The TA technique is clear, direct and effective. Patients can identify Ego-States and transactions just as well as therapists can. Even when it comes to the profound Script Analysis of a particular patient, the process soon becomes intelligible to other group members. Thereby, therapy is demystified, and the activity of the therapist herself is openly scrutinized. Her contract requires her to maintain her Adult (while patients are encouraged to free their Spunky Children) and her patients can keep tabs as to whether the therapist is operating usefully. This, in itself, represents a major advance in psychotherapy.

by Irene Kassorla

FOR CATATONIA:

Smiles, Praise, and a Food Basket

IN MAY 1967, several British newspapers carried a story with headlines to this effect: "SCHIZOPHRENIC PATIENT SPEAKS AFTER 30 SILENT YEARS." This was a major event in the life of the patient, and it was also another kind of milestone. Operant conditioning, which has been used experimentally with psychotics in this country a number of times during the last few years, had never been tried before in Britain with such a severely regressed human subject.

Partly for that reason I decided, when I went to England to direct the project, to work with the "sickest" patient I could find. A group of psychiatrists recommended Mr. B., a catatonic and mute schizophrenic living in a ward at Springfield Hospital, just south of London. According to the psychiatrists, this man showed fewer fragments of normal behavior than any other patient in a British mental hospital.

Mr. B's history showed that he had been under unusual stress from an early age. He quit school at 11 in order to earn additional income for his family, which was on public assistance. His mother was fatally ill; his father, who had been a milkman, was severely depressed and had not worked for years. Mr. B. held a series of short-term, unskilled jobs in the neighborhood.

When he was 18, he became very attracted to a girl who lived next door. She was a beautiful girl, blonde and fair, but Mr. B. was afraid to confront her because "she was so much better than me." Instead, he watched her through the window. He did this secretly, and without incident, for about a year. Then the girl's father caught him. He reprimanded Mr. B., loudly and severely, in the presence of the surprised girl.

This was an extremely painful and humiliating experience for Mr. B. He became very depressed, stopped eating, and had trouble sleeping. One night he awoke in a sweat, screaming that he had murdered the girl's father. His fantasy persisted, and his verbal behavior became increasingly hallucinated. His father, unable to care for him, had him admitted to a mental hospital.

Once in the hospital, Mr. B. got worse instead of better. His speech ceased to have meaning; he refused to bathe or dress; he would not take part in the normal hospital routines set up for patients; he often became violent. After two years, he withdrew into total silence. Many therapies were tried, including electric shock and drugs, but Mr. B.'s behavior did not change. Month after month, for the next 30 years, his hospital record read: "mute, negativistic, sits motionless for much of the day, needs full nursing care."

Early in 1967, Jag Behrgold, Ian Evans, Rosemary Nelson, Ronnie Balmforth, Bernard Perloff and I began our experimental project with this man. Our method of training, operant conditioning, is based on the principle that behavior which is reinforced is likely to occur again, but that brief description makes the training sound considerably easier than it was. With Mr. B, our first problem was to find a bit of behavior that bore some resemblance to speech, so that we would have something to reinforce.

On the first day of the experiment, we asked Mr. B. a series of 120 questions that most seven-year-old children can answer: "What is your name?" "Where do you live?" "How old are you?" During 89 percent of the questioning he remained silent, head down. He didn't move, and seemed to be sleeping with his eyes open. The rest of the time he responded with a barely audible "ugh," and twice with something that sounded like "crack 'em." We gave the same series of questions to two other schizophrenics, men who showed almost as little normal behavior as Mr. B., and they responded almost as infrequently.

These results gave us a baseline by which we could judge Mr. B's progress, and a baseline for the control pair, who would not receive training. Mr. B.'s responses also helped us over our first hurdle: they told us what to reinforce. We planned to begin with an imitative paradigm, in which the experimenter would say a word and then reinforce the patient for repeating it, or even for moving his mouth in the slightest way. As the word, we chose "crack 'em."

In starting with a sound that was already part of the patient's verbal repertoire, we did much the same thing that parents do with infants just before they begin to talk. As first, when a baby babbles, his parents simply imitate the meaningless sounds, This babbling back and forth is the earliest form of verbal communication between parent and child. Later, the parents are more selective. They choose a sound which resembles one that has meaning in their language and say it to the child, inviting him to repeat it and smiling and nodding happily when he does. As this process continues, the child gradually increases his repertoire of meaningful sounds and drops the nonsense ones. It is extremely important that the parents choose for reinforcement a sound they have already heard the baby make. A mother who urges her baby to say "father" or "mon père" instead of "da-da" or "pa-pa" is likely to have a long wait.

With our severely withdrawn patient, we could not expect intangible reinforcements to have much effect, especially at first. So, although we did smile and praise him at every opportunity, the reinforcement we relied on was food. In spite of considerable resistance from the hospital staff, which felt that Mr. B. was too sick to talk and should not be treated "unkindly," we took full control of the patient's feeding.

Initially, we gave food to him if he so much as moved his lips when the experimenter said "crack 'em." But by the fifth day of the experiment Mr. B. was repeating "crack 'em" about 10 percent of the time. From then on, any attempt to speak was rewarded with verbal praise, but only "crack 'em" was reinforced with food. Again, this is similar to the way parents act with their children. At first the infant is praised profusely for all approximations of speech, but as the child becomes more expert the parents begin to take his earlier accomplishments for granted, and to reinforce only improvements and new additions.

On the 14th day of training, Mr. B. was saying "crack 'em" after the experimenter about 92 percent of the time. This may not sound like much, but it was, for it meant that we had established control over the patient's verbal behavior. He was taking part in a verbal exchange—a primitive one, meaningless in terms of normal speech, but an exchange nonetheless—at a high, reliable rate.

In daily life, each of us has considerable control over the speech of other people. If you ask a child what his name is, he usually tells you; if you ask a woman in the supermarket where the meat counter is, she usually answers, even if she says no more than "Sorry, I don't know." Normal speech is like a game of catch: verbal stimuli are thrown back and forth, back and forth, like balls. Our patient, who had refused to play for 30 years, could now be counted on nine-tenths of the time to return at least this one ball.

It was time to add another word. We chose a real one this time, "dog," and we trained Mr. B. to say it by means of an imitative paradigm, as before. Now, however, the meaningless grunts that we had praised during the first phase of the experiment were ignored. Only "dog" was reinforced with food, and only "dog" and other verbalizations were praised. To add complexity and also, we hoped, meaning, the experimenter held up a picture of a dog each time he said the word to Mr. B.

This phase went faster than the first. After nine days of training, the patient was imitating the experimenter appropriately 90 percent of the time.

Working toward a higher level of speech, we showed the picture to Mr. B. and said, "What's this?" Mr. B. was quite used to saying "dog" and the picture was the same as before, but the patient was unable or unwilling to answer correctly. Instead, he said "I don't know." Although we were delighted that he was using a three-word sentence, it was difficult to believe him, for he had responded appropriately with "dog" before.

After seven days of "I don't know," we decided that this negativistic behavior was interfering with the patient's progress and we deliberately set out to extinguish it. According to operant conditioning theory, negativistic behavior and apparent nonbehavior (such as withdrawal and muteness) are forms of behavior nonetheless; like more obvious behavior, they continue because they are reinforced. If reinforcement is withdrawn, they die out.

So each time Mr. B said "I don't know" when we asked him to identify the picture of the dog, he was briskly and firmly removed from the room we were working in. This maneuver was something of a gamble. Its success would depend on whether Mr. B. did, as we thought he must, regard the experimental setting (where he had received food and praise) as positively reinforcing. But it worked. Within four days, the patient had stopped saying "I don't know," and soon he was answering "dog" almost all the time.

We began pointing to other objects in the room and asking "What's that?" We continued to usher Mr. B. out of the room whenever he said "I don't know." For appropriate answers we gave food. However, as Mr. B. had just shown us, a second reinforcement also seemed to be operating, in the form of the attention involved in training itself. Possibly he enjoyed not only being fed and praised, but found the experimental setting reinforcing.

On the 31st day of this phase, Mr. B. labeled more than 150 objects correctly, without a single case of negativism. At first we trained him systematically on each object. However, after the 31st day this labeling became less controlled, and we worked with magazines, newspapers and objects from the hospital grounds. We even took Mr. B. into the neighborhood shopping center, where he labeled items on the store counters. His vocabulary increased more spontaneously, as an infant's vocabulary often does once he has mastered the first few words.

Mr. B. had made considerable progress. As this point we needed to transfer control of his behavior to reinforcements that were likely to occur under ordinary (rather than experimental) conditions.

Without this vital step, a new repertoire of behavior often dies out when the experimenter packs his food basket and leaves. Transferring the control of behavior to natural reinforcers is an especially difficult problem for those who work with psychotic children, because children are so often dependent on adults for reinforcement. Frequently, disturbed children live in settings where parents may be preoccupied, ill, or themselves disturbed and therefore unable to deliver the reinforcements necessary to maintain new repertoires. An experimenter may, for example, train an autistic child to put on his coat, using a strong reinforcement such as food. He may then fade out the food, replacing it with a reinforcement that is more likely to occur when the child puts his coat on, such as going outside to the sandbox in the yard. But if the child then returns to a home where no one takes him outside, or indeed responds in any way, when he puts his coat on, he is not likely to continue the new behavior very long.

One reason that so many psychotics regress after they are hospitalized is that mental hospitals often are understaffed and unable to offer a reliable schedule of positive reinforcements. This is hardly surprising. Experts at operant conditioning, working in the ideal one-to-one relationship, often have a hard time identifying approximations of desirable behavior in psychotics and figuring out what they will find reinforcing; for an untrained, overworked ward nurse, the task is almost impossible.

However, we had some hope for Mr. B. For one thing, once behavior has been established, it can be maintained by intermittent reinforcement, and this we thought he could expect to get. For another, speech is basic to so much human behavior that it tends to be subject to a wide variety of reinforcements. The Occupational Therapy Department had become very interested in the research, and they were now regularly reinforcing Mr. B.'s speech.

We trained him to make direct demands, first in imitation of the experimenter and then merely in response to the sight of food. He would say "I want some tea," "I want some eggs," and so forth, and when he did, we gave them to him. Near the end of this phase of training, he began to generalize the behavior to areas not trained: "I want cigarettes"; "I want sweets"; "I want the magazine."

As a final step, we trained him to ask questions—a form of speech that is also likely to get some sort of response. During this phase, we moved from one part of the hospital to another, so that Mr. B. would not associate speech with just one room. We also encouraged the other patients to talk with him.

At the end of the experiment, we re-administered the series of 120 questions with which we began. The two schizophrenics who served as our control group answered rarely and inappropriately, as before. Mr. B., after 138 days of training, responded appropriately a full three-quarters of the time. He also answered, out loud, the rest of the time, but with minor errors.

Although Mr. B.'s speech lacked spontaneity, his catatonic behavior was gone and he was talking. As his occupational therapist described it, "Mr. B. isn't satisfied to sit back any more—he's right up front now. He's interested in everything. He'll run to you from across the room if you give him the slightest nod. We don't feed him for talking now—we just talk." At last report, received a year after the training stopped, Mr. B. was working with occupational therapists and still talking.

Group Therapy:
Let the Buyer Beware

Everett L. Shostrom

A shortage of professional manpower has resulted in programs to train students, housewives, grandmothers, and even hospitalized patients to serve as therapists. These nonprofessional therapists have learned to use a variety of approaches, ranging from behavior modification to psychodynamic therapy. Such programs have had remarkable success; clearly, certain individuals can act as effective therapists with only a minimum of training and supervision. However, there is nothing to show that powerful confrontation forms of therapy can be conducted successfully by persons with absolutely no training.

Despite this dearth of evidence, leaderless encounter groups and groups with untrained "facilitators" are becoming more and more popular. Perhaps this trend grows out of the attempt to discard the doctor-patient model and view the group leader as "one of the guys." The results of this approach have at times been humorous, at times disastrous. In his warning to the public, Everett Shostrom brings attention to the increasing problems of nonprofessional commercialism in the area of group therapy.

Joan was a fine scholar and teacher. She was fat and difficult, and had a grotesque limp, but true students loved her. She had made brilliant contributions to the High Minoan period, and her colleagues trembled as they waited to see what or whom she would demolish next. Joan was also pathologically sensitive about certain episodes of her adolescence. In a moment of distraction—she had been gleefully rebuked for a serious bibliographical error—Joan responded to an ad in the local underground paper; this ad promised an "encounter" group, and Joan was eager to encounter something. To her surprise, she found that two of the three other participants, including the leader, were university people whom she knew. Uncharacteristically, Joan said what the hell, and plunged into those interactions she had heard about. She found herself under cruel attack by the other participants, all of them therapeutically sophisticated; they quickly located and probed into the most painful segments of her life.

Initially, Joan felt herself rather better for the experience. In the weeks that followed, however, she thought she heard allusions to her deeply classified torments, even at the most superficial of faculty gatherings. Soon she began to suspect her most valued students of noninnocent, nonprofessional slyness—a quizzical smile here, a cool "Don't *you* think" there, a chuckle running through the lecture hall. . . . Three weeks later, on a bright afternoon, Joan drove her dusty and heretofore sluggish sedan into a bridge abutment.

They said she had been driving eighty miles an hour.

Doug worked in personnel, and his corporate star was rising. His people—applicants he had recommended—were turning out very well in the jobs he had selected them for. Doug was, however, bored and uneasy about his job—he felt that this "gift" his superiors were always talking about was overvalued. Doug went to an "attack-in" organized by his church; he was encouraged to give vent to his hostilities and critical scorn, and he did. It was great fun, and Doug carried the techniques back to his job. He got into a number of violent shouting matches with applicants and superiors, and was suddenly, and violently, fired.

Mr. and Mrs. Wassail had been married twenty-three years; they had done a commendable job of raising their children; they maintained respect for each other; and they had intelligent friends, eclectic but solid. On the advice of one of these close and trusted friends, they went to a sensory-awareness seminar. They arrived at a spectacular estate where very quickly they and some other persons very much like them abandoned themselves to systematic depravity. Mr. and Mrs. Wassail enjoyed themselves for a while but found that they were literally unable to face each other or their children. After a few months, they separated, with a great deal of oblique bitterness.

Bill was a slender, handsome young man who had been fighting clearsightedly what he had identified—correctly, but on principle and without professional

303

help—as homosexual panic. Bill read a newspaper ad that promised awareness and self-expansion. He signed up for sessions and was told—or rather shown—that everybody was really homosexual. Bill promptly, and with great relief, became a screaming queen. He alienated his parents and friends and found himself committed to a world in which he was by breeding, interests, and insight, truly and hopelessly alien.

Carl Rogers has said that the encounter group may be the most important social invention of the century, and he is probably right. The group experience has invaded every setting—industry, the church, universities, prisons, resorts. Corporation presidents have become group members, along with students, delinquents, married couples, dropouts, criminals, nurses, educators.

The demand for group experience—whether in the form of actualization groups, as I call them, or of T-groups, Synanon-like attack-ins, sensitivity-training groups, or marathons, nude and otherwise—has grown so tremendously that there are not now enough trained psychologists, psychiatrists, or social workers to meet it directly. As a result, groups organized by lay leaders have proliferated. While some of these lay groups have honestly and efficiently fulfilled their almost miraculous promises, others have been useless, stupid, dangerous, corrupt, and even fatal. I shall make it clear later that I am not arguing against lay leadership but rather for lay leadership that has been trained in such a way that the public will be protected. What I'd like to do at this point is suggest a few practical guidelines for choosing an encounter group, and then later take up a few general whys, maybes, and what-to-dos.

Each of the four examples with which I began this article contains elements that may be taken as fairly strict nos:

| 1. | Never respond to a newspaper ad. Groups run by trained professionals, or honestly supervised by them, are forbidden by ethical considerations to advertise directly. Modest and tasteful informational brochures are circulated among professionals in relevant disciplines, and referral by a reputable and well-informed counselor is one of the surest safeguards. Cheap mimeographed flyers promising marvels, especially erotic ones, are danger signals, as are donations or fees of less than $5.00. A good group is backed by a lot of labor and experience, which are today in very short supply.

| 2. | Never participate in a group of fewer than a half-dozen members. The necessary and valuable candor generated by an effective group cannot be dissipated, shared, and examined by too small a group, and scape-goating or purely vicious ganging-up can develop. Conversely, a group with more than sixteen members generally cannot effectively be monitored by anyone, however well trained or well assisted.

| 3. | Never join an encounter group on impulse—as a fling, binge, or surrender to the unplanned. Any important crisis in your life has been a long time in prepara-

tion and deserves reflection. If you are sanely suspicious of your grasp on reality, be doubly cautious. The intense, sometimes apocalyptic experience of the group can be most unsettling, particularly for persons who feel that they are close to what one layman calls "controlled schizophrenia." A trained person responsible for a meaningful session would not throw precariously balanced persons into a good encounter group. Nor would he allow persons who are diabolically experienced in the ways of group dynamics to form a group. If you find yourself in a group in which everybody talks jargon, simply walk out.

| 4. | Never participate in a group encounter with close associates, persons with whom you have professional or competitive social relations. Be worldly wise, or healthily paranoid, about this. As a corollary, never join a group that fails to make clear and insistent distinctions between the special environment of the group and the equally special environment of society. You should be told crisply that everything occurring within the group must be considered vitally privileged communication. You should always feel that the warm, vigorous dis-alienation that flowers in a good group is to a certain extent designed to suggest the richness of possibilities—in terms of self-knowing and other-knowing—and does not by any means imply a rigid code of behavior. In these matters, consult your common sense—it probably is one of the worst enemies you have, but it still is an entirely internalized enemy, hence deserving of notice.

| 5. | Never be overly impressed by beautiful or otherwise class-signaled surroundings or participants. Good group sessions can be held in ghetto classrooms, and all good sessions will include persons and life styles with which you do not identify intimately or on a day-to-day basis. Social or intellectual homogeneity in a group usually suggests an unimaginative, exploitative hostess mentality. A good group session should, I think, eventually unfold itself to every member as a kind of externalization or dramatization of himself—himself as fawner and snob, weakling and bully, villain and victim, poet and bureaucrat, critic and nice guy—himself as a small but complex galaxy of contraries. If you have a strong feeling that, as Huck Finn said, you've "been there before," you most probably have.

| 6. | Never stay with a group that has a behavioral ax to grind—a group that seems to insist that everybody be a Renaissance *mensch*, or a devotee of *cinéma vérité*—or a rightist or leftist, or a cultural, intellectual, or sexual specialist. This is narrow, destructive missionary zeal, or avocational education, and it has nothing to do with your self, your sweetest goals, or your fullest life as a self-knowing, self-integrating human being.

| 7. | Never participate in a group that lacks formal connection with a professional on whom you can check. Any reputable professional has a vital stake in any group he runs or in any group whose leader he has trained and continues to advise and consult. Such a professional

may be a psychiatrist (M.D.), a psychologist (M.A. or Ph.D. in psychology), a social worker (M.S.W.), or a marriage counselor (Ph.D.). One of the most significant questions to ask is, *Are you, or is your professional consultant, licensed to practice in this state?* If he has a Ph.D. and is not licensed, find out why not. Most reputable professionals are members of local, usually county, professional organizations; such organizations in many instances determine who may be listed where and how in your local Yellow Pages. If you can't find your group leader or the group's adviser in the Yellow Pages, check with the professional organization to find out why. It must be said at this point that all the training and accreditation in the world will not guarantee that every man in every place will be a good, efficient, worthy, or honest practitioner. Everyone knows that, but I am after all talking about rules of thumb, and rules and thumbs will take us just so far.

Any encounter group that uses the words *psychologist, psychiatrist, psychotherapy, psychotherapist, psychology,* or *therapy* in describing itself is usually subject to regulation by state laws and by the American Psychological Association, the American Psychiatric Association, or the National Association of Social Workers. In the past decade or so, however, humanistic psychology has explicitly and implicitly deemphasized therapy, at least in the sense of curing or treating people who are, on the analogy with physical medicine, mentally sick. Humanistic psychology, from whose passionate forehead the encounter group has sprung, tends to talk about *emotional growth, fulfillment of one's potential, feeling, contact,* and the participative *experiencing* of one's self and others with *honesty, awareness, freedom,* and *trust.* It has dealt usually with persons who are performing within socially acceptable parameters of legality, productivity, and success. It speaks usually to those who are not sick but rather normal—normally depressed, normally dissatisfied with the quality of their lives, normally tormented by irrelevance, meaninglessness, waste, loneliness, fear, and barrenness. Anyone can appropriate this humanistic vocabulary, set up shop as a lay encounter leader, and evade all professional and legal regulation by omitting psychological, psychiatric, and therapeutic terms from his descriptive catalogue or notice.

There are dangers in all group encounters—groups are crucibles of intense emotional and intellectual reaction, and one can never say exactly what will happen. It can be said generally, however, that well-trained people are equipped to recognize and deal with problems (and successes) before, while, and after they happen, and that ill-trained or untrained people often are not. Yet training—in the sense of specialized, formally accredited education—will not guarantee that a man or woman will be a helpful or successful group leader. Indeed, such researchers as Margaret Rioch have shown that natural group leaders with almost no training can facilitate precisely the kind of ideal, joyful, alive, tender, and altogether marvelous self-learning that the most highly trained leaders strive for. Since there are not enough trained professionals to go around, the problem is to get good group leaders—to develop a set of standards that will allow us to enroll good people, teach them the necessary skills, and send them out with some formal approval that will give the public a fair chance to stay out of trouble.

Such well-selected, well-trained leaders should have a title and a certificate of some sort indicating that they have met certain nationally accepted standards. They would stand in some fairly well-defined relationship to professionals and to other licensed counselors. The analogy that most quickly, and perhaps most unhappily, comes to mind is the relationship of registered nurses to physicians.

A good model for the kind of nation-wide programmatic training I have in mind should be developed by such groups as the national psychological and psychiatric associations. (The California State Psychological Association is considering legislation that would permit nonlicensed persons to practice group leadership only when they are supervised by trained psychologists.) Research is badly needed to evaluate and measure competence and codify standards. In the meantime, there is a pilot program that can serve as an example at the National Center for the Exploration of the Human Potential in La Jolla, California, which sponsors a one-year course for adults who want to be encounter-group leaders. The center is advised by Abraham Maslow, Jack Gibb, Gardner Murphy, and Herbert Otto, among others.

Applicants for this training must have, among other things, a bachelor's degree. They must have some leadership experience (as a teacher or administrator, for example), and extensive encounter-group experience. They also must be evaluated by a psychologist or a psychiatrist. Then they are trained intensively and intelligently.

I'd like to propose that persons with such training call themselves facilitators and refer to their work in such a way that they distinguish themselves from certified counselors who work in institutional settings, and from licensed psychotherapists in professional practice. The National Center program is just an example, and it appears that many similar programs are developing. I think that the public is entitled to some ready means for distinguishing a rigorously selected and coached facilitator from, for instance, a member of Esalen Association. (Anyone may become a *member* of Esalen Association by paying annual dues; this indicates no other connection with Esalen Institute.)

Encounter groups in all their forms are far too valuable—and the demand for such groups is far too clamorous and desperate—for us to let ignorance, psychosocial greed, or false prophecy tarnish them.

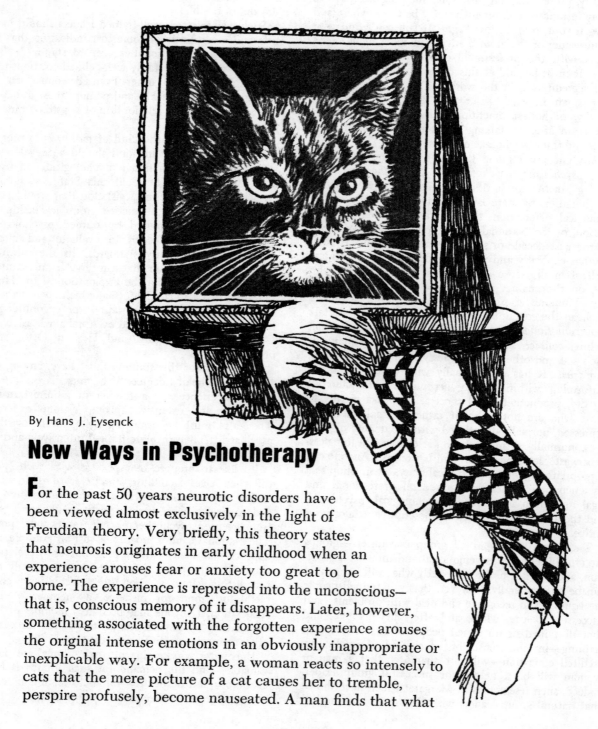

By Hans J. Eysenck

New Ways in Psychotherapy

For the past 50 years neurotic disorders have
been viewed almost exclusively in the light of
Freudian theory. Very briefly, this theory states
that neurosis originates in early childhood when an
experience arouses fear or anxiety too great to be
borne. The experience is repressed into the unconscious—
that is, conscious memory of it disappears. Later, however,
something associated with the forgotten experience arouses
the original intense emotions in an obviously inappropriate or
inexplicable way. For example, a woman reacts so intensely to
cats that the mere picture of a cat causes her to tremble,
perspire profusely, become nauseated. A man finds that what

he has regarded as a natural though unusual fastidiousness has gradually been transformed into an obsession that makes it impossible for him to touch anything handled by others—money, doorknobs, tableware, books.

According to prevailing Freudian theory, neurosis can be cured only through a therapy which, by painstaking probing in the course of many sessions, uncovers the repressed experience as well as the unconscious motives and conflicts associated with it. Now able to understand why the experience aroused such overwhelmingly painful emotions, the patient is cured. Without treatment, it is claimed, neurotic disorders will persist or get worse. Ridding the patient of the symptoms while ignoring the underlying causes will only complicate matters: There will be a relapse, or the underlying fears and anxieties will attach themselves to a different object, or a different set of symptoms will appear. The patient may, for example, be relieved of a neurotic fear of rats only to find himself even more seriously incapacitated by a fear of automobiles; the patient cured of his claustrophobia may be plunged into a deep depression.

It is generally believed that even though psychotherapeutic treatment may take years, it is thorough and will eventually lead to a permanent cure. These beliefs have seldom been con-

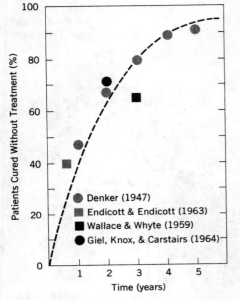

Spontaneous remission occurs when the symptoms of neurotic patients disappear of their own accord—without the "benefit" of psychotherapy. Here a curve of the spontaneous remission rate (dotted line) is fitted to the combined data of four independent studies of patients cured without treatment.

tested and there is virtually unanimous agreement—even among adherents of non-analytic psychotherapy—that neurotic disorders can best be understood and treated on the basis of Freudian or neo-Freudian theory.

The casual reader of modern textbooks of psychiatry or clinical psychology is scarcely aware that there is, in fact, no evidence to support Freudian theory, while there is considerable evidence that all the foregoing beliefs are actually false.

I wish to discuss only briefly some of the studies which disprove psychoanalytic dogma, and to focus on "behavior therapy," a new approach which offers an effective alternative, both in theory and in practice, to conventional "insight" or "dynamic" psychotherapy, and that promises at long last to bring scientific method to bear on a field until now ruled by faith and dogma.

Does Psychoanalysis Cure?

One of the most striking features of neurotic disorders is the fact that in the majority of cases they are subject to spontaneous remission—that is, in time the symptoms disappear without therapy. I have combined the results of four independent studies to show the percentage of severely neurotic patients whose symptoms disappeared without any psychiatric treatment whatsoever [see illustration this page].

In three of the studies, spontaneous remissions occurred in from 65 to 75 percent of the cases over the passage of two to three years; in the fourth, a long-term study, 90 percent of the patients were free of symptoms at the end of five years. There is much other evidence in the literature to substantiate the claim that neurotic symptoms sooner or later disappear spontaneously in a great number of cases.

This raises a serious question about the effectiveness of psychotherapy. To prove its worth, proponents of pychotherapy must show that the percentage of cures following treatment is significantly greater than the percentage of spontaneous remissions. In 1952 I analyzed a number of reports on the effects of psychotherapy and found that the figures for cures did not differ from those for spontaneous remissions. Statistically speaking, therefore, treatment had contributed nothing. Analyses of later studies on adults and children, including much more data, tended to support this conclusion.

It might nevertheless be argued that even though psychotherapy does not produce more cures than does the passage of time alone, the cures it does achieve are more permanent—that is, there are fewer relapses. However, a 10-year follow-up study by Johannes Cremarius showed that this is not the case. Of more than 600 neurotic patients treated by various methods, including psychoanalysis, 73 percent were considered to be improved or cured when treatment ended. Eight to ten years later, only 25 percent of this group were still considered improved or cured. In other words, of those patients declared to have benefited from treatment, two out of three suffered a relapse.

To date, then, there is no real evidence for the effectiveness of psychotherapy—as is now admitted even by leading psychoanalysts and psychotherapists—though with further search such evidence might be uncovered.

Pavlov's Dogs

The theory and practice of behavior therapy are grounded on modern knowledge of learning and conditioning. Classical behaviorist theory holds (1) that behavior can be understood as a response to a stimulus, and (2) that most behavior is learned through a process called conditioning by which links are established between certain stimuli and responses.

To illuminate the meaning of these terms, let us recall Pavlov's salivating dogs. A hungry dog responds to food in its mouth (an unconditioned stimulus) by salivating (an unconditioned response). This is but one example of the many "built-in" responses or reflexes over which the organism has little or no control. Pavlov found that if an experimenter consistently rings a bell (a neutral stimulus) just before he puts the food into the dog's mouth, the dog will gradually associate the sound of the bell with the presence of the food. Eventually the sound of the bell (the conditioned stimulus) will alone be sufficient to cause the dog to salivate (now a conditioned response).

Much behavior is learned through conditioning of this sort; it is involuntary and may take place without the organism's being aware of it. But it must be reinforced; if it is not, the conditioned response will extinguish. In other words if, after the dog is conditioned to salivate at the sound of the bell, the bell is repeatedly rung but no food appears, the association between the conditioned and the unconditioned stimuli will extinguish and the dog will no longer salivate at the sound of the bell. These prin-

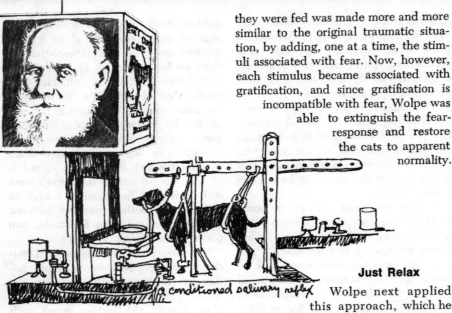

a conditioned salivary reflex

they were fed was made more and more similar to the original traumatic situation, by adding, one at a time, the stimuli associated with fear. Now, however, each stimulus became associated with gratification, and since gratification is incompatible with fear, Wolpe was able to extinguish the fear-response and restore the cats to apparent normality.

ciples of conditioning and extinction are fundamental to classical conditioning, the basis for much of behavior therapy.

"Unscaring" Scared Cats

Behavior therapy has its roots in the early studies of John B. Watson, Mary Jones, and other behaviorists, but it may be said to date from the end of the 1950's with the publication of Joseph Wolpe's book, *Psychotherapy by Reciprocal Inhibition*, and my paper, "Behavior Therapy." Since Wolpe's method is an important part—though only a part —of the general theory and practice of behavior therapy, it serves as an excellent starting point for discussion.

Increasingly dissatisfied by his lack of results with conventional psychotherapy, Wolpe set out to see if the behaviorist approach, so successful in changing the behavior of laboratory animals, could erase neurotic behavior in humans. In a series of exploratory experiments with cats, Wolpe gave them a mild electric shock at the same time he presented them with a variety of neutral stimuli such as a toy mouse, a rubber ball, flashing lights. Thus he was able to induce a "neurotic" fear of the previously neutral stimuli. He then conducted another series of experiments to see if he could erase their neurotic fear by reversing the conditioning process. He concluded that the most satisfactory treatment was to expose them to the fear-provoking stimuli under conditions which were incompatible with fear.

He began by feeding his cats in a "safe" environment in which there were no fear-provoking stimuli. Gradually, through a series of carefully worked-out stages, the safe environment in which

Just Relax

Wolpe next applied this approach, which he called *desensitization,* to problems of human neurosis. To start with, he looked for a practicable method of desensitizing his patients. He needed to find a response which would be incompatible with fear or anxiety. His search led him to the work of E. Jacobson who had developed a method for relaxing patients, and who recommended it as a treatment for neurotic disorders. Because it is impossible to be relaxed and anxious at the same time, Wolpe decided to use relaxation as the essential response which might damp down anxiety reactions in his patients.

At first he attempted to relax his patients in the presence of the objects which were producing their fear. But it was soon evident that this procedure would be both tedious and impractical. Not only would it involve gathering a large collection of objects to meet his patients' varied needs, but what of the patient who was terrified of horses, or was compelled to dive under a table at the sound of an airplane? Furthermore, in some patients the anxiety was not associated with an object but with an experience—for example, riding in an elevator or a subway.

Wolpe therefore began to experiment with the imaginary evocation of the anxiety-provoking stimuli, a method which was easy to manipulate in the consulting room and allowed a great deal of flexibility in planning treatment. In practice, Wolpe's desensitization technique works as follows. Before the desensitization treatment is begun, the therapist takes a general history of the patient and a complete history of the disorder. Next, he attempts to reduce or eliminate any conflicts or anxiety-producing situations in the patient's life which do not directly bear on his neurotic symptoms. Then he trains the patient in Jacobson's method of progressive relaxation where the subject is taught to relax first one muscle, then another, progressing from one part of the body to other parts. Finally, patient and therapist discuss all the stimuli and situations which might possibly produce anxiety, grading them in a hierarchy ranging from the most to the least disturbing.

a kitten playing with a ball of wool.. pounces on it

The Lady and the Cat

Now the patient is ready for desensitization. Let us illustrate this process through the story of a woman who suffers unbearable anxiety at the sight of a cat. In the course of discussions with her, the therapist has found that she is least disturbed at seeing a small kitten in the arms of a child. When treatment begins she is asked therefore to imagine this sight as clearly and vividly as she can. Though she feels some anxiety, it is bearable. Still keeping the picture firmly in mind, she is instructed to relax as she has been taught. She finds that when she is thoroughly relaxed her anxiety disappears. She repeats this exercise in subsequent sessions until she never experiences any anxiety while imagining a kitten in the arms of a child. Now the therapist asks her to imagine a slightly more disturbing situation—a kitten playing with a ball of wool, pouncing on it, biting it, and so on—while she relaxes. When this imaginary situation ceases to provoke anxiety, the therapist asks her to evoke a still more disturbing image, moving up the hierarchy which had been established prior to treatment. Eventually she is able to imagine with tranquility a big black tom cat stalking through the grass or curled up on her bed. And finally at the end of treatment, she is able to confront cats in real life as tranquilly as she can evoke their images in the consulting room.

Indeed, at each stage of treatment she finds she can transfer to real life her new ability to tolerate the stimulus. Thus when our hypothetical patient reaches the stage at which she can evoke the image of a playful kitten without anxiety in the therapist's office, she no longer experiences anxiety at the actual sight of a kitten frolicking in the neighbor's yard.

In behaviorist terms desensitization, as well as the other therapeutic procedures used by Wolpe, is based on a general principle which he states as follows: "If a response antagonistic to anxiety can be made to occur in the presence of anxiety-provoking stimuli so that it is accompanied by a complete or partial suppression of the anxiety responses, the bond between the stimuli and the anxiety responses will be weakened." In somewhat simpler terms, we can say that because relaxation suppresses, or inhibits anxiety, the lady was desensitized to cats by gradually conditioning herself to respond with relaxation. The "cat-anxiety" association has been replaced by a "cat-relaxation" association.

Does Behavior Therapy Work?

Wolpe claimed that desensitization was not only much more effective than psychotherapy, but was also quicker. In an unselected series of more than 300 cases he found that 90 percent were improved or cured after an average of 30 sessions. Reports by his students and followers on the whole corroborate his findings. None of these clinical studies, however, included the proper control groups—patients with similar disorders who were not treated, or patients treated by other methods. Thus questions about the superiority of desensitization to psychotherapy could not be effectively an-

swered in terms of percentages, treatment-times, and so on.

Recently, however, James Humphery carried out a study specifically designed to compare the results of behavior therapy with those of traditional psychotherapy. Formerly director of a child guidance clinic and a psychotherapist of many years' experience, Humphery was trained in behavior therapy specifically in order to conduct the investigation. His subjects were 71 children who

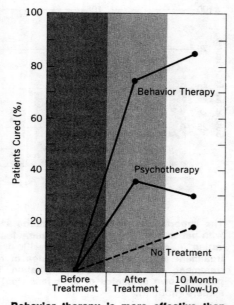

Behavior therapy is more effective than psychotherapy in curing psychiatric disorders. Follow-up diagnoses indicate that the cures produced by behavior therapy are more permanent than those produced by psychotherapy.

had been referred to London child guidance clinics for all types of disorders except brain damage and psychosis. The children were divided into matched groups: The 34 in the control group received no treatment of any kind; the 37 children in the treated group were then divided into two groups, one of which received behavior therapy and the other traditional psychotherapy. A five-point rating scale was used to establish the severity of each child's disorder (his clinical status) and to evaluate the success of the treatment. Each child was rated on this scale at the beginning of the study; the children in the treatment group were rated immediately after treatment, while those in the control group were rated 10 months after the start of the experiment. Experienced psychiatrists, who did not know to which group a child had been assigned, did the rating. The decision to end treatment was made in consultation between Humphery and the psychiatrist assigned to the case. A rise of two or more points

on the clinical rating scale was taken as an arbitrary criterion of "cure."

All children were again rated 10 months later. Seventy-five percent of the children who received behavior therapy were rated cured at the close of treatment, as compared with only 35 percent of those who received psychotherapy. At the 10-month follow-up, 85 percent of those who had received behavior therapy were rated as cured—an increase of 10 percentage points—but only 29 percent of those in the psychotherapy group were still considered cured. Of those who had received no treatment at all, 18 percent were found to be cured [see illustration this page].

These results are even more impressive when differences in the length of treatment are taken into account. The children receiving psychotherapy required 21 sessions spread over 31 weeks before it was thought that treatment could be terminated, but those receiving behavior therapy required only nine sessions during 18 weeks. Thus behavior therapy cured twice as many cases as did psychotherapy, and in less than half the number of sessions. By happenstance, moreover, the children assigned to the behavior therapy group were the more seriously ill, which would seem to militate against the success of behavior therapy. On the other hand, since the children given psychotherapy began treatment with a higher clinical-status rating they were less likely to achieve the two-point rise necessary to denote cure. These factors were undoubtedly important in accounting for the startling difference between the two groups. It should be noted, however, that the percentage of cures resulting from psychotherapy in this experiment did not differ from that usually obtained in the clinics involved in the study.

Interesting as the study may be, it can be criticized on various grounds. From the standpoint of this article, however, the most interesting focus for examination is the assumption that the crucial therapeutic element for the children treated with behavior therapy was the *combination* of desensitization and relaxation. This may not have been the case. At least three alternative hypotheses could be put forward. One, simple extinction might be involved. According to the laws of conditioning, if the anxiety-provoking stimulus is repeatedly evoked without any distressing consequences, the response should eventually be extinguished; thus we might conclude that desensitization—without relaxation—is sufficient to produce a cure. Two, since relaxation lowers the intensity of all responses (drive level), this in itself would reduce the intensity of the conditioned fear-response and might suffice to bring about a cure. Hence relaxation—without desensitization—might be the crucial therapeutic element. Three, it might be that the sympathetic attention of a person in authority is, by itself, all that is needed. Indeed, this view has often been expressed by those who claim that behavior therapy embodies important but standard psychotherapeutic procedures. For example, during the preliminary interviews the behavior therapist, despite his radically different approach to treatment, in fact employs such elements of psychotherapy as sympathy, acceptance of deviant behavior, and movement toward insight.

Clearly, questions such as these cannot be answered in the "clinical trial" type of investigation but must be dealt with in formal experimental studies. Fortunately, a number of such studies have been made in the last 10 years.

Neurosis in the Laboratory

Behavior therapists, taking these problems into the laboratory, have designed experimental studies previously thought impossible in so complex a field as human emotion and interaction. To compare the effects of differing treatments, it is essential that the pre- and post-treatment states of the patient be measured as accurately as possible. Studies have usually focused therefore on such relatively simple disorders as phobias for snakes and spiders.

Is it possible to measure fear with any degree of precision? To be sure, the patient confronted by a snake can be asked to rate his own fear on a numbered scale ranging from "intense" to "slight." But while his subjective feelings are certainly relevant, they are not objectively "observable" enough to meet scientific criteria. Objective measures of fear, based on involuntary physiological reactions, have therefore been devised. We are all aware that fear is accompanied by a temporary increase in heartbeat (our hearts "pound"), by a temporary restriction or collapse of capillary blood vessels (we "turn white"), by profuse sweating, a dry mouth, and other changes—all of which can be measured with suitable instruments. Indeed the polygraph, or so-called lie detector, does nothing more than measure several physiological concomitants of changes in emotional reaction.

In addition, it is possible to measure a patient's actual behavior vis-a-vis the

fear object—his *approach-avoidance* behavior. Fright is accompanied by an involuntary retreat from stimulus. How near will the patient approach the feared object? Will he touch it for a moment only? Will he handle it?

We can thus measure with some degree of accuracy the behavior we wish to modify and the degree of our success. This approach has enabled researchers

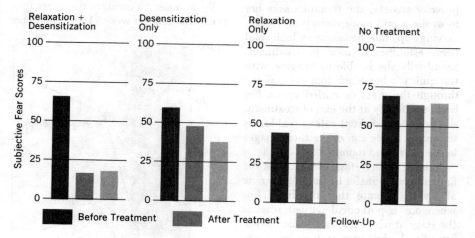

The importance of both desensitization and relaxation in behavior therapy is shown with patients suffering from an extreme fear of spiders. The effectiveness of desensitization + relaxation is compared with desensitization only, relaxation only, and no treatment at all (controls). Estimates of fear were obtained before treatment, after treatment, and in a follow-up evaluation. Two measures of fear were employed: the patients' own estimates of their fear (top) and a scale of the physical avoidance of spiders (bottom).

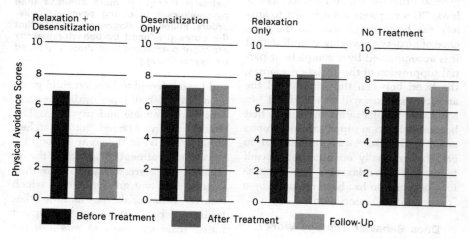

to isolate specific components of behavior therapy and see which is the active ingredient. A study conducted by Stanley Rachman at Maudsley Hospital illustrates how this can be accomplished.

Rachman attempted to answer some of the questions posed by Wolpe's "reciprocal inhibition" theory, using as subjects a number of persons who feared spiders. He divided his subjects into four groups. One received behavior therapy (desensitization plus relaxation), a second desensitization only, a third relaxation only, and a fourth no treat-

ment at all. Rachman used two independent measures of anxiety: the subjects' own estimates of their fear and a scale based on the subjects' physical avoidance of spiders [*see illustrations on this page*].

The results show very clearly that only the *combination* of desensitization and relaxation significantly decreased the fear of spiders.

Behavior Therapy vs. Psychotherapy

In addition to testing out the effectiveness of different components of behavior therapy, recent laboratory experiments have enabled us to compare different treatments. The work of Gordon Paul at the University of Illinois is an example. Persons suffering from severe stage fright were divided into four groups: some received the desensitization-relaxation therapy, some received conventional psychotherapy, some received a placebo (in this case, non-therapy-oriented meetings between patient and

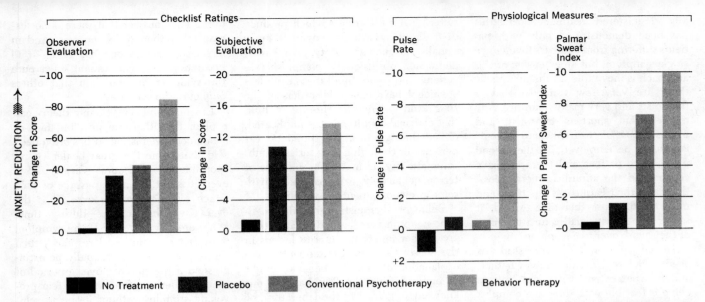

Observer Evaluation   Subjective Evaluation   Pulse Rate   Palmar Sweat Index

ANXIETY REDUCTION
Change in Score

No Treatment   Placebo   Conventional Psychotherapy   Behavior Therapy

Groups of patients suffering from anxiety caused by severe stage fright were given conventional psychotherapy, behavior therapy (desensitization + relaxation), placebo treatment (non-therapy oriented meetings with a therapist), or no treatment at all (controls). Anxiety was measured before and after treatment by observer and subjective checklist ratings and by pulse rate and palmar sweating physiological measures. (Scale values are not identical.) In all cases, behavior therapy produced the greatest amount of anxiety reduction.

therapist), and an untreated control group. Paul used four general measures of anxiety: (1) observable manifestations of anxiety during public speaking, as rated by trained observers; (2) the subjects' own ratings of their experienced anxiety; (3) pulse rate; and (4) palmar sweating.

Ratings made before and after treatment demonstrated that on all four criteria the group receiving behavior therapy showed the greatest average reduction of anxiety [see illustration above]. Indeed, only in this group was there a noticeable reduction in pulse rate after treatment, while pulse rate actually increased in the control group. Results with psychotherapy and the placebo were about the same, while the control group showed little change. It should be added that the behavior therapy was carried out by psychotherapists (specially trained in Wolpe's method for this experiment) who continued to prefer psychotherapy and its associated doctrines.

Gordon Paul and Donald Shannon later carried out a similar study in which they added a fifth experimental condition: Five patients were given behavior therapy as a group. This treatment was as effective as individual treatment. In addition, it was found that the academic performance of those given behavior therapy greatly improved, indicating that the specific reduction in anxiety achieved in the experiment may have generalized to other life situations.

Many more questions raised by behavior therapy are being studied in sim-

ilar experiments, questions such as: Which is more effective, the presentation of the actual anxiety-producing stimulus or its imaginary evocation? Is it better to space the treatments or to compress them into short periods of time? How quickly does desensitization transfer to real-life situations?

These questions have not yet been definitively answered. Nor can it yet be claimed that the experiments I have described clearly show the superiority of behavior therapy. What may, I think, be claimed is that for the first time therapeutic methods are being tested in properly designed and controlled experiments, using objective criteria of known reliability. Vital questions which were until now discussed only in a subjective and anecdotal fashion are being brought under experimental control.

"Treatment Machines"

Psychoanalysts hold that an essential element in therapy is the transference—the interaction in which the patient transfers to the analyst his feelings toward significant persons in his life. Ex-

perimental studies of Wolpe's method suggest, however, that since the important ingredient in behavior therapy is the combination of conditioned stimulus and relaxation, the presence of the therapist may not be necessary. Could learning machines be substituted for the therapist? Properly programmed, they might be used both to teach the patient how to relax and to carry him through the desensitization process, based as it is on the patient's visualization of the fear-provoking stimulus.

Machines may indeed replace the therapist. Peter Lang, at the University of Wisconsin, has shown not only that behavior therapy can be programmed, but that it can be as effective as personally administered treatment. So far this has been demonstrated only with patients suffering from neuroses involving a single symptom, but an extension of this approach is inevitable. In the first place, there are very few trained behavior therapists and very many neurotics. Any method that shortens treatment and makes it possible to treat more patients is sure to be employed. In the second place, once patient and therapist have constructed the stimulus "hierarchies," the rest of the treatment is repetitive and mechanical. Most therapists would, it seems safe to say, gladly turn this part of their work over to a machine.

To be sure, much more study is needed before we can know whether, and to what extent, treatment by machine is feasible with the more complex neuroses, or with psychoses. It is possible, too, that the use of machines will be governed by the patient's personality-type or emotional needs. It might be that introverts would do well with programmed treatments while extroverts, or those particularly in need of personal support and human contact, would prefer to work only with the therapist.

Neurotic Symptoms or Bad Habits?

So far in this discussion we have dealt only with one type of neurotic disorder and with one type of behavior therapy. This is justifiable because most neurotic patients who seek psychiatric help are suffering from disorders which produce distressing symptoms—negative emotional states such as anxiety, phobic fear, depression, obsessional or compulsive reactions, and so on. In all these disorders—which I have called "disorders of the *first* kind"—behavior therapists hold that classical conditioning is implicated, either through a single traumatic experience or through a long series of sub-traumatic events in which emotions of terror or anxiety are associated with some previously neutral stimulus.

Behavior therapists agree that neurotic symptoms are learned. That is, they are neither innate nor due to lesions in the nervous system. Consequently, any explanation of neurotic behavior ought to proceed from the firm basis of our knowledge, gained in the laboratory, of learning and conditioning. According to these theories, there is no "neurosis" or "complex," as such, which causes the symptoms. There are only symptoms. A patient's response of overwhelming anxiety to so neutral a stimulus as the picture of cat is, for example, in a real and literal sense *learned*. It is a "bad" (or maladaptive) habit, acquired through the processes of classical conditioning. The so-called symptom *is* the neurosis—I say "so-called" because the anxiety-response is not in fact symptomatic of anything. Behavior therapists are not pained, therefore, when psychoanalysts accuse them of curing only the symptoms. They answer that there is no disease other than the symptoms. And in any case, as someone has said, "It ill becomes those who cannot *even* cure the symptom to complain that others *only* cure the symptom."

Learning and conditioning theory can explain the otherwise puzzling fact of spontaneous remission. It has often been said that "time the great healer" is responsible for such cures. Clearly, however, it is not the mere passage of time which alone works the cure. It is the events which transpire during time. What are those events? If the symptom is in fact a conditioned response, then the response should gradually be extinguished if the sufferer, over a period of time, encounters the original fear-provoking stimulus without its being reinforced by a traumatic event. The woman who is terrified of cats will, from time to time, encounter cats, and if nothing happens to reinforce her fear it should gradually die away.

In many cases, however, this cannot come about because the patient refuses to encounter the conditioned stimulus. By taking great pains to avoid it he evades the possibility of testing reality. Furthermore, each time he avoids the stimulus he is consolidating the very behavior pattern which is the neurosis.

A striking example of this is the case of a woman we recently treated for a cat phobia so severe she was unable to leave her room. The phobia had developed when, as a very young girl, her father drowned her favorite kitten before her eyes. So traumatic was the experience that every time she saw a cat

she ran away. Doing so reduced her anxiety—and reinforced her avoidance behavior. The conditioned habit, feeding on itself, became so dominating that eventually she immured herself in her room. Behavior therapy, by gradually exposing her to the sight of cats while she was thoroughly relaxed, completely restored her to a normal life within a few weeks; there was no relapse, nor was there any indication that her anxiety had been transferred to some other object or had expressed itself in some other form.

what a pretty shoe

This freedom from relapse and symptom-substitution after behavior therapy has also been observed many times by other therapists, even by some who were unsympathetic to this approach. Nevertheless, long-term, follow-up studies are needed to put this point beyond argument.

Aversion Therapy

In addition to disorders of the first kind involving distressing symptoms such as anxiety, phobic fear, or depression, there are neurotic disorders of the *second* kind. They may arise when some socially desirable conditioning has failed to occur, as with psychopaths or sociopaths. Such people are characterized by an almost complete lack of social responsibility; they are the pathological liars, or those who steal or murder regardless of the fact that they will almost certainly be found out and punished.

Disorders of the second kind also arise when some socially undesirable or

unacceptable behavior has become associated with positive emotions such as pleasure, comfort, happiness, sexual arousal. The most obvious examples are associated with the sexual impulse—homosexuality, fetishism, transvestism, among others. For instance, an ordinarily neutral stimulus such as a shoe may accidentally become associated with sexual pleasure and through subsequent reinforcement come to serve as a conditioned stimulus which calls forth a sexual response (shoe fetishism).

In cases of this kind the aim of the therapist is to break the association between the conditioned stimulus—a woman's shoe, for example—and the conditioned response—aberrant sexual satisfaction. The dissociation process is often called "aversion therapy," and is the opposite of desensitization. In desensitization therapy, the link between the conditioned stimulus (a cat) and the conditioned response (fear) is replaced by a new link between the conditioned stimulus and a pleasant response (relaxation). In aversion therapy, the link between the conditioned stimulus (a woman's shoe) and the pleasant sexual response is broken by linking the shoe-stimulus to an unpleasant experience.

The classic example of aversion therapy is the use of apomorphine to cure alcoholism. The patient takes the drug, which causes nausea and vomiting. Just before the onset of nausea, he is given a drink of liquor. The drink (conditioned stimulus) is now followed by a very distressing conditioned response—nausea. Behaviorist theory predicts that after many such repetitions, the mere sight of a drink will evoke the newly conditioned response.

In spite of its apparent crudity, aversion therapy works surprisingly well if properly carried out. However, research reports show that much useless effort has been expended by medical people with little knowledge of conditioning procedures. To take but one example: In treating alcoholism many would-be therapists have administered the drink *after* nausea has set in. Behaviorists know that conditioning will be effective only if the conditioned stimulus *precedes* the response to be conditioned; backward conditioning just does not occur.

Modern behavior therapists prefer to use electric shock rather than drugs in aversion therapy. The intensity of the unconditioned stimulus (the shock) can be much better controlled; it is less messy; and it can be administered at a precisely chosen moment. Where the patient urgently requests such treatment, electric shock has been used to cure certain sexual deviations, including homosexuality and transvestism.

Typically in such treatment, while the male homosexual is looking at pictures of nude males, he is given a moderately intense shock. The combination of the male picture (conditioned stimulus) with shock (unconditioned stimulus) should lead to an aversion to men as sex objects (conditioned response).

The treatment is not yet complete, however. The next step is to condition a positive response to women: the picture of the nude male is suddenly replaced by the picture of a nude female—and the shock is terminated. Since the cessation of shock is pleasurable, a favorable response to women is now established.

Techniques such as these offer a potentially powerful therapeutic approach. However, the effectiveness of these conditioning methods cannot as yet be judged because too few cases have been studied and there have not been enough long-term, follow-up studies.

"Operant" Conditioning

No article on behavior therapy would be complete without some discussion of *operant conditioning* as a technique for changing behavior. Because the theories of operant conditioning underlie such revolutionary new pedagogical methods as the use of teaching machines, as well as new approaches to therapy, I should like to describe this method briefly.

Operant conditioning was originally worked out by B. F. Skinner who succeeded in shaping the behavior of pigeons by reinforcing bits of behavior that were originally quite random. In one of Skinner's early experiments, he fed a hungry pigeon whenever it happened to stretch its neck above a predetermined point. Gradually it "caught on" and spent most of its time raising its head just as high as it could. This method of changing behavior is also called "instrumental conditioning," since the organism's behavior is instrumental itself in obtaining the "reward."

The notion that psychotics can learn to control their delusions or their unacceptable behavior is rejected by almost all knowledgeable people. Nevertheless, the technique of shaping behavior, originally worked out with pigeons, has been used with startling success to change the behavior of psychotic adults and disturbed children. Hardcore schizophrenics, considered hopeless, who had been vegetating for years in the back wards of mental hospitals, have been taught to relinquish the behavior which identified them as insane. An example is reported by Colin Blakemore of the Maudsley Hospital.

A middle-aged woman, suffering from severe paranoid delusions that communists were following her everywhere trying to kill her, was asked to wear earphones during her meetings with the therapist. Every time the woman mentioned her paranoid ideas, the therapist pressed a button which enabled him to deliver an unpleasant noise into the earphones. Whenever she talked normally, the therapist turned off the noise. Gradually the paranoid topic dropped out of her conversation completely—not only in the presence of the therapist, but in the ward as well.

As further proof of the efficacy of this technique, Blakemore reversed the process. He brought back her paranoid talk by punishing her whenever she spoke of normal topics; then he again taught her to leave communists and persecution out of her conversation. Thus he showed that by employing this technique he could bring her talk under complete experimental control.

This experiment, like many similar operant conditioning experiments with mental patients, raises more questions than it answers. Hopefully, these questions will be answered in the future with more experiments using many subjects and rigorous controls. In the meantime, however, operant conditioning has opened many new and undreamed-of avenues to the therapist.

Action Before Thought?

Some of the most important consequences of behavior therapy are its effects on theory. For example, it has long been held that thought precedes and controls action. Behavior therapy suggests that the contrary may often be true, so that changing a person's behavior through some form of conditioning process may actually change his thought or mental set.

For example, Teodoro Ayllon, at Anna State Hospital in Illinois, reports the case of a woman who was committed to a mental hospital because she would not eat for fear her husband would poison her. She refused to feed herself in the hospital and had to be fed by a nurse. Finding that she was very fastidious about her personal appearance and her clothing, Ayllon told the nurse to spill food on the woman's dress whenever she fed her, and to explain that it was very difficult to feed another person. Gradually the patient began to feed herself—and at the same time her delusions about being poisoned began to disappear. Her *actions* in feeding herself had changed her *thought* that she would be poisoned.

Of course, not too much should be read into isolated experiments of this sort. On the other hand, when we keep in mind that psychotherapists have had almost no success with cases such as these, it seems reasonable to suggest that behavior therapists are opening doors and windows, bringing fresh air into a room in which the atmosphere has grown very heavy, stale, and musty.

Science and Psychotherapy

The work of the behavior therapists has important implications for the treatment of neurotic and psychotic disorders, and has opened new paths toward understanding them. I would like to suggest, though, that their chief contribution has been to bring this hitherto mysterious realm under the discipline of scientific method. It is possible, though unlikely, that all the theories of conditioning discussed in this paper are wrong. But by insisting that both theory and practice be experimentally tested, behavior therapists are trying to insure that errors will be exposed, and that new evidence will be obtained on which new

and better theories can be based.

Behaviorist objections to psychoanalysis and its allied psychotherapeutic theory and practices are not based solely on opposition to Freudian *theory*. They are based on an opposition to the Freudian *approach* as well; it must be ruled out of court, as far as science is concerned, on two grounds. In the first place, Freudian theories are not stated in terms that permit them to be tested and verified; indeed it is almost impossible to think of experiments by which they could be either confirmed or disproved. In the second place, practitioners have made no effort to gather the kind of data, based on experience and observation with patients, that alone could give us a factual basis for evaluating their work. They demand belief, but they do not offer proof.

Behavior therapy is based on applying fundamental discoveries gained in the laboratory to practical problems—curing neurotic patients. The Freudian approach reversed this process. Freud's dynamic psychology was based on "discoveries" made in the course of treating patients. He and his followers universalized these ideas by applying them to all human beings. They manufactured new theories to bolster the original assumptions and attempted to fit all aspects of human behavior into their untested theoretical framework.

Behavior therapists hold that theories which attempt to explain behavior, neurotic or otherwise, should be based on fundamental scientific knowledge which is susceptible to experimental proof. They are attempting to test how well learning and conditioning theory can be applied to human problems, and they ask that judgment be suspended until the proof is conclusive. If their experiments are subject to criticism, better experiments will be designed in accordance with the criticism. If the theories do not stand up to experimental test, then better theories will be put forward to fit the established facts. As I see it, this is nothing more—nor less—than the long-delayed introduction of scientific method into the murky and emotion-ridden field of psychotherapy. In essence, psychotherapy involves changing those maladaptive emotional states and behavior patterns that interfere with adequate functioning. The new approaches and results I have described hold promise that, after 50 years in the twilight zone of unverified claims, unjustified beliefs, and passionately held dogma, psychotherapy will at last become truly scientific.

THERE ARE TWO frequently quoted and contradictory legends about the outcome of psychotherapy. One maintains that one third of treated patients get better, one third remain the same and one third get worse. The other asserts that two thirds of neurotics get better on their own, without treatment. Neither belief is supported by acceptable evidence. No one has established a reliable rate of cure for persons who have therapy or a rate of recovery for persons who have not had it. Nevertheless, contrary to prevailing beliefs, adequately controlled, fully scientific experiments have demonstrated repeatedly that psychotherapy does bring about positive changes.

These experiments have been done with patients whose maladjustments ranged widely in severity, who were treated by therapists of varied theoretical persuasions who used many different therapeutic techniques. It is true that some research efforts have shown no more benefits from psychotherapy than from neutral, nontherapeutic procedures or from the simple passage of time. But these instances are by far overshadowed by studies that reveal psychotherapy's positive results.

Doubts. Sustained and often tumultuous debate over the effectiveness of psychotherapy has raged among psychologists since Freud's day. The doubts of researchers and academic psychologists are entirely appropriate; it is their responsibility to question beliefs and to search for evidence. Practicing psychotherapists, on the other hand, continue to be convinced by good clinical experiences that their craft is a valid one. They are understandably prepared to give their therapy credit for the positive changes in their patients and to discount or find good reasons for their failures.

The testimonials and individual case studies of former patients, however, fail to prove to the satisfaction of the scientific community that recovery is causally related to the efforts of psychotherapists. Many psychologists feel that therapists are like rain dancers who usually will succeed if they have the energy to dance long enough. Rain dancers, like therapists, can furnish abundant instances of success following upon their ministrations. To true believers the causality of their efforts is self-evident; to skeptics it is equally obvious that they merely take credit for natural events that would have occurred in any event. Fortunately for psychology, the effectiveness of any procedure does not have to be left to faith. Success is not decided by authoritarian decree or by democratic vote. It can be assessed impartially by scientific methods.

Fear. Many therapists bridle at the thought of scientific appraisal, however. They object to the cold impersonality of research technique and they dislike transmuting the rich, warm exchange of the consulting room into patterns of unfeeling numbers. Scientifically oriented psychologists, in turn, are suspicious when therapists are reluctant to cooperate in research on psychotherapy. They take it as evidence that therapists fear exposure of their ineffectiveness. H.J. Eysenck, for example, concluded in his influential paper [*see "New Ways in Psychotherapy," on page 306*] that existing research did not successfully reveal conventional psychotherapy and psychoanalysis to be more effective than the recovery that comes with time alone. Eysenck's conclusion, first stated in 1952, confirmed already-existing doubts and aroused further misgivings about the alleged benefits of therapy. Some psychologists went beyond Eysenck's statement to inference that psychotherapy was at best a cult or meaningless ritual; they called for a moratorium on practice. Others defen-

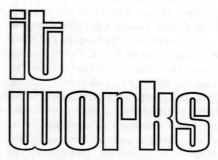

it works

"The person who needs help should know that if he goes to a skilled therapist who applies techniques that have an established record of success, and if the two of them work together on achieving goals that are relevant and realistic, then there is a good chance for improvement."

by Julian Meltzoff
& Melvin Kornreich

sively accused Eysenck of saying things that he had never said and they refuted arguments he had never made.

How have firm advocates of psychotherapy responded to these embarrassing data found by reputable and conscientious investigators? One sweeping answer has it that research cannot be done in psychotherapy because of its highly individual nature. Unfortunately, this attitude places therapy outside the realm of testability and out of science altogether. Some believe that the psychotherapeutic experience is important, possibly essential, whether or not any effects can be shown outside the therapist's office. Like vitamins, it is supposed to be good for all of us. Others argue that the testimony of large numbers of patients confirms the value of the enterprise. However, unsupported testimonials are as poor at proving the efficacy of psychotherapy as they are at proving the curative power of patent medicines. Testimonials tell us nothing of how patients would have made out without therapy, or how those who do not testify have fared.

Zero. Still other writers believe that the favorable effects of psychotherapy have been obscured in research data. They say that while some patients improve in treatment, others, for a variety of reasons, become worse and the rest remain unchanged. The average for a group of individuals is a deceptive zero. The implication, however, is that therapy causes deterioration in as many persons as it helps—hardly a comforting thought if true. Other therapy advocates began to make a new point. They accepted the conclusion that psychotherapy in general has not proved to be effective—with the exception of the kind of therapy that they themselves advocated. What a relief! There was light at the end of the darkness. If they could not present a relevant experiment to support their point of view, they offered selected case studies in evidence. They even explained "spontaneous" cures—in persons who had no formal therapy: friends, relatives or associates of the subject unwittingly applied the therapeutic method.

Of course this assertion can never be proven or disproven. Therapeutic social contacts are chancy, and we never know what is done, what succeeds, and with whom. When we discuss psychotherapy, we mean the informed and deliberate application of established psychological principles by trained and experienced specialists. The therapist's knowledge and skills are addressed to specific emotional, attitudinal and behavioral problems of the client.

Some researchers interested in demonstrating the effectiveness of therapy have used improvement in untreated patients as a baseline against which to measure the effects of treatment. As the argument goes: if the number of persons who recover from emotional disturbance without treatment is as great as the number of persons who recover *with* treatment, then perhaps therapists should close up shop.

Unfortunately no really valid baseline data are available. The questionable technique used so far has been to compare surveys of clinical results with a speculative baseline. The clinical literature is glutted with such surveys. Most of them are conducted after the patient has left treatment. Standards of recovery or improvement vary markedly from survey to survey, as do the results that are reported. The judgments usually depend upon the therapist's written records which are inspected long afterward by the therapist or by an independent investigator. Surveys cannot validly be compared with each other; criteria, patient populations and treatment conditions differ. Moreover, surveys cannot reliably be repeated. To average the findings of many surveys is impressive because they contain hundreds, even thousands, of cases. But the net effect is misleading and the procedure yields an uninterpretable average of disparates. It is like trying to compute the average beauty of many groups of girls, some judged by their own mothers and others judged by others' mothers.

The most obvious way to get dependable data on the effects of psychotherapy is to measure the status of patients carefully, both before and after therapy. This is an improvement, but it leaves us looking for a way to prove that any measured gains were *caused* by the therapy and not just coincidental to it. We do not know how these patients would have done without treatment. It is therefore necessary to compare the progress of the treated group with that of another group of individuals who match the treated group in all important characteristics but who do not receive specialized treatment.

Another, more popular, approach is to start with a patient population and at random select half of them to receive treatment. The remainder, the control group, receive no treatment at all or undergo some experience not designed to be therapeutic.

Booby Traps. How one measures improvement is of course a crucial issue, and one must take care to see that the measures are reliable, relevant and free from bias. Researchers have been reasonably successful in developing such measures. The simplest and most basic research design is to compare a treated group and an untreated group, equivalent in all other respects, on measurements that are specified in advance and taken objectively before and after a preestablished period of time. Then we can determine whether the treated group has changed more than the control group and apply statistical procedures designed to estimate whether the change is of sufficient magnitude and consistency to be considered a result of therapy rather than of chance. These procedures are conceptually simple and straightforward, but subject to all kinds of booby traps in execution. Nonetheless, if psychotherapists are to continue offering services to the public it is vital for the public to know if these services are usually beneficial.

More than a score of research projects have weighed the value of psychotherapy for those who were diagnosed as psychoneurotic or who had personality disorders. For example, R. B. Morton checked the effectiveness of short-term individual psychotherapy on 40 Ohio State University students who had severe personal problems and were doing poor work. He randomly divided the traffic of students who applied for help; he assigned half to immediate therapy and deferred treatment of the other half for 90 days. He assessed progress on a variety of ratings and tests. The treated group showed significantly more improvement than did those whose treatment had not begun. The study was designed in such a way that the differential improvement could not be attributed to chance or to the mere passage of time.

A study by George A. Shouksmith and James W. Taylor showed the value of psychotherapy with underachieving early-adolescent boys of above-average intelligence. After six months of individual counseling sessions and some group discussion, students showed significantly more improvement on four of six achievement tests than comparable untreated boys did. After the study, almost all of the untreated boys continued to be classified as underachievers, while 67 per cent of those who had been treated attained functioning levels commensurate with their capacities. Secondary to this improvement were gains in social adjustment, peer-group acceptance and favorable reports from their teachers.

Match. A study by J.E. Exner in a community mental-health clinic assessed the effects of group therapy upon female patients who had psychoneurosis and personality disorders. He compared various groupings with a control group that met without a therapist for a comparable period of time. He found some improvement in 92 per cent of the treated patients and in only 33 per cent of the controls. In the treated groups 75 per cent improved enough to be discharged, but only 17 per cent of the controls were considered to be well enough for discharge.

In another investigation, at the Uni-

versity of Chicago Counseling Center and the Alfred Adler Institute, John M. Shlien, Harold H. Mosak and Rudolf Dreikurs studied the effectiveness of three different therapeutic approaches. Improvement in patients who received all three of these types of treatment (client-centered time-limited therapy, client-centered time-unlimited therapy, and time-limited Adlerian therapy) was clearly greater than improvement in patients in a control group who received no treatment.

Phobia. A number of successful scientific investigations have demonstrated that the techniques of behavior therapy can eliminate phobic symptoms. The work of A.A. Lazarus at Witwatersrand University, South Africa, is an outstanding example of the successful elimination of pathological fears of heights and closed places, sex fears and other phobias. To prove the efficacy of this form of treatment, former acrophobics climbed a fire escape to the roof of an eight-story building, looked over the parapet, and for two minutes counted cars passing below. Formerly claustrophobic patients remained in a closed cubicle for five minutes. If a subject showed any signs of anxiety or hesitation, the treatment was considered as having failed with him. With these rigorous stress-tolerance tests as criteria, this form of therapy achieved a remarkable level of success in contrast to other treatments that served as controls. Controlled experiments by other investigators have confirmed the relief of phobias for such animals as snakes, rats and spiders, and for such anxiety-provoking situations as public-speaking and the taking of examinations.

Psychosomatic disorders, long resistant to standard medical regimens, have also been shown to yield to various psychotherapeutic approaches. At New York Hospital, Cornell Medical Center, W.J. Grace, R.H. Pinsky, and H.G. Wolff studied patients with ulcerative colitis who participated in group therapy, comparing them with control patients whom they matched for age, sex, duration and severity of

illness, age at onset of illness, and X-ray changes. The control group had only diet and medication for treatment. Consideration of such criteria as number of deaths, operations required, complications, X-ray changes, and time spent in the hospital showed the relative benefits of group therapy. Other controlled studies conducted in England, the Netherlands, the Soviet Union and the United States have demonstrated the efficacy of psychotherapy in such diverse ailments as bronchial asthma, neurodermatitis, peptic ulcer, warts and enuresis.

Drink. Earl J. Ends and Curtis W. Page at Willmar State Hospital, Minnesota, made a rigorous test of the effectiveness of psychotherapy in alcoholism. They considered a patient "greatly improved" only if he showed no evidence of alcoholic episodes over an 18-month period after his treatment. The patients they considered "possibly improved" displayed one or two brief episodes of drinking during their first three months after treatment, but no further reversion. The experimenters tried three different types of group therapy and compared them. Control subjects met socially in groups for a period of time comparable to the time that the subjects spent in therapy. One of the therapies limited reversion to old drinking patterns to 33 per cent. There was a 77 per cent reversion rate in the control group.

A number of research projects have shown the effectiveness of psychotherapy in improving institutional adjustment and returning severely disturbed hospitalized patients to the community.

M.B. Jensen, at the Salisbury, North Carolina, Veterans Administration Hospital, demonstrated the positive effects of group therapy with psychotic women patients. He compared them with a group of patients who did not have therapy, although the experimenters discussed their cases with the social workers, nurses and other personnel who were in direct contact with them. A third group had no psychotherapy and experimenters avoided any discussion of their cases during the research period. The criteria used for progress were movement of a patient from a closed ward to open-ward status and discharge from the hospital. The women who had group therapy showed the greatest progress.

In evaluating treatment of patients who were out of the hospital and back in the community, Meltzoff and R.L. Blumenthal, at the Veterans Administration Outpatient Clinic, Brooklyn, New York, demonstrated that patients in a therapy program benefited more than controls. The criteria of benefit included lowered rehospitalization rates, higher back-to-work rates and better ratings on such personal-adjustment variables as use of community facilities, dependency, mood, motivation, interpersonal relations, self-concept, emotional control and adjustment to family.

Youths. Research with antisocial-behavior problems, long thought to be impervious to treatment, has yielded surprisingly positive results. Psychotherapy has improved patients' adjustments in and out of institutions. R.T. Snyder and L.B. Sechrest compared three groups at the Huntington, Pennsylvania, Institution for Defective Delinquents. All were in their late teens or early 20s and of well-below-average intelligence. One of the three matched groups had group therapy. A second group met as a group for the same amount of time, but the discussion was not therapeutically oriented. The third group did not meet and received no treatment. There were significantly fewer reports of behavioral violations within the institution by members of the treated group than there were for members of the other groups.

R.W. Persons at the Fairfield, Connecticut, School for Boys applied a more demanding test of adjustment—functioning outside an institution. The teen-age male subjects of this research were serving indeterminate sentences for such offenses as automobile theft and breaking and entering; they averaged four offenses each. Treated boys showed more improvement on a variety of psychological test measures after 40 sessions of group therapy and 20 sessions of individual therapy than did a control group who had no treatment. The treated boys also had fewer disciplinary violations, obtained passes sooner, and did better school work. A follow-up check, run some 10 months after each boy's release, found fewer back in institutions, fewer parole violators and significantly more employment among the treated boys than among those who were not treated. The experimenter thoroughly investigated and ruled out the possibility that these boys had returned to better home environments.

Help. We could cite many more studies. The ones we have described are meant only to illustrate the research approaches that have been used and the diversity of the problems that have been studied. Prior to 1970, more than 100 studies compared treated patients with control cases; 80 per cent of these yielded positive results. This percentage runs even higher in the more carefully done studies. Each year brings more well-designed studies that make the same point: that psychotherapy produces improvements in personal adjustment above and beyond those that can be accounted for by unpredictable life events or by the healing power of time. No one method or approach has been shown to be successful with all types of problems. Nor do the positive findings guarantee that any particular person will find a solution to his problems: results are generally reported for groups, collectively.

But the person who needs help should know that if he goes to a skilled therapist who applies techniques that have an established record of success, and if the two of them work together on achieving goals that are relevant and realistic, then there is a good chance for improvement.

In the past, psychotherapists' efforts were based on their good intentions, personal convictions and best hopes. Now that the accumulated research of the past 15 years appears to support their beliefs, practitioners may be tempted to say, *We told you so. You have simply demonstrated what we knew all along. Was all this research necessary?* It most certainly was necessary, and it will continue to be. The history of science and medicine is littered with dead bodies of knowledge surrounded by discredited "facts," ideas and procedures that were at one time thought to be self-evident. Scientific appraisal of the effectiveness of psychotherapy has been necessary to help us resolve, in some measure at least, the conflicting faiths, convictions and prejudices that have always attended it.

The researcher emerges not as an obtrusive intruder in psychotherapeutic affairs, but as a collaborator working ultimately toward the same ends as the psychotherapist. Closer cooperation between them is in order. The researcher can help the psychotherapist to refine the tools of his craft. Together, one hopes, they can find out what kinds of techniques are most effective and most economical for what kinds of problems and persons and further improve the efficiency of the procedure. ∎

THE CRIME OF COMMITMENT

Do we banish them to Bedlam for society's convenience?   by Thomas Szasz

PHYSICIANS AND LAYMEN ALIKE generally believe persons are involuntarily confined in mental hospitals because they are mentally ill, but don't know they are sick and need medical treatment. This view, to put it charitably, is nonsense. In my opinion, mental illness is a myth. People we label "mentally ill" are not sick, and involuntary mental hospitalization is not treatment. It is punishment.

Involuntary confinement for "mental illness" is a deprivation of liberty that violates basic human rights, as well as the moral principles of the Declaration of Independence and the U.S. Constitution. In short, I consider commitment a crime against humanity.

Any psychiatrist who accepts as his client a person who does not wish to be his client, who defines him as "mentally ill," who then incarcerates his client in an institution, who bars his client's escape from the institution and from the role of mental patient, and who proceeds to "treat" him against his will—such a psychiatrist, I maintain, creates "mental illness" and "mental patients." He does so in exactly the same way as the white man created slavery by capturing the black man, bringing him to America in shackles, and then selling and using the black man as if he were an animal.

To understand the injustice of commitment it is necessary to distinguish between *disease* as a *biological condition* and the *sick role* as a *social status*. Though a simple one, this distinction is rarely made in articles on mental illness, and there is a good reason for this. For once this distinction is made, psychiatry ceases to be what it is officially proclaimed, namely a medical specialty, and becomes, instead, social engineering.

Strictly speaking, *illness* is a biological (physicochemical) abnormality of the body or its functioning. A person is sick if he has diabetes, a stroke, or cancer.

The *sick role,* on the other hand, refers to the social status of claiming illness or assuming the role of patient. Like husband, father or citizen, the *sick role* denotes a certain relationship to others in the society.

A person may be ill, but may prefer not to assume the sick role, as when we have a severe cold but go about our business. Conversely, a person may be healthy, but choose to assume the sick role, as when we feel perfectly well but offer illness as an excuse for avoiding an obligation to go to the office or a party. Soldiers often assume the sick role --called "malingering"—to avoid the dangers of combat.

Where does the distinction between illness and sick role leave the alleged mental patient? He is said to be "very sick" by his relatives and the psychiatrists retained by them, but the patient maintains he is perfectly well and rejects medical or psychiatric help. Society then uses the police power of the state to force such a person into the sick role: this is done by calling the person a "mental patient," by incarcerating him in a "mental hospital" and by "treating" him for his "mental illness" whether he likes it or not. The underlying issue, however, is whether or not an individual has the right to refuse to be cast into the role of mental patient.

To answer this question, it is necessary to consider the problem of what mental illness is. Mental illness is not a physicochemical abnormality of the body, that is, an organic illness. If it were, we would simply call it illness and have no need for the qualifying adjective "mental." Actually, what we call "functional" mental diseases are not diseases at all. Persons said to be suffering from such disorders are socially deviant or inept, or in conflict with individuals, groups or institutions.

Not only does mental illness differ fundamentally from physical illness, but mental hospitalization differs from medical hospitalization. Mental hospitalization is typically involuntary, whereas medical hospitalization is typically voluntary. In a free society, a person can't be committed and treated against his will for cancer or heart diseases, but he can be committed for depression or schizophrenia.

Should future research establish that certain so-called functional mental illnesses are actual physical disorders, they would then be treated like other organic disorders and the question of involuntary hospitalization for them would become irrelevant.

If schizophrenia, for example, turns out to have a biochemical cause and cure, schizophrenia would no longer be one of the diseases for which a person would be involuntarily committed. Pellagra once sent many persons to mental hospitals with symptoms resembling schizophrenia until a vitamin deficiency was found to cause pellagra.

A person is said to be mentally ill if he behaves in certain "abnormal" ways. Since what is abnormal to one person is normal to another, mental illness is

319

> "But even if a mental patient has expert legal advice,
> what facts can *he* offer to prove that he is not potentially dangerous...
> it is impossible to *prove* that a person is not dangerous."

a kind of loose-fitting, quasi-medical synonym for bad or undesirable behavior. To a Christian Scientist, going to a doctor is abnormal. To a hypochondriac, *not* going is. To a Roman Catholic, using artificial birth control is abnormal. To a non-Catholic eager to avoid pregnancy, *not* using it is abnormal. The fact that mental illness designates a deviation from an ethical rule of conduct, and that such rules vary widely, explains why upper-middle-class psychiatrists can so easily find evidence of "mental illness" in lower-class individuals; and why so many prominent persons in the past 50 years or so have been diagnosed by their enemies as suffering from some type of insanity. Barry Goldwater was called a "paranoid schizophrenic"; Whittaker Chambers, a "psychopathic personality"; Woodrow Wilson, a "neurotic," frequently "very close to psychosis" (by no less a psychiatrist than Sigmund Freud!). Jesus himself, according to two psychiatrists quoted by Dr. Albert Schweitzer in his doctoral thesis, was a "born degenerate" with a "fixed delusional system"; manifesting a "paranoid clinical picture [so typical] it is hardly conceivable people can even question the accuracy of the diagnosis."

My argument that commitment is a crime against humanity is opposed on the grounds that commitment is necessary for the protection of the healthy members of society. To be sure, commitment does protect the community from certain threats. But the question should not be *whether* the community is protected, but precisely *from what,* and *how.*

Commitment shields nonhospitalized members of society from having to accommodate to the annoying or idiosyncratic demands of persons who have *not* violated any criminal statutes. The commitment procedure has already been used against General Edwin Walker and Ezra Pound. Conceivably it could be used against a Stokely Carmichael or an Eldridge Cleaver.

But what about those persons who are actually violent? Society could, if it were willing, protect itself from violence and threats of violence through our system of criminal laws, which provides for the imprisonment of violators in correctional institutions.

What about so-called emotionally disturbed persons who have not violated any statute but are believed to be violence-prone? Everything possible should be done to give them help, but is it just to hospitalize or treat them involuntarily for being "potentially dangerous"?

To be judged potentially violent, a patient must be interviewed by a psychiatrist, which in effect violates the patient's right under the Fifth Amendment to refuse to incriminate himself. Few "mental patients" receive legal advice prior to being committed, but if they refused to be seen or interviewed by a physician, commitment would be impossible.

Psychiatrists cannot predict whether a person will be violent. Many "mental patients" who lose their liberty never have been and never will be violent.

Being "potentially dangerous" is not a crime. Most of us equate emotional disturbance with being violence-prone. Studies show, however, that "mental" patients are no more violence-prone than "normals."

To further clarify the political dimensions and implications of commitment practices, let us note some of the fundamental parallels between master and slave on the one hand and the institutional psychiatrist and involuntarily hospitalized mental patient on the other. In each instance the former member of the pair defines the social role of the latter, and casts the latter in that role by force. The committed patient must accept the view that he is "sick," that his captors are "well," that the patient's own view of himself is false and his captors' view of him is true, and that to effect any change in his social situation, the patient must relinquish his "sick" views and adopt the "healthy" views of those who have power over him. By accepting himself as "sick" and the institutional environment and the various manipulations imposed by the staff as "treatment," the patient is compelled to authenticate the psychiatrist's role as that of benevolent physician curing mental illness. The patient who maintains the forbidden image of reality—that the psychiatrist is a jailer—is considered paranoid. Since most patients (like oppressed people generally) eventually accept the ideas imposed on them by their superiors, hospital psychiatrists are constantly immersed in an environment in which their identity as "doctor" is affirmed. The moral superiority of white men over black was similarly authenticated and affirmed.

Suppose a person wishes to study slavery. He might start by studying slaves—and he would then find that slaves are, in general, brutish, poor and uneducated. The student of slavery might

> "Mental illness is a myth. People we label 'mentally ill' are not sick, and involuntary mental hospitalization is not treatment. It is punishment."

then conclude that slavery is the slave's natural or appropriate social state. Such, indeed, have been the methods and conclusions of innumerable men through the ages. For example, Aristotle held that slaves were naturally inferior and hence justly subdued.

Another student, biased by contempt for slavery, might proceed differently. He would maintain there can be no slave without a master holding the slave in bondage. This student would accordingly consider slavery a type of human relationship, a social institution, supported by custom, law, religion and force. From this perspective, the study of masters is at least as relevant to the study of slavery as is the study of slaves. I hold that the study of institutional psychiatrists is as relevant to the study of involuntary hospitalization as is the study of mental patients.

Mental illness has been investigated for centuries, and continues to be investigated today, in much the same way slaves were studied in the antebellum South and before. Men took for granted the existence of slaves. Scientists duly noted and classified the biological and social characteristics of the slaves. In the same way, we take for granted the existence of mental patients. Indeed, many Americans believe the number of such patients is steadily increasing. And it is generally believed that the psychiatrist's task is to observe and classify the biological, psychological and social characteristics of mental patients.

The defenders of slavery claimed the Negro was happier as a slave than as a free man because of the "peculiarities of his character." As historian S. M. El-

kins has said, "The failure of any free workers to present themselves for enslavement can serve as one test of how much the analysis of the happy slave may have added to Americans' understanding of themselves." The failure of most persons with so-called mental illness to present themselves for hospitalization is a test of how much current analysis of mental health problems may have added to our understanding of ourselves.

Today, of course, involuntary mental hospitalization is a universally accepted method of social control, much as slavery was in the past. Our unwillingness to look searchingly at this problem may be compared to the unwillingness of the South to look at slavery. "A democratic people," wrote Elkins, "no longer reasons with itself when it is all of the same mind." Today the Supreme Court of Iowa can say: "Such loss of liberty [as is entailed in commitment of the insane] is not such liberty as is within the meaning of the constitutional provision that 'no person shall be deprived of life, liberty or property without due process of law.'" I submit, however, that just as slavery is an evil, so is hospitalizing anyone without his consent, whether that person is depressed or paranoid, hysterical or schizophrenic.

Commitment practices flourished long before there were mental or psychiatric "treatments" for "mental diseases." Indeed madness, or mental illness, was not always a requirement for commitment. The Illinois commitment laws of 1851 specified that, "Married women . . . may be entered or detained in the hospital on the request of the husband of the woman . . . *without* the evidence of in-

sanity required in other cases." Regulations for the Bicètre and Salpêtrierè, the two Parisian "mental hospitals" that became world famous, made it possible in 1680 to lock up children (of artisans and poor people) who "refused to work or who used their parents badly." Girls "debauched or in evident danger of becoming so," and prostitutes or "women who ran bawdy houses" were also considered fit subjects for incarceration.

Today, commitment laws usually specify that, for involuntary hospitalization, a person not only must be mentally ill, but must also be dangerous to himself or to others. But even if a mental patient has expert legal advice, what facts can *he* offer to prove that he is not dangerous, when a psychiatrist claims he is? Clearly, it is impossible to *prove* that a person is not dangerous.

Involuntary mental hospitalization remains today what it has been ever since its inception in the 17th Century: an extra-legal, quasi-medical form of social control for persons who annoy or disturb others and whose nonconformity cannot be controlled through the criminal law. To be sure, the rhetoric has changed. Formerly, a housewife's commitment could be justified by her husband's disaffection and his unsupported complaints. Today, commitment must be justified by calling the housewife "mentally ill." The locus of confinement has changed. The Bedlams of old have been replaced by state mental hospitals and community mental-health centers. But the social reality remains the same: commitment is still punishment without trial, imprisonment without time limit, and stigmatization without hope of redress.

VIII. social psychology

The study of social psychology focuses on the individual in society and investigates such topics as interpersonal attraction, attitude formation and propaganda, conformity and obedience to authority, leadership, and the influence of social class. The very nature of the subject matter often forces the social psychologist to confront issues that have political, moral, and ethical implications. Whether social-psychological studies surrounding these issues are performed in the laboratory or in the real world, they are likely to have immediate practical applications.

Strangers who meet and find that they have a mutual acquaintance may exclaim, "My, it's a small world!" This aphorism started Stanley Milgram searching for an objective evaluation of the size and extent of the social network. He wanted to find, given any two people at random, how many intermediate acquaintances link the two. Milgram's results show that, far from being alienated from one another, people are bound together in a tightly knit social fabric. This small-world study demonstrates a novel approach to field research in social psychology.

If the world is small, does familiarity breed contempt? Robert Zajonc shows that, on the contrary, repeated exposure to unfamiliar stimuli, whether words or people, may be enough to increase a person's attraction to those stimuli. He makes clear the implications for advertising and politics through several unsettling examples.

Although increased exposure may lead to liking, once a person has learned to expect love and praise from a close associate, that associate may become less potent than a stranger as a source of reward. Elliot Aronson reaches this conclusion as he examines the factors that affect interpersonal attraction. He shows how increasing levels of reward or punishment from a person may have more impact on his or her attractiveness than will constant, invariant reward or punishment. The mechanisms that cause these gains or losses in attractiveness are a critical factor in successful relationships.

Attitudes toward people, then, are alterable. But how does one alter people's values on issues of freedom, equality, or civil rights? Milton Rokeach reports a procedure that did, in fact, alter such attitudes in a forty-minute psychological experiment, and the changes persisted for more than a year after the laboratory experience. Rokeach's findings strongly suggest that social control and the shaping of political institutions are possible and must be guarded against.

William McGuire offers ways for people to protect themselves against persuasion techniques. Borrowing from the terminology of medical biology, he suggests a vaccine against brainwash; he shows how resistance to persuasion can be built up through inoculation with a weak dose of the attacking arguments. A well-integrated series of experiments leads McGuire to conclude that the ideal prescription for building resistance to persuasion consists of first attacking a person's belief and then reassuring the person that the belief is right after all. However, immunization against persuasion is not in itself a guarantee of safety from cognitive corruption, because the technique could as well be used by malevolent forces.

Interpersonal attraction and personal attitudes are two factors that determine whether people respect their leaders. Pondering the determinants of successful qualities in kings, Shakespeare wrote in *Twelfth-Night,* "Some are born great, some achieve greatness, and some have greatness thrust upon them." Recent studies by Fred Fiedler on what makes a leader do not include research on kings, but they do contradict traditional views on leadership of all varieties. The notion that some people are endowed with certain identifiable personality traits that make them "born leaders" is a myth, according to Fiedler. It also seems unlikely that short-term training programs could alter the basic personality traits assumed to characterize good leaders. Studies in a group-effectiveness laboratory have shown that people are effective leaders only when they function in situations compatible with their own characteristics. The effectiveness of a leader may be enhanced by modifying the group itself, the structure of the group's task, or the leader's position of power. Successful leaders are those who learn to recognize the situations in which they can operate most effectively and to avoid those situations in which they are likely to fail.

In emergency situations witnessed by groups of strangers a leader may emerge, but often individual responsibility is diffused because of the presence of other bystanders. In response to a growing number of incidents in which victims were beaten, raped, and murdered in the presence of bystanders, John Darley and Bibb Latané began studying how people react to emergencies. To find what it is that inhibits people in groups from coming to the aid of the victim—and to find if it is true that the more people who watch a victim in distress, the less likely it is that someone will help—the investigators arranged laboratory experiments that simulated crisis situations, and they watched the responses of subjects acting alone or in groups. The findings of Darley and Latané's research program, coupled with field research on bystander intervention, are having a noticeable effect on the American public. Knowing that the presence of others tends to inhibit the response of any given individual, many people are now assuming leadership roles and taking responsibility for protecting others.

By Stanley Milgram

the small world problem

Fred Jones of Peoria, sitting in a sidewalk cafe in Tunis, and needing a light for his cigarette, asks the man at the next table for a match. They fall into conversation; the stranger is an Englishman who, it turns out, spent several months in Detroit studying the operation of an interchangeable-bottlecap-factory. "I know it's a foolish question," says Jones, "but did you ever by any chance run into a fellow named Ben Arkadian? He's an old friend of mine, manages a chain of supermarkets in Detroit…"

"Arkadian, Arkadian," the Englishman mutters. "Why, upon my soul, I believe I do! Small chap, very energetic, raised merry hell with the factory over a shipment of defective bottlecaps."

"No kidding!" Jones exclaims in amazement.

"Good lord, it's a small world, isn't it?"

Almost all of us have had the experience of encountering someone far from home, who, to our surprise, turns out to share a mutual acquaintance with us. This kind of experience occurs with sufficient frequency so that our language even provides a cliché to be uttered at the appropriate moment of recognizing mutual acquaintances. We say, "My it's a small world."

Random dispersement of people in the small world.

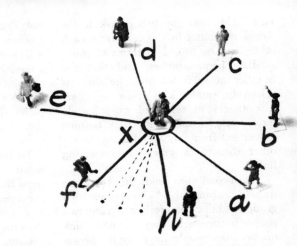

Each person's first-hand acquaintances are shown, A through N.

The simplest way of formulating the small-world problem is: Starting with any two people in the world, what is the probability that they will know each other? A somewhat more sophisticated formulation, however, takes account of the fact that while persons X and Z may not know each other directly, they may share a mutual acquaintance—that is, a person who knows both of them. One can then think of an acquaintance chain with X knowing Y and Y knowing Z. Moreover, one can imagine circumstances in which X is linked to Z not by a single link, but by a series of links, X-*a-b-c-d* . . . *y*-Z. That is to say, person X knows person *a* who in turn knows person *b*, who knows *c* . . . who knows *y*, who knows Z.

Therefore, another question one may ask is: Given any two people in the world, person X and person Z, how many intermediate acquaintance links are needed before X and Z are connected?

Concern with the small-world problem is not new, nor is it limited to social psychologists like myself. Historians, political scientists, and communication specialists share an interest in the problem. Jane Jacobs, who is concerned with city planning, describes an acquaintance chain in terms of a children's game:

When my sister and I first came to New York from a small city, we used to amuse ourselves with a game we called Messages. I suppose we were trying, in a dim way, to get a grip on the great, bewildering world into which we had come from our cocoon. The idea was to pick two wildly dissimilar individuals—say a head hunter in the Solomon Islands and a cobbler in Rock Island, Illinois—and assume that one had to get a message to the other by word of mouth; then we would each silently figure out a plausible, or at least possible, chain of persons through which the message could go. The one who could make the shortest plausible chain of messengers won. The head hunter would speak to the head man of his village, who would speak to the trader who came to buy copra, who would speak to the Australian patrol officer when he came through, who would tell the man who was next slated to go to Melbourne on leave, etc. Down at the other end, the cobbler would hear from his priest, who got it from the mayor, who got it from a state senator, who got it from the governor, etc. We soon had these close-to-home messengers down to a routine for almost everybody we could conjure up . . .

The importance of the problem does not lie in these entertaining aspects, but in the fact that it brings under discussion a certain mathematical structure in society, a structure that often plays a part, whether recognized or not, in many discussions of history, sociology, and other disciplines. For example, Henri Pirenne and George Duby, important historians, make the point that in the Dark Ages communication broke down between cities of western Europe. They became isolated and simply did not have contact with each other. The network of acquaintances of individuals became constricted. The disintegration of society was expressed in the growing isolation of communities, and the infrequent contact with those living outside a person's immediate place of residence.

There are two general philosophical views of the small-world problem. One

The network spreads, with complicated inter-connections.

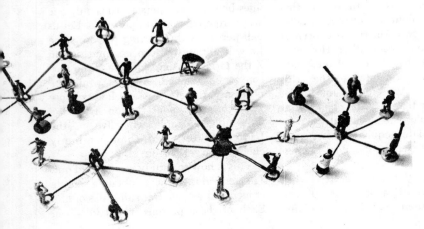

With group inbreeding, X's acquaintances feed back into his own circle, normally eliminating new contacts.

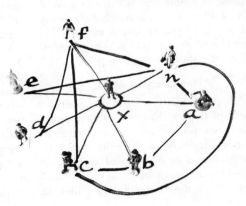

view holds that any two people in the world, no matter how remote from each other, can be linked in terms of intermediate acquaintances, and that the number of such intermediate links is relatively small. This view sees acquaintances in terms of an infinitely intersecting arrangement that permits movement from any social group to another through a series of connecting links.

The second view holds that there are unbridgeable gaps between various groups and that therefore, given any two people in the world, they will never link up because people have circles of acquaintances which do not necessarily intersect. A message will circulate in a particular group of acquaintances, but may never be able to make the jump to another circle. This view sees the world in terms of concentric circles of acquaintances, each within its own orbit.

The Underlying Structure

Sometimes it is useful to visualize the abstract properties of a scientific problem before studying it in detail; that is, we construct a model of the main features of the phenomenon as we understand them. Let us represent all the people in the United States by a number of blue points. Each point represents a person, while lines connecting two points show that the two persons are acquainted. [*See top illustration, previous page.*] Each person has a certain number of first-hand acquaintances, which we shall represent by the letters $a, b, c, \ldots n$. Each acquaintance in turn has his own acquaintances, connected to still other points. The exact number of lines radiating from any point depends on the size of a person's circle of acquaintances. The entire structure takes on the form of a complex network of 200 million points, with complicated connections between them [*see bottom left illustration, previous page.*] One way of restating the small-world problem in these terms is this: Given any two of these points chosen at random from this universe of 200 million points, through how many intermediate points would we pass before the chosen points could be connected by the shortest possible path?

Research at M.I.T.

There are many ways to go about the study of the small-world problem, and I shall soon present my own approach to it. But first, let us consider the important contributions of a group of workers at The Massachusetts Institute of Technology, under the leadership of Ithiel de

Sola Pool. Working closely with Manfred Kochen of IBM, Pool decided to build a theoretical model of the small-world, a model which closely parallels the idea of points and lines shown. However, unlike my own model, which is purely pictorial, Pool and Kochen translate their thinking into strict mathematical terms.

To build such a model they needed certain information. First, they had to know how many acquaintances the average man has. Surprisingly, though this is a very basic question, no reliable answers could be found in the social science literature. So the information had to be obtained, a task which

The beginning of a typical chain (#111) in the Nebraska Study.

STARTING PERSON
Widowed clerk in Omaha, Nebraska

Michael Gurevitch, then a graduate student at M.I.T., undertook. Gurevitch asked a variety of men and women to keep a record of all the persons they came in contact with in the course of 100 days. It turned out that on the average, these people recorded names of roughly 500 persons, so that this figure could be used as the basis of the theoretical model. Now, if every person knows 500 other people, what are the chances that any two people will know each other? Making a set of rather simple assumptions, it turns out that there is only about one chance in 200,000 that any two Americans chosen at random will know each other. However, when you ask the chances of their having a mutual acquaintance, the odds drop sharply. And quite amazingly, there is better than a 50-50 chance that any two people can be linked up with two intermediate acquaintances. Or at least, that is what the Pool-Kochen theory indicates.

Of course, the investigators were aware that even if a man has 500 acquaintances, there may be a lot of in-

breeding. That is, many of the 500 friends of my friend may be actually among the people I know anyway, so that they do not really contribute to a widening net of acquaintances; the acquaintances of X simply feed back into his own circle and fail to bring any new contacts into it [*see bottom right illustration, previous page*]. It is a fairly straightforward job to check up on the amount of inbreeding if one uses only one or two circles of acquaintances, but it becomes almost impossible when the acquaintance chain stretches far and wide. So many people are involved that a count just isn't practical.

So the big obstacle one runs up against is the problem of social structure. Though poor people always have acquaintances, it would probably turn out that they tend to be among other poor people, and that the rich speak mostly to the rich. It is exceedingly difficult to assess the impact of social structure on a model of this sort. If you could

think of the American population as simply 200 million points, each with 500 random connections, the model would work. But the contours of social structure make this a perilous assumption, for society is not built on random connections among persons but tends to be fragmented into social classes and cliques.

A Harvard Approach

The Pool and Kochen mathematical model was interesting from a theoretical standpoint, but I wondered whether the problem might not be solved by a more direct experimental approach. The Laboratory of Social Relations at Harvard gave me $680 to prove that it could. I set out to find an experimental method whereby it would be possible to trace a line of acquaintances linking any two persons chosen at random.

Let us assume for the moment that the actual process of establishing the linkages between two persons runs only one way: from person A to person Z. Let us call person A the *starting* person, since he will initiate the process, and person Z the *target* person, since he is the person to be reached. All that would be necessary, therefore, would be to choose a starting person at random from the 200 million people who live in the United States, and then randomly choose a target person.

This is how the study was carried out. The general idea was to obtain a sample of men and women from all walks of life. Each of these persons would be given the name and address of the same target person, a person chosen at random, who lives somewhere in the United States. Each of the participants would be asked to move a message toward the target person, using only a chain of friends and acquaintances. Each person would be asked to transmit the message to the friend or acquaintance who he thought would be most likely to know the target person. Messages could move only to persons who knew each other on a first-name basis.

As a crude beginning, we thought it best to draw our starting persons from a distant city, so we chose Wichita, Kansas for our first study and Omaha, Nebraska for our second. (From Cambridge, these cities seem vaguely 'out there,' on the Great Plains or somewhere.) To obtain our sample, letters of solicitation were sent to residents in

1st REMOVE
Self-employed friend in Council Bluffs, Iowa

these cities asking them to participate in a study of social contact in American society. The target person in our first study lived in Cambridge and was the wife of a divinity school student. In the second study, carried out in collaboration with Jeffrey Travers, the target person was a stockbroker who worked in Boston and lived in Sharon, Massachusetts. To keep matters straight, I will refer to the first study as the Kansas Study, and the second as the Nebraska Study. These terms indicate merely where the starting persons were drawn from.

Each person who volunteered to serve as a starting person was sent a folder containing a document, which served as the main tool of the investigation. Briefly, the document contains:

1. The name of the target person as well as certain information about him. This orients the participants toward a specific individual.

2. A set of rules for reaching the target person. Perhaps the

most important rule is: *"If you do not know the target person on a personal basis, do not try to contact him directly. Instead, mail this folder . . . to a personal acquaintance who is more likely than you to know the target person . . . it must be someone you know on a first-name basis."* This rule sets the document into motion, moving it from one participant to the next, until it is sent to someone who knows the target person.

3. A roster on which each person in the chain writes his name. This tells the person who receives the folder exactly who sent it to him. The roster also has another practical effect; it prevents endless looping of the folder through participants who have already served as links in the chain, because each participant can see exactly what sequence of persons has led up to his own participation.

In addition to the document, the folder contains a stack of 15 business reply, or "tracer" cards. Each person receiving the folder takes out a card, fills it in, returns it to us, and sends the remaining cards along with the document to the next link.

Several other features of the procedure need to be emphasized. First, each

2nd REMOVE
Publisher in Belmont, Mass.

participant is supposed to send the folder on to one other person only. Thus the efficiency with which the chain is completed depends in part on the wisdom of his choice in this matter. Second, by means of the tracer card, we have continuous feedback on the progress of each chain. The cards are coded so we know which chain it comes from and which link in the chain has been completed. The card also provides us with relevant sociological characteristics of the senders of the cards. Thus, we know the characteristics of completed, as well as incompleted, chains. Third, the procedure permits experimental variation at many points.

In short, the device possesses some of the features of a chain letter, though it does not pyramid in any way; moreover

it is oriented toward a specific target, zeroes in on the target through the cooperation of a sequence of participants, and contains a tracer that allows us to keep track of its progress at all times.

Would It Work?

The question that plagued us most in undertaking this study was simply: Would the procedure work? Would any of the chains started in Kansas actually reach our target person in Massachusetts? Part of the excitement of experimental social psychology is that it is all so new we often have no way of knowing whether our techniques will work or simply turn out to be wispy pipe dreams.

The answer came fairly quickly. It will be recalled that our first target person

3rd REMOVE
Tanner in Sharon, Mass.

was the wife of a student living in Cambridge. Four days after the folders were sent to a group of starting persons in Kansas, an instructor at the Episcopal Theological Seminary approached our target person on the street. "Alice," he said, thrusting a brown folder toward her, "this is for you." At first she thought he was simply returning a folder

4th REMOVE
Sheet metal worker in Sharon, Mass.

that had gone astray and had never gotten out of Cambridge, but when we looked at the roster, we found to our pleased surprise that the document had started with a wheat farmer in Kansas. He had passed it on to an Episcopalian minister in his home town, who sent it

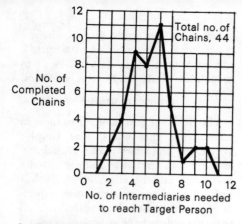

No. of Completed Chains

Total no. of Chains, 44

No. of Intermediaries needed to reach Target Person

In the Nebraska Study the chains varied from two to 10 intermediate acquaintances with the median at five.

to the minister who taught in Cambridge, who gave it to the target person. Altogether the number of intermediate links between starting person and target person amounted to *two!*

How Many Intermediaries?

As it turned out, this was one of the shortest chains we were ever to receive, for as more tracers and folders came in, we learned that chains varied from two to 10 intermediate acquaintances, with the median at five [see illustration above]. A median of five intermediate persons is, in certain ways, impressive, considering the distances traversed. Recently, when I asked an intelligent friend of mine how many steps he thought it

5th REMOVE
Dentist in Sharon, Mass.

would take, he estimated that it would require 100 intermediate persons or more to move from Nebraska to Sharon. Many people make somewhat similar estimates, and are surprised to learn that only five intermediaries will—on the average—suffice. Somehow it does not accord with intuition. Later, I shall try to explain the basis of the discrepancy between intuition and fact.

On a purely theoretical basis, it is reasonable to assume that even fewer links are essential to complete the chains. First, since our participants can send

the folder to only one of their 500 possible contacts, it is unlikely that even through careful selections, they will necessarily and at all times, select the contact best able to advance the chain to the target. On the whole they probably make pretty good guesses but surely, from time to time, they overlook some possibilities for short cuts. Thus, the chains obtained in our empirical study are less efficient than those generated theoretically.

Second, by working on a highly rational basis, each intermediary moves the folder toward the target person. That is, a certain amount of information about the target person—his place of employment, place of residence, schooling, and so forth—is given to the starting subject, and it is on the basis of this information alone that he selects the next recipient of the folder. Yet, in real life, we sometimes know a person because we chance to meet him on an ocean liner, or we spend a summer in camp together as teenagers, yet these haphazard bases of acquaintanceship cannot be fully exploited by the participants.

There is one factor, however, that could conceivably have worked in the opposite direction in our experiments, giving us the illusion that the chains are shorter than they really are. There is a certain decay in the number of active chains over each remove, even when they do not drop out because they reach the target person. Of 160 chains that started in Nebraska, 44 were completed and 126 dropped out. These chains die before completion because on each remove a certain proportion of participants simply do not cooperate and fail to send on the folder. Thus, the results we obtained on the distribution of chain lengths occurred within the general

6th REMOVE
Printer in Sharon, Mass.

drift of a decay curve. It is possible that some of the incompleted chains would have been longer than those that were completed. To account for this possibility, Harrison White of Harvard has con-

structed a mathematical model to show what the distribution of chain lengths would look like if all chains went through to completion. In terms of this model, there is a transformation of the data, yielding slightly longer chains.

Examining the Chains

Several features of the chains are worth examining, for they tell us something about the pattern of contact in American society. Consider, for example, the very pronounced tendency in our Kansas Study for females to send the folder on to females, and males to send it on to males. Of the 145 participants involved in the study, we find:

Female	⟶	Female	56
Male	⟶	Male	58
Female	⟶	Male	18
Male	⟶	Female	13

Thus participants were three times as likely to send the folder on to someone of the same sex as to someone of the opposite sex. Exactly why this is so is not easy to determine, but it suggests that certain kinds of communication are strongly conditioned by sex roles.

7th REMOVE
Clothing merchant in Sharon, Mass.

Participants indicated on the reply cards whether they were sending the folder on to a friend, a relative, or an acquaintance. In the Kansas Study, 123 sent the folder to friends and acquaintances, while only 22 sent it to relatives. Cross-cultural comparison would seem useful here. It is quite likely that in societies which possess extended kinship systems, relatives will be more heavily represented in the communication network than is true in the United States. In American society, where extended kinship links are not maintained, acquaintance and friendship links provide the preponderant basis for reaching the target person. I would guess, further, that within certain ethnic groups in the United States, a higher proportion of familial lines would be found in the data. Probably, for example, if the study were limited to persons of Italian extraction, one would get a higher proportion of relatives in the chain. This illustrates, I hope, how the small world technique may usefully illuminate varied aspects of social structure.

Spaced throughout the preceding text is a series of illustrations showing the kinds of people found in a typical chain (number 111) from the Nebraska Study.

Common Pathways

Each of us is embedded in a small-world structure. It is not true, however, that each of our acquaintances constitutes an equally important basis of contact with the larger social world. It is obvious that some of our acquaintances are more important than others in establishing contacts with broader social realms; some friends are relatively isolated, while others possess a wide circle of acquaintances, and contact with them brings us into a far-ranging network of additional persons.

Referring to our Nebraska Study, let us consider in detail the pattern of convergence crystallizing around the target person—the stockbroker living in Sharon, Massachusetts, and working in Boston [*see top illustration on next page*]. A total of 64 chains reached him. (44 chains originated in Nebraska and 20 chains, from an auxiliary study, originated in the Boston area). Twenty-four of the chains reached him at his place of residence in the small town outside of Boston. Within Sharon, 16 were given to him by Mr. Jacobs, a clothing merchant in town. Thus, the clothing merchant served as the principal point of mediation between the broker and a larger world, a fact which came as a considerable surprise, and even something of a shock for the broker. At his place of work, in a Boston brokerage house, 10 of the chains passed through Mr. Jones, and five through Mr. Brown. Indeed, 48 percent of the chains to reach the broker were moved on to him by three persons: Jacobs, Jones, and Brown. Between Jacobs and Jones there is an interesting division of labor. Jacobs mediates the chains advancing to the broker by virtue of his residence. Jones performs a similar function in the occupational domain, and moves 10 chains enmeshed in the investment-brokerage network to the target person.

More detail thus fills in the picture of the small world. First, we learn that the target person is not surrounded by acquaintance points, each of which is equally likely to feed into an outside contact; rather, there appear to be highly popular channels for the transmission of the chain. Second, there is differentiation among these commonly used channels, so that certain of them provide the chief points of transmission in regard to residential contact, while others have specialized contact possibilities in the occupational domain. For each possible realm of activity in which the target person is involved, there is likely to emerge a sociometric star with specialized contact possibilities.

Geographic and Social Movement

The geographic movement of the folder from Nebraska to Massachusetts

TARGET PERSON
Mr. Jones, a Stock broker living in Sharon, Mass.

is striking. There is a progressive closing in on the target area as each new person is added to the chain. [*See bottom illustration on next page.*] In some cases, however, a chain moves all the way from Nebraska to the very neighborhood in which the target person resides, but then goes round and round, never quite making the necessary contact to complete the chain. Some chains died only a few hundred feet from the target person's house, after a successful journey of 1000 miles. Thus we see that social communication is sometimes restricted less by physical distance than by social distance.

The next step is to see what happens when we change the relationship between the starting person and the target person. That is, if the two are drawn from different class backgrounds, does this then decrease the probability of completing the chain? Does it increase the number of links?

In collaboration with Charles Korte, I am now applying the small-world method to the study of communications between subgroups in American society

—Negro and white. We will have both Negro and white starting persons, but only Negro target persons, and try to trace the lines of communication between them. First, we want to ask: In what degree are the racial lines surmounted? Can any sizeable fraction of the communications get through the racial barrier? If the answer is yes, we then want to identify the typical locus of transmission. Does it occur at the neighborhood level, or at the place of work? We are particularly interested in the persons who serve as links between Negro and white groups. In what way do they differ from others in the chain? Do they tend to occupy particular professional categories, such as minister, teacher, and so forth? Is the communication flow between Negroes and whites easier in Northern or in Southern locales? Perhaps some new light can be cast on the structural relationships between Negro and white communities by probing with the small-world method.

Intuition and Fact

As we saw above, many people were surprised to learn that only five intermediaries will, on the average, suffice to link any two randomly chosen individuals, no matter where they happen to live in the United States. We ought to try to explain the discrepancy between intuition and fact.

The first point to remember is that although we deal directly with only five intermediaries, behind each of them stands a much larger group of from 500 to 2500 persons. That is, each participant has an acquaintance pool of 500 to 2500 persons from which he selects the person who, he thinks, is best able to advance the chain. Thus we are dealing only with the end product of a radical screening procedure.

The second thing to remember is that geometric progression is implicit in the search procedure, but nothing is more alien to mathematically untutored intuition than this form of thinking. As youngsters, many of us were asked the question: If you earned a penny a day and the sum were doubled each day, how much would you have earned by the end of a 30-day working period? Most frequently people give answers on the order of $1.87 or $6.45, when in fact the sum is more than $10 million for one 30-day working period, the last day alone yielding $5,368,709.12. Elements of geometric progression with an increase rate far more powerful than mere doubling underlie the small-world search procedure, and thus, with only a few removes, the search extends to an enormous number of persons.

Finally, when we state there are only five intermediate acquaintances, this connotes a closeness between the position of the starting person and the target person. But this is in large measure misleading, a confusion of two entirely different frames of reference. If two persons are five removes apart, they are far apart indeed. Almost anyone in the United States is but a few removes from the President, or from Nelson Rockefeller, but this is true only in terms of a particular mathematical viewpoint and does not, in any practical sense, integrate our lives with that of Nelson Rockefeller. Thus, when we speak of five intermediaries, we are talking about an enormous psychological distance between the starting and target points, a distance which seems small only because we customarily regard "five" as a small manageable quantity. We should think of the two points as being not five persons apart, but "five circles of acquaintances" apart — five "structures" apart. This helps to set it in its proper perspective.

There is a very interesting theorem based on the model of the small world. It states that if two persons from two different populations cannot make contact, then no one within the entire population in which each is embedded can make contact with any person in the other population. In other words, if a particular person, *a*, embedded in population A (which consists of his circle of acquaintances), cannot make contact with a particular person, *b*, embedded in population B, then:

1. No other person in A can make contact with *b*.
2. No other person in A can make contact with any other person in B.

Funneling occurs in the last remove. Several persons serve as key links in completing chains.

JONES (10)

(2)

(2)

TARGET PERSON

JACOBS (16)

BROWN (5)

(3)

(3)

(3)

(3)

(3)

(17)

3. In other words, the two sub-populations are compeltely isolated from each other. Conceivably, this could happen if one of the populations were on an island never visited by the outside world. In principle, any person in the United States can be contacted by any other in relatively few steps, unless one of them is a complete and total hermit, and then he could not be contacted at all.

In sum, perhaps the most important accomplishment of the research described here is this: Although people have talked about the small-world problem, and have even theorized about it, this study achieved, as far as I know, the

first empirically-created chains between persons chosen at random from a major national population.

Although the study started with a specific set of questions arising from the small-world problem, the procedure illuminates a far wider set of topics. It reveals a potential communication structure whose sociological characteristics have yet to be exposed. When we understand the structure of this potential communication net, we shall understand a good deal more about the integration of society in general. While many studies in social science show how the individual is alienated and cut off from the rest of society, this study demonstrates that, in some sense, we are all bound together in a tightly knit social fabric. ◨

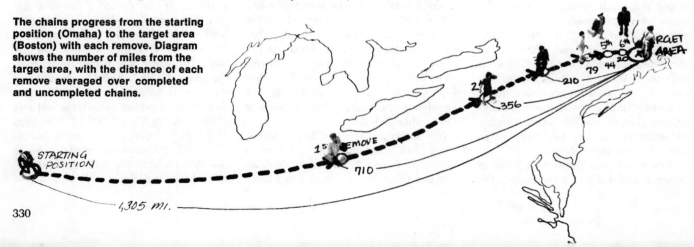

STARTING POSITION

1 ST REMOVE
710

356

210

79 44

5th 6th TARGET AREA

1,305 mi.

by Robert Zajonc

Brainwash: Familiarity Breeds Comfort

But if you be nice to foul your fingers, which good anglers seldom are, then take this bait . . .
—Izaak Walton, *The Compleat Angler*

The word *nice* comes from the Latin word *ignorant*. By the time it got into Middle English, *nice* meant *foolish;* and in the 17th Century English sentence above it meant *fastidious* or *finicky*. Today, of course, *nice* has a nicer meaning. A similar evolution is true for the word *pretty*, which can be traced to the Old English *praetig*—deceitful or sly. In its Middle English form, *prati* meant *cunning*, a usage which soon gave way to *ingenious*.

A vast number of words have changed their meanings over the centuries to become more positive. This mysterious process can, in some of its aspects, be reproduced in a laboratory in a much shorter period of time—about five minutes. Take a word your subject has never seen before, such as the Turkish word *dilikli*. Show it to the person a number of times and ask him whether it means something good or something bad. The more times the person has seen *dilikli*, the more likely he is to say it means

something good. Subjects who have seen the word only once or twice don't like it much at all.

I don't wish to imply that etymology is simply a matter of repetition and that word meanings always improve. There are many words whose meanings have deteriorated over time. But the above example does illustrate a phenomenon that is vastly more universal, and whose consequences are more profound and diverse, than it would at first appear. The proposition holds that the *mere repeated exposure of an unfamiliar stimulus is enough to increase one's attraction to that stimulus*. Repeated exposure makes words more positive, food more appetizing, strangers more acceptable. Repeated exposure will increase the attraction between two people or two animals. I am not saying that exposure is always necessary for attraction or attachment to occur. Many other psychological processes are equally efficient in getting people to like each other. But exposure

Preference and Frequency of Antonym Pairs

Preference	Word	Frequency	Preference	Antonym	Frequency
100%	Able	930	0%	Unable	235
99	Good	5,122	1	Bad	1,001
99	Peace	472	1	War	1,118
98	Friend	2,553	2	Enemy	883
98	Love	5,129	2	Hate	756
97	On	30,224	3	Off	3,644
97	Remember	1,682	3	Forget	882
95	Most	3,443	5	Least	1,259
94	Leader	373	6	Follower	49
92	Up	11,718	8	Down	5,534
91	Always	3,285	9	Never	5,715
85	In	75,253	15	Out	13,649
77	Usually	718	23	Unusually	91
63	Answer	2,132	37	Question	1,302
58	Husband	1,788	42	Wife	1,668
52	Play	2,606	48	Work	2,720

(Thorndike and Lorge, 1944)

Preference Rank and Frequency Counts for Ten Countries and Ten Cities

Preference	Country	Frequency	Preference	City	Frequency
1	England	497	1	Boston	255
2	Canada	130	2	Chicago	621
3	Holland	59	3	Milwaukee	124
4	Greece	31	4	San Diego	9
5	Germany	224	5	Dayton	14
6	Argentina	15	6	Baltimore	68
7	Venezuela	9	7	Omaha	28
8	Bulgaria	3	8	Tampa	5
9	Honduras	1	9	El Paso	1
10	Syria	4	10	Saginaw	2

Preference Ratings and Frequency of Fruits and Flowers (from Zajonc, 1968)

Rank	Fruits	Frequency	Average Pref. Rating*	Rank	Flowers	Frequency	Average Pref. Rating*
1	Apple	220	5.13	1	Rose	801	5.55
2	Cherry	167	5.00	2	Lily	164	4.79
3	Strawberry	121	4.83	3	Violet	109	4.58
4	Pear	62	4.83	4	Geranium	27	3.83
5	Grapefruit	33	4.00	5	Daisy	62	3.79
6	Cantaloupe	1.5	3.75	6	Hyacinth	16	3.08
7	Avocado	16	2.71	7	Yucca	1	2.88
8	Pomegranate	8	2.63	8	Woodbine	4	2.87
9	Gooseberry	5	2.63	9	Anemone	8	2.54
10	Mango	2	2.38	10	Cowslip	2	2.54

* Preference Rating Scale, 0 = dislike, 6 = like

"We then told them that they had just seen a list of Turkish adjectives, and shamelessly asked them to guess what the words meant."

itself, under certain conditions, is enough to increase attraction.

The first support for this hypothesis came from semantics—specifically, data on word frequencies. That is, in many languages there are counts of how often certain words occur. E. L. Thorndike and Irving Lorge did such a count for English during the Depression. They determined how often each of 30,000 words appears in a total of 4.5 million. In 1960 R. C. Johnson, C. W. Thomson and G. L. Frincke observed that words with "positive" meaning occur much more frequently than words with "negative" meaning. *Love*, for example, occurs 5,129 times, while *hate* appears only 756 times; *beauty* outscores *ugliness* by 776 to 18; and *happiness* is 25 times as frequent as *unhappiness*. These observations are also true for such innocent members of our vocabulary as prepositions, pronouns and adverbs. We prefer to be *in* rather than *out*—*up* occurs twice as often as *down*, and *in* five times as often as *out*. And in anticipation of recent modes of entertainment, Thorndike and Lorge counted 1,674 instances of *high* to 1,224 of *low*.

Unfortunately for us, word frequencies are clearly fickle in representing reality. But they are extraordinarily accurate in representing real values: words that stand for good, desirable and preferred aspects of reality are more frequently used. This frequency-value rela-

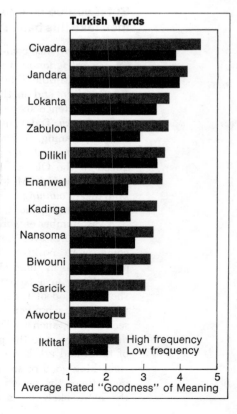

Turkish Words

Civadra
Jandara
Lokanta
Zabulon
Dilikli
Enanwal
Kadirga
Nansoma
Biwouni
Saricik
Afworbu
Iktitaf

High frequency
Low frequency

1 2 3 4 5
Average Rated "Goodness" of Meaning

tionship, I suggest, is one case of the exposure effect.

My colleagues and I gave a list of 154 antonym pairs to a large number of subjects and asked them to judge which member of each pair had the more favorable meaning — which word "represented the more desirable object, event or characteristic." The subjects showed remarkable agreement in their preferences. And it is clear, above all, that they preferred the member of the pair that is most frequently used. For instance, 97 of the 100 student subjects thought *on* was more desirable than *off; on* occurs 30,224 times, *off* a mere 3,644.

One interesting exception is the *war-peace* pair. Our students unquestionably preferred *peace*, but the Thorndike-Lorge count (which presumably represents the feelings of the entire population) shows that *war* is favored and occurs more often. I will add that the frequencies of *war* and *peace* in German are about the same as in English. But in French and Spanish, *paix* and *paz* occur much more often than *guerre and guerra*. I shall leave you to draw your own conclusions about national character.

The frequency effect is not limited to the meanings of words. It also applies to a person's attitudes toward what the words stand for. Our subjects' liking for cities and countries, for example, related quite closely to the frequencies with which the names of these places occur in the written language. Their attitudes toward trees, fruits, flowers and vegetables show the same effect.

Since these findings are correlational, one cannot speculate about casual directions. We do not know whether we rate *sweet* more favorably than *bitter* because *sweet* is used more frequently or because it means something more pleasant than *bitter*. We can argue that many roses are grown because people like roses, or we can argue that people like roses because there are many roses around. Still there are some studies that get around this problem.

Ordinarily we do not think of numbers as being pleasant or unpleasant. Yet I have found that contrary to the cultural values of "the bigger the better" and "the more the merrier," it seems that people like smaller numbers best—the numbers that occur most frequently. William Johntz, a mathematics teacher, once asked some children whether they liked even or odd numbers best. The children overwhelmingly preferred the even numbers—and also thought there were many more evens than odds! The frequency effect is true of letters as well as numbers. In 1962, E. A. Alluisi and O. S. Adams found that some letters—the more frequent ones—are consistently better liked than others. Since it would be hard to argue that the letter E and the number 2 occur often because for some peculiar reason they are well-liked, we had best assume that they are well-liked because they occur often. In this case at least, frequency determines attractiveness.

Good experimental evidence supports these studies. Johnson, Thomson and Frincke were the first to find that the preference ratings of nonsense words can be enhanced if the words are presented repeatedly. My colleagues and I have similar evidence. We exposed our subjects to a number of three-syllable Turkish words, such as *iktitaf, afworbu* and *jandara*. They saw some of these words frequently (25 times), some occasionally (five or 10 times), others rarely (once or twice). The words were randomized so that each had a different frequency for each subject. We then told them that they had just seen a list of Turkish adjectives and shamelessly asked them to guess what the words meant. (They were Turkish words indeed, but not all adjectives.) We said we appreciated how nearly impossible this task was, given their unfamiliarity with Turkish, but we insisted that they try. To help, we told them that each adjective meant something good or something bad, and all they had to do was guess which. The results clearly supported the prediction: the more often the subject had seen the word, the more likely he was to think that the word meant something good. We repeated this experiment using Chinese ideographs and men's faces instead

"Repeated exposure will enhance liking primarily when we show the person something he has never seen before. Probably the effect won't work at all on familiar objects, such as Aunt Martha."

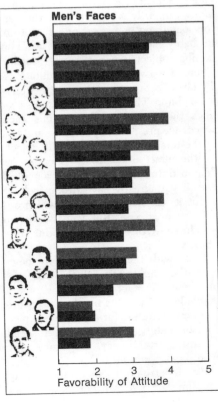

Chinese-like Characters

Average Rated "Goodness" of Meaning

1 2 3 4 5

Men's Faces

Favorability of Attitude

1 2 3 4 5

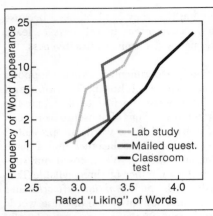

MERE exposure increases liking of words.

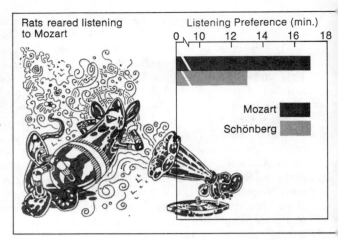

"I would like to stress, with some sympathy, that animals reared with Mozart became true Mozart lovers, while the Schönberg group merely learned to prefer Schönberg."

and the exposure-liking effect remained.

Don Rajecki and I tried the Turkish-word study in a more natural situation. We printed the same set of words in two college papers, one at the University of Michigan, at Ann Arbor, and the other at Michigan State, at East Lansing. For several weeks these words appeared every day without explanation. We "advertised" some of the words once, others twice, the rest five, 10 or 25 times. Those shown frequently in one paper were shown infrequently in the other. The word appeared in a rectangle one column wide and one inch deep. After the ad campaign we went to several classes with our scales and asked for the same kinds of ratings that we took in the lab experiments. We also sent out hundreds of questionnaires by mail to the subscribers of the newspapers. The results confirmed the earlier studies. Readers liked the words that had appeared most often, although they had no idea what the words meant or why they were in the paper.

Why does repeated exposure increase the attractiveness of an object? Albert Harrison suggests an explanation that may be fairly simple. Consider something a person encounters for the first time: obviously he has no ready response to it. But in some ways this new object will be similar to others that he has encountered in the past; the word or face may be unfamiliar, but he has certainly seen words and faces before. Generalizing from experience, the person will want to respond to the stimulus in several different ways. Some of these response tendencies may be incompatible and the individual will feel mild stress. Since this stress is associated with the unfamiliar object, the person is not likely to consider the object attractive. But as the stimulus is exposed more, it becomes more familiar; the incompatible

responses drop out and the person establishes a stable way of responding. The initial stress and discomfort are reduced greatly and the object becomes more attractive.

Harrison and Margaret Matlin have done independent experiments that support this explanation. Both have shown that novel stimuli elicit several conflicting responses, and that this causes discomfort. As a result, new objects are less well liked than familiar objects to which single responses have been attached. Novelty apparently is associated with uncertainty and with conflict, which are likely to produce tension and negative feelings. Familiarity, on the other hand, is comfortable.

The novelty explanation puts a critical limit on the applicability of the exposure effect. Repeated exposure will enhance liking primarily when we show the person something he has never seen before. Probably the effect won't work at all on familiar objects, such as Aunt Martha. There are two other such limitations. 1) The effect of exposure on attraction is logarithmic. That is, early exposures produce the strongest effects, while each successive presentation adds less and less to the total attractiveness of the object; 2) the effect of exposure is easiest to demonstrate when the object is a neutral one. If you already have strong feelings about it, the exposure effect will probably be overcome. But you usually do not have strong feelings about new objects.

Even with these qualifications, however, the implications of the exposure phenomenon reach far. Almost every psychological process involves exposure of a new stimulus—for example, acquisition of habits, perceptual and social learning, attachment. Exposure may even help form attitudes. Consider a study of persuasion aimed at changing a person's attitude. Most of these studies

attempt to change opinions in a positive direction; the subject hears a lot of arguments designed to make him like chocolate grasshoppers, teaching machines, or even Spiro Agnew. But for every argument in favor of Agnew there is also an exposure of the name Agnew. In this case the number of arguments works along with increased exposure to produce a more favorable attitude. Theoretically, this should be easier to do than to make attitudes more unfavorable. In that case, every argument given against Spiro Agnew would be counteracted by exposure to his name. And, in fact, studies of persuasion seldom try to effect a negative change.

In one recent study, P. H. Tannenbaum and R. W. Gengel could get only positive shifts of opinion, although they had tried to get negative ones as well. Or recall the AMA's propaganda campaign against Medicare — a compelling case in point. Richard Harris, writing in *The New Yorker* in 1966, concluded that "the medical profession's immense outlay may have brought about precisely what it least wanted — increased public interest in some form of national health insurance."

The exposure effect applies not only to human beings, but also to a wide variety of animals. Consider imprinting, a form of attachment of young animals to objects or to other animals, typically the mother.

Imprinting has long been considered the crowning example of the interaction between instinct and learned habit. The process itself, say the ethologists, is generated by an innate disposition; but the target and onset of the process are determined or "triggered" by experience.

However, it is entirely plausible that imprinting is not at all instinctive. In contrast to the well-established instinctual bases of mating, nest-building and hoarding, imprinting has not been traced

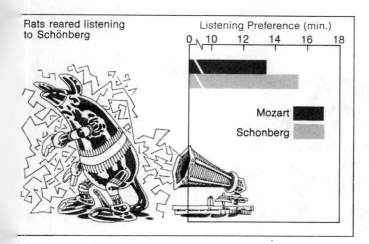

Rats reared listening to Schönberg

Listening Preference (min.)

Mozart
Schönberg

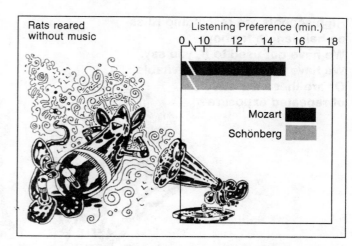

Rats reared without music

Listening Preference (min.)

Mozart
Schönberg

to any specific neuro-anatomic structures, to endocrine processes or to other physiological functions. These functions may yet be discovered, but for now the evidence for an instinct theory rests on three observations. 1) Imprinting occurs nearly universally among some species; 2) it occurs in a most compelling and dramatic fashion; 3) it is particularly likely to occur during a short time of the animal's life, shortly after birth. (For example, John Scott considers the period between the third and seventh weeks as the only time during which a puppy can become attached to people ["A Time to Learn," *PT, 3/69*].) These facts are not proof that imprinting is necessarily a matter of instinct.

Suppose that imprinting is nothing more than a special case of mere exposure. The young animal likes whatever he sees most often, whether it is his mother, a milk bottle, a cardboard box or a human being. In all cases this attachment can be explained in terms of early social experience alone.

Typically, of course, this experience is with members of the animal's species. The normal Oregon fruitfly, for instance, grows up with other Oregon fruitflies, and at mating time an Oregon male will court an Oregon female in preference to other species. But as M. Mainardi showed, fruitflies raised in isolation do not discriminate between Oregon females and yellow ones. They have not learned the difference.

But mere exposure is enough to attach an animal to members of a different species. R. B. Cairns did an experiment with lambs that had lived for several weeks with their mothers and other lambs. He then separated the lambs from the flock and each lamb lived for 71 days with one of four possible companions: a dog in the same cage, a dog in an adjacent cage, an unfamiliar ewe, or a continuously operating television

set. At various times during this period Cairns put each lamb in a maze and allowed it to choose between an empty compartment or one containing the companion. Each lamb chose the cohabitant, and this preference increased over time. Dogs, ewes, and television sets were all equally effective in gaining the lambs' affections.

Nine weeks later, Cairns let each lamb choose between his companion and a tethered ewe. Most still chose the companions. Television didn't fare quite as well; lambs raised with the TV sets generally chose the ewe. Still this preference was not overwhelming, and reliably lower than that shown by control animals.

Imprinting is not even limited to animate targets. In fact, almost any object or repeated event will do. Chicks and ducklings have been imprinted to small red boxes, colored balls and sponges, a plastic milk bottle mounted on an electric train, and wooden decoys. (In our own laboratory, David Reimer exposed chicks to four styrofoam shapes for differing amounts of time. He found a clear exposure effect—the birds later approached the most familiar shapes.) Experience also has a lot to say about food preferences. Gulls raised on cat food will prefer that to worms, a food closer to their natural diet.

Animals can even become attached to sounds. H. A. Cross, C. G. Halcomb and W. W. Matter tried an ingenious musical experiment with three groups of rats. One group grew up with Mozart; 12 hours a day for 52 days, these rats listened to such pieces as the *Violin Concerto No. 5, The Magic Flute* and *Symphonies No. 40 and 41.* The second group heard only Schönberg: *Pierrot Lunaire, Chamber Symphonies No. 1 and 2, Verklarte Nacht,* and so on. The third group was totally deprived of music. After 52 days the experimenters gave all the rats a two-week rest, then

tested their musical preferences. They put each rat in a chamber with a floor that was hinged in the center and suspended over two switches, one on each side of the hinge. A rat's weight was enough to push down one side or other of the floor and thus activate a switch. As you might guess, one switch turned on music by Mozart, the other turned on music by Schönberg. Let me add that Cross and his colleagues used selections that the rats had not heard before.

It is clear from the results that experience with one kind of music led the animals to prefer that kind. But I would like to stress, with some sympathy, that animals reared with Mozart became true Mozart lovers, while the Schönberg group merely learned to prefer Schönberg. And the rats that had grown up with no music at all preferred Mozart. (Incidentally, the Thorndike-Lorge count for Mozart is 8. There is no entry for Schönberg.)

The studies show not only that the rat may have a more tender soul than we have come to believe, but also that it takes little more than mere exposure to produce affection and attachment. But if we consider imprinting as a special case of the exposure effect we must still explain two important findings. First, why are certain critical periods especially favorable for the formation of these attachments? Second, if a lamb can love a TV set, why shouldn't a newly hatched chick become enamored of a nearby twig or rock instead of its mother?

The existence of critical periods is due in part to the maturation process of the animal. For example, a three-day-old puppy simply cannot see well enough to distinguish between possible objects of attachment. To the extent that the animal cannot make fine discriminations, his behavior toward his surroundings will be very generalized. Only when his

"High schools are rescinding rules on hair length for boys. We have got used to it, you say. We have accepted the inevitable. Or are these the effects of repeated exposure?"

senses have developed sufficiently will he be able to imprint. For puppies this development takes about three weeks; for ducklings no more than seven hours.

But sensory development cannot explain why the critical period *ends*. This stage is not as inflexible as we had once thought; it can be restricted or extended. But it always has a clear termination point; animals do not form attachments easily after this period. One explanation is that imprinting, like marriage, exercises a priority right. Once an attachment has been made, others are less likely to form. The tendency to approach new objects will begin to conflict with the affection for the original target.

This explanation must be extended to encompass two additional facts. Animals kept in isolation during the critical period still show a subsequent inability to form attachments. In addition, these inexperienced and isolated animals will prefer members of their own species even on a first encounter. Both of these occurrences can be explained by assuming self-exposure and self-attachment. That is, consider an animal reared in isolation. This poor fellow will be deprived of social experience and a rich physical environment, but his sensory development is not delayed. So he cannot prevent being exposed to many things about himself. He can hear himself bark or chirp or squeak; he can see his legs or wings or feet or tail; he can smell his own odor and feel his own texture, and so on. There must be thousands of cues associated with his own body and behavior that are obviously like the bodies and behavior of members of his species.

Thus an isolated animal may develop some form of attachment to the only objects and events to which it is exposed: its own body and its own behavior. The critical period, then, ends when

a primary attachment has been made. That attachment, whether it is to the animal itself, to another animal, or to an inanimate object, enjoys the privilege of priority over subsequent objects of liking. If the animal has been raised with others of his species, he will prefer them as targets of imprinting because of their similarity to himself. If he has been reared alone, he may become attached to himself. To the extent that isolation leads to self-imprinting, the likelihood of the animal's forming other attachments is severely curtailed. Given a choice, he may later prefer to associate with others of his species: after all, they have some of his characteristics.

In short, imprinting and attachment can be explained as examples of the effects of mere exposure. We do not need to resort to an instinct theory, for which there is no convincing evidence thus far.

By now it should be obvious that I believe the exposure effect has a wide range of applicability for animals and people alike. No one doubts that human attitudes and attachments are motivated by a complex variety of factors. But it is also clear that some of them are a result of mere exposure.

A few years ago when young men began to grow their hair long, many of us on the other side of the generation gap were aghast. Some treated the phenomenon as a passing fad, a few said it was a protest against the war, others regarded it as a symptom of the utter perversity of the Dr. Spock generation. It simply did not seem proper for honors scholars in our universities to wear the hairstyles of Louis XIV while adorning their feet with moccasins. We were extremely critical. But now more and more of our children look that way, and fewer and fewer adults are appalled. Those of us who still can grow longer hair do so. High schools are rescinding rules on hair

length for boys. We have got used to it, you say. We have accepted the inevitable. Or are these the effects of repeated exposure?

Not long ago a mysterious student, totally enveloped in a big black bag, attended a speech class at Oregon State University. Only the professor knew his identity. The professor later said, in describing the feelings of other students in the class, that their attitude changed from hostility toward the Black Bag to curiosity and finally to friendship. The effect of repeated exposure?

A man by the name of Hal Evry will elect you to office if you can follow his formula. You must not make speeches, not take a stand on issues. In fact, you must not appear at all in the campaign. But his organization guarantees that your name will be as familiar to voters as Tide or Ford. Evry mounted an extensive saturation campaign on behalf of one unknown fellow, by flooding the city with signs saying *three cheers for Pat Milligan.* That was all. The voters saw those words on billboards, in full-page newspaper ads, on facsimile telegrams sent through the mails. The advertisement of this slogan went on for months, and on election day Pat Milligan was the undeniable winner. What else but the effects of mere exposure?

With this evidence in mind, consider the advertising community. Clearly they believe that effective salesmanship requires exposure of the product, but they aren't convinced that *mere* exposure is enough. They insist on *attractive* exposure. Thus few products appear without a seductive woman. I wonder, however, about the effects of this strategy. Associating so many products with sex gives sex an unprecedented amount of exposure. Does this really increase sales, or does it only make potential customers more interested in sex? ◪

336

ONCE WE HAVE LEARNED TO EXPECT LOVE, FAVORS AND PRAISE
FROM A PERSON CLOSE TO US, THAT PERSON MAY BECOME
LESS POTENT THAN A STRANGER AS A SOURCE OF REWARD.

WHO LIKES WHOM AND WHY

by Elliot Aronson

mr. and Mrs. Doting, who have been married for 10 years, are preparing to leave their house for a cocktail party. He compliments her—"Gee, honey, you look great." She yawns. She already knows that her husband thinks she is attractive.

Mr. and Mrs. Doting arrive at the cocktail party. A male stranger begins to talk to Mrs. Doting and after a while he says, with great sincerity, that he finds her very attractive. She does not yawn. The compliment increases her liking of the stranger.

This little episode is an example of what some of my students have called Aronson's Law of Marital Infidelity. Once we have learned to expect love, favors and praise from a person close to us, that person may become less potent than a stranger as a source of reward.

The reason for this is that someone close is already operating near ceiling level as a source of rewards. It is not likely that he can provide much more. But the closer the person and the more he has been a constant source of reward, then the greater is his potential as a punisher. Withdrawal of his approval constitutes a loss of esteem. In effect, then, he has the power to hurt the one he loves, but very little power to reward him. In the words of the well-known ballad, you always hurt the one you love.

During the past several years, my students and I have been happily engaged in an investigation of what affects interpersonal attraction. Most persons act as

if they like to be liked. They seek friendships, try to impress others with their abilities, they entertain, smile a lot, they are happy when told someone likes them, unhappy when someone ignores them or acts unkindly.

What are some of the conditions that lead us to like other persons? The research of psychologists has confirmed beyond doubt several important if obvious antecedents.

Propinquity—we like persons who are physically close to us more than people who are not near because it costs less in terms of time and effort to receive a given amount of benefit from those who are nearby.

Similar values and beliefs—we like those persons who agree with us more than those persons who disagree with us.

Similar personal traits—we like persons who are like us.

Complementary needs—we like persons who can satisfy our needs and whose needs are such that we can easily satisfy them.

High ability—we like able and competent persons more than incompetent ones, perhaps because we expect to gain more through association with highly competent persons.

Pleasant or agreeable behavior—we like persons who are nice or who do nice things.

Being liked—we like persons who like us, a reward in itself because most persons think rather highly of themselves.

All of these could be loosely summarized under a general reward-cost kind of theory. It may be that we like persons

who bring us maximum gratification at minimum expense. But there are some phenomena that cannot be squeezed under the rubric of reward theory. For example, several researchers have shown that we like other persons for whom we have suffered. Reward in such instances is extremely difficult to define.

Moreover, certain behaviors that would seem to be highly rewarding at first glance do not always lead to a high degree of attraction. For example, though it does seem reasonable that we would like persons of extremely high ability more than we like those who are poorly endowed with ability, there is evidence that this is not always the case. It has been shown that persons who initiate most of the ideas and are acknowledged as the best idea men of a group are most often not the best-liked group members.

How can one account for these data? It may be the case that ability, in and of itself, might make a person seem to be too good, unapproachable, distant, nonhuman, and thus less attractive. If this is the case, then some manifestation of fallibility might actually increase the attractiveness of the gifted person.

We performed an experiment in order to test this proposition. We had individuals listen to a tape recording. They were told that they would be listening to a candidate for a television quiz show and that they were to rate him in terms of the impression he made and how much they liked him.

On one tape, the candidate was virtually perfect. He answered 92 per cent

337

of the questions correctly. Moreover, in the interview he modestly admitted that in high school he had been an honor student, yearbook editor and a track-team member.

On another tape, using the same voice, the candidate answered only 30 per cent of the questions correctly and during the interview admitted that he had average grades and had been a proofreader on the yearbook, and that he failed to make the track team. On tape number three, we had the superior person again but this time he committed an embarrassing blunder. Near the end of the interview, he clumsily spilled a cup of coffee over himself. On the tape, this blunder was accompanied by a great deal of noise, clatter and anguished talk.

The fourth tape was the candidate with the average ability and the coffee-spilling blunder.

The results were clear-cut: the most attractive candidate was the superior person who committed a blunder, while the least attractive was the person of average ability who committed a blunder. Thus, although a high degree of competence is probably rewarding and, therefore, attractive, some evidence of incompetence in high-ability persons leads to higher ratings of attractiveness.

Further tentative support of this notion is found in the case of John F. Kennedy. According to the Gallup Poll, Kennedy's personal popularity increased immediately after the Bay of Pigs fiasco. Here is a situation in which a President commits one of history's truly great blunders, and lo and behold, people like him more. The explanation? Perhaps President Kennedy was too perfect. He was young, handsome, bright, witty, a war hero, wealthy, charming, athletic, a voracious reader, a master political strategist, an uncomplaining endurer of physical pain. He has a perfect wife, two cute kids and a talented, powerful, close-knit family. Some evidence of fallibility, like the Bay of Pigs fiasco, could have served to make him appear more human, hence more likeable.

In order to obtain a more precise matrix of predictions it may be necessary to abandon the attempt to apply a loose global theory and instead construct limited, small-scale "mini-theories."

In recent years, a mini-theory I have been working on is the gain-loss theory: *increasing rewards and punishments from a person have more impact on his attractiveness than constant, invariant rewards and punishments.*

As Spinoza wrote 300 years ago in Proposition 44 of *The Ethics:*

Hatred which is completely vanquished by love passes into love, and love is thereupon greater than if hatred had not preceded it. For he who begins to love a thing which he was wont to hate or regard with pain, from the very fact of loving, feels pleasure. To this pleasure involved in love is added the pleasure arising from aid given to the endeavor to remove the pain involved in hatred accompanied by the idea of the former object of hatred as cause.

Thus, a person whose liking for us increases over time will be better liked by us than a friend who has always liked us. Also, a person whose liking for us decreases over time will be disliked more

"THE MALES DID NOT SEEM TO CARE MUCH ABOUT THE IMPRESSIONS THEY MADE ON THE UGLY WOMAN."

than one who has always disliked us.

Imagine that you are back at the cocktail party with the Dotings. You have a conversation with a person whom you have never met before. After several minutes he excuses himself and drifts into another group. Later that evening, while standing behind a potted palm, you overhear him talking about you. Now suppose you run into this person at several consecutive parties, talk to him at each, and chance to overhear his comments about you each time.

There are four possibilities that I find interesting: 1) you overhear the person saying only positive things about you, 2) you overhear him saying only negative things about you, 3) he begins with negative comments but gradually they become increasingly positive, 4) he begins with positive comments but gradually they become increasingly negative. Our theory, if correct, should be able to predict the circumstances in which you would find this stranger most attractive to you.

To test this theory I set up an experimental analogue of the cocktail situation in collaboration with Darwyn Linder. In our experiment college stu-

dents interacted during seven sessions with a student who was actually a paid confederate. After each session the subject was surreptitiously allowed to overhear the confederate evaluate her to the experimenter.

The results confirmed the predictions of our gain-loss theory. A person who began with negative comments about the subject and gradually became more positive was liked more by the subject than persons who made only positive comments. Also, a person who began with positive comments that gradually became negative was liked less than a person who made only negative comments about the subject.

Why does a gain or loss of liking have more effect than either constant positive liking or constant disliking? When a person expresses negative feelings toward us, we probably experience anxiety. If the person gradually becomes more positive in his feelings toward us, this is reward in itself and it also reduces the prior anxiety he has aroused. Thus the attractiveness of an individual who has first created and then reduced anxiety is increased.

The same reasoning applies to the loss part of the theory. When negative feelings follow positive ones, they not only punish but they wipe out the reward of the earlier positive behavior.

The anxiety-reduction explanation is further supported by another finding in my experiment with Darwyn Linder. When the overheard comments were first neutral and then increasingly positive, the eavesdropper liked the talker almost precisely the same as she liked the talker who made only positive comments. Thus a negative evaluation seems essential to maximize the effect.

Next, in collaboration with Harold Sigall I did an experiment to further ascertain the importance of prior anxiety on attraction. We reasoned that if a person is aware that he is about to be evaluated, he will experience anxiety. All other things being equal, the more attractive the evaluator the greater the anxiety— because it is more important to receive a high evaluation from an attractive person.

Thus, according to our theory, if a beautiful woman were to evaluate a male favorably, she would be liked more than a homely woman who evaluated him favorably. If a beautiful woman were to give a negative evaluation, she would be disliked more than a homely woman who had evaluated him unfavorably, because the beautiful woman would leave the male with more anxiety.

Sigall and I took a naturally attractive young woman and, in one set of experiments, made her look homely by dressing her in loose, ill-fitting clothes, providing her with a rather ugly wig, and giving her complexion a rather oily, unappetizing look. Thus, we showed that while only God may make a woman truly beautiful, all it takes is a couple of diabolical experimenters to make a beautiful woman look ugly.

In the experiment, our confederate posed as either a "beautiful" or an "ugly" graduate student in clinical psychology who was interviewing and testing a number of men. She then gave each man her personal clinical judgment, which was either favorable or unfavorable. The results confirmed our predictions: the beautiful-positive woman was best liked; the beautiful-negative woman was least liked. The males did not seem to care much about the impressions they made on the ugly woman.

We also had an unexpected finding. Despite the fact that they said they disliked the beautiful woman who evaluated them negatively, many of the males expressed great desire to return and be in another experiment with the woman. Our interpretation is that the males wanted to see the beautiful woman again because they hoped to be able to change her impression of them from unfavorable to favorable.

This experiment demonstrated that anxiety is an important component of the gain-loss phenomenon. But it may not be the only component. There may be another reason for our liking a person whose attitude toward us begins by being negative and gradually becomes positive. It may be that we like him because, by inducing him to change his opinion of us, we enable him to give us a feeling of competence or effectiveness. Since this is a good feeling, it increases our liking for the person who provided it. In his Ph.D. thesis, Harold Sigall investigated this possibility in what we have called the conversion effect. The question is: does a missionary feel more kindly disposed toward someone he has converted to the faith than toward someone who has always been a loyal member of the flock? On the basis of our theory, we would predict that the missionary would like the convert more because there is a greater gain involved.

Sigall speculated that the degree of effectiveness in shifting opinion and the extent of the missionary's ego involvement would both affect attractiveness. Suppose you felt that marijuana should be made available to everyone, all the time, and you were presenting your argument to a person who believed that all marijuana and marijuana seeds should be destroyed. After hearing your argument, this person comes to believe that marijuana could be used on Saturday nights under supervised conditions by persons over 35. On a scale from −10 to +10, his position has moved from say −10 to −2. He still disagrees with you, but you have shifted his position and have every right to feel proud and effective.

In his experiment, Sigall manipulated both the degree of opinion shift and the involvement. In the low-involvement condition, the missionary-type was given a prepared speech to read without dramatics. In the high-involvement condition, he had to organize the argument himself and present it as effectively as possible.

When there was low involvement, subjects liked best the persons who agreed with them and had no opinion shift. They liked least the persons who disagreed even though they shifted their opinions slightly. When there was high involvement, the findings were just the opposite. Thus persons like similar persons better than converts unless they are ego-involved in converting them. Then they like the converts better.

It is difficult for me to summarize the major thrust of my results without becoming depressed—for my data do suggest a rather dismal picture of the human condition. Like Mrs. Doting, we seem to be forever seeking compliments from strangers and being hurt by those we love.

Before we become too pessimistic about the human condition, however, let us look at a different dimension—namely, what action does a person take when he is hurt by another person? On this score the evidence suggests that the more important the relationship, the more likely a person will try to maintain it—in spite of the hurt. Some support for this contention can be gleaned from the experiment we reported on beautiful and homely women. Recall that our subjects expressed greatest dislike for the beautiful woman who treated them badly—but, at the same time, it was these very subjects who expressed the greatest desire to return to that situation—perhaps to try to make a better impression on her. This phenomenon receives still stronger support from an experiment by one of my students, Joanne Floyd. Floyd placed two young children in a room together—either close friends or strangers. She assigned one a task for which he was allowed to earn several trinkets. The child was instructed to share the trinkets with his partner (the subject). The experiment was rigged so that the subjects would get different impressions of the generosity of their partners. Some subjects were led to believe that the friend (or stranger) was treating them in a stingy manner, others were led to believe that he was treating them in a generous manner. Floyd then allowed the subject to earn several trinkets of his own and instructed him to share them with his partner. She found, as predicted, that subjects showed the most generosity in both the gain and the loss conditions—i.e., they were most generous toward either a generous stranger or a stingy friend. In short, they were relatively stingy to the stingy stranger (why not?—the stranger had behaved as they might have expected) and to the generous friend ("Ho-hum, so my friend likes me—what else is new?"). But when it looked as though they might be gaining a friend (the generous stranger), they reacted with generosity—and likewise, when it looked as though they might be losing a friend (the stingy friend), they responded once again with generosity.

Personally, I find this last datum a touching aspect of the human condition. While it appears to be true, as the line goes, that "you always hurt the one you love," the hurt person appears to be inspired to react kindly rather than in kind in an attempt to reestablish the intensity of the relationship. This suggests the comforting possibility that individuals have some motivation toward the maintenance of stability in their relationships. To return to Mr. and Mrs. Doting for a moment, while Mr. Doting has great power to hurt his wife (by telling her that he thinks she's ugly), if he does so, Mrs. Doting is apt to be very responsive to this criticism, striving to win back what she has lost by once more making herself attractive in the eyes of her husband. Carrying this speculation a step further, I would suggest that the more authentic a relationship is, the less the possibility of reaching the plateau that the Dotings appear to be stuck on. In short, if marriage partners do not dote on each other but remain honest and open, it may be the case that their relationship will stay close to the "gain" condition of our gain-loss experiment. My current research is aimed at testing this proposition. ∩

PERSUASION THAT PERSISTS

"It now seems to be within man's power to alter experimentally another person's basic values and to control the direction of the change."

by Milton Rokeach

SUPPOSE YOU COULD TAKE a group of people, give them a 20-minute pencil-and-paper task, talk to them for 10 to 20 minutes afterward, and thereby produce long-range changes in core values and personal behavior in a significant portion of this group. For openers, it would of course have major implications for education, government, propaganda and therapy. Suppose, further, that you could ascertain quickly and that you could predict accurately the nature and direction of these changes.

Scientists have urged us all to consider the consequences of research in this area, warning that we are on the brink of breakthroughs that will demand new levels of social responsibility. According to these predictions we will soon face several major ethical questions that have to be answered.

My colleagues and I have in the last five years achieved the kinds of results suggested in the first paragraph of this article. As a result we must now face up to the ethical implications that follow from the fact that it now seems to be within man's power to alter experimentally another person's basic values, and to control the direction of the change.

Dissonance. Contemporary social psychologists generally agree that before changes in attitudes or in value-related behavior can occur, there must first exist what John Dewey had called a "felt difficulty" and what social psychologists nowadays call a state of psychological imbalance or dissonance.

There are two major experimental methods for doing this: 1) You can force a person to act in a way that is incompatible with his professed or real attitudes and values, or 2) You can expose him to conflicting attitudes or values held by persons who are in some way important to him.

We used a third method. We exposed a person to information designed to make him consciously aware of inconstancies within his own value-attitude system, inconsistencies of which he is normally unaware.

We have also differed in our definition and measurement of dissonance itself. Dissonance requires at least two elements—let us call them X and Y—that stand in some dissonant or unharmonious relationship with each other. Leon Festinger's theory and other similar theories usually identify X and Y as two "ideas" (beliefs, attitudes, values, or rationalizations) about some particular situations or actions that will occasionally differ from or be incompatible with one another.

In contrast, we identified X and Y in such a way that they are not two ideas that vary from one situation to another, but rather are elements that remain invariant across all situations. In our hypothesis, X was equivalent to self. We defined Y as a person's interpretation of his own performance or behavior in any given situation.

Gauge. Dissonance occurs whenever a person's behavior in any given situation, Y, leads him to become dissatisfied with himself, X. Conversely, if a person is pleased with himself in any given situation, we consider that X and Y are nondissonant or harmonious. We can measure such states of dissonance

Importance of Values As Ranked in Previous Tests

1 freedom
2 happiness
3 wisdom
4 self-respect
5 mature love
6 a sense of accomplishment
7 true friendship
8 inner harmony
9 family security
10 a world at peace
11 equality
12 an exciting life
13 a comfortable life
14 salvation
15 social recognition
16 national security
17 a world of beauty
18 pleasure

Average Rankings of Freedom and Equality for and Against Civil Rights in Previous Tests

	Yes, sympathetic and have participated in a demonstration.	Yes, sympathetic but have not participated in a demonstration.	No, not sympathetic to civil rights.
freedom	6	1	2
equality	5	11	17
difference	+1	−10	−15

and self-satisfaction in any experiment simply by asking the subject how he feels about what he may have said or done in a given situation.

It might be objected that such a question really tests the subject's general self-esteem; self-confident persons would probably report satisfaction with their behavior, while a person with low self-esteem would probably report chronic dissatisfaction with his achievement, no matter how acceptable that achievement might be in some objective sense. Although a number of psychiatric theories seem to predict such an outcome, it is nevertheless also true that self-confident persons are not always satisfied with what they do and say in certain situations, and, conversely, that persons of low self-confidence are not always dissatisfied with what they do or say.

We also made a firm operational distinction between attitudes and values, and, unlike many researchers in the field of social psychology, we focused on the latter. We also defined values as more fundamental to human personality than attitudes for values serve as determinants of attitudes as well as of behavior.

Hotpants. For the purposes of our research we identified an attitude as a more or less enduring organization of interrelated thoughts and feelings called into being by a specific object or situation. Thus an attitude always has a historical context as well as a personal one—toward the Pill, for instance, or civil-rights demonstrations, hotpants, or J. Edgar Hoover. Assuming that values are less embedded in particular temporal or socioeconomic contexts, we used the word *value* to describe either a desirable end-state of existence (a terminal value) or a desirable mode of behavior (an instrumental value). In a sense, values are the source and foundation of attitudes and behavior toward specific events, people, or situations. A person can have thousands of attitudes but only a few values that transcend and dynamically determine these thousands of attitudes.

My colleagues and I performed a number of experiments in which we induced in our subjects feelings of self-dissatisfaction about specific values and behavioral situations, and we measured the long-range effects that such self-dissatisfaction produced.

We took two groups of college students—usually 20 to 25 in a group—and asked them to rank 18 terminal values in an order of perceived importance. The 18 values were:

A comfortable life, an exciting life, a sense of accomplishment, a world at peace, a world of beauty, equality, family security, freedom, happiness, inner harmony, mature love, national security, pleasure, salvation, social recognition, self-respect, true friendship and wisdom.

Grade. We asked each subject to rank each value from one to 18 in order of its personal importance. We then asked members of both groups to state in writing their attitudes toward civil-rights demonstrations, after this was done, we dismissed one group, which became our control group.

Members of the remaining or experimental group then viewed a chart that showed the average rankings of the 18 terminal values obtained from students in a previous experiment conducted at their school. We drew their attention especially to the data concerning two of the 18 values shown in the chart—equality and freedom—pointing out that students in previous tests had ranked freedom first and equality 11th. We interpreted these findings to mean that "students are, in general, much more interested in their own freedom than other people's." We then invited students to compare their own value rankings with those of their peers.

To raise levels of self-dissatisfaction further, we asked students to indicate the extent of their sympathy with the aims of civil-rights demonstrators by agreeing to one of the following phrases: "Yes, I am sympathetic, and I have personally participated in a civil-rights demonstration"; "Yes, I am sympathetic, and I have not participated in a civil-rights demonstration"; or "No, I am not sympathetic."

After this, students viewed a second table from previous tests that showed correlations between rankings of freedom and equality and positions on civil-rights issues. The main finding brought out in this table is that those who are unsympathetic with civil rights rank freedom high and equality low, while those who are sympathic rank both freedom and equality high. We explained that the findings of this table can be interpreted to mean that persons who are against civil-rights are really saying that they are indifferent to other people's freedom, while they care a great deal about their own. Those who are *for* civil rights want freedom not only for themselves, but for other people too. We then invited students to compare their own rankings of equality and freedom and their own positions on the civil-rights issue with those on the table.

Dismay. In this procedure, many of the experimental subjects—about 40 per cent—became aware of certain inconsistencies within their own value and attitude systems. Some students discovered to their dismay that they had placed a high value on freedom but a low value on equality. Others discovered that they cared about civil rights but had ranked equality low in their scaling values. Many thus discovered that they had been doing their liberal thing because it was fashionable rather than because of principle.

At the end of the experiment, we asked students to rate—on a scale ranging from one to 11—how satisfied or dissatisfied they were in general with what they had found out about their values and attitudes. More importantly, we asked them to indicate whether they were satisfied or dissatisfied with their ranking of each of the 18 values considered separately. This latter, more specific rating proved to be a significant predictor of subsequent changes in the value hierarchy.

Members of the control group, you will recall, had no opportunity to think about their values or possible conflicts among them; they did not see the tables that the experimental subjects saw. Sessions for the control group lasted only about 20 minutes, and the experimental session ran from 30 to 40 minutes.

Change. Follow-ups on the experimental and control groups indicated that the experimental groups experienced highly significant changes in values and attitudes, increases in the value placed on equality and freedom, and increases in favorable attitudes toward civil rights that were evident three to five months after the 10-to-20-minute experimental "treatment." Further, the self-ratings on satisfaction-dissatisfaction obtained at the end of the experimental sessions predicted the value changes that were to be observed three weeks and three to five months afterward.

We were extremely reluctant to accept these experimental findings as evidence of genuine, long-range changes in values and attitudes. It seemed unlikely that any single, brief experimental session could produce such effects. We therefore did more experi-ments—II and III—to monitor the long-term effects more closely and in more detail.

Subtlety. Experiments II and III were basically identical in procedure to the initial series. However, this time we used more subtle measures of behavioral effects in addition to paper-and-pencil tests of change in value and attitude. We extended post-testing to include more intervals, among them three-week, three-to-five-month and 15-to-17-month intervals.

The subjects of Experiments II and III were newly entering freshmen of two small new residential colleges at Michigan State University, James Madison College and Lyman Briggs College. Both experiments were identical in all respects; only the students were different. In both cases, we aroused feelings of self-dissatisfaction by making the subjects aware that certain of their values or attitudes were possibly incompatible with one another. As in previous experiments, the only difference between the experimental and the control groups was that we exposed the experimental students to tables, along with a brief commentary on the tables, and did not do so with the control students.

Join. Pre-testing showed no significant differences between the two groups. On the average both groups ranked equality and freedom approximately the same, and took the same range of civil-rights positions toward black Americans. Post-testing techniques included unobtrusive measurements of behavior along with questionnaires. For example, three to five months and 15 to 17 months after the experiment, each subject received a direct solicitation through the mails from the National Association for the Advancement of Colored People (on N.A.A.C.P. stationery). The letter in-vited the student to join the N.A.A.C.P. To do this, the student had to fill out an application blank, enclose $1.00, and mail back a prestamped return envelope.

We found significant increases in ranking for both equality and freedom in the experimental students on all the post-tests. After 15 to 17 months, for example, the experimental group had increased its ranking of equality an average of 2.68 units (on the 18-point scale) while the control group had increased its ranking by only .32 units. Freedom also rose in value. Within the same period, the experimental ranking of freedom increased an average of 1.59 units, while the control ranking increased only .22 units. This suggests that significant changes in bedrock standards or broad normative beliefs about social ends and means took place as a result of a relatively short experimental session.

Backlash. The findings in relation to attitude-change (how do you think-feel about civil rights for blacks?) also were significant. Three weeks after the session, we noticed what might be called a sleeper effect among the experimental students. There was no positive change in attitude toward civil rights. In fact there was a slight backlash. However, we did find significant increases in pro-civil-rights attitudes among these same experimental subjects three to five months later, and 15 to 17 months later. These results point to long-range attitude change, and the time-lag suggests that a change in the ordering of values preceded the change of attitude.

In contrast to the findings for the experimental group, there were no significant changes in value hierarchy or attitude among the control students at any of the post-test intervals. After 15 to 17 months' exposure to the college

The teacher exposes himself to the danger of being accused by the community in which he lives and by his colleagues that he is unethically manipulating his students' values, attitudes and behavior without their informed consent.

environment, the students in the control groups had essentially the same value and attitude profiles they started with.

Range. I come now to the long-range behavioral effects of the experimental session. In the first N.A.A.C.P. solicitation of all experimental and control subjects, undertaken three to five months after the experimental session, 40 students responded by joining N.A.A.C.P., and 13 more responded by writing sympathetic letters asking for more information. In all, 53 of 366 students responded; of these, 39 were experiment subjects and 14 were control subjects.

A full year after the first solicitation—and 15 to 17 months after the experimental sessions—each experimental and control subject received another invitation to join N.A.A.C.P., (or to renew his membership) by paying another dollar. The second letter resulted in six new memberships—five experimental and one control. In addition there were 11 favorable letters, seven from experiment subjects, four from controls, one of whom had also written after the first solicitation. There were six renewals, half of them by experimental students and half by control students. There were two indignant letters—both from experimental students complaining about the N.A.A.C.P.'s year-long silence. In all, 17 experimental subjects responded as against eight controls. When the results of both N.A.A.C.P. solicitations are combined, we find that a total of 69 persons out of 366—about 20 per cent—responded to the letters. Of these 69 persons, 51 were from the experimental group and only 18 were from the control group. This represents a statistically significant response rate of about one out of 10 for the control group and one out of four for those

students who had been in the briefing.

The data produced by the satisfaction-dissatisfaction ratings throw some light on the basic psychological processes that underlie the long-range changes seen in the experimental groups. Experimental subjects substantially revised their rankings of equality and freedom over the long haul, whether they reported themselves initially satisfied or dissatisfied. But it is apparent that those students who reported themselves dissatisfied with parts of their original value hierarchy changed more significantly than those who reported themselves satisfied. Reports of specific satisfaction or dissatisfaction predicted changes in value rankings that could be observed three weeks after the experiment, three to five months afterward, and 15 to 17 months afterward. Any value that caused dissatisfaction typically changed place in latter rankings. On the other hand, reports of general dissatisfaction did not predict as reliably, although they had some predictive value.

Ethnics. In the very process of conducting our experiment we caused an unsolicited reordering of people's value systems and behavioral choices. It might be argued that no scientist should be permitted or required to cause such changes without some broad social or consensual ethical framework to refer his work and its effects to. We should remember that institutions—such as public schools—are based upon the assumption that such changes are not only desirable but do in fact occur.

Every teacher I have ever met who takes professional pride in his work would like to think that his teaching somehow changes the values, attitudes and behavior of his students in some significant way. So long as he cannot

prove that what he does in the classroom actually results in such change, none will bother him, or raise questions about the ethics of changing other people's values. But when the day comes that he can demonstrate that certain changes in values, attitudes and behavior have in fact occurred, the teacher exposes himself to the danger of being accused, by the community in which he lives and by his colleagues, of unethically manipulating his students' values, attitudes and behavior without their informed consent.

I believe that educational institutions have always been in the business on the one hand of transmitting knowledge and, on the other, of shaping the values of students in certain directions. Psychologists like Jerome Bruner and B. F. Skinner have spent a good deal of their professional lives trying to figure out better ways of transmitting knowledge from one generation to succeeding generations, and we all applaud such efforts. But if we agree that educational institutions are also in the business of shaping values then we should encourage scientific research on better ways of shaping values.

But which values, and in which directions?

Market. If it is possible to alter the process of valuation so that freedom and equality go up in value market, it is also possible to short-sell them. We obviously need safeguards to ensure that the values we choose to change in our students and the direction we choose in changing them are consistent with the values of our educational and scientific institutions, and are consistent with the values of political democracy and, above all, with interests of all humanity.

What exactly are the values of education, science, democracy, and humanity? ♻

343

A Vaccine for BRAINWASH

by William J. McGuire

The TV stations of one city carried, in one week, 7,887 acts of violence. One episode of a Western series garnished Christmas night with 13 homicides. Between the ages of five and 14, your children and mine may, if they are average viewers, witness the annihilation of 12,000 human beings.
—LOOK *December 2, 1969*

It seems unlikely that those who communicate explicitly mean to prompt people to feelings, thoughts or acts of violence. But they apparently do just that; studies by Albert Bandura of Stanford and Leonard Berkowitz of the University of Wisconsin suggest that they do influence their audiences in this direction. But if the mass media, without meaning to, can prompt viewers to violence, it seems likely that when they really set their minds to it they can be truly effective in bending the public's buying habits and its politics.

Since there are both technical means and political and economic motives for trying to influence masses, researchers have inevitably been drawn into the study of social-influence processes. Twenty years of assiduous research on these processes have given us an impressive knowledge of how to manipulate human thought and behavior, though it is far from complete.

Reaction to this rapid growth in the study of persuasion was equally inevitable. The preoccupation of many social scientists with techniques for social influence has provoked increasing interest in techniques for developing resistance to persuasion. For some years my own research was on the side of the persuaders. When I realized that social scientists had neglected the ways to immunize people against persuasion, I redirected my research—with more than a little feeling of virtue and relief.

Barrage. We are all—except for the catatonic schizophrenic—susceptible in some degree to peer-group pressure or to the mass-media barrage. Ideally each person would be open to outside influences that are correct, yet able to cling to his own position when it is more valid. My research cannot help us achieve this selective openness and resistance, but it does help, by presenting a small advance in the relatively neglected area of immunization against persuasion.

The guiding idea behind our approach is the selective-exposure postulate. When Joseph Klapper produced the first review of communication literature in 1949, he called the selective-exposure tendency the most basic principle yet revealed by communication research. The postulate is really a double one:

People tend to seek out information that will confirm their preconceptions and they actively avoid information that might conflict with what they already believe.

This principle clearly implies, first, that people try to defend their beliefs by maintaining them in an ideologically germ-free environment, never exposed to attacking arguments. Second, it implies that one's belief system shows strengths and weaknesses comparable to the health of an animal raised in a germ-free environment. That is, the belief system appears extremely strong and healthy as long as the environment is aseptic, but it turns out to be extremely vulnerable when it is attacked. The third implication is that we can develop belief resistance in people as we develop disease resistance in a biologically overprotected man or animal: by exposing the person to a weak dose of the attacking material, strong enough to stimulate his defenses but not strong enough to overwhelm him.

The notion is such a beautiful one that it really deserves to work. Unfortunately, the whole approach is based on an apparently false premise. It now appears that the selective-avoidance notion has little empirical validity. The tendency is not, it seems, particularly powerful. What is more, in a wide range of conditions a person will expose himself to discrepant material in preference to material that conforms to his already accepted conclusions.

When the social and behavioral scientist has a provocative set of principles, he seldom permits their lack of general empirical validity to inconvenience him. He simply finds some sub-area of the environment in which the principles do hold true—or else he creates such conditions in the laboratory.

Truisms. Because the theory that people maintain their beliefs in a germ-free ideological environment seems to be highly questionable, we felt it would be rash to apply the inoculation approach to beliefs in general. Instead we sought some special sub-area of the ideological universe in which beliefs are maintained in an aseptic environment. The germ-free beliefs we needed appeared to be cultural truisms. Cultural truisms are beliefs that are so generally accepted that most individuals are unaware of attacking arguments. Indeed, they are unaware that there could be any serious opposition to the beliefs. Once we had found our cultural truisms, we would be dealing with beliefs that had been maintained in a germ-free environment, not because of any psychological tendency to avoid discrepant material, but because almost no such material had been available.

It was difficult to find beliefs that were monolithically accepted by our college sophomore subjects. Our initial surveys indicated that such promising candidates as "God is good" or "Capitalism is better than Communism" drew no more than 50 per cent of the students into a strong, affirmative stand—choosing among the top three levels of a 15-point agreement scale. Slight editing—"God, if he exists, is good" or "John Birch Society members think that capitalism is better than Communism"—raised the number of extreme agreers to 60 or 70 per cent, but this was still not the monolithic assent required by cultural truisms.

X-Ray. At last we uncovered an area in which cultural truisms abound, even among college students: health and medicine. Well over 90 per cent of college students agreed completely with such propositions as "It is a good idea to get a chest x-ray every year to check on possible TB symptoms." We selected four truisms to attack: the belief in annual chest x-rays; the merits of penicillin; the value of frequent toothbrushing; and the annual medical checkup.

Armed with these truisms, we set up a series of experiments to determine what kind of defense best prepares a person to meet attacks on cultural truisms. It often is suggested that young Americans should hear more about the virtues of their cultural traditions so that they could resist attacks. To approximate this condition we prepared a reassuring defense of each health truism. This is analogous to preparing the germ-free animal against attack by giving him vitamins and a good diet. To create a situation analogous to inoculation, we prepared a *threatening* defense that pre-exposed the individual to weak attacking arguments that would stimulate his defenses but not overwhelm them.

Attack. Every student took part in several experimental conditions, each on a different health truism. When he faced the first truism, he received one kind of defense and then an attack; on the second, a different kind of defense and then an attack; on the third, an attack without a preliminary defense; and on the fourth, neither an attack nor a defense. These last two conditions served as controls for the study. We told the students that we were studying the relation between verbal skills and emotional and personality traits. In each experiment, two sessions were required. During the first, defensive session, the participants received different defenses of the various cultural truisms. In most experimental conditions, the students read 600-word essays defending the truisms, but in some conditions they wrote essays.

The attacking session followed the defensive session by an interval that varied from a few minutes to one week. This time the students read 600-word essays presenting a series of strong and plausible arguments against the four truisms. After they read the essays, we measured their final belief levels by asking each student to indicate on a 15-point scale his degree of agreement or disagreement with four statements about each truism.

Defense. In the first experiment we used two kinds of defensive material: reassuring and threatening. The reassuring

Everyone should see his doctor at least once a year.

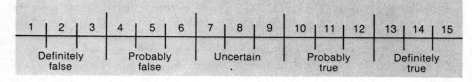

If everyone were to get a complete physical checkup once every year more harm than good would result.

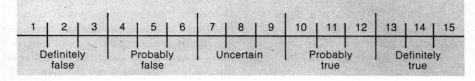

defense presented a series of arguments in favor of each truism and ignored all arguments against it. For example, one of the truisms we tested was "Everyone should get an annual physical checkup, even when he is not bothered by any symptom of illness." The reassuring defense discussed the possibility of preventing serious illness by early detection and the relief from anxiety the patient receives on being told by the physician that his health is good.

The threatening defense ignored arguments in favor of the truism and dealt only with arguments against it, first mentioning and then refuting these hostile arguments. Students who were to receive the threatening defense of annual physical checkups read an essay that put forth—and then refuted—the argument that routine medical visits tend to make people into hypochondriacs and the argument that, faced with an expensive annual checkup, people might risk going without immediate treatment for specific symptoms that appeared a month or so before the scheduled examination. The immediate refutation weakened the strength of these attacking arguments, as a biological inoculation uses a weakened form of the attacking material.

We began by measuring the level of student belief at the end of the first session, when the students had been exposed only to defenses of the truisms. At this time the reassuring defense left the beliefs stronger than did the threatening defense. But when we measured the beliefs again after the second, attacking, session—when the arguments against the truisms were presented and in full strength, without any refutation—we found that the greater strength of the reassuring defense had been more apparent than real. When the truisms were vigorously attacked, the effectiveness of the two defenses was reversed: now the beliefs that had received the threatening defenses were less affected by the full-strength attacks on the truisms than were beliefs that had received the reassuring defenses.

Best Threat. In our first experiment, students who received the threatening defense had been given refutations of the very arguments we later used in the attack session.

It could be argued that the greater resistance they conferred came from the

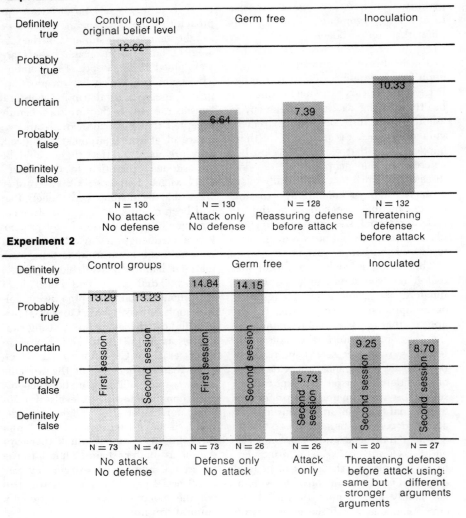

refutations we provided, not from their stimulating the believers' defenses. To clear up this ambiguity, we conducted a second experiment in which we tested two types of threatening defense. One, which we called "threatening-same," was identical to the threatening defense of the first experiment. The same arguments mentioned and refuted in the first session were used as attacks in the second session. The "threatening-different" defense presented the students with one set of attacks and refuted them, but in the second session an entirely different attack was used against the truism. In this case, the specific refutations that the students had received during the first session were of little use during the final attack.

When we tested the belief level after the second session, we found that stu-

dents exposed to the same arguments against the truisms in both sessions did show stronger belief than the students who encountered a completely new set of arguments during the second session. But the difference was trivial—just over half a point on the scale of 15 and both types of threatening defenses conferred considerable resistance over the attack-only control condition. Apparently, threatening defenses are effective even when the arguments they refute are different from the arguments used in later attacks.

This experiment again demonstrated the extreme vulnerability of overprotected cultural truisms exposed to sudden attack. Students who had encountered strong attack without a preparatory session again showed great susceptibility to the attacking arguments.

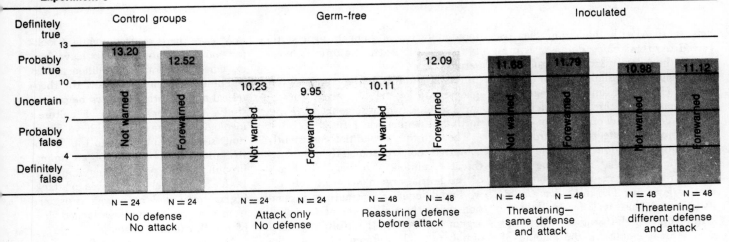

Forewarning. In our third experiment, we added extrinsic threat to the truisms. At the first session we warned half the students that they would have a chance to read defenses of the truisms, but that later there would be strong attacks on these beliefs. In this study we used all three defenses: reassuring, threatening-same and threatening-different.

In line with our inoculation theory, we expected that the warning of attack would make all the defenses more effective because our extrinsic threat would motivate the students to assimilate the defenses we presented for these overprotected truisms. We also expected that the warning would be especially effective with the reassuring defense because the two threatening defenses already contained some intrinsic threat—the hostile arguments.

The results were in line with our expectations. At first glance it appeared that the significantly higher belief level in the forewarned group could be attributed either to increased motivation

—in line with our prediction—or simply to a weakening of the attack by the warning. But the results in our control group ruled out the theory that a warning of attack is enough to stimulate an individual's defenses. Those members of the control group who were warned of the attack showed a slightly lower level of belief than did those who believed we were testing verbal skills.

Prior Reassurance. Our fourth experiment was the mirror-image of the one just described. Instead of warning the students that we planned to attack the truisms, we used extrinsic reassurance. At the beginning of the first study, all participants indicated their belief in the truisms. We then informed half of the students that almost everyone in the group completely agreed with them. The other half were told nothing about the group consensus. Then all students received the defenses and attacks on the truisms. As in the previous study all three types of defenses (reassuring, threatening-same and threatening-differ-

ent) were used with both the reassured and the non-reassured believers.

If the inoculation theory held true, we expected that, because their defenses would be lulled, the reassured believers would show a lower resistance to persuasion than the non-reassured believers. Our reassurance should further lower the overconfident believer's already low motivation to assimilate the defenses. We also predicted that the detrimental effects of extrinsic reassurance would be more pronounced with the reassuring defenses than with the threatening, since the hostile arguments in the latter did contain some motivation-stimulating threat.

Our prediction that the reassurance of peer support would weaken the defenses' efficacy was confirmed. The overall belief level after defenses and attacks was significantly higher among the students who had received no reassurance. While the detrimental effect of reassurance was more pronounced with the group that received the reassuring

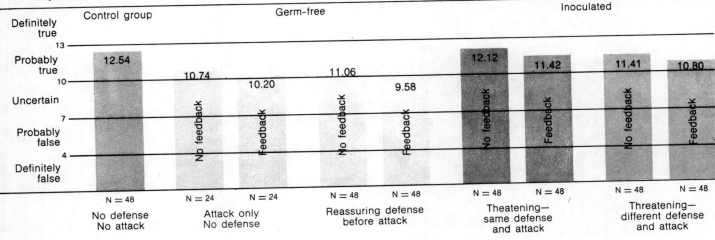

defense than with the group that received the threatening defense, as predicted, the difference was *not* significant.

Unraveling. We designed a fifth experiment to clear up an ambiguity regarding the effects of the threatening defenses. We wanted to find out to what extent the immunizing effect comes from the threatening mention of hostile arguments, and to what extent the effect comes from the reassuring refutation of these arguments. The threatening quality of the defense was manipulated by setting up a high-threat condition and a low-threat condition; the amount of reassurance was manipulated by setting up a high-reassurance condition and a low-reassurance condition.

One-fourth of the students were subjected to high-threat, high-reassurance: they encountered four hostile arguments and refutations of two of the arguments.

Another fourth of the students were in the high-threat, low-reassurance group: they met four hostile arguments, but none of the arguments was refuted.

That fourth of the students in the low-threat, high-reassurance group encoun-

Experiment 5

	High threat	Low threat	Overall
High Reassurance	11.07	10.54	10.75
Low Reassurance	10.97	9.75	10.23
Overall	11.02	10.14	

tered only two arguments against the truisms and both arguments were refuted.

The last fourth of the students were placed in a low-threat, low-reassurance group: only two arguments were put forth, but neither was refuted.

The high-threat condition consistently conferred more resistance than the low-threat condition. Whether or not any of the hostile arguments were refuted, we found superior resistance to persuasion when the defense mentioned four arguments against the truisms instead of only two. The difference between the resistance of the high-threat condition and the low-threat one was significant at the .01 level.

But reassurance also plays a role in conferring resistance. Under conditions of high reassurance—when two of the arguments were refuted during the defensive session—the subsequent attacks on the truisms were not as effective as when the arguments went unchallenged. Reassurance does help an individual resist persuasion. When we examine the results under all conditions, it appears that the ideal prescription for conferring resistance to persuasion consists of first threatening a person's belief in a cultural truism and then reassuring him that his belief is correct after all.

Paper Tiger. In several of our studies we found the paper-tiger effect that turned up in the first experiment when we measured the belief level after the first session. Those defenses that seem to leave beliefs the strongest—reassurance without any threat whatsoever—actually confer the least resistance to subsequent attacks. This finding is in keeping with our biological analogy: treatments that

may leave the germ-free organism looking most healthful tend to leave him extremely vulnerable to sudden attack.

These experiments support the theoretical notion with which we began our study. A believer's faith in his culture's ideological truisms tends to have a spurious strength, analogous to the deceptive physical robustness of an animal brought up in a germ-free environment. Both are extremely vulnerable to attacking material and both gain resistance from pre-exposure to a weakened dose of the threatening material.

We have continued to follow the inoculation theory in exploring resistance to persuasion. In later studies we have found that just as vaccinated persons require several days to develop resistance to disease, so a person who has been immunized against persuasion requires several days to build up resistance to propaganda.

The feeling of virtue that developed when I dropped techniques of persuasion and took up immunization against persuasion may have been somewhat premature. The study of how to make people resistant to persuasion can be misused just as readily as studies on how to persuade them to overcome these resistances can be. One day I received a phone call from an advertising executive who had heard about my research. I virtuously told him that he would not be interested since his job was to persuade people while my work, on the other hand, was on how to make them resistant to persuasion.

"Don't underrate yourself, Professor," he replied. "Your stuff might be of use against our competitors."

Style or Circumstance: The Leadership Enigma

By Fred E. Fiedler

WHAT IS IT that makes a person an effective leader?

We take it for granted that good leadership is essential to business, to government and to all the myriad groups and organizations that shape the way we live, work and play.

We spend at least several billions of dollars a year on leadership development and executive recruitment in the United States. Leaders are paid 10, 20 and 30 times the salary of ordinary workers. Thousands of books and articles on leadership have been published. Yet, we still know relatively little about the factors that determine a leader's success or failure.

Psychologists have been concerned with two major questions in their research on leadership: How does a man become a leader? What kind of personality traits or behavior makes a person an *effective* leader? For the past 15 years, my own work at the University of Illinois Group-Effectiveness Research Laboratory has concentrated on the latter question.

Psychologists used to think that special personality traits would distinguish leaders from followers. Several hundred research studies have been conducted to identify these special traits. But the search has been futile.

People who become leaders tend to be somewhat more intelligent, bigger, more assertive, more talkative than other members of their group. But these traits are far less important than most people think. What most frequently distinguishes the leader from his co-workers is

that he knows more about the group task or that he can do it better. A bowling team is likely to choose its captain from good rather than poor bowlers, and the foreman of a machine shop is more likely to be a good machinist than a poor one.

In many organizations, one only has to live long in order to gain experience and seniority, and with these a position of leadership.

In business and industry today, the men who attain a leadership position must have the requisite education and talent. Of course, as W. Lloyd Warner and James C. Abegglen of the University of Chicago have shown, it has been most useful to come from or marry into a family that owns a large slice of the company's stock.

Becoming a leader, then, depends on personality only to a limited extent. A person can become a leader by happenstance, simply by being in the right place at the right time, or because of such various factors as age, education, experience, family background and wealth.

Almost any person in a group may be capable of rising to a leadership position if he is rewarded for actively participating in the group discussion, as Alex Bavelas and his colleagues at Stanford University have demonstrated. They used light signals to reward low-status group members for supposedly "doing the right thing." However, unknown to the people being encouraged, the light signal was turned on and off at random. Rewarded in this unspecified, undefined manner, the low-status member came to regard himself as a leader and the rest

of the group accepted him in his new position.

It is commonly observed that personality and circumstances interact to determine whether a person will become a leader. While this statement is undoubtedly true, its usefulness is rather limited unless one also can specify how a personality trait will interact with a specific situation. We are as yet unable to make such predictions.

Having become a leader, how does one get to be an effective leader? Given a dozen or more similar groups and tasks, what makes one leader succeed and another fail? The answer to this question is likely to determine the philosophy of leader-training programs and the way in which men are selected for executive positions.

There are a limited number of ways in which one person can influence others to work together toward a common goal. He can coerce them or he can coax them. He can tell people what to do and how to do it, or he can share the decision-making and concentrate on his relationship with his men rather than on the execution of the job.

Of course, these two types of leadership behavior are gross oversimplifications. Most research by psychologists on leadership has focused on two clusters of behavior and attitudes, one labeled autocratic, authoritarian and task-oriented, and the other as democratic, equalitarian, permissive and group-oriented.

The first type of leadership behavior, frequently advocated in conventional supervisory and military systems, has its philosophical roots in Frank W. Taylor's *Principles of Scientific Management* and other early 20th Century industrial engineering studies. The authoritarian, task-oriented leader takes all responsibility for making decisions and directing the group members. His rationale is simple: "I do the thinking and you carry out the orders."

The second type of leadership is typical of the "New Look" method of management advocated by men like Douglas McGregor of M.I.T. and Rensis Likert of the University of Michigan. The democratic, group-oriented leader provides general rather than close supervision and his concern is the effective use of human resources through participation. In the late 1940s, a related method of leadership training was developed based on confrontation in unstructured group situations where each participant can explore his own motivations and reactions. Some excellent studies on this method, called T-group, sensitivity or laboratory training, have been made by Chris Argyris of Yale, Warren Bennis of State University of New York at Buffalo and Edgar Schein of M.I.T.

Experiments comparing the performance of both types of leaders have shown that each is successful in some situations and not in others. No one has been able to show that one kind of leader is always superior or more effective.

A number of researchers point out that different tasks require different kinds of leadership. But what kind of situation requires what kind of leader? To answer this question, I shall present a theory of leadership effectiveness that spells out the specific circumstances under which various leadership styles are most effective.

We must first of all distinguish between leadership style and leader behavior. Leader behavior refers to the specific acts in which a leader engages while directing or coordinating the work of his group. For example, the leader can praise or criticize, make helpful suggestions, show consideration for the welfare and feelings of members of his group.

Leadership style refers to the underlying needs of the leader that motivate his behavior. In other words, in addition to performing the task, what personal needs is the leader attempting to satisfy? We have found that a leader's actions or behavior sometimes does change as the situation or group changes, but his basic needs appear to remain constant.

To classify leadership styles, my colleagues and I have developed a simple questionnaire that asks the leader to describe the person with whom he can work least well:

LPC—Least-Preferred Co-worker

Think of the person with whom you can work least well. He may be someone you work with now, or he may be someone you knew in the past. Use an X to describe this person as he appears to you.

helpful :_:_:_:_:_:_:_:_: frustrating
        8 7 6 5 4 3 2 1
unen-   :_:_:_:_:_:_:_:_: enthusiastic
thusiastic 1 2 3 4 5 6 7 8
efficient :_:_:_:_:_:_:_:_: inefficient
        8 7 6 5 4 3 2 1

From the replies, a Least-Preferred-Co-worker (LPC) score is obtained by simply summing the item scores. The LPC score does not measure perceptual accuracy, but rather reveals a person's emotional reaction to the people with whom he cannot work well.

In general, the high-scoring leader describes his least-preferred co-worker in favorable terms. The high-LPC leader tends to be "relationship-oriented." He gets his major satisfaction from establishing close personal relations with his group members. He uses the group task to gain the position of prominence he seeks.

The leader with a low score describes his least-preferred co-worker in unfavorable terms. The low-LPC leader is primarily "task-oriented." He obtains his major satisfaction by successfully completing the task, even at the risk of poor interpersonal relations with his workers.

Since a leader cannot function without a group, we must also know something about the group that the leader directs. There are many types of groups, for example, social groups which promote the enjoyment of individuals and "counteracting" groups such as labor and management at the negotiating table. But here we shall concentrate on groups that exist for the purpose of performing a task.

From our research, my associates and I have identified three major factors that can be used to classify group situations: (1) position power of the leader, (2) task structure, and (3) leader–member personal relationships. Basically, these classifications measure the kind of power and influence the group gives its leader.

We ranked group situations according to their favorableness for the leader. Favorableness here is defined as the degree to which the situation enables the leader to exert influence over the group.

Based on several studies, leader–member relations emerged as the most important factor in determining the leader's influence over the group. Task structure is rated as second in importance, and position power as third. [*See illustration, upper right, page 351.*]

Under most circumstances, the leader who is liked by his group and has a clear-cut task and high position power obviously has everything in his favor. The leader who has poor relationships with his group members, an unstructured task and weak position power likely will be unable to exert much influence over the group.

The personal relationships that the leader establishes with his group members depend at least in part upon the leader's personality. The leader who is loved, admired and trusted can influence the group regardless of his position power. The leader who is not liked or trusted cannot influence the group except through his vested authority. It should be noted that a leader's assessment of how much he is liked often differs markedly from the group's evaluation.

Task structure refers to the degree the group's assignment can be programmed and specified in a step-by-step fashion. A highly structured task does not need a leader with much position power because the leader's role is detailed by the job specifications. With a highly structured task, the leader clearly knows what to do and how to do it, and the organization can back him up at each step. Unstructured tasks tend to have more than one correct solution that may be reached by any of a variety of methods. Since there is no step-by-step method that can be programmed in advance, the leader cannot influence the group's success by ordering them to vote "right" or be creative. Tasks of committees, creative groups and policy-making groups are typically unstructured.

Position power is the authority vested in the leader's position. It can be readily measured in most situations. An army general obviously has more power than a lieutenant, just as a department head has more power than an office manager.

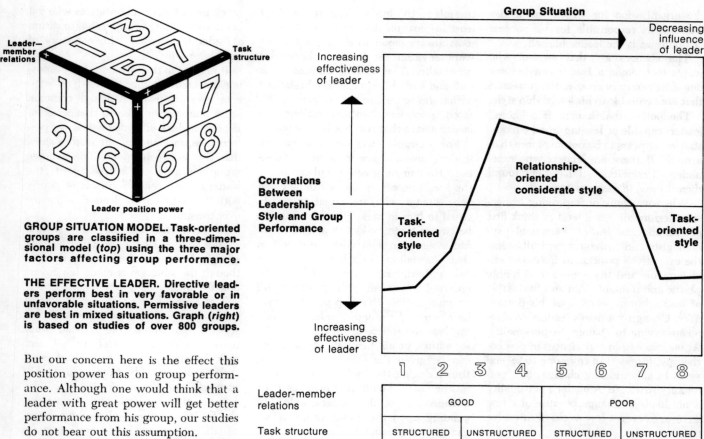

GROUP SITUATION MODEL. Task-oriented groups are classified in a three-dimensional model (*top*) using the three major factors affecting group performance.

THE EFFECTIVE LEADER. Directive leaders perform best in very favorable or in unfavorable situations. Permissive leaders are best in mixed situations. Graph (*right*) is based on studies of over 800 groups.

But our concern here is the effect this position power has on group performance. Although one would think that a leader with great power will get better performance from his group, our studies do not bear out this assumption.

However, it must be emphasized that in some situations position power may supersede task structure (the military). Or a very highly structured task (launching a moon probe) may outweigh the effects of interpersonal relations. The organization determines both the task structure and the position power of the leader.

In our search for the most effective leadership style, we went back to the studies that we had been conducting for more than a decade. These studies investigated a wide variety of groups and leadership situations, including basketball teams, business management, military units, boards of directors, creative groups and scientists engaged in pure research. In all of these studies, we could determine the groups that had performed their tasks successfully or unsuccessfully and then correlated the effectiveness of group performance with leadership style.

Now by plotting these correlations of leadership style against our scale of group situations, we could, for the first time, find what leadership style works best in each situation. When we connected the median points on each col-

umn, the result was a bell-shaped curve. (*See illustration, directly above.*)

The results show that a task-oriented leader performs best in situations at both extremes—those in which he has a great deal of influence and power, and also in situations where he has no influence and power over the group members.

Relationship-oriented leaders tend to perform best in mixed situations where they have only moderate influence over the group. A number of subsequent studies by us and others have confirmed these findings.

The results show that we cannot talk about simply good leaders or poor leaders. A leader who is effective in one situation may or may not be effective in another. Therefore, we must specify the situations in which a leader performs well or badly.

This theory of leadership effectiveness by and large fits our everyday experience. Group situations in which the leader is liked, where he has a clearly

defined task and a powerful position, may make attempts at nondirective, democratic leadership detrimental or superfluous. For example, the captain of an airliner can hardly call a committee meeting of the crew to share in the decision-making during a difficult landing approach. On the other hand, the chairman of a voluntary committee cannot ask with impunity that the group members vote or act according to his instructions.

Our studies also have shown that factors such as group-member abilities, cultural heterogeneity and stressfulness of the task affect the degree to which the leader can influence members of the group. But the important finding and the consistent finding in these studies has been that mixed situations require relationship-oriented leadership while very favorable and very unfavorable job situations require task-oriented leaders.

Perhaps the most important implication of this theory of leadership is that the organization for which the leader works is as responsible for his success or failure as is the leader himself.

The chances are that *anyone* who wants to become a leader can become one if he carefully chooses the situations that are favorable to his leadership style.

The notion that a man is a "born" leader, capable of leading in all circumstances, appears to be nothing more than a myth. If there are leaders who excel under all conditions, I have not found them in my 18 years of research.

When we think of improving leadership performance, we tend to think first of training the leader. Personnel psychologists and managers typically view the executive's position as fixed and unchangeable and the applicant as highly plastic and trainable. A man's basic style of leadership depends upon his personality. Changing a man's leadership style means trying to change his personality. As we know from experiences in psychotherapy, it may take from one to several years to effect lasting changes in a personality structure. A leader's personality is not likely to change because of a few lectures or even a few weeks of intensive training.

It is doubtful that intensive training techniques can change an individual's style of leadership. However, training programs could be designed to provide the opportunity for a leader to learn in which situations he can perform well and in which he is likely to fail. Laboratory training also may provide the leader with some insights into his personal relationships with group members.

Our theory of leadership effectiveness predicts that a leader's performance can be improved by engineering or fitting the job to the leader. This is based, at least in part, on the belief that it is almost always easier to change a leader's work environment than to change his personality. The leader's authority, his task and even his interpersonal relations within his group members can be altered, sometimes without making the leader aware that this has been done.

For example, we can change the leader's position power in either direction. He can be given a higher rank if this seems necessary. Or he can be given subordinates who are equal or nearly equal to him in rank. His assistants can be two or three ranks below him, or we can assign him men who are expert in their specialties. The leader can have sole authority for a job, or he may be required to consult with his group All communications to group members may be channeled through the leader, making him the source of all the inside information, or all members of the group can be given the information directly, thus reducing the leader's influence.

The task structure also can be changed to suit the leader's style. Depending upon the group situation, we can give the leader explicit instructions or we can deliberately give him a vague and nebulous goal.

Finally, we can change the leader–member relations. In some situations it may be desirable to improve leader–member relations by making the group homogeneous in culture and language or in technical and educational background. Interdisciplinary groups are notoriously difficult to handle, and it is even more difficult to lead a group that is racially or culturally mixed. Likewise, we can affect leader–member relations by giving a leader subordinates who get along well with their supervisor or assign a leader to a group with a history of trouble or conflict.

It may seem that often we are proposing the sabotaging of the leader's influence over his group. Although common sense might make it seem that weakening the leader's influence will lower performance, in actuality our studies show that this rarely happens. The average group performance (in other words, the leader's effectiveness) correlates poorly with the degree of the leader's influence over the group.

In fact, the findings from several studies suggest that a particular leader's effectiveness may be improved even though the situation is made less favorable for him.

The leader himself can be taught to recognize the situations that best fit his style. A man who is able to avoid situations in which he is likely to fail, and seek out situations that fit his leadership style, will probably become a highly successful and effective leader. Also, if he is aware of his strengths and weaknesses, the leader can try to change his group situation to match his leadership style.

However, we must remember that good leadership performance depends as much upon the organization as it does upon the leader. This means that we must learn not only how to train men to be leaders, but how to build organizations in which specific types of leaders can perform well.

In view of the increasing scarcity of competent executives, it is to an organization's advantage to design jobs to fit leaders instead of attempting merely to fit a leader to the job.

Kitty Genovese is set upon by a maniac as she returns home from work at 3:00 a.m. Thirty-eight of her neighbors in Kew Gardens come to their windows when she cries out in terror; none come to her assistance even though her stalker takes over half an hour to murder her. No one even so much as calls the police. She dies.

Andrew Mormille is stabbed in the stomach as he rides the A train home to Manhattan. Eleven other riders watch the 17-year-old boy as he bleeds to death; none come to his assistance even though his attackers have left the car. He dies.

An 18-year-old switchboard operator, alone in her office in the Bronx, is raped and beaten. Escaping momentarily, she runs naked and bleeding to the street, screaming for help. A crowd of 40 passersby gathers and watches as, in broad daylight, the rapist tries to drag her back upstairs; no one interferes. Finally two policemen happen by and arrest her assailant.

Eleanor Bradley trips and breaks her leg while shopping on Fifth Avenue. Dazed and in shock, she calls for help, but the hurrying stream of executives and shoppers simply parts and flows past. After 40 minutes a taxi driver helps her to a doctor.

WHEN WILL PEOPLE HELP IN A CRISIS?

By John M. Darley and Bibb Latané

The shocking thing about these cases is that so many people failed to respond. If only one or two had ignored the victim, we might be able to understand their inaction. But when 38 people, or 11 people, or hundreds of people fail to help, we become disturbed. Actually, this fact that shocks us so much is itself the clue to understanding these cases. Although it seems obvious that the more people who watch a victim in distress, the more likely someone will help, what really happens is exactly the opposite. If each member of a group of bystanders is aware that other people are also present, he will be less likely to notice the emergency, less likely to decide that it is an emergency, and less likely to act even if he thinks there is an emergency.

This is a surprising assertion—what we are saying is that the victim may actually be less likely to get help, the more people who watch his distress and are available to help. We shall discuss in detail the process through which an individual bystander must go in order to intervene, and we shall present the results of some experiments designed to show the effects of the number of onlookers on the likelihood of intervention.

Since we started research on bystander responses to emergencies, we have heard many explanations for the lack of intervention. "I would assign this to the effect of the megapolis in which we live, which makes closeness very difficult and leads to the alienation of the individual from the group," contributed a psychoanalyst. "A disaster syndrome," explained a sociologist, "that shook the sense of safety and sureness of the individuals involved and caused psychological withdrawal from the event by ignoring it." "Apathy," claimed others. "Indifference." "The gratification of unconscious sadistic impulses." "Lack of concern for our fellow men." "The Cold Society." All of these analyses of the person who fails to help share one characteristic; they set the indifferent witness apart from the rest of us as a different kind of person. Certainly not one of us who reads about these incidents in horror is apathetic, alienated or depersonalized. Certainly not one of us enjoys gratifying his sadistic impulses by watching others suffer. These terrifying cases in which people fail to help others certainly have no personal implications for us. That is, we might decide not to ride subways any more, or that New York isn't even "a nice place to visit," or "there ought to be a law" against apathy, but we needn't feel guilty, or re-examine ourselves, or anything like that.

Looking more closely at published descriptions of the behavior of witnesses to these incidents, the people involved begin to look a little less inhuman and a lot more like the rest of us. Although it is unquestionably true that the witnesses in the incidents above did nothing to save the victims, apathy, indifference and unconcern are not entirely accurate descriptions of their reactions. The 38 witnesses of Kitty Genovese's murder did not merely look at the scene once and then ignore it. They continued to stare out of their windows at what was going on. Caught, fascinated, distressed, unwilling to act but unable to turn away, their behavior was neither helpful nor heroic; but it was not indifferent or apathetic.

Actually, it was like crowd behavior in many other emergency situations. Car accidents, drownings, fires and attempted suicides all attract substantial numbers of people who watch the drama in helpless fascination without getting directly involved in the action. Are these people alienated and indifferent? Are the rest of us? Obviously not. Why, then, don't we act?

The bystander to an emergency has to make a series of decisions about what is happening and what he will do about it. The consequences of these decisions will determine his actions. There are three things he must do if he is to intervene: *notice* that something is happening, *interpret* that event as an emergency, and decide that he has *personal responsibility* for intervention. If he fails to notice the event, if he decides that it is not an emergency, or if he concludes that he is not personally responsible for acting, he will leave the victim unhelped. This state of affairs is shown graphically as a "decision tree" (*see illustration, right*). Only one path through this decision tree leads to intervention; all others lead to a failure to help. As we shall show, at each fork of the path in the decision tree, the presence of other bystanders may lead a person down the branch of not helping.

Noticing: The First Step

Suppose that an emergency is actually taking place; a middle-aged man has a heart attack. He stops short, clutches his chest, and staggers to the nearest building wall, where he slowly slumps to the sidewalk in a sitting position. What is the likelihood that a passerby will come to his assistance? First, the bystander has to *notice* that something is happening. The external event has to break into his thinking and intrude itself on his conscious mind. He must tear himself away from his private thoughts and pay attention to this unusual event.

But Americans consider it bad manners to look too closely at other people in public. We are taught to respect the privacy of others, and when among strangers, we do this by closing our ears and avoiding staring at others—we are embarrassed if caught doing otherwise. In a crowd, then, each person is less likely to notice the first sign of a potential emergency than when alone.

Experimental evidence corroborates this everyday observation. Darley and Latané asked college students to an interview about their reactions to urban living. As the students waited to see the interviewer, either by themselves or with two other students, they filled out a preliminary questionnaire. Solitary students often glanced idly about the room while filling out their questionnaires; those in groups, to avoid seeming rudely inquisitive, kept their eyes on their own papers.

As part of the study, we staged an emergency: smoke was released into the waiting room through a vent. Two-thirds of the subjects who were alone when the smoke appeared noticed it immediately, but only a quarter of the subjects waiting in groups saw it as quickly. Even after the room had completely filled with smoke one subject from a group of three finally looked up and exclaimed, "God! I must be smoking too much!" Although eventually all the subjects did become aware of the smoke, this study indicates that the more people present, the slower an individual may be to perceive that an emergency does exist and the more likely he is not to see it at all.

Once an event is noticed, an onlooker must decide whether or not it is truly an emergency. Emergencies

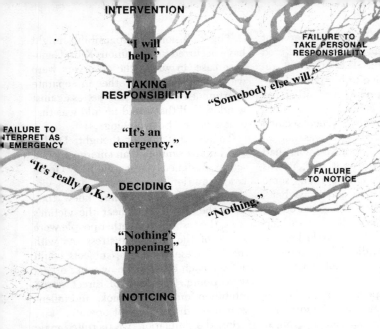

INTERVENTION

"I will help."

FAILURE TO TAKE PERSONAL RESPONSIBILITY

TAKING RESPONSIBILITY

"Somebody else will."

FAILURE TO INTERPRET AS AN EMERGENCY

"It's an emergency."

"It's really O.K."

FAILURE TO NOTICE

DECIDING

"Nothing."

"Nothing's happening."

NOTICING

THE DECISION TREE. In an emergency, a bystander must: 1) notice something is happening; 2) interpret it as an emergency; 3) decide that he has a personal responsibility for intervention.

are not always clearly labeled as such; smoke pouring from a building or into a waiting room may be caused by a fire, or it may merely indicate a leak in a steam pipe. Screams in the street may signal an assault or a family quarrel. A man lying in doorway may be having a coronary or be suffering from diabetic coma—he may simply be sleeping off a drunk. And in any unusual situation, Candid Camera may be watching.

A person trying to decide whether or not a given situation is an emergency often refers to the reactions of those around him; he looks at them to see how he should react himself. If everyone else is calm and indifferent, he will tend to remain calm and indifferent; if everyone else is reacting strongly, he will become aroused. This tendency is not merely slavish conformity; ordinarily we derive much valuable information about new situations from how others around us behave. It's a rare traveler who, in picking a roadside restaurant, chooses to stop at one with no other cars in the parking lot.

But occasionally the reactions of others provide false information. The studied nonchalance of patients in a dentist's waiting room is a poor indication of the pain awaiting them. In general, it is considered embarrassing to look overly concerned, to seem flustered, to "lose your cool" in public. When we are not alone, most of us try to seem less fearful and anxious than we really are.

In a potentially dangerous situation, then, everyone present will appear more unconcerned than they are in fact. Looking at the *apparent* impassivity and lack of reaction of the others, each person is led to believe that nothing really is wrong. Meanwhile the danger may be mounting, to the point where a single person, uninfluenced by the seeming calm of others, would react.

A crowd can thus force inaction on its members by implying, through its passivity and apparent indifference, that an event is not an emergency. Any individual in such

a crowd is uncomfortably aware that he'll look like a fool if he behaves as though it were—and in these circumstances, until someone acts, no one acts.

In the smoke-filled-room study, the smoke trickling from the wall constituted an ambiguous but potentially dangerous situation. How did the presence of other people affect a person's response to the situation? Typically, those who were in the waiting room by themselves noticed the smoke at once, gave a slight startle reaction, hesitated, got up and went over to investigate the smoke, hesitated again, and then left the room to find somebody to tell about the smoke. No one showed any signs of panic, but over three-quarters of these people were concerned enough to report the smoke.

Others went through an identical experience but in groups of three strangers. Their behavior was radically different. Typically, once someone noticed the smoke, he would look at the other people, see them doing nothing, shrug his shoulders, and then go back to his questionnaire, casting covert glances first at the smoke and then at the others. From these three-person groups, only three out of 24 people reported the smoke. The inhibiting effect of the group was so strong that the other 21 were willing to sit in a room filled with smoke rather than make themselves conspicuous by reacting with alarm and concern—this despite the fact that after three or four minutes the atmosphere in the waiting room grew most unpleasant. Even though they coughed, rubbed their eyes, tried to wave the smoke away, and opened the window, they apparently were unable to bring themselves to leave.

These dramatic differences between the behavior of people alone and those in a group indicate that the group imposed a definition of the situation upon its members which inhibited action.

"A leak in the air conditioning," said one person when we asked him what he thought caused the smoke. "Must be chemistry labs in the building." "Steam pipes." "Truth gas to make us give true answers on the questionnaire," reported the more imaginative. There were many explanations for the smoke, but they all had one thing in common: they did not mention the word fire. In defining the situation as a nonemergency, people explained to themselves why the other observers did not leave the room; they also removed any reason for action themselves. The other members of the group acted as nonresponsive models for each person—and as an audience for any "inappropriate" action he might consider. In such a situation it is all too easy to do nothing.

The results of this study clearly and strongly support the predictions. But are they general? Would the same effect show up with other emergencies, or is it limited to situations like the smoke study involving danger to the self as well as to others—or to situations in which there's no clearly defined "victim"? It may be that our college-age male subjects played "chicken" with one another to see who would lose face by first fleeing the room. It may be that groups were less likely to respond because no particular person was in danger. To see how generalizable these results are, Latané and Judith Rodin set up a second experiment, in which the emergency would cause no danger for the bystander, and in which a specific person was in trouble.

Subjects were paid $2 to participate in a survey of game and puzzle preferences conducted at Columbia by the Consumer Testing Bureau (CTB). An attractive young woman, the market-research representative, met them at the door and took them to the testing room. On the way, they passed the CTB office and through its open door they could see filing cabinets and a desk and bookcases piled high with papers. They entered the adjacent testing room, which contained a table and chairs and a variety of games, where they were given a preliminary background information and game preference questionnaire to fill out. The representative told subjects that she would be working next door in her office for about 10 minutes while they completed the questionnaires, and left by opening the collapsible curtain which divided the two rooms. She made sure the subjects knew that the curtain was unlocked, easily opened and a means of entry to her office. The representative stayed in her office, shuffling papers, opening drawers, and making enough noise to remind the subjects of her presence. Four minutes after leaving the testing area, she turned on a high fidelity stereophonic tape recorder.

If the subject listened carefully, he heard the representative climb up on a chair to reach for a stack of papers on the bookcase. Even if he were not listening carefully, he heard a loud crash and a scream as the chair collapsed and she fell to the floor. "Oh, my God, my foot....I...I...can't move it. Oh...my ankle," the representative moaned. "I... can't get this...thing...off me." She cried and moaned for about a minute longer, but the cries gradually got more subdued and controlled. Finally she muttered something about getting outside, knocked over the chair as she pulled herself up, and thumped to the door, closing it behind her as she left. This drama was of about two minutes' duration.

Some people were alone in the waiting room when the "accident" occurred. Seventy per cent of them offered to help the victim before she left the room. Many came through the curtain to offer their assistance, others simply called out to offer their help. Others faced the emergency in pairs. Only 20 per cent of this group—eight out of 40—offered to help the victim. The other 32 remained unresponsive to her cries of distress. Again, the presence of other bystanders inhibited action.

And again, the noninterveners seemed to have decided the event was not an emergency. They were unsure what had happened but whatever it was, it was not too serious. "A mild sprain," some said. "I didn't want to embarrass her." In a "real" emergency, they assured us, they would be among the first to help the victim. Perhaps they would be, but in this situation they didn't help, because for them the event was not defined as an emergency.

Again, solitary people exposed to a potential emergency reacted more frequently than those exposed in groups. We found that the action-inhibiting effects of other bystanders works in two different situations, one of which involves risking danger to oneself and the other of which involves helping an injured woman. The result seems sufficiently general so that we may assume it operates to inhibit helping in real-life emergencies.

Diffused Responsibility

Even if a person has noticed an event and defined it as an emergency, the fact that he knows that other bystanders also witnessed it may still make him less likely to intervene. Others may inhibit intervention because they make a person feel that his responsibility is diffused and diluted. Each soldier in a firing squad feels less personally responsible for killing a man than he would if he alone pulled the trigger. Likewise, any person in a crowd of onlookers may feel less responsibility for saving a life than if he alone witnesses the emergency.

If your car breaks down on a busy highway, hundreds of drivers whiz by without anyone's stopping to help; if you are stuck on a nearly deserted country road, whoever passes you first is apt to stop. The personal responsibility that a passerby feels makes the difference. A driver on a lonely road knows that if he doesn't stop to help, the person will not get help; the same individual on the crowded highway feels he personally is no more responsible than any of a hundred other drivers. So even though an event clearly is an emergency, any person in a group who sees an emergency may feel less responsible, simply because any other bystander is equally responsible for helping.

This diffusion of responsibility might have occurred in the famous Kitty Genovese case, in which the observers were walled off from each other in separate apartments. From the silhouettes against windows, all that could be told was that others were also watching.

To test this line of thought, Darley and Latané simulated an emergency in a setting designed to resemble Kitty Genovese's murder. People overheard a victim calling for help. Some knew they were the only one to hear the victim's cries, the rest believed other people were aware of the victim's distress. As with the Genovese witnesses, subjects could not see each other or know what others were doing. The kind of direct group inhibition found in the smoke and fallen-woman studies could not operate.

For the simulation, we recruited male and female students at New York University to participate in a group discussion. Each student was put in an individual room equipped with a set of headphones and a microphone and told to listen for instructions over the headphones. The instructions informed the participant that the discussion was to consider personal problems of the normal college student in a high-pressure urban university. It was explained that, because participants might feel embarrassed about discussing personal problems publicly, several precautions had been taken to insure their anonymity: they would not meet the other people face to face, and the experimenter would not listen to the initial discussion but would only ask for their reactions later. Each person was to talk in turn. The first to talk reported that he found it difficult to adjust to New York and his studies. Then, very hesitantly and with obvious embarrassment, he mentioned that he was prone to nervous seizures, similar to but not really the same as epilepsy. These occurred particularly when he was under the stresses of studying and being graded.

Other people then discussed their own problems in turn. The number of other people in the discussion varied. But whatever the perceived size of the group —two, three or six people—only the subject was actually present; the others, as well as the instructions and the speeches of the victim-to-be, were present only on a pre-recorded tape.

When it again was the first person's turn to talk, after a few comments he launched into the following performance, getting increasingly louder with increasing speech difficulties:

"I can see a lot of er of er how other people's problems are similar to mine because er er I mean er it's er I mean some of the er same er kinds of things that I have and an er I'm sure that every everybody has and er er I mean er they're not er e-easy to handle sometimes and er I er er be upsetting like er er and er I er um I think I I need er if if could er er somebody er er er er er give me give me a little er give me a little help here because er I er I'm er h-h-having a a a a a real problem er right now and I er if somebody could help me out it would it would er er s-s-sure be sure be good be . . . because er there er er a cause I er *uh* I've got a a one of the er seiz—er er things coming *on* and and and I c-could really er use er some h-help s-so if somebody would er give me a little h-help uh er-er-er-er-er c-could somebody er er help er uh uh uh (choking sounds) . . . I'm gonna die er er I'm . . . gonna . . . die er help er er seiz-ure er er . . ." (chokes, then quiet).

While this was going on, the experimenter waited outside the student's door to see how soon he would emerge to cope with the emergency. Rather to our surprise, some people sat through the entire fit without helping; a disproportionately large percentage of these nonresponders were from the largest-size group. Eighty-five per cent of the people who believed themselves to be alone with the victim came out of their rooms to help, while 62 per cent of the people who believed there was one other bystander did so. Of those who believed there were four other bystanders, only 31 per cent reported the fit before the tape ended. The responsibility-diluting effect of other people was so strong that single individuals were more than twice as likely to report the emergency as those who thought other people also knew about it.

The Moral Dilemma Felt by Those Who Do Not Respond

People who failed to report the emergency showed few signs of apathy and indifference thought to characterize "unresponsive bystanders." When the experimenter entered the room to end the situation, the subject often asked if the victim was "all right." Many of these people showed physical signs of nervousness; they often had trembling hands and sweating palms. If anything, they seemed more emotionally aroused than did those who reported the emergency. Their emotional arousal was in sharp contrast to the behavior of the nonresponding subjects in the smoke and fallen-woman studies. Those subjects were calm and unconcerned when their experiments were over. Having interpreted the events as nonemergencies, there was no reason for them to be otherwise. It was only the subjects who did not respond in the face of the clear emergency represented by the fit, who felt the moral dilemma.

Why, then, didn't they respond? It is our impression that nonintervening subjects had not decided *not* to respond. Rather, they were still in a state of indecision and conflict concerning whether to respond or not. The emotional behavior of these nonresponding subjects was a sign of their continuing conflict; a conflict that other people resolved by responding. The distinction seems an academic one for the victim, since he gets no help in either case, but it is an extremely important one for arriving at an understanding of why bystanders fail to help.

The evidence is clear, then, that the presence of other bystanders and the various ways these other bystanders affect our decision processes, make a difference in how likely we are to give help in an emergency. The presence of strangers may keep us from noticing an emergency at all; group behavior may lead us to define the situation as one that does not require action; and when other people are there to share the burden of responsibility, we may feel less obligated to do something when action is required. Therefore, it will often be the case that the *more* people who witness his distress, the *less* likely it is that the victim of an emergency will get help.

Thus, the stereotype of the unconcerned, depersonalized *homo urbanis*, blandly watching the misfortunes of others, proves inaccurate. Instead, we find a bystander to an emergency is an anguished individual in genuine doubt, concerned to do the right thing but compelled to make complex decisions under pressure of stress and fear. His reactions are shaped by the actions of others—and all too frequently by their inaction.

And we are that bystander. Caught up by the apparent indifference of others, we may pass by an emergency without helping or even realizing that help is needed. Aware of the influence of those around us, however, we can resist it. We can choose to see distress and step forward to relieve it.

biographies

Elliot Aronson ("Who Likes Whom and Why") was influenced while at Brandeis University by humanistic psychologist Abraham Maslow. At Wesleyan University, where he received an M.A., his interest in research was encouraged by David McClelland. Dr. Aronson took his Ph.D. in 1959 at Stanford University, where he designed and conducted pioneering experiments on cognitive dissonance theory under the guidance of Leon Festinger. He taught at Harvard University and the University of Minnesota before going to the University of Texas, where he now teaches psychology and directs the social psychology program. His research on attraction was awarded the 1970 Socio-Psychological Prize by the American Association for the Advancement of Science. He is also working to facilitate racial integration in the elementary schools of Austin, Texas. Dr. Aronson is coauthor, with G. Lindzey, of the *Handbook of Social Psychology* (Addison-Wesley) and author of *The Social Animal* (W. H. Freeman).

Richard C. Atkinson ("The Computer as a Tutor") joined the faculty of Stanford University in 1956, after receiving his Ph.B. from the University of Chicago and his doctorate from Indiana University. He is a professor of psychology at Stanford and holds courtesy appointments in the schools of Education and Engineering. Dr. Atkinson is coauthor of the fifth edition of E. Hilgard's textbook *Introduction to Psychology* (Harcourt Brace Jovanovich) and is a frequent contributor to scholarly and professional journals. His chief research interest is memory and perception.

David Bakan ("Psychology Can Now Kick the Science Habit" and "Is Phrenology Foolish?") received his B.A. from Brooklyn College of the City of New York, his M.A. from Indiana University, and his Ph.D. (1948) from Ohio State University. He has held teaching positions at Ohio State, the University of Missouri, Harvard University, and the University of Chicago; he is presently a professor of psychology at York University in Toronto. Dr. Bakan is a past president of the Division of the History of Psychology of the American Psychological Association. He has written many articles and several books, including *Duality of Human Existence* (Beacon Press); *Disease, Pain, and Sacrifice: Toward a Psychology of Suffering* (Beacon Press); and *On Method: Toward a Reconstruction of Psychological Investigation* (Jossey-Bass). His most recent book, *Slaughter of the Innocents: A Study of the Battered Child Phenomenon* (Beacon Press) deals with child abuse. Dr. Bakan's research interests include the history of psychology, the psychology of religion, and research methods.

Theodore Xenophon Barber ("Who Believes in Hypnosis?") did research in hypnosis as part of his doctoral dissertation (1956) at American University. At Harvard University's Laboratory of Social Relations, he conducted research for three years, under William Caudill and Clyde Kluckhohn, in the cross-cultural aspects of hypnosis. He has continued his investigations during more than twelve years at the Medfield State Hospital and Foundation in Medfield, Massachusetts, where he is director of psychological research. A prolific writer, Dr. Barber has published more than 130 articles in professional journals and has published several books, including *Hypnosis: A Scientific Approach* (Van Nostrand Reinhold); *LSD, Marijuana, Yoga, and Hypnosis* (Aldine); and *Biofeedback and Self-Control* (Aldine).

Ralph J. Berger ("Morpheus Descending") did his undergraduate work at Cambridge University. He received a Ph.D. from the University of Edinburgh for his dissertation on sleep and dreaming, a topic he studied under Ian Oswald. Dr. Berger then went to Puerto Rico, where he was a research associate in the Laboratory of Perinatal Physiology of the National Institute of Neurological Diseases and Blindness. He spent eighteen months there studying the development of sleep patterns in newborn monkeys. He then went to the University of California, Los Angeles, where he spent three years in the anatomy department and the Brain Research Institute. Since January 1968, Dr. Berger has been an associate professor of psychology and biology at the University of California, Santa Cruz. His research has been almost entirely devoted to studies of sleep and dreaming in humans and animals and has provided the material for about thirty articles.

Leonard Berkowitz ("Impulse, Aggression and the Gun") is Vilas Research Professor at the University of Wisconsin, where he has been a faculty member since 1955. He did his undergraduate work at New York University, and, after receiving his doctorate from the University of Michigan (1951), he was a research psychologist at Crew Research Laboratory of the Human Resources Research Center. Dr. Berkowitz is primarily interested in experimental social psychology, especially aggression and altruism. He is the author of *Aggression: A Social-Psychological Analysis* (McGraw Hill); editor of the seven-volume *Advances in Experimental Social Psychology* (Academic Press); and coeditor, with J. Macaulay, of *Altruism and Helping Behavior* (Academic Press).

Sidney W. Bijou ("The Mentally Retarded Child") is director of the Child Behavior Laboratory and a professor of psychology at the University of Illinois. Before joining the Illinois faculty, he taught psychology and served as director of the Developmental Psychology Laboratory at the University of Washington for almost twenty years. Dr. Bijou received his B.S. from the University of Florida, his M.A. from Columbia University, and his Ph.D. from the University of Iowa. He is on the editorial boards of the *Journal of Experimental Child Psychology*, the *International Review of Research in Mental Retardation*, the *Journal of Abnormal Child Psychology*, and the *Journal of Behavior Therapy and Experimental Psychiatry*. He has written many articles for professional journals and has coauthored several books. Dr. Bijou is a member of the Research Advisory Board for the National Association for Retarded Children, of the American Psychological Association, and of the Society for Research in Child Development.

Gordon H. Bower ("How to ... Uh ... Remember!") went to Case Western Reserve University to study in the premedical program. Dr. Bower, who attended college on a baseball scholarship, changed career ambitions after a college job in a state mental hospital. He did his graduate work at Yale University under Neal E. Miller and received a Ph.D. (1959) in experimental psychology. As a professor of psychology at Stanford University, he conducts research on learning, including mathematical models of learning, information processing, and memory. One of his hobbies is mnemonic devices. Dr. Bower has published more than eighty research papers and four books, among them *Human Associative Memory* (Halsted Press), with J. Anderson, and the third edition of *Theories of Learning* (Appleton-Century-Crofts), with E. R. Hilgard. Dr. Bower was elected last year to the National Academy of Science.

Jerome Bruner ("Up from Helplessness") helped to found Harvard University's Center for Cognitive Studies in 1960 and was the Center's director from 1965 to 1972. He received his B.A. from Duke University and his Ph.D. (1941) from Harvard. He was for many years a professor of psychology at Harvard, although in the past he has served temporarily at other institutions of higher learning. Dr. Bruner is currently a professor of psychology at Oxford University. Among the many books and articles on the nature of cognitive processes that he has written are *On Knowing: Essays for the Left Hand* (Atheneum) and *Toward a Theory of Instruction* (Norton). Dr. Bruner has served on committees advising the White House, the State Department, the United Nations, the Department of Defense, the National Science Foundation, and the National Institutes of Health. He is a founding member of the National Academy of Education and a past president of the American Psychological Association, which honored him with its Distinguished Scientific Award in 1962.

Raymond Bernard Cattell ("Are I.Q. Tests Intelligent?") has just retired from the position of Distinguished Research Professor in the Department of Psychology at the University of Illinois, where he directed the Laboratory of Personality and Group Analysis. He is now director of the Institute for Research in Morality and Adjustment in Boulder, Colorado, where he is investigating the individual and cultural dynamics of morality. His study of intelligence began more than forty years ago when he did his Ph.D. research under the direction of Charles Spearman and Sir Cyril Burt at the University of London. This university later awarded him a D.Sc. Dr. Cattell came to the United States at the invitation of E. L. Thorndike, and he has taught at Clark and Harvard universities. He has published 335 articles, has contributed 34 chapters to books, and has written 30 books of his own.

Jean Chapman (coauthor, "Test Results Are What You Think They Are") is presently a lecturer in psychology at the University of Wisconsin. She received her Ph.D. from Northwestern University in 1960, and has worked on psychology research with her husband, Loren J. Chapman, for more than fifteen years. Her special interests are experimental design and statistics. With support from the Public Health Service, Dr. Chapman and her husband are engaged in a long-term study of schizophrenic thought disorder.

Loren J. Chapman (coauthor, "Test Results Are What You Think They Are") is a professor of psychology at the University of Wisconsin. He and his wife, Jean Chapman, have worked as a husband-wife research team for over fifteen years. Dr. Chapman received a Ph.D. in clinical psychology from Northwestern University in 1954. His primary research has been on schizophrenic thought disorder, psychodiagnosis, and cognitive error. The Public Health Service supports the Chapmans' long-term study of schizophrenic thought disorder.

Michael H. Chase ("The Matriculating Brain") is director of the Brain Information Service at the University of California, Los Angeles, and conducts his own research at the Brain Research Institute there. He spent his college years at UCLA and the University of California, Berkeley, in the prelaw and premedical programs. After two years of medical school in New York, he returned to UCLA to take a Ph.D. in neurophysiology and anatomy at UCLA. Dr. Chase edited *The Sleeping Brain* (Brain Information Service), and he is studying brain areas that control motor activity during sleep. Although primarily interested in the brain mechanisms that control sleep and wakefulness, he also studies the control of feeding behavior and motor behavior by the central nervous system and operant conditioning of electrical brain impulses. In addition, Dr. Chase is an impressionist artist.

Noam Chomsky ("Language and the Mind") holds the Ferrari P. Ward Professorship of Modern Languages and Linguistics at the Massachusetts Institute of Technology. He received his Ph.D. in linguistics from the University of Pennsylvania; the subject of his dissertation was transformation analysis. Dr. Chomsky is the author of books and articles not only on linguistics but also on philosophy, intellectual history, and contemporary issues.

Stephan L. Chorover ("Big Brother and Psychotechnology") attended the Bronx High School of Science and graduated from the City College of New York in 1955. Four years later he received a Ph.D. in physiological psychology from New York University, where he conducted research on the physiological effects of mescaline. He then went to England for two years and studied brain-injured humans and brain-lesioned monkeys at the National Hospital in London and at Cambridge University. In 1961 he became a research associate at the Massachusetts Institute of Technology, and he is now a professor of psychology and brain science there. Dr. Chorover has been primarily interested in exploring the disorders that produce seizures and in the effects of such physical treatment as electroconvulsive shock on learning and memory. He is currently completing a book on research methods in physiological psychology.

Michael Cole (coauthor, "Russian Nursery Schools") was a postdoctoral fellow in the Soviet-American Exchange Program from 1962 to 1963. He studied with Alexander Luria at Moscow University, where he was introduced to cross-cultural research on the development of cognitive processes. Dr. Cole received his B.A. from the University of California, Los Angeles, and his Ph.D. (1962) from Indiana University, where he began his research on human learning. He is presently a professor of ethnopsychology at Rockefeller University. Among Dr. Cole's recent publications are interviews with Russian psychologists, which have appeared in *Psychology Today*.

Sheila Cole (coauthor, "Russian Nursery Schools") spent the summers of 1962 and 1966 in the Soviet Union with her husband, Michael Cole, gathering information on Soviet nursery schools. An experienced education writer, she has a B.A. from Indiana University and an M.S. from the Columbia Graduate School of Journalism.

John M. Darley (coauthor, "When Will People Help in a Crisis?") is a professor of psychology at Princeton University. He completed his undergraduate work at Swarthmore College; he took his M.A. and Ph.D. at Harvard University after a year's leave of absence for study at the University of Minnesota. He taught four years at New York University, where a good deal of the research for this article was done. In addition to bystander intervention, Dr. Darley is studying determinants of conforming behavior and the relationships of subgroups (including experimentally created deviate subgroups) with the majority.

José M. R. Delgado ("ESB") has recently accepted the chairmanship of the Department of Physiological Sciences at the New Autonomous Medical School in Madrid, where he will also be director of Research at the National Institute, now under construction. For many years, Dr. Delgado was a professor of physiology at the Yale University Medical School. He has written more than 200 articles for scientific journals. His book *Physical Control of the Mind: Toward a Psychocivilized Society* (Harper & Row) has been translated into six languages. Dr. Delgado's research explores the neurophysiological bases of behavior, using techniques developed in his laboratory for radio stimulation of the brain. His recent investigations involve the interaction of mobil-

ity recorders, computers, and brain pacemakers. In Madrid, Dr. Delgado plans to continue his research with primates and to explore clinical applications of his findings to man.

J. Anthony Deutsch ("Brain Reward, ESB & Ecstasy" and "Neural Basis of Memory") has been a professor of psychology at the University of California, San Diego, since 1966. After his undergraduate and doctoral studies at Oxford University, where he received the D.Phil. degree in 1956, he was a member of the Oxford faculty for eight years. He went to Stanford University as a fellow of the Center for Advanced Study in the Behavioral Sciences and has also been a faculty member at Stanford, the University of California, Los Angeles, and New York University. Dr. Deutsch has been concerned with physiocranial psychology—specifically, the mechanism of thirst, intracranial self-stimulation, and the physical basis of memory and learning. He is the author of *Structural Basis of Behavior* (University of Chicago Press) and is coauthor—with Diana Deutsch, his wife—of a textbook, *Physiological Psychology* (Dorsey).

Theodosius Dobzhansky ("Differences Are Not Deficits"), one of the world's most respected and famous geneticists, graduated from the University of Kiev in the Soviet Union. He has taught and studied at Kiev's Polytechnique Institute and at the University of Leningrad. In 1927 he moved to the United States to work at the Rockefeller Foundation and to teach at the California Institute of Technology, at Rockefeller University, and, for twenty-two years, at Columbia University. He is now adjunct professor of genetics at the University of California, Davis. Dr. Dobzhansky has been president of most of the prestigious societies in the field of evolution and genetics, and he has honorary doctor of science degrees from universities in eight nations. Among his books, *Genetics and the Origin of Species* (Columbia University Press) and *Mankind Evolving: The Evolution of the Human Species* (Yale University Press) are basic reading for anyone interested in genetics and evolution. He possesses the National Medal of Science, the Darwin Medal, the Kimber Genetics Award, and the D. G. Elliot Medal of the National Academy of Sciences.

Fanita English ("Transactional and Script Analysis Today") moved from Rumania to Turkey and studied in Paris before studying child development at Columbia University and receiving a master's degree in social work from Bryn Mawr College. In Illinois she worked in family-service agencies and with emotionally disturbed children and then opened a clinical practice in Chicago. She became interested in transactional analysis after she read Eric Berne's first book on the subject. Finding Dr. Berne's clinical approach lucid and practical, she entered training in transactional analysis. She moved to Philadelphia to practice psychotherapy and to conduct transactional-analysis seminars. She is currently director of The Eastern Institute for Transactional Analysis and Gestalt in Philadelphia.

Hans J. Eysenck ("New Ways in Psychotherapy") is a professor of psychology at the University of London and director of the Psychological Department at the Institute of Psychiatry, Maudsley and Bethlem Royal Hospitals. He left Germany in 1934 to study French and English history and literature at the University of Dijon and Exeter University and received his Ph.D. in psychology from the University of London in 1940. Dr. Eysenck's experimental research in the field of personality has earned him international recognition. He has published more than 300 articles as well as 20 books, which include *Structure of Human Personality* (Methuen); *IQ Argument: Race, Intelligence and Education* (Library Press); and *Psychology of Politics* (Humanities). He is also proud to have had material published in *Punch* magazine.

C. B. Ferster ("The Autistic Child") is a professor of psychology and director of the University Learning Center at the American University in Washington, D.C. After undergraduate work at Rutgers University, Dr. Ferster received M.A. and Ph.D. degrees from Columbia University. For five years he was a research fellow at Harvard University, and he has also been affiliated with the Yerkes Regional Primate Research Center at Emory University, the Institute of Psychiatric Research at Indiana University, and Georgetown University. He served for several years as director and as senior research associate at the Institute for Behavioral Research in Silver Spring, Maryland, working under a research career development award from the National Institute of Health. He is coauthor, with M. C. Perrott, of *Behavior Principles* (New Century, Meredith) and, with B. F. Skinner, of *Schedules of Reinforcement* (Appleton-Century-Crofts). He has written more than fifty articles for professional journals.

Fred E. Fiedler ("Style or Circumstance: The Leadership Enigma"), after nineteen years as director of the Group Effectiveness Research Laboratory at the University of Illinois, was appointed a professor of psychology and of management and organization at the University of Washington, where he directs the Organizational Research Group. Dr. Fiedler, who received his Ph.D. in psychology from the University of Chicago in 1949, was awarded the 1953 Award for Outstanding Research by the American Personnel Association and received honorable mention in 1960. He was also awarded the 1971 Consulting Psychology Research Award by the American Psychological Association. In 1958–1959 he received a Fulbright Research Scholarship, which enabled him to become a visiting professor at the University of Amsterdam; in 1963–1964 he was a guest professor at the University of Louvain in Belgium under a Ford Faculty Research Fellowship. Dr. Fiedler is the author of *Leadership and Effective Management* (Scott, Foresman), with M. M. Chemers; *Boards, Management, and Company Success* (Interstate), with E. P. Godfrey and B. M. Hall; and *Theory of Leadership Effectiveness* (McGraw-Hill).

John Garcia ("IQ: The Conspiracy") is a professor of psychiatry and psychology at the University of California, Los Angeles. He has done research in social psychology and education, but his main contribution has been in the area of biological constraints on learning. He believes that the environment and the organism interact to shape behavior, and he opposes an analysis that attempts to separate the two. During World War II he served in the Army. He then studied at the University of California, Berkeley, where he received B.A. and M.A. degrees in psychology. Later he completed a Ph.D. there also. Dr. Garcia has worked as a biologist at the Harvard University Medical School and has been a professor of psychology at the State University of New York at Stony Brook and at the University of Utah.

Joanne L. Hager (coauthor, "Biological Boundaries of Learning: The Sauce–Béarnaise Syndrome") completed two years of Ph.D. research in philosophy at the University of Rochester before receiving her Ph.D. in psychology from Cornell University. Dr. Hager does research on the physiological correlates of stress and anxiety; her thesis research focused on respiratory responses to anxiety. She has received a postdoctoral fellowship in psychophysiology from Harvard University's Medical School and will work in David Shapiro's laboratory. Martin E. P. Seligman and Dr. Hager share an interest in learning theory and physiology, which led them to collaborate on this article. They are also joint editors of *The Biological Boundaries of Learning* (Appleton-Century-Crofts).

Harry Harlow (coauthor, "The Young Monkeys") received his Ph.D. from Stanford University. He has previously served as president of the American Psychological Association and director of the Regional Primate Research Center at Madison, Wisconsin. He is currently a professor of psychology and director of the Primate Laboratory at the University of Wisconsin. Dr. Harlow and his wife, Margaret Harlow, are famous for their studies of the effects of isolation and the influence of surrogate mothers on the social development of young primates.

The late Margaret Harlow (coauthor, "The Young Monkeys") received her Ph.D. from Iowa State University in 1944. Before expanding her interests to include the social development of primates, which her husband, Harry Harlow, was studying, she specialized in child development and learning. She also served as managing editor of publications for the American Psychological Association.

Donald O. Hebb ("The Mind's Eye" and coauthor, "A DMZ in the Language War"), a neuropsychologist, has been a professor of psychology at McGill University in Montreal since 1947 and the University's chancellor since 1970. He received a B.A. from Dalhousie University in Nova Scotia, an M.A. from McGill, and a Ph.D. (1936) from Harvard University. He has been a research assistant at Harvard, a fellow of the Montreal Neurological Institute, and a lecturer and assistant professor at Queen's University; he was also a researcher for five years with K. S. Lashley at the Yerkes Regional Primate Research Center at Emory University. Dr. Hebb has continued Lashley's goal: to contribute to the understanding of the human mind. Much of his work has focused on brain-damaged humans and animals. Dr. Hebb's *Organization of Behavior* (Wiley) is still selling in paperback and has become a standard work; A *Textbook of Psychology* (W. B. Saunders) went into its third edition in 1972. A new book that Dr. Hebb is writing provided the material for his article in this edition of *Readings in Psychology Today*.

Matina Horner ("Fail: Bright Women") received her B.A. from Bryn Mawr College, with honors in psychology, and a Ph.D. from the University of Michigan (1968). She went to Harvard University as a lecturer in the Department of Social Relations in 1969 and is now president of Radcliffe College and an associate professor of psychology and social relations at Harvard. Her research interests are achievement motivation (particularly the intrinsic motivational factors), the psychology of women, the psychological impact of internalized sex- and race-role stereotypes, and the effects of psychological interference on population planning and changing family structures. Dr. Horner is a member of Phi Beta Kappa and Phi Kappa Phi honorary societies.

Kenneth I. Howard (coauthor, "Inside Psychotherapy") did his undergraduate work at the University of California, Berkeley, and received his Ph.D. from the University of Chicago. He spent several years as a research associate at the University of Chicago and at the Loyola University School of Medicine. The article in this edition of *Readings in Psychology Today* is based on research done while Dr. Howard was a staff therapist at the Katharine Wright Mental Health Clinic. At the present time he is a professor of psychology at Northwestern University, has a small private practice, and is an administrative research scientist at the Institute for Juvenile Research.

Murray E. Jarvik ("The Psychopharmacological Revolution") is an associate professor of pharmacology at the Albert Einstein College of Medicine in New York City, a position he has held since 1956. His interest in drugs

was first aroused in 1949 when, as a second-year medical student, he taught a course in pharmacology at the University of California, Berkeley. After receiving his M.D. and Ph.D. from Berkeley, he joined the staff of Mt. Sinai Hospital in New York City as a research associate in the department of neurology. Dr. Jarvik's chief professional interests are the influence of drugs on behavior and the physiological basis of memory.

Jerome Kagan ("The Many Faces of Response" and "Check One: ☐ Male ☐ Female") is a professor of developmental psychology at Harvard University. Doctoral studies at Yale University and a position at Ohio State University preceded his Army service, during which Dr. Kagan did a research study on attrition at West Point. Later research at the Fels Research Institute of Antioch College resulted in *Birth to Maturity: A Study in Psychological Development* (Wiley), with H. A. Moss, which was awarded the 1963 Hofheimer Prize by the American Psychiatric Association. Dr. Kagan has written numerous articles and, with E. Havemann, a textbook, *Psychology: An Introduction* (Harcourt Brace Jovanovich).

Joe Kamiya ("Conscious Control of Brain Waves") is a lecturer in medical psychology at the Langley Porter Neuropsychiatric Institute of the University of California Medical Center in San Francisco. Dr. Kamiya received his A.B., M.A., and Ph.D. degrees from the University of California, Berkeley, and he has taught social psychology at the University of Chicago. It was there that he became interested in sleep and dream research and in studies of alpha waves. He is also interested in introspection and in the trained self-control of psychophysiological stages.

Irene Kassorla ("For Catatonia: Smiles, Praise and a Food Basket") studied for three years in Europe, initially at the invitation of Hans J. Eysenck of the University of London's Institute of Psychiatry. Four British Broadcasting Corporation documentaries on her work with severely disturbed psychotic patients have been widely distributed; one of them, released in Great Britain in 1974, chronicles her life. A documentary was made from tapes of the research on which the article in this book is based; the documentary, which had first been presented as a forty-minute radio science program, was awarded the international Prix Italia in Rome. At the University of California, Los Angeles, Dr. Kassorla worked with autistic children. She is now in private practice, conducting five group-therapy sessions a week (with a minimum of eighteen members in each group) and consulting with other patients. Dr. Kassorla is the only psychologist to have a nationally syndicated weekly television program, which consists of actual group-therapy sessions.

Lawrence Kohlberg ("The Child as a Moral Philosopher") received his Ph.D. in psychology from the University of Chicago. A postdoctoral residence at Children's Hospital, Boston, "confirmed my opinion that psychoanalysis had little to offer the systematic study of the development of moral ideas and feelings." Dr. Kohlberg then spent two years at Yale University studying psychosexual development and identification in early and middle childhood. A year at the Center for Advanced Study in the Behavioral Sciences was followed by five years at the University of Chicago. After a year at Harvard University's Human Development Laboratory, Dr. Kohlberg has settled at Harvard as a professor of education and social psychology.

Melvin Kornreich (coauthor, "It Works") did his undergraduate work at the City College of New York, received an M.A. from Columbia University, and received a Ph.D. in 1950 from New York University. He is now assistant chief psychologist at the Veterans Administration Outpatient Clinic in Brooklyn and teaches in the graduate and undergraduate programs of Brooklyn College at the City University of New York. Dr. Kornreich is coauthor, with J. Meltzoff, of *Research in Psychotherapy* (Aldine). As a clinical psychologist, he has specialized in marital and family psychotherapy and in the development of training programs for young psychologists. As a teacher, he has concentrated on the late bloomer who returns to school for a second try and on the student who never had a first chance.

Stanley Krippner (coauthor, "ESP in the Night") is director of the Maimonides Dream Laboratory. After undergraduate work at the University of Wisconsin, he received his Ph.D. from Northwestern University in 1961. Dr. Krippner has worked as a research assistant to Gardner Murphy at the University of Hawaii. He was selected by the New York University Metropolitan Leadership Program as an adjunct professor. Dr. Krippner has also supervised a research program for Harlem preschool children at the New York Institute for Child Development. He is currently the president of the Association for Humanistic Psychology and vice-president for the Western Hemisphere of the International Association for Psychotronic Research. Dr. Krippner has written more than 200 articles, many of them dealing with altered states of consciousness. He is coauthor, with M. Ullman and A. Vaughan, of *Dream Telepathy: An Experimental Odyssey* (Macmillan) and coeditor, with Rubin, of *Galaxies of Life: The Human Aura in Acupuncture and Kirlian Photography* (Gordon & Breach).

W. E. Lambert (coauthor "A DMZ in the Language War") left Nova Scotia, Canada, to study in the United States and received a Ph.D. in psychology from the University of North Carolina in 1953. The next year he returned to Canada to teach and to do research at McGill University. Since 1964 he has been a professor of psychology at McGill. Dr. Lambert considers himself to be a social-experimental psychologist. He has conducted research on attitudes, socialization, the psychology of language, and bilingualism. He has written a social psychology text with his older brother, psychologist William Lambert, and his papers on linguistics have been published as *Language, Psychology and Culture: Essays by Wallace E. Lambert* (Stanford University Press).

Peter J. Lang ("Autonomic Control") is a professor of psychology at the University of Wisconsin and a National Institute of Mental Health career research scientist. Before joining the Wisconsin faculty, he taught psychology at the University of Pittsburgh. He received an M.A. in romance languages and a Ph.D. in psychology from the University of Buffalo. Dr. Lang is a consulting editor of *Psychophysiology*; he is also on the editorial boards of *Behavior Therapy* and *Behavior Therapy and Experimental Psychiatry*. Dr. Lang is a fellow of the American Association for the Advancement of Science and of the Division of Comparative and Physiological Psychology of the American Psychological Association. His research interests include psychophysiology, schizophrenia, and behavior modification.

Bibb Latané (coauthor, "When Will People Help in a Crisis?") took his Ph.D. in psychology at the University of Minnesota and then taught for six years in the Department of Social Psychology at Columbia University. He is now a professor of psychology and head of the social psychology program at Ohio State University. Dr. Latané's research efforts span the general area of social and emotional behavior. In the

course of his research, he has worked with such diverse subjects as psychopathic criminals, albino rats, Navy enlisted men, gerbils, sky divers, and college sophomores.

James B. Maas is an associate professor of psychology and director of the Center for Improvement of Undergraduate Education at Cornell University. He received his B.A. from Williams College and his M.A. and Ph.D. from Cornell. He is director of the Cornell Candid Camera Collection, which produces educational films based on the *Candid Camera* television program footage. He has also produced educational films and slides for introductory psychology courses. One of these films, *The Maze*, recently won an American Film Festival Award for outstanding educational documentary. In 1970 Dr. Maas received a Fulbright Senior Lectureship, which enabled him to teach at Uppsala University in Sweden. In 1972 he received the Clark Award for Distinguished Teaching at Cornell University. The American Psychological Association gave him the Distinguished Teaching Award for 1973 and he was elected president of the APA's Division on Teaching in the same year. Dr. Maas is currently working on a textbook, *The Frontiers of Psychological Inquiry*. His research focuses on the observation and evaluation of teaching, the production and evaluation of multi-media educational materials, and research on psychophysical variables influencing the nature of sleep and dreams.

Brendan A. Maher ("The Shattered Language of Schizophrenia") was born in England and did his undergraduate work at the University of Manchester. A Fulbright Scholarship took him to Ohio State University, where he received his Ph.D. in 1954. After serving briefly as a psychologist at Her Majesty's Prison in Wakefield, England, Dr. Maher returned to the United States. He has taught at Northwestern University, Louisiana State University, Harvard University, the University of Wisconsin, and Brandeis University. He is currently a professor of psychology and chairman of the Department of Psychology at Harvard. Dr. Maher is the author of *Principles of Psychopathology* (McGraw-Hill) and *Introduction to Research in Psychopathology* (McGraw-Hill) and has published a selection of the writings of the late George Kelly. He is the editor of *Progress in Experimental Personality Research* (Academic Press).

William J. McGuire ("A Vaccine for Brainwash") received his Ph.D. from Yale University in 1954. Since then he has taught at Yale, the University of Illinois, Columbia University, and the University of California, San Diego. After taking a leave at the London School of Economics, he rejoined the Yale faculty as chairman and professor of psychology. Dr. McGuire was a Fulbright Scholar in 1950–1951 at Louvain University in Belgium. He won the 1963 Socio-Psychological Prize awarded by the American Association for the Advancement of Science and delivered the Hovland Memorial Lecture at Yale in 1964. His professional interests include persuasion, selective perception, cognitive structure, and the psychology of history. Dr. McGuire is the author of more than forty articles and was editor of the *Journal of Personality and Social Psychology* from 1967 to 1970.

Roger W. McIntire ("Spare the Rod, Use Behavior Mod") received his Ph.D. from Louisiana State University in 1962. He is an associate professor of psychology at the University of Maryland and is active in parent-counseling programs. His work includes individual therapeutic strategies for, as well as formal research on, the behavior problems of children in

schools and those of adults in institutions. Dr. McIntire is the author of *For Love of Children: Behavioral Psychology for Parents* (CRM Books).

Frank B. McMahon Jr. ("Personality Testing—A Smoke Screen Against Logic") is a professor of psychology at Southern Illinois University, Edwardsville, where he was nominated for the teacher of the year award in 1972. Dr. McMahon worked for four years as a therapist and counselor at Washington University Counseling Center, and he received his Ph.D. in clinical psychology from Washington in 1965. He then became a counselor and psychology teacher for the St. Louis Junior College District, where he was named teacher of the year in 1965. Dr. McMahon is the author of *Psychology: The Hybrid Science* (Prentice-Hall) and *Psychology: Perspectives on the Hybrid Science* (Prentice-Hall). He is currently writing textbooks on abnormal psychology and personality.

Julian Meltzoff (coauthor, "It Works") was graduated from the City College of New York, received an M.Litt. from the University of Pittsburgh, and, after a semester at the Université de Nancy in France, obtained a Ph.D. from the University of Pennsylvania. Since 1954 he has been chief of the psychology section of the Veterans Administration Outpatient Clinic in Brooklyn, where he designed and introduced the concept of the Day Treatment Center. The program, a form of milieu therapy for outpatients of mental hospitals, has been adopted by some thirty to forty Veterans Administration Clinics throughout the United States. Dr. Meltzoff, with R. L. Blumenthal, reports on the success of the program in *The Day Treatment Center: Principles, Application and Evaluation* (Charles C. Thomas). He has also coauthored, with M. Kornreich, *Research in Psychotherapy* (Adline-Atherton).

Ronald Melzack ("How Acupuncture Works: A Sophisticated Western Theory Takes the Mystery Out") received his B.S., M.S., and Ph.D. degrees from McGill University in Montreal. D. O. Hebb was adviser for his 1954 doctoral dissertation on pain perception; this study indicated that raising dogs in a sheltered, restricted environment could dramatically reduce their reactions to ordinarily painful stimuli. At the Massachusetts Institute of Technology Dr. Melzack met Patrick D. Wall, with whom he formulated the gate-control theory of pain. He returned to McGill, where he is now a professor of psychology, in 1963. Dr. Melzack has published more than sixty journal articles, most of them on pain or on early experience, and he has written a book, *Pain: Revolution in Theory and Treatment* (Basic Books), which describes recent advances in pain research. His interest in Eskimo legends led him to write two children's books, *The Day Tuk Became a Hunter and Other Eskimo Stories* (Dodd, Mead) and *Raven: Creator of the World* (Little, Brown).

Stanley Milgram ("The Small-World Problem") is now a professor at the Graduate Center of the City University of New York. In 1960 he received his Ph.D. in social psychology from Harvard University. After spending three years at Yale University as an assistant professor of psychology, Dr. Milgram returned to Harvard, where he taught experimental social psychology. His publications have been translated into French, German, and Italian, and in 1964 he was awarded a prize for research in social psychology by the American Association for the Advancement of Science. In 1972 he was awarded a Guggenheim Fellowship and a silver medal (documentaries) at the International Film and Television Festival of New York for his collaborative work in the film *The City and the Self*.

George A. Miller ("On Turning Psychology Over to the Unwashed") received a B.A. in speech from the University of Alabama, then began work in voice-communication systems. After the war, he enrolled at Harvard University and received his Ph.D. in psychology in 1946. He has taught at Harvard and at the Massachusetts Institute of Technology, and he served as chairman of Harvard's psychology department from 1964 to 1968. He is now a professor of psychology at Rockefeller University. Dr. Miller has received the American Psychological Association's award for distinguished scientific contribution and is a past president of the APA. His work with Noam Chomsky on a mathematical analysis of language and psychology became part of the *Handbook of Mathematical Psychology, Vol. II* (Wiley). In addition, Dr. Miller is the author of a number of articles and books, including *Language and Communication* (McGraw-Hill); *Psychology: The Science of Mental Life* (Harper & Row), with R. Buckhout; *Mathematics and Psychology* (Wiley); and *Psychology of Communication* (Penguin Books).

Ashley Montagu ("Chromosomes and Crime"), noted anthropologist and social biologist, was born in England and came to the United States in 1930. He received his Ph.D. from Columbia University in 1937. He has written extensively on race, genetics, and human evolution, and he was responsible for drafting the UNESCO statement on race. Among his forty-five books are *Human Heredity* (World Publishing) and *Natural Superiority of Women* (Macmillan). Dr. Montagu's hobbies are gardening and collecting rare books—in particular private press books, books on the history of science and medicine, and first editions of selected nineteenth- and twentieth-century authors.

Gardner Murphy ("Parapsychology: New Neighbor or Unwelcome Guest") received his doctorate from Columbia University in 1923 and taught psychology there until 1940, when he became chairman of the Department of Psychology at the City College of New York. While at CCNY, he published his chief systematic work, *Personality: A Biosocial Approach to Origins and Structure* (Basic Books). Dr. Murphy is a past president of the American Psychological Association. At the invitation of the Indian government, he participated in a 1950 UNESCO project directed at reducing social tensions in India, particularly those between Hindus and Muslims. He is now retired from a teaching position at George Washington University, and he spends time on writing connected with his earlier research at the Menninger Foundation. There he held the Henry March Pfeiffer Research-Training Chair in Psychiatry and was director of research from 1952 to 1967. Dr. Murphy oversees much of the parapsychological experimentation conducted by the American Society of Psychical Research, of which he was president from 1961 to 1971.

David E. Orlinsky (coauthor, "Inside Psychotherapy") is a staff therapist at the Katharine Wright Mental Health Clinic in Chicago, where the research project described in his article was conducted. Dr. Orlinsky also serves as senior research associate at the Institute for Juvenile Research in Chicago and teaches at the University of Chicago, where he obtained his bachelor's degree and his doctorate. He is now an assistant professor of social science.

Karen Rabkin (coauthor, "Children of the Kibbutz") received her B.S. in education from the State University of New York. After teaching emotionally disturbed and slum children, she studied anthropology at the University of Washington under Melford Spiro. She has been continuing her anthropological studies at Hebrew Union College in Jerusalem.

Leslie Y. Rabkin (coauthor, "Children of the Kibbutz") and Karen Rabkin are preparing a study of child personality development based on their eighteen-month stay at a kibbutz. Dr. Rabkin received a B.A. in dramatic literature and history from Columbia University and earned his Ph.D. in psychology from the University of Rochester. He has held grants from the National Institute of Mental Health for his work in Israel.

Irvin Rock ("Perceptual Adaptation") is a professor at the Institute for Cognitive Studies at Rutgers University. After completing his B.S. and M.A. degrees at the City College of New York, he received his Ph.D. from the New School for Social Research. Dr. Rock has taught at CCNY, Kansas State University, and Yeshiva University.

Milton Rokeach ("Persuasion That Persists") is a professor of sociology and psychology at Washington State University. He received an M.A. degree from Brooklyn College, served in the U.S. Army as an aviation psychologist, and then received his Ph.D. (1947) from the University of California, Berkeley. As a professor of psychology at Michigan State University, he was a fellow at the Center for Advanced Study in the Behavioral Sciences in 1961 and received the Michigan State Distinguished Faculty Award in 1968. In 1970 he went to teach at the University of Western Ontario. As a cultural exchange fellow for the National Academy of Sciences, Dr. Rokeach worked for two months in his native Poland. He is a former president of the Society for the Psychological Study of Social Issues and a fellow of the American Association for the Advancement of Science. Dr. Rokeach has recently written *The Nature of Human Values* (Free Press), which describes his work on the theory and measurement of values, particularly American values.

B. G. Rosenberg ("Psychology Through the Looking Glass") is a social psychologist whose interests center on personality and developmental psychology. He took B.A., M.A., and Ph.D. degrees, the latter in personality theory, at the University of California, Berkeley. He has taught at Southern Methodist University, the University of Alabama, Berkeley, and Bowling Green State University. He is now a visiting professor at Berkeley. Dr. Rosenberg is the author of sixty-five articles and three books. His books are widely used in personality and developmental psychology courses, as well as in courses on the psychology of women. At present Dr. Rosenberg is in the midst of a developmental psychology textbook and is finishing a new book, *One Half the Human Experience: The Psychology of Femininity*, with J. Hyde. His current research deals with the effects of a mother's personality on her infant, personality development and fertility rates, and longitudinal studies of children's fantasies and adult leisure activities.

Robert Rosenthal ("Self-Fulfilling Prophecy") is a professor of social psychology at Harvard University. He left Germany, where he was born, in 1938 and received his Ph.D. from the University of California, Los Angeles, in 1956. In 1960 he was awarded the Socio-Psychological Prize (with Kermit Fode) by the American Association for the Advancement of Science for research on experimenter expectancy effects. In 1967 he received (with Lenore Jacobson) the Cattell Fund Award from the American Psychological Association for work on teacher expectancy effects in the classroom. Dr. Rosenthal has written many articles and several books, among them *Pygmalion in the Classroom: Teacher Expectation and Pupil's Intellectual Development* (Holt, Rinehart & Winston), with L. Jacobson. With R. Rosnow, he edited *Artifact in Behavioral Research* (Academic Press). Dr. Rosenthal's current research interests include methods to control experimenter effects, differences in the responses of volunteers and nonvolunteers in behavioral research, nonverbal communication, and expectancy effects in everyday life.

Ralph L. Rosnow ("When He Lends a Helping Hand, Bite It") received a Ph.D. in social psychology from American University in 1962. He taught for four years at Boston University and is currently a visiting professor at the London School of Economics, although his principal affiliation remains with Temple University. He is coeditor, with E. J. Robinson, of *Experiments in Persuasion* (Academic Press) and, with R. Rosenthal, of *Artifact in Behavioral Research* (Academic Press). He is coauthor, with R. E. Lana, of *Introduction to Contemporary Psychology* (Holt, Rinehart & Winston) and is preparing, with R. Rosenthal, *The Volunteer Subject*. Dr. Rosnow has also published a number of articles on methodological problems. He is now doing research on the mediation of artifacts in human behavioral research and on the social psychology of rumors and gossip.

Julian B. Rotter ("External Control and Internal Control") received a Ph.D. from Indiana University in 1941. Dr. Rotter practiced clinical psychology at Norwich State Hospital in Ohio and then became a U.S. Army aviation psychologist. After the war he joined the Ohio State University faculty and directed the psychological clinic there. In 1963 he moved to his present position as a professor of psychology and director of the clinical-psychology training program at the University of Connecticut. Dr. Rotter now concentrates on psychological theory and research that has included studies on interpersonal trust. He has recently published, with J. Chance and E. J. Phares, *Applications of Social Learning Theory of Personality* (Holt, Rinehart & Winston).

Zick Rubin ("Jokers Wild in the Lab") received a Ph.D. from the University of Michigan in 1969. He is now a lecturer in social psychology at Harvard University. Dr. Rubin's central research interest is romantic love, which he explores through survey and laboratory studies of dating couples. His initial study of love won the 1969 Socio-Psychological Prize of the American Association for the Advancement of Science. He has written a book, *Liking and Loving* (Holt, Rinehart & Winston).

Floyd L. Ruch ("Personality: Public or Private") is founder and president of Psychological Services, Inc. He is also a professor emeritus of psychology at the University of Southern California. A pioneer in the field of aptitude and temperament testing, he developed the first "lie detector" for a personality test. Dr. Ruch is a past president of both the California State Psychological Association and the Western Psychological Association, a past president of the Business and Industrial Division of the American Psychological Association, and a two-time past president of the APA's Division on Teaching. He is best known to generations of college students as the author of *Psychology and Life* (Scott, Foresman), a widely used psychology textbook.

Martin E. P. Seligman (coauthor, "Biological Boundaries of Learning: The Sauce—Béarnaise Syndrome" and author, "For Helplessness: Can We Immunize the Weak?") is an associate professor in the Department of Psychology at the University of Pennsylvania. He received his B.A. in philosophy *summa cum laude* from Princeton University in 1964 and his Ph.D. from the University of Pennsylvania in 1967. Dr. Seligman's major research interests are motivation, learning, and psychopathology. He has written about forty articles on the effects of uncontrollable and unpredictable trauma, depression, fears, and phobias, on the nature/nurture question, and on the conditioning of drinking. He is the coauthor, with J. L. Hager, of *Biological Boundaries of*

Learning (Appleton-Century-Crofts) and the author of *Helplessness* (W.H. Freeman).

Everett L. Shostrom ("Group Therapy: Let the Buyer Beware") received his Ph.D. from Stanford University and a diploma in clinical psychology from the American Board of Professional Psychology. He has taught at Stanford University, Oregon State University, and Pepperdine College. He is currently on the training staff of the Institute of Industrial Relations at the University of California, Los Angeles, and is a professor of clinical psychology at the United States International University in San Diego. Dr. Shostrom recently was the recipient of the PSI Award for distinguished achievement in professional psychology. He has authored or coauthored seven books, many of which are published in foreign languages, including *Man, the Manipulator: The Inner Journey from Manipulation to Actualization* (Abingdon Press). He is the author of three tests: the Personal Orientation Inventory, the only published test of self-actualization; the Caring Relationship Inventory; and the Pair Attraction Inventory. He is also the producer and director of many psychological films. Currently he is the director of the Institute of Therapeutic Psychology in Santa Ana, California, and president of Psychological Films.

James A. Simmons ("The Sonar Sight of Bats") carried out his research on echolocation under E. G. Wever at the Princeton Auditory Research Laboratories; experiments with bat sonar were the subject of his doctoral dissertation. Dr. Simmons did much of his undergraduate work in chemistry, and he hopes someday to study behavior from the point of view of chemical events in the central nervous system. Dr. Simmons is currently an assistant professor of psychology at Washington University in St. Louis. The National Science Foundation supports his research on bat sonar, which employs two computers to study in detail the properties of the bat's sonar receiver. He moved to St. Louis to work with Nobuo Suga, a neurophysiologist famous for his studies of the bat's auditory nervous system, and to be associated with the large community of scientists studying hearing at the Central Institute for the Deaf and at Washington University.

Charles F. Stromeyer III ("Eidetikers") was graduated from Dartmouth College, where he worked on figure after-effects under Gestalt psychologist Wolfgang Köhler. After receiving a Ph.D. from Harvard University,

Dr. Stromeyer spent a year a a postdoctoral fellow in Richard Held's laboratory at the Massachusetts Institute of Technology. He is presently at Stanford University as a postdoctoral fellow in the laboratory of Karl Pribram and is a member of the sensory- and perceptual-processes department at Bell Telephone Laboratories, where he does research on spatial-analyzing mechanisms in human vision with psychophysical techniques.

Thomas Szasz ("The Crime of Commitment") is a professor of psychiatry at the State University of New York Upstate Medical Center in Syracuse. He has also served as a visiting professor at the University of Wisconsin and at Marquette University, and he has lectured to professional and lay groups in the United States and many foreign countries. He obtained his M.D. degree from the University of Cincinnati. After that he worked as an intern, resident, and training-research fellow at several clinics and universities before earning a certificate from Chicago's Institute for Psychoanalysis. Dr. Szasz is the author of nine books, among them *The Myth of Mental Illness* (Harper & Row) and *Manufacture of Madness: A Comparative Study of the Inquisition and the Mental Health Movement* (Harper & Row). Due soon is his tenth book, *Ceremonial Chemistry* (Doubleday). He is a member of the board of consultants for *The Psychoanalytic Review* and of the editorial boards of several journals and magazines. Dr. Szasz has been associated with and has received awards for efforts in behalf of persons charged with mental illness, including the designation "Humanist of the Year" by the American Humanist Association in 1973.

G. Richard Tucker (coauthor, "A DMZ in the Language War") received a Ph.D. in psychology from McGill University, then became an associate professor of psychology there. His primary research interest is language acquisition and usage. Dr. Tucker has been an English-language consultant for the Ford Foundation in Southeast Asia and the Middle East and has been a visiting associate professor at the English Language Institute of The American University in Cairo.

Montague Ullman (coauthor, "ESP in the Night") received an M.D. from New York University in 1938. He trained in neurology, psychiatry, and psychoanalysis and was for twelve years a member of the psychoanalytic faculty of New York Medical College. He has headed the Maimonides Community Mental

Health Center, where in 1962 he established the first dream laboratory for the study of extrasensory communication and dreaming. He is now director of psychiatry at the Maimonides Medical Center, professor of psychiatry at Downstate Medical Center of the State University of New York, and a consultant in mental health at Skidmore College. Dr. Ullman is current president of the American Society for Psychical Research and a fellow of the American Association for the Advancement of Science. He has written extensively on the theoretical and clinical aspects of dreaming; among his recent books is *Dream Telepathy* (Macmillan), with S. Krippner and A. Vaughan.

Joachim F. Wohlwill ("The Mystery of the Prelogical Child") is a professor in the Division of Man-Environment Relations at Pennsylvania State University. He graduated from Harvard University and received his Ph.D. in 1957 from the University of California, Berkeley. Dr. Wohlwill has worked with Jean Piaget at the Institut Rousseau in Geneva; he has been a fellow of the Center for Advanced Study in the Behavioral Sciences and a research fellow at Educational Testing Service. From 1958 to 1970 he directed the Graduate Training Program in developmental psychology at Clark University, and his research on the development of perception and thinking in the child—including the work reported in this edition of *Readings in Psychology Today*—dates from this time. He has more recently become interested in the individual's response to the physical environment and in the effect that environment has on individual behavior.

Robert Zajonc ("Brainwash: Familiarity Breeds Comfort") came to the United States from Poland in 1948 and received a Ph.D. in psychology from the University of Michigan in 1955. He is now a professor of psychology, program director of the Research Center for Group Dynamics, and chairman of the social psychology program in the psychology department at Michigan. Dr. Zajonc's research on the effects of mere exposure was preceded by studies of the effects of the mere presence of others. His research has included humans, rats, chickens, pigeons, and cockroaches. Dr. Zajonc is a past associate editor of the *Journal of Abnormal and Social Psychology* and of the *Journal of Personality and Social Psychology*. He is the author of *Social Psychology: An Experimental Approach* (Brooks/Cole) and the editor of *Animal Social Psychology: A Reader of Experimental Studies* (Robert E. Kreiger).

bibliographies

PSYCHOLOGY: THE SCIENCE OF BEHAVIOR

On Turning Psychology Over to the Unwashed

Ashton-Warner, Sylvia. *Teacher.* New York: Simon and Schuster, 1963.

Bennett, C.C. *Community Psychology.* Boston: Boston University, 1966.

Davis, Kingsley. "The Perilous Promise of Behavioral Science," in *Research in the Service of Man: Biomedical Knowledge, Development, and Use.* Washington, D.C.: U.S. Government Printing Office, 1967, 23-32.

Hofstadter, Richard. *Social Darwinism in American Thought.* Rev. ed. New York: Braziller, 1959.

Kuhn, T. S. *The Structure of Scientific Revolutions.* Chicago: University of Chicago Press, 1962.

Ladd, E. C., Jr. "Professors and Political Petitions," *Science,* 163 (1969), 1425-1430.

McGregor, Douglas. *The Human Side of Enterprise.* New York: McGraw-Hill, 1960.

Sanford, F. H. "Creative Health and the Principle of Habeas Mentem," *American Psychologist,* 10 (1955), 829-835.

Varela, J. A. *Psychological Solutions to Social Problems: An Introduction to Social Technology.* New York: Academic Press, 1971.

White, R. W. "Motivation Reconsidered: The Concept of Competence," *Psychological Review,* 66 (1959), 297-333.

Zimbardo, P. G., and E. B. Ebbesen. *Influencing Attitudes and Changing Behavior.* Reading, Mass.: Addison-Wesley, 1969.

Psychology Through the Looking Glass

Baldwin, Alfred L. *Theories of Child Development.* New York: Wiley, 1967.

Bandura, Albert, and R. H. Walters. *Social Learning and Personality Development.* New York: Holt, Rinehart and Winston, 1963.

Cohen, Morris R., and Ernest Nagel. *Introduction to Logic and Scientific Method.* New York: Harcourt Brace, 1934.

Conant, James B. *On Understanding Science: A Historical Approach.* New Haven, Conn.: Yale University Press, 1947.

Goldstein, Kurt. *The Organism.* Boston: Beacon Press, 1963.

Kohlberg, Lawrence. "State and Sequence: The Cognitive-Developmental Approach to Socialization," in *Handbook of Socialization Theory and Research,* David A. Goslin (ed.). Chicago: Rand-McNally, 1969.

Maslow, Abraham H. *Toward a Psychology of Being.* 2nd ed. Princeton, N.J.: Van Nostrand, 1968.

Werner, Heinz. *The Comparative Psychology of Mental Development.* Rev. ed. New York: International Universities Press, 1966.

Psychology Can Now Kick the Science Habit

Bakan, David. "The Mystery-Mastery Complex in Contemporary Psychology," *American Psychologist,* 20, (1965), 186-191.

_____. "Behaviorism and American Urbanization," *Journal of the History of the Behavioral Sciences,* 2, 1 (1966), 5-28.

_____. "The Influence of Phrenology on American Psychology," *Journal of the History of the Behavioral Sciences,* 2, 3 (1966), 200-220.

_____. "The Test of Significance in Psychological Research," *Psychological Bulletin,* 66 (1966), 423-437.

_____. *On Method: Toward a Reconstruction of Psychological Investigation.* San Francisco: Jossey-Bass, 1967.

_____. "Psychology's Research Crisis," *Illinois Psychologist* (April-June 1967).

_____. "The Social Context of America Psychology." (Presidential Address to the Division of the History of Psychology, American Psychological Association Convention, September 1971).

Self-Fulfilling Prophecy

Beez, W. Victor. "Influence of Biased Psychological Reports on Teacher Behavior and Pupil Performance," *Proceedings of the 76th Annual Convention of the American Psychological Association,* 3 (1968), 605-606.

Burnham, J. Randolph, and Don M. Hartsough. *Effect of Experimenter's Expectancies (The "Rosenthal Effect") on Children's Ability to Learn to Swim.* Chicago: Midwestern Psychological Association, May 1968.

Pfungst, Oskar. *Clever Hans, The Horse of Mr. Von Osten.* C. L. Rahn (tr.). New York: Holt, Rinehart and Winston, 1965.

Rosenthal, Robert. *Experimenter Effects in Behavioral Research.* New York: Appleton-Century-Crofts, 1966.

_____. "Interpersonal Expectations," in *Artifact in Behavioral Research,* R. Rosenthal and R. L. Rosnow (eds.). New York: Academic Press, 1969, 181-277.

Rosenthal, Robert, and Lenore Jacobson. *Pygmalion in the Classroom: Teacher Expectation and Pupils' Intellectual Development.* New York: Holt, Rinehart and Winston, 1968.

When He Lends a Helping Hand, Bite It

Friedman, Neil. *The Social Nature of Psychological Research: The Psychological Experiment as a Social Interaction.* New York: Basic Books, 1967.

Rosenthal, Robert, and Ralph L. Rosnow (eds). *Artifact in Behavioral Research.* New York: Academic Press, 1969.

Rosnow, Ralph L. "Experimental Artifact Research," in *Encyclopedia of Education.* New York: Macmillan, in press.

Rosnow, Ralph L., and Robert Rosenthal. "Volunteer Effects in Behavioral Research," in *New Directions in Psychology IV.* New York: Holt, Rinehart and Winston, in press.

Schultz, Duane P. "The Human Subject in Psychological Research," *Psychological Bulletin,* 72 (1969), 214-228.

Jokers Wild in the Lab

Baumrind, Diana. "Some Thoughts on Ethics of Research: After Reading Milgram's 'Behavioral Study of Obedience,'" *American Psychologist,* 19 (1964), 421-423.

Kelman, Herbert C. "Human Use of Human Subjects: The Problem of Deception in Social Psychological Experiments, "*Psychological Bulletin,* 67 (1967), 1-11. Reprinted in Kelman, Herbert C. *A Time to Speak: On Human Values and Social Research.* San Francisco: Jossey-Bass, 1968.

McGuire, William J. "Some Impending Reorientations in Social Psychology: Some Thoughts Provoked by Kenneth Ring," *Journal of Experimental Social Psychology,* 3 (1967), 124-139.

Milgram, Stanley. "Issues in the Study of Obedience: A Reply to Baumrind," *American Psychologist*, 19 (1964), 848-852.

Ring, Kenneth. "Experimental Social Psychology: Some Sober Questions About Some Frivolous Values," *Journal of Experimental Social Psychology*, 3 (1967), 113-123.

BRAIN AND BEHAVIOR

ESB

Bishop, M. P., S. T. Elder, and R. G. Heath. "Intracranial Self-stimulation in Man," *Science*, 140 (1963), 394-396.

Delgado, José M. R. "Evolution of Physical Control of the Brain." (James Arthur lecture on the evolution of the human brain, American Museum of Natural History, 1965).

_____. "Brain Technology and Psychocivilization," in *Human Values and Advancing Technology*. Cameron P. Hall (ed.). New York: Friendship Press, 1967.

_____. *Physical Control of the Mind*. New York: Harper & Row, 1969.

Delgado, José M. R., V. Mark, *et al.* "Intracerebral Radio Stimulation and Recording in Completely Free Patients," *Journal of Nervous and Mental Disease*, 147 (1968), 329-340.

Delgado, José M. R., W. W. Roberts, and Neal E. Miller. "Learning Motivated by Electrical Stimulation of the Brain," *American Journal of Physiology*, 179 (1954), 587-593.

Heath, Robert G. "Electrical Self-stimulation of the Brain in Man," *American Journal of Psychiatry*, 120 (1963), 571-577.

Olds, James, "Hypothalmic Substrates of Reward," *Physiological Reviews*, 42 (1962), 554-604.

Brain Reward, ESB & Ecstasy

Deutsch, J. Anthony. *The Structural Basis of Behavior*. Chicago: University of Chicago Press, 1960.

_____. "Behavioral Measurement of the Neural Refractory Period and Its Application to Intracranial Self-stimulation," *Journal of Comparative and Physiological Psychology*, 58 (1964), 1-9.

Deutsch, J. Anthony, and Diana Deutsch. *Physiological Psychology*. Homewood, Ill.: Dorsey, 1966.

Deutsch, J. Anthony, and Leo DiCara. "Hunger and Extinction in Intracranial Self-stimulation," *Journal of Comparative and Physiological Psychology*, 63 (1967), 344-347.

Deutsch, J. Anthony, and C. I. Howarth. "Some Tests of a Theory of Intracranial Self-stimulation," *Psychological Review*, 70 (1963), 444-460.

Deutsch, J. A., D. W. Adams, and R. J. Metzner. "Choice of Intracranial Stimulation as a Function of Delay Between Stimulations and Strength of Competing Drive," *Journal of Comparative and Physiological Psychology*, 57 (1964), 23-34.

Gallistel, C. R. "Electrical Self-stimulation and Its Theoretical Implications," *Psychological Bulletin*, 61 (1964), 23-24.

_____. "Intracranial Stimulation and Natural Reward: Differential Effects of Trial Spacing," *Psychonomic Science*, 9, 3 (1967), 167, 168.

_____. "The Incentive of Brain-Stimulation Reward," *Journal of Comparative and Physiological Psychology*, 69 (1969), 713-721.

The Psychopharmacological Revolution

Barron, F., M. E. Jarvik, and S. Bunnell, Jr. "The Hallucinogenic Drugs," *Scientific American*, 210 (April 1964), 3-11.

Jarvik, M. E. "The Influence of Drugs Upon Memory," in *Animal Behaviour and Drug Action*, H. Steinberg, A. V. S. de Reuck, and J. Knight (eds.). London: Churchill, 1964.

_____. "Drugs Used in the Treatment of Psychiatric Disorders," in *The Pharmacological Basis of Therapeutics*, L. S. Goodman and A. Gilman (eds.). 3rd ed. New York: Macmillan, 1965, 159-214.

Steinberg, Hannah. "Drugs and Animal Behaviour," *British Medical Bulletin*, 20 (1964), 75-80.

Wikler, A. *The Relation of Psychiatry to Pharmacology*. Baltimore: Williams & Wilkins, 1957.

Conscious Control of Brain Waves

Bagghi, B. K., and M. A. Wenger. "Electrophysiological Correlates of Some Yogi Exercises," *EEG Clinical Neurophysiology*, Supplement No. 7 (1957), 132-149.

Kamiya, J. "Trained Self-Control of the EEG Alpha Rhythm," in *Altered States of Consciousness*, C. Tart (ed.). New York: Wiley, 1969.

Kasamatsu, A., and T. Hirai. "An Electroencephalographic Study on the Zen Meditation (Zazen)," *Folia Psychiatrica et Neurologica Japonica*, 20 (1966), 315-336.

Sterman, M., and W. Wrywicka. "EEG Correlates of Sleep: Evidences for Separate Forebrain Substrates," *Brain Research*, 6, Part 1 (1967), 143-163.

Stoyva, J., and J. Kamiya. "Electrophysiological Studies of Dreaming as the Prototype of a New Strategy in the Study of Consciousness," *Psychological Review*, 75 (1968), 192-205.

Autonomic Control

Lang, Peter J. "Fear Reduction and Fear Behavior: Problems in Treating a Construct," in *Research in Psychotherapy*, John M. Shlien, *et al.* (eds.). Washington, D.C.: American Psychological Association, 1968, Vol. 3.

_____. "The Application of Psychophysiological Methods to the Study of Psychotherapy and Behavior Modification," in *Handbook of Psychotherapy and Behavior Change*, A. E. Bergin and S. L. Garfield (eds.). New York: Wiley, 1971.

Lang, Peter J., and Barbara G. Melamed. "Case Report: Avoidance Conditioning Therapy of an Infant With Chronic Ruminative Vomiting," *Journal of Abnormal Psychology*, 74 (1969), 1-8.

Miller, Neal E. "Learning of Visceral and Glandular Responses," *Science*, 163 (1969), 434-445.

Rosenfield, J. P., A. P. Rudeil, and S. S. Fox. "Operant Control of Neural Events in Humans," *Science*, 165 (1969), 821-823.

Shapiro, David, Bernard Tursky, Elliot Gershon, and Melvin Stern. "Effects of Feedback and Reinforcement on the Control of Human Systolic Blood Pressure," *Science*, 163 (1969), 588-590.

The Matriculating Brain

Barber, Theodore X., *et. al.* (eds.). *Biofeedback and Selfcontrol*. Chicago: Aldine, 1971.

Benson, Herbert, *et al.* "Decreased Systolic Blood Pressure Through Operant Conditioning Techniques in Patients with Essential Hypertension," *Science*, 173 (1971), 740-742.

Chase, Michael H. (ed.). *Operant Control of Brain Activity; Perspectives in the Brain Sciences*. Los Angeles: Brain Information Service, UCLA, in press, Vol. 2.

DiCara, Leo V. "Learning in the Autonomic Nervous System," *Scientific American*, 222 (January 1970), 30-39.

_____. "Learning of Cardiovascular Responses: A Review and a Description of Physiological and Biochemical Consequences," *Transactions of the New York Academy of Sciences*, 33 (1971), 411-422.

Karlins, Marvin, and Lewis M. Andrews. *Biofeedback: Turning on the Power of Your Mind*. Philadelphia, Pa.: Lippincott, 1972.

Malmo, Robert B. "Emotions and Muscle Tension," *Psychology Today*, 3, 10 (March 1970), 64-67, 83.

Miller, Neal E. "Learning of Visceral and Glandular Responses," *Science*, 163 (1969), 434-445.

Miller, Neal E., *et al.* "Psychological Aspects of Hypertension: Learned Modifications of Autonomic Functions: A Review and Some New Data," *Circulation Research*, 27, Supplement 1 (July 1970), 3-11.

Rosenfeld, Joel P., Alan P. Rudell, and Stephen S. Fox. "Operant Control of Neural Events in Humans," *Science*, 165 (1969), 821-823.

Schwartz, Gary E. "Voluntary Control of Human Cardiovascular Integration and Differentiation Through Feedback and Reward," *Science*, 175 (1972), 90-93.

Shearn, Donald W. "Operant Conditioning of Heart Rate," *Science*, 137 (1962), 530-531.

Morpheus Descending

Berger, Ralph J. "Oculomotor Control: A Possible Function of REM Sleep," *Psychological Review*, 76 (1969), 144-164.

Clemente, Carmine D. (ed.). "Physiological Correlates of Dreaming," *Experimental Neurology*, Supplement 4 (1967).

Hartmann, Ernest. *The Biology of Dreaming*. Springfield, Ill.: C. C. Thomas, 1967.

Kleitman, Nathaniel. *Sleep and Wakefulness*. Rev. ed. Chicago: University of Chicago Press, 1963.

Oswald, Ian. *Sleeping and Waking: Physiology and Psychology*. New York: American Elsevier, 1962.

ESP in the Night

Bleksley, A. E. H. "An Experiment on Long-Distance ESP During Sleep," *Journal of Parapsychology*, 27 (1963), 1-15.

Freud, Sigmund, and James Strachey (eds.). *New Introductory Lectures on Psychoanalysis*. New York: Norton, 1965, Chapter 2.

Globus, G., *et al.* "An Appraisal of Telepathic Communication in Dreams," *Psychophysiology*, 4 (January 1968), 365.

Hall, Calvin S. "An Experiment on Telepathic Influence in Dreams," *Zeitschrift für Parapsychologie und Grenzegebiete der Psychologie*, 10 (1967), 18-47.

Murphy, Gardner. "Trends in the Study of Extrasensory Perception," *American Psychologist*, 13 (1958), 69-76.

Ullman, Montague, and Stanley Krippner. *Dream Studies and Telepathy: An Experimental Approach*. Durham, N.C.: Parapsychology Foundation, 1970.

Who Believes in Hypnosis?

Barber, Theodore X. *Hypnosis: A Scientific Approach*. Princeton, N.J.: Van Nostrand, 1969.

_____. *LSD, Marihuana, Yoga, and Hypnosis*. Chicago: Aldine, 1970.

Chavis, John F. "Hypnosis Reconceptualized: An Overview of Barber's Theoretical and Empirical Work," *Psychological Reports*, 22 (April 1968), 587-608.

Dalal, Abdulhuseins. "An Empirical Approach to Hypnosis," *Archives of General Psychiatry*, 15 (August 1966), 151-157.

Gordon, Jesse E. *Handbook of Clinical and Experimental Hypnosis*. New York: Macmillan, 1967.

Meeker, William B., and Theodore X. Barber. "Toward an Explanation of Stage Hypnosis," *Journal of Abnormal Psychology*, 77 (1971), 61-70.

Moss, C. Scott. *Hypnosis in Perspective*. New York: Macmillan, 1965.

Parapsychology: New Neighbor or Unwelcome Guest

Margenau, Henry. "ESP in the Framework of Modern Science," *Journal of the American Society for Psychical Research*, 60 (1966), 214-228.

Moss, Thelma, and J. A. Gengerelli. "Telepathy and Emotional Stimuli: A Controlled Experiment," *Journal of Abnormal Psychology*, 72 (1967), 341-348.

Murphy, Gardner. *Challenge of Psychical Research.* New York: Harper & Row, 1961.

Schmeidler, Gertrude. "The Influence of Belief and Disbelief in ESP Upon Individual Scoring Level," *Journal of Experimental Psychology*, 36 (1946), 271-276.

Schmeidler, G. R., and R. A. McConnell. *ESP and Personality Patterns.* New Haven, Conn.: Yale University Press, 1958.

Ullman, Montague. "An Experimental Approach to Dreams and Telepathy," *Archives of General Psychiatry*, 14 (1966), 605-613.

Big Brother and Psychotechnology

Fuller, Watson (ed.). *The Biological Revolution—Social Good or Social Evil?* Garden City, N. Y.: Doubleday, 1972.

Kittrie, Nicholas N. *The Right to Be Different: Deviance and Enforced Therapy.* Baltimore: Penguin, 1973.

Medvedev, Zhores A., and Roy A. Medvedev. *A Question of Madness.* New York: Random House, 1972.

Montagu, Ashley (ed.). *Man and Aggression.* 2nd ed. New York: Oxford University Press, 1973.

Ryan, William. *Blaming the Victim.* New York: Random House, 1972.

Wertham, Fredric. *A Sign for Cain: An Exploration of Human Violence.* New York: Paperback Library, 1969.

THE SENSORY WORLD

The Mind's Eye

Boring, Edwin G. *A History of Experimental Psychology.* 2nd ed. New York: Appleton-Century-Crofts, 1950.

_____. "A History of Introspection," in *Psychologist at Large.* New York: Basic Books, 1961.

Humphrey, George. *Thinking* (Science Editions series). New York: Wiley, 1963.

James, William. *Principles of Psychology.* New York: Dover, 1950.

Solomon, Philip, Philip Kubzansky, *et al.* (eds.). *Sensory Deprivation.* Cambridge, Mass.: Harvard University Press, 1961.

Perceptual Adaptation

Gibson, J. J. "Adaptation, Aftereffect, and Contrast in the Perception of Curved Lines," *Journal of Experimental Psychology*, 16 (1933), 1-31.

Held, Richard. "Plasticity in Sensory-Motor Systems," *Scientific American*, 213 (November 1965), 84-94.

Kohler, Ivo. "The Formation and Transformation of the Perceptual World," *Psychological Issues*, 3, 4 (1964), 1-173.

Kohler, Wolfgang. *Gestalt Psychology.* New York: Liveright, 1947.

Rock, Irvin, and Charles Harris. "Vision and Touch," *Scientific American*, 216 (May 1967), 96-104.

Stratton, George. "Vision Without Inversion of the Retinal Image," *Psychological Review*, 4 (1897), 341-360, 463-481.

Eidetikers

Haber, Ralph Norman. "Eidetic Images," *Scientific American*, 220 (April 1969), 36-44.

Jaensch, E. R. *Eidetic Imagery and Typological Methods of Investigation.* New York: Harcourt Brace, 1930.

Julesz, Bela. "Experiment in Perception," *Psychology Today*, 2, 2 (July 1968), 16-23.

Land, Edwin H. "Experiments in Color Vision," *Scientific American*, 200 (May 1959), 38, 84-94.

Luria, A. R. *The Mind of a Mnemonist.* New York: Basic Books, 1968.

Stratton, George M. "The Mnemonic Feat of the 'Shass Pollak,' " *Psychological Review*, 24 (1917), 244-247.

Stromeyer, C. F., and J. Psotka. "The Detailed Texture of Eidetic Images," *Nature*, 225 (January 24, 1970), 346-349.

How Acupuncture Works: A Sophisticated Western Theory Takes the Mystery Out

Beecher, Henry K. *Measurement of Subjective Responses: Quantitative Effects of Drugs.* Fair Lawn, N.J.: Oxford University, 1959.

Brown, P. E. "Use of Acupuncture in Major Surgery," *Lancet*, 1 for 1972 (June 17, 1972), 1328-1330.

Dimond, E. G. "Acupuncture Anesthesia," *Journal of the American Medical Association*, 218 (1971), 1558-1563.

LeCron, Leslie M. *Experimental Hypnotism.* Englewood Cliffs, N.J.: Prentice-Hall, 1964.

Mayer, David J., *et al.* "Analgesia from Electrical Stimulation in the Brainstem of the Rat," *Science*, 174 (1971), 1351-1354.

Melzack, Ronald. "Phantom Limb Pain: Implications for Treatment of Pathological Pain," *Anesthesiology*, 35 (1971), 409-419.

_____. *The Puzzle of Pain.* Baltimore: Penguin, 1973.

Melzack, Ronald, and P. D. Wall. "Pain Mechanisms: A New Theory," *Science*, 150 (1965), 971-979.

Nathan, P. W. "Reference of Sensation at the Spinal Level," *Journal of Neurology, Neurosurgery and Psychiatry*, 19 (1956), 88-100.

Travell, Janet, and Seymour H. Rinzler. "The Myofascial Genesis of Pain," *Postgraduate Medicine*, 11 (1952), 425-434.

_____. "Relief of Cardiac Pain by Local Block of Somatic Trigger Areas," *Proceedings of the Society For Experimental Biology and Medicine*, 63 (1946), 480-482.

Wall, P. D., and W. H. Sweet. "Temporary Abolition of Pain in Man," *Science*, 155 (1967), 108-109.

The Sonar Sight of Bats

Griffin, Donald. *Listening in the Dark.* New Haven, Conn.: Yale University Press, 1958.

Marler, Peter, and W. J. Hamilton. *Mechanisms of Animal Behavior.* New York: Wiley, 1966.

Simmons, James. "Echolocation: Auditory Cues for Range Perception by Bats," *Proceedings of the 76th Annual Convention of the American Psychological Association*, 3 (1968), 301-302.

Vincent, F. "Acoustic Signals for Auto-Information or Echolocation," in *Acoustic Behavior of Animals*, René Busnel (ed.). New York: American Elsevier, 1963.

LEARNING, MEMORY, AND LANGUAGE

Spare the Rod, Use Behavior Mod

Ayllon, Teodoro, and Nathan H. Azrin. *The Token Economy.* New York: Appleton-Century-Crofts, 1968.

McIntire, R. W. *For Love of Children: Behavioral Psychology for Parents.* Del Mar, Calif.: CRM Books, 1970.

Patterson, G. R., and M. E. Gullion. *Living with Children.* Madison, Wis.: Research Press, 1968.

Reese, Ellen P. *The Analysis of Human Operant Behavior.* Dubuque, Iowa: William C. Brown, 1967.

Smith, J. M., and D. E. P. Smith. *Child Management: A Program for Parents.* Ann Arbor, Mich.: Ann Arbor Publishers, 1966.

Whaley, D. L., and R. W. Malott. "Elementary Principles of Behavior," *Behaviordelia*, 1969.

Biological Boundaries of Learning: The Sauce-Béarnaise Syndrome

Breland, Keller, and Marian Breland. *Animal Behavior.* New York: Macmillan, 1966.

Manning, Aubrey. *An Introduction to Animal Behavior.* Reading, Mass.: Addison-Wesley, 1968.

Seligman, Martin E. P., and Joanne Hager (eds.). *The Biological Boundaries of Learning.* New York: Appleton-Century-Crofts, 1972.

For Helplessness: Can We Immunize The Weak?

Lefcourt, Herbert M. "Internal vs. External Control of Reinforcement: A Review," *Psychological Bulletin*, 65 (1966), 206-221.

Richter, Curt P. "On the Phenomenon of Sudden Death in Animals and Man," *Psychosomatic Medicine*, 19 (1967), 191-198.

Seligman, Martin. "Chronic Fear Produced by Unpredictable Electric Shock," *Journal of Comparative and Physiological Psychology*, 66 (1968), 402-411.

Seligman, Martin, and S. F. Maier. "Failure to Escape Traumatic Shock," *Journal of Experimental Psychology*, 74 (1967), 1-9.

Seligman, Martin, S. F. Maier, and James H. Geer. "Alleviation of Learned Helplessness in the Dog," *Journal of Experimental Psychology*, 73 (1968), 256-262.

Seligman, Martin, S. F. Maier, and R. L. Solomon. "Unpredictable and Uncontrollable Aversive Events," in *Aversive Conditioning and Learning*, F. R. Brush (ed.). New York: Academic Press, 1971.

The Computer as a Tutor

Atkinson, R. C. "Instruction in Initial Reading Under Computer Control: The Stanford Project," in *Education Technology Research Reports Series.* Englewood Cliffs, N.J.: Educational Technology Publications, 1971.

Atkinson, R. C., and D. N. Hansen. "Computer-Assisted Instructions in Initial Reading," *Reading Research Quarterly*, 2 (1966), 5-25.

Atkinson, R. C., and R. M. Shiffrin. "Human Memory: A Proposed System and Its Contract Processes," *The Psychology of Learning and Motivation: Advances in Research and Theory*, K. W. Spence and J. T. Spence (eds.). New York: Academic Press, 1968, Vol. 2.

Neural Basis of Memory

Asimov, Isaac. *The Human Brain: Its Capacities and Functions.* Boston: Houghton Mifflin, 1964.

Deutsch, J. A. *The Structural Basis of Behavior.* Chicago: University of Chicago Press, 1960.

Deutsch, J. A., and D. Deutsch. *Physiological Psychology.* Homewood, Ill.: Dorsey Press, 1966.

How to . . . Uh . . . Remember!

Bower, Gordon H. "Analysis of a Mnemonic Device," *American Scientist*, 58 (September/October 1970), 496-510.

_____. "Mental Imagery and Associative Learning," in *Cognition in Learning and Memory*, Lee W. Gregg (ed.). New York: Wiley, 1972.

Bower, Gordon H., and Michal C. Clark. "Narrative Stories as Mediators for Serial Learning," *Psychonomic Science*, 14, 4 (1969), 181, 182.

Bower, Gordon H., and Judith S. Reitman. "Mnemonic Elaboration in Multilist Learning," *Journal of Verbal Learning and Verbal Behavior*, 11 (August 1972), 478-485.

Bower, Gordon H., and David Winzenz. "Comparison of Associative Learning Strategies," *Psychonomic Science*, 20, 2 (1970), 119,120.

Paivio, Allan, "Mental Imagery in Associative Learning and Memory," *Psychological Review*, 76 (1969), 241-263.

Ross, John, and Kerry A. Lawrence. "Some Observations on Memory Artifice," *Psychonomic Science*, 13, 2 (1968), 107, 108.

Language and the Mind

Chomsky, N. *Aspects of the Theory of Syntax*. Cambridge, Mass.: M.I.T. Press, 1965.

————. *Cartesian Linguistics*. New York: Harper & Row, 1966.

Chomsky, N., and M. Halle. *Sound Pattern of English*. New York: Harper & Row, 1968.

Fodor, J., and T. Bever. "The Psychological Reality of Linguistic Segments," *Journal of Verbal Learning and Verbal Behavior*, 4 (1965), 414-420.

Fodor, J., and J. Katz (eds.). *Structure of Language: Readings in the Philosophy of Language*. Englewood Cliffs, N.J.: Prentice-Hall, 1964.

Katz, J. *The Philosophy of Language*. New York: Harper & Row, 1966.

Savin, H., and E. Perchonock. "Grammatical Structure and the Immediate Recall of English Sentences," *Journal of Verbal Learning and Verbal Behavior*, 4 (1965), 348-353.

A DMZ in the Language War

Bever, Thomas, J. A. Fodor, and William Weksel. "On the Acquisition of Syntax: A Critique of Contextual Generalization," *Psychological Review*, 72 (1965), 467-482.

Braine, M. D. S. "On Learning the Grammatical Order of Words," *Psychological Review*, 70 (1963), 323-348.

Brogden, W. J. "Sensory Preconditioning," *Journal of Experimental Psychology*, 25 (1939), 323-332.

Gardner, R. Allen, and Beatrice T. Gardner. "Teaching Sign Language to a Chimpanzee," *Science*, 165 (1969), 664-672.

Hebb, D. O. *Organization of Behavior*. New York: Wiley, 1949.

————. "Heredity and Environment in Mammalian Behavior," *British Journal of Animal Behavior*, 1, 2 (1953), 43-47.

Hebb, D. O., W. E. Lambert, and G. R. Tucker. "Language, Thought and Experience," *Modern Language Journal*, 55 (1971), 212-222.

Hubel, David H., and Torsten N. Wiesel. "Receptive Fields and Functional Architecture of Monkey Striate Cortex," *Journal of Physiology*, 195 (1968), 215-243.

Lambert, W. E. *Language, Psychology and Culture*. Stanford, Calif.: Stanford University, 1972.

Leeper, R. W. "A Study of a Neglected Portion of the Field of Learning—The Development of Sensory Organization," *Journal of Genetic Psychology*, 46 (1935), 41-75.

Lenneberg, Eric H. *Biological Foundations of Language*. New York: Wiley, 1967.

Smith, Frank, and George A. Miller (eds.). *The Genesis of Language*. Cambridge, Mass.: M.I.T. Press, 1968.

Tucker, G. R., and Alison D'Anglejan. "Language Learning Processes," in *Britannica Review of Foreign Language Education*, D. Lange (ed.). Chicago: Encyclopaedia Brittanica, Inc., 1971, 163-182, Vol. 3.

Tucker, G. R., W. E. Lambert, A. Rigault, and N. Segalowitz. "A Psychological Investigation of French Speakers' Skill with Grammatical Gender," *Journal of Verbal Learning and Verbal Behavior*, 7 (1968), 312-316.

PSYCHOLOGICAL DEVELOPMENT

The Mystery of the Prelogical Child

Flavell, J. H. *The Developmental Psychology of Jean Piaget*. Princeton, N.J.: Van Nostrand, 1963.

Hunt, Joseph McV. *Intelligence and Experience*. New York: Ronald Press, 1961.

Piaget, J. *The Child's Conception of Number*. New York: Norton, 1965.

Piaget, J., B. Inhelder, and A. Szaminska. *The Child's Conception of Geometry*. New York: Basic Books, 1960.

Sigel, I. E., and F. H. Hooper (eds.). *Logical Thinking in Children*. New York: Holt, Rinehart and Winston, 1968.

Wallace, J. G. *Concept Growth and the Education of the Child*. England and Wales: National Foundation for Educational Research, 1966.

Wohlwill, J. F. "The Place of Structured Experience in Early Cognitive Development," *Interchange*, 1, 2 (1970), 13-27.

The Mentally Retarded Child

Bijou, S. W. "Behavior Modification in the Mentally Retarded: Application of Operant Conditioning Principles," *Pediatric Clinics of North America*, 15 (1968), 969-987.

————. "Environment and Intelligence: A Behavioral Analysis," in *Contributions to Intelligence*, Robert Cancro (ed.). New York: Appleton-Century-Crofts, in press.

Bijou, S. W., and D. M. Baer. *Child Development*. Vols. I and II. New York: Appleton-Century-Crofts, 1961, 1965.

Davis, Kingsley. "Final Note on a Case of Extreme Isolation," *American Journal of Sociology*, 57 (1947), 432-457.

Dennis, Wayne, and Pergouchi Najarian. "Infant Development Under Environmental Handicap," *Psychological Monographs General and Applied*, 71, 7 (1957), 436.

Ferster, C. B. "Reinforcement and Punishment in the Control of Human Behavior by Social Agencies," *Psychiatric Research Reports*, 10 (1958), 101-118.

————. "Positive Reinforcement and Behavior Deficits of Autistic Children," *Child Development*, 32 (1961), 437-456.

Sayegh, Yvonne, and Wayne Dennis. "The Effect of Supplementary Experiences Upon the Behavioral Development of Infants in Institutions," *Child Development*, 36 (1965), 81-90.

Wolf, M. M., T. R. Risley, and H. L. Mees. "Application of Operant Conditioning Procedures to the Behavior Problems of an Autistic Child," *Behavior Research and Therapy*, 1 (1964), 305-312.

Zimmerman, D. W. "A Conceptual Approach to Some Problems in Mental Retardation," *Psychological Record*, 15 (1965), 175-183.

Up from Helplessness

Bruner, J. S. *Processes of Growth in Infancy*. Worcester, Mass.: Clark University Press and Barre Publishers, 1968.

Levi-Strauss, Claude. *Structural Anthropology*. New York: Basic Books, 1963.

McNeill, D. "The Development of Language," in *Carmichael's Manual of Child Psychology*, P. A. Mussen (ed.). 3rd ed. New York: Wiley, 1970.

Twitchell, T. E. "The Automatic Grasping Responses of Infants," *Journal of Neurophysiologia*, 3 (1965), 247-259.

The Child as a Moral Philosopher

Kohlberg, Lawrence. "The Development of Children's Orientations Toward A Moral Order: 1. Sequence in the Development of Moral Thought," *Vita Humana*, 6 (1963), 11-33 (b).

————. "Development of Moral Character and Ideology," in *Review of Child Development Research*, M. L. Hoffman, (ed.). New York: Russell Sage Foundation, 1964.

Wilson, John. *Equality*. Nashville, Tenn.: Hutchison, 1966.

The Many Faces of Response

Kagan, J. "Impulsive and Reflective Children: Significance of Conceptual Tempo," in *Learning and the Educational Process*, J. D. Krumboltz (ed.). Chicago: Rand McNally, 1965.

————. "Personality and the Learning Process," *Daedalus*, 94 (1965), 553-563.

————. "Personality, Behavior, and Temperament," in *Human Development*, Frank Falkner (ed.). Philadelphia: Saunders, 1966.

————. "On the Need for Relativism," *American Psychologist*, 22 (1967), 131-142.

Kagan, J., and R. B. McCall. "Stimulus-Schema Discrepancy and Attention in the Infant," *Journal of Experimental Child Psychology*, 5 (1967), 381-390.

Kagan, J., and H. A. Moss. *Birth to Maturity: A Study of Psychological Development*. New York: Wiley, 1962.

Kagan, J., B. A. Henker, A. Hen-Tov, J. Levine, and M. Lewis. "Infants' Differential Reactions to Familiar and Distorted Faces," *Child Development*, 37 (1966), 519-532.

The Young Monkeys

Harlow, H. F. "Love in Monkeys," *Scientific American*, 200 (June 1959), 68-74.

Harlow, H. F., and M. K. Harlow. "Learning to Love," *American Scientist*, 54 (1966), 244-272.

Harlow, M. K., and H. F. Harlow. "Affection in Primates," *Discovery*, 27 (1966), 11-17.

Harlow, H. F., M. K. Harlow, R. O. Dodsworth, and G. L. Arling. "Maternal Behavior of Rhesus Monkeys Deprived of Mothering and Peer Association in Infancy," *Proceedings of the American Philosophical Society*, 110 (1967), 329-335.

Harlow, H. F., W. Danforth Joslyn, M. G. Senko, and A. Dopp. "Behavioral Aspects of Reproduction in Primates," *Journal of Animal Science*, 25 (1966), 49-67.

Check One: ☐ Male ☐ Female

Bennett, E. M., and L. R. Cohen. "Men and Women: Personality Patterns and Contrast," *Genetic Psychology Monographs*, 60 (1959), 101-153.

Kagan, Jerome, and Howard Moss. *Birth to Maturity*. New York: Wiley, 1962.

Kagan, Jerome, Barbara Hosken, and Sara Watson. "Child's Symbolic Conceptualization of Parents," *Child Development*, 32 (1961), 625-636.

Kagan, Jerome. "The Child's Sex Role Classification of School Objects," *Child Development*, 35 (1964), 1051-1056.

Kagan, Jerome, Irving L. Janis, George Mahl, and Robert Holt (eds.). *Personality: Dynamics, Development and Assessment*. New York: Harcourt Brace Jovanovich, 1969.

Osgood, C. E. "The Cross-Cultural Generality of Visual-Verbal Synesthetic Tendencies," *Behavioral Science*, 5 (1960), 146-169.

Children of the Kibbutz

Darin-Drabkin, Haim. *The Other Society.* New York: Harcourt, Brace & World, 1963.

Neubauer, Peter B. (ed.). *Children in Collectives.* Springfield, Ill.: Thomas, 1965.

Rabin, A. I. *Growing Up in the Kibbutz.* New York: Springer, 1965.

Rabkin, L. Y. "A Very Special Education: The Israeli Kibbutz," *Journal of Special Education,* 1 (1968), 251-261.

Spiro, Melford. *Kibbutz: Venture in Utopia.* New York: Schocken, 1963.

_____. *Children of the Kibbutz: A Study in Child Training and Personality.* New York: Schocken, 1965.

Russian Nursery Schools

Bronfenbrenner, Urie. *Children of Two Worlds.* New York: Russell Sage, 1969.

Cole, Michael, and Irving Maltzman (eds.). *A Handbook of Contemporary Soviet Psychology.* New York: Basic Books, 1968.

Usovoi, A. P., and N. P. Sakulinoi (eds.). *Teoriia I Praktika Sensornovov Vocpitania V Detskom Sadu [The Theory and Practice of Sensory Training in Nursery School].* Moscow: Proveshcheniia, 1965.

Zaluzhskaia, M. V. (ed.). "Programma Vospitaniia V Detskom Sadu [The Program of Education in Nursery School]," *Gosidarstvennoe Uchebno-Pedagogicheskoe Izdatel 'stvo Ministerstua Prosveshcheniia [Ministry of Education, RSFSR].* Moscow, 1962.

INDIVIDUAL DIFFERENCES AND PERSONALITY

Is Phrenology Foolish?

Bakan, D. "The Influence of Phrenology on American Psychology," *Journal of the History of the Behavioral Sciences,* 2 (1966), 200-220.

Boring, E. G. *A History of Experimental Psychology.* New York: Appleton-Century-Crofts, 1950, 50-60.

Curti, M. "Human Nature in American Thought: The Age of Reason and Morality, 1750-1860," *Political Science Quarterly,* 48 (1953), 354-375.

Davis, J. *Phrenology, Fad and Science: A 19th Century American Crusade.* New Haven, Conn.: Yale University Press, 1955.

Spurzheim, J. K. *Phrenology.* Philadelphia: Lippincott, 1908.

Are I.Q. Tests Intelligent?

Anastasi, A. "Culture Fair Testing," *Educational Horizons,* 43 (1964), 26-30.

Cattell, I. R. "A Culture Free Intelligence Test," *Journal of Educational Psychology,* 31 (1940), 161-179.

Cattell, R. "Some Theoretical Issues in Adult Intelligence Testing," *Psychological Bulletin,* 38 (1941), 592.

_____. "Theory of Fluid and Crystallized Intelligence: A Critical Experiment," *Journal of Educational Psychology,* 54 (1963), 1-22.

_____. *Abilities: Their Structure, Growth and Action.* Boston: Houghton Mifflin, 1971.

Eells, K., A. Davis, R. J. Havighurst, *et al. Intelligence and Cultural Differences.* Chicago: University of Chicago Press, 1951.

Feingold, S., R. Cattell, and S. Sarason. "A Culture Free Intelligence Test, II. Evaluation of Culture Influence on Test Performance," *Journal of Educational Psychology,* 32 (1941), 81-100.

Hunt, J. McV. *Intelligence and Experience.* New York: Ronald Press, 1961.

McArthur, R. T., and W. B. Elley. The Reduction of Socio-Economic Bias in Intelligence Testing," *British Journal of Educational Psychology,* 33 (1963), 107-119.

Spearman, C. *The Abilities of Man.* New York: Macmillan, 1932.

IQ: The Conspiracy

Anastasi, Anne. *Individual Differences.* New York: Wiley, 1965.

Atlantic, "Answers to Herrnstein," 228 (September 1971), 43-52.

Bloom, B. S. "The Jensen Article" (letter to the editor), *Harvard Educational Review,* 39, (Spring 1969).

Burt, Cyril. "The Genetic Determination of Differences in Intelligence: A Study of Monozygotic Twins Reared Together and Apart," *British Journal of Psychology,* 57, 1 and 2 (1966), 137-153.

Christie, Richard, and John Garcia. "Subcultural Variation in Authoritarian Personality," *Journal of Abnormal and Social Psychology,* 46 (1951), 457-469.

Garcia, John, *et al.* "Biological Constraints on Conditioning," *Classical Conditioning Two: Current Research and Theory,* A. H. Black and W. F. Prokasy (eds.). New York: Appleton-Century-Crofts, 1972.

Herrnstein, Richard. "I.Q.," *Atlantic,* 228 (September 1971), 53-58.

Jensen, Arthur R. "How Much Can We Boost IQ and Scholastic Achievement?" *Harvard Educational Review,* 39 (Winter 1969).

Kagan, Jerome S., J. McV. Hunt, James F. Crow, Carl Bereiter, David Elkind, Lee J. Cronbach, and William F. Brazziel. "How Much Can We Boost IQ and Scholastic Achievement? A Discussion," *Harvard Educational Review,* 39 (Spring 1969).

Lenontin, Richard C. "Race and Intelligence," *Bulletin of the Atomic Scientists,* 26, 3 (March 1970), 2-8.

Differences Are Not Deficits

Darlington, C. D. *The Evolution of Man and Society.* New York: Simon and Schuster, 1970.

Davis, Kingsley, and Wilbert E. Moore. "Some Principles of Stratification," in *The Logic of Social Hierarchies,* E. O. Laumann, *et al.* (eds.). Chicago: Markham, 1970.

Dobzhansky, Theodosius. *Genetic Diversity and Human Equality.* New York: Basic Books, 1973.

Eckland, Bruce K. "Genetics and Sociology: A Reconsideration," *American Sociological Review,* 32 (April 1967), 173-194.

Jencks, Christopher, *et al. Inequality.* New York: Basic Books, 1972.

Muller, Herbert. *Freedom in the Western World.* New York: Harper & Row, 1963.

Scarr-Salapatek, Sandra. "Unknowns in the I.Q. Equatioh," *Science,* 174 (1971), 1223-1228.

Personality: Public or Private

American Psychologist. "Special Issue on Testing and Public Policy," 20, 11 (November 1965), 857-1004.

Berdie, R. F. "The Ad Hoc Committee on Social Impact of Psychological Assessment," *American Psychologist,* 20 (1965), 143-146.

Gleser, G. G. "Projective Methodologies," *Annual Review of Psychology,* 14 (1963), 391-422.

Gross, M. L. *The Brain Watchers.* New York: Random House, 1962.

Ruch, F. L., and W. W. Ruch. "The K Factor as a (Validity) Suppressor Variable in Predicting Success in Selling," *Journal of Applied Psychology,* 51 (1967), 201-204.

Ruebhausen, O. M., and O. G. Brim. "Privacy and Behavioral Research," *American Psychologist,* 21 (1966), 423-437.

Ward, L. B. "Problems in Review: Putting Executives to the Test," *Harvard Business Review,* 38 (1960), 6.

Westin, A. F. *Privacy and Freedom.* New York: Atheneum, 1967.

Winkler, R. C., and T. W. Mathews. "How Employees Feel About Personality Tests," *Personnel Journal,* 46, 490-492.

Personality Testing—A Smoke Screen Against Logic

Anastasi, Anne. "Self-Report Inventories," in *Psychological Testing.* New York: Macmillan, 1961.

Anderson, G. L., and H. H. Anderson (eds.). *An Introduction to Projective Techniques.* Englewood Cliffs, N.J.: Prentice-Hall, 1951.

Cronbach, L. J. "General Problems in Personality Measurement," *Psychological Testing.* New York: Harper & Row, 1960.

Eysenck, H. J. "Can Personality Be Measured? " in *Sense and Nonsense in Psychology.* Baltimore: Penguin Books, 1964.

Forty-Eight Item Test, The. Los Angeles: Western Psychological Services, 1963.

Hall, Prentiss. *Psychology: The Hybrid.* New York: Science House, 1970.

McMahon, F. B. "A Contingent-Item Method for Constructing a Short Personality Questionnaire," *Journal of Applied Psychology* (1964), 197-200.

Miller, G. A. *Psychology: The Science of Mental Life.* New York: Harper & Row, 1962.

Test Results Are What You Think They Are

Chapman, Loren J. "Illusory Correlation in Observational Report," *Journal of Verbal Learning and Verbal Behavior,* 6 (1967), 151-155.

Chapman, Loren J., and Jean Chapman. "Genesis of Popular but Erroneous Psychodiagnostic Observations," *Journal of Abnormal Psychology,* 72 (1967), 193-204.

_____. "Illusory Correlation as an Obstacle to the Use of Valid Psycho-Diagnostic Signs," *Journal of Abnormal Psychology,* 74 (1969), 271-280.

Machover, Karen. *Personality Projection in Drawing of the Human Figure.* Springfield, Ill,: C. C. Thomas, 1962.

Sundberg, Norman D. "The Practice of Psychological Testing in Clinical Services in the United States," *American Psychologist,* 16 (1961), 79-83.

Wheeler, William M. "An Analysis of Rorschach Indices of Male Homosexuality," *Rorschach Research Exchange,* 13 (1949), 97-126.

External Control and Internal Control

Battle, Esther S., and Julian B. Rotter. "Children's Feelings of Personal Control as Related to Social Class and Ethnic Group," *Journal of Personality,* 31 (1963), 482-490.

Gore, Pearl Mayo, and Julian B. Rotter. "A Personality Correlate of Social Action," *Journal of Personality,* 31 (1963), 58-64.

Katz, Harvey A., and Julian B. Rotter. "Interpersonal Trust Scores of College Students and Their Parents," *Child Development,* 40 (1969), 657-661.

Jessor, Richard, *et al.* (eds.). *Society, Personality and Deviant Behavior: A Study of a Tri-Ethnic Community.* New York: Holt, Rinehart and Winston, 1968.

Phares, E. Jerry. "Changes in Expectancy in Skill and Chance Situations," *Dissertation Abstracts,* 16 (1956), 579, 580.

Rotter, Julian B. "Generalized Expectancies for Internal Versus External Control of Reinforcement," *Psychological Monographs: General and Applied,* 80, Whole No. 609 (1966), 1-28.

_____. "A New Scale for the Measurement of Interpersonal Trust," *Journal of Personality,* 35 (1967), 651-665.

Fail: Bright Women

Atkinson, J. W. (ed.). *Motives in Fantasy, Action, and Society: A Method of Assessment and Study.* Princeton, N.J.: Van Nostrand, 1958.

Atkinson, J. W., and N. T. Feather (eds.). *A Theory of Achievement Motivation.* New York: Wiley, 1966.

Farber, S. M., and R. H. L. Wilson (eds.). *The Potential of Woman.* New York: McGraw-Hill, 1963.

French, E. G., and G. S. Lesser. "Some Characteristics of the Achievement Motive in Women," *Journal of Abnormal and Social Psychology,* 68 (1964), 119-128.

Freud, Sigmund. "Femininity, Lecture XXXIII," in *New Introductory Lectures on Psychoanalysis.* New York: Norton, 1965.

Horner, M. S. *Sex Differences in Achievement Motivation and Performance in Competitive and Non-Competitive Situations"* (Unpublished Ph.D. dissertation, University of Michigan, 1968).

McClelland, D. C., J. W. Atkinson, R. A. Clark, and E. L. Lowell. *The Achievement Motive.* New York: Appleton-Century-Crofts, 1953.

Mead, Margaret. *Male and Female.* New York: Morrow, 1957.

Impulse, Aggression and the Gun

Berkowitz, Leonard. *Aggression: A Social-Psychological Analysis.* New York: McGraw-Hill, 1962.

——— (ed.). *Roots of Aggression: A Re-Examination of the Frustration-Aggression Hypothesis.* New York: Atherton, 1968.

Buss, A. H. *Psychology of Aggression.* New York: Wiley, 1961.

Clemente, C. D., and D. B. Lindsley (eds.). *Aggression and Defense.* Berkeley: University of California Press, 1967.

Masotti, L. H., and D. R. Bowen (eds.). *Riots and Rebellion: Civil Violence in the Urban Community.* Beverly Hills, Calif.: Sage, 1968.

DISORDERS AND THERAPY

The Autistic Child

Ferster, C.B. "Positive Reinforcement and Behavioral Deficits of Autistic Children," *Child Development,* 32 (1961), 437-456.

———. "Perspectives in Psychology: XXV, Transition from Animal Laboratory to Clinic," *The Psychological Record,* 17 (1967), 145-150.

———. "Arbitrary and Natural Reinforcement," *The Psychological Record,* 17 (1967), 341-347.

———. "Operant Reinforcement of Infantile Autism," in *An Evaluation of the Results of the Psychotherapies,* S. Lesse (ed.). Springfield, Ill.: C.C. Thomas, 1968.

Ferster, C. B., and Jeanne Simons. "An Evaluation of Behavior Therapy with Children," *The Psychological Record,* 16 (1966), 65-71.

Rimland, Bernard. *Infantile Autism.* New York: Appleton-Century-Crofts, 1964.

The Shattered Language of Schizophrenia

Chapman, L.J., L. Chapman, and G.A. Miller. "A Theory of Verbal Behavior in Schizophrenia," in *Progress in Experimental Personality Research,* B. Maher (ed.). New York: Academic Press, 1964, Vol. 1.

Critchley, MacDonald. "The Neurology of Psychotic Speech," *British Journal of Psychiatry,* 110 (1964), 353-364.

Laffal, Julius. *Pathological and Normal Language.* New York: Atherton Press, 1965.

Maher, Brendan. "Schizophrenia: Language and Thought," in *Principles of Psychopathology.* New York: McGraw-Hill, 1966.

Maher, Brendan, K.O. McKean, and B. McLaughlin. "Studies in Psychotic Language," in *The General Inquirer: A Computer Approach to Content Analysis,* P.J. Stone, D.C. Dunphy, M.S. Smith, and D.M. Ogilvie (eds.). Cambridge, Mass: M.I.T. Press, 1966.

Chromosomes and Crime

Asimov, Isaac. *The Genetic Code.* New York: Grossman, 1963.

Brown, W.M. Court. *Human Population Cytogenetics.* New York: Wiley, 1967.

Glass, David C. (ed.). *Genetics.* Biology and Behavior Series. New York: Rockefeller University Press and Russell Sage Foundation, 1968.

Lancet. "The YY Syndrome" (March 12, 1966), 583-584.

Montagu, Ashley. *Human Heredity.* Cleveland: World Publishing, 1964.

Inside Psychotherapy

Howard, K.I., D.E. Orlinsky, and J.A. Hill. "The Patient's Experience of Psychotherapy: Some Dimensions and Determinants," *Multivariate Behavioral Research,* Special Issue (1968), 55-72.

———. "The Therapist's Feelings in the Therapeutic Process," *Journal of Clinical Psychology,* 25 (1969), 83-93.

Orlinsky, D.E., and K.I. Howard. "Dimensions of Conjoint Experiential Process in Psychotherapy Relationships," *Proceedings of the 75th Annual Meeting of the American Psychological Association* (1967), 251-252.

———. "The Good Therapy Hour: Experiential Correlates of Patients' and Therapists' Evaluations of Therapy Sessions," *Archives of General Psychiatry,* 16 (1967), 621-632.

———. "Communication Rapport and Patient Progress," *Psychotherapy: Theory, Research and Practice,* 5 (1968), 131-136.

Transactional and Script Analysis Today

Berne, Eric. *Transactional Analysis in Psychotherapy.* New York: Grove Press, 1961.

———. *Games People Play.* New York: Grove Press, 1964.

———. *Principles of Group Treatment.* New York: Oxford University Press, 1966.

———. *What Do You Say After You Say Hello?* New York: Grove Press, 1972.

English, Fanita. "Episcript and the 'Hot Potato' Game," *Transactional Analysis Bulletin,* 8 (October 1969), 77-82.

———. "Strokes in the Credit Bank for David Kupfer," *Transactional Analysis Journal,* 1, 3 (July 1971), 27-28.

———. "The Substitution Factor: Rackets and Real Feelings," Part 1, *Transactional Analysis Journal,* 1, 4 (October 1971), 27-32; Part 2, *Transactional Analysis Journal,* 2, 1 (January 1972), 23-32.

———. "Sleepy, Spunky and Spooky," *Transactional Analysis Journal,* 2, 2 (April 1972), 64.

Harris, Thomas A. *I'm OK, You're OK.* New York: Harper & Row, 1969.

James, Muriel, and Dorothy Jongeward. *Born to Win.* Reading, Mass.: Addison-Wesley, 1971.

Piaget, Jean. *Judgment and Reasoning in the Child.* Totowa, N.J.: Littlefield, Adams, 1968.

Steiner, Claude M. *Games Alcoholics Play.* New York: Grove Press, 1971.

For Catatonia: Smiles, Praise and a Food Basket

Ayllon, Teodoro, and Jack Michael. "The Psychiatric Nurse as a Behavioral Engineer," *Journal of Experimental Analysis of Behavior,* 2 (1959), 323-334.

Eysenck, Hans J. "New Ways in Psychotherapy," *Psychology Today,* 1, 2 (June 1967), 39-47.

Krasner, Leonard, and Leonard P. Ullman (eds.). *Research in Behavior Modification.* New York: Holt, Rinehart and Winston, 1965.

Lovaas, O. Ivar, Gilbert Freitag, Vivian Gold, and Irene Kassorla. "Experimental Studies in Childhood Schizophrenia: Analysis of Self-Destructive Behaviors," *Journal of Experimental Child Psychology,* 2 (1965), 67-83.

Ullman, Leonard P., and Leonard Krasner (eds.). *Case Studies in Behavior Modification.* New York: Holt, Rinehart and Winston, 1965.

Group Therapy: Let the Buyer Beware

Brammer, Lawrence, and Everett Shostrom. *Therapeutic Psychology: Fundamentals of Actualization Counseling and Therapy.* 2nd ed. Englewood Cliffs, N.J.: Prentice-Hall, 1968.

Bugenthal, James. "The Process of the Basic Encounter Group," in *Challenges of Humanistic Psychology.* New York: McGraw-Hill, 1967.

Dunham, Maxie, Gary Herbertson, and Everett Shostrom. *The Manipulator and the Church.* New York: Abingdon Press, 1968.

Rogers, Carl. "The Increasing Involvement of the Psychologist in Social Problems," *The California State Psychologist,* 9, 7 (1968), 29.

Shostrom, Everett. *Man, the Manipulator.* New York: Abingdon Press, 1967.

New Ways in Psychotherapy

Bandura, A. *Principles of Behaviour Modification.* New York: Holt, Rinehart and Winston, 1969.

Chapman, L.J., L. Chapman, and G.A. Miller. "A Theory of Verbal Behavior in Schizophrenia," in *Progress in Experimental Personality Research.* New York: Academic Press, 1964, Vol. 1.

Eysenck, H.J., and H.R. Beech. "Counter Conditioning and Related Methods," *Handbook of Psychotherapy and Behaviour Change,* A.E. Bergin and S. Garfield (eds.). New York: Wiley, 1971, 543-611.

Stone, P.J., D.C. Dunphy, M.S. Smith, and D.M. Ogilvie (eds.). *The General Inquirer: A Computer Approach to Content Analysis.* Cambridge, Mass.: M.I.T. Press, 1966.

Yates, A.J. *Behavior Therapy.* New York: Wiley, 1969.

It Works

Eysenck, Hans J. "The Effects of Psychotherapy: An Evaluation," *Journal of Consulting Psychology,* 16 (1952), 319-324.

———. *Handbook of Abnormal Psychology.* New York: Basic Books, 1961.

———. "The Effects of Psychotherapy," *International Journal of Psychiatry,* 1 (1965), 99-142.

———. "New Ways in Psychotherapy," *Psychology Today,* 1, 2 (June 1967), 39-47.

Meltzoff, Julian, and Melvin Kornreich. *Research in Psychotherapy.* New York: Atherton Press, 1970.

The Crime of Commitment

Chekhov, Anton P. "Ward No. 6 [1892]," in *Seven Short Stories by Chekhov.* New York: Bantam, 1963, 106-157.

Goffman, Erving. *Asylums: Essays on the Social Situation of Mental Patients and Other Inmates.* Garden City, N.Y.: Doubleday-Anchor, 1961.

Guttmacher, Manfred S., and Henry Weihofen. *Psychiatry and the Law.* New York: Norton, 1952.

Kesey, Ken. *One Flew Over the Cuckoo's Nest.* New York: Viking, 1962.

Lindman, F.T., and D.M. McIntyre, Jr. *The Mentally Disabled and the Law: The Report of the American Bar Foundation on the Rights of the Mentally Ill.* Chicago: University of Chicago Press, 1961.

SOCIAL PSYCHOLOGY
The Small-World Problem

Harary, Frank, Robert Z. Norman, and Dorwin Cartwright. *Structural Models: An Introduction to the Theory of Directed Graphs*. New York: Wiley, 1965.

Kemeny, John G., and J. Laurie Snell. *Mathematical Models in the Social Sciences*. Waltham, Mass.: Blaisdell, 1962.

Korte, Charles, and Stanley Milgram. "Acquaintance Networks Between Racial Groups: Application of the Small World Method," *Journal of Personality and Social Psychology*, 15 (1970), 101-108.

Rapoport, Anatol. "Mathematical Models of Social Interaction," in *The Handbook of Mathematical Psychology*, D. Luce, R. Bush, and E. Galanter (eds.). New York: Wiley, 1963, Vol. 2.

Travers, Jeffrey, and Stanley Milgram, "An Experimental Study of the Small World Problem," *Sociometry*, 32 (December 1969), 425-443.

Brainwash: Familiarity Breeds Comfort

Cairns, R.B. "Attachment Behavior of Mammals," *Psychological Review*, 73 (1966), 409-426.

Collias, Nicholas E. "Social Development in Birds and Mammals," in *Roots of Behavior*, Eugene L. Bliss (ed.). New York: Harper & Row, 1962.

Harrison, Albert A. "Response Competition, Frequency, Exploratory Behavior, and Liking," *Journal of Personality and Social Psychology*, 9 (1968), 363-368.

Johnson, R.C., C.W. Thomson, and Gerald Frincke. "Word Values, Word Frequency, and Visual Duration Thresholds," *Psychological Review*, 67 (1960), 332-342.

Salzen, Eric, and Cornelius Meyer. "Reversibility of Imprinting," *Journal of Comparative and Physiological Psychology*, 66 (1968), 269-275.

Scott, J.P. *Animal Behavior*. Chicago: University of Chicago Press, 1958.

_____. "Critical Periods in Behavioral Development," *Science*, 138 (1962), 949-958.

Sluckin, Wladyslaw. *Imprinting and Early Learning*. Chicago: Aldine, 1965.

Thorndike, E.L., and Irving Lorge. *The Teacher's Workbook of 30,000 Words*. New York: Columbia University Press, 1944.

Zajonc, R.B. "Attitudinal Effects of Mere Exposure," *Journal of Personality and Social Psychology Monograph Supplement*, 9, Part 2 (1968), 1-27.

_____ (ed.). *Animal Social Psychology: A Reader of Experimental Studies*. New York: Wiley, 1969.

Who Likes Whom and Why

Aronson, Elliot. "Some Antecedents of Interpersonal Attraction," *Nebraska Symposium on Motivation*, W.J. Arnold and D. Levine (eds.). Lincoln: University of Nebraska Press, 1970.

Aronson, Elliot, and Vernon Cope. "My Enemy's Enemy is My Friend," *Journal of Personality and Social Psychology*, 8 (1968), 8-12.

Aronson, Elliot, and Darwyn Linder. "Gain and Loss of Esteem as Determinants of Interpersonal Attractiveness," *Journal of Experimental Social Psychology*, 1 (1965), 156-171.

Aronson, Elliot, and Judson Mills. "The Effect of Severity of Initiation on Liking for a Group," *Journal of Abnormal and Social Psychology*, 19 (1959), 177-181.

Aronson, Elliot, and Harold Sigall. "Liking for an Evaluator as a Function of Her Physical Attractiveness and Nature of the Evaluations," *Journal of Experimental Social Psychology*, 5 (1969), 93-100.

Aronson, Elliot, Ben Willerman, and Joanne Floyd. "The Effect of a Pratfall on Increasing Interpersonal Attractiveness," *Psychonomic Science*, 4, 6 (1966), 227-228.

Berscheid, Ellen, and Elaine Walster. *Interpersonal Attraction*. Reading, Mass.: Addison-Wesley, 1969.

Bramel, Dana. "Interpersonal Attraction, Hostility and Perception," in *Experimental Social Psychology*, J. Mills (ed.). New York: Macmillan, 1969.

Persuasion That Persists

Feather, N.T. "Educational Choice and Student Attitudes in Relation to Terminal and Instrumental Values," *Australian Journal of Psychology*, 22 (1970), 127-144.

Homant, Robert. "Semantic Differential Ratings and the Rank-Ordering of Values," *Educational and Psychological Measurement*, 29 (1969), 885-889.

Rim, Y. "Values and Attitudes," *Personality*, 1 (1970), 243-250.

Rokeach, Milton. *Beliefs, Attitudes and Values*. San Francisco: Jossey-Bass, 1968.

_____. "Faith, Hope and Bigotry," *Psychology Today*, 3, 11 (April 1970), 33-37, 58.

_____. "Long-Range Experimental Modification of Values, Attitudes and Behavior," *American Psychologist*, 26 (1971), 453-459.

Rokeach, Milton, Martin G. Miller, and John Snyder. "The Value Gap Between Police and Policed," *Journal of Social Issues*, in press.

Shotland, R.L., and W.G. Berger. "Behavioral Validation of Several Values from the Rokeach Value Scale As an Index of Honesty," *Journal of Applied Psychology*, 54 (1970), 433-435.

A Vaccine for Brainwash

McGuire, William J. "Inducing Resistance to Persuasion," in *Advances in Experimental Social Psychology*, Leonard Berkowitz (ed.). New York: Academic Press, 1964, Vol. 1.

_____. "Personality and Susceptibility to Social Influence," in *Handbook of Personality Theory and Research*, E.F. Borgatta and W.W. Kambert (eds.). Chicago: Rand McNally, 1968.

_____. "The Nature of Attitudes and Attitude Change," in *Handbook of Social Psychology*, G. Lindzey and E. Aronson (eds.). Reading, Mass.: Addison-Wesley, 1969, Vol. 3.

Sears, D.O., and R.P. Abeles. "Attitudes and Opinions," *Annual Review of Psychology*, 29 (1969), 253-288.

Tannenbaum, Percy H. "The Congruity Principle Revisited: Studies in the Reduction, Induction and Generalization of Persuasion," in *Advances in Experimental Social Psychology*, Leonard Berkowitz (ed.). New York: Academic Press, 1967, Vol. 3.

Zimbardo, Philip, and E.B. Ebbesen. *Influencing Attitudes and Changing Behavior*. Reading, Mass.: Addison-Wesley, 1969.

Style or Circumstance: The Leadership Enigma

Bavelas, Alex, A.H. Hastorf, A.E. Gross, and W.R. Kite. "Experiments on the Alteration of Group Structure," *Journal of Experimental Social Psychology*, 1 (1965), 55-70.

Fiedler, Fred E. "Engineer the Job to Fit the Manager," *Harvard Business Review* (September 1965).

_____. *A Theory of Leadership Effectiveness*. New York: McGraw-Hill, 1967.

Herzberg, Frederick. "Motivation, Morale & Money," *Psychology Today*, 1, 10 (March 1968), 42-45, 66.

Likert, Rensis. *New Patterns of Management*. New York: Wiley, 1961.

McGrath, J.E., and Irwin Altman. *Small Group Research: A Synthesis and Critique of the Field*. New York: Holt, Rinehart & Winston, 1967.

McGregor, Douglas. *Leadership and Motivation*. Cambridge, Mass.: M.I.T. Press, 1966.

Schein, Edgar H. "The First Job Dilemma," *Psychology Today*, 1, 10 (March 1968), 26-37.

When Will People Help in a Crisis?

Darley, J.M., and Bibb Latané. "Bystander Intervention in Emergencies: Diffusion of Responsibility," *Journal of Personality and Social Psychology*, 8 (1968), 377-383.

Latané, Bibb, and J.M. Darley. "Group Inhibition of Bystander Intervention in Emergencies," *Journal of Personality and Social Psychology*, 10 (1968), 215-221.

_____. *The Unresponsive Bystander: Why Doesn't He Help?* New York: Appleton-Century-Crofts, 1970.

Latané, Bibb, and Judy Rodin. "A Lady in Distress: Inhibiting Effects of Friends and Strangers on Bystander Intervention," *Journal of Experimental Social Psychology*, 5 (1969), 189-202.

Milgram, Stanley, and Paul Hollander. "Murder They Heard," *The Nation*, 198 (1964), 602-604.

Rosenthal, A.M. *Thirty-Eight Witnesses*. New York: McGraw-Hill, 1964.

index

a

butyrophenones, 37
bystander intervention, 353–357

C

Cairns, R. B., 335
Calverley, David, 67
cannabis sativa, 38
carbachol, 139
Carroll, Lewis, 10
Carp, Abraham, 243
Cartwright, Samuel A., 75
cataplexy, 56
catatonia, 300–302
Catch-22 (Heller), 14
catecholamines, 40, 41
Cattell, Raymond Bernard, 226–231
Cavalli-Sforza, L. L., 239
central nervous system, 56, 154
Chalmers, Derel, 67
Chambers, Robert, 224
Channing, William Emery, 222
Chapman, Jean, 249–252
Chapman, Loren J., 249–252, 273
Chapman, Richard, 105
Chase, Michael H., 54–57
Chhina, G. S., 47
Chiang, Han Two, 105
children
    in kibbutzim, 207–211
    mental development of, 161,
        162–164, 165–166, 169, 170–176
    mentally retarded, 177–181
    moral development of, 186–191
    sex-role development in, 204–206.
        See also infant development
Chimera, Thomas C., 105
Chinese Acupuncture (Wei-P'ing), 105
chloral hydrate, 39
chlordiazepoxide, 40
chloroform, 39
chloropromazine, 37, 39, 40
Chomsky, Noam, 118, 125, 146–151,
    152
Chorover, Stephan L., 74–81
chromosomes, and criminal behavior,
    275–280. *See also* genetics
Claparède, Edouard, 167
Clark, Brant, 84
Clark, Michael, 141
class, social, 194–197
classical conditioning, 122, 307–308.
    See also operant conditioning
Clever Hans, 19–20
Client-Centered Therapy (Rogers), 284
cocaine, 38, 41, 45
Cocteau, Jean, 38
Cohen, Larry, 205
Cohen, Maimon, 41
Cole, Michael, 210, 212–217
Cole, Sheila, 210, 212–217
Coleridge, Samuel, 41
colleges, role of, in development of
    psychology, 13–15
Collins, John, 66
color, Land phenomenon, 99
Combe, Andrew, 224
Combe, George, 222, 224
commitment, of mental patients,
    319–321
communication, social, 324–330. *See
    also* language
computer teaching, 129–134
computers, use of, in therapy, 53
concrete operations, stage of (Piaget),
    172

conditioning. *See* classical condi-
    tioning; operant conditioning
Confessions of an English Opium Eater
    (Quincy), 38
Conn, Lane K., 17
conservation, 162–163, 164, 170–171,
    172–173, 215
constancy, perceptual, 90
contrapreparedness, in learning,
    123–125
conventional level of morality (Kohl-
    berg), 187
Cook, Leonard, 40
Corita, Sister Mary, 286
Cordus, Valerius, 39
Cottle, Tom, 286
Counseling and Psychotherapy
    (Rogers), 284
counterirritation, 102–103
Cowie, John, 279
Cremarius, Johannes, 307
criminal behavior
    genetics and, 275–280
    psychotechnology and, 80. *See also*
        deviance, social
Cronbach, Lee, 246
Crodd, H. A., 335
Crowne, Douglas, 17, 22, 23, 254, 255,
    257
crystallized intelligence, 227–230
culture, effect of, on attitudes, 348
    on infant development, 194–197
    on IQ testing, 232–236
    on moral development, 190–191
curare, 38, 51, 52
cyclohexamide, 45
Cyrano de Bergerac (Rostand), 286

d

Dale, Laura A., 62
Damaser, Esther, 67
Darley, John M., 353–357
Darwin, Charles, 5, 6, 13, 15, 224
Davis, Kingsley, 4, 180
Davis, R. C., 51
Davison, Gerald, 26
Davy, Sir Humphrey, 59
deep structures, linguistic, 149–150,
    152
Delgado, José M. R., 30–34, 36
delta waves, 46, 55
Dement, William, 56, 61
Dennis, Wayne, 179
depression, treatment of, with drugs,
    40
Depression, Great, role of psychology
    during, 13–14
depth perception
    eidetic imagery and, 99
    relationship of, to REM sleep, 61
Deutsch, J. Anthony, 35–36, 135–139
development
    infant, 182–185
    mental, 161, 162–164, 165–166, 169,
        170–176
    moral, 186–191
    sex-role, 204–206
deviance, social, 74–81. *See also* crimi-
    nal behavior; mental illness
Dewey, John, 164, 225, 340
*Diagnosis of Reasoning in the Mentally
    Retarded, The* (Inhelder), 167
dibenzazepine, 37, 40, 41
diethyl ether, 39
digitalis, 45

dihydroxyphenylalanine (DOPA), 40
diisopropyl fluorophosphate (DFP),
    136, 139
Dimond, E. G., 101
Dixon, George, 242
Dobzhansky, Theodosius, 237–240
Dodge, Raymond, 44
dopamine, 40
Down's syndrome, 280
Draw-a-Person test, 249–252
dreaming
    ESP studies during, 62–65, 71
    REM sleep and, 58–60
Dreikurs, Rudolf, 317
drives, effects of ESB on, 35–36
drugs, 37–45
    as analgesics, 102
    effects of, on alpha waves, 48
    effects of, on REM sleep, 61
    use of, with hyperactive children,
        79–80
    memory and, 135–139. *See also spe-
        cific names of drugs*
Duby, George, 325
Dudek, Stephanie, 67
Dugdale, Richard L., 275
Durkheim, Emile, 16
Dysart, Willis N., 142

e

Ebbinghaus, Hermann, 140
echolocation, in bats, 106–111
Eckland, Bruce K., 240
ECS. *See* electroconvulsive shock
education
    in kibbutzim, 210–211
    Piaget's views of, 163–164
    Rogers' views of, 285–286
    in Soviet Union, 212–217
Edwards, Carl N., 17
EEG. *See* electroencephalograph
Efran, Jay, 257
ego states (transactional analysis),
    292–299
eidetic imagery, 97–100
electrical stimulation of the brain
    (ESB), 30–34, 35–36
electroconvulsive shock (ECS), 42
electroencephalograph (EEG), 46, 54
Elkins, S. M., 321
Ellsberg, Daniel, 76
emergencies, bystander intervention
    during, 353–357
Emlen, Stephen T., 125
emotion, nature of, 53
empiricism, 15, 146
encounter groups, 281–287, 304
Ends, Earl J., 317
Engel, Bernard, 53
English, Fanita, 292–299
epilepsy, 56
epistemology, in Piaget's work,
    160–162
Epstein, Joyce, 20
Erikson, Erik, 296
Erismann, T., 93, 94
Ervin, Frank, 78
Erwin, William, 63
ESB. *See* electrical stimulation of the
    brain
ESP. *See* extrasensory perception
Essentials of Psychological Testing
    (Cronbach), 246
Estabrooks, George, H., 71
Estes, William K., 122

ether, 39
ethics
    and bystander intervention, 357
    of ESB, 33
    experimental, 25–27. *See also* moral-
        ity
Ethics, The (Spinoza), 338
Evans, Ian, 300
Evans, John, 256
Evans, Judy, 17
Evans, Oliver, 13
Everts, Kenneth V., 292
evolution, 6, 122–125, 166. *See also*
        Darwin, Charles
Exner, J. E., 317
expectancy, effects of, 17–21
experimentation, 15, 22–24, 25–27
extinction, 122
extrasensory perception, 70–73
    alpha waves and, 48
    studies of, during dreaming, 62–65,
        71
Eysenck, Hans, 246, 306–314, 315–316

f

familiarity, 331–336
fantasy, 10–11
Fantz, Robert, 192
fear
    effects of electrical stimulation of
        the brain on, 31
    in primates, 198, 200–202
Fedorn, Paul, 296
Feingold, S., 230
Ferster, Charles B., 178, 266–269
Festinger, Leon, 340
Fetz, Eberhard, 52, 56–57
Fiedler, Fred E., 349–352
Fielding, Lewis, 76
Finch, Frank, 231
Finley, Gordon, 195
5-hydroxytryptamine, 41, 45
Flourens, Pierre, 221
fluid intelligence, 227–230
Fodor, Jerry, 149, 156
Forster, Francis M., 53
Foulkes, David, 59
Fox, John W. C., 105
Fox, Stephen, 57
Franklin, Benjamin, 13
Freedman, Jonathan, 27
French, John, 227
Freud, Sigmund, 15, 16, 38, 41, 118,
    160, 161, 245, 258, 289, 297, 315
Freudian psychology, 4–5, 14, 187,
    245, 306–307, 314. *See also* Freud,
        Sigmund
friendship, 337–339
Frincke, G. L., 332–333
Fuchs, Natalie, 287
Fulton, J. F., 33

g

g factor, 226–231
gain-loss theory, 338
Galambos, Robert, 107
Gall, Franz Joseph, 220–225, 275
Gallagher, Cornelius, 242–243
Gallistel, Charles R., 36
Galston, Arthur, 104
Games People Play (Berne), 296, 297
Garcia, John, 123–124, 232–236
Gardner, Beatrice, 153
Gardner, R. Allen, 153

credits

Cover. Design by Tom Suzuki, photograph by Stephen Wells.

I. Psychology: The Science of Behavior. 18–21—Karl Nicholason.

II. Brain and Behavior. 32, 34—Nat Antler; 37–39—Mercury Archives; 38—(bottom) courtesy University of Pennsylvania Medical Library and Photo Illustrators, Inc.; 40, 41—(top) John Oldenkamp; 42, 43—Al Limpo; 44—photographs courtesy of Murray Jarvik; 46–48—photographs by John Waggaman; 52—Richard Oden; 58—design by Tom Gould, art and lettering by Arline Thompson; 71—drawing courtesy of Gardner Murphy; 72—painting by Marc Chagall, courtesy of Montague Ullman.

III. The Sensory World. 91—Karl Nicholason; 92—Karl Nicholason, (bottom) Paul Weller (prior publication in *Scientific American*); 93—John Oldenkamp; 94–96—Karl Nicholason; 98, 100—courtesy of Charles F. Stromeyer III; 107—(left) James Simmons, (right) Joseph Tobias; 108—(top) James Simmons, (bottom) John V. Conover; 109—Robert Watts.

IV. Learning Memory, and Language. 115, 117–119—Ted Polubaum; 126–127—construction by Joyce Fitzgerald, photograph by Stephen Wells; 129—John Oldenkamp; 130—courtesy of Richard C. Atkinson; 135—John Oldenkamp; 137—(top) depiction of nerve cell redrawn from Anthony Ravielli illustration in *The Human Brain: Its Capacities and Functions* by Isaac Asimov, Houghton Mifflin Co., 1964; 143—Joe Garnett.

V. Psychological Development. 161—Gerri Blake; 162—Eric Shaal; 163—Gerri Blake; 164–166—Eric Shaal; 168—Gerri Blake; 169—Eric Shaal; 175, 176, 179—John Oldenkamp; 189, 191—construction by Joyce Fitzgerald, photograph by John Oldenkamp; 192—John Oldenkamp; 193–195—photographs courtesy of Jerome Kagan; 200, 201, 203—courtesy of Harry and Margaret Harlow; 206—Gerri Blake; 209—(from top left, clockwise) Leni Sonnenfeld, Ann Zane Shanks, Ann Zane Shanks, Leni Sonnenfeld, Ann Zane Shanks, (center) Ann Zane Shanks; 212–217—courtesy of Michael and Sheila Cole.

VI. Individual Differences and Personality. 200—John Oldenkamp; 221—(top) Mercury Archives, (bottom) Bob Kinyon/Millsap and Kinyon; 222–225—Mercury Archives; 235—"Genetics and Intelligence: A Review," L. Erlenmeyer-Kimling and L.F. Jarvik, *Science*, Vol. 142, pp. 1477–1479, Fig. 1, Dec. 13, 1963. © 1963 American Association for the Advancement of Science; 241—John Isely.

VII. Disorders and Therapy. 268, 269, 281–287—John Oldenkamp; 288—Karl Nicholason; 306, 308, 311 (bottom), 312, 313—John Dawson.

VIII. Social Psychology. 325—photograph by John Oldenkamp; 326–329—illustrations by Don Wright; 330—photograph by John Oldenkamp; 331—John Green; 332, 333—charts from *Journal of Personality and Social Psychology Monograph Supplement*, Vol. 9, No. 2, Part 2, copyright © 1968 by the American Psychological Association, Inc., reproduced by permission; 333—(right) John Green; 334—(right) John Green; 335, 336—John Green.

A special thanks for the contributions of: Alice Harmon, Pamela Morehouse (design assistance); David Estrada (index); Patricia Campbell (bibliographies); Amy Barnett, Rolande Angles (typing).

READINGS IN PSYCHOLOGY TODAY, THIRD EDITION/BOOK TEAM

Harvey A. Tilker, Ph.D., *Publisher*
Sherred Lane, *Publishing Coordinator*
Nancy Hutchison Sjöberg, *Project Manager*
Rebecca Smith, *Editor*
Linda Higgins, *Designer*
Sandra Marcus, *Production*
Lyn Smith, *Permissions Assistant*
John Ochse, *Psychology Marketing Manager*

CRM BOOKS

Charles C. Tillinghast III, *President*
Russ Calkins, *Marketing Manager*
Brian Sellstrom, *Director of Finance and Administration*
Trygve E. Myrhen, *Vice-President, Marketing*
Tom Rotell, *National Sales Manager*